MAINE

Portland

Cape Elizabeth

SACO BAY

Biddeford Pool

Kennebunkport

Piscataqua R.

Ogunquit

HAMPSHIRE

Kittery

York Harbor

Rye Harbor

Portsmouth

ISLES OF
SHOALS

Gulf of Maine

ATLANTIC OCEAN

Merrimack R.

Plum I.

Plum I. Sound

CAPE
ANN

Gloucester

Salem

Marblehead

SETTS

Boston

*MASSACHUSETTS
BAY*

N

W   E

S

Provincetown

Race Pt.

Plymouth

*CAPE COD
BAY*

RHODE

Providence

ISLAND

Cape
Cod
Canal

Marion

CAPE   COD

Chatham

New
Bedford

NARRAGANSETT BAY

BUZZARDS BAY

Woods
Hole

Hyannis

Monomoy
Pt.

*NANTUCKET
SOUND*

Newport

Sakonnet
Pt.

Vineyard Sound

Pt.
Judith

Watch Hill
Pt.

MARTHA'S
VINEYARD

BLOCK
ISLAND

NANTUCKET
ISLAND

Montauk Pt.

Nautical Miles

0   5   10   15   20   25

Jane Crosen, Mapmaker — 1994

The Cruising Guide
to the

NEW ENGLAND
COAST

The Cruising Guide

to the

NEW ENGLAND COAST

INCLUDING THE HUDSON RIVER,
LONG ISLAND SOUND, AND
THE COAST OF NEW BRUNSWICK

Roger F. Duncan,

Paul W. Fenn, W. Wallace Fenn,

and John P. Ware

COMPLETELY REVISED AND
UPDATED ELEVENTH EDITION

W. W. NORTON & COMPANY

NEW YORK · LONDON

The text and display of this book are composed in Adobe Caslon
Composition by The Sarabande Press
Manufacturing by R. R. Donnelley
Book design by Joe Marc Freedman
Cover illustration credit: James L. Mairs

Library of Congress Cataloging-in-Publication Data

The cruising guide to the New England coast: including the Hudson
River, Long Island Sound, and the coast of New Brunswick / Roger F.
Duncan . . . [et. al.].—Completely rev. and updated 11th ed.
p.   cm.
Includes bibliographical references (p.   ) and index.
1. Yachting—New England—Guidebooks.   2. Yachting—New Brunswick—
Guidebooks.   3. Harbors—New England.   4. Harbors—New Brunswick.
5. New England—Guidebooks.   6. New Brunswick—Guidebooks.
I. Duncan, Roger F.   95-9312
GV815.C87   1995
797.1'246'0974—dc20
ISBN 0-393-03639-1

W. W. Norton & Company, Inc., 500 Fifth Avenue, New York, NY 10110
W. W. Norton & Company Ltd., 10 Coptic Street, London WC1A 1PU

2   3   4   5   6   7   8   9   10

*This edition is dedicated to all those who,
cruising the coast, love it
and seek to preserve it.*

Contents

Apologia Pro Sua Vita by Robert F. Duncan   ix
Foreword   xi
The Origin and History of This Guide   xiii
Acknowledgments   xv
List of Illustrations   xvii

PART ONE
INTRODUCTORY

1. Introduction to the Coast   3
2. General Conditions, Suggestions, and Advice to the
   Eastward-Bound Mariner   8

PART TWO
HARBORS

*Whitehall, New York to the Headwaters of the
Saint John River, New Brunswick*

3. The Hudson River and the Passage from
   Long Island Sound   31
4. North Shore of Long Island Sound   87
5. South Shore of Long Island Sound   178
6. Fishers Island to Buzzards Bay, Including
   Narragansett Bay   242

7. Buzzards Bay, the Elizabeth Islands, and the
   Cape Cod Canal   302
8. Vineyard and Nantucket Sounds and the Voyage
   around Cape Cod   338
9. Cape Cod Canal, Massachusetts, to
   Cape Elizabeth, Maine   378
10. Portland to Rockland   449
11. Rockland to Schoodic Point   563
12. Schoodic Point to West Quoddy Head   665
13. Grand Manan   704
14. West Quoddy Head to Calais, Maine   714
15. The Coast of New Brunswick and the
    Saint John River   734
    Appendix A. Wildlife from the Deck:
        An Introduction to the Birds and
        Mammals of the New England Coast   759
    Appendix B: A Guide to the Geology of the
        Maine Coast   769
    Appendix C: New England Coastal Pumpout Stations   780
    Appendix D: Hospitals   783
    Appendix E: Fog   784
    Index   789
    Cruising Notes   801

The following Apologia written over half a century ago by Robert F. Duncan, who was principally responsible for the conception and first publication of this *Guide,* is an appropriate tribute to the past.

Apologia Pro Sua Vita

"The first boat I ever owned was a beautiful, fast but ancient racing sloop some 30 feet overall. My choice, dictated by a shallow purse, was influenced by the saying of a famous Irishman that 'an ugly yacht is no more attractive than an ugly woman, no matter how fast she may be.' The *Dizzy* had lovely lines, but on her first cruise, from Boston to Cape Cod, she sprang a bad leak, and we put into Scituate where she nearly sank in the night. My wife, unsympathetic with this adventure, which had also involved two of her brothers, waxed sarcastic and referred to the boat as having had 'a severe sinking spell.'

"Through several other misadventures the *Dizzy* survived her first summer in Buzzards Bay. In September I entrusted her welfare, with much misgiving, to one Archibald Butts who owned a small yachtyard at Hen Cove, Pocasset, Mass. The following spring I wrote Mr. Butts suggesting several important improvements. In reply, I received a pencilled note which, ignoring my suggestions, simply read, 'What your boat needs is a can of kerosene and a match.' Thus ended my first adventure as a boat owner. I never saw the *Dizzy* again.

"But the capacity for punishment on the part of those who take to small boats is, to landsmen, beyond belief. You have cranked a certain self-willed gasoline engine for almost as many revolutions as it has run voluntarily. Stripped to a running suit, you have scraped gallons of heavy grease and mud from the bilge of numerous boats, a generous portion of the mixture adhering to your anatomy and the clothes which your wife had to wash. For five hours in a lively gale you have fed alternately beef stew to a man at the tiller and oil to an irresolute engine. You have, according to *The Boston Herald,* been picked up by the Coast Guard in a sinking condition in Ipswich Bay in a Spring blow, when, as a matter of fact, the Coast Guard had only helped you change from a dangerous anchorage to the snug security of Annisquam Harbor. Having left the water jug on the beach, you have been becalmed for a day in a broiling sun with one tomato, an uncooked steak, and a quart of gin between four of you. Fending off a dock, you have slipped and plunged overboard into the icy waters of Maine in late May only to be pulled out by the collar and held over the side to drain—all at the hands of a giant companion with a grip like a bear trap. Mistaking the clearance under a drawbridge, you have hit the top of your mast and severed the forestay, so that it whipped down and sunk the shackle three inches into the pine deck—at the exact spot where a beloved classmate had stood a few minutes before. This, and a whole lot more grief.

"Why will a man of normal intelligence put up with much discomfort and run some little danger for the privilege of living for days at a time in an unsteady compartment no bigger than a good-sized linen closet? I have often been asked this question—particularly by anxious wives of men whom I have lured from comfortable, safe homes to go cruising. This question cannot be answered in a few hundred words, but at least a hint can be offered.

"To those who like it, the sea and cruising thereon offer adventure close at hand—a taste of romance—the thrill of discovery—and occasional battle with the elements on something like equal terms.

"I know of no quicker way to catapult oneself, like the hero of 'Berkeley Square,' back into the seventeenth century than to get on a small boat without an engine and cruise off the New England Coast."

This piece was first published in *Block Island to Nantucket* by Fessenden S. Blanchard.

Foreword

The purpose of this *Guide* is to make your cruise safer, easier, and more interesting. The *Guide* is intended to supplement, not replace the *Coast Pilot*, NOAA charts, *Eldridge*, and the invaluable corresponding Canadian publications. We, who have "been there before," seek to cruise with you, to try to keep you out of trouble, to suggest courses and harbors which might be convenient, to head you toward anchorages which you may always remember with delight. We will tell you something of history, of folklore, and of our own experiences which will make islands, sounds, and capes more than mere landmarks. We want this to be a memorable cruise.

We write largely from our own experience and record our own observations seen through our eyes. Under different conditions you may see the same things differently. What to us is a roll hole may be to you a delight. We may see the tide running hard to the southwest. On another day you may find it negligible. Write us and tell us about it. This book could not have been put together by four people working alone. We have had a great deal of help and we need as much as we can get.

We have tried very hard to be accurate, but we are not infallible and we write of a coast which is constantly changing, afloat and ashore. Therefore it is important to remember that **the information contained herein cannot be guaranteed and must be used with due caution. Charts reproduced or sketched herein are not for navigational purposes but are illustrations of the text.**

The astute reader may notice we have omitted a few attractive and secluded anchorages. We have done this in the spirit of Descartes, who wrote in the introduction to his *Geometry,* "I hope that posterity will judge me kindly, not only for those things which I have included but also for those which I have purposely omitted that others may share in the joy of discovery." May we meet in those harbors.

Roger F. Duncan
Box 66
East Boothbay, Maine
04544

Paul W. Fenn
Coastline Sailing School
Eldridge Yard, Marsh Road
Noank, Connecticut 06340

W. Wallace Fenn
169 Seneca Drive
Noank, Connecticut 06340

John P. Ware
9 Ridgecrest West
Scarsdale, New York 10583

The Origin and History of This Guide

In 1934 Fessenden S. Blanchard planned a cruise from Woods Hole eastward. He asked his friend and neighbor Robert F. Duncan, who had cruised New England waters since boyhood, to give him some notes on interesting places to visit. Thus was the *Guide* conceived.

Mr. Blanchard added to the notes. The Cruising Club of Scarsdale, New York, of which both men were members, added further. A mimeographed edition was circulated among fellow cruising men for comment and emendation, and in 1937 the First Edition was published by David Kemp in New York. Dodd, Mead & Company took it over from Kemp, Mr. Blanchard became coauthor, and through successive editions the book grew in scope and detail.

In 1960 Mr. Duncan turned the book over to his son, Roger F. Duncan, who, with the coauthorship of Mr. Blanchard and of Mr. Blanchard's son-in-law John P. Ware, published a Fifth Edition. Duncan and Ware presided over five more editions. The Ninth Edition, published in 1987, celebrated the *Guide*'s fiftieth anniversary. G. P. Putnam's Sons published a Tenth Edition in 1990. W. W. Norton & Company is the publisher of the current edition.

Resolved to produce the best *Guide* ever and aware that a great many important changes have occurred in recent years, the authors enlisted the help of W. Wallace Fenn and his son, Paul W. Fenn, as additional coauthors to cover the waters between Rye, New York, and Provincetown. Paul Fenn started the Coastline Sailing School in Noank, Connecticut, and has conducted his "students" on cruises from New York to Maine, particularly in the region south of Cape Cod. Wallace Fenn has sailed and cruised in Long Island Sound and other New England waters for many years, and for this edition has visited most of the harbors of Long Island Sound, Rhode Island, and other related areas. Mr. Ware continued to write about the waters of the Hudson River, New York Harbor, and the Sound to Rye. Mr. Duncan covered the coast from Provincetown to Grand Lake in New Brunswick, visiting most of the harbors by sea and some by land. All the authors were materially assisted by Roger S. Duncan, great-grandson of the founder of the *Guide*, who visited by automobile some of the harbors which the others found it difficult to get to. Never has a cruising guide been more thorough. However, we are reminded that a wise man wrote, "Perfection is a plant that does not grow on this earth."

Acknowledgments

Special thanks are due to our wives, Mary Duncan, Carol Fenn, and Molly Ware, for bearing with the priorities necessary to this project and for their unfailing support throughout, both afloat and ashore. Then to Gerry Peer for extended help on New Brunswick harbors, Edward Myers for writing the article on the Damariscotta River, Joan Welsh for the article on Hurricane Island, David Pierson for help on the Isles of Shoals, Michael Doane for an extended tour of Cape Ann, Donald Duncan for research on South Shore harbors, Clark Thompson for extended help with aerial photographs, and Bob and Barbara Ireland for extended notes on the Maine coast. Peter Worrell wrote postcards on almost every harbor he visited for three years—of inestimable help. William Hancock and Olcott Gates reviewed and improved their appendices on wild life and geology.

In addition, we must thank Hartley Lord, David Brown, Philip Davis, Hugh G. Williams, Robert and Alexander Duncan, George Hall, John Church, Richard Salter, Dr. J. B. Heiser, Fred Muehl, David Lusty, Joel White, Farnham Butler, Larry Pritchett, Neil Corbet, Anne Miller, Alfred Beck, Vivien and Lillian Lunt, Chuck Loring, Jim Baker, Daniel Bickford, Peter Bradley, Anthony Codding, Warren Colby, Grenville Henthorne, James Connolly, Michael Grey, Ellen Higgins, John Higgins, Philip Conkling, Tom Kiley, Mary and Robert Lappeus, Carol Macaulay, Sune Noreen, Herbert Parson, Steven Parsons, Eric Roos, Oscar Simpson, Eugene Thurston, Peter Toppan, John Winder, Debbie

Holmes, Peter Haddock, Jerry Merser, Herb Duncan, Capt. Parrot, Dean Crosman, Liz Duncan, John Totman, Mal Saxton, Carl Corson, Bigelow Crocker, Mr. and Mrs. Robert Tilney, Den Bancroft, Ken Eaton, Janet and Helmut Kohl, Angela LeBlanc, Marla Katz, Capt. Ted Brown, D. A. Noonan, Thomas Osowski, Carl Magee, Charles Burnham, John Brewer, David Hulburt, Gerry Gamage, Dick Cook, Steve and Earl Moore, Charles and Barbara Jenness, Leverett Davis, Betty Roberts, Rusty Court, Jack Halliday, Dr. Harry Quick, Anne Vaughan, Pat Curtis, Paul Klienhans, Lydia Lyman, Scott Davis, Herbert Macaulay, Jennifer Ware Ellis, Leslie Ware Caputo, Dr. Charles Arnold, Edward M. Roberts, William Byers, Charles Gould, John Thompson, John Anderson, Christopher Gross, Robert Shiekel, Al Stuckles, Richard Hall, Cliff Mitchell, Donald Greene, William Pearson, Noreen Litchfield, Richard Stewart, J. C. Dempsey, Richard Nye, Elliott Keezner, Rick Batt, A. W. Thomson, William Roman, Mel Kantor, Tim Noble, Jeffrey Eng, Daniel Siegel, Stephen DeLay, Robert Butt, Anthony Saline, Ethan Fenn, Abbott Fenn, David Fenn, Norman Dudziak, Demaris Dudziak, Axel Westerberg, Robert MacIntyre, Kimberlee Cornett, Gale Beyea, Madeline Clem, Jeanne Garant, Catherine Crawford, Glen MacLeod, John Wojcik, Neal Cornell, Bayard Hooper, John Church, Bill Cavanaugh, Anthony Zane, Rita Nelson, Irwin Donenfeld, David Roberts, Robert Seiferman, John Campbell, Raymond Farrow, Joseph Imhoff, Leslie Crandall, Michael Camarata, Earle Bragdon, The Staff of the Coastline Sailing School and Yacht Charters, Ellen Barbour, Jake Farrel, Richard Goodwin, Sumner Simmons, Kenneth Barbour, George K. Hansen of the New York State Dept. of Environmental Conservation, Ms. Lynn S. Beman, Executive Director of the Hudson River Maritime Museum, Arthur Lindo of the South Street Seaport, William Kavanaugh, U.S. Army Corps of Engineers, Waltham, MA, Ms. Lisa D. Ryan, New York City Dept. of Transportation, Melville P. Cote, Jr., Water Management Division, U.S. Environmental Protection Agency, Boston, MA, Carl G. Boutilier who sent us many engineers reports on harbor surveys, Russell C. Mt. Pleasant, Tom Rohan, and Ken Goss.

Illustrations

East River (Hell's Gate) — 33
Hudson Highlands — 36
Some Ports along the Hudson River — 76
New Rochelle — 93
Stamford Harbor — 110
Branford — 135
The Thimble Islands — 139
The "Sand Hole" at Lloyd Point — 187
Mt. Sinai — 202
Mattituck Inlet — 205
Shelter Island — 209
Mystic Seaport — 247
Stonington — 253
Port Judith — 265
Newport Harbor and Narragansett Bay — 281
Sippican Harbor, Marion — 312
West Falmouth — 324
Quisset — 325
Woods Hole — 326
Cuttyhunk Harbor — 333
Menemsha — 343
Lake Tashmoo — 345
Edgartown — 348

Courses to the Head of the Harbor at Nantucket   355
Lewis Bay   366
Wychmere   369
Chatham   372
Annisquam   411
Newbury Port   421
Porstmouth   426
The Isles of Shoals   429
Gosport Harbor   432
York River and York Harbor   436
Portland   451
Small Point   466
The Kennebec River   469
Boothbay Harbor   488
Damariscove   494
Pemaquid Harbor   509
New Harbor   515
Muscongus Bay   522
Muscongus Sound   524
Friendship with Morse's Bay and the St. George River   527
An Early Friendship Sloop   529
A Modern Friendship Sloop   531
Georges Harbor   534
Monhegan Harbor   543
Port Clyde   551
Muscle Ridge   556
Achorages in Muscle Ridge Channel   558
Camden   572
Castine   584
Horseshoe Cove   589
Vinalhaven   606
Matinicus Harbor   611
Northeast Harbor   652
Corea Harbor   671
Anchorages in Eastern Bay   679
The Mud-Hole   682
The Main Channel Way to Steele Harbor   683
Roque Island Thorofare   686
Haycock Harbor   699

Drawing of Haycock Harbor   701
Tide at Lubec Narrows Bridge   717

Part One

INTRODUCTORY

Chapter I

Introduction to the Coast

Fortunate indeed is the man or woman, boy or girl, who can cruise the waters covered by this volume. Nowhere else in the United States are greater and more lovely contrasts to be found so close together. Spread on the table before you National Ocean Survey Chart 13006. Within a few hundred miles lie the protected waters of the Hudson River, the lively racing activities of Long Island Sound, the sportfishing grounds from Montauk to Cape Cod, the sand dunes of the Cape. From the Cape it is but a day's sail to rocky Cape Ann and an overnight run to the Maine coast, where granite islands form sheltered and uninhabited harbors. The gray and tide-churned waters of the Bay of Fundy run over the Reversing Falls at Saint John into the placid Saint John River.

The old charts showed in the margins vignettes of the coast from offshore, little steel engravings showing church steeples rising from wooded hills or a lighthouse on the end of a point, to help the mariner recognize the landmarks of a harbor entrance. A few sketches from different parts of the coast may help to suggest which regions the yachtsman may choose to explore.

The Hudson River flows between low, rounded mountains forested with hardwoods and rising quite sharply from the water. Along the edge of the stream run a road and a railroad. A tug with several barges in tow comes down the middle, taking advantage of the current. Against the shore a little beacon on the end of a breakwater signals an anchorage in the mouth of a creek out of the tide. A power cruiser spreads a wide V on the smooth surface. Perhaps *Clearwater,* the replica of an old Hudson

3

River sloop, rounds a distant headland, her enormous mainsail using all of the light air it can catch.

Shift the scene to Long Island Sound on a July Sunday. There must be over a hundred sailing craft in sight. Here is a class of Internationals racing, everyone keyed up, getting every bit out of the boat, and alert to the tactics of the competition. Over on the Connecticut shore a cruising ketch slides along before the gentle westerly, her crew sunning on top of the cabin house, the helmsman with the tiller in one hand and a cool can in the other. Ahead is an ocean racing yawl—you have seen her picture in *Yachting*—exercising the crew. A great yellow-and-blue spinnaker blossoms ahead of her. The low line of the Connecticut shore is hazy with smoke, but the harbors are clearly marked by white lighthouses or beacons and by throngs of anchored yachts. The Long Island shore looks much the same, but our contemplation of it is distracted by an airplane gliding in toward LaGuardia and then by a gleaming power cruiser, all white enamel, chrome, and varnish. From a flying bridge shaded by a striped awning, two men in swimming trunks wave down at us. If we put into one of the harbors tonight, we will find moorings crowded closely together and tiers of boats in finger piers at the marina.

Passing inside of Block Island in a fresh southerly, we feel the heave of the open Atlantic and see around us fishermen with pulpits manned for the sight of a fin or with baits on long outriggers, the fishermen lounging in the fighting chairs. Yonder is a party boat from Montauk, anchored and rolling heavily in the tide while the customers catch ground fish or mackerel. Passing a commercial dragger, we are lucky enough to see off Newport a great crowd of sails, perhaps a yacht club "cruise" with formal races from port to port. As the leaders sweep down on the committee boat at the finish line, almost hidden under spinnakers of every hue and pattern, the finish gun booms.

Milling about watching are schooners, little sloops with outboards, cruisers, steamers crowded with sightseers, even a seagoing automobile complete with horn and windshield wiper! After the race, the whole fleet will run up into Newport, filling Brenton Cove, lining the wharves, and thronging Newport's bars and restaurants.

With East Chop astern, we find a very different scene. Last night we lay in Hadley Harbor, lucky to find a quiet berth. Some who came too late had to lie outside. We shot through Woods Hole this morning, and with a fair wind and 2 knots of tide, we are running down Nantucket Sound for the Cross Rip horn buoy. The water is a light-greenish color, for it is shallow here. The sea is short and choppy, the wind quite fresh all of a sudden. There is no land in sight, although we aren't far from the low shore. Cape Poge Light is a pencil on the southern horizon, and several water towers on the south shore of Cape Cod show above the horizon to port. As it breezes up rapidly, we overtake a small sloop lugging a Genoa jib too big for the breeze, burying her bow, yawing wildly, and leaving a wide wake. Coming toward us is a power cruiser leaping half out of the water on almost every sea, being driven hard against the steepening chop. Astern, a ferry bound for Nantucket is overtaking us, her high decks crowded with vacationers. We have called ahead for a slip in the Nantucket Marina. The old whaling town is profoundly changed but in many ways we will find much to remind us of the early days. The cobbled streets lead up the hill past the whale-oil mansions of Coffins and Macys and Starbucks, and on across the bleak moors and barren beaches the whalemen knew.

Far to port are the sandy little harbors of the south shore, protected by jetties and constantly dredged—crowded, quiet little places, the shores teeming with refugees from metropolitan heat and humidity.

Look again and see us off Plymouth, north of Cape Cod. The water is dark green and much colder. The shore is a long yellow ribbon of sand, backed by yellow dunes sparsely grown over with grass. Astern is the high hill of Manomet. Abeam is Gurnet Point with the light on top, and just visible behind it is the dark cylinder of Duxbury Pier Light. The low hills inland are quite distant, but on Captains Hill in Duxbury is the unmistakable Pilgrim Monument. Far off to starboard another Pilgrim Monument rises over the dunes of Provincetown. We are running under power, for it is calm and, short of Scituate nearly 15 miles ahead, there is no harbor fit for a vessel of our draft. Inshore is a fleet of small powerboats fishing. One of them, a light aluminum outboard, circles us. Like an advertisement in a magazine, a girl in a bikini waves. Astern are several power cruisers drumming steadily up the shore for the suburban ports of Cohasset and Hingham. Ahead lies a sloop becalmed, rolling in the uneven wash, her skipper preferring to sail all night rather than use the power. The air is vibrant with internal combustion.

Off Cape Ann we see the Marblehead racing fleet, and late in the afternoon the procession of heavy draggers heading for Gloucester after several days' fishing. A container ship out of Boston passes astern on a course for Cape Sable and European ports. Inshore are the first high, rocky shores we have seen, with elaborate summer homes at intervals along the cliffs. Thacher Island with its tall twin towers keeps us clear of the wicked ledges ahead, now gently washing in the easy swell. A whale may startle us here with his hoarse blow and the majestic roll of back and fin. Fifteen feet high go the flukes and he sounds, leaving only a slick in the water and our quickened pulse.

Eastward we sail, past miles of exposed beach, here and there speckled with summer cottages or broken by river mouths. At Isles of Shoals, our first offshore harbor, we spend the night, scarcely aware of the easy motion.

The next day we are into Casco Bay; and with the fair southwest breeze astern we find a new world of islands and ledges between long points of mainland until the Maine fog shuts down, cold and gray. Our world is a circle, two waves wide. We listen carefully for the distant roll of surf. We hear Halfway Rock bleating regularly astern and far ahead the horn on Seguin—otherwise only the swash of water along the lee side. The navigator, alert for pot buoys to judge the tide, watches the fathometer and loran and keeps an eye on clock and compass. The radar reflector swings in the rigging and drops of fog dew patter on deck. But with the powerful foghorns on Seguin and the Cuckolds, with bells, whistles, and bold shores to run for, there is no need for worry. Snug anchorages lie ahead.

Across Penobscot Bay we catch a brisk northwester. The Camden Hills stand sharply behind us. The water is cold and a bright blue-green, whitecaps and dark puffs rushing across it. A lobster fisherman hauling a trap waves as we rush by, our lee rail awash. In Deer Island Thorofare we thread our way among islands wooded to the water's edge and fragrant with the sun on raspberry, sweet fern, wild rose, and spruce. Crossing Jericho Bay, we meet the *Roseway,* a former Portland pilot boat, close-hauled and leaning to the puffs. We count fifteen sails, some running east with us for Mount Desert, others beating up for Eggemoggin, and three working up under Isle au Haut. A motor yacht slashes by, throwing clean spray from her bow and dragging a turbid wake, which only for a moment interrupts the rhythm of our running. A gull swings under our stern and an eider duck hustles her fleet of ducklings off Long Ledge. As the wind eases late in the afternoon, we have a wide choice of harbors. We can run up Blue Hill Bay toward Prettymarsh and tuck in under Western Mountain for the night. Ahead is Swans Island with a quiet spruce-ringed anchorage at Buckle Harbor. Or we can go down to Burnt Coat, where we will find a telephone and a wharf at which we can buy gas and lobsters. Or we can press on for Mount Desert, where we will arrive after dark, the mountains black against the sky and the harbors starred with anchor lights.

East of Mount Desert the character of the coast changes again. Off Petit Manan, everything is far away. To the westward is the low profile of Mount Desert. Schoodic, left astern two hours ago, shows blue already. Petit Manan Lighthouse abeam is a lonesome shaft, gray and forbidding above the bleak deserted dwelling, the shore behind it scarcely showing in the distance. Far up Narraguagus Bay is Cape Split and the white spot of Nash Island Light. Ahead the great cliffs of Crumple Island, Great Wass Island, and Mistake Island have not yet risen above the horizon. The tide is running hard, and the sea is lumpy and irregular. It is a bare and lonely spot with not a lobsterman or yacht anywhere in sight. Porpoises roll and a guillemot skitters off, the white patches on his wings flashing. But we are by 'Tit Manan, and a libation to the gods of wind and tide is due. They have favored us thus far, but they may test us at any time.

From the blue Passamaquoddy we are shot out through Letite Passage on a swirling tide into the icy gray Bay of Fundy and a mighty tidal stream funneling up toward Saint John. A puffin may burst out of water nearby and splash into flight. To port are cliffs, flat topped and sheer, with the rolling hills of New Brunswick behind them. Harbors are few and exposed, protected by massive government wharves. Few yachtsmen ever see this coast, usually shrouded in fog.

But if we make it through busy Saint John Harbor and up the Reversing Falls, we find the hospitable Canadian yachtsmen sailing the long reaches of the river in clear, warm sunshine. Salmon roll, the water is clean enough to swim in, and even, in places, clean enough to drink. Pleasant farms, gentle hills, green islands grazed by cows and sheep make this a paradise after the fog and chill outside.

Start where you will. Go as far as you want and as fast. Run offshore from one big lighthouse and fog signal to another or work your way among the islands, anchoring in quiet coves, yarning with fishermen, or visiting country stores. Sail with the racing fraternity from yacht club to marina or fish the rips and ledges. The coast is to be enjoyed by each in his own way and at his own pace. By virtue of no authority whatsoever, the authors welcome you to the coast and hope that this *Guide* will add to the safety and pleasure of your cruise.

Chapter II

General Conditions, Suggestions, and Advice to the Eastward-Bound Mariner

1. Weather. I have often asked a fisherman about the safety of some harbor or the advisability of an offshore run and been told, "Take *summertime,* they ain't nothin' to hurt ya." In relation to winter weather, this is true. Nevertheless, a few observations on coastal summer weather may be helpful.

Throughout the whole coastal area covered by this book, the prevailing summer wind is southwest. This is due partly to the presence of a large high-pressure area between the Azores and Bermuda and partly to the effect of the heated land close to water cooled by a branch of the Labrador Current.

In midsummer, day after day will repeat the following pattern: In the morning it will be warm and quiet. Not a ripple will break the surface. The sky will be cloudless or thinly veiled with high cirrus. Later in the morning, as the land heats up, small, puffy clouds will appear over the land. Soon zephyrs from south or even southeast will come in, hauling soon to south-southwest or southwest. Then on the glassy water will appear cat's-paws and the ripples of the daily southwester. The southwester may come at any time from shortly after dawn until noon, often coming earlier when the flood tide makes in the morning. Meteorologists deny the connection between wind and tide, but the writers are backed by local fishermen in believing that a phenomenon so frequently observed has some foundation. The arrival of this breeze is often dramatic. You may lie becalmed, sweltering in the heat and slow roll for an hour. Then in the space of five minutes the sails fill, the temperature drops comfortably, and you are under way doing 3 or 4 knots with the calm forgotten. Close astern may lie another vessel, still becalmed. This breeze may increase to as much as 25 knots in some places. Buzzards Bay is notorious for its vigorous afternoon southwesters, which, with a strong ebb tide, can become dangerous for small craft and "high-charged" powerboats.

Many cruising men have noticed that, contrary to what we might expect, the southwest wind is stronger under the lee of an island or point and is likely to have a bit more westerly in it than offshore. Conversely, off a point or close to windward of the land, the breeze is sometimes quite feeble.

The late Dr. Charles F. Brooks of the Blue Hill Observatory in Milton explained the phenomenon thus: The southwest wind as it blows over the open sea has vertical stability. That is, it is flowing like a great river of air with the air on the bottom staying on the bottom. This lower air is slowed by friction with the water, so the upper air is traveling considerably faster. When this air approaches an island warmed by the sun, the rising currents of warm air and the interference of the land itself stir up the air, and the speed of the upper air is imparted to the whole mass. Hence Massachusetts Bay, Ipswich Bay, upper Penobscot Bay, and the northeast sides of Mount Desert and Isle au Haut are renowned for having plenty of wind even when it is much quieter offshore. It is often better to beat to the westward through the Maine islands, where one finds a good breeze and smooth water, than it is to slat about offshore in a light air.

As the sun drops in the afternoon and the land cools, the breeze moderates. Sometimes it just quits, cut off as though someone had turned a celestial switch. The evening is likely to be calm, although sometimes the land may cool enough to produce a light northerly drawing down a harbor. By dawn, conditions will have become stable again and the pattern may repeat itself.

This schedule, however, may be interrupted by a cyclonic disturbance. This is often heralded by a murky afternoon and the southwester continuing into the evening. When this happens, the next day is usually showery and sometimes is followed by a northwester.

These northwest days are the ones we wait for all winter. Usually the early morning will be crystal clear, with a gentle northerly breeze increasing in dark little puffs. As the sun gets up and the day develops, the breeze increases. By noontime it may be blowing a reefing breeze, with the puffs rushing out to sea, dark green and silvery. Houses 10 miles away still stand out sharply. As one runs offshore, the puffs become more moderate and the wind steadies. Hard, flat-based, or lenticular clouds suggest that the wind will hold or even increase. Puffy cumulus clouds over the land usually indicate that the breeze will moderate and even shift to the southwest or west-southwest later in the day. However, toward sunset the northerly will often reassert itself and provide a fine chance to make a harbor well to the westward. These are great days to travel, especially for the westward-bound vessel. Such a vessel should ease sheets and stand offshore to make all the westing and southing possible if the glass is rising rapidly. Otherwise it is well to hang under the shore, where there is more wind and where it is likely to last longer.

One cruising skipper turned his crew out and got under way before breakfast when he awoke at dawn in Camden Harbor and saw an easterly breeze and a clear sky. "A bird's nest in the grass," he termed it as he made long legs of it to the westward. Occasionally during the summer these dry easterlies come in and are indeed a gift to the westward-bound skipper. Later in the day the sky usually clouds up, visibility shortens, and the day may end in rain or fog, but 40 or 50 miles of beating up toward Boston may have been saved.

Fog. The entire area covered by this book is subject to summertime fog. In general, the farther east you go, the more likely and more lasting is the fog. However, even in the worst places, the odds based on climatological records are about two to one that you will not encounter fog on any particular day. In general, an August day is a little more likely to be clear than a July day. June and September have only about half as much fog as July and August.

For a more complete discussion of fog, see Appendix E in this volume.

Thunderstorms. These storms in eastern New England are seldom severe offshore and always provide adequate warning. Occasionally, however, a really heavy one will cause considerable damage. Long Island Sound and Salem Bay are renowned "hot spots" for thunderstorms.

A thunderstorm first shows as a thunderhead, a heavy, towering, cumulus cloud with a dark base. If it is north of northwest, it will usually pass over the land, but the ones to the west or west-northwest will probably come aboard.

As the cloud builds up, the top flattens and becomes anvil shaped. The bottom is blue-black. As it approaches, flickers and grumbles come out of it and a veil of rain appears. The usual southerly wind dies out.

By this time the wise skipper has dropped all sail and tied it down tightly. He has taken a long look to the southeast to be sure he has no lee shore close by, and if he cannot quickly make a sheltered anchorage under power, he will jog along easily, feeling rather like a nail awaiting the hammer.

Often there will be only a capful of wind, a slash of rain, and a few snaps of lightning as the storm blows over. Sometimes, if the squall is bringing in the front of a cooler air mass, an arch of tightly rolled cloud will appear against the black of the storm and the low clouds will be boiling and ragged. Such a squall will surely blow very hard for a short time and is nothing with which to take a chance.

Once in a long time a squall may produce a "miniburst," a very violent downrush of cold air in the middle of the storm. It apparently comes straight down, plastering flat to the water whatever is under it, and spreads out in all directions, losing velocity as it does so. It is suspected that minibursts caused the loss of the *Pride of Baltimore,* the *Marquesa* off Bermuda, and the *Albatross* in the Gulf of Mexico. Minibursts give no warning and can be lethal to a yacht carrying sail.

Yachts have been struck by lightning and survived. Most yacht designers ground mast and rigging to neutralize the air around the boat by draining off its charge. This seems to work pretty well, but no grounding system will protect a yacht should she for some reason encounter a full-scale lightning bolt. It is wise during a thunderstorm to disconnect all electronic gear lest a surge of current blow it apart.

Usually, however, no disaster strikes. You will soon see light under the clouds in the west, a rainbow appears in the east as the rain thins, and the sky blows clear for a lovely northwest evening.

Hurricanes. Occasionally a tropical hurricane will depart from the usual course and churn up the New England coast. Usually the radio provides more than adequate warning. There is no need to be concerned about a hurricane in Florida; but if it continues a northerly course beyond Cape Hatteras, seek out a snug harbor with good holding ground. If it hits New Jersey, look to your ground tackle.

Bowditch and Eldridge give good explanations of the meteorology of hurricanes, and the *Coast Pilot* explains them with a strength of feeling lacking in its usual factual style. However, it is sufficient to remember that if the center is to pass inland, to the west and north, the wind will begin from the east or southeast and pull around into the south, southwest, and west. If the center is to pass offshore, the wind will work from east through northeast and north to northwest. If the center is to pass overhead, the wind will not shift at all but blow from the southeast or east until the calm eye passes. Then it will slam around into the west or northwest.

If it seems at all likely that the storm will strike, make every preparation you can think of. Even then, it may not be enough. Unbend sails and stow them below. Stow all movable deck gear below. Lash down the dinghy on deck. Double lash it. Do not rely on someone else's mooring. Lay out all your ground tackle in the direction from which the anchorage is exposed and from which the wind is expected. Protect all lines with chafing gear at the chock. Consider sliding a pig of ballast down the anchor line to act as a spring and help to prevent yawing. It is said that an automobile tire hung over the stern will have the same good effect. Very careful use of the engine in the heaviest gusts may take some of the strain off the ground tackle, but be careful not to surge ahead on the lines lest an extra strain come on them when the bow falls off and is driven back.

Pay particular attention to avoid anchoring in a position which will be to leeward of one likely to drag. There is little defense against a barge adrift.

If you are to get the full force of the storm, you will have noticed a very long roll offshore the day before, followed by thickening clouds. Rainsqualls will become more frequent and heavier as the storm approaches, until it is blowing unbelievably hard, raining out straight, and blowing clouds of spray off the surface of the water, even in a protected anchorage. Anything loose will go off to leeward and the barometer will dive. To move about on deck, even in a protected anchorage, can be very difficult and possibly dangerous.

However, these things pass. With thorough preparation and a dash of good luck, you should weather a hurricane at anchor in a snug harbor. But don't be caught at sea, in an open roadstead, or in an exposed bight or you may lose more than your boat.

2. Tides. The moon, assisted by the sun at new and full moon, picks up a wave and carries it westward along the shore from the Bay of Fundy.

High water is one-half to one hour before the moon crosses the meridian. The water, released by each previous wave, runs east to join the next one coming, so the tidal current east of Long Island, in general, runs *east on the flood and west on the ebb.* This rule is subject to many exceptions caused by configurations of land. For instance, the tide ebbing out of Blue Hill Bay runs east across Bass Harbor Bar. There seems to be a constant westerly set of current off Two Bush at the entrance to Penobscot Bay, and the tide seems to set almost northwest into Saco Bay on both ebb and flood. (See notes in the text under those places.)

In general, the farther east one goes, the higher the tide rises and the more vigorous the current. The exceptions to this generality are so many that one need call attention only to Hell Gate in the East River, The Race in Long Island Sound, and Cape Cod Canal, by way of illustration. But these are "tide holes," and the generality still stands.

West of Cape Elizabeth the tidal current nearly parallels the course of the coastwise cruiser, but on the Maine coast the tide also sets in and out of the bays, running nearly across one's course. The current is strong enough to make a considerable difference to a sailing yacht or slow auxiliary. The writer's experience has been that for the bays west of Schoodic Point about one-quarter mile should be allowed for tide for every hour one will be in the current. At the full strength of a moon tide, however, this will not be enough. Watch the tide running by lobster buoys and remember that your first guess at the velocity of the current should be divided in half. Most people overestimate the speeds of both wind and tide.

The draggers and sardiners move so fast that they make very little if any allowance for tide.

If you keep a record in your logbook of the time of high water and the way the tide sets at different times and places relative to it, you will doubtless become badly confused because you will find through the years considerable inconsistency in your evidence. Tides are often influenced by winds, a tide running against the wind often turning early and one running to leeward turning late. In some places the tide works around in a circle, running east, for instance, at three hours before high water but east-southeast an hour later and perhaps south at low-water slack. This seems to be the situation in Jericho Bay. The writer started across one foggy day and allowed for a flood tide he supposed to be running north into Eggemoggin Reach and Blue Hill Bay. Between Egg Rock and Long Ledge the tide must have been running east, for we sailed across

Potato Ledge and made Shabby Island far to the south. Careful observation, good luck, and a habit of hedging loran and radar with log, lead, and lookout—these you need for successful navigation anywhere on the New England coast.

3. Silting. Harbors and their channels have a bad habit of silting up and then requiring dredging. This is particularly true of most of the harbors along the southern shore of Cape Cod and the areas to the south and west. Usually the silting continues for several years before it seriously affects accessibility, and we try to warn you of it in this *Guide;* but sometimes a severe storm will produce a great acceleration in this process and leave a lot of places much shallower than before. Permits for dredging usually take a year or more to obtain, so a dangerous condition can persist. Public sources of information do not help much unless you keep a very close watch on *Notices to Mariners.* If you have any concerns about being able to navigate a harbor or channel, contact a local harbormaster, marina operator, or Power Squadron port captain. Then proceed slowly on a rising tide so you won't hit *too* hard and the coming tide will float you clear.

4. Navigating Equipment. Compass and Clock. The first and single most important instrument to be provided is a first-class compass in good condition. It should be permanently mounted in a solid binnacle where it is easily read from the wheel and where it can be used to take bearings. Secondly, it must be properly compensated and frequently checked in clear weather. Not only must iron and steel be kept away from it, but also instruments like light meters and transistor radios, for they have powerful little magnets in them.

Almost as important as the compass is a clock firmly mounted where it is visible from chart table and wheel. In the fog, your runs are made in terms of time at a known—or estimated—speed. Obviously you must always use the same timepiece. When you run out your time, don't just keep going in the hope something will turn up. Stop and listen, take a sounding, or make a square. See Appendix E.

Charts. An old and reliable friend of the writer's was anchored in Rockland Harbor one foggy morning, cleaning up after breakfast and waiting for the fog to scale up, when he heard the motors of a power cruiser approaching. Presently a large varnished and bechromed cruiser churned out of the fog, threw both motors into reverse, and came to a stop close by. The owner, clad picturesquely in a yachting cap and shorts, appeared from the wheelhouse and hailed.

"Hey, which way to Bar Harbor?"

Somewhat startled by the apparition and by the question, he was tempted to reply, "Follow the yellow brick road," but instead invited the "captain" aboard. As the visitor squeezed down the hatch, the downeaster unrolled the chart of Penobscot Bay on the bunk.

"Say," ejaculated the motorboater, "that's a swell map. Where do you get those? And what's all the numbers?"

It appeared later that he had come up from Marblehead in his new boat, navigating from the map in a railroad timetable.

This story, which comes to the surface over and over again with different corroborative details, leads one to believe that there is a special providence which watches over the ignorant. The rest of us need to provide ourselves with proper charts before we start.

Charts are published by the National Ocean Survey and are sold at outlets in almost every maritime city and in a great many smaller harbor towns frequented by yachtsmen. However, inventories are limited, especially late in the season, so it is well to provide yourself with those charts you will need before you start. Recently, appropriations for charts have been sharply cut. Charts will become more expensive and will be issued less frequently. Charts may be ordered by mail or telephone from the following outlets: Hagstrom Map and Travel Center, 57 West 43rd Street, New York, NY 10036; L. J. Harri, Nautical Booksellers, 120 Lewis Wharf, Boston, MA 02110; Chase-Leavitt & Co., 10 Dana Street, Portland, ME 04112. Charts can also be ordered by mail from National Ocean Survey, Distribution Branch (N/CG33), 6501 Lafayette Avenue, Riverdale, MD 20737. A check should accompany the order. Chart catalogs are free upon request.

First you will need a small-scale chart of the whole coast such as 13006 or 13260. You can use it for planning your trip, for orienting your guests, and for offshore runs. Then you will need a set of the 1:80,000 scale charts for planning a day's run or for selecting alternate routes. The 1:40,000 scale charts and the 1:20,000 scale are essential for navigating harbors, intricate channels, and the bays and passages not covered by the smaller-scale charts. The "SC," small-craft, versions are more detailed and more frequently updated than the standard version.

The date of publication of the chart is the latest date at which corrections have been made. You can keep your portfolio of charts up to date by subscribing to *Notices to Mariners,* published free by your local Coast Guard District. To make these corrections weekly can be a nuisance and often one gets behind. Another solution is to buy the *Light List,* published annually, and update charts from that. A more expensive but less time-consuming solution is to buy a *Chart Kit* from Better Boating Associates, 10 Commerce Road, Rockland, MA 02370, telephone (800) 242-7854. This is a spiral-bound book containing about 80 charts or sections of charts. Region 3 contains charts from Cape May to Nantucket, Region 2 from Block Island to the Canadian border. In 1994 the price for each was $94.95, far less than the NOS charts necessary to cover the same territory. The chart sections are well selected and cover almost everything covered by the NOS charts. These *Kits* are published about every two years and corrections are issued at least annually. The *Kits* can be used as they come, or used to update the NOS charts. *Chart Kits* covering smaller areas are available at lower cost.

Another Better Boating development is the electronic chart. This can be keyed in to your loran or GPS receiver to show on a screen a section of a chart and your position on it second by second.

A new and less expensive method is to buy "smart charts" through Boat/U.S. These are NOAA charts updated by computer to within a week of date of purchase. In 1994 all corrected East Coast charts were available at $19.95 each to members and $24.95 each to non-members. Call (800) 937-2628. International Sailing Supply, 320 Cross Street, Punta Gorda, FL 33950, sells updated waterproof charts printed on both sides at about the same price.

Canadian charts can be obtained from the outlets listed above. They can also be ordered from the Hydrographic Chart Distribution Office, Department of Fisheries and Oceans, 1675 Russell Road, P.O. Box 8080 Ottawa, Ontario, CANADA K1G 3H6.

Some charts, both United States and Canadian, show soundings in meters. A table of equivalents is useful, but for quick work, 1 fathom is roughly equivalent to 2 meters, and one meter equals 3 feet.

The alert navigator will notice that charted buoys are occasionally not in the position charted and, further, that they sometimes wind themselves up in their own mooring chains and submerge completely. Nevertheless, the ledges and islands don't move and are, for the most part, very accurately charted. Floating aids are to be regarded with suspicion.

Publications. The navigator's shelf should include among others the following reference books:

United States Coast Pilot. Volume I covers the coast from Eastport to Cape Cod, and Volume II from Cape Cod to Sandy Hook. The books are corrected and republished annually and contain many details not included in this *Guide.* The first two chapters are particularly valuable for specific information on drawbridges, anchorage areas, radiotelephone rules, pollution regulations, and emergency Coast Guard procedures.

Eldridge Tide and Pilot Book. This almost indispensable compendium of valuable information is published annually by Marion Jewett White, 34 Commercial Wharf, Boston, MA 02110, and is available at many marine stores along the shore. It contains tide tables for the region covered by this *Guide* and, most importantly, tidal current charts for each hour of the tide for Buzzards Bay, Vineyard and Nantucket Sounds, Boston Harbor, Narragansett Bay, Long Island Sound, and New York Harbor. There are also current tables for the Cape Cod Canal, Woods Hole, Pollock Rip, Newport, The Race, Bridgeport, Willets Point, Hell Gate, the Narrows, and the Battery.

Other useful and interesting information fills the book's more than 250 pages. It is wise to purchase the book early in the season and to become familiar with what it contains. It has been constructed by an experienced navigator and is constantly being improved.

Reed's Almanac. This book does much the same thing and includes more astronomical data.

Light List, Volume I. Published by the Department of Transportation, U.S. Coast Guard, this book contains all lights, fog signals, buoys, day beacons, radio beacons, racons, and loran stations between the St. Croix River in Maine and Little River in South Carolina. It is published annually and contains more information about each aid to navigation than can be shown on the chart.

Navigation Rules. In 1977 the United States adopted new international rules of the road and changed the boundaries of inland waters to put under international rules almost the entire coast, except for major commercial harbors used by foreign vessels, and in 1993 made further changes. It would be well to have a copy of the new rules aboard and to become familiar with them. They differ in some significant details from the old rules, particularly as they concern sailing vessels, whistle signals, and fog signals.

Logbook. Although this is not a publication, it deserves a prominent place on the navigator's bookshelf. Do not buy a fancy yacht log, all ruled in columns, at vast expense. Get a hardbound blank book such as law students use.

If kept up to date, the logbook is a legal document concerning the vessel's operation should a "regrettable incident" occur. The skipper should enter in it the time of arrival and departure at various buoys and landmarks, and his course and speed. Especially on a run in the fog he should record every detail of the run, including set of the tide, sounds of surf or gulls, soundings, loran readings, or whatever may be useful. If he fails to find a buoy or mark, he can rework his course and make a good guess as to his location.

Record in the back of the logbook the serial numbers of engine, radio, and other expensive equipment. Include the capacity of tanks; height of mast above the water; amount of copper paint needed to cover the bottom; location of the heel of the rudder relative to something on deck, in case it is necessary to go on a strange railway; size, pitch, and rotation of the propeller; radio call letters; names, addresses, and telephone numbers of the yacht's insurance agent and of all people aboard— whatever vital statistics are likely to be needed in short order.

Most importantly, however, the logbook should contain the things you want to remember about the trip. Names of people, vessels, and places that you want to remember you will, of course, include. Also write about your crew—what they did and said, how they felt, what they particularly enjoyed. Have a good time writing the book and you will enjoy reading it.

5. Electronic Equipment. For centuries men have sailed the New England coast without the aid of electronics, and some people still do. Nevertheless, there are a few relatively inexpensive aids that may be of great help.

Fathometer. This instrument saves the picturesque but cold, wet, and slow operation of sounding with a lead. The fathometer is especially useful in fog navigation. The chart indicates contour lines at 18, 30, 60, and 120 feet. You can follow one of these with the fathometer, often right into a harbor. In Maine, especially, ends of points make off a long way underwater. And on the back of Cape Cod, the bottom slopes evenly off the beach. You can often locate your position from the depth.

The fathometer is not as useful in shallow water as one might think, for it gives the depth under the boat only and gives no hint of what is ahead.

Radio Direction Finder (RDF). This is a useful instrument, if not as precise as radar and loran machines. You can use it to "home in" on a station, but remember in approaching a radio beacon that you may be on a converging course with a 100,000-ton tanker. Be alert to sounds from astern as well as from both sides. *Eldridge* gives the frequencies of the RDF stations and so does the *Light List.* If not dead accurate, at least the machine gives a useful indication.

VHF Radiotelephone. This is now almost a necessity. Most yachts and almost all commercial vessels are so equipped and many of them monitor channel 16 consistently. In case of sickness, injury, or accident, a call on channel 16 to the Coast Guard will bring quick advice or assistance.

Channel 16 is now reserved primarily for emergency use. Channel 9 is now the hailing channel. It is overcrowded. Shift to another immediately.

In case of doubt concerning the exact location, course, and speed of a vessel that appears threatening, a call on channel 13 or 16 will clarify the situation in a moment's quiet conversation. It can save a lot of horn blowing.

Bridgetenders monitor channels 13 and 16. When they can't hear your little horn, they will respond to a radio call.

Because many harbors are now very crowded, moorings for transients are not always available and there is little or no room to anchor, a call to a harbormaster or marina on channel 9 may secure you a berth for the night.

By calling the Marine Operator on channel 26 or 28, you can be connected through the telephone system with anyone ashore with whom you wish to talk. You can tell your friends ashore at what time you will be listening and they can call you through the Marine Operator. But remember that everything you say on the radio is public.

Bear in mind that the instrument is not for casual chatter although it is too often so used. Call on channel 9, shift to a working channel, say what you have to say, and sign off.

The rules and conventions for the use of the radiotelephone are clearly set forth in *How to Use Your Marine Radiotelephone*, a pamphlet published by the Federal Communications Commission and available for $14 from Radio Technical Commission for Marine Services, Box 19087, Washington, DC 20036.

Many vessels, cars, and trucks carry citizens-band sets. These have a short range but are very widely used. A great many fishermen have them and keep them turned up to a maximum volume to keep in touch with each other and with a home base. A call for help on CB may be the quickest way to get assistance.

Cellular telephones are now increasingly common and increasingly useful.

Many vessels carry an EPIRB, an Emergency Position Indicating Radio Beacon. This little long-range radio will utter a call for help when activated and is entirely independent of the vessel's power supply or antenna. Therefore, it can be used in case of fire, dismasting, stranding, or collision and can be thrown into the dinghy or life raft if one must abandon the vessel. It broadcasts on frequencies monitored by commercial airplanes, by larger Coast Guard vessels, and by some shore stations. Search planes can home in on it and find a distressed vessel quickly. It is an expensive gadget, but it may make all the difference. Be sure your EPIRB is registered with NOAA so your signal can be identified.

Radar, GPS, and Loran. For any of these to be of real use in the fog, the skipper must practice with it in clear weather until he knows its strengths and weaknesses. Once one has learned to sort out the patterns on the radar screen, he must learn to interpret them accurately. One yacht, running for a buoy on her radio screen, came bow to bow with another. Each had missed the buoy and was running for the other.

Loran is most valuable after you have kept a record of the readings at important buoys as you go along. The readings are highly repeatable. If you record the reading at an important buoy or punch it into the machine's memory, when you return to that reading, the buoy will be there. The TD readings are more accurate than the latitude-longitude readings. It is worthwhile to learn to use them. As long as the machine is working, it seems highly reliable.

The latest miracle machine is GPS. If it does what it is said to do, it is a great source of comfort to the navigator.

The principal danger with these aids is that they can allay anxiety to the point of carelessness. The responsible navigator will rely steadfastly on clock and compass, on log, lead, and lookout, and use electronics as a helpful supplement.

6. Safety Equipment. Anyone taking command of a vessel is responsible for the safety of those aboard. This is a legal and a moral obligation sanctioned by long tradition. The skipper, before he drops the mooring, should be sure that he has the required government equipment, consisting of a life preserver for each person aboard, adequate fire extinguishers, bell, horn, and proper running lights in working order. The provident skipper will add an efficient bilge pump, at least two good anchors with 200 feet of anchor rode for each, a complete first-aid kit and a copy of Dr. Paul Sheldon's *First Aid Afloat*, a ring buoy or horseshoe buoy carried loosely on deck with a strobe light attached, and a tall pole weighted to float upright. A pole in the water is much easier to see from the yacht than a man, and a man in the water can see the pole and perhaps make his way to it to await rescue. The yacht should be provided with a dinghy and a quickly inflatable rescue raft big enough to accommodate all hands. Next to fire, the greatest danger to a cruising yacht is a huge commercial vessel. In a locker handy to the helmsman should be a powerful electric light that will bring the mate out on the bridge of a tanker at a range of a mile. Some yachts carry strobe lights at the masthead. It may not be legal, but it may save your life. Flares are also useful scarers. Probably the best defense in all weather, however, is a good radar reflector. Some skippers keep one aloft at all times. A radar reflector can be improvised by hanging up a pie plate or frying pan, but one composed of three planes intersecting at right angles is better.

Seldom is a well-equipped cruising boat lost, and seldom are yachtsmen injured. Compared to driving a car, sailing is the epitome of safety. Nevertheless, accidents do happen at sea; and if the proper equipment is on hand, serious loss or injury may be averted.

Recent studies by the Coast Guard and Boat/U.S. based on increasingly accurate reports of accidents suggest that alcohol is far too often a significant cause. One of the best safety precautions the yachtsman can take is to do his serious drinking over an anchor.

7. Pollution. The major issues on this topic are enormously important and affect the entire population of the world. Jacques Cousteau, who ought to know, gives the oceans only forty years to live. If life in the ocean is seriously damaged, yachting won't be a problem. In this volume we cannot hope to deal with the major issues of pollution, but we might consider what yachtsmen can do to keep their own environment clean and improve coastal conditions as much as possible.

In the last few years considerable progress has been made in cleaning up the waters on which we sail. In the old days, you could throw overboard a paper bag or a paper plate, knowing that in half an hour it would disintegrate. Now, however, with the wide use of plastics, most things you throw overboard will float forever. Most of us know this, and although we have been distressed to see plastic-foam drinking cups floating jauntily 30 miles offshore and beer cans bobbing in the Fundy tide rips, in general there is nothing like the mess afloat there used to be. The trash cans ashore are stuffed and running over. Two little boys came alongside one night in a skiff and offered to carry ashore our garbage and sold us some of their mother's blueberry tarts instead of asking payment, in an effort to make cleanliness both attractive and profitable.

Sewage from yachts has become a sufficient problem to attract federal attention. All yachts are required to carry a holding tank. Many harbor towns, especially those frequented by live-aboards and cruising yachts, have found pollution intolerable and have established no-discharge zones in which one *must* use a holding tank. Places in which shellfish are harvested are also protected in this way. Therefore, necessarily, pumpout stations have been established in a great many harbors. A list by states and harbors as of 1994 appears in Appendix C, and locations of pumpout services are listed in the accounts of many individual harbors.

One can also provide a means for pumping the accumulation overboard, but one must go well offshore to do it. Still, an offshore run may be preferable to waiting in line at a marina.

More serious than sewage is the problem of municipal and industrial pollution, including the danger of oil from tankers and refineries.

Until a solution to this problem is found, about all a yachtsman can do is to take his trash ashore where it came from and to support, both morally and financially, the organizations that are working on the problem of pollution.

8. Conservation. Various groups, including Friends of Nature, the National Audubon Society, the Island Institute, and the Nature Conservancy in particular, are raising money by subscription to buy and preserve wild areas of the coast. It is not our purpose to list these places, for the list would be out of date in a month. Rather, we call on all those who love the coast to do three things:

First, whenever you land, especially on an island, be sure to leave nothing there but your footprints. Build no fires! The soil on some islands is composed of rotted vegetation built slowly through centuries. The soil is thin, and in late summer it dries out right down to the bedrock. In this condition it is inflammable. A fire that gets into the soil will smolder, flaring up perhaps when the wind fans it, and will in a week reduce the island to an ash heap.

Second, be careful of wildlife. The ecological balances are very delicately adjusted. To walk through a meadow where terns are nesting may destroy some eggs and chicks, however careful you are, and also may drive mothers away from the nests either permanently or for so long as to damage the young. Petrels nest in holes. Tread on the ground over the hole and you may cave it in. Your pet dog, glad of a run ashore, may do serious damage to sheep or small animals.

Lastly, consider devoting 10 percent of your fitting-out bills to one of the organizations mentioned above.

Those interested in a nationwide analysis of conservation problems and progress and their solution should read *Islands of America,* published by the U.S. Department of the Interior, Bureau of Outdoor Recreation, Washington, DC 20240, and *Islands in Time* by Philip W. Conkling, Down East Publishing, Camden, ME 1981.

9. The Authors' Prejudices. Should anyone have the hardihood to read this book through, he will doubtless become aware of some of the writers' prejudices. Even with the best intentions, it is impossible to comment helpfully on so many places without occasionally making judgments with which others disagree. We admit to preferring sail to power and have made various comments about prevailing winds that powerboat men may find irrelevant. However, we hold no hard feelings toward those who prefer to motor and indeed have noted places that they may find uncomfortable or even dangerous and other places accessible to them alone.

Perhaps our most violent prejudice we would do well to air at once.

We are strongly prejudiced in favor of the people who live in coastal communities the year round. The towns are theirs. They pay the taxes, provide the facilities, do the work. Yachtsmen are at best uninvited guests and should behave themselves accordingly. The local people, I suppose, are "natives" in that we all are natives of some town, but we should not speak of them as if they lived in grass huts. Local people, even in this standardized age, still have a characteristic manner of speech, still use colloquialisms that we consider picturesque, still dress in a way different from ours. Nevertheless, they are not living isolated lives in a part of the world little known to city people. They listen to the same radio programs, see the same TV shows, hear the same weather reports, go to the same movies that yachtsmen do. They also deposit their money in the same banks and own shares of the same stocks. In some cases they are far ahead of their visitors.

I am reminded of the story about the city man who accosted a resident of Cape Cod and asked him the way to West Dennis. The old gentleman eyed the young city man thoughtfully, pondered a moment, and admitted that he didn't know the way to West Dennis. The city man said, patronizingly, "You don't get around much, do you, Grampa?"

"Well," answered the old gentleman, "I've been to Hong Kong, Singapore, and Manila, but I never had any reason to go to West Dennis."

One proud moment in the life of one writer came when a Maine lady said, "You aren't a summer fellow; you're a local resident who goes away winters."

Most of these people, at least the ones who make their livings afloat, have poured more salt water out of their boots than we have ever sailed over. They know what is dangerous, and their advice is worth taking. Although you may not know it, they are watching out for one another and for you. If you ever get into trouble, you may be amazed at how fast help comes. My father and I in a skiff were run down by a seiner. Before the seiner could circle back to us, a lobsterman was alongside helping us out of the water. If a fisherman gives you advice, take it and thank him. If he helps you in a difficult crisis, thank him and offer him a drink in the cockpit; and if he has spent time, gasoline, or gear in your behalf, you can offer to pay for it. You can pay most effectively, however, with your affection and respect.

One more piece of gratuitous and prejudiced advice: don't ruin a cruise by hurrying. Early starts can be delightful. Anchoring by starlight can be magical. But to start early and run late, using the engine whenever the wind drops or hauls ahead, can be grueling. You will ruin your own disposition and your crew's. Vary your activities. Get in early and take a walk ashore. If the breeze falls off, ghost along or lie becalmed. You will appreciate the breeze when it comes in. If you find it thick or raining when you put your head out the hatch in the morning, pull it in again and lay over for half a day or a day. Read a book or play cards or go up to the store to see who's there. Those who like to cook can profitably be encouraged.

On a cruise with my son and my new daughter-in-law, I nearly ruined her cruising life by running all day in the fog from Cutler outside Moose Peak and up to Trafton Island. It was no fun, there was no need of it, and had the lady been anything less than saintly, she never would have gone to sea again. Don't let it happen to you.

10. Changes. Fundamental changes are taking place on the New England coast and the rate of change is accelerating. The islands, capes, and ledges still lie where they were moored centuries ago, but the harbors and the shores around them are not the same.

I was once asked, seriously, by a Power Squadron member who had just completed a course in seamanship whether he could count on marinas and moorings on a cruise to Maine or whether he should take an anchor. I almost choked on that one! But now I am not so sure that for a Long Island Sound or Cape Cod sailor it is such a foolish question.

There are many more yachts afloat now than there used to be, perhaps because the salesman is such an important member of the "boating industry," perhaps because there are more people in megalopolis than there used to be and more of them have discovered either the joys or the social distinction of owning a yacht. Residents of waterfront communities own so many boats that the harbors are choked with their moorings. No longer is there room for a visitor to anchor in scarcely any harbor west of Portland, Maine. Consequently, marinas have been established where one lies in a slip with water, electricity, telephone, and TV laid on and privacy a commodity unobtainable. The demand for these slips has grown so that in many places there are long waiting lists for slips whose annual rental is a significant percentage of the cost of the boat. So what is the transient to do, circling the harbor in search of mooring or slip like a Saturday shopper in a parking lot?

Conversations with harbormasters in 1994 revealed a growing frustration. Already the Buzzards Bay yachtsman knows that he will seldom find swinging room in Hadley Harbor and that if he arrives at Cuttyhunk after 3 o'clock, he will have to lie outside. There are harbors farther west where one cannot get in at all after early afternoon.

The cruising skipper has three choices. He can make reservations ahead by telephone or radio, so planning his cruise and his day that he arrives at a mooring every night. To tie a cruise to such a schedule rather takes the bloom off the rose. Or he can cruise in June or September, when the crowds are somewhat reduced and his chances of being accommodated are much better. Or he can head offshore for the coast east of Portland, where most of the harbors are still comparatively uncrowded and the shores, if not deserted, are at least less densely populated. With the development of increasingly less expensive loran, radar, and GPS, some of the terrors of fog are reduced, and the coast of Maine is only an overnight run from Cape Ann.

Another change, becoming increasingly obvious now in Maine, is that shore property is being bought up, subdivided, and developed. The cruising man, returning to a secluded anchorage, perhaps intentionally omitted from this *Guide,* where he has been accustomed in years past to dig a bucket of clams and boil a few lobsters, finds a new cottage overlooking the cove. And the inhabitants of that cottage, looking at a yacht anchored in their front yard, are a bit discouraged to find that after having come so far for seclusion, they have not come far enough.

Yet another change is the increase of "tourism" ashore. More and more motorists come to waterfront communities to seek local color. They find that their arrival has stimulated the growth of motels, fast-food chains, gasoline stations, and innumerable gift shops and has completely submerged the atmosphere they came to find. They have only each other to look at. This presents a poor prospect ashore for the cruising man as well. Further, the increase in automobile transportation has made first the coastwise steamers, then the railroads, and now the bus lines unprofitable, although in 1994 buses still ran from Portland east.

Fuel and fresh water are more difficult to find. The new environmental laws make the installation, renewal, and maintenance of underground tanks so difficult and expensive that many owners of marinas and wharves are giving them up. Very few Canadian harbors offer fuel in small quantities. If you need over 100 gallons, you can call a tank truck to the wharf, but otherwise you must lug it from the gasoline station in cans.

The same is increasingly true in Maine, New Hampshire, Massachusetts, Rhode Island, Connecticut, and New York harbors.

Water, too, is in some cases a problem as increased tourism is putting greater demands on water supplies in shore communities. This is especially true on Cape Cod where the only source of water is rain which soaks into the sand and thence runs into wells. For instance, in Round Pond and in Jonesport, Maine, no water hose is available. In Cutler, water coming from a well piped to the shore was sharply curtailed. When a careless yachter used the hose to wash down decks, the owner of the well shut off water to all yachts. In most harbors, water is available still, but it may not be so for long.

Every town used to have its grocery store carrying the necessaries of life and a cheering selection of the luxuries. It was also a social center and, for the visiting yachtsman with a modicum of humility and tact, a source of local information and colorful reminiscence. Lately local people have taken to driving 10 miles or more inland to a supermarket with a wider selection and lower prices. Fishermen on Matinicus, Swans Island, Isle au Haut, and Frenchboro sell their lobsters and buy fuel, bait, and groceries at mainland towns. One should provision one's vessel for several days ahead.

The era of the "gentleman's yacht" is almost over. One sees alongshore now very few 50-foot schooners, yawls, or ketches shining with brass and varnish, flying the proper flags at the proper time, and having a paid skipper and deckhand to row the owner ashore in a varnished cedar skiff. There are a great many more fiberglass sloops of standard design motoring about or sailing under jib alone. More people are getting on the water and enjoying it, but at the expense of a style recollected with nostalgia.

Before World War II when we sailed past lighthouses, we often got a wave from the keeper or from his wife's laundry on the line. Since then, the lights have all been automated, and now many of them are being turned over to the Island Institute, which is passing them on to organizations that will preserve them as historic and picturesque additions to the coastal scene. The Coast Guard reserves the right to maintain the machinery but threatens to discontinue even that in some cases. Lighthouses are antiques.

Another change is reflected in the fishing industry. There are almost no active fish weirs in Maine and few in New Brunswick. With planes to spot schools, herring and menhaden are being seined offshore. Cod and haddock are seriously depleted. You will see few active draggers now, and what they catch is small. No longer can one becalmed drop a line overside with any hope of jigging up a codfish. There is a sharp quota on tuna and a limit on the size of a striped bass one can keep. The deficit is being made up with sea urchins for the Japanese market and farmed salmon in pens. And in many towns you now need a license to go clamming.

Old-timers half a century ago complained that "stink pots" had taken all the fun out of yachting, and old men twenty-five years ago growled that "Clorox bottles" had permanently perverted yacht design. Changes are inevitable and they are inevitably distressing to some. Yet as long as the islands hold fast to their moorings and the brave west wind still blows, there will be those who will sail the coast and love it.

Part Two

HARBORS

Whitehall, New York to the Headwaters of The Saint John River, New Brunswick

Chapter III

The Hudson River and the Passage from Long Island Sound

Let me transport you to those wild blue mountains
That rear their summits near the Hudson's wave
Though not the loftiest that begirt the land,
They yet sublimely rise, and on their heights
Your souls may have a sweet foretaste of heaven . . .*

Introduction to the Hudson

Before embarking upon the Hudson, we might first gain a sense of its beauty and majesty from vivid impressions written long ago by famous men closely associated with this great river of history.

Let us therefore start at the source, its discovering in 1872 by Verplanck Colvin, mountain explorer and engineer. Standing by Lake Tear of the Clouds, a 2-acre pond on the southwest slope of Mount Marcy in the Adirondacks, Colvin described his view. It is "a minute, unpretending tear of the clouds, as it were, a lonely pool, shivering in the breezes of the mountains, and sending its limpid surplus through Feldspar Brook and to the Opalescent River, the wellspring of the Hudson."

Fifty years earlier, Thomas Cole, the acknowledged leader of the Hudson River school of painting, brilliantly described a sunrise in the Catskills reflecting the lure the river held for him:

*By Thomas Cole in *Picturesque Catskills—Greene County*, by R. Lionel De Lisser (Northampton, Mass.: Picturesque Publishing Co., 1894).

31

The mists were resting on the vale of the Hudson like drifted snow: tops of distant mountains in the east were visible—things of another world. The sun rose from bars of pearly hue: above there were clouds light and warm, and the clear sky was of a cool grayish tint. The mist below the mountains began first to be lighted up, and the trees on the tops of the lower hills cast their shadows over the misty surface—innumerable streaks. A line of light on the extreme horizon was very beautiful. Seen through the breaking mists, the fields were exquisitely fresh and green. Though dark, the mountainside was sparkling; and the Hudson, where it was uncovered to the sight, slept in deep shadow.

Our third pathfinder is the author Washington Irving, whose writing has always closely identified him with the Hudson. Sailors can readily share his enthusiasm for its grandeur in reading these stirring words from the diary of his first voyage up the Hudson in 1800:

What a time of intense delight was that first sail through the Highlands! I sat on the deck as we slowly tided along at the foot of those stern mountains, and gazed with wonder and admiration at cliffs impending far above me, crowned with forests, with eagles sailing and screaming around them; or listened to the unseen stream dashing down precipices or beheld rock, and tree, and cloud, and sky reflected in the glassy stream of the river. And then how solemn and thrilling the scene as we anchored at night at the foot of these mountains, clothed with overhanging forests; and everything grew dark and mysterious; and I heard the plaintive note of the whippoorwill from the mountain-side, or was startled now and then by the sudden leap and heavy splash of the sturgeon.

The Hudson River with all its delights for us still flows along majestically at the very back door of Long Island Sound. It is only 18 miles to the Hudson from City Island by way of the East and Harlem rivers, through Hell Gate. And don't let the name of that gate discourage you from leaving the Sound by the back door. Because, if it does, you will miss one of the most beautiful river cruises on the Atlantic Coast, perhaps *the* most beautiful.

Note the current through Hell Gate where the East and Harlem
Rivers Meet. *Aero Graphics Corp.*

From the point where the Harlem River enters the Hudson (which is
12 miles above the Battery) to the Federal Dam and Lock at Troy, New
York, is a distance of about 120 nautical miles. From the Battery at the
south end of Manhattan to what is generally called the head of navigation on the Hudson, it is 132 miles. Please note that throughout the
Guide, all miles on water will be nautical miles and all miles on land will
be "land" miles. But for cruising yachting people who want to explore
further, perhaps go to lovely Lake Champlain, the Troy Lock is not the
head of navigation but the beginning of a further cruise of 54 miles to
Whitehall at the foot of Lake Champlain. Beckoning farther, above
Lake Champlain, is the Richelieu River leading into the St. Lawrence;
but that is another story. Still another story is a cruise along the Mohawk
River and the subsequent canals, westward from the Hudson, starting

just above Troy, at Waterford. This leads to Lakes Ontario and Erie, and our chapter is about the Hudson River.

While, except in the vicinity of Albany, almost all of the Hudson River is attractive, the most beautiful part, in our opinion, is below Catskill, which is 85 miles north of the Harlem River and 97 miles from the Battery. But include Catskill in this, for Catskill Creek is our favorite port on the entire Hudson. The parts of the Hudson that are most impressive are: (1) *along Manhattan Island,* where the grandeur is humanmade; (2) *along the Palisades,* which begin in New Jersey, opposite New York City, and continue a short distance north of the New York State line; and (3) most beautiful of all, the section of the river that lies *between Stony Point* (where there is a first-class yacht basin at Grassy Point, 22¹/₂ miles above the Harlem River) *and Newburgh,* 41 miles above the Harlem. Along this last stretch of 18¹/₂ miles are such famous landmarks as Bear Mountain (1305 feet) and St. Anthony's Nose (900 feet) on the other side; the United States Military Academy at West Point, part of it perched on a high cliff; Storm King Mountain (1,355 feet), and Bull Hill (1,425 feet), on the east shore, less well known but higher.

If you can't make the whole Hudson trip, go as far as Newburgh anyway; but we'd hate to have you miss Catskill, where the steep hills are reflected in the still water. It is only 85 miles above the Harlem, as we noted. We shan't soon forget a night spent there in October with our boat lying quietly at the dock and the moon reflected on the glassy water. This was the time of year when the banks of the Hudson were of red, yellow, and gold as well as green, adding a new beauty to the scene as we went "Cruising down the river on a Sunday afternoon."

Through James Fenimore Cooper's writings, we can receive an impression of what a Hudson River cruise was all about more than 150 years ago:

In 1803, the celebrated river we were navigating, though it had all the natural features it possesses today [1844], was by no means the same picture of moving life. The steamboat did not appear on its surface until four years later. . . . In that day, the passenger did not hurry on board . . . he passed his morning saying adieu, and when he repaired to the vessel it was with gentlemanlike leisure, often to pass hours on board previously to sailing. . . . There was no jostling of each other . . . no impertinence manifested, no swearing about missing the eastern or southern boats, or Schenectady, or Saratoga, or Boston trains, on account of a screw being loose. . . . On the contrary, wine and fruit were provided, as if the travellers intended to enjoy themselves; a journey in that day was a *festa*. . . . The vessel usually got aground once at least, and frequently several times a trip; and often a day or two were thus delightfully lost, giving the stranger an opportunity of visiting the surrounding country.

The Hudson River rises in Tear of the Clouds, a small lake in the Adirondack Mountains, in the northeastern section of New York State. It flows in a general southerly direction and empties into New York Bay, about 300 miles from its source. Most of it is deep, though there are some shoals to avoid. Navigation is not at all difficult, for the river is extremely well buoyed. But above Kingston it is more challenging because of the numerous steep shoals and middle grounds. River barges usually follow the shoreline that is most favorable with regard to wind and current; with a strong northwest wind, they will favor the west shore, plying either north or south. While tide water extends to Albany, the river is generally fresh above Poughkeepsie. The mean range of tide is 4.5 feet at the Battery, 3.7 feet at Yonkers, 2.8 feet at Newburgh, 3.1 feet at Poughkeepsie, 3.7 feet at Kingston, and 4.6 feet at Albany. Currents for different parts of the river are given in the *Tidal Current Tables for the Atlantic Coast of North America* and range from 0.6 knot average velocity at strength of current to 2.0, the strongest currents being in the lower Hudson off Manhattan (where it runs 1.4 knots flood and 1.4 knots ebb at the Battery), 1.3 and 1.6 knots at Kingston, and 0.3 knot flood and 0.8 knot ebb at Albany. Around the entrance to Spuyten Duyvil and the Harlem River currents are swift and erratic. Numerous fish traps are planted each spring in the lower Hudson, usually from about the middle of March to the middle of May, during the seasonal running of shad to the spawning grounds in the upper Hudson. In general, the traps extend from one-fourth to two-thirds the distance across the river from the west side of the channel to the New Jersey shore. Your charts also show the fish-trap areas in the 30-mile stretch beginning about 5 miles above the Battery and extending upriver to Stony Point. Outer limits of the nets usually are marked by flags during the day and by lights at night. Caution is advised when navigating a fish-trap area, since broken-off poles from previous traps may remain under the surface.*

*Data in this paragraph from the *Coast Pilot*.

From the point of its southward turn into the old glacial channel the Hudson flows through a gorge within an old valley. The floor of the gorge from almost as far north as Albany to its mouth lies below the level of the sea, creating a fiord or estuary where the fresh waters are ever subject to the invasion of salty ocean tides. . . . For thousands of years the great stream ran, constantly lowering its level and digging one of the deepest canyons the world has ever known. From a shallow beginning, as scientists have discovered by soundings, the floor of the gorge dropped steeply until in some places it reached a depth of 3600 feet, a thousand feet deeper than the Royal Gorge of the Colorado. Had there been human life then, a traveler in a boat on the Hudson might have looked up to the blue sky between walls more than two miles high.*

But the sea came back and buried the canyon.

Once many great private estates lined the Hudson. Some still do, but now a considerable number of them have been taken over by various

*From *The Hudson,* by Carl Carmer, in "The Rivers of America" series (Rinehart & Co., Inc., New York)—a very interesting book for those who cruise the Hudson.

The Hudson Highlands taken northward from Plum Point. *Charles Porter.*

institutions: Catholic colleges and monasteries, Protestant organizations, museums, sanitaria, schools, etc.

There have been many changes since Giovanni da Verrazano, Floren-
tine explorer, wrote to his employer, Francis I of France, in July 1524:
"We have found," he said, "a pleasant place below steep little hills. And
from those hills a mighty deep-mouthed river ran into the sea." Eighty-
five years later, on September 2, 1609, an English sea captain, employed
by the Dutch East India Company to find the Northwest Passage to
China, sailed his *Half Moon* into the river that bears his name and came
to anchor near the mouth.

There are many good docks or sheltered anchorages in the 132 miles
of the Hudson River from the Battery to the Troy Lock. In the pages that
follow we have described the ones that we consider the most important,
thirty in all to Troy. We don't pretend to have covered all of them, and
even if we did, we should soon be out of date, for new ones are constantly
being developed, as the Hudson becomes more and more popular among
cruising yachtsmen. Evidence of the size of the boating population
traversing these waters comes from the New York Throughway Authority Department of Canals. In 1992, for instance, a total of 132,381
pleasure boats were lifted or lowered within the 57 locks interspersed
throughout the New York State Canal System.

Here is a table of the distances in nautical miles, most of them upriver
from the point where the Harlem River joins the Hudson. Distances are
given to a spot on the Hudson opposite each port. It may take ¹/₂ mile to
a mile or so to reach the dock.

Tidewater Area

Distance above the Battery

Weehawken (west shore)	4.
79th Street Marina (east shore)	6.
Edgewater (west shore)	8.5
Englewood Boat Basin (west shore, across from Harlem River)	12.
Harlem River (enters from east shore)	12.

Distance above Harlem River

Alpine Boat Basin (west shore)	4.

Hastings-on-Hudson (east shore, Tower Ridge Yacht Club)	7.
Tarrytown Harbor (east shore)	12.
Upper Nyack (west shore, Julius Petersen Inc., boatyard)	13.
Ossining (east shore)	16.5
Haverstraw (west shore)	20.5
Grassy Point (town Stony Point— west shore)	22.5
Montrose (east shore)	23.5
Peekskill (east shore, Peekskill Yacht Club)	26.
Garrison (east shore)	33.
Cold Spring (east shore)	35.4
Cornwall-on-Hudson (west shore)	37.5
Newburgh (west shore, Newburgh Yacht Club)	41.
New Hamburg (east shore)	46.5
Poughkeepsie (east shore)	53.5
Staatsburg, Indian Kill (east shore, Norrie Park Boat Basin)	61.5
Kingston, Rondout Creek (west shore, 2 miles to dock)	67.
Saugerties, Esopus Creek (west shore)	76.
Catskill, Catskill Creek (west shore)	85.
Athens (west shore)	89.
Coxsackie (west shore)	95.5
New Baltimore (west shore)	100.5
Coeymans (west shore)	102.
Castleton-on-Hudson (east shore)	105.5
Rensselaer (east shore, Albany Yacht Club)	112.5
Watervliet (west shore)	118.
Troy (east shore, Federal Lock)	120.

Above Tidewater Area
From (Federal Troy) Lock

North Troy	2.
Lock 1. Canalized, Upper Hudson	2.5
Mechanicsville	10.

Schuylerville	24.
Fort Edwards (beginning of Champlain Barge Canal)	34.
Smith Basin	41.
Whitehall (lower end of Lake Champlain)	54.
Total—the Battery to Lake Champlain	186.

We are hoping that the fellow who asked us if there were any good stopping places on the Hudson will read the above and then study our descriptions of these ports below. But first we must get to the Hudson.

City Island to the Hudson River, New York
(12366) (12339) (12342) (12335) (12341) (12345)

1. The Current. The important thing about the passage through the East River and its famous Hell Gate is to pick the current right. Unlike Long Island Sound, the ebb current here sets westward, the flood eastward. A good plan is to start from City Island about an hour before the ebb turns westward at Rikers Island (6 miles from City Island) and then carry the ebb through the East River and Hell Gate. From Whitestone Bridge to North Brother Island the current at mean velocity is $1\frac{1}{2}$ knots. In Hell Gate, off Mill Rock, the mean velocity at strength of current is about $3\frac{1}{2}$ knots for the eastward current and $4\frac{1}{2}$ knots for the westward (ebb current). In the Harlem River the *north* current toward the Hudson from Hell Gate flows while the *west* or ebb current is flowing through East River and Hell Gate—and vice versa. Thus, if you carry a favorable ebb current from Long Island Sound to Hell Gate (westward), you will also carry a favorable current (northward) through the Harlem River. The northerly current in the Harlem is considered the ebb, for after passing under the bridge at Hell Gate on its way to New York Bay, it swings around Ward and Randall Islands into the Harlem River and later joins the ebb current on the Hudson at Spuyten Duyvil. This is an added reason for picking the current right if you are headed for the Hudson from City Island. Currents in the Harlem River range from 2.8 opposite Little Hell Gate to 1.1 in other parts.

The authors are indebted to James Gordon Gilkey, Jr., who, as an experienced Hudson River skipper, provides us here with additional information on tidal currents. His description has been approved by the

Chief of Currents Section, Oceanography Division of the U.S. Department of Commerce.

Because the Hudson River between Manhattan Island and Troy, below the Federal Lock, for a distance of approximately 120 miles, is influenced both by the flow of tidal currents and by the downstream flow of the river, taking advantage of the current when cruising on the Hudson is a somewhat tricky business. Particularly going upstream, however, the alert cruising man can save both time and fuel by giving a little consideration to the flow of the current.

Under ordinary summer conditions, when most pleasure cruisers will be making the trip, the downstream flow of the Hudson River, eliminating the effect of tidal action, is approximately one-half a knot. There is, of course, considerable local variation, depending upon the width of the river at a given point, the fresh water flowing into the Hudson from tributary streams, and the location of the navigation channel with respect to the channel the current of the river follows.

Because of the flow of the river current downstream, the tidal current floods upstream for only a bit over five hours between slack waters, whereas the ebb current flows downstream for approximately seven hours. This discrepancy will puzzle a skipper the first time he travels up or down the Hudson River. Table #1 of the *Current Tables,* published by the National Ocean Survey, gives the times of slack water and the times and velocities of maximum current for a calendar year at various points along the coast. From this Table of Daily Current Predictions, giving the time when slack water occurs at the Narrows, New York Harbor, the cruising navigator can calculate, by using Table #2 in the same publication, the difference in the time slack water occurs at thirty different points along the Hudson between the Battery and Troy Lock. For every 20 miles traveled up the Hudson, slack water occurs at approximately an hour later than downstream. This rough generalization means that slack water at the Battery comes an hour and a half later than slack water in the Narrows; at the Thruway Bridge over the Tappan Zee just below Tarrytown slack water comes two and a half hours later than at the Narrows, at Poughkeepsie four and a half hours later, at Catskill about six hours later, and at Albany seven and a half hours later.

If one is cruising *up* the Hudson, if the time of departure can be scheduled for a couple of hours *after* the time of maximum *ebb* current, as given in Table #1 for the Narrows, and corrected in Table #2 for the point of departure on the Hudson, the current the cruiser will have to buck going upstream will diminish and after slack water will then for about five hours be in his favor before once again turning against him. The buoys marking the channel in the Hudson will quickly show whether or not his calculations are accurate. Since the ebb current flows at an average rate of 1 to 2 knots, and the average flood current flows between .8 and 1.6 knots, the advantage of going with the current is considerable. During times of spring tides (new and full moon) the velocities will be about 20 percent stronger; and at certain periods of the year (around October 15) the velocity of flood could be up to 2 knots and the ebb might run as strong as 3 knots. The effect upon fuel consumption of such currents, obviously, becomes a significant factor in any trip up or down the Hudson River.

It frequently happens that the difference of a few hours in departure time, in cruisers moving along at a speed of about 10 knots (which is maximum speed in any case in the canals for which the trip is planned), makes the difference between bucking the current or having a favorable current for much of the day. Since there are plenty of sights to see all along the Hudson while waiting for a favorable current, and since pleasure cruising is intended to be just that, adjusting the hour of departure to take advantage of the current is a game well worth the candle, and the price of fuel.

2. Distances. From City Island, the distances toward the Hudson are about as follows:

To Rikers Island, east end	6.
To Mill Rock, Hell Gate, where Harlem River comes in	11.

Via Harlem River

To the Harlem River entrance on the Hudson	18.

Around Manhattan Island

To the Battery	17.
To the Harlem River entrance on the Hudson	29.

Thus, it is about 11 miles farther if you go around Manhattan Island. But if you have time, it is an entrancing trip, which can also be made exciting by tides, traffic, and floating debris. Don't try it at night, when the driftwood may be invisible.

3. Bridges. Should you decide to reach the Hudson via the Harlem River, however, be advised that of the fifteen fixed and movable bridges that span the Harlem, separating the Bronx from Manhattan, nine have a clearance under 35 feet.

The draws of all the city-owned movable bridges on the Harlem River have been placed on Advance Notice Status by the U.S. Coast Guard. Also be advised that boat owners requiring a bridge opening to pass through the Harlem River should realize that all movable bridges will open on signal only between 10 A.M. and 5 P.M., except for the following: the Ward's Island, Willis Avenue, Madison Avenue, Third Avenue, 145th Street, Macombs Dam, University Heights, Broadway, 103rd Street, and Triboro bridges, which require a six-hour advance notice. The Park Avenue and Spuyten Duyvil bridges both open on demand.

Requests for openings of any of the bridges requiring six-hour notice should be directed to the City of New York Department of Transportation's Hot Line: (212) 566-3406. Of course, all bridges must open on demand for United States Government and City of New York vessels.

Once you have entered the Harlem River, having passed through Hell Gate or up the East River, the first bridge you will reach is a foot bridge at 103rd Street (55 feet, lift). After the 103rd Street Bridge come, in order, the Triboro Bridge (54 feet, lift), Willis Avenue Bridge (25 feet, swing), Third Avenue Bridge (26 feet, swing), Park Avenue Bridge (35 feet, lift), Madison Avenue Bridge (25 feet, swing), 145th Street Bridge (25 feet, swing), Macombs Dam Bridge (29 feet, swing), High Bridge (102 feet, fixed), Alexander Hamilton Bridge (103 feet, fixed), Washington Bridge (134 feet, fixed), University Heights Bridge (25 feet, swing), and then the Broadway Bridge, which is a lift bridge (24 feet high).

Now let Parton Keese describe the Harlem as he did in *The New York Times:*

> The Broadway Bridge operator, as all operators are required to do, keeps a record of the vessels passing through, as well as the time, and if he cannot make out the name on the hull (many times it is on the stern and impossible to see), he will shout for the skipper to tell him. . . .
>
> The Broadway Bridge is followed by a fixed bridge, the Henry Hudson (141 feet high), and then at last comes a railroad bridge of

the swing type, only 5 feet high but usually left in an open position, as trains seldom run on its tracks.

There are three types of bridges in the metropolitan waterways system that open for tall vessels: a swing bridge, which rotates on a mechanized turntable; a bascule, or draw, bridge, which breaks in the center and raises upward; and a lift bridge, which goes up like an elevator.

On the Harlem, however, there are only the swing and lift types, besides the fixed bridges, which are all more than 100 feet above water level.

Bridges are governed by federal law, which states that each skipper shall signify his request to have a bridge opened for him by signaling with one prolonged blast followed by one short blast of his horn or whistle.

Also, boat owners with vessels having appurtenances unessential to navigation, such as fishing outriggers, radio and television antennas, false stacks, and masts that are hinged, adjustable, or collapsible, are expected by the Coast Guard to lower such appurtenances, so as to avoid requests for bridge openings.

Here's a final word of caution to the boat owner planning a cruise through the Harlem River: Make sure you plan your trip in accordance with the tide schedules and bridge operating hours so that you don't get stranded between bridges.

4. Anchorages, City Island to Hudson River. After one passes between Throgs Neck and Willets Point, there are several places of anchor, of which we'll mention only those we consider fairly good. However, the anchorages or docks in the Hudson may be considered better and we'd recommend keeping on if there is still daylight.

a. Flushing Bay—World's Fair Marina (12339). As you approach College Point to port, you head in a southwesterly direction into Flushing Bay. Note that the Rikers Island channel's eastern entrance is completely obstructed by a lighted runway approach to LaGuardia Field and that just beyond, to the west, a bridge spans across this channel from the mainland to the island. The main channel into the bay is very clearly marked, and from lighted buoy 3 it is a straight run to the special anchorage and facilities at the World's Fair Marina, operated by Vinco Marine Management Corp. under the supervision of Jim Gardella of the Norwalk Cove Marina. Here is a moderately good anchorage, though somewhat exposed to the north and distant from the main passage. There are 350 deep-water slips, some of which can accommodate yachts 100 feet in length. Channel 71 is monitored for reservations and Pier 1, located farthest to the east, is reserved primarily for transient vessels. Gas, diesel fuel, ice, water, showers, mechanics, and a tight security system can all be found here. The independently run Grand Bay Marina Restaurant on the premises serves lunch and dinner. Subways to New York pass nearby but so does the noisy air traffic to and from the airport. This is one of the largest permanent facilities in the area and as such can probably serve most of your boat's needs.

b. East River—New York Skyports Marina (12335). This marina, overwater parking garage, and seaplane base, jutting out 350 feet from the west bank of the East River at 23rd Street, is easily identified by a large blue building. This is the river's only marina. The dockmaster, Captain Giulio Paties, who is on duty from April 1 to October 31, offers gas, diesel fuel, water, and electricity at the ten slips, which can accommodate vessels up to 120 feet overall. Since this is a unique spot, which is handy to the center of Manhattan, we suggest reserving your slip in advance by calling on VHF-13 or phoning (212) 686-4548.

Just to the north, along the riverfront, stands the United Nations International School. Farther up rises the attractive Waterside Plaza, on the third floor of which is a large open patio bordered by a bank, a liquor store, a hair stylist, a cleaner, and a general food store where supplies may be purchased. The intimate River Caper Restaurant, with a bar and a reasonably priced menu, is also right off this patio. Other food stores and restaurants may be found on nearby First and Third avenues.

c. East River—South Street Seaport (12335). The only tie-up for transient boats at the South Street Seaport is at the floating dock located between Piers 14 and 15. To obtain a slip for which there are either hourly or overnight fees, call ahead on VHF-72 or phone the dockmaster at (212) 425-0167. No services are provided. Make sure you put out plenty of fenders for boats here are widely exposed to the river traffic's wash.

South Street Seaport provides both an extraordinary maritime museum and a thriving marketplace housing more than 100 shops and restaurants. Historic ships, fine-art exhibitions, children's programs, a maritime craft center, a nineteenth-century print shop, a hands-on workshop, and tours—these and more bring New York City's maritime heritage to life for those fortunate enough to visit here.

The Visitors' Center is located at 12 Fulton Street, where you can gather information or make sailing reservations—phone (212) 669-9400. The Seaport is open daily from 10 A.M. to 5 P.M., with summer hours running daily from 10 A.M. to 6 P.M.

South Street Seaport, chartered by the New York State Board of Regents in 1967, set as its goal the restoration of this area officially designated as a State Historic Preservation Site. Twelve blocks of Old New York waterfront in Lower Manhattan, known as the "Street of Ships," have been beautifully restored. Other buildings of the early 1800s still survive and have been saved in the old Fulton Fish Market section. Nearby, northernmost Pier 17 was developed in 1985 into a lively shopping and restaurant mall. All this attracted 8 million visitors in 1985; for 1994 this number had increased to over 12 million.

During the last century, South Street was also a busy place, a home of packet ships, fishing schooners, clippers, and Long Island Sound steamers. It swarmed with seamen, merchants, travelers, and people bustling their way to market.

Today, these ships of the Seaport Museum are berthed at Piers 15 and 16, foot of Fulton Street: *Wavertree*, a 293-foot, full-rigged ship of 1885, undergoing restoration; the Lightship *Ambrose* of 1908; *Pioneer*, a cargo schooner of 1885, still actively cruising, and the *W. O. Decker*, a 43-foot tugboat (these last two vessels are available for charter); and one of the main attractions, the 347-foot, four-masted bark *Peking*, which joined this fleet in 1975.

The 84-foot *Lettie G. Howard*, a Gloucester fishing schooner of 1893, completed her restoration here in time for her centennial and celebrated by cruising home waters along the New England coast. Her future role may be as a sail training vessel providing enriching educational experiences for disadvantaged youth.

Ashore on Water Street is found the Museum Gallery and Library as well as the Chandlery selling fascinating nautical books, charts, and prints. Nearby is the Titanic Memorial Lighthouse, which for years rose atop the Seamen's Church Institute in New York. It dropped a time ball every day precisely at noon so that mariners on watch 6 miles at sea could set their chronometers accurately. Over at 16 Fulton Street there's a museum display open daily from 11 A.M. to 6 P.M. Nearby Sweet's Restaurant has the distinction of being New York's oldest seafood restaurant, whose doors first opened on Schermerhorn Row in 1845. Serving meals from 11:30 A.M. to 8:30 P.M. weekdays, it accepts no reservations; be prepared to line up! The Yankee Clipper Restaurant at the corner of John and South Streets is also recommended.

The South Street Seaport is like no other. Museum President Peter Neill describes it as "the cultural heart of an area now a vital part of contemporary New York, where city-dwellers and visitors alike can discover the maritime origin of America's culture and economy and the link all of us have to the sea."

Hudson River Ports below the Harlem River
(Going upriver, leave green buoys to port, red to starboard.)

Robert H. Boyle, author of the now-classic book *The Hudson—a Natural and Unnatural History,** is "an outspoken friend of this great but manhandled river." Considering the Hudson's future, he gives two alternatives:

The first is that of a clean and wholesome river from the Adirondacks down to the harbor; a wild unfettered stream in its forested mountain headwaters; productive tidewater from Troy south. Useful for both navigation and drinking water, the Hudson will be a river toward which millions of people can turn with pride and expectation. In recreation alone, the Hudson will be worth billions to the communities along its banks.

The second vision is not pleasant. Dammed and strangled in the Adirondacks to serve as a draw-down reservoir, the upper river trickles to the estuary. Overloaded with sewage and industrial wastes and cooked by cooling water from power plants, the lower Hudson is bereft of the large forms of life except for a few stray catfish or carp in isolated "zones of recovery." At night, the mountains of the Highlands thrum to the noise of pumped storage plants

*Published in 1969 by W. W. Norton, New York.

sucking part of the river uphill. Discovery of a dead sturgeon or a striped bass along the shore is cause for excitement and a front-page story in the *Times* on the wonder of it all. Here and there, between the transmission towers and stacks, a few breathtaking views of the valley landscape are still to be seen, if you look quickly while speeding behind a truck over a six-lane highway built on filled-in river bottom. In essence, the valley is jammed with sense-less sprawl, and the river is a gutted ditch, an aquatic Appalachia, a squalid monument to greed.

The future of our "American Rhine," however, may appear to be brighter than its present waters, which Henry Hudson once found "clear, blue, and wonderful to taste." The state and federal governments, with special assigned funds, are now committed to a major effort toward reducing pollution in the Hudson. True, it will take years to clean up the river and remove many of the eyesores along its waterfront, but the Scenic Hudson Preservation Conference located in New York City, the Hudson River Sloop Restoration, Inc., in Poughkeepsie, the Hudson River Maritime Museum on Rondout Creek in Kingston, as well as other dedicated conservation groups, have taken united action toward maintaining its heritage and majestic scenery.

River people all up and down the Hudson agree with the writer that the water looks and smells better than it did in recent decades, this being the result of years of effort to provide adequate wastewater treatment facilities near industrial and sewage discharges under the 1965 New York Pure Waters Program. A letter written to us from George K. Hansen, Chief, Evaluation Section, Monitoring and Assessment Bureau, New York State Department of Environmental Conservation, tells some of the latest steps being taken in continuing to clean up the river.

Water quality conditions in the Lower Hudson River Basin, below Troy, have improved considerably due to the installation of secondary sewage treatment plants in Albany, Rensselaer, and lower Saratoga counties. These facilities replaced the previously untreated individual discharges from surrounding municipalities and industries.

Ten years after the recognition of the PCB contamination of the Hudson River, PCB concentrations in the water column, fish, and surficial sediments are substantially lower than the very high levels observed during the late 1970s. However, PCB levels in water and fish still exceed acceptable concentrations.

Bans on commercial striped bass fishing in the lower river and all forms of fishing in the upper river between Troy and Fort Edward, New York, have been maintained.

Monitoring demonstrates the persistence of a contamination gradient along the length of the river and implicates the region near Fort Edward, New York, as a major contributor of the continued load of PCB to the lower Hudson.

In 1979, Congress authorized the Hudson River PCB Reclamation/ Demonstration Project, perhaps the last in a series of actions in the remedial strategy for the river's PCB contamination.

In 1989, the U.S. Environmental Protection Agency called for a reassessment of the remedial strategy for the river's PCB contamination. This reassessment is in progress and should be completed in the mid-1990s.

Boaters should check on fishing restrictions and health advisories that may be in effect. Such information is included in materials received with a New York State fishing license. Boaters should minimize contact with sediments from the upper river between Troy and Fort Edward, New York.

At the time of writing, the Coast Guard was proposing a plan to overhaul the Aids to Navigation (AtoN) system on the Hudson River, beginning at the George Washington Bridge and continuing north to the end of the estuary at Troy. The proposal calls for Aids to Navigation to start with number 1 at the Battery and then to be sequentially numbered north to Troy. Once the plan is approved and fully funded, the Corps of Engineers will be relocating existing buoys to mark the best water at the time. It will probably take a long period of time to complete the task.

Also being considered is the improvement of the range system along the river to provide consistency and to help vessels navigate safely through the many narrow reaches the year round. Five-degree Direction Lights, each with a range of 4 nautical miles, will consist of three different-colored sectors. The center of each light will display a white light on a 1-degree arc if you are approaching on the correct course. The two side sectors will display either red or green on a 2-degree arc. If you see green, you steer to starboard; if you see red, you steer to port.

With so many potential changes taking place, one may not fully rely on even the latest charts of the Hudson. It is recommended that boaters keep up to date with copies of the *Local Notice to Mariners* or contact Commander (OAN), First Coast Guard District, 408 Atlantic Avenue, Boston, MA 02110-3350, phone (617) 223-8363.

1. The Battery (east shore—12335). There is more life on and in the waters of New York Harbor than there has been for decades. Six companies now run more than a dozen ferry routes, and well over a thousand new marina slips have been created in recent years along the Jersey shore.

Across the river on Manhattan's western shore, the Chelsea Piers project was deliberating the possibility of constructing a 100-slip marina for mid-size boats between 17th and 22nd streets at Piers 59, 60, 61, and 62. New York State environmental officials were reviewing this proposal before granting approval to build.

Meanwhile, just to the south and identified on Chart 12335 lies a prominent, deep-water basin behind a breakwater with two lighted markers at its entrance. Facing the twin towers of the World Trade Center, North Cove was designed specifically to tend megayachts from 80 to 150 feet at a location like none other on the entire East Coast. Here at the heart of the World Financial Center is the acclaimed Winter Garden, the finest hotels, and a dozen highly rated restaurants. With such a convenient berth and affluent clientele, you can expect the overnight dockage fee to be unusually high, but for several-hour tie-ups it is considerably less. We were told to make a slip reservation by phoning (212) 938-9000.

2. Jersey City, New Jersey (west shore—12335). The most dramatic improvements for cruising yachts in the lower Hudson have taken place on its western shore along a $6^2/_3$-mile stretch from Jersey City to Edgewater. The four upscale complexes we soon describe have made this shoreline a veritable marina gold coast. There may be only one drawback. If you are short of fuel in New York Harbor, be reminded that only the Port Imperial Marina has both gas and diesel and that Lincoln Harbor pumps just diesel. If necessary, one can run up the Morris Canal Basin north of the Liberty State Park complex to fill up at the very protected fuel dock of the Liberty Harbor Marina.

The 180 well-maintained slips of the Newport Yacht Club and Marina for boats 35 to 200 feet lie just south of the green-topped Holland Tunnel "Ventilator." The marina is further identified by a large illuminated sign dockside. A protective breakwater stretches across the basin's entrance, where 10 feet MLW is reported. Greater depths are found farther in.

On arrival here, boat owners should report to the dockmaster on the main pier to be assigned a slip with electrical, water, and phone hookups.

You can give him advance notice by calling him on VHF-9. An expert mechanic is always on hand.

Newport is another example of several year-round, upscale developments providing cruising visitors with breathtaking views of Manhattan's towers. Here one can find a full range of convenient services, including minutes-away access to the big city via nearby PATH trains which run every 15 minutes or by an on-site ferry. The attractiveness of Newport is enhanced by its conversion of a 150-year-old ferry terminal into a 400-seat dockside restaurant called Cafe Newport. It offers modestly priced Italian fresh seafood for lunch and dinner served in a casual setting. A short walk will also take you to the 100-shop Newport Centre Mall, a 9-screen movie theater, a supermarket, and a fancy deli. As they claim, Newport Marina is pretty much "a self-contained community."

Just above Newport lies the Colgate Pier, long identified by a prominent neon clock that can be seen from downtown Manhattan across the river. Here, the Colgate-Palmolive Company is proceeding with plans to add a marina to its 42-acre office, retail, and residential high-rise project. The marina will join a 550-foot office building, a 1,000-foot riverfront park, a restaurant, and mooring space for at least 100 small and medium-size boats beginning in 1994. With the PATH train only two blocks away, boat owners staying at this newest complex will find easy access to Manhattan's World Trade Center.

3. Weehawken, New Jersey (west shore—12341). Directly across the river from the Empire State Building, the Lincoln Harbor Yacht Club can be identified by a large blue-and-white building, red and green lights at its entrance, and a prominent sign on its outer 775-foot breakwater. On hailing them on VHF-74, you will be met by a steward at one of 250 slips furnished with electricity, water, and phone lines. Other services provided dockside include the free delivery of provisions and laundry pickup.

Set in the midst of an urban environment is a ship's store, a concierge, a tight security system, diesel refueling, a pump-out station, a Ramada Hotel, a ferry to Manhattan, and five nearby restaurants including recommended Shanghai Red's and also Ruth Chris Steak House.

Lincoln Harbor reportedly prides itself on the efficiency and courtesy of its staff members. Apparently this is confirmed by a number of yacht club members whose boats have berthed here taking advantage of this marina's special rate to club fleets.

Four miles above the Battery at Weehawken is found Port Imperial, the most extensive marina along the lower Hudson shore. The 36-acre pristine property lies directly across the river from the permanently stationed aircraft carrier *Intrepid*. It is further identified by its sign, lighted at night, set atop this marina's large, five-star restaurant, Arthur's Landing. Two breakwaters, protecting six piers, almost surround Port Imperial's boat basin. To the south, the piers are concrete; the others to the north are wood. Go through the narrow entrance at the south end and once inside proceed north to the gas-diesel fuel dock to be assigned one of the 300 slips. Slips record 8 to 10 feet MLW. It will save time if you can alert the dockmaster on VHF-88A/9 before your arrival.

The amenities here seem almost endless. There is full mechanical and hull repair and in the main office is located the manager, a concierge, a marine store, a laundromat, and immaculate showers. Grocery deliveries dockside are a convenience. The Port Imperial Ferry operates between the marina and midtown Manhattan (38th Street and Twelfth Avenue) every 15 minutes, and during the week it runs on rush hours to Wall Street. Once in Manhattan, passengers are provided complimentary bus service to the theatre district and other popular destinations. Special half-day ferry tours travel to the Statue of Liberty or to historic Tarrytown.

Port Imperial's well-tended landscaping and its distinctive Golf Center add to the spectacular setting here.

4. Edgewater, New Jersey (west shore—12341). Formerly Richmond Marina, Grand Cove Marina and Yacht Club can be found 2 miles south of the George Washington Bridge and opposite the large sewage treatment plant on the Manhattan shore. It is further identified by a white, flat-roofed building behind which is the marina's office. Almost one hundred protected slips in three separate basins record 5 feet at low water. The usual dockside services are on tap. The other advantages that may appeal to transients include full repair service, a 50-ton travelift whose lift capacity is rarely found in a hoist in this area, nearby restaurants, and pleasant-looking surroundings.

On our latest visit, Manager Peter Monte told us of Grand Cove's plans for future expansion. These include new showers, a laundry room, a ship's store, and the installation of a fuel dock. It was suggested that slip reservations be made by phoning (201) 944-2628.

Any marina which has served the boating public for almost ninety continuous years and is now under third-generation family ownership must have been doing something right and deserves comment here. Joseph Von Dohln says its clue to survival is just "old-fashioned, caring, personal service to our customers."

A mile before you reach the George Washington Bridge, you can spot on the Jersey shore his guest mooring and two long, newly constructed piers jutting out into the Hudson with finger slips accommodating boats up to 35 feet in 6 feet low water. Do not expect the numerous services or the ambience of a Port Imperial or a Lincoln Harbor here at Von Dohln's, or a docking fee as pricey. But if repair work is your objective and you don't need extra frills, head in to meet Joseph Von Dohln. We think you will have his complete and undivided attention. It seems to have become a tradition.

5. Hudson Harbor—79th Street Marina, New York (east shore— 12341). This longtime facility operated by the New York Parks Commission is approximately 6 miles north of the Battery and clearly identified on the chart. It has been called, somewhat wryly, "Armageddon on the Hudson." One close look at this faded marina and it is hard to picture that its docks once berthed some of the finest yachts that cruised the Hudson. At low tide, 14 feet is recorded at the outer seawall, while houseboats and power craft, many permanently moored at weathered docks, are seen sitting on the mud flats inside the basin. Obviously, deep-draft vessels can only tie up and remain afloat along the seawall. The mean range of tide here is about 5 feet.

Not only is this marina's water depth limited. It provides few services and no fuel, although 24-hour security exists. The dockmaster, Ron Boudreau, monitors VHF-9 and 68 and can also be reached by telephoning (212) 408-0264.

The management here apparently agrees with most boaters that a city like New York should have a full-service marina worthy of its name. In a recent discussion with the dockmaster about the future of his marina, we learned that with the approval of a capital improvement plan the following steps may be completed in 1995: docks will be rebuilt, restrooms and showers installed, and transient moorings set outside the basin, which will be dredged to 8 feet MLW. Meanwhile, this place still has one drawing card. It is conveniently located, with ready access to Riverside Park. Broadway is also only three blocks away, where restaurants and supply sources abound, and the subway makes a stop at 79th Street to take you most anywhere in the Big Apple.

Approximately 5¹/₂ miles beyond the 79th Street Marina, on the east shore at Tubby Hook, marked on the chart north of the George Washington Bridge, Dyckman Marina may be a convenient, alternative stop, with slips available for boats up to 35 feet. Larger craft can be accommodated at moorings with launch service provided from 8 A.M. to midnight. The usual amenities, except fuel, are provided transients, who may reserve space by calling manager John Boldt on VHF-9. Stores for provisions are only three blocks away, and the subway at Broadway and Dyckman Street runs an express to downtown Manhattan.

For added protection from the river's wash, this marina was planning at the time of writing to construct a 500-foot floating dock to serve as a breakwater, including another 200-foot offshore breakwater with finger floats.

6. Englewood Boat Basin, New Jersey (west shore—12345). This is slightly below the point where the Harlem River joins the Hudson and is one of the best yacht basins on the river. Located under the shadow of the Palisades, as the sun goes down in the west, the surroundings are pleasant, and a wooden breakwater supplemented by sunken barges gives good protection in 5 feet at MLW from the confused waters of the much-traveled Hudson. This large and well-kept marina opens annually on May 1 and is operated by the Palisades Interstate Park Commission. A steward is on duty from 10 A.M. to 6 P.M. on weekdays and from 9 A.M. to 7 P.M. on weekends. Most of the slips are rented for the season, but one is reserved for transients, and there also may be vacancies while boats are away. Gas, diesel fuel, showers, water, and electricity are provided, but supplies are obtainable only by phoning a taxi, and no repairs or moorings are available. Make sure of your depths in this basin and in the one at Alpine, for, although there is a 4¹/₂-foot rise and fall of tide here, the bottom tends to silt up, requiring frequent dredging.

Hudson River above the Harlem River
(12345, 12346, 12343, 12347, 12348)

1. Alpine Boat Basin, New Jersey (west shore—12345). Like the Englewood Boat Basin, this is run by the Palisades Interstate Park Commission and has similar facilities and prices, except that there is no adequate breakwater and yachts are subject to almost continuous motion. Gas, showers, water, and electricity are available, with two slips reserved for transients. We prefer the basin at Englewood, with its greater depths, where the Palisades rise up steeply behind in a totally uncommercial setting.

Designated a National Natural Landmark in 1983, the Palisades are considered "the best example of a thick diabase sill in the United States." The term "palisade" means "fence of stakes" and derives from the long, vertical columns' resemblance to a stockade.

Extending from Staten Island about 50 miles northwest to Haverstraw, these cliffs formed about 190 million years ago when hot molten rock or "magma" was squeezed horizontally between layers of sandstone and shale. Sandwiched between these sedimentary rocks, the magma cooled and solidified into the igneous material known today as diabase.

Because of its durability and compact nature, diabase was quarried during the late nineteenth century for buildings, cobblestone roads, and ships' ballasts.

2. Hastings-on-Hudson, New York (east shore—12346). Approximately 4.2 miles south of the Tappan Zee Bridge lies the basin of the small, unpretentious, and friendly Tower Ridge Yacht Club, protected by the battered and ancient remnants of a once-active brigantine. Steel-and-stone breakwaters give the docks here added protection from the north.

At the time of writing, plans were being made to dredge the club's basin to 6 feet MLW. Ice, electricity, and water are available at the slips, and showers can be found in the clubhouse. The sale of gas is limited to members only except in case of emergency. The club may have an extra mooring available north of the breakwater. For overnight slip space, the Hastings Yacht Club, a few hundred yards downriver, is also a possibility.

The wooden breakwater was once the brigantine *City of Beaumont*, which carried lumber by sail during World War I and then roosted for years at a New York City pier. When Prohibition came, she was renamed the *Buccaneer* and anchored off Tarrytown, where she functioned as a floating speakeasy and showboat until the authorities interceded. The late Mayor Jimmy Walker is said to have entertained his friends there. Now her task is more prosaic and her keel rests firmly on the ground.

3. Tarrytown, New York (east shore—12343). With the availability of the Tappan Zee Bridge and dredging to 12 feet in its channel, Tarrytown Harbor has become extremely convenient for boats up to 70 feet overall as a rendezvous from either side of the Hudson. Tarrytown Marina is located on a narrow point shown on the chart. The westernmost walkway contains its own built-in breakwater. Leave red nun 6 to starboard before heading for the main dock to the north of the point. You will approach a large basin with 180 slips located offshore of the Tarrytown Boat Club. There is 6 feet MLW in the slips and at the gas dock where the dockmaster, Ted Tenenzapf, will assign you a slip and give you the marina's rules and a folder entitled "The Best of Boat Worlds," a visitor's guide to local historic sites ashore. They offer ice, water, electricity, fuel, showers, a laundromat, free pumpout service, marine charts and supplies, a 25-ton travelift, 24-hour security, but no moorings. A Grand Union store is nearby.

Located at the marina but belonging to the Tarrytown Boat Club is Dockside at Tarrytown, a bar and restaurant serving continental lunch and dinner daily on the waterfront to patrons in casual dress. They offer guest docking for several vessels up to 40 feet in length.

Close by is the Tarrytown railroad station, with trains to New York, and the convenient Tarrytown Hilton offers limousine service to all local airports. Slip reservations for weekends and holidays should be made by phoning (914) 631-1300 or by calling over VHF-16.

The Washington Irving Boat Club, which is located just to the south, is best suited for boats under 30 feet but is less comfortable due to its close proximity to the railroad. It has limited transient space.

In leaving this harbor heading north, be sure to follow closely the buoys marking the north connecting channel. You'll pass the restored Kingsland Point Lighthouse. Constructed in 1883, it guided boats past these shores until the mid-1950s, when the completion of the Tappan Zee Bridge made it obsolete. Farther up, close along the river's eastern shoreline, keep a sharp eye out and note on your chart a rock marked just south of Scarborough and approximately 1,000 yards ENE of flashing buoy 5. This is infamous Bishop's Rock. Without any navigational marker, submerged at high water, it has over the years staved in many a hull and bent many a prop.

A short distance south of the junction of the bridge and the New York Thruway stands "one of the great houses of America—uniting in its walls the beginning and culmination of Hudson River Gothic." Here is

Lyndhurst, a huge baronial castle of dazzling beauty, built in 1938 and for a time the home of Jay Gould. Visiting hours at this historic preservation are from 10 A.M. to 5 P.M. daily.

Settled as a Dutch trading post in the seventeenth century, Tarrytown was developed as farmland with the rest of the rich Hudson Valley by Dutch and English manor lords. Of historic interest in this "Sleepy Hollow" country is Philipse Castle, the seventeenth-century home of Frederick Philipse, First Lord of the Manor, who once owned most of Westchester. Recently his old gristmill was rebuilt by Sleepy Hollow Restoration, offering visitors a good opportunity to see what a center of commerce looked like over two hundred years ago. One can also pay a visit to Sunnyside, the gabled and turreted home of Washington Irving, who peopled these slumbering hills with gnomes, trolls, and comic Dutchmen.

4. Nyack, New York (west shore—12343). At upper Nyack is Julius Petersen, Inc. The dock is easy to identify by a number of large, gray boat sheds. There's a functional look about this place which gives one an impression of what old traditional yacht yards should resemble. However, Petersen's rates are comparatively low, and they promise, "We'll guarantee you a quiet night's sleep.

Visiting yachts up to 120 feet can find excellent repair work of all types with mechanics on full-time duty. Although they have no fuel, they provide a 20-ton crane and a 60-ton travelift; a splendidly equipped marine supply store with quick delivery of marine parts; electronic, rigging, and one-day sail repair; and even welding facilities. There is 10 feet dockside and 15 MLW at its moorings.

Bus service to the New York Port Authority runs on an hourly basis from the top of the hill above Petersen.

The Nyack Boat Club is above the old ferry. The club is said to have 6 feet of water at its dock.

Nyack was the hometown of America's First Lady of the Theater, the late Helen Hayes, so it is fitting that the Tappan Zee Playhouse up on nearby Main Street has a first-class repertoire. Famous artists such as Faye Dunaway, Eli Wallach, Barbara Britton, Maureen O'Sullivan, and Hume Cronyn have appeared onstage here from time to time in major Broadway hits.

Dowe Harmensen Tallman first settled in this hamlet of the Nyack Indians in 1684. Now it's known as the Art, Antiques, and Handcrafts

Village of the Hudson Valley, with a hodgepodge of quaint little shops offering collectibles from the nineteenth century. Here also, on South Broadway in the center of town, is the Old Fashion Chop House Tavern, whose splendid table draws people from miles around. This section of town is mapped in a free descriptive brochure, *Discover Nyack,* available at any of the stores. Every Wednesday, there is held a popular open-air farmers' market in the center of town, and with some 32 restaurants and bars, Nyack now has a thriving night life.

Perhaps some night off Nyack's shore you'll also discover the Unresting Oarsman. A young Dutchman, he stayed too long at a Saturday party on the shore of the Tappan Zee, and though warned, he recklessly started rowing home after midnight, breaking the Sabbath. He rows there yet. Listen . . .

5. Ossining, New York (east shore—12343). The Shattemuc Yacht Club is the preferable stopover point at Ossining. The derivation of its name came from the Mohican Indians, who called the Hudson "great waters in motion." The club property is located on the northernmost projection of land on the Ossining waterfront, where an L-shaped pier shows on the chart. The old clubhouse burned down in 1973 and was replaced by a ferryboat formerly run by the Circle Line. At the time of writing, plans were being made to replace the ferryboat with a new clubhouse similar to that of the San Diego Yacht Club and to build a new dinghy dock. There are gas, water, ice, showers, and electricity—in season—at the slips, which have 5 feet at low water on both sides. Members of other recognized yacht clubs are welcome, and the new club facilities may include a bar and snack bar. The swimming pool still exists.

The club usually has spare dock space for guests. At night, the signal is a flashing green and white light at the end of a barge just to the south of the entrance to the basin. The takeoff point for the club is from Hudson lighted buoy 8. If coming from the north, give Tellers Point a wide berth of at least 1/4 mile, as the gravel-bottomed shoal projects southward farther than the chart indicates. In approaching from the south, be sure to stay well outside of the dolphins; and as you enter the basin keep the stake marking a sunken barge in the channel well to starboard. Some moorings lie north of the breakwater but there is no launch service to them.

During our latest visit here, the club was a swarming beehive of activity while hosting a weekend regatta composed of sailing fleets from clubs along the river. Shattemuc has become a major sailing center, boasting a fine fleet of cruising auxiliaries and one-design racing classes tied up snugly behind a 300-foot breakwater of steel barges.

If you look westward across the river, this spot is attractive, but it is wide open, except from the southeast to northwest, in one of the widest parts of the Hudson.

Just south of the club lies the entrance to Westerly Marina, immediately beyond several prominent storage tanks and at the stern of a large steel barge. The inland slips here offer 6 feet MLW. Having acquired the properties of Samalot Marine and Ship Store, Westerly with its open-end lift and 35-ton travelift performs engine and hull repairs on both sail and power craft. It also offers gas, electricity, ice, and the usual services to transients, including a well-stocked marine store. Sellazzo's Marina Restaurant, serving delicious Italian meals, and the Metro North station are both nearby.

On heading north from the Shattemuc Yacht Club, be sure to give Croton Point a wide berth as Potato Rock lies closely offshore its northwestern tip and a very popular, crowded anchorage is located along its northern shore.

Beyond, on Haverstraw Bay's eastern shore looms an impressive-looking, brown-shingled condominium complex named the Half Moon Bay Yacht Club. Enter its deep-water basin from the south end of the breakwater marked by a white light. An orange light designates the northern end where the transient dock is located. Club moorings are seen to the north. The dockmaster monitors VHF-9 from 10 A.M. to 8 P.M. Although there are few marina-type services here, its non-commercial makeup, sparkling new appearance, and serene protection make this a recommended layover. In any case, most visitors' needs can be filled by taking a ten-minute walk to the shops in Croton-on-Hudson.

The famous Sing Sing Prison was established at Ossining in 1824 with the intention of using convict labor on marble quarries. Once a prison in which severe repression was the norm, Sing Sing has now become known for its enlightened penal practices.

6. Haverstraw, New York (west shore—12343). Nestled below the craggy cliffs of High Tor, Little Tor, and Pnygyp (so named because it resembles a Dutch loaf of bread) lies a little cove shown on the chart just southwest of can 15. Hug this can close to port in heading into the shallow cove entrance marked by a prominent concrete plant at its southern end. Two markers to be kept to starboard will guide you by a low concrete breakwater into depths of $4^1/_2$ feet at MLW.

The docks to port belong to the friendly Rockland-Bergen Boat Club where boats of up to 4-foot draft can tie up. There is no clubhouse, but what this organization may lack in facilities, it makes up in consideration of others out on the water. A member has said, "No boats in trouble have ever been turned away, and we have always been able to find some dockage for them." Here is an example of the unselfish spirit one often finds at small boating clubs whose members follow the adage of "one for all and all for one." The cove provides excellent shelter in rather pleasant surroundings.

Another extremely protected basin, the year-round "home" of the Haverstraw Marina, which is the largest boating installation on the Hudson, lies just $1^1/_2$ miles upriver on the west shore almost due west of red flashing buoy 16. Furthermore, the long white pier of the U.S. Gypsum Company extends out into the Hudson and runs just to the north and parallel to this marina's entrance channel. There are no markers in the deep-water channel, but red and green range lights at its head will help guide you in at night. The basin records a 24-foot average depth throughout and has a 1,000-slip capacity. There are no moorings. As a source of clay, this basin made Haverstraw a major brickmaking center in the early 1800s.

A 230-foot gas and diesel dock runs along the basin's northern shore where craft up to 150 feet can be accommodated. The services seem endless. A 30-ton travelift is on hand as well as these facilities: ice, showers, a laundromat, a trailer ramp, a machine shop, and a pumpout facility. Bright, airy, and inviting Hudson's Landing Restaurant located on the premises offers casual dining with superb views of the Hudson from almost every seat, either in the house or from its patio deck. The Samalot Marine and Ship Store monitors VHF-16 and handles all sailboat and sail repairs, including the stepping of masts. Powerboats requiring repairs can call on B & J, a major marine-service center. There is a surcharge for the use of the tennis courts and swimming pool on the property as well as a fee for golf; transportation is furnished to the course a few miles distant.

With all these conveniences at one's disposal here, we suggest a call for reservations to the manager, Courtlandt Herbert, at (914) 429-2001. The marina also monitors VHF-9 and 16. How does Herbert describe his complex? "It's a summer resort, a one-stop vacation place for boaters."

Mayor Frank Haera, in commenting on his village to the press, was quoted as saying, "I think people are beginning to take notice of Haverstraw." The very same, and more, could be said for the Haverstraw Marina.

Here it was, on September 22, 1780, that Benedict Arnold met Major John André to plot the betrayal of West Point. James Wood later discovered the modern process of making brick and established an industry that at one time included forty brickyards producing over 325,000 bricks a year here.

Although the river is arguably cleaner than it has been in decades, its health is not why the Hudson attracts exotic wanderers, especially to Haverstraw Bay. Other characteristics make this river irresistible— location, oceanography, and food. Its mouth is a natural catch basin for fish swimming north along New Jersey's coast or east along Long Island. The Gulf Stream, sweeping past New York, also carries trop- ical fish north. And the Hudson with its wide range of temperatures and salt content is loaded with food—shrimp, crabs, algae, and other organisms.

Recently a local fisherman pulled from his net a lumpfish, a species common in the frosty waters of Hudson's Bay but never reported here before. Other foreign fish include a silver perch and a mangrove snapper—"the only fish species that's ever been taken in the Hudson and the Congo," according to Robert H. Boyle, author of *The Hudson River: A Natural and Unnatural History*. Other naturalists have turned up other firsts: a ladyfish, a popular gamefish in Florida; a permit, a member of the pompano family; and wedge clams, native to the Gulf of Mexico but now found in abundance in the mud flats of Haverstraw Bay.

Now the tiny, pestiferous zebra mussel has finally invaded the salty regions of the Hudson between Westchester and Rockland counties. Mussels have been found in 6 feet of water near a dock off Haverstraw. According to James Carlton, director of maritime studies at Mystic Seaport, "it may represent the first record in the United States of zebra mussels settling in detectable salt."

7. Grassy Point—at town of Stony Point (west shore—12343). This is one of the best ports on the Hudson River and certainly the most attractive in the area. Its location can be spotted from the river by a prominent church spire and the U.S. Gypsum watertower nearby. One can enter by following a 6-foot channel about 150 feet off the shore of Grassy Point until red and green buoys are reached opposite the entrance between the breakwaters. A flashing red buoy marks the channel to a snug-looking basin. Go in between the buoys, keeping about 10 feet away from the eastern bulkhead. Here is a dredged-out clay hole with a 20-foot depth running almost to the shore. Opposite the entrance is the attractive Minisceongo Yacht Club, which was founded by the High Tor Sailing Fleet and whose name is derived from an Indian phrase, "winding waters."

The clubhouse was built entirely by the members with their own hands. Visiting yachtsmen from other recognized yacht clubs may use the floats and facilities "as long as they behave themselves." Upon entering the basin, all boats should go to the gas dock to starboard where a pumpout station is also located. You may tie there temporarily until you are assigned a slip. Dropping your anchor is not permitted. Water, ice, electricity, gas, showers, and snacks are available from 9 A.M. to 4 P.M. Minor repair work can be done and there is one small marine railway.

We have often enjoyed our visits to this quiet little harbor with its friendliness and rather rustic atmosphere. Since it appeals to so many yachts cruising along the river, it is suggested that slip reservations be made ahead by phoning (914) 786-8767.

To reach the following full-service marinas on the west side of shallow Stony Point Bay, one must follow the previously mentioned channel and observe the white-pipe-lined markers. The first marina you will come to is Belle Harbor with slips for boats of 55-foot length and moorings for visitors. Willow Cove Marina, the largest and most impressive of all three, has a deep-water, sheltered basin formed by two river barges identified by a prominent mast and boom. This is not your average marina but somewhat of an elegant, upscale retreat with its swimming pool, tennis court, Jacuzzi, picnic grounds, a fully stocked marine store, and what you will. Pickup transportation is provided by local restaurants. Willow Cove also handles complete repairs as does the Stony Point Marina and Yacht Club located beyond. The depth at the slips here, the home of the Seaweed Yacht Club, is 3 feet low water. None of these three marinas supply fuel. Willow Cove monitors VHF-16 and 12; Stony Point Bay Marina may be reached on 16 and 71.

The village of Stony Point and the rocky bluff on the shore of the Hudson bear a name familiar to American schoolboys. Be sure to visit the Stony Point Battlefield Reservation. Here, on July 16, 1779, 1,200 Continentals under General "Mad" Anthony Wayne stormed and captured a fort held by British forces. In the daring charge, General Wayne was wounded and borne forward over the rampart to victory on the shoulders of his men. A story is told that during the discussion of Hudson River tactics, Washington asked Wayne if he thought he could storm Stony Point. The general replied: "I'll storm Hell, sir, if you'll make the plans!" Washington looked at him meditatively for a moment, then replied: "Better try Stony Point first." On one of the highest points on the promontory is the Stony Point Museum.

At the Battlefield Reservation, you can experience the sights and sounds of the battle through exhibits and an audiovisual program. Or you can take an historic walking tour. Up on the summit of the Stony Point peninsula stands an 1826 lighthouse that guided Hudson River traffic for one hundred years. It still affords a splendid sweeping panorama of Haverstraw Bay.

8. Montrose, New York (east shore—12343). On the eastern shore opposite Stony Point Bay, Georges Island juts out in the Hudson as an unspoiled peninsula, ideal for hiking, picnicking, and nature study. The 175 acres that make up this Westchester County–owned park have been carefully preserved for the recreation and enjoyment of boatmen and local residents. A popular launching ramp located on the peninsula's southern shore has been built to accommodate boats up to 20 feet overall and leads directly to a 60-foot-wide channel dredged to a depth of 4 feet below mean low water extending some 430 feet into the river. Do not attempt to tie up to the many buoys you will see in this area. We poked along this sylvan shore in our boat of 3-foot draft and found the best anchorage with the most beautiful setting in the bight on the peninsula's north side. If you enjoy visiting places that are different, you will not be disappointed here. The park closes at sunset.

Almost a mile northward along the innermost shore of Greens Cove southeast of Verplanck Point lies the home of the Cortland Yacht Club sheltered behind a small but prominent island and a line of barges forming a breakwater protecting an inner basin. A buoyed channel leads to a narrow entrance marked by a red flashing light placed at the end of the centermost barge. Here you may find water, electricity, showers, slip space in 4 feet at MLW, engine repairs, a travelift, but no fuel. A snack bar is next to one of the few swimming pools on the Hudson. Free swims are included in the dockage fee. Commodore Don Gelfer introduced us to Cortlandt's proud new clubhouse whose lofty porch presents a striking view across the river.

This place has won lots of boating devotees over the years so it is suggested that slip reservations be made by phoning (914) 737-9483 or calling on VHF-9. Few visitors here perhaps realize that this cove is reportedly the first anchorage Henry Hudson made after leaving the mouth of the Hudson.

Just to the north of the yacht club an unmarked channel leads to a protected basin belonging to the Viking Boatyard. Its narrow entrance, marked by two small buoys, is located between a string of barges. Since there are varying depths within this basin for boats up to 40 feet, yachts should check in first at the gas dock to be assigned a floating slip. Fred and Molly Johannsen, who have a nice setup here, provide electricity, water, ice, a small marine store, a 60-ton open-end lift, a competent mechanic on call, but no gas. Their phone number is (914) 739-5090 and they also monitor VHF-9.

Another Point of View, a restaurant offering casual family dining in a nautical setting, is located at Viking with slips available for its patrons.

9. Peekskill, New York (east shore—12343). Peekskill's chief new attraction among boaters is the Charles Point Marina nestled in secluded, idyllic Lent's Cove due east of lighted buoy 19. Anchorage in the cove is not advised. At mean low water there is 6 feet in the marked channel and 4 feet at the many floating slips with a 3-foot tide range. This marina, monitoring VHF-9, has the advantage of being the only local facility as an on-site full-service, full-security center. Here for seven days a week they can fill almost any need for any vessel or crew cruising the Hudson. A five minute cab drive can take you to the Peekskill train station.

Crystal Bay Seafood, located in the very charming Gin House, is one of the finest restaurants and caterers in the region, as we know from our recent visits. The National Maritime Historical Society's headquarters, art gallery, and library are also housed there.

In 1898 the Fleischman brothers purchased Lent's Cove Landing.

Brother Charles renamed the locale Charles Point after his son and began making Fleischman's baking yeast, white vinegar, and gin. After a merger, Standard Brands took over the distillery in 1929, and the plant finally closed in 1985 to become what it is today.

"Everybody is welcome" is always the greeting we receive when we stop at the Peekskill Yacht Club, founded in 1908 as the Peekskill Motorboat Club and identified by a shingled clubhouse perched on top of a barge. The best way to get there is to go in from Hudson River beacon 19, whose flashing light is white. The beacon itself is green and white with its number unpainted. Leave this to port and nun channel buoy 2 to starboard. Round nun 4, farther in, and head for the club dock on Travis Point. The chart indicates 4^1/$_2$ feet in the south channel with only 3 feet MLW in the north channel beyond. There is 4 feet at the dock where a predominance of powerboats are tied up. Enter on the north end of the barges. Unless the space is already occupied, yachts may be permitted to tie up on the north side of the dock, where they are out of the way of entering boats, and can take lengthwise any wash that comes in from the river. Only water, ice, electricity, and showers are supplied. After 5 P.M. the club is usually closed except on weekends.

While the Peekskill waterfront is what might be expected in a good-sized commercial city, the view across the river to Dunderberg (930 feet) is pleasant. The Peekskill Motor Inn nearby is an excellent spot for meals, and shops are not far away. In ordinary quiet summer weather this port is O.K., but it is open to the river for some distance to the northwest and southwest.

To the south on Indian Point, you will see Consolidated Edison's nuclear power plant #2 which energizes an impressive 985,000 megawatts. Indian Point #3 adds another 980,000 megawatts to Con Edison's capacity to meet the energy needs of New York and Westchester. Special guided tours and exhibits at plant #2's Nuclear Information Center are available to the public from 8:30 A.M. to 4:30 P.M., Mondays through Fridays.

On the run through "The Race" to Garrison, passing by Iona Island just south of the Bear Mountain Bridge, bird lovers may observe an aerial spectacle. During recent years, a small but growing number of bald eagles, as many as a dozen, have been nesting at this island, an old Indian campground. The eagles reportedly like the island because the river narrows there. It acts as a funnel, concentrating whatever finned and feathered corpses float by into a relatively small area of water close to the eagles' roosts.

10. Garrison, New York (east shore—12343). As you proceed north to Garrison you will behold the magnificent Gothic spectacle that is West Point rising from the west bank of the river.

Across the river is the basin of the Garrison Yacht Club, identified by two red-lighted bulkheads. There is 13 feet at the gas dock and sufficient water in the protected basin for boats of 3-foot draft. The mean range of tide here is about 3 feet. Deep-draft vessels may tie up along the outer edge of the bulkheads but will be subject to river wake. The quaint, old Guinan's Country Store in back of the marina may help you "replenish the larder or pick up that item that was forgotten." Here we learned from a native fisherman that leaping carp, so often seen on the Hudson, usually designate shallow water of 2- to 3-foot depths.

The film *Hello, Dolly!* was shot at Garrison, since its surroundings so closely resemble the Yonkers of the 1890s. Art fans from miles around come here annually in late August to attend the colorful Garrison art festival.

If you can obtain transportation, a memorable experience may be had by visiting nearby Boscobel, a beautiful eighteenth-century restored mansion originally built by States Morris Dyckman for his beloved wife.

Railroad buffs may be interested to learn that Garrison has restored its antique depot, where railroad tycoons used to wait for their private cars in style. The depot is now the theatrical home of the Hand to Mouth Players. Across from the station is the Garrison Art Center.

Many Continental troops were stationed here during the Revolution so it is likely that a ferry service crossing over to West Point began during that period. Later on, ferry boats named the *Highland* and the *Garrison* began operations, and the remains of their slips may be seen to this day.

Should you and your crew wish to visit the U.S. Academy at West Point, you can dinghy across the river from the Garrison Yacht Club or contact the West Point harbormaster on VHF 13 and 16 or at (914) 938-2137 for the latest information.

Along the academy's shoreline, there is the restricted North Dock and the 175-foot South Dock, which only has pilings for a limited number of transient tie-ups, no floating slips, and minimum services. There is a small anchorage north of the South Dock, but it is also widely exposed to river traffic. The water off the nearby West Point Yacht Club, being quite shoal, is to be avoided by boats of deep draft.

The best step for one intent on going to the academy's Visitors Center and the world's largest military museum is to put in at the Highland Falls Marina, located near a lighted marker to the south off Highland Falls. A long, steep hike will bring you to the center, which is open daily from 9 A.M. to 4:45 P.M. The museum behind the center is open daily from 10:30 A.M. to 4:15 P.M.

11. Cold Spring, New York (east shore—12343). Passing Constitution Island heading for Cold Spring, you may sight to starboard a sizable inlet identified on the chart as Foundry Cove. Here was located America's first arsenal, the West Point Foundry, established in 1817. Throughout the nineteenth century, it served as an important center of technology; it built America's first iron ship and developed the Parrott gun, the Union's major artillery piece during the Civil War. All this helps to remind us that the Hudson River Valley formed the cradle of the American iron industry.

The village of Cold Spring is included for it offers its visitors a certain uniqueness among Hudson River ports. Having just passed Constitution Island, one cannot miss the sight of a picturesque bandstand and village green set behind a prominent dock. The dock, being reconstructed by the Corps of Engineers at the time of writing, will have an estimated length of 300 feet with pilings set in deep water. Look out for signs suggesting a possible tie-up. From here, the magnificent views of West Point, Cro'nest, Storm King, and Constitution Island have probably been painted and photographed more frequently than any other scenes along the Hudson Valley.

The Cold Spring Boat Club, just to the south, has facilities for shoal-draft boats to tie up for a visit, or there is a possibility of a temporary mooring at the dock already mentioned, but tie up "at your own risk." If you can arrange to get ashore, an anchorage just off of it can be made in deeper water, but you'll be exposed to the river's wash.

Next to the bandstand rises the former Hudson View Hotel, which used to be the third-oldest hostelry in New York State—only the Beekman Arms in Rhinebeck and the Canoe Place Inn on Long Island predated it. Built in 1837, it housed the famous Gus's Antique Bar, filled with the pungent atmosphere of a German ale house and a wild display of stains, military insignia, and weapons of the American past. One hundred and forty years later it sold out to new owners, who have given the place a pleasant colonial decor, an expensive bill of fare, and a new name, the Hudson House, A Country Inn. Just to the north lies the

Dockside Harbor Restaurant which offers a fine view of the river but has no dockage facilities. Both places permit casual dress.

A stroll up the town's steep main street lined with antique shops is a pleasant diversion. All kinds of supplies may be found at the top of the hill.

Although history doesn't record that George Washington slept at Cold Spring, it is a fact that in frequent visits to his American Revolutionary troops encamped nearby, he often drank from the local spring that gives the village its present name.

12. Cornwall-on-the-Hudson, New York (west shore—12343). As you proceed north to Cornwall, you will behold some impressive wonders both natural and historic. Just above West Point there is a sharp bend in the river named Worlds End, with depth exceeding 150 feet. At this point, through which you should move cautiously, the colonials strung a wrought-iron chain during the Revolution to prevent British advance upriver. No British ship ever tested the 1,700-foot chain with its 1,200 iron links. It was attached to rocks on the West Point shore, stapled to logs that held it in place as it was stretched across to Constitution Island. Each link weighed between 90 and 122 pounds. Thirteen of these still exist and can be seen at West Point's Trophy Point.

Then you may see from the river the old battlements of Fort Constitution peeking out from the jagged cliffs on the northwestern side of Constitution Island. Farther along on the western shore rises magnificent 1,400-foot Storm King Mountain, which natives years ago believed to be the haunt of hobgoblins and elves.

On the western shore across from Pollepel Island, on which Bannerman's Castle rises in medieval splendor, lies the Cornwall Yacht Club, identified by a small white building flanked by a stone breakwater forming a very protected basin. Transients are advised to tie up or swing by the gas dock, located at the northern outer end of the breakwater, to get permission from the dockmaster before entering the basin. The stern of the prominent black barge marks the entrance, which should be approached from due east. Keep the fixed marker to port on entering the basin. Sound your horn as you enter and avoid the lighted spar to starboard marking the southern end of the outer breakwater. Once past the spar, swing sharply to starboard to enter the basin. Check with the steward to be assigned a slip with a sufficient depth to carry your boat's draft. Depths vary in the basin from 3 to 6 feet MLW, with the deepest water found along the inner rim of the outer bulkhead. Gas, water, ice, and electrical connections are all available but no meals are served. The warm reception we often receive here, the quiet anchorage, and the pleasant surroundings make Cornwall a recommended stop.

Bannerman, who began as a munitions dealer at the end of the Civil War, built his Rhine-type castle in 1900 as a storehouse for his supply of guns, armor, and ammunition. After his death in 1918, the arsenal was abandoned and the business moved to Long Island. A fire raged through this castle in 1969, gutting the interior but fortunately leaving its "ramparts" intact. The island's unusual name is derived from two possible sources. A prickly pear called the Polypus, a form of cactus, once grew abundantly here. But the closest origin is best traced to the Dutch, in whose language "polopel" means "spoon" or "potladle."

Nowadays, one approaches the state-owned island very carefully. It is closed to the public due to extremely hazardous conditions. Bannerman's nevertheless still draws the curious like a magnet.

13. Newburgh, New York (west shore—12343). At the upper end of what we consider the most spectacular passage on the Hudson is the well-equipped and hospitable Newburgh Yacht Club, where there is a basin with many slips protected by sunken barges marked by a prominent fuel sign. It is located just below the Newburgh fixed bridge, at the foot of a steep hill.

The club's gas dock is off nun 38A and lies outside the basin. Here you will be assigned a slip and sign a "rental agreement." You will then proceed to the basin's entrance located at the southern end of a line of barges formerly used to carry coal and freight along our Eastern Seaboard. Keep to starboard of the dolphin on entering. Slips are usually available for visiting yachts, and gas, diesel fuel, water, ice, and electricity are on tap. There is an average of about 6 feet in the basin. Use of the swimming pool is included in the dockage fee. Showers are available, and lunch and dinner are served in the attractive clubhouse seven days a week. Advance reservations can be made by phoning 565-3920 or call on VHF-16.

Although the immediate surroundings are not beautiful, this is a very convenient and well-protected place to stop, and if you have the climbing ability of a mountain goat or the cash for a taxi, you can reach some movies and good stores in the city. Hanaford Marine (561-2771) has all sorts of marine supplies and may deliver them at the yacht club on call.

The club was founded in 1883 as a rowing club under the name "Newburgh Dock Rats."

14. New Hamburg, New York (east shore—12347). To enter White's Hudson River Marina basin from the south, turn sharply to starboard at the midchannel light marking Diamond Reef and run a course close and parallel to the barges forming the basin's southern edge. With only 3 feet of water at the basin's western side, this place is best suited for powerboats under 30 feet. The venerable owner, John White, offers marine supplies, all types of engine repair work, a mobile lift, gas, and ice, but limited transient space. John is a very personable marina owner "of the old school" who goes out of his way to please his customers. At the time of writing he was hoping to dredge his basin to 6 feet MLW.

Although the surroundings are far from scenic and the whole place has a topsy-turvy look, there is excellent protection, especially from the north, and we were told that boats here have been safe even in storms of hurricane strength. Light sleepers beware, however. You may not appreciate the trains that rumble by only a few hundred yards away.

White's often recommends that boats of deep draft proceed north to the nearby slips of the New Hamburg Yacht Club, which are on an "as-available" basis and have from 8 to 20 feet MLW. Water and electricity are dockside while showers, restrooms, and a snack bar can be found in the inviting clubhouse surrounded by a picnic area. VHF-16 is monitored here on the weekends. Club members are usually around.

The clubhouse opens on Thursdays and Fridays at 4 P.M. and on weekends at 2 P.M. Within easy walking distance you will find the Metro North train station and River Cafe North, a deli serving meals. They will deliver provisions to the club if phoned at 297-6129.

On our most recent visit, former Commodore Daynor White graciously showed us around and handed us a booklet giving useful information and a history of the New Hamburg Yacht Club. "It was incorporated in 1869 making it the sixth oldest yacht club in the United States. It originally was formed for the purpose of ice yacht racing and created the 'Ice Yacht Challenge Cup of America' in 1880. The Challenge Cup remains the premier prize for ice boat racing in the U.S. and Canada and has been held by various clubs in Minnesota and Wisconsin since the 1930s." Perhaps the club will get it back some day!

15. Poughkeepsie, New York (east shore—12347). About halfway between New York and Albany, Poughkeepsie is well known as the location of Vassar College and also for the intercollegiate rowing championships formerly held here. Huge college letters painted on boulders and now barely visible are the only trace of these regattas, first held in 1895.

Just above the Hudson River at Highland Landing on the west shore lies the Mariner's Harbor Marina with limited dock facilities in deep water. Ice, gas, diesel fuel, water, and showers are furnished here. The main attraction is its nautical-looking restaurant, patio, and bar, claiming "gracious riverside dining." It's fairly peaceful here except for an occasional passing train and considerable wake from passing vessels—hardly the place for an overnight stay.

Poughkeepsie's urban renewal project forced the Poughkeepsie Yacht Club to move from its former location in the shadow of the Mid-Hudson Bridge. This turn of events has been fortunate for all concerned. Now the club has enjoyed a rebirth at its appealing present location on the east shore just south of Esopus Island and 1 mile below Indian Kill. On our latest visit we were greeted by two congenial club members, John Kraus and former Commodore Einar Reves, who reminded us how the members had pitched in to improve the new layout, including filling in the land, on which has arisen a splendid-looking clubhouse complete with bar, showers, and a laundromat. Founded in 1892, it is one of the oldest yacht clubs on the Hudson.

The club's facilities also include water, electricity, ice, repair work, a launching ramp, travelift, pumpout facilities, and all the depth you'll need off its outer slips. Although this location lies near the railroad and is exposed to river wake, it offers fair protection and a breathtaking view of the Hudson from the clubhouse porch. A special anchorage area has been established off the club's shore to the north, but be reminded that no launch service is provided.

Here you will find an active social and junior program; it's also a choice spot for a night's layover.

16. Indian Kill, Staatsburg (east shore—12347). In our opinion, this is one of the two best overnight stopping places on the Hudson—the others being Catskill and Rondout Creeks. The Mills-Norrie State Park Boat Basin, with plans for its dredging by 1994 to a depth of at least 6 feet MLW, is one of the most beautiful basins we have seen and is located at the mouth of Indian Kill, where two lights are shown on the chart a short distance north of Esopus Island. You come in between two lighted spars, red and green, on the north side of the inlet, and the dockmaster will show you where to tie up, giving you a docking permit. Water and 50-amp electricity are included in the dockage fee. A permit to supply gas and diesel fuel to boats at the outer end of the dock was being reviewed at the time of writing. At the inner end are showers and a small office where soft drinks are sold. Although VHF-9 is monitored here, we were advised to phone ahead for a slip reservation, making sure to give our boat size. The number to call is (914) 889-4200.

A short walk from the basin will take you to the Dutchess Community College Environmental Museum whose exhibits will give you a unique opportunity to study the natural resources of the Mid-Hudson region. For those who might prefer a round of golf, there are two 9-hole courses only a mile distant.

The port captain pointed out to us a fine concrete launching ramp and presented us with some of the regulations established and strictly enforced by the Taconic State Park Commission of the New York State Office of Parks, Recreation and Historic Preservation, which administers the marina. We have abbreviated them somewhat:

1. The dockmaster assigns slips.
2. Don't waste water.
3. Unnecessary noise, loud talking, playing of musical instruments or radios between the hours of 10 P.M. and 7 A.M. are prohibited.
4. Storage on dock is prohibited.
5. Fitting-out or major repair work in berths is prohibited.
6. Disposal of garbage or trash must be in receptacles provided for the purpose.
7. Laundry shall not be exposed to public view at any time.
8. No beer drinking is permitted in the park.
9. Since this boat basin is run by New York, all visiting craft must be equipped with state-approved holding tanks. Here are pumpout facilities similar to those at Catskill, Hudson, and Troy.
10. Swimming is not permitted off docks or boats.

On all sides and across the river the surroundings and view are lovely. The Gothic-style turrets of the Mount St. Alphonse Monastery rise high along the western shore. Some of the most lordly estates along the Hudson are within easy reach of Indian Kill. Just to the south, one of them with its own dock is the Vanderbilt Mansion National Historic Site, commanding a magnificent view of the river. The fifty-room dwelling contains many masterpieces of Italian art and is open to the public daily. In nearby Hyde Park is the home of Franklin D. Roosevelt, another National Historic Site with many fascinating collections and relics acquired by the late President. Roosevelt's grave in the rose garden is marked by a simple and impressive white marble monument. Adjacent is the Roosevelt Library, with much material of historic interest and also some unusual gifts sent to the White House. About 1 mile north of Indian Kill at Dinsmore, you will note the Ogden Mills and Ruth Livingston Mills Memorial State Park—the 200-acre estate of the former Secretary of the Treasury. The sixty-five room Mills mansion in French Renaissance style is open Wednesday through Saturday 10 A.M. to 5 P.M. and on Sunday noon to 5 P.M.

17. Kingston, Rondout Creek, New York (west shore—12347). On entering Kingston, be sure to keep in the middle of the entrance between the lighthouse and green tower 1 since shoal water extends for a considerable distance from the shores on both sides. Maximum speed permitted through the entire channel is 5 mph and the tide range is $3^1/2$ feet.

Its entrance is marked by two partially submerged jetties set with day beacons. A fog signal is at the north jetty light. The controlling depth in the creek records 13 feet from the entrance to the highway bridge, 10 feet to the southwest tip of Gumaer Island, and thence 7 feet to the head of the channel at Eddyville.

Rondout II Lighthouse, built in 1913 and still standing at the creek's entrance, is maintained as a satellite museum facility by the Hudson River Maritime Museum under a long-term lease from the Coast Guard. Rondout II continues to light the way for vessels plying the river, and visitors are able to wander through the former living quarters (which contain period furnishings), enjoy an exhibit on the history of the Kingston lighthouses and the keepers, and climb to the top of the lantern tower for breathtaking views of the Hudson River. If you are interested in learning more about the life of the old full-time keepers of the light and their families, take the tour boat which departs from the Museum.

From New York City north, the remaining lighthouses besides Rondout II are at Jeffrey's Hook under the George Washington Bridge, Tarrytown, Stony Point, Esopus Meadows, Hudson-Athens, and Saugerties. State, municipal, and conservancy groups are active in trying to preserve them. All seven are listed on the National Register of Historic Places.

The Hudson River Maritime Museum was organized in 1980 at Rondout Landing to help preserve the fast disappearing maritime heritage of the Hudson River. The museum has an active program of special events and educational programs which interpret the history of the Hudson, its major tributaries, and the industries which developed along the river's shores. The museum offers transient dockage *to its Boating Members with advance reservations.* Boating Membership is $40 a year and includes one night free docking. The museum's docks offer a quiet place to tie up for a night in a secure facility, dockside electricity, and an onshore head, shower, washer, and dryer—all within walking distance of a variety of excellent restaurants, boutiques, and antique shops. The museum is located on the starboard (north) side of the creek across from Sleightsburg, where the museum buildings and the drydocked 1898 steam tug *Mathilda* dominate the shore.

A nostalgic treat is to visit the Trolley Car Museum across the street from the museum and on the weekends to board a trolley for a 1¹/₂-mile ride to the old Hudson River Day Line dock. In the old days, steamers would come up here from New York City, where trains also picked up vacationers bound for Catskill Mountain resorts.

Just beyond the museum on the same shore between the two fixed bridges, you will come upon the Kingston Municipal Dock where a tie-up at a reasonable fee will provide easy access to local restaurants and the restored downtown area.

Farther up on the same shore nestled up a narrow inlet, sailing craft have found the Hideaway Marina to be a favored and secure haven, free of the wash from the main channel. Low water at the slips averages 5 feet MLW. Although there is no fuel here, Hideaway offers the usual conveniences to visitors.

Proceeding up the main channel beyond the first fixed bridge at Sleightsburg, you will note on the southern shore the first of the two full-service marinas on Rondout Creek. The Rondout Yacht Basin, located in quiet, attractive surroundings, provides gas and diesel fuel, showers, tight security, a store for provisions, a laundromat, a 35-ton travelift, pierports, pumpout, and an ability to handle large yachts up to 140 feet overall.

Views of the shoreline are lovely until you reach a unique structure right out of the Hudson's past. Built in 1847, this is a restored, privately owned, Gothic-style "weigh lock." How ironic that it now signals the beginning of a section of Rondout defiled by commercial interests—traprock excavation to port and a long string of barges to starboard.

But a comparatively pleasant rustic anchorage finally awaits you at creek's end at Eddyville. Make sure to hug closely to the starboard bank on the way. You'll have good water in the marked channel as far as the fourth and final bridge at Eddyville. About 500 yards beyond Gumaer Island, you will reach the Goose Roost Marina, set forward on a small peninsula. There is 10 feet MLW along 500 feet of dock space here, and transients can find the usual conveniences. The Goose Roost Saloon has a casual, fun menu and musical entertainment on the weekends. If no space is open here, slips might be open at next-door Anchorage Marina whose attractive restaurant serves Italian and seafood specialties. Lou's Boat Basin is the only local source for gas.

The best anchorage may be found along the shore across from Lou's. Here there is 8 feet of water, literally alive with bass, perch, pickerel, stripers, and carp. There is a small general store nearby. The swimming is reported fine just below the dam, and close by one can see the ruins of the first lock of the abandoned Delaware and Hudson Canal, on whose waters barges used to be drawn from the Pennsylvania coal mines. The mountains surrounding Eddyville have furnished much of the stone toward the construction of some of New York's highest skyscrapers.

The "Queen of the River," the *Mary Powell*, built in 1861, was broken up in 1920 and left on a bank to rot about halfway up Rondout Creek, along the southern shore. Little remains of her. She had been sold for scrap at a price of $3,250. Without a doubt, she captured the hearts of more people than any other steamboat in the history of Hudson River steamboating, and even today, many years since she last ran, you will find her mentioned in articles on the river or hear her name on the lips of old-timers. She launched her long career of service here in Rondout Creek.

18. Saugerties, Esopus Creek (west shore—12347). This is one of the best natural anchorages on the Hudson, and boats entering the creek should stay in mid-channel and not exceed a speed of 5 mph. A few years ago, the channel was dredged to a depth of 12 feet as far as the Coast Guard station a short distance up on the starboard shore. It is the only station between Albany and Governor's Island and is mainly responsible for maintaining the buoyage along the river. It monitors VHF-16. Across from this station lies the white clubhouse of the Saugerties Power Boat Association. We have always enjoyed our many visits here. Electricity, ice, and water are at the slips. The clubhouse provides showers and a weekend bar. One small example of this club's conviviality is the special ceremony of launching any member's boat in return for two pitchers of beer to wet the whistle of the workers. We were cautioned to stay well clear of the dam situated at the head of the creek.

We put into Saugerties Marine next to the club for gas and marine supplies, then looked over Lynch's Marina just beyond the port bank. Here you'll find equally pleasant surroundings, a bit more privacy, and good water. A recommended anchorage lies just beyond Lynch's where the creek widens. This marina is the winter home of the Hudson River sloop *Clearwater*.

Although attractive homes border the channel, some ruins are reminders that once there was a Saugerties Line that maintained daily passenger service to New York. Saugerties is Dutch for "saw mills."

The renovated Saugerties Lighthouse, originally built in 1867, returned to operation in 1990 and is now open to visitors on weekends and holidays from 3 to 5 P.M. during the summer. Its dock can be reserved only by special permission from the Lighthouse Conservancy, phone (914) 246-9170.

19. Catskill, Catskill Creek (west shore—12347). Along the entire Hudson, this is still one of our favorite spots. It was first visited by Hendrick Hudson and his crew on September 15, 1609, in his vain search for a northwest passage to the Indies. "Now," according to a Catskill native, "if the river could be cleaned up, we would have to string a velvet rope across the channel and let boats in two at a time." With a large shallow mud bank covering much of the southern part of the creek entrance, it is wise to keep flashing green buoy 67 well to port and on entering the channel swing wide to the east and north of green can 1. Catskill Creek has a controlling depth of 6½ feet to the highway bridge located 1 mile upstream, with a 5-foot rise and fall of tide. Keep in mid-creek, especially at the first bend, to avoid a rock with 4 feet over it located about 50 feet off the southern bank. This is part of a projected

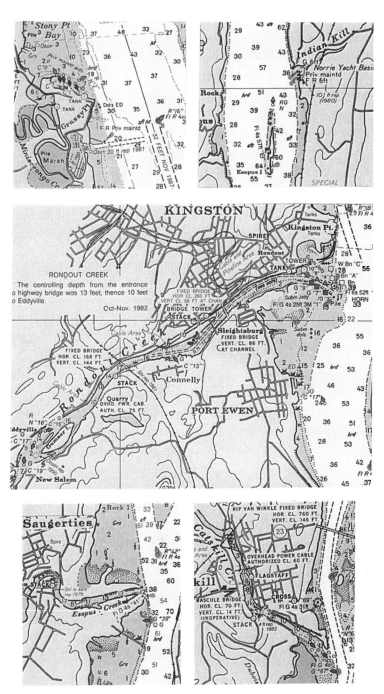

Some ports along the Hudson River. Upper left, refer to Chart 12343; other refer to Chart 12347.

rock formation named Hop-O-Nose after the prominent nose of a local Indian named Hopp. It reportedly caused many steamboat collisions.

The first facility you will come to, located not far from the creek's entrance on the starboard shore, is Riverview Marine, providing several berths for transients, gas, diesel fuel, a well-equipped marine store, and a pumpout station. It reportedly claims fast and complete services on inboards and outboards, including towing operations, and prop replacements seven days a week. The local sheriff's patrol boat, stationed here, monitors VHF-9 and 16, and Riverhead can be reached on 16. Not much beyond, you can tie up at the Catskill Marina, nestled on the edge of the same shore, where the hills rise steeply on both sides and are mirrored in the glassy water. It affords a picturesque view of the creek; Manager Dolores Pegaz pointed out telephones, gas, diesel fuel, ice, water, and electric connections along the floats. There's a small swimming pool for the kids but no repair service for your boat. Showers, a laundromat, rental cars, and a ship's store complete the services here. Certainly it would be difficult to find a more scenic, safe, and friendly anchorage, convenient to the churches, stores, and theater on Main Street in Catskill. Ask to receive a copy of this marina's complete guide to all local restaurants, stores, services, and historic sites.

Across the creek on the south shore is Hop-O-Nose Marine with gas, diesel fuel, water, ice, showers, a marine railway, cookout facilities, a ship's store offering nautical charts and limited groceries, a mast-stepping rig, engine repairs, and a bar and restaurant recognized for its Italian fare. Motel arrangements can be made for you, and transportation to town for supplies is available; people come here from miles around to enjoy the restaurant's very palatable pizzas. Don Edwards reminded us that Riverview is a designated pumpout station and that it monitors VHF-16. Since Catskill is an extremely popular point of call during the summer season, it is advisable to phone ahead for slip space. Catskill Marina can be reached at (518) 943-4170 and Hop-O-Nose is at (518) 943-4640.

At the end of the creek to port you will find the long dock of the well-maintained Catskill Yacht Club. With a modest number of services to transients, its greatest advantage is its close proximity to the village.

Once known as Catskill Landing and before then called Kaatskill by the Dutch in the days of river and turnpike transportation, this port was a busy and prosperous shipping point. Early tavernkeepers in this community were known as "retailers of liquid damnation." Catskill mountain-brewed applejack was a staple during the Prohibition era, and shady characters once established hideouts in the hills. And it was at a spot near Catskill that Rip Van Winkle is supposed to have indulged in his legendary sleep. Things are different now, for in summer many vacationists descend on Catskill and yachts come and go. But so far, nothing seems to have spoiled the quiet charm of this snug harbor, except possibly occasionally lively freshets in the spring.* Both Night and Day Line steamers landed here until the final Day Line sailing in 1953.

20. Athens, New York (west shore—12347). As you approach Hudson, you will pick up the Hudson Island Lighthouse, one of the two remaining midstream lighthouses on the Hudson. The other is at Esopus Flats. Leaving the lighthouse to starboard, you will leave the main channel and pass by the town of Athens, making sure to keep well off of Middle Ground Flats. Near the mouth of Murderers Creek, approximately 1 1/2 miles beyond Hudson Island Lighthouse, you can make out Hagar's Harbor, identified by a white building behind a floating dock. This location is extremely well protected from the main channel, although very open to winds from the north and southwest. The owner, Dot Richardson, has gone out of her way in providing visiting yachtsmen with a modest-sized stopping place that is spanking clean and set in peaceful surroundings. Their intimate-looking restaurant and bar alone offer a refreshing change. Food and ice for your galley will be delivered to your slip on call. Don't count on having major repair work performed here, but you will find limited dockage space in good water with electricity provided. Amazingly, Time-Warner's 170-foot yacht, *Papa*, tied up here for a visit in the summer of 1993.

Few of us may know that the town of Hudson, across the river from Athens, thrived as an important whaling center in the early 1800s. The War of Independence had disastrous effects on the highly vulnerable Nantucket whaling fleet, and, according to *Surveyor*, a periodical of the American Bureau of Shipping, Seth Jenkins left Nantucket and in 1784 led a parade of whaling ships to Claverack Landing, renamed Hudson in 1785. Situated 100 miles from New York City, this deep-water port became a safe haven from marauders during the American and French Revolutions and the War of 1812. By 1830 the Hudson Whaling Company, consisting of 20 ships, was formed. In 1831–32, the Pough-

*From *New York*—American Guide Series (Oxford University Press, New York).

keepsie and Newburgh Whaling Companies added their 10 ships to the river's fleet; whaling fever was running high. A reminder of those halcyon days may be rekindled in us today on viewing the tall, stately Nantucket-style houses in Hudson and nearby towns.

By the 1840s, the wars with Britain had ended and the need for special protection of the whaling fleets was no longer required. New Bedford, with ships twice as large as those on the river, began to usurp the place of the Hudson River whalers. The Hudson Whaling Company was forced to sell the last of its ships in 1845.

Among Hudson's other distinctions is that it was the first city chartered in the United States after the adoption of the Declaration of Independence. In addition, what has been called "The Friendly City" was almost selected as the capital of New York State in 1797, losing out to Albany by only one vote in the State Legislature.

21. Coxsackie, New York (west shore—12348). There is a good anchorage in 12 feet of water off the main channel to the west of Coxsackie Island. Should you be making your approach from the south, however, note that the sandbar due south of the island and marked on the chart has now shifted dangerously westward across the channel's mouth, resulting in periodic groundings. Therefore, if you are unfamiliar with these waters, we advise you to reach your anchorage by passing through the channel north of Coxsackie Island. In doing so, do not be tempted into the treacherous shoals behind Rattlesnake Island.

The pretty surroundings promise you pleasant picnicking or walking tours. On the western shore is the Coxsackie Yacht Club, with floats, ice, water, electricity, gas, and showers, about a third of the way above the lower end of the island. The club, which monitors VHF-9, has limited dock space in 9 feet MLW for boats up to 40 feet in length. Former Commodore Leonard Jump told us on our most recent visit that his club operates a snack bar Saturday and Sunday from 11 A.M. to 5 P.M., and its traditional pig roast, held each Labor Day, is still going strong. Groceries may be obtained at the Grand Union in town. There is no charge for overnight dockage, but a "little brown jug" at the club's bar invites volunteer contributions both large and small.

Coxsackie is an Indian name meaning "hoot of an owl," and tribes from miles around used to gather here to make arrowheads. It is no wonder, therefore, that the club's burgee is identified by a red arrowhead on a field of white. The surrounding countryside has been one of the largest mushroom-growing centers in the world—an industry that was first developed in huge icehouses formerly supplying natural ice to New York City.

On your run north to New Baltimore, you may find a popular spot to explore or anchor for the night. It is in the creek to the east of Houghtaling Island. The creek, whose entrance lies off nun 34A, carries ample depths for 3 miles north. But remember, if you are tempted to venture up this peaceful, pastoral byway beyond the Hook Boat Club on the eastern shore, there is no northern passage back into the main channel.

22. New Baltimore, New York (west shore—12348). Many years ago, when we first put into the Shady Harbor Marina, just north of flashing buoy 41, the original owner, Walter Stansfield, stretched out his hand in greeting and declared, "We're the friendly people. When we built this marina in 1970, we had some definite goals in mind. We thought that it was high time this part of the Hudson had a facility that you could call modern, clean, and efficiently run. We wanted to offer our cruising customers, mostly family groups, a sense of security during their visits plus some old-fashioned peace and quiet to be enjoyed in a natural setting."

Although Stansfield has long since retired, our recent tour around this marina, now run by Tony and Marie Brock, convinced us that his goals have been maintained. At the floating docks with 6-foot depths, gas, diesel fuel, electricity, ice, and water are supplied, and ashore there are showers, washers and dryers, a fine marine store, a launching ramp, a 20-ton travelift, and a swimming pool. There's a sizable demand here for propeller repair and orders for mast unstepping on sailing craft heading for the canals. Minivan transportation is also available, for buying provisions from local stores. At the time of writing, the Brocks were planning the building of an on-site restaurant serving a light fare to marina visitors.

Shady Harbor may well offer you the most convenient stopover you'll experience until you and your boat have reached the Troy Lock. The Awenke Yacht Club, whose Indian name means "on the water" and which is reported to be the only nonworking club on the river, finds its home here.

New Baltimore as early as 1800 was the center for building sloops, schooners, and river barges.

23. Coeymans, New York (west shore—12348). Hug the west shore until you pick up flashing-light marker 45, marking the southernmost extension of a treacherous 1,500-foot dike facing the harbor. If you do not wish to join the disreputable "Coeyman's Dike Club," be sure to leave this lighted marker 45 well to starboard, keeping off the dike at least 100 feet at all times. The five Coeyman's dike day beacons, marked on the chart, are equipped with diamond-shaped white daymarks with orange reflective borders in whose center are the words, "Danger— Submerged Jetty." The entire area inside the dike continues to shoal up alarmingly. Years ago, we spotted a small sloop drawing 4 feet firmly aground on her beam's end in mud just inside the dike; we're sure there'll be many more hapless craft to follow until this channel is completely dredged to its former depths.

Should you decide to stop at the docks ahead to port, keep inside of any line of moorings and you'll arrive safely before a blue concrete building. Hedy and Carl Allen are the friendly new owners here of the Coeyman Landing Marina, formerly Finke Marine. They have done a fine job in improving their marina's appearance and facilities. It now offers complete services to transients, new docks in 6 feet MLW, a full-line marine store, a 35-ton travelift, a pumpout station, even propane gas. Hail them on VHF-16 to get a slip.

Boats stopping over at Ravena Coeyman's Yacht Club face the same dilemma in attempting a safe, dockside approach. This club, situated just to the north, offers reciprocal privileges and similar protection including gas, electricity, and adequate dock space. If you don't need supplies and you are lucky enough to obtain a slip, a stop here where there is an attractive clubhouse nestled midst shady picnic grounds will be enjoyable.

Coeymans, pronounced Queeman's, was first settled in 1673 and later became a foremost ice harvester, one of the major industries along the Hudson during the last century.

The Tri-City Yacht Club formerly located at Cedar Hill has moved to a new location on the west shore almost 2 miles north of Ravena Coeyman's Yacht Club and just south of the fixed highway bridge. Its entrance is marked by a buoy forming a break in a low stone breakwater running north-south. Favor the lighted pole as you enter the basin with your bow on line with the club's range lights. Watch for shoaling inside the breakwater since the basin proper has a depth of only about 3 feet at low water. Once inside the basin, keep the docked boats close aboard. The clubhouse, which one might consider chalet style, offers showers, water, and overnight dockage, if available, to members of other recognized yacht clubs. We were cautioned not to enter or anchor anywhere north of the docks. Tri-City is one of 18 member yacht clubs belonging to the Mohawk Hudson Council concerned with boating activities along the Hudson.

24. Castleton-on-Hudson, New York (east shore—12348). Just above nun 54 lies the progressive Castleton Boat Club. There is a fine concrete launching ramp, floats with gas, ice, a picnic table, moorings, a restaurant and bar, a laundromat, showers, and a nearby grocery store. The club is housed in a small, well-located white building. Though there is a considerable stretch of open Hudson to the north and south, the river is narrow enough here to prevent waves from making up in stiff winds from the west. The wash from the passing boats may not trouble you half so much as the noise from the trains nearby.

It was suggested that transient craft call ahead on VHF-9 for a possible slip. The club, founded in 1952, serves food on weekends and holidays. Just Richie's, a recommended restaurant open everyday except Monday, is only a few blocks away.

Let William Storandt give us his impression of this club, as expressed in his article in *Cruising World.*

> We have encountered boats as far away as Trinidad with spars stepped in Castleton. I'm sure one could find—nestled in the logbooks of a thousand sailboats—amused but glowing accounts of this seat of hospitality. Again, it is a powerboat club. But these jovial tinkerers have created a perfect symbiosis—they have built a large, hand-operated crane for handling spars. It's the lifeblood of the shoestring club and a great deal for sailors.

25. Rensselaer, New York (east shore—12348). Here right below the fixed bridge to Albany at Mill Creek, is located the white, one-story clubhouse of the Albany Yacht Club founded in 1873. The dockmaster told us that they have gas, diesel fuel, ice, water, electricity, pumpout service, and supplies nearby. Although he monitors VHF-16, he advises that you reserve ahead for a slip by phoning (518) 445-9587. There is deep water at their long line of floating docks, and the clubhouse offers as complete facilities inside as you will find along the upper Hudson. Behind the club are stores and eating places in the city of Rensselaer.

You will find that a 20-minute walk across the bridge to the Empire State Plaza is a rewarding experience. Here you can see special exhibits at the New York State Museum, take interesting tours, and view the surrounding area for miles from the 42-story Tower Building. The plaza celebrates each Fourth of July with a variety of musical events and a display of electrifying fireworks.

Two blocks south of the club is restored Fort Crailo, a museum and national landmark, where the famous song "Yankee Doodle" was written in 1758. A visit here any time between 10 A.M. and 5 P.M. Wednesday through Saturday and Sunday from 1 to 5 P.M. is well worthwhile.

26. Watervliet, New York (west shore—12348). This shoreline is now covered by a busy waterfront highway with no boating facilities.

Troy and Watervliet are both important industrial centers, and the latter has a large arsenal. According to our historical source of information:

> The War of 1812 brought the settlement one of the largest arsenals in the United States, now the Watervliet Arsenal, and immortalized Samuel Wilson, who supplied the soldiers quartered nearby with what they called "Uncle Sam's beef," as the original "Uncle Sam."
>
> In 1825 Mrs. Hannah Lord Montague, a Troy housewife, developed a detachable collar for men's shirts; according to tradition, she cut the dirty collars off her husband's shirts to save herself the trouble of washing the entire garment, and thereby created a new industry.*

The Federal Lock, Troy (east shore—12348)

A quarter-mile south of the Federal Lock and just north of the Green Island Lift Bridge, you will approach Troy Town Dock and Marina, a full-service, round-the-clock facility providing berths for transient yachts up to 200 feet overall. It is a recommended stop for any vessel and

---

*From *New York*—American Guide Series (Oxford University Press, New York).

crew preparing to enter the lock system. The dockmaster monitors VHF-16 or he can be contacted by phoning (518) 272-5341. Even sailboat masts up to 55 feet can be stepped with prior notification and fenders for use in the locks are available here.

Another advantage this marina offers is its proximity to historic downtown Troy and various restaurants serving daily luncheon and dinner to patrons dressed casually. The New Castaway Restaurant, with an outdoor deck and dancing in its lounge, is located immediately south of the Green Island Bridge. Directly overlooking the marina the multi-story Brown and Moran Restaurant and Brewery serves varied pub-style food with beer actually brewed on the premises. North of the bridge, the River Street Cafe prepares a continental cuisine. Dockage for the patrons of these establishments can usually be arranged at the Troy Town Dock and Marina.

On powering up to the Federal Lock, hug the east shore to avoid shoal water below the dam. You will notice a mooring wall installed in 1970 for use by boats awaiting the opening of the lock. Proceed to the lock's entrance when the green light shows, while avoiding being swept westward by the current. No permit is required for this lock, and as with the other locks above, there is no charge for transit. This is the biggest lock in the system, but the lift is only 14 feet. At the time we were there the schedule called for opening the lock for pleasure craft on the hour, but should a lockage for commercial vessels be made at any other time, it is possible to follow along provided there is sufficient room. Lock personnel monitor VHF-13.

The Canalized Hudson and the Champlain Barge Canal
(Book of Charts of New York Canals)

Above the Troy Lock, as previously noted, the "road" forks. One fork begins with the Mohawk River and leads westward through canal, river, and lake into Lakes Ontario and Erie. The other fork begins as a continuation of the Hudson River—called the Canalized Hudson—and leads northward for about 34 miles. It then becomes the Champlain Barge Canal and continues northward for 20 more miles (making 54 in all) until it reaches Whitehall, at the southern end of Lake Champlain. Although the westward fork is beyond the scope of this *Guide,* and involves a long trip, the northern passage offers the possibility of reaching beautiful Lake Champlain from the Troy Lock in about a day. For those who want to cruise farther than Lake Champlain, there is the possibility of continuing northward by the way of the Richelieu River into the St. Lawrence and thence eastward into the Gulf of St. Lawrence, then around (or through) Cape Breton, and then south and west around Nova Scotia and across the Bay of Fundy to the New England coast.

Between the Troy Lock and Lake Champlain are several stopping places that we can only mention here, with their approximate distances in miles from the Troy Lock (in parentheses): Mechanicville (10); Schuylerville (24); Fort Edward, beginning of the Champlain Barge Canal (34); Smith Basin (41). There are undoubtedly other places for overnight tie-up and supplies, but these are also beyond the range of our explorations for this *Guide*.

The upper Canalized Hudson is pretty and pastoral but lacking in the spectacular beauty found in the Hudson below Albany. Progress is slow on the voyage to Lake Champlain, because of the eleven locks (numbered to 12 with 10 omitted), each of which may cause delay, and also because of the speed limit between the locks: 10 miles an hour in the Canalized Hudson and 6 in the Champlain Barge Canal. The route is well marked and covered to Lake Champlain by Chart 14786, New York State Barge Canal System, obtainable at a cost of $28 from NOAA, National Ocean Service; N/CG33, Distribution Branch, Riverdale, MD 20737 or through its local chart agencies. There is no official chart covering the Erie Canal from Lyons to Tonawanda, since this section is a land-cut for which charts are not necessary.

A few basic rules and regulations for pleasure boaters are outlined in the free pamphlet *Cruising the Canals*, obtained by writing to the Director, Waterways Maintenance Subdivision, New York State Department of Transportation, 1220 Washington Ave., Albany, NY 12232. An important leaflet entitled *Your Key to the Lock*, describing the operation of the Federal Lock and Dam at Troy, is available from U.S. Army Engineer District, New York, Attn: Public Affairs Office, 26 Federal Plaza, New York, NY 10278-0090. There is no charge for this.

The Federal Lock at Troy is toll-free but requires boat registration for passage. Motorboats and sailboats with auxiliary power, which are used principally in New York State, must be registered with the Department of Motor Vehicles, Empire State Plaza, Albany, NY 12228.

Recently, user fees have been imposed on recreational vessels passing through the locks and lift bridges of the New York State Canal System.

Chapter IV

North Shore of Long Island Sound

Throgs Neck, New York, to New London, Connecticut

Throgs Neck, New York (12366). At the western end of Long Island Sound a long and narrow peninsula, known as Throgs Neck, marks the place where the Sound ends and the East River begins. On the east side of this peninsula between the northern end of the neck and Locust Point is one of the snuggest harbors on Long Island Sound—a fine overnight-stopping place for cruising boats on their way to or from Manhattan or the Hudson River. The Locust Point Yacht Club, around "the corner" to starboard as one enters, is hospitable to visiting yachtsmen and will help them to find a mooring if one is available. A club burgee, one of the friendly members told us, is all the introduction needed. Ice and water are obtainable at the club during the season. From the club, buses connect with the Manhattan subway at Westchester Square.

At the end of the harbor is the Locust Point Marina where you will find a marine store, ice, water, and nearby restaurants. They handle small repairs but supply no fuel and have a limited number of overnight slips.

As the chart shows, there is plenty of water inside the harbor, but one must use care in getting past several outlying rocks off Locust Point at the entrance. However, during the summer the yacht club has a pole on the outermost rock, which must be left to starboard going in. The narrow channel, marked by red and green pilings, records only 4 feet at MLW.

Although the inner harbor beyond the yacht club is congested with moored powerboats, it is over 1/4 mile long and usually some room can be found somewhere. The Throgs Neck Bridge from the Bronx to Long Island passes over the entrance between Locust Point and Throgs Neck, but all except auxiliaries with fairly tall masts will have no difficulty in getting through. Yachts inside the harbor, we have been told, have ridden out hurricanes without difficulty.

At the end of Throgs Neck is Fort Schuyler, erected over a hundred years ago, with Fort Totten on the opposite shore, to protect New York City from enemy attack from the Sound. Now it is the home of the New York State Maritime Academy. Those standing at the end of Throgs Neck on a fateful day in October 1776 might have watched the passage of a flotilla loaded with redcoats on their way to land on the northern shore of Eastchester Bay. The British attempt to cut off the retreat of General Washington and his army from Manhattan to White Plains failed, thanks in part to a withering cross fire from Colonel John Glover and his fishermen of Marblehead.

Little Neck Bay, New York (12366). The fetch of water between Fort Totten to the west and the U.S. Merchant Marine Academy on Kings Point to the east forms the mouth of Little Neck Bay, where there is plenty of deep water due to dredging, as illustrated on the latest chart. However, as you pull up on the west shore to the 300-foot pier with floating docks of the Bayside Marina, identified by a flagpole marked on the chart, depths decrease to less than 4 feet at MLW. This modest marina is under the jurisdiction of the New York City Parks and Recreation Department. It offers water, overnight moorings, launch service, a snack bar, but no fuel.

In 1969, 350 acres of mud were dredged out of much of the bay to attain controlling depths of 7 feet for anchoring. Such depths can be found now in mid-channel to a point where you come abeam the southeastern tip of Willet's Point marked by black-and-white can LN. From that point, 7 feet can be safely carried to starboard into a special anchorage area forming almost two-thirds of the western part of the lower bay. But, also from that point, only about 3 feet can be carried to port into another sector lying immediately east and south of nun A. At low ebb, no boat of 3-foot draft or greater should venture closer than 300 yards from the bay's shoreline. A popular anchorage for boats of fairly shoal draft is in the bight formed on the chart near Udalls Mill Pond on the eastern shore.

It is estimated that 500 recreational boats are moored in Little Neck Bay, and the figure is growing. Although there are limited facilities and it's wide open to the north, yachtsmen often use the bay as a convenient jumping-off point for cruising east or west. The unusual tidal currents here form a continual flushing action, which many believe gives this bay the cleanest water in western Long Island Sound.

City Island, New York (12366). City Island is New York headquarters for yacht building and repair. Rimmed from end to end with four yacht clubs, seven marinas, a half-dozen full-service yacht yards, and two sailmakers, it serves as home port to nearly 2,000 boats. The island is about a mile long, connected with the mainland by a fixed bridge with a vertical clearance of 12 feet and accessible to New York by bus, taxi, and subway.

No yachtsman should miss a visit to City Island, but it is not the place for a quiet, secure anchorage. The best anchorage for large boats is to the east, approximately off the middle of the island. The holding ground, however, is reported to be only fair, and the anchorage is exposed to northeasterly and southeasterly blows. In such storms, it is well to run over to the shore of Hart Island and anchor off the upper half of that island, where the holding ground is said to be good. There is also a possibility of tying up at a slip at one of the large docks that run along the eastern shore of City Island. The mean range of tide is $7^1/_4$ feet.

For boats drawing less than 7 feet, the western side of the island is preferred, though it is exposed to southerly winds. The yacht clubs are on this side and as a rule have moorings and launch service available to members of other recognized clubs. The Morris Yacht and Beach Club is on the southerly point, near the dock used by the pilots and Coast Guard.

The City Island Yacht Club is in a white building marked by a flagpole a short distance to the north along the westerly shore. It has a long dock with shear legs, and over 6 feet of water at low tide. The club, which monitors VHF-68, is especially popular among the sailing fraternity and maintains a few guest moorings. The Stuyvesant Yacht Club is a little farther north, and the Harlem Yacht Club, the oldest on City Island, is in a cove on the northwest side of the island.

There are also a number of good yards and marinas on the western shore, most of them catering to smaller craft and located at the northern end. Two of the popular ones on this side of the island from south to north are Kretzer Boat Works (which can take care of fairly large boats, does welding and rigging work, and has been favorably known for many years) and Royal Marina (formerly Maritime Landings). The latter, run by Richard Reardon, is marked by long, very sheltered finger docks and a prominent dockhouse. It offers general repairs, ice, showers, and a laundromat and is very close to the Manhattan bus line which runs from 6 to 9 A.M. and from 4 to 7 P.M. Although neither of these facilities provide fuel, they are accessible to all types of stores, including these upscale seafood restaurants that provide free docking to their patrons along the western shore: Anna's Harbor Inn, Sea Shore Restaurant, and Crab Shanty. Portofino, next door, serves an excellent northern Italian cuisine.

The one source of fuel on City Island is at Bridge Boat Sales at the northeast end of the island. It only sells gas; the nearest diesel fuel is in Manhasset Bay.

On the east shore, the leading yards are, from south to north, Yacht Services International, Consolidated Yachts, and the Minniford complex. The latter is at the site of the former builders of a long line of victorious America's Cup 12-meters: *Columbia* (1958), *Constellation* (1964), *Intrepid* (1967 and 1970), *Courageous* (1974 and 1977), and *Freedom* (1980).

Consolidated Yachts, managed by Wesley Rodstrom for over twenty-five years, may have a few slips open for transient yachts. A good plan to gain a berth is to phone (718) 885-1900 or radio ahead on VHF-9 up to 4 P.M. The mean tidal range here at City Island docks is 7 feet. Here they have ice, showers, and a marine-parts store, and restaurants and stores for supplies are within walking distance.

Minneford's City Island Marineland handles engine and hull repairs with some accommodations for visiting yachts while the South Minneford Yacht Club primarily serves local residents. It is suggested that the most pleasant stop for transients at the Minneford complex is at the North Minneford Yacht Club, which monitors VHF-71. Minneford derives its name from its original inhabitants, the Minnewit Indians.

Unfortunately, few yachts are being built here now. High costs and foreign competition have taken care of that. But few ports have as much to offer in terms of maintenance, repair, storage, and marine equipment of all kinds. Leading sailmakers have their lofts on City Island. Ulmer Kolius Sails is located near Consolidated Yachts, and Herb Hild of Hild Sails can be found at the end of Fordham Street, on the eastern shore. Both these lofts enjoy a worldwide reputation among yachtsmen.

The age of the coastal condominium has come to the island, as it has to a large portion of the New England shoreline. The famous old Nevins yard has been converted into a school building and the former United Boatyard is now the site of a cluster of gray clapboard condominiums called "The Boatyard." Some of the over 4,000 islanders think there will be more condos to come. But one native, in considering this new age, seems to sum up the public's outlook. "City Island changes and yet it doesn't. The people who are moving in have basically the same value system as the old-timers. I know we have to move ahead, but I just wish that we do it cautiously." Retired sea captain Skippy Lane expresses his feelings this way. "I love City Island. I went to sea for 40 years and I went all over the world. I saw beautiful places but I didn't want to live anywhere but City Island. To me it's the best part of New York."

Perhaps City Island's greatest hidden treasure today is the North Wind Undersea Institute, a fascinating museum to visit at 610 City Island Avenue. Situated in an old sea captain's house, the museum houses collections devoted to whaling, whale and marine mammal rescue programs, diving and treasure hunting, marine-life exhibits, and the effects of pollution on the local waters. Some 30,000 New York children tour the museum and participate in its educational shows each school year.

The island got its name in 1761, when some early settlers devised a plan to develop the area into a booming seaport that would some day outrival New York. Now many of the island's permanent residents, all very community minded, but linked to the Bronx by a bridge and taxes, are more interested in keeping the island the way it is than in competing with any other place. It's so geographically isolated that one can believe the remark recently made by a native islander: "You daren't say anything to anybody about somebody here because the chances are they're somebody's cousin."

Neighboring Hart Island has an interesting history. After the Civil War, during which it served as a prison camp, it was purchased for $75,000 with the plan to use it as a New York City burial ground. Six hundred thousand dead have been interred on the island, with burials continuing to this day. In the 1950s, the northern end of the island was a Nike missile base; several empty silos are still in place there.

In the early summer of 1614, Captain Adriaen Block, Dutch fur trader, sailed past City Island in his 44^1/$_2$-foot "jacht" *Onrust,* (Restless), and thus began the first cruise on Long Island Sound ever made by white men. Many thousands of yachts have followed the path of the *Onrust*, and on a weekend in summer the waters to the south of that famous island are in a perpetual state of confusion from conflicting wakes.

What Block might have observed with fearful eye as he entered the channel between Sands Point, Long Island, and New Rochelle has since become a familiar and respected beacon to thousands of seamen approaching New York Harbor from the Sound. Yet no light was erected upon the perilous shoals of Execution Rocks until 1850. Ed Hine of Sea Cliff, a Corinthian yachtsman, adds this interesting bit of historical lore:

> With such a forbidding name, several speculations have been made about the origin of Execution Rocks. Probably no one now knows why the place got that name, but one good reason is shown on a chart in the Raynham Hall Museum in Oyster Bay, Long Island. It is called the "Chart of Oyster Bay, Published in London in 1777 for His Majesty's Ships of War."
>
> This chart shows the north shore of Long Island from Cow Bay (now Manhasset Bay) to Eatons Neck. What we call Execution Rocks has neither light nor beacon and is named bluntly "The Executioners." Certainly no name could be more apt for an unmarked hazard practically in the fairway, and this origin seems more likely than the stories of pirate hangings or other mass executions.

The Execution Rocks lighthouse became automated in 1979 and is a key navigational aid. This 62-foot structure with its 600,000-candlepower light flashing every 10 seconds is visible for 13 miles along the Sound, can emit a foghorn blast in thick weather every 15 seconds, and issues a radio signal every 6 minutes to help the modern navigator.

New Rochelle, New York (12366). This is one of two harbors serving the New Rochelle area. The other is Echo Bay. The two do not connect. There is a well-protected anchorage in attractive surroundings inside of Glen Island to the southwest of the bascule bridge connecting Glen Island Park to the mainland. At one prolonged blast of your horn followed by one short blast the bridge will open promptly. Here on the northwest shore just inside the bridge is located the excellent Huguenot

New Rochelle Harbor, showing Bascule Bridge connecting to Glen Island Park. *Aero Graphics Corp.*

Yacht Club, which extends the use of its facilities to members of other recognized yacht clubs offering reciprocal privileges. In 1965 this third-oldest yacht club on the Sound was swept by fire but, like a phoenix, it has sprung anew from its own ashes with a clubhouse that once belonged to Lillian Gish, over 1,200 feet of docks, and improved depths at dockside to 8 feet. There is a fine bar in the clubhouse. The club's facilities include launch service, possible moorings, water, electricity, ice, showers, a laundromat, and supplies when requested of the dockmaster. Don't tie up on the outside of the front floats; these are reserved for the club launches.

On May 25, 1895, the *New York World* carried this momentous announcement:

> There is one thing that our Regatta Committee eagerly desires to impress upon the members, and that is that each boat will be required to carry at least one lady.

This is quite the proper caper, as there are hosts of sailor girls at New Rochelle who desire to have their nautical education completed. And who can do it better than the festive and gallant Huguenot boys?

Just beyond Huguenot is located West Harbor Yacht Service which is specially equipped to repair sailing craft.

Across the channel on Glen Island is a conversation piece—the remains of John Starin's "Rhine castle," built in 1880. Starin, a shipping magnate, ran excursions from New York City to the beer garden he operated on what is now the site of the casino built by the Westchester Park Commission in 1924. The comparative prices paid for the island by Starin in 1880 and by the county in 1924 offer an interesting footnote— from $18,000 the price jumped to $500,000. Westchester County's Department of Parks has built a fine launching ramp next to the picturesque castle on the northern perimeter of the island. It is limited to boats up to 21 feet overall and requires that their owners have a Westchester County resident permit.

The county-owned Casino, a mecca for the "Swing Generation," has been renovated and is not only rented out for weddings and banquets but open as a restaurant on Saturday evenings.

Still farther to the southwest is the large and well-equipped New York Athletic Club Yacht Club and service center. Members of other recognized clubs are welcome and slips or moorings are usually available. It is best to phone ahead at (914) 738-9716 to seek a possible reservation. Here it is not as crowded as farther to the east. Launch service and other facilities are offered. Beyond the N.Y.A.C. the channel is tricky and should not be attempted without a local pilot. Speed limit in the harbor is 4 knots. Both Huguenot and N.Y.A.C. monitor VHF-9.

Although Glen Island Park is reserved for residents of Westchester County, it provides a pleasant outlook for visiting yachts anchored in the harbor. From the other side, access to the heart of the city of New Rochelle is obtained by bus from the Fort Slocum Dock.

There are two main channels into New Rochelle Harbor, one between Glen and Davids Islands and the other north of Davids Island. They are both well marked, but don't skip any of the buoys; there are many outlying rocks. Especially dangerous are the rocks between Columbia and Pea Islands and Davids Island.

In 1637, Davids Island was sold by the Siwanoy Indians to the Dutch East India Company. Later it was used for cattle grazing, until 1856, when it was bought by Thaddeus Davids as the site for an ink factory which was never built. During the Civil War, wounded from both sides were treated here, and in 1896 the island was named Fort Slocum to become the outer defense of New York Harbor. Now that its most recent owner, Consolidated Edison, has returned the island to the city of New Rochelle, we can expect its 80 acres to be further developed. We have been told to look for the possible private development by the end of this decade of a 2,000-unit condominium complex on Davids Island including the construction of a marina with an 850-boat capacity. But strong opposition continues to come from the local residents and environmentalists who foresee many problems including the possibilities of monstrous traffic and pollution.

Beside the harbor in back of Glen Island there is also a northeast channel behind Davenport Neck. Caution is necessary here as there are no markers inside the harbor entrance. Just to port on entering this channel with its 8-foot depth, you will note the docks of Wright Island Marina, which specializes in powerboats, gives fairly complete services to transients, and presents to the eye a rather commercial image. As a contrast, up the channel to starboard you may reach the alluring Imperial Yacht Club, whose many facilities are open all year round to cruising people and live-aboards. It claims to be "the most luxurious, largest, and modern marina in the New York metropolitan area." This is evidenced perhaps by its offerings not only of all types of fuels and full repair services but of a completely manicured layout, including laundromat, heads and showers, overnight dockage with electricity, a restaurant, a 70-ton open-end lift with 24-hour emergency hauling, the use of its tennis court included in the transient fee, and the major attraction—a 75-foot swimming pool. The owners, Johanna and Anthony Giacobbe, who live on the property, enthuse about the great protection here. "You can tie up a boat to our docks with a shoelace!" Reservations are suggested by phoning (914) 636-1122 or using VHF-9. The Castaways, just beyond, is also a new but smaller, more exclusive marina complex, which is apparently trying with some success and considerable bustle to emulate its competitor next door. A five-minute cab ride from either of these two facilities will take you to the New Rochelle Mall, railroad station, movies, and stores for provisions.

The small, trim-looking Neptune Boat Club lies between these two major clubs, and its use is reportedly for members only.

If the anchorages of the Huguenot Yacht Club or the N.Y.A.C. are crowded or hot and moorings are unavailable, the best place to anchor is in the stretch of water between Goose and Glen Islands. This spot offers fair protection in all but northeast storms and is apt to be cooler than inside.

First settled by Huguenot refugees in 1689, New Rochelle is said to have been the scene of George M. Cohan's *Forty-five Minutes from Broadway*.

Echo Bay, New Rochelle, New York (12367). This harbor behind Beaufort Point is too commercial and crowded to be appealing for an overnight stop, though it is well protected from all winds. On entering this harbor at night, carefully note that the extreme left limit of the outer channel is on a line straight between green flasher 3BR, northeast of Bailey Rock, and a flashing green light on a flagpole set near the southeastern end of Beaufort Point.

As you enter the inner harbor, you will come up to the large Municipal Marina on the starboard shore. Concessions here include boat and engine repair shops, showers, ice, a laundromat, and a gas dock with diesel fuel. Dockage is available for 750 boats, including 300 moorings and 450 slips with electrical connections for those over 18 feet. However, slips are usually reserved for local residents. Harbormaster Pat Barrett, who monitors VHF-16 at this dock, will assign you one if it is available. He reports that "this place is big enough that we can absorb just about anybody." The On the Waterfront Restaurant is conveniently located back of the marina office.

The basin with its 7-foot depth is too congested for suitable anchorage and there is shoaling to 6 feet along its southern section.

One suggested anchorage area for large craft in Echo Bay is in the western part inside of a line from can 5 off Duck Point to the flashing buoy off Bailey Rock. This is open from northeast to south. Other space for anchoring, which is much used, is between Beaufort Point and Echo Island to the east of the channel. This anchorage is, however, wide open to the southeast, and any wind between east and south may make it uncomfortable for a small boat.

The Echo Bay Yacht Club on Echo Island has a crowded anchorage with moorings exclusively assigned to its fleet.

Echo Bay is a convenient anchorage, because it is only a short distance from the center of New Rochelle, which is about thirty minutes from Grand Central Station, New York. Except for shoal-draft boats, it does not provide a comfortable or safe anchorage in northeasterly to southerly winds, and is much less secure than New Rochelle or Mamaroneck harbors nearby. However, in a storm, shelter can be found in the inner harbor.

Larchmont, New York (12367). Like Marblehead, Massachusetts, this is one of the most important yacht racing centers on the coast; it is attractive for that reason, rather than for the excellence of its harbor. During Race Week several hundred boats are anchored off Larchmont or race from there. The harbor is protected from easterlies by a breakwater but is open from approximately southeast through south. The breakwater has a flashing red light which, being rather dimly lit, may be difficult to pick up against a confusing background of lights ashore. Can 7 marks Umbrella Rock and a daymark stands on North Ledge. In making your final approach at night, line up your stern on this breakwater light and then head directly for the club's flagpole outlined by three vertical lights colored blue-red-blue.

The large and well-equipped Larchmont Yacht Club is on the westerly shore. The club float and launch service are available to members of recognized yacht clubs. There's a Cruising Club mooring and guest moorings are also occasionally obtainable. Anchor in the southern part of the harbor, or fairly close to the breakwater if moorings are unavailable. There is no public gas dock in the harbor, though the yacht club supplies gas, diesel fuel, and ice at the work dock to the east where there is $5^1/_2$ feet MLW. But do not tie up at either of the club's two docks. Skippers must register first with the club's launchman who is often seen covering the harbor. He will assign you a mooring and present you with the rules visiting yachts and their crews should follow. Several good eating places over on the Post Road are a short ride from the harbor but the restaurant in the clubhouse is far more convenient. The nearest boatyards are in Rye and Mamaroneck.

A tour of Larchmont's clubhouse will soon reveal how highly established it has become as a hub of our yachting heritage. Interclub dinghy racing first began here in 1946. Another contribution was Larchmont's convincing demonstration that the Marconi rig was a more efficient racing rig than the old gaff. In 1917, in a series of ten informal regattas, the Marconi-rigged *Varuna* won eight out of ten races against four gaff-rigged one-design competitors in the O-boat class, designed by William Gardner. The S class and the Victory class, still seen on the Sound today, are said to be the two first one-design Marconi-rigged yacht classes to be built.*

In 1980, the 100th anniversary of the club's founding, Commodore William Luckett expressed in its centennial book how sailing and people who are dedicated to the sport have kept Larchmont alive. "Over the years the membership has enjoyed good sailing, good friendships and our children, as a result of our junior programs, have learned much of the discipline needed to succeed in life."

Larchmont is famous for its frostbite dinghy racing, carried on all winter by the yacht club, which remains active the year round. It is said that more than half of the total adult population of Larchmont commutes daily to New York.

Mamaroneck, New York (12367). Mamaroneck (Indian for "he assembles the people") was first settled in 1650 by English farmers. Apparently some of the neighboring cities did not always approve of what went on there later for in 1704 Colonel Caleb Heathcote, Lord of the Manor of nearby Scarsdale, wrote as follows: "The most rude and heathenish country I ever saw in my life, which call themselves Christian; there being not so much as the least marks or footsteps of religion of any sort; Sundays being the only time set apart by them for all manner of vain sports and lewd diversion."†

We are afraid that Mamaroneck must plead guilty, not to the absence of churches, for there are many, but to being—even on Sunday—a very active center for many sports and diversions, though neither vain nor lewd—especially yachting. Believe it or not, in this small harbor, the home port for about 1,700 boats, there are 6 boat yards, 6 yacht, beach, or tennis clubs, numerous marine retail businesses, and Harbor Island Park with 2 public marinas and a Coast Guard Auxiliary Station. According to Mamaroneck's waterfront revitalization report, an estimated 10,000 people use the harbor each year and marina activity contributes more than $18 million annually to the local economy.

*From *Long Island Sound,* by Fessenden S. Blanchard (D. Van Nostrand Co., Princeton, N. J., 1958).

†Quoted in the section on Mamaroneck from *New York*—American Guide Series (Oxford University Press, New York).

Mamaroneck is a splendid example of what a community is doing to protect the attractiveness and value of its 9 miles of coastline and to maintain its harbor as a "working port." Through its waterfront-revitalization program and marine-rezoning plan, the village is setting an example for other waterfront communities to emulate—communities which are being subjected to pressures to deface their existing shorelines by developing new high-density construction.

Chart House, a national restaurant chain, has been negotiating with town officials to build a first-class restaurant overlooking the harbor in Harbor Island Park. If and when it opens, it is expected to enhance the attractiveness of the 45-acre parkland.

The West Basin recorded a controlled depth of 6 feet at the time of writing, and Harbor Island (which isn't really an island) between East and West basins is an attractive park with beach facilities and a town dock. The dock is on the westerly shore of the island about halfway up the basin. Here Harbormaster Jim Mancusi, who monitors VHF-16 daily from 8 A.M. to 5 P.M. in the large brick building, will assign a guest mooring to a visiting yacht if one is available, since there is no anchoring in the harbor. For advance reservations, he suggests a phone call to (914) 777-7744. Just beyond, Flotilla 63 of the Coast Guard is housed in a small beige headquarters. We learned from the officials here that all incoming vessels should use engine power from the time they reach lighted buoy 5, at Outer Steamboat Rock, until they make their final mooring.

Mamaroneck offers much better protection from wind and sea than its neighbors, Milton Harbor at Rye, or Larchmont Harbor. Here are two snug, if crowded, landlocked basins, fully protected from all directions. However, the other two harbors mentioned offer considerably more privacy, and have their own particular assets. There is also an outer harbor at Mamaroneck, where many boats are moored during the summer months but which is open from southeast to southwest. During the winter, boating continues at Mamaroneck—now active in "frostbiting."

The entrance to the inner harbor is narrow and a speed-limit sign outside warns boats to slow down on entering. The place where the channel forks is marked by a red-and-green buoy. Follow the channel carefully, whichever way you go, as there are closely bordering shoals. The mean range of tide here is 7.3 feet.

The West Basin, with its 6-foot depth at MLW, is prettier and quieter than the East Basin, and not close to the Boston Post Road and its heavy traffic, as is the latter. At the same time, however, it is less convenient to the city center with its many fine stores.

For overnight, we much prefer the West Basin, the best tie-up being to port halfway up the basin at the dock of the Nichols Yacht Yard headed up by Chris Heraghty. The dock records 6 feet of water, and water, electric connections, ice, telephones, and showers are available. It is safer to arrange for dock space by placing an advance reservation; phone (914) 698-6065 or try VHF-9. The yard, as we know from experience, has good repair service, including engine, electronics, and sail.

At the entrance to the West Basin, just beyond the small dock of Total Yacht Sales, a fine assortment of small craft is on display and for sale, from dinghies to outboard cruisers, boat trailers, and marine hardware.

In 1993 we recorded a controlled depth of 6 feet at low water for a midwidth of 80 feet. You can carry this depth up to the entrance of the East Basin if you stay in the middle. The extension of the channel once inside records $5^1/2$ feet with a 65-foot width. There is 4 to 7 feet in the crowded basin itself but be careful to avoid a dangerous rock, covered at high water, which is located right off nun 16 and is marked by a prominent stake. At the basin's north end are gathered over half of the boatyards and yacht clubs in Mamaroneck, all crowded together. From west to east the first is the popular Post Road Boatyard, the flagship of the Brewer fleet of yacht yards, which was founded in 1879 and has been home to some of the most distinguished yachts ever to sail the Sound. Open daily from 8 A.M. to 8 P.M., it has 6 feet at its gas dock plus diesel fuel, ice, water, electricity, showers, slips, and a laundromat nearby. Then appears the R. E. Derecktor Shipyard, the birthplace of many a 12-meter contender. Next comes the Orienta Yacht Club, which has two guest moorings, and finally McMichael Yacht Yard #1. Nearby on the Post Road is Brewer's, established over eighty years ago and a first-rate marine hardware emporium, sometimes open on Sundays in summer. Next door to Brewer's, the atmosphere is informal at Charlie Brown's, where entrees posted on a blackboard rarely exceed $10. All these are fine facilities, but our advice to visiting yachts is still to spend the night if possible in the West Basin, on an assigned mooring, not on your hook!

A pumpout station has been installed at an East Basin dock since the harbor is being proposed as a "no-discharge" zone. Use of this facility is free and operational 24 hours a day. Check with the harbormaster for its operation.

James Fenimore Cooper married a Mamaroneck girl in 1811 and lived in his wife's ancestral home for a while after the wedding. The original building was eventually sold at auction for $11 and then moved. Today, this black-and-white gabled house overlooks the harbor near the corner of the Post Road and Fenimore Road. It now serves as a restaurant called The Landmark. And over in Harbor Island Park a small outdoor stage forms the scene for free cultural events in the opera, dance, and theater during the summer.

Rye (Milton Harbor), New York (12367). If you are coming from the direction of Lloyd Harbor, a tall office building in New Rochelle with a square knob on the top is a good guide for the Scotch Caps buoys and the entrance to Rye. On entering at night, it is important to give the Scotch Caps a wide berth, as the entrance is deceptive, the lighted buoy being much farther west than the contour of the coast would seem to require. After leaving the Scotch Caps lighted bell buoy to starboard, run toward the north until the two red range lights on the club grounds are in sight, and then run in. Note that on West Rock, at the south end of the Caps, there's a white day beacon extremely difficult to spot both from seaward and from the chart. This is privately maintained from April 1 to November 1 and should be kept well to starboard on entering the harbor.

The anchorage, to the west and southwest of the American Yacht Club, is fair except in a southwester when, if desired, one can quickly run over to Mamaroneck. It is frequently rough in the harbor, and uncomfortable when the tide is against the wind. If drawing more than 5 feet, anchor in the deep water between the southern end of Hen Island and the end of Milton Point if possible, either to the north or to the south of the gut that runs between the clubhouse point and the first of three islets forming the Scotch Caps chain. A tide rip runs through this gut, and in a storm the sea comes through. The bottom is soft, sticky mud.

Over on Hen Island, thirty-four families enjoy the isolation of spartan island living surrounded by many species of bird and marine life. This little Shangri-La was first occupied by Indians of the Apaqquaminis tribe, whose sachem sold Rye to John Budd in 1662.

The American Yacht Club float, with diesel fuel, gas, ice, water, and a depth of 8 feet at low tide, is available to visitors from accredited yacht clubs, as is the club launch service running on weekdays from 8 A.M. to 10 P.M. and on weekends from 8 A.M. to midnight. Contact the launch over VHF-71 or give three blasts of the horn while displaying code flag

T during daylight hours and turning on spreader lights at night. All guests must register with the dockmaster. The launch will direct you to a mooring vacated by a club member off cruising. American has an excellent restaurant in its very attractive clubhouse overlooking the Sound as well as a swimming pool as fine as you'll see at any yacht club.

Supplies can be obtained from the Dockside Deli almost a mile down the road on Milton Point near the end of the channel; it is open evenings and part of the time on Sunday. Nearby there is a formal restaurant named La Panetière with a three-star rating.

Proceeding up the harbor, one can see the Shenorock Shore Club just beyond the stone town dock to starboard. At the harbor's head is a boatyard in a basin, reached by a narrow, 1-mile-long channel marked by #5 class buoys and dredged throughout its length in 1993 to 8 feet MLW. The mean range of tide here is about 7 feet. Gone is the Nichols Yacht Yard, formerly located on the west fork, where there is shoaling to a depth of 4 feet MLW. This inlet was the site over a century ago of David Kirby's boatyard which built the 1876 America's Cup defender, *Madeleine,* and originated the Wee Scot class. On the east fork is Shongut Marine, the only spot for gas and possible overnight dockage, and beyond that the Municipal Boat Basin, open only to residents of Rye and not set up to handle transients. Rye's harbormaster, who monitors VHF-16 to handle emergencies, is located here and offers free pumpout service.

The American Yacht Club is one of the oldest yacht clubs in the United States, founded in May 1883 by a small group of steam-yacht enthusiasts headed by Jay Gould. It became one of the leaders in the middle 1920s in establishing a Junior Yacht Club and instructional program that is now one of the most active on the Sound. This program has turned out young sailors who have captured the Midget Championship Trophy at Larchmont Race Week and have distinguished themselves in 420 and interclub competition.

In recent years, the American Yacht Club has hosted the 420 North American Championships and the New York 36 Class National Championships. Its race committee runs, among others, the AYC Annual Spring Regatta in May with over 150 entries, making it one of the premier racing events on the East Coast. It is sailed over the demanding Olympic course. Many of the club's members have competed successfully in winning racing honors on Long Island Sound and in international events.

After a horrendous fire destroyed it in 1951, the venerable Victorian clubhouse, built in 1887, was replaced on its original site by a handsome brick clubhouse. But the original flagpole still stands. It serves as a prominent landmark looking out from Milton Point on one of the busiest scenes on Long Island Sound. In 1983, American celebrated its centennial anniversary with a host of memorable activities.

Playland, Rye, New York (12367). This is an artificial harbor made by two converging breakwaters at Rye Beach. The narrow entrance is open to the southeast, but the harbor offers a good shelter from all other winds. The jetty lights are operated by the Westchester County Playland Commission. Playland is a summer harbor, so if one is entering out of season, a careful check on the neighboring buoys and lights should be made in advance. There is from 6 to 10 feet of water in the anchorage at low tide, with 10 feet at the pier.

The park, which is well worth a visit as an outstanding example of community enterprise, is operated efficiently and like Spotless Town by the commission. There is an excellent beach of imported sand, and plenty of music, expansive-picnic grounds, and restaurants—a complete change for people on a cruise, except possibly for the roller coasters. However, one's privacy is about equal to that of a goldfish, as in summer the beach is crowded and swimmers are apt to line the log boom nearby. Don't try to drink soup, for it may land in your lap from the waves of a passing speedboat. A beautiful 80-acre salt-water lake lying behind the amusement area offers a wildlife sanctuary that attracts bird-watchers and boating enthusiasts from seven to seventy.

In entering at night, watch for a line of heavy log booms parallel with the beach and well out from it. The nearest boatyard is the Tide Mill Yacht Basin in Port Chester. The Rye railroad station is about 2 miles away, reached by bus from Playland.

Scheduled to open at Rye Playland in late 1995, Scienceport will be a hands-on museum dedicated to science education and committed to fostering an enthusiasm for science and love of discovery in both the children and adults of Westchester and visitors to the park.

Playland is still the largest, and one of the finest, municipally owned amusement parks in the world, with over 270 acres. If you want an evening of fun, go there. Playland was designated a National Historic Landmark in 1987.

Port Chester, New York (12367). The best place here for overnight anchorage or tie-up is not in the crowded and commercial Byram River, where oil barges and tankers come and go. There are two better choices: one is an anchorage (if there is room) in the deep water south of the green beacon with the flashing green light and west of the main channel. Another possibility is to tie up in a slip (if one is available) in a yard the existence of which you might never suspect from looking at the chart. This is the Tide Mill Yacht Basin in the bight at the edge of Kirby Pond and behind Manursing Island. The basin is separated from Kirby Pond by a dam, and the dockhouse, which was originally a flour mill, is built over the sluiceway through which the tidal currents flowed to power the mill. The basin has been dredged to a depth of 7 feet and is reached by following private green and red markers lining a 7-foot dredged channel. The approach is through the charted deep water south and southwest of the green beacon mentioned earlier. This marina is identified by a prominent red dockhouse offering gas, diesel fuel, ice, showers, telephone, slips with electrical connections, a mechanic, various marine supplies, and arrangements for grocery delivery. The dockhouse is part of the original Old Tide Mill built in 1770 by Wright Frost and owned and operated for 50 years by David Kirby. With the basin protected from all winds and seas, an overnight tie-up is desirable at this unique marina which can be reached at (914) 967-2995.

The Port Chester Yacht Club is on the north shore, at the entrance of the Byram River, and will let you tie up at their float for emergencies. It is home base for Flotilla 61 of the Coast Guard Auxiliary. For medical emergencies, victims can be picked up at the ramp/main float and quickly transported to nearby United Hospital. Fuel and supplies are available farther up the river. Excessive silting is reported and strict adherence to the channel is suggested. Tugs and barges use the river mostly at high tide.

Port Chester has improved its name as well as its harbor. It was once known as Saw Log Swamp, and later as Saw Pit.

Byram Harbor, Port Chester, New York (12367). Byram Harbor is attractive mainly if the tide is high enough for boats to go into the shallow cove to the west of Huckleberry Island. Byram Park is a pretty place and the Byram Shore Boat Club in the cove is most hospitable. The best place to anchor is to the east of the line between Huckleberry Island

and Wilson Head, but this is only for shoal-draft boats and is open from east to south.

The depth in the cove is about 3 feet at mean low water. There is a guest mooring just outside of the narrow channel to the cove, but no gas or supplies are available at the club. Check in with the harbormaster before picking up this mooring. Slips in the cove are reserved for local residents.

For deeper-draft craft, the best anchorage is north of Calf Island between the tower and the flashing red-lighted buoy south of Otter Rocks. Enter between this buoy and green can 1 north of Bowers Island. A reef, bare at low water, connects the two islands. Southern Calf, owned by the Greenwich YMCA, has become, partly because of its natural charm, a favorite rendezvous spot for many local yacht club fleets, including the Westchester Power Squadron. Groups wishing to go ashore for a picnic should first place their reservations with the YMCA officials. Another possibly quiet anchorage, except in southerlies, can be found in the bight formed by the western shore of Calf Island and the small private island to the northwest on which is located the stone tower. This latter island is now owned by the Greenwich Land Trust and is off limits except for education and scientific study.

Greenwich, Connecticut (12367). Captain Harbor, north of Great and Little Captain Islands, affords fair shelter for large boats in the open area east of Field Point and the channel into Greenwich Harbor. The harbor has no space for anchoring. Guest moorings are available at the attractive and well-equipped Indian Harbor Yacht Club, which stands on the point to the east of the main channel, whose depth all the way to the head of the harbor is reported to be 8 feet at the time of writing. The Captain Harbor anchorage is exposed to the south and southeast, although the islands afford some protection. It is comfortable only for large yachts or in calm weather.

In bad weather the best entrance is the easterly one, as courses can be laid from flashing bell 1 to can 1A (located just north of dangerous Hen and Chickens Reef) and from there to the end of the harbor's channel off Field Point. Be sure to keep can 1A at least 50 yards to port as you proceed from the east. From Field Point on to the yacht club the harbor is filled with boats in summer and the visitor may find it very difficult to find a secure anchorage with sufficient swinging room within the vicinity of boats about his own size. The outer or larger yachts usually carry mooring lights.

In a storm, a moderate-draft boat can find a snug anchorage in Chimney Corner north of Tweed Island, though it may be crowded.

There is seldom any weather to which the inner harbor is exposed. The Indian Harbor Yacht Club float, launch service, and guest moorings are open to members of recognized yacht clubs. Before you do anything, make sure to check in on VHF-68 with the waterfront manager who will assign you a mooring or a slip if one is available. Depth at the float is about 8 feet but you'll find no gas on tap here. Long considered one of the "prestige" clubs on Long Island Sound, Indian Harbor also has one of the most beautiful, busy, and interesting locations. It offers an impressive schedule of yachting events during the summer and is active in winter frostbiting. Some of its events include an invitation cruise in July and the Stratford Shoal Race in October.

Above the yacht club stretches the 800-foot bulkhead of the smart-looking Greenwich Harbor Inn which serves up fine food and music whether you're dressed in boating denims or a Dior. The Showboat is still tied up at the dock. A $25 fee for dockage with electricity is credited toward any food or drink partaken at the Inn. On a busy night boats are tied up three deep along the bulkhead. You might also try the widely acclaimed Italian cuisine found at Manero's Restaurant inshore to starboard halfway up the channel.

Across the channel on the east side of Grass Island, ferries leave from the town dock for trips to Great Captain Island and Island Beach. Here, too, is Greenwich Fuel Dock, with 8 feet at MLW, gas and diesel fuel, pumpout facility, water, ice, and two slips for transient boats.

Tucked away in the small bight south of Grass Island lies the well-groomed Greenwich Boat and Yacht Club, founded in 1938. It is identified by a sizable amount of dockage, a prominent flagpole, and a small white clubhouse. There is 6 feet in this cove but we were advised by club member Don Hoffkins to stay clear of a red stake marking a rock to starboard coming in and also to be aware of a submerged rock close off the port shore. This cove will offer you excellent protection should you be granted one of the club's two guest moorings. We were warmly received here. In the spring of 1992 there were plans to dredge a 250- by 320-foot basin to a depth of 7 feet MLW to allow continued use of this club, but as of this writing, it hasn't happened yet.

Greenwich is a convenient place to meet people coming from New

York as the Indian Harbor Yacht Club is only ¹/₂ mile from the railroad station and ³/₄ mile from the post office. It is a less convenient harbor to obtain fuel and supplies.

The town, just north of the depot, offers excellent shops and restaurants. The country back of Greenwich, with many large estates on high land enjoying wide views of the Sound, is most attractive and well worth a motor ride. It was at Greenwich that General Putnam of Revolutionary War fame escaped the British by riding down the face of a cliff.

Cos Cob or Riverside, Connecticut (12367). Many yachtsmen prefer this harbor to Greenwich. The buoys should be watched carefully on entering, as there are numerous rocks and shoal spots. The beginning of the 50-foot entrance channel appears to be even narrower between can 1 and nun 2, so make sure you give ample berth to ominous Hitchcock Rock. There is no space for anchoring now as the good areas are all taken up with moorings. Past nun 8, mud flats rise sharply on both sides. Recent dredging in the channel up to the Riverside Yacht Club has improved its depth to 8 feet MLW.

The Riverside Yacht Club is one of the most attractive clubs on the Sound and welcomes yachtsmen from other clubs with whom privileges are exchanged. It is on the point to the starboard (just before reaching nun 10), and has a long pier, with 10 feet of water along its edge, reaching to the channel. The dockmaster monitors VHF-74 and suggests that a visitor, prior to his arrival, obtain an invitation from a member of this club in order to secure an overnight mooring. Ice, water, and showers are available, but fuel is sold to members and guests only. Launch service runs from 8 A.M. to 11 P.M. on weekends, to 10 P.M. on weekdays. Both the Yardarm Bar, with its nautical ambience, and the club's dining room command a splendid view of the harbor.

In spite of the dredging, the channel running north from nun 10 reflects shoaling to 4 feet at MLW all the way up to the fixed highway bridge, so this part of the Mianus River is used primarily by powerboats. The bascule bridge will open, theoretically, on your signal from 5 A.M. to 9 P.M. Actually, there are now so many trains that there is often a very long wait before the bridge opens. The mud flats on either side of the narrow channel at the bridge are a real hazard at low tide. We went aground three times waiting for the bridge to open. Our conclusion was that visitors who can't get under the bridge should not plan to go through it at all. The November 1993 issue of *Soundings* newspaper has an article saying that the railroad had requested that the Coast Guard eliminate bridge openings on weekdays during the times 6:30 to 10 A.M., 4:30 to 6:45 P.M. and 7 to 8 P.M. If the current AMTRAK plan to add additional express trains is approved, this bridge will be impossible to use.

The Mianus River Boat and Yacht Club just north of the bridge will rent you a slip if one is available. Their guest facilities are a little primitive, but they do have a pumpout station. Just north of the club is the Chart House Restaurant which we enjoyed very much.

The upper western shoreline of the river is giving way to the construction of dockominiums. Gone is McMichael Yacht Yard No. 3, and only Palmer Point Marina, Harbor Marine Center, and Drenckhahn Boat Basin remain to offer service mostly to small local craft. They are all close together, so, if you can't find what you want at one, try another.

They are also not far from a Howard Johnson Motel on U.S. Route 1 and a fine shopping center where fresh supplies can be gathered.

Greenwich Cove, Riverside, Connecticut (12367). Here is an attractive, cool anchorage, popular and more crowded than ever, without shore facilities or supplies. The swimming is first-rate. There is fairly good protection from all sides if you anchor northeast of Pelican Island; another anchorage is farther up the harbor opposite Greenwich Island. Both anchorage areas are full of moorings. With great care, you may find space to fit yourself in, but be sure there isn't a rock in that open space. The bottom is mud, providing poor holding ground.

Come in toward Cove Rock and its nun, numbered 2, keeping south of the line between this buoy and the red flasher on Newfoundland Reef in order to avoid Finch Rock, marked by a privately maintained can buoy. Depths decrease from 8 feet in the outer cove to less than 3 feet in its eastern sector at the end of the buoyed channel.

The Old Greenwich Yacht Club has a dock with 6 feet of water at the end of a marked channel just to the east of the northern tip of Greenwich Point, south of Pelican Island. There are no guest moorings and the launch service is primarily reserved for club members and their guests.

Julius Wilensky, author of the very useful guide *Where To Go; What To Do; How To Do It on Long Island Sound*, gives us some background on this area:

> The whole of Greenwich Point, Flat Neck Point, and the narrow neck north of Greenwich Point is a public park, much of it left wild.

Ducks and swans are at home here. It is known locally as Tod's Point, not to be confused with the point of the same name at the south end of Riverside. The Tod family had a huge three-story Victorian mansion on the point, which wasn't torn down until 1961. Greenwich had bought the peninsula for $550,000 early in World War II, and used the mansion to house returning veterans. The park includes an arboretum.*

Recently a piece of good news was received. The waters in this part of the Sound have improved so that it is possible to take shellfish legally from Greenwich Point. Out at the rocky southern end, there are large beds of mussels waiting to be picked off the rocks at low tide.

Don't get caught outside the park after dark, for everything locks up at 8 P.M. We tried every password in the book to get past the guard at the front gate. One of them finally worked, and we were faced with a long trudge in pitch blackness back to our anchorage.

Stamford, Connecticut (12368). Stamford Harbor is easy to enter and the channel inside the breakwaters is simple to follow. But outside of the channel there are a few rocks, in inconvenient places, to be avoided in looking for an anchorage. The two breakwaters have greatly improved the harbor as a place of refuge, though it is still large enough in the outer harbor for many "local" whitecaps, and boats may drag in a southwester. The Stamford Yacht Club is noted on the chart and is about halfway up Shippan Point, an attractive residential section of Stamford. In case you approach the channel in poor visibility, as we did on one visit, we might note that the fog signal at the west breakwater light has been changed from a siren to a horn sounding one blast for a two-second duration every twenty seconds. The light itself is now a green flasher, equal-interval, six seconds. Eighty-foot-high Harbor Ledge Light, which is automated to flash every four seconds, stands off the west breakwater, also helping to mark the channel's entrance. This century-old lighthouse was privately purchased for $230,000 in 1985.

For boats not wishing to land, a convenient and easy anchorage is just behind the western breakwater, east of the rocks shown on the chart. Farther up the channel, a course taken from nun 8 directly for the end of

*From *Where To Go: What To Do: How To Do It on Long Island Sound,* by Julius M. Wilensky (Snug Harbor Publishing Co., 1968).

Stamford Harbor, showing Yacht Haven East and West on the East and West Branch channels. *Aero Graphics Corp.*

the Stamford Yacht Club dock will give at least 5 feet of depth all the way in; but don't stray from this "straight and narrow path," for there are some rocks close to the north side of the channel and on the south side, too. Head in for the club dock by passing through the fleet slowly and then between the private red and green buoys; the green one to port marks a hidden rock and the red marker to starboard identifies a dangerous reef extending seaward. Also note that moored boats here often swing to block the club's channel. That orange ball buoy floating to the north marks a shallow rock ledge extending 40 feet to the southeast.

There is a depth of about 5 feet at mean low water at the outer end of the Stamford Yacht Club dock. Diesel fuel, water, and ice are available. The club facilities, including guest moorings when not in use, are available to members of recognized yacht clubs who come here by boat and to others who make reservations by calling (203) 323-3161 or on VHF-14. This is one of the Sound's leading clubs, host of the annual Vineyard Race, and very active in both the yachting and social life of the community.

Earlier editions of this *Guide* in describing Stamford Harbor claimed that here "the facilities and opportunities available to visiting yachtsmen are among the best on the Sound." If one considers the facilities that now remain, the Stamford Yacht Club, Yacht Haven East and West, the new Stamford Landing Marina, and Harbour Square Marina, this claim still rings true. But "the old order changeth, yielding place to new" and, for cruising yachts entering this harbor, not always toward improvement. Recently, real estate developers have discovered and capitalized on Stamford's waterfront, turning a half-dozen boatyards into luxury condominiums, dockominiums, and office buildings.

A clear example of this shoreline transformation may be seen as one enters the East Branch channel to starboard, now "condominium row." However, Yacht Haven East—(203) 359-4500—which you come to first, still remains. It has about everything a yachtsman could want in ranking as one of the largest marinas on the East Coast. A breakwater offering good protection has been constructed from Jack Island eastward to the mainland. Dredging has taken place just above this breakwater to provide fill for the building up of the southern shore of Ware Island, permitting the formation of additional piers. There are now twelve piers with a total of about five hundred slips having depths of 9 feet, and the transient dockage charge includes water, electricity, use of showers, and a laundromat. Boats requiring all types of hull and engine work are sent across the harbor to a joint subsidiary, Yacht Haven West—(203) 359-4500—which is set up to handle repairs efficiently. Yacht Haven East, on the other hand, is preferable for an overnight stop if you can find space among the throng of local boats. It's quiet after dark, a bit more residential, and offers 24-hour security. Both marinas monitor VHF-9. Farther up to starboard, the Rusty Scupper is housed in a white building sandwiched between two large brick office buildings. One may tie up at this recommended restaurant's dock for lunch or dinner. The Harbor Deli is a good source for sandwiches.

In 1967 a hurricane barrier was constructed across the East Branch channel just beyond Yacht Haven East. Its 90-foot-wide gate is equipped with lights. At the head of this 100-foot-wide channel along the west bank lies Stamford's newest complex—Harbour Square Marina. Attractively designed, efficiently run, and well protected, it caters to king-sized yachts, providing them with every service except repair work. A high-priced restaurant and a provision store are close at hand. They can be reached for reservations at (203) 324-3331 and VHF-9. The dockmaster can be found running the deli by the fuel pumps.

Adjacent to this and just south is the Stamford Harbor Park Marina, with slips for boats up to about 45 feet and about 6-foot depth. They monitor VHF-9 and can be reached at (203) 978-1053.

Across, on the east bank and a little farther south, is the extensive Harbor House Marina, whose dockmaster can be reached at (203) 967-9600. Below that are the docks belonging to a large set of condominiums.

The whole region north of the floodgate is very protected in a storm when the gate is closed, but there are no repair facilities along the East Branch.

Back at the fork separating the East and West Branches, note the two range lights to guide you in at night. The West Branch is the wider and deeper of the two. Depths in this channel run as much as 12 feet at MLW, with average readings of 8 feet MLW up in the turning basin. Halfway up to starboard looms the prominent dockhouse of Yacht Haven West, home of the annual North Atlantic All Sailboat Show, and claiming to be the "best bet for the cruising yachtsman on Long Island Sound." Check in here for gas, diesel fuel, ice, showers, electricity, a laundromat, marine supplies, and a travelift with a 60-ton capacity. On the property, electronics repair is handled by Electra-Yacht, rigging work is performed by MacDonald Yacht Rigging, and diesel service is offered by Marine Diesel of New England. Just outside this marine center's gate is a deli for the purchase of supplies. The Ponus Yacht Club here reportedly serves good meals.

Yacht Haven West is home port for the Eagle, a three-masted gaff-rigged shoal-draft schooner which belongs to Sound Waters, an environmental educational organization. They run short trips mostly for schoolchildren throughout that part of the Sound.

In 1986, a promising new marina was constructed on the west shore just beyond Yacht Haven West. It is called Stamford Landing, previously the site of a chocolate factory. Although many of its floating slips with 9 feet MLW are leased, we were assured by the congenial dockmaster that he will accommodate visiting yachts whenever space is open. A call on VHF-9 or phoning (203) 965-0065 may help reserve a slip for you. Check in with him at "A" dock, the first you will meet to port coming upchannel. This is more of a residential than a working yard and has condominiums instead of repair shops.

Stamford Landing provides its guests with the Dolce and Crabshell restaurants, a laundromat, showers and heads, ice, electricity dock-side, and a pumpout station. In listening to his story, we had to agree with him that "you won't find many marinas around with the pleasant yacht club atmosphere that people here enjoy." No doubt this attractive development will be welcomed by boaters using Stamford as a port of call.

Nearby express trains run between Stamford and New York City, making it a convenient place for picking up crews or reaching Manhattan.

Westcott Cove, Stamford, Connecticut (12368). Westcott Cove has a completely sheltered "lagoon," as it is called locally. It has a well-marked channel of 100-foot width and a controlling depth of 3 feet at mean low water and 7 feet within the basin. Enter around Shippan Point, east of Stamford Harbor, leaving the green flasher entrance buoy to port. Follow the channel carefully; it is very shoal on either side, especially to port entering, near the end of the jetty. Thus favor the nuns all the way and, once inside, hug the docks to port.

Now gone are the old docks and former property of Muzzio Bros. Yacht Yard, having been replaced by slips belonging to Marina Bay Condominiums and Dock Services, Inc. A new office building has been added to this complex, but the services to transient yachts are minimal. At the northwest corner of the lagoon, in Cummings Park, is the Halloween Yacht Club, which offers its facilities to yachtsmen from recognized clubs with whom reciprocal privileges are extended. The club, we were told, may have a spare slip or berth for visiting boats. Mention was also made of a large rock that lies off and between the first and second of the club's docks. This can be avoided by keeping well to port. Tie-up is fore-and-aft, as the harbor is too small and busy to permit swinging at anchor.

There are several good grocery stores about ¼ mile from the club, and fast-food restaurants are nearby. The vicinity is apt to be crowded and busy on weekends, and there is less privacy than in a larger, more isolated harbor.

Goodwives (Darien) River, Noroton, Connecticut (12368). This is one of the numerous "made" harbors on Long Island Sound, located off the Noroton Yacht Club and along the western shore of Long Neck Point. Be sure to keep well east of flashing buoy 1 and then nun 2 to starboard in entering. About midway between this nun and the end of the yacht club there was a bar across the channel, as the chart indicates, but it is reported by Manager Jeffrey Eng to have been eliminated. There are range lights to mark the channel at the club from Memorial Day to Labor Day. One of these is located at the end of the dock and the other stands at the right edge of the attractive clubhouse.

In entering, head from nun 2, following the club's small red and white mid-channel markers to the yacht club dock with 6 feet of water. There is plenty of water to the pier, where a guest mooring is sometimes obtainable. The club monitors VHF-72 or can be called at (203) 655-7686. Beyond the pier there is also good water to the gut opposite Peartree Point, but not beyond the Darien Boat Club docks to starboard where it has shoaled considerably. Not shown on the chart is some fairly deep water, reported at 8 feet, in the dredged but congested basin to the west of the pier, where it is well protected; but space may be hard to find. Large boats anchor close to Pratt Island or in the anchorage area, where it is deeper and less crowded, though more open. This special anchorage area, as shown on the chart, is established off the southwesterly side of Long Neck Point. The town's mooring supervisor or his representative can usually be reached on VHF-72.

There is a large and impressive-looking estate at the end of Long Neck Point. Once the estate of Anson Phelps Stokes, it was subsequently occupied by the Convent of the Sacred Heart. Now it has been split up to make separate private residences.

The Noroton Yacht Club has a large, active fleet of Blue Jays, Lasers, Sonars, J-24s, and Ensigns and the anchorage is often full. The weekend racing is hotly contested. The club has an outstanding reputation in yachting circles, largely due to its philosophy that there is nothing more important than sailing. Its excellent junior program has produced some great sailors, such as Bob Bavier, helmsman of the winning America's Cup defender *Constellation,* and Bill Cox, skipper of the almost-defender *American Eagle.* In more recent years, Noroton has won the Queens Cup Women's Sailing Championship of Long Island Sound and its junior sailing program has been ranked among the top ten along our East Coast.

The club is most hospitable to members of recognized yacht clubs and has a snack bar but no bar, and water but no gasoline. Its launch service runs from 9 A.M. to 10 P.M. every day and monitors VHF-72. Pumping of heads within the harbor is forbidden. Repair facilities are available at nearby Fivemile River or at Stamford. It is about 1 mile to the village of Noroton. There is a good beach at Peartree Point, open only to local residents. However, a small, pleasant beach spreads out in front of the clubhouse. This harbor is a good destination in normal summer weather and provides a most appealing natural setting.

Hay Island, Noroton, Connecticut (12368). North of Hay Island, on the east side of Long Neck Point, was once one of the most popular and attractive harbors on the Sound, but it is now overcrowded—choked with permanent mooring owned by local residents. It is well protected from all but strong winds from northeast to southeast, when an unpleasant roll penetrates. Shallow-draft yachts, however, can escape most of this by going south behind the island. An anchorage along the cove's northern shore may provide more space to swing at anchor. This inlet with its low, rocky cliffs and lush foliage is known locally as Ziegler's Cove, since the Ziegler family has owned the surrounding property for many years.

The approach to this cove is devoid of buoys, but the chart shows a way. Follow along the eastern shore of Long Neck Point, steering to pass to the east of the exposed rock just east of Hay Island. Go north of the rock at least 200 yards, leaving the charted rock in 5 feet of water to port, turn west into the cove along the southern shore of Great Island, and anchor, preferably near the 8-foot spot. The harbor is surrounded by private estates, and no supplies or public landing facilities are available. You'll think you are in Maine until you go swimming, and then you'll be glad you aren't.

The harbor is apt to be crowded on weekends, so get in early if you want to find swinging room. Fortunately, some boats come there to fish—and often do very well at it—but leave in the early evening, so the overnight flotilla is reduced considerably. One of our writers has been there at least ten times but currently has failed to find satisfactory anchorage. It is one of his favorite ports on the Sound.

Fivemile River, Rowayton, Connecticut (12368). This anchorage between Roton Point and Darien, rates high on the following counts: (1) convenience; (2) protection from all winds; (3) docks from which groceries, gasoline, ice, and water can be obtained; (4) boatyards and machine shops. The nun 28 off Greens Ledge Light is a good guide to the entrance, about 1 mile distant. The entrance is well buoyed, though narrow.

This harbor is attractive, with perfect shelter from all winds, but very crowded. On our last visit we saw no anchoring space and the channel was so narrow between moorings and the docks that we barely had room to turn around. Butler Island, at the left of the entrance, is wooded and high. There is a dredged basin on the westerly shore opposite nun 6 beyond Butler Island. This may be a possible anchorage, but the congested harbor makes a tie-up preferable. Four to five feet can be carried in mid-channel all the way up to Conel's dock and two to three feet beyond to the head of the dredging. New dredging is expected soon. The mean range of tide is about seven feet. All moorings must be on line with other boats.

The first dock you reach to starboard is the Town Dock where there is no overnight dockage. The next dock beyond is Fivemile Landing, where you can pick up gas, ice, and water and which offers the best possibility for transient yachts. Just beyond lies The Boatworks, composed of the South and North Yards. It supplies diesel fuel, does all types of repair work on boats up to 25 tons, and houses a fine little marine store. The dockmaster is located in the prominent barn-red building and handles visitors to both Fivemile Landing and The Boatworks. He can be reached at (203) 866-9295 or on VHF-68.

Next to The Boatworks, the Bait Shop specializes in the sale and repair of outboard motors; Rowayton Lobster dishes out fresh clams and lobsters. For first-class repair work on all types of electronic gear, you might try Conel, Inc., up at the head of the harbor where the river begins to shoal to a depth of 3 feet MLW. The B and G Marina is also up here. The main street, which runs behind the docks, displays antique stores, a general market, an art center, a package store, and Fivemile River Grill specializing in the "freshest of the fresh" seafood served in a cheerful publike atmosphere.

Fivemile River is a friendly and intimate place, and the writer has rarely been in there without finding friends along the boat-lined waterfront. Though there is no yacht club on the river, the clubby mood makes one seem unnecessary. However, the Norwalk Yacht Club is just across the point.

Rowayton has well been called "a delicious and crazy hodgepodge of boat yards, lobster fishermen, artists, writers, boating enthusiasts and just plain local people."*

South and East Norwalk, Connecticut (12363, 12368, 12364SC).

Much of this section on South and East Norwalk is presented by Donald P. Relyea, Norwalk's harbormaster, and by Thomas Reidy, Commanding Officer, Norwalk Marine Police. We are grateful for their contribution.

Like Stamford, here is another case where man has stepped in to improve one of New England's best-protected (barrier-island) natural harbors. There are now at least eleven possible anchorages or tie-ups, but the snuggest and, in our opinion, the most desirable of all is the human-made dredged harbor adjacent to the west side of Calf Pasture Point just outside the entrance to the Norwalk Cove Marina. Many boats pass by this way but always at slow speed. If it's not blowing, use short scope in this excellent holding ground to avoid too much swing into traffic. BE SURE to avoid the mud flats on the Peach Island side of the main channel. All references to anchorages in the harbor are optimistic to say the least. In 1992 we saw no easily accessible and protected spots, but these references will show you where to look. You may find an open spot among the moorings.

Because of a complete dredging of Norwalk Harbor and its channels in 1980–81, charted depths are generally accurate. The preferred entrance to Norwalk Harbor is via the main west passage from Green's Ledge Light, north of Sheffield Island, to the well-marked channel entrance. At night, care must be exercised to identify carefully each lighted aid on the right side of the channel (inbound) since some of the lights may be overpowered by back-lighting from the public park/beach at Calf Pasture Point.

*From *The Exurbanites*, by A. C. Spectorsky (J. B. Lippincott Company, Philadelphia, 1955.)

The east approach from Peck's Ledge Light is not a federally maintained channel. It carries a natural 6 to 8 feet MLW and is well marked. Some consider this approach more formidable than the main channel, but it need not be so. A good helmsman and a sharp lookout can run from Peck's Ledge to the red spindle (8) at Grassy Hammock, then fairly close to cans 9 and 11 (reflector tape at night), and thence to the channel junction spindle (14) west of Round Beach. CAUTION: The east approach is only formidable if one passes north of the spindle at Grassy Hammock or too close to Round Beach.

Moving in a more or less easterly direction, as we are in this book, the eleven anchorages or tie-ups are as follows:

1. Off the Norwalk Yacht Club in what is locally known as Wilson Cove, located roughly between Noroton Point, Tavern Island, and Wilson Point. The club landing, located on the west shore of Wilson Point (east side of the cove), has 5 feet at MLW, and club moorings are usually available with tender service. Approach toward the eastern side of the moored boats and find a channel between the moored boats to approach the club. The club, organized in 1894, boasts a large fleet of good-looking cruising and racing boats and is very active in dinghy and frostbite racing. Its launch service runs from 8 A.M. to 9 P.M. weekdays and from 8 A.M. to 10 P.M. on weekends during the season. Ice and water may be had at the landing. The modern one-story clubhouse is open to members of other recognized yacht clubs. The protection in Wilson Cove is not good in a blow from the south to the west, but in normal summer weather this is a most pleasant and convenient place to stop. Continuing north through Wilson Cove following the markers lining a 5-foot (MLW) channel, one can reach the docks of Wilson Cove Marina and Yacht Club. A quieter, more secluded place than this would be hard to find. Unfortunately, the entrance channel is tending to silt-in slightly, but 5 feet can be carried with little difficulty. If you get stuck, it will be in very soft mud. Wait a few minutes for the tide or back up and try again on a slightly different line.

2. The north shore of Sheffield Island is the place to anchor for those who want to "get away from it all" south of the main channel or in the small bight at the western end of the island north of the old, abandoned (now privately owned) unlighted lighthouse. There is good holding ground throughout. A popular anchorage is off an old stone pier at the northerly point of the island. However, this is exposed to the southwest and some wash from powerboats in the main channel. The eastern end of the island is publicly owned and is a wildlife preserve, not yet posted, while the western end is privately owned and is posted. Exploring is permitted on the eastern end, especially of a large burned-out home on the north shore near the pier. Beware the poison ivy and consider picking up and removing from the island some of the rubbish discarded by your fellow human—if everyone picked up, think how nice it would be.

3. The area between Calf Pasture Point and Peach Island (see introduction to this section) on the east side of the main channel off the pier (shown on the chart) and a scuttled barge is exposed to the south and west for some distance but is partially protected by the Norwalk Islands. It is also close to the traffic in a busy channel as well as to traffic into Cove Marina and to several shorefront condominiums.

4. In the anchorage triangle (locally known as South Anchor Basin— no one knows where the north one is!) north of Gregory Point, one is on the edge of traffic in the main channel (usually at 5 mph and no wake) and must anchor among an increasing number of permanently moored boats, some free swinging (northerly end) and some moored fore and aft (southerly end). Excellent holding ground in relatively shallow water (mostly 6 feet MLW) may compensate for less privacy than mooring out at the islands. Here one is a relatively short row or putt-putt by dinghy to the commercial marinas to the north or into the East Branch of Norwalk Harbor (see 10) where one can get ashore for a short walk to downtown South Norwalk near the drawbridge across the Norwalk River. In the South Anchor Basin, one may find a vacant mooring to pick up for overnight (at skipper's risk since some private moorings are not always well maintained).

5. South Norwalk Boat Club on the west side of the river just above the South Anchor Basin is a hospitable club, founded in 1900, with a loyal and remarkably large membership of 850 who come from hither, thither, and yon. The club sports about 99 percent small and mid-sized power-boats. It started out in an old barge afloat in the channel and then moved to a barn on the present location. They still laugh about the "hay falls" sprinkling down from a musty loft onto the heads of the Saturday night jitterbugs. A new club with an impressive bar and restaurant, including showers, was built in 1960. On our latest trip here, we followed protocol and reported in at the bar where the commodore, at the time, brought us up to date on his club. He couldn't have been more obliging. You'll find 6 feet off the club's docks.

6. Vinco Marine—(203) 853-0771, VHF-9—just north of the SNBC, is a small but well-found, full-service marina with gas, diesel, water, electricity, and showers. Dock space and rental moorings are usually available. The yard specializes in engine repairs, both gas and diesel. Their haulout service carries to 35 tons, unlimited length, but limited in beam to 16′6″. Beware the approach to their gas dock, close ashore upland of their slips, which carries only about 3 feet at MLW. It's scheduled to be dredged, but ask for local knowledge.

7. Rex Marine Center—(203) 831-5234—next upstream from Vinco and SNBC, has berths for transients, a well-stocked marine store, and sales and service on inflatables and outboards (Mercury and Yamaha) as well as sailboards and marine electronics.

No fuel is available here but Rex claims that it is the best source for marine parts and supplies in Norwalk. This marina is run by the Gardella family, as is Cove Marina (see 11). The renowned Pier Restaurant lies on the waterfront at Rex but has been condemned as unsafe because the pilings supporting it have become old and tired, so it is not now in operation.

Historic South Norwalk's recently restored Washington Street is an ideal and nearby place to go for dinner, a stroll, or food supplies. Lining the street are numerous eateries whose very names whet one's appetite in offering a wide variety of seafood dishes. Places like Shenanigan's Irish Pub, Pasta Nostra, and Sono Seaport Seafood Restaurant—(203) 854-9483—which is on the river can give your crew a complete change of scene and taste. The latter has a couple of dockage spaces.

Just to the south lies the Maritime Center, Norwalk's newest major attraction. This multimillion-dollar aquarium/maritime history/IMAX theater complex is devoted to the maritime history and marine life of Long Island Sound. It offers both entertainment and a range of educational programs. The center is open Sunday through Wednesday from 11 A.M. to 6 P.M. and Thursday through Saturday from 11 A.M. to 10 P.M.

Just below the first bridge, on the east side of the river, is the brand-new visitors' dock with a launching ramp and large parking area. The city is still deciding how to use it. It has a free pumpout station and a dockmaster.

8. Norwest Marine—(203) 253-2822, VHF-68—is a smaller marina and full-service yard catering to powerboats and outboard service (OMC). A well-stocked marine store and neat, clean service shop attest to quiet competency. Dock space is limited but one may try there for overnight space. They do have fuel.

9. Maurice Marine, smaller yet than the others, is the last commercial marina before the drawbridge in South Norwalk. It is now looking very old and worn with its dock in need of major repair and activity at a very low ebb.

Returning to our main, eastward migration, we find:

10. East Branch of Norwalk Harbor can be entered from the South Anchor Basin (see 4) through a 6-foot (MLW) channel at the eastern tip of the triangular anchor basin between the spindle (FLG1) and the nun 2 and thence to cans 3 and 5. This recently dredged channel and anchor basin is quite full of privately owned moorings, several of which are empty at any given time. The slightly adventurous skipper could enter the basin through the well-marked channel and then keep to the right of the moored boats (inbound) around into the body of the basin opposite a three-story condominium. Pick up a vacant mooring (at the risk of being dislodged if the owner returns). From here it is a short dinghy trip to the city docks (north shore of the basin) or to a public right-of-way (dirt and gravel ramp) opposite the city docks at the south end of the condominium. N.B.: The city docks are locked from landward so access is limited to those with keys. If you go ashore by this route, check with the locals to see if the constable is on duty (brick building opposite northerly city dock) or wait until a local boater comes along; either of these can let you back onto the docks (if they like the cut of your jib). If you are going ashore at off hours, the public right-of-way, which is Second Street in East Norwalk, is surer and not too long a walk around the basin to Veterans Park and thence to South Norwalk itself. In the East Branch, Cross Channel Outboard, first place on the starboard hand inbound, offers engine repairs, specializing in outboard, and fuel (gas).

11. Norwalk Cove Marina is behind Calf Pasture Point, entrance between Calf Pasture Point and Gregory Point northeast of can 17. A draft of 8 feet MLW may be carried into the marina to 8- to 10-foot depths inside. On the right side, inbound, is the Skippers Restaurant, specializing in seafood (open year-round except Mondays in the off-season) with limited free dockage for patrons. Just inside the cove one finds the gas dock (gas, diesel, ice, and water) and the well-stocked ship's store. Here too find the dockmaster who will assign transient dock space. Electricity is available at all dockside space. Telephone, laundromat, showers, mopeds for rent, amusement arcade, miniature golf, and a swimming pool (fee charged) round out the features of this fully equipped marina. Three travelifts, at 15, 70, and 150 tons, and a full-service yard can handle just about anything and any job that can get into the cove. Nearby, Norwalk's public beach is free for those who walk in.

Cruisers who prefer anchoring out will find suitable crannies here and there in the outer harbor. Unfortunately, most of the good anchorages are well known and prone either to surge or to wash from the main channel. Some boats anchor between Grassy and Goose Islands; go in slowly with depth sounder on. Exploring Grassy, which is town property, is fine, but Goose Island is a bird sanctuary and it, like all the other islands, is a nesting place for such northern shorebirds as herons, egrets, Canada geese, and pheasants. Be sure to tread lightly if you go ashore during nesting season. Also, help clean up these areas when you run across culch (great down-east word which means "garbage") while exploring.

Shea Island is also publicly owned, so many Norwalkers camp here on summer weekends. The landing place, for small boats only, is the eastern tip of the island; elsewhere is foul. It is the only Norwalk island with a warden, Alice Cingolani. Each summer she "hosts" about 1,500 visitors who enjoy the wild strawberries, blackberries, raspberries, and poison ivy which abound on the island, as well as the red, pink, and white roses, daisies, honeysuckle, beach peas, and yellow cactus blossoms.

To the northeast lies Chimon Island, the largest of the Norwalk island group. Its 70 unspoiled acres make it a unique sanctuary for many forms of marine life and numerous kinds of land and water birds. To lie off this island, many shoal-draft boats anchor due north of Copps Island—but beware the poor holding ground and the narrow, rock-strewn entrance from the southeast.

Both Chimon and Sheffield Islands are scheduled to be included in the Connecticut Coastal National Wildlife Refuge as bird sanctuaries. Other refuges joining them are Milford Point and Falkner Island, whose automated lighthouse will continue to be maintained by the Coast Guard.

Another way to view these islands is to board the *Lady Joan* out of Cove Marina for day or evening tours of the harbor. In season, the evening tours frequently feature a (loud) band and are a favorite of singles and young couples.

On July 11, 1779, Calf Pasture Point was used as a landing place for 2,500 British troops carried in twenty-six vessels. Both a Congregational and an Episcopal church as well as many houses and barns were burned by the British. The Indians used the point as a pasture.

Norwalk was formerly one of the major transatlantic oyster-shipping ports in the country. Today, it is the center of a dramatically revitalized shellfishing industry in Connecticut and boasts one of the largest shell-fish areas on the East Coast. Tallmadge Brothers of Norwalk is a major oyster shipper in the United States.

Saugatuck, Connecticut (12368). Compo Yacht Basin has been dredged in the lee of Cedar Point at the east of the entrance to the Saugatuck River. However, they do not have facilities for transients.

The channel to this basin is well marked on both sides by privately maintained buoys. It has range lights also for entrance after dark. To enter this harbor, do not attempt the channel passage that leads from the west from Peck Ledge Light northward around Cockenoe Island to the Saugatuck River. It is not marked, and at low tide the best draft obtainable is not more than 2 feet. Instead, enter this harbor from the east, carrying the can off Georges Rock and the lighted buoy off Cedar Point on your port. Having just passed Saugatuck River nun 8, you will spot the channel to the yacht basin. Be sure to carry nun 8 on your starboard when entering this narrow channel.

The 50-foot channel has been dredged to a 10-foot depth, except where it has begun to shoal along the small sandspit to starboard almost at channel's end. Just before reaching this point, stay well to the port. "If the *Clearwater* can come in here, so can you," hailed the harbormaster as we came alongside. Protection from all winds may be found in the oval basin, 400 yards long by 100 yards wide, with a depth of about 9 feet, but extremely shallow along its entire southern shore. The basin is very congested, over 230 boats, large and small, being moored there on any summer weekend. Anchoring is impossible, so it is necessary to obtain a mooring, usually fore and aft. A depth of 7 feet at low water can be carried to the float, where gasoline, ice, and water may be obtained. There is no overnight dockage. The dockmaster, is on duty seven days of the week from 9 A.M. to 8 P.M. and is usually spotted in the small white building housing the Minuteman Yacht Club which operates the Compo Basin. Any Westporter with a boat is eligible to join this club.

Commodore Daniel Siegel of the Cedar Point Yacht Club writes:

In approaching the Cedar Point Yacht Club, located on the northeastern shore of Saugatuck Shores, follow the buoys leading to the west past a fleet of boats moored beside the channel. While the channel buoys are moved periodically, stay in mid-channel as there has been some shoaling. Anchoring among the boats is not advisable as there is very little space that also has adequate depth.

The modern two-story clubhouse of Cedar Point Yacht Club was built in 1966 on Bluff Point just south of can 15. The upper deck of the clubhouse offers a panoramic view of the area and on clear days Long Island can be seen across the Sound. The whole area sparkles with lighted buoys and lighthouses at night. A narrow channel, running southeast from nun 16, leads to Cedar Point's dredged basin. While anchoring is not permitted, there are over 100 slips, and, according to club manager Rick O'Rourke, no visitor has ever been turned away. The slips can accommodate boats up to 45 feet and offer water and electricity. The facilities include gas, diesel, ice, water, showers, and a neat snack bar open from 11 A.M. to 2 P.M. daily and 11 A.M. to 6 P.M. weekends and holidays. There are tennis courts and a beach for swimming. You will always see a preponderance of sailboats here, since the club has a rich sailing heritage; recently it hosted Atlantic Class and J-30 Class National Championships as well as Star Class and Thistle Class District Championships. The club runs a very active Junior Program.

Cedar Point extends reciprocal privileges to members of other recognized clubs. It is best to make reservations by calling Rick O'Rourke at (203) 226-7411. When registering, pick up a copy of a visitor's guide to Cedar Point and the excellent shopping and dining out available in nearby Westport. Congenial club members can usually be found who will offer a ride to town. Taxi service is available. The Cedar Point basin is a closed-head area.

Farther up the Saugatuck River channel on the western shore lies the Saugatuck Harbor Yacht Club's dock at the head of Duck Creek, affording a quiet, appealing, but crowded shelter. As you approach the narrow entrance, go between the two privately maintained channel markers and line up on the two range lights standing close ashore. The facilities here include gas, diesel fuel, water, ice, use of the swimming pool (included in the dockage fee), and electricity at the slips with reported 8-foot depths. This private club had its beginning in 1960 and is established in a 100-year-old Victorian carriage garage and horse stable. If you are a member of a recognized yacht club, it is suggested you phone ahead to the manager at (203) 454-3004 for a reservation. He also monitors VHF-71. They also welcome non-yacht club people if space permits. Whenever leaving the creek, make sure to stand off until incoming boats have cleared the "narrows" at the entrance.

The nearest restaurants lie 2¹/₂ miles to the north at Westport.

The channel up the Saugatuck River to the railroad bridge is marked as far as Stony Point but is subject to shoaling with a 3-foot depth at low water reported just beyond nun 26. Above the bridge the channel is not marked and strangers are advised not to attempt it. However, just above the railroad bridge on the west bank is Coastwise Marine, run by Irwin Donenfeld, who promises that "Coastwise will repair anything." So if you are in trouble anywhere in the harbor, give him a call from Compo or either yacht club and he'll send a pilot to direct you up the river. For major repairs, however, contacting a marina in Norwalk may be your best bet.

Southport, Connecticut (12369). Here is another instance of a community's improving its waterfront to form a perfect shelter, under any conditions. By means of a breakwater and dredging, the entrance to Mill River has become an appealing, fully protected though narrow harbor. The channel has a width of 50 feet and a depth of 7 feet at low water down its center all the way to the head of the harbor, and then 4 to 6 feet in the area beyond the Pequot Yacht Club's fuel dock. However, at the present writing, the harbor is badly in need of dredging. Silting has reduced the number of moorings and there is no room for transients unless someone is out cruising. Dredging is awaiting approval of a harbor management plan, money, and priority with the Army Corps of Engineers.

Though the channel is marked by two flashing lights and eight can and nun buoys, it is somewhat tricky. For instance, on our latest visit, we were advised by a local authority not to go too close to the outer nun buoys but to favor the green cans until the last nun, number 10, was reached; that nun should be favored closely. Enter with caution if the tide is low. We don't advise strangers to enter after dark. Watch for oyster stakes off the entrance.

Southport has a quaint public marina, (203) 259-1384, a boat shack which used to have a sign reading "Ye Yacht Yard" located on the west side of the entrance channel near where the chart shows White Rock. Water is available there, or a possible tie-up or mooring. Beyond, also to port, where the harbor widens, is the well-known Pequot Yacht Club, (203) 255-5794, one of the leading clubs on the Sound. The club offers a helpful visiting yachtsmen's guide and reciprocal privileges to members of other recognized yacht clubs and may be able to provide a mooring on a first-come, first-served basis. It is necessary to tie up fore and aft, because the river is crowded and narrow, with no room to swing at anchor. Launch service runs from 8 A.M. to 10 P.M. and monitors VHF-69. We suggest taking a possible mooring for a small fee per night since the slips here are for the use of the club's members.

Gasoline, diesel fuel, ice, and water can also be procured at Pequot's float, where there is 7 feet at low tide. Showers and daily luncheons are available in the clubhouse. It's a short walk to the small village center located inland from the fountain outside the club entrance. Here you will find such stores as a pharmacy, a coffee shop, and a grocery, as well as hardware, gift, and liquor stores. A newspaper store supplying limited groceries is open Sundays. The best meal in town is reportedly served at the Pepper Mill Steakhouse, reached by taxi.

Southport is one of the most delightful harbors on the Connecticut shore. In Revolutionary times, crews were organized here to protect the town from numerous Tory depredations suffered by settlements along the Sound. Southport was once a famous onion-shipping point. Onion fields spread out over the land to the east of the harbor at the turn of the century, and an old wharf used for transshipment of crops can still be seen facing the club. Southport is part of the town of Fairfield.

On October 21, 1799, the town voted that it was willing to allow the

General Assembly to grant a lottery to raise money for "Sinking the channel of Mill River harbor."

Black Rock Harbor, Bridgeport, Connecticut (12369). This harbor, west of Bridgeport, is easy to make both day and night, on account of the lights and buoys at the north and south of the entrance. A white tower on the sandspit to the east of the entrance is a good guide in the daytime from far out in the Sound. Penfield Reef Light, converted to automatic operation, is a sure guide to the entrance at night. But day or night, make sure to keep well off of Black Rock, out of water at low tide and located 600 yards to the northeast of this light. It is identified by a white triangular daymarker with red borders marked "Danger."

The Black Rock Yacht Club is in a white building to the west, inside of Grover Hill, where a pier is indicated on the chart. In approaching this pier through the deeper water, head due west, keeping directly on your stern the highest stand of trees on Fayerweather Island. The best anchorage for all but small and shoal-draft boats is across the channel from this yacht club north of nun 8 although it seemed pretty full of moorings on our last visit. This, however, is exposed from southeast to southwest and offers a considerable roll. In a blow it is possible to run for shelter into Cedar Creek, where complete protection is found in the dredged channel. If you must come up to the club's dock, be aware of a long strip of rocky shoal 50 yards north of it and running parallel to it. This is exposed at low water.

The Black Rock Yacht Club is both a lively social club and a yacht club. Besides its pier in 3-foot depth, it has a swimming pool, tennis courts, a fine restaurant, and a handsome clubhouse, all open during the summer months. Across the channel, an impressive fleet of yachts may be seen anchored or moored. An overnight mooring is available for a fee with launch service provided until 10 P.M. Signal the dockmaster, John Lucas, who monitors VHF-9, for a mooring and register later in the clubhouse. Ice and water are available dockside where there is $3^1/2$ feet MLW. Showers and a swimming pool are found on the property. Members of recognized yacht clubs are warmly welcomed by this club whose Sunday buffet, served from 5:30 to 7:30 P.M., we have found delectable.

Black Rock Yacht Club traces its origins back to 1874. In that year, George A. Wells, an associate of P. T. Barnum, purchased its present building from the Penfield family, and it became part of the George

Hotel, known the world over for its elegance and charm. The clubhouse was used as the bar and for shore dinners. During that period it was called the "Pleasure Hall."

Farther up the harbor on the west shore of Cedar Creek, across from Fayerweather Island and on the point where Black Rock is indicated on the chart, is the Fayerweather Yacht Club, with a large membership and open the year round. Its large barroom was bustling with activity during our latest stopover. Unlike many of the other yacht clubs visited, in this club more men of our own age were around than younger people, and the convivial aspects of the club were much in evidence among the hospitable members who were on hand. There is 5 or 6 feet of water at the dock, and the club usually has spare moorings for visitors, and provides gas, ice, and water. But if there's space, boats up to 40 feet can tie up to a floating club dock across the channel in 7-foot depth. Visiting yachtsmen are always welcome, the commodore told us, whether members of other clubs or not. "We aren't fussy," said one of the members. "We like to be friendly to everyone." And they certainly have been to us. There are more sailboats than powerboats here, and the docks and moorings offer better protection than Black Rock.

One of the strongest signs of Bridgeport's increasing yachting activity is the success of Captain's Cove Seaport, formerly Burr Cove Marina up in Burr Creek. During the seventies, this old marina went from bad to worse—an embarrassment to the waterfront. Finally, the city of Bridgeport asked Kaye Williams, a native of Black Rock and longtime marine businessman and lobsterman, to take over the marina on a long-term lease, and he did. Since 1983, Williams has restored new docks and slips and built a boardwalk lined with brightly colored shops, a fish market, a boat repair shop, and a 450-capacity seafood restaurant overlooking the harbor. Above the restaurant is a big hall with a bar that has become a popular local night spot, especially on weekends. The disco music stops at 11 P.M. The whole place is frequented by a great many non-boaters. We were informed that the city of Bridgeport has also established a marine high school adjunct where area students can get a taste of the sea. All this probably makes it the largest boat basin in Fairfield County. Williams has also added a picturesque, historic touch by docking at the cove H.M.S. *Rose,* a 150-foot replica of a Revolutionary War British frigate which he picked up for $70,000.

It is obviously crowded here and often noisy; the number of boats docked has jumped dramatically in recent years. Captain's Cove has certainly changed boating people's old image of Bridgeport as a port of call. Entrepreneur Williams says it all: "It's finally coming alive." Across the channel is a long series of floating slips at reduced rates, serviced by a small ferry during the day. It is a fun place to visit, and we were treated very well there. Fuel, ice, showers, and repairs are available.

Bridgeport, Connecticut (12369). The best anchorage is up Johnson's Creek just beyond the large gas tanks on the western point as one enters the creek. The Miamogue Yacht Club is here with increased dockage space and will advise yachtsmen as to moorings and where to get gasoline and supplies.

Although this is a fully protected anchorage, it is very unattractive and commercial, with tankers coming and going nearby. Not much can be said for going up the long channel into Bridgeport. One will probably meet barges and collect much coal dust and soot. Bridgeport is useful to cruisers chiefly as a protection in a storm. Anchoring inside the breakwaters is a definite possibility.

Note to navigators: That tall red-and-white stack which is visible for miles out in the Sound is located on the west bank of the Pequonnock River just below the I-95 bridge in Bridgeport.

Stratford, Connecticut (12370). Here is another river entrance cutting into the Connecticut shore that is no place to enter at night if it can be avoided. There is a strong current in the river, and sometimes, when the wind is against an outgoing tide, a short, hard sea breaks in the channel and the buoys are dragged under. However, dredging of the channel to a 100-foot width and an approximate depth of 18 feet, at least as far north as can 29 below Popes Island, has helped to minimize the current and make river navigation easier. The mean range of tide at Stratford is 5$^{1}/_{2}$ feet.

A cluster of tall black chimneys at Devon, up the Housatonic, stand out prominently as a good guide in clear weather from far out in the Sound for both Milford and the entrance of the Housatonic River. The ebb tide swirls and eddies about, so power is a necessity. The flood sets strongly to the west; this tends to set you toward the shoal running along the entire length of the entrance channel's western shore. Housatonic means "land beyond the mountains."

We have stayed at the hospitable Housatonic Boat Club which is just above nun 16 on the west shore and is lodged in a porch-lined white building. Here they offer no gas, ice, showers, or slips, but they do have a swimming dock, guest moorings, and launch service from 8 A.M. to 9 P.M. Anchoring is not permitted in their mooring area where you will find a large fleet of sailing craft across the river. This club, built in 1887, is conveniently near the impressive-looking American Shakespeare Theater at the Connecticut Center for the Performing Arts, which is not operating at present. They welcome all cruising sailors.

Just beyond lies Stratford Marina run by Dave Olsen, with 200 slips and the most complete services around. Should you need any repair work on your boat, have it done here; special attention is given to inboards at Marine Systems and to electronic gear at Maritronics. Dockmaster Lew Cella, who monitors VHF-9 for advance reservations, catered to theatergoers since his facility claims to be the official marina for the Shakespeare Theater. He offers each skipper a marina guidebook which mentions their snack bar, canvas repair work, laundromat, a well-stocked ship's store, pumpout station, fuel dock, the only showers in the area, nearby stores for supplies, and such fine restaurants as Fagan's and Blue Goose. The only down side is the "Housatonic no-see-ums" which appear in swarms at dusk from the marsh area to the east, but they disappear after an hour or so. They probably afflict the whole area.

The Pootatuck Yacht Club can be spotted in its red building, a short distance farther up the same shore about 2 1/2 miles from the river's entrance. Here you can obtain gas, water, and ice, sometimes a slip but rarely a mooring. Longtime club steward Andy Pavlucik showed us around their refurbished dining room where credit cards in payment for tasteful meals are accepted.

The American Festival Theater, formerly the American Shakespeare Theater, is mothballed while the state of Connecticut pursues private lessors. Its resemblance to London's Globe Theatre evoked the pageantry of Elizabethan England.

The anchorage off the Pootatuck Yacht Club is exposed to the southward and northeast for some distance along the river, and most of the nearby land is low and marshy. While the yacht facilities, stores, and other conveniences are at Stratford, the beauty of the Housatonic is up the river where dredging has been authorized for an 8- by 75-foot minimum channel to Shelton and Derby.

If you decide to explore further, it is a run of about 9 miles from the yacht club, along a well-marked channel, to the head of navigation at Derby and Shelton. Make this passage on a rising tide and you should have little trouble in carrying 5 feet all the way up if you stay in mid-channel. Note, however, that in early 1993 depth at MLW at N"32" shoals to 2 feet before dredging. The shoreline scenery is impressive as you approach Derby, with hills of 200 to 300 feet sloping down to the river's edge. The two bascule bridges at Devon demand our attention. They usually open on signal daily from 5 A.M. to 9 P.M.; but on Monday through Friday from 7 to 9 A.M. and from 4 to 5:45 P.M., these draws need not open for vessels.

Although Adriaen Block, the Dutch fur trader, stopped at Stratford in 1614, the first settlers were English. They came there in 1639 and named it for Stratford-on-Avon.

Milford, Connecticut (12370). Should you put in to this well-protected but crowded port of Milford on one of its interclub race days, you will probably find a busy yachting center swarming with attractive young boys and girls who have gathered from far and near. Some of the boats will be on trailers getting a final going-over; others will be in the water or on the way in. Blue Jays, Lightnings, 210s, Thistles, 420s, and Lasers will be teeming with youngsters aboard. Such liveliness confirms a Milford Yacht Club officer's comment that "We're probably the most active sailing club on the Sound."

Across the Wepawaug River, above the yacht club, are the attractive condominiums with docks which replaced the oyster operations of the former Cedar Island Corporation. The National Marine Fisheries Service has a laboratory at Milford to advise oyster "farmers," and the Connecticut Aquaculture Division has its headquarters here. Oysters and other shellfish may be found along the beaches on either side of the Gulf and taken without a license.

The harbor is formed by two jetties at the mouth of the Wepawaug River, completing the protection of the anchorage from all winds. In 1988 the 75-foot channel, lined by buoys with reflectors, carried about 8 feet all the way to the Milford Yacht Club on the west side of the entrance, on Burns Point to port, and thence to the head of navigation just above the Milford Boat Works. Members of other recognized yacht clubs who register in the clubhouse are welcomed hospitably; Dockmaster Ted Halat, located in his office next to the club's swimming pool, will assign, if available, a guest mooring or a slip for a fee. The pool is open to transients. On a recent visit, Vice-Commodore Frank Batchelor helped bring us up to date on his club and on Milford, the sixth-oldest town in

Connecticut. Water, ice, telephones, showers, a bar, and meals are all available at the club, and there are stores, including a laundromat, just 5 minutes away. Regular launch service is provided.

Congestion is the chief difficulty at this otherwise splendid harbor. The outgoing tide sweeps in under a bridge from the east, making it unwise to anchor behind the eastern jetty, where it is also shoal. There is 6 feet at the club float at low tide. Milford is a good place to visit, but is quieter on weekdays or nights than on weekends. The late Captain Bradley, a local authority, told us, "The ducks may wake you up if you are fool enough to feed them." And don't be foolish enough to try to anchor along the river.

A Corps of Engineers survey in 1992 showed 10 feet draft up to half a mile beyond nun 6, and 8 feet thence to the head of the harbor. The west side is a little less so avoid that side if you have a deep keel.

There are three marinas and a boatyard on the Wepawaug River, all providing slips and other facilities and thus helping to lessen the congestion in the lower river: Port Milford Marina which monitors VHF-9 (in buildings that are to port just below the first creek that runs among the marshes and that have been rebuilt since Hurricane Gloria visited); Spencer's (housed in a barn-red building to starboard a short distance up); and just beyond to port a unique boating complex composed of Milford Harbor Marina, Milford Boat Works, and Milford Yacht Sales. To pick up provisions, a 7-11 store is located straight down from Fibbers Saybrook Fishhouse beyond the railroad bridge, a short walk from the marina.

We have often tied up at Spencer's Marina, but those were during the days when they faced less competition. Flourishing Milford Harbor Marina has much going for it now. Their facilities include diesel fuel, gas, ice, heads, and showers, and the "Ship's Store" is one of the best on the Connecticut shore. Close by are town shops and the popular Fibbers, Milford Seafood, and The Gathering restaurants. They are knowledgeable about boats here, as well as the needs of boating people, and specialize in the repair of engines found in auxiliary vessels.

At the turn of the century, Milford was, strangely, a center for the manufacture of straw hats. Now it's a popular and attractive summer resort with pleasantly shaded streets and lovely homes. There is a railway station on the main line of Amtrak, with express trains to New York or Boston that stop at nearby New Haven.

"On a quiet night a pleasant place to anchor if bound east or west," writes a yachtsman, "is just to the north of Charles Island. The bottom is sand and good-holding. At low water a bar connecting Charles Island with the mainland is dry, so don't anchor to the northwest of the island. This, also, is a good spot to duck into for a quick bite if the going is rugged on the Sound."

Charles Island, now owned by the state of Connecticut, is rich in historic lore and was originally purchased in 1639 by Milford settlers from Ansantawae, chief of the local Paugusset tribe, for 6 coats, 10 blankets, 1 kettle, 12 hatchets, 12 hoes, 24 knives, and 12 small mirrors. Its peaceful, rustic appearance is deceptive, for down through the years it has borne three mysterious curses, harbored the secret hiding place of two unfound treasures (one of them Captain Kidd's), and served as the proving ground for America's first submarine, *The Turtle,* which served conspicuously in an American Revolutionary naval battle. At various times in its history, it has housed a mansion, a hotel, a factory, and a Dominican retreat, whose foundations may still be seen. The island was also once considered by the American Yacht Club for its original clubhouse site but was rejected in favor of Milton Point, Rye. If you enjoy exploring ashore, don't miss a stop here.

New Haven, Connecticut (12371). This harbor has seen big changes in the past few years, and many more are anticipated in the near future. The third-busiest commercial port in New England, New Haven is known as a place of refuge, a place to secure supplies, and an interesting place to visit. The entrance, outside of which stand numerous oyster stakes, is well marked by the strobe lights on the United Illuminating Company tower and range lights on the West Haven shore and is easy to enter at night or in fog or storm. With the numerous buoy changes throughout this area, it is important to observe all navigational aids.

The usual anchorage for yachts is at Morris Cove, which is accessible to the Sound and where depths are in the 10- to 12-foot range. But it is not always peaceful here. A sea roll from the southwest frequently makes in by the breakwaters, and the cove is rough in westerly winds. The New Haven Yacht Club—(203) 469-9608, VHF-68—first chartered in 1882, is housed in a small gray building set behind a pier jutting out from the cove's southern shore. Do not approach this pier, at which there is only 2 feet or less at low water. This sailing club, open from noon to sunset Mondays through Fridays and from 9 A.M. to sunset on weekends, has a few guest moorings set out in good holding ground with launch service provided. These are free to any cruiser, and although their shoreside facilities are limited, there are restaurants and supplies nearby.

Just to the west, the New Haven Marina does some engine and hull repairs in a tiny, shallow basin behind a prominent stone jetty. The Lighthouse Marina, located on Morris Creek just west of Morgan Point, is too small and shallow to be considered except in dire emergencies at high tide.

On the chart, note that a Coast Guard station with a marked channel is located at the north end of Fort Hale Park just to the east of lighted bell 15. They monitor VHF-9 and 16 here. What is not shown on the chart is a deep hole south of Forbes Bluff so avoid dropping an anchor here.

The West River channel leads from the New Haven Reach to City Point and then around to the West River. The channel which is 75 feet wide is used primarily for transporting fuel barges and is federally maintained to a depth of 12 feet MLW up to the Kimberly Avenue bridge beyond nun 18. Although it is tempting to cut across the harbor because it is wide and open looking, do not stray from the channel. Many a skipper has sat red-faced awaiting the tide just feet from the channel while wiser boaters passed by with a knowing nod.

Located on the southern shore of City Point, just before can 11, is a new facility appropriately called the Oyster Point Marina—(203) 624-5895, VHF-9. This is the location where Indians and settlers alike came for oysters and is the former site of the City Point Boat Yard and Traders' Dock Marina. With low-water depths of 12 feet at the service docks and 7 feet to all slips, there is adequate water for most boats. Rental slips are available. In northerly or westerly winds you will be more protected here than in Morris Cove where there is better shelter in southerly or easterly winds. Gas, diesel fuel, showers, and a laundromat are among the marina's facilities, and protection from wakes is provided by timber-and-board breakwaters. It is not unusual to see visiting crews enjoying a delectable evening dinner or Sunday brunch at the nearby Charthouse Restaurant overlooking the harbor. For those who prefer a lighter snack, sandwiches are ordered at the basin's store and fast food is within a seven-minute walk. Basic food supplies, ice, and deli goods may be purchased at a small grocery store on the premises. Oyster Point is about five minutes from downtown by taxi; a bus stop is one block from the marina. Once in New Haven, one can take a walking tour of the Yale University campus and visit museums and the Long Wharf Palace and Shubert theaters.

Directly to the east of the marina basin is the Connecticut Marine Studies Center. Used during the school year as a marine high school called "The Sound School," it serves as a research and laboratory center for the Connecticut Marine Studies Consortium. The consortium is composed of the four Connecticut universities, the New Haven Board of Education, and Schooner, Inc., a non-profit marine educational organization. This is the home for their marine research vessels which include the *J. N. Carter,* the 66-foot research ketch, flagship of the city of New Haven.

One may also venture farther up the harbor to anchor in the charted area south of can 1 or dock and dine at the Rusty Scupper located on New Haven Long Wharf. Here the Long Wharf Maritime Center is planning the construction of hundreds of slips for use by local and visiting craft.

Entrance to Branford. Lovers Island, with its sandspit, is on the lower left, Big and Little Mermaid just to the northeast. *Aero Graphics Corp.*

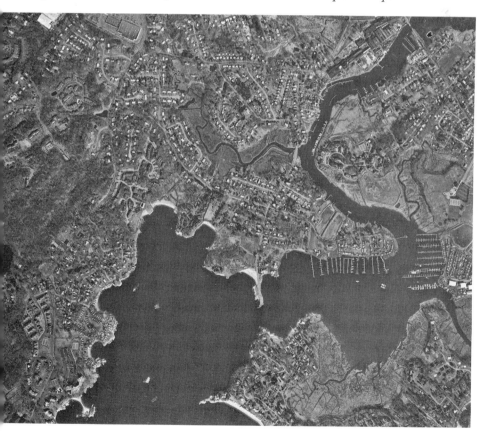

In 1985, the West River channel recorded a depth of 8 feet at low water up to nun 18, thence a depth of 5 feet to the Connecticut Turnpike crossover. The West Cove Marina—(203) 933-3000—with showers, ice, laundry, clubhouse, and pool and the City Point Yacht Club lie just above the fixed bridge with a vertical clearance of 23 feet. If you can get under the bridge and find space, this is the place to come in case of a blow.

Branford, Connecticut (12373). Chart 12373 shows a large shallow bay 4 miles east of New Haven, fully exposed to the south. But, like so many other places on the Connecticut shore, the farther in one goes, the better the anchorage for small boats.

The 100-foot-wide channel was surveyed in 1990 with a depth of 8.2 feet or more up to about Bruce Johnson Marina. The entrance must be made under power by all except very small boats. Don't attempt it at night. If you must enter by night, we would like to advise that the flashing green light on Big Mermaid's pipe tower is difficult to pick up. A good anchorage offering a bottom of mud and rock can be found in the charted 7-foot depth area between Big Mermaid and Lamphier Cove to the north.

With dredging and filling, and new docks at the yacht club located on the north shore, this harbor was transformed prior to "Branford Day," which came on August 18, 1954. Now Branford has become, in its facilities for yachtsmen, one of the finest ports on Long Island Sound. Yachting activities revolve around the Branford Yacht Club, which was organized in 1909 and is now equipped with a first-class marina containing many slips. Members of recognized yacht clubs offering reciprocal privileges are welcomed there. Report when you come in to the dockmaster at the long gas dock to your port after you have kept well clear of the nearby mud flats running along the northern edge of the channel. He will assign you a slip or a tie-up between mooring stakes across the channel if one is available. No reservations are taken by the club.

Besides gas, diesel fuel, ice, and a telephone at the main dock, electricity and fresh water are provided at the slips. At the large piers, depths of up to 8 feet are available. Supplies may be purchased at a store about 1/2 mile away.

Not only has the Branford Yacht Club concentrated on maintaining its fine dockage, but its clubhouse is spic and span and the manicured grounds with numerous picnic tables afford a splendid view of the river.

Pier 66, just beyond the yacht club, is an enterprising marina which has been built up from a mountain of mud to a facility that includes 350 floating slips, a ship's store, a gas dock, and a snack bar featuring home-style Italian cooking. While it has apparent appeal for powerboat people, we still prefer the setup at Bruce & Johnson's.

The channel, marked in part by stakes on both sides as one proceeds upriver, winds its way among the marshes. Hug these stakes closely. In the middle of the bend on the east shore, on now-filled land, is Bruce & Johnson's Marina—(203) 488-8329—a Brewer Yard, with slips, ice, water, a marine store, full repair work, showers, and a swimming pool. A little restaurant called Sam's Place with outdoor tables serves good sandwiches near the pool and is a cut above most snack bars. Bruce & Johnson's is popular with sailing people, and their rigging shop is very good and accommodating. After rounding the bend and heading westward beyond the stakes, keep in the middle. Below some large buildings on the west shore is the Dutch Wharf Boat Yard Marina. Here are slips and moorings, a supply store, but no gas. Hauling and repair work are done here, and we saw some fine-looking yachts tied up. A package and grocery store may be found nearby.

Branford is an attractive residential community, deservedly popular among cruising men. There are many fine old houses. Yankee traders were once very active there. When West Indies rum didn't pay, some took up slave trading and on occasion procured slaves for some very pious people. One of the pious was Reverend Ezra Stiles, president of Yale.*

Pine Orchard, Connecticut (12373). Pine Orchard is a delightful summer resort between Branford and the Thimble Islands. In making your approach at night, line up on the club's range lights marking the outer end of a breakwater. East of Brown Point and behind this breakwater lies a basin with depths that vary from time to time according to the dredging. The approach channel and this basin inside of St. Helena Island were dredged in 1993. On entering, make a sharp turn to port just after passing the eastern end of the breakwater that marks the short channel to the basin. Stay well off of a chain of rocks that extends southward from St. Helena Island.

On the west shore of the basin is the Pine Orchard Club, with a fine clubhouse, docks, tennis courts, a nine-hole golf course, a freshwater

*From *The Yankees of Connecticut,* by W. Storrs Lee (Henry Holt & Co., New York).

swimming pool, a dining room, and yacht facilities that include slips, guest moorings, water, ice, electric connections, gas, telephone, etc. An enthusiastic member once told us that this was the "only club on Long Island Sound that has everything." Judging from what we have seen, he wasn't far off. Guest privileges, we were told by the dockmaster, are granted to yachtsmen who are members of recognized clubs that accord reciprocal privileges. All visiting yachts must adhere to the club's published rules and regulations governing dockage and should leave port by 11 A.M. the day after their arrival or be charged for another day's stay.

You'll pay a fee for a tie-up at one of the slips or for a mooring, with an extra fee for use of the swimming pool and tennis courts with permission of the swim or tennis pro. The inner moorings lie in 5-foot depths but there's 7 feet farther outside. Anchoring in the basin is not permitted, due to very limited swinging room. The Pine Orchard Market, 1/2 mile distant, has been recommended as a good source for supplies.

Large yachts can anchor outside the island, but with little protection from south or east winds and from the frequent crying of the seagulls nesting. The charted channel running northeastward by St. Helena leads to a cove just east of Juniper Point. This is busily used by traprock barges so you'll find no suitable anchorage here.

During the summer months, an active group of attractive people of all ages keep the club and nearby waters very busy.

Pine Orchard, in spite of its tendency to shoal up, has become one of the more appealing ports of call on the Sound, except in easterlies.

Thimble Islands, Stony Creek, Connecticut (12373). "Like a section of the Maine Coast, drifted into Long Island Sound,"* the Thimbles offer a good, picturesque anchorage between Money Island and West Crib Island.

"One leaves the mainland," wrote a summer resident of one of these islands, "and trouble is left behind. The world is forgotten, and the clean air sweeps one to absolute ecstasy."†

We have previously advised the reader to disregard the cable warning

---

*Quotation from *Connecticut*—American Guide Series (Houghton Mifflin Co., Boston).
†Mrs. Gertrude G. Single, as quoted by Robert Froman in *One Million Islands For Sale* (Duell, Sloan and Pearce).

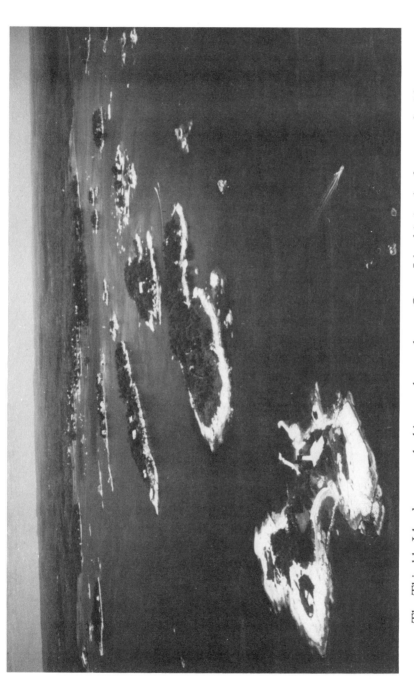

The Thimble Islands as seen looking to the northeast. Outer Island is in the foreground with Horse Island in center. Just beyond, from left to right, are High Island, Pot Island, and Money Island. Boats lie at anchor northwest of Money Island. *Better Boating Association.*

marked by red lines on the chart, suggesting that the anchorage areas around the islands were safely clear. With the laying of new, underwater power lines, however, this is no longer true. Anchorage sites should be selected with discretion and anchors handled with caution to avoid fouling. The Thimbles have a 6½-foot rise and fall of tide.

Here are some other words of caution. Although this anchorage is preferable to Sachem Head, being larger and better protected, it is a difficult place to enter at night or in fog. In the daytime, a shoal boat under power can approach through the narrow passage from the east, but it is not recommended without power. We have been told that some dredging is planned for spring 1995. The anchorage is apt to be rough in a storm or strong sou'wester, and a roll frequently comes in from the Sound while the tide runs strong through the cuts between Money and High Islands. Also, be aware of small-boat traffic darting day and night in the maze of waterways threading throughout the islands. We have found that the most scenic spots to anchor, offering good holding ground, are either northwest of Money Island just to the south of the Cribs or along the shore southeast of High Island.

The village of Stony Creek lies about 1 mile north of the anchorage. With caution, the draft of 4 feet can be carried at low tide to the public dock, which is on the point east of Burr Island. Gas and supplies can be had here. Near this dock, the Thimble Island Cafe (previously America's Cup Restaurant) offered an appealing and extensive lunch and dinner menu for its patrons who could arrive informally dressed, but on our last visit it was not in operation.

Stony Creek has more characters per square acre than you might find anywhere except down east. It is an eccentric, simple place with a special flavor all its own. Captain Dwight Carter, former skipper of the ferryboat *Volsunga III*, is not only a local factotum whose family has lived in the Thimbles several generations but a salty personification of the village's individuality.

> I've been a banker, carpenter, clothing salesman, actor. We carry just about everything you can imagine on my boat—all kinds of freight, people, animals. The only thing we've never delivered on the *Volsunga* is a baby, although once a young lady in great distress just managed to get ashore in time. I don't mind having children aboard, but I'd rather not have a baby bouncing on my deck.

Captain Bob Milne has bought Carter's *Volsunga*, which runs frequently between the islands in summer and will transport one to the public landing at Stony Creek. Thus it is possible for visiting crews without powered dinghies to obtain supplies or a shore meal in the village while their boats lie at anchor among the islands. This ferry leaves the landing at a quarter before the hour from 6:45 A.M. to 7:45 P.M. and will pick up passengers from yachts for the return trip if signaled or called from the phones at the public dock harborside—(203) 488-9978. *Volsunga* monitors VHF-16 and 68 and its launch, *Charley More*, which carries residents to the islands, can be reached over VHF-68.

The enchanting Thimble Islands anchorage is a good stopping place for the first night on the way east from the various yachting centers at the western end of Long Island Sound. But on approaching the islands from the west, make sure to give Dick Rocks and Goshen Rock, just west of High Island and marked by nun 6, a very wide berth. Otherwise, in good weather and during the daytime, it is an easy anchorage to enter and very little off the direct course eastward. If you sail around among the islands, keep track of where you are on the chart so you don't get into foul water by mistake. The islands look a lot alike and it is easy to get confused. We left a little bottom paint on a rock on a recent trip.

Wayne Allen Hall, in an article in *The New York Times*, presents us here with an interesting story about the Thimbles:

Named by the Stony Creek Indians for the lowly thimble berry, second cousin to the gooseberry, the Thimble Islands consist of 365 islands, 32 of them habitable, the largest being Horse Island, 17 acres, and the smallest, Dogfish Island, three-quarters of an acre.

The islands are glacial deposits of pink granite, which was quarried at the turn of the century to make sturdy foundations for the Statue of Liberty and the Brooklyn Bridge. Even the Indians discovered that the rocks made excellent arrowheads.

Captain Kidd had his observation headquarters on High Island, providing him with a semilandlocked cove, where he hid from American sloops of war. Across the narrow channel on Pot Island, he found a cavern, reachable only from under the water.

It is rumored that Kidd left a substantial amount of gold in the cavern, but to this day no one has been able to find the underwater entrance.

Pot Island gained fame in the 1880s when a fat-men's club used the island's glacially formed potholes for a drinking rite. The club filled one pothole 30 feet deep with their punch and didn't leave the island until the hole had been drained.

Little Harbor, Leetes Island, Connecticut (12373). For yachts drawing under 4 feet here is a very pretty "little harbor," protected by jetties on both sides of the entrance of Harrison and Clark points. Although no depths are given on the chart, our soundings indicated depths of 7 feet or more leading up to the entrance, 6 feet at the entrance, 5 feet just inside, and 4 feet at mean low water in most of that section of the harbor that is south and west of the point that separates the two inner branches. Most of the bottom is fairly hard, and we would expect the holding ground to be only fair. If you are so lucky as to find enough free-swinging room, an anchorage here is satisfactory in ordinary summer weather, through likely to be uncomfortable in strong southerlies.

For those who don't need supplies or want to land, this is a pleasant variation from the usual, better-known anchorages and appeal especially to those who like poking into new places. The surrounding land and docks are privately owned, so there are no landing facilities for visiting yachts.

Sachem Head, Connecticut (12373). This is a small harbor open to the west and southwest, at the outer end of Sachem Head, with 6 to 10 feet of water at low tide. In entering, keep well off the southerly side of the point. The anchorage is difficult for strangers at night, but in the morning they will be won over by the charming scene of a rock-ribbed shoreline on which lovely residences are perched.

The Thimble Islands anchorage is less crowded, larger, and better protected. Sachem Head is highly recommended for shelter in easterlies if you are lucky enough to find a mooring for the night. In northwesters it can be very unpleasant, and in hard southwesters a correspondent warns, "It is a regular saucer bowl and is apt to roll the sticks out of you."

The Sachem Head Yacht Club maintains a well-sheltered float at the shore end of the lighted breakwater extending northwestward from the small island to the south of the entrance. A flashing red light is on the breakwater's outer end, and across the harbor below Joshua Point there's a privately maintained flashing white beacon. Guest moorings are no longer available to transient yachts here, although you might be assigned one should a member's boat be off on a cruise. Boats should not remain at the club docks for any reason other than to load or unload. Gas and ice are unavailable but a snack bar and showers can be found within the clubhouse.

The nearest boatyard is at Branford. The town of Guilford, where there are good restaurants and all manner of supplies can be purchased, is only 3 miles distant. A house built in 1639 is extant.

On Sachem Head a bloody battle of the Pequot War was fought in 1637. Tradition says that the head of an Indian, slain in combat, was placed by Uncas in the fork of a tree, where the skull remained for many years, giving the point its present name.*

Guilford, Connecticut (12373). Interestingly, Guilford is considered a harbor of refuge. Of course, this is provided you can enter safely in the first place, assuming you are blessed with a skillful skipper at the helm of a boat of fairly shoal draft. The entrance acts as a delta, taking the mud silt coming down from East River and Sluice Creek and building up currents of at least 3 knots in the channel. It is subject to continual shoaling. A major hurdle in entering can be found between nun 10 and can 9. Four powerboats, on separate occasions, have struck a rock just inside of nun 10. A recent report says that Guilford Harbor was scheduled by the Corps of Engineers for dredging in the fall of 1992. The 100-foot entrance channel and 60-foot Sluice Creek channel were to be restored to a 6-foot depth. The inshore part of that has been done, and the remainder should be completed by the time this edition is printed.

Up in shallow Sluice Creek, the town marina's slips to starboard are all rented to local boaters; there is one transient dock. A Coast Guard auxiliary station can be found next to the office of the dockmaster, who may be able to rent you a slip in 6 feet MLW or possibly an East River mooring if the regular occupant is out cruising.

Another alternative is to anchor up the East River between cans 7 and 9 in 5-foot depths with lines out fore and aft to cope with the current. We spent a night at anchor there in 1992 and found it very pleasant. On the way upriver you will note to port a launching ramp and float. Here you

*From *Connecticut*—American Guide Series (Houghton Mifflin Co., Boston).

might leave your dinghy while eating at either the Dock House or the Little Stone House nearby.

You can wear your sailing duds to the Dock House which specializes in seafood. The Little Stone House, where you can select your own lobster for dinner or to take out, requires more formal attire and is considered one of the finest dining spots on the Connecticut shore. Everything along the creek shuts down on Mondays. To obtain all kinds of supplies or to visit the charming, historic Guilford Town Green, a mile away, you can phone Guilford Taxi at 453-2264. Or you may prefer to explore the extensive marshland and its bird life by dinking nearly a mile up the East River or the Neck River—both ecologically intriguing. Jacobs Public Beach, which stretches to port at the harbor's entrance, is reported to have good clean water and always looks extremely inviting to us.

Previous editions of this guide have recommended against going up the West River to the Guilford Yacht Club, but the channel has recently been dredged to 4 feet MLW and the slips to 6 feet MLW, and the whole establishment has been improved since then. Stay in the channel indicated with the privately maintained buoys and you should have no trouble. The club accepts all visitors and monitors VHF-71 and answers (203) 458-3048. Browns Boat Yard along this channel does repairs.

Clinton, Connecticut (12374). In 1984, the Army Corps of Engineers fortunately dredged this channel from its entrance to a width of 100 feet and a depth of 8 feet at low water for a distance of 1 mile. A 1991 survey found 4.7 feet MLW in the left outside quarter and less elsewhere up to nun 8, 8 feet all across the channel for another 1,430 feet, and then 6 feet to the end only in the left quarter. We are advised by Mike Camarata, a Power Squadron port captain, to stay in the center or favor the green side of the channel and to remember that the channel is curved and not go buoy to buoy in straight lines.

In the vicinity of nun 16 is the friendly Port Clinton Marina with fairly low prices and pleasant facilities. They monitor VHF-9 and answer (203) 669-4563. A little farther upstream is the town dock which controls all the stakes serving as fore and aft moorings. These are the least expensive tie-ups in the harbor, and the facilities are also the least (porta-johns on shore). Just to the east is the modest-looking Harborside Marina, which specializes in all types of engine repair work and has an excellent store.

For those who prefer a dockage demonstrating an efficient operation and promising much ado ashore, we can recommend the attractive Cedar Island Marina, seen spread out beyond Holiday Dock, with a 400-berth capacity. They have protected floating docks handling boats up to 120 feet, with complete services including refueling, hauling, and repairs, a pumpout facility, showers, swimming pool, ship's store, The Crew's Closet selling nautical attire, a grocery store, a family recreational area, and the popular Dead Eye Dick Restaurant. But for a meal change aboard, pick up a freshly cooked lobster or other seafood at J & J Lobster.

Since the Hammonasset River begins to shoal beyond these marinas, boats of deep draft are advised not to proceed farther upriver without local knowledge. However, Clinton Yacht Haven, accommodating many powerboats, is located on York Haven Inlet, going northeastward from the Hammonasset River, well out of the current. It has full services plus a swimming pool. In 1990, after dredging, there were $4^1/2$ feet to the docks at MLW, but caution is advised. There is no place to anchor at Clinton.

Among the old dwellings in Clinton is Stanton House, built in 1789 and now a Colonial museum. In the center of the green is a monument commemorating the early years of the Collegiate School, later Yale. The first Yale students attended classes at this school until the opening of the college of Saybrook.

Duck Island Roads, Clinton, Connecticut (12374). To some yachtsmen (not including the writers) this is the most appealing harbor on Long Island Sound, although designated by the *Coast Pilot* as a harbor of refuge. It is formed by two long breakwaters extending north and west from Duck Island. Another breakwater to the westward offers additional protection from the southwest.

One determined yachtsman, who is obviously on our side, presents his impression of this questionable retreat:

> Who has not chilled, at least once, to the aubade of a wifely voice saying, "Goodness, I didn't think we had anchored that close to the breakwater!" For me, this summarizes this place. Avoid it. Either your anchor drags or it fouls among the lobster pots and it's a damn tide hole. If caught here, look up the Patchogue River for a berth.

There is a strong run of tide off Kelsey Point Breakwater. When you are making Duck Island Roads from mid-Sound, with no direct bearings, the cottages on Hammonasset Beach and the elevated tank shown well to the east are helpful. An experienced cruising man writes as follows (consult Chart 12374 in reading these directions, although gong 8 may have been changed to nun 8 on current charts):

If approaching from the west at night with a slight to medium haze, and sailing fairly close in along the Connecticut shore, having left Falkner Island well astern (roughly 4 miles) and bearing about east a quarter north to gong 8 (roughly 2¹/₂ miles ahead), it is then well to know of certain confusion which has been experienced by others under similar circumstances because of the varying intensity of the lights on the three breakwaters.

As one approaches closer, with the white light appearing to be very close at hand, one should also begin to pick up the flashing (every four seconds) red light on the west end of the longer breakwater on Duck Island proper (one half of the intensity of the white light). It is then wise to note that the white Kelsey Point Breakwater light is probably dead ahead, mingled in the background of shore lights running all the way eastward from Hammock Point to the Patchogue River entrance. Don't fear that this 2¹/₂ sec. white light is past or lies well to port, but hold on, bearing off somewhat to starboard (south), and await your approach close aboard the Kelsey Point Breakwater until this white light comes into distinct view.

The danger lies in attempting to go farther inshore in the hope of running in closer to, and thus picking up, this white light, which in reality has little brilliance and is probably dead ahead clouded by the shore lights. To run in may present the danger of entering the foul waters surrounding Stone Island Reef.

Having held on, picked up the white light, and passed it close abeam on the port hand, one will find the entrance to Duck Island Roads simple. Swing the bow to port (north) and run close past the red light of the longer Duck Island Breakwater to starboard.

It might be appropriate here to remind the reader that changes in aids to navigation are constantly being made on the Sound as well as along our entire coast. To cite an example, Kelsey Point Breakwater Light, Branford Reef Light, and Seaflower Reef Light have all been given new daytime appearances. They have been changed to pipe towers and equipped with diamond-shaped daymarks divided into four diamond shapes which are colored so that the horizontal diamonds are white and the vertical diamonds are green with white reflective borders.

Good anchorage will be found in the V of the breakwater, with only fair holding ground. But don't get so near to the breakwater that you haven't plenty of room to swing and let out more scope on your anchor in case of a northwester or a northwest squall. The lights on the breakwater make Duck Island Roads extremely easy of access at night, with no particular dangers. However, lobster pots sprinkled throughout the area have become an annoyance to many a skipper. (On a visit in 1992, the number of lobster pots seemed smaller than was indicated in earlier accounts.)

A large fleet can be accommodated, and everything is lovely if it doesn't start blowing from the northwest. There is some privacy, and the very desolateness of the place has a charm.

On the northeast end of the shorter breakwater on Duck Island proper there is a brilliant flashing (every four seconds) white light. This has four times the intensity of one of the other breakwater lights, and can under most conditions be picked up long before the flashing (every two and one-half seconds) white light on the Sound end of Kelsey Point Breakwater. In midsummer this condition is aggravated by the mass of lights in the background, at Kelsey Point and along the beaches to the north. This white light is well out to sea and some 2 miles nearer a vessel approaching from the west than the aforementioned white light that flashes at four-second intervals.

There has been considerable shoaling in the last few years, and the chart at the time of writing showed depths of 5 or 6 feet, even 2-foot spots, in the angle between the breakwaters, where 15 to 19 feet were shown in 1948.

Patchogue River, Westbrook, Connecticut (12374). Here is another developed human-made channel and harbor, the most convenient alternative to Duck Island Roads. For those who prefer to anchor in the Roads for the night, it is a nearby place for gassing up or obtaining supplies. The entrance channel was dredged in 1985 to a width of 150 feet and a 10-foot depth at MLW, but this river has had a history of silting up especially at two specific locations. The first is at charted can 5 marking the entrance to the Menunketesuck River. If you should enter this tributary, favor can 5 closely and then hug the starboard shore proceeding upriver. The second localized trouble spot is in the Patchogue River channel just beyond nun 6. In early 1993 two local marinas had these dredged to eliminate the bottleneck; the Corps of Engineers plans to dredge the channel to a 9-foot depth when they get the money.

There is a privately maintained green buoy, which has a red top, marking the southern end of a sandbar coming out from the point of land separating the two rivers. To enter the Menunketesuck, go between this buoy and the one just to its south and favor the side of the river with the slips.

Brewers Pilot's Point Marina consists of three sections, North, South, and East, all served by the same dockmaster who can be reached on VHF-9 or (203) 399-7906. They have a courtesy van for short local trips, available through the dockmaster.

The full-service Pilot's Point Marina South, consisting of four separate bulkheaded basins, each dredged to 8 feet, is located to starboard as you enter. Report to the gas dock there to be assigned a slip. Their services include gas, diesel fuel, water, ice, electricity, showers, electronic repairs, travelifts, pool, pumpout, and a ship's store with charts available. The Gourmet Galley is open until 7 P.M. on weekends and 5 P.M. on weekdays. It also has volleyball and basketball courts and a clubhouse with Ping-Pong. We can promise you a secure berth for a week or perhaps more here, in case your cruise plans include some layover time.

To the west and up on the starboard shore of the Menunketesuck River can be found Pilot's Point Marina North, with full facilities plus pool, tennis courts, volleyball court, playground, barbecue grills, and pumpout station, with restaurants nearby. Its only drawback is that although its river approach carries about 5 feet, there tends to be bad shoaling at its entrance off the Patchogue River channel, as mentioned earlier. Proceed cautiously through this very narrow entrance, favoring the docks in making your approach. Finding good restaurants, easily accessible, may come as a welcome surprise. Frankie's Restaurant sets a good table and is within easy walking distance. The Hungry Lion is a bit more plush and expensive. And upstairs in the marina's building, you'll find the home of the convivial Menunketesuck Yacht Club, founded in 1968.

Up the Patchogue River beyond Pilot's Point Marina South, is Harry's Marine Repair—(203) 399-6165—offering pumpout service. Facing the latter, you can spot Pilot's Point Marina East, whose Marina Village provides nautical supplies but no fuel. It has the usual people facilities but is not as complete as the other two parts of this complex. At the channel's end, below the bridge, are gas dock and slips belonging to Westbrook Harbor Marina, where there's an excellent lobster pound, the recommended Bill's Restaurant, and a market for supplies 1/2 mile away. But this area is congested and not nearly as attractive as downstream.

Connecticut River, Connecticut (12375, 12377)

Entrance, Saybrook (12375). Yachtsmen with a love of exploring rivers and creeks and poking their way into fascinating byways should not miss the Connecticut River. Some of its byways between Essex and Middletown have a beauty and charm reminiscent of the Upper Hudson or the coast of Maine. Long a mecca for motorboats, the Connecticut, because of the depths of some of its coves and creeks and the speed with which the drawbridges are opened, is also attractive for sailing craft. It is not recommended, however, for boats without power except for purposes of refuge near the entrance and with favoring tides. The Connecticut state boating law restricts speed limits to 6 mph within 100 feet of anchored boats, docks, or marinas.

We might advise those who are planning a cruise up the Quinnehtqut, the Indian term for "long tidal water," that the Connecticut River Watershed Council publishes *A Complete Boating Guide to the Connecticut River.* It covers the entire 410-mile river from its source on the Canadian border to Long Island Sound. It provides guidance for boat owners and canoeists, along with information on the cultural and natural history of the region. Maps and descriptions of the river in 15- to 20-mile sections are provided. Copies of this guide are available in local bookstores and equipment supply stores or by writing to the Connecticut Watershed Council, Inc., 1 Ferry Street, Easthampton, MA 01027.

Charles A. Goodwin, in his very interesting *Connecticut River Pilot* (1944), explains that, although Adrian Block discovered the river, it was King Charles and his bishops who forced the settlement at Saybrook. Lord Say and Lord Brook got together with Pym and decided to resist the King and to prepare in the wilderness a place of refuge for the conspirators, in case their plans miscarried.

In 1797, Timothy Dwight, president of Yale College, looked upon the land bordering the Connecticut River and wrote this description: "In its extent, it is magnificent. In its form, it is beautiful. Its banks possess uncommon elegance, almost universally handsome, with a margin entirely neat and commonly ornamented with a fine fringe of shrubs and trees." At the same time, he reported the river's water to be "remarkably pure and light . . . everywhere pure, potable, perfectly salubrious."

Rising in the extreme northern part of New Hampshire, 375 miles from the entrance, the Connecticut River is one of the most important rivers in New England. Hartford, 45 miles upriver, is the head of navigation for all but very shoal-draft boats, except in times of high water, though the most beautiful part of the river is below Middletown. At Deep Water, 10$\frac{1}{2}$ miles from the Sound, and above, the water is fresh. High water occurs at Hartford 4$\frac{3}{4}$ hours after it does at the entrance at Saybrook, and low water 6$\frac{1}{4}$ hours later. Some of the principal towns or entrances to the best anchorages are at the following distances from the Saybrook Breakwater Light:

Nautical Miles

Saybrook Point	1.4
Essex	6.0
Hamburg Cove entrance	7.5
Selden Creek entrance	9.0
Salmon River entrance	15.0
Middletown	28.0
Wethersfield	42.0
Hartford	45.2

With 4 or 5 knots of power, there is no difficulty in entering for shelter or to explore. Any smart sailing boat can negotiate the river without power with favorable winds. Tidal current is a factor as far as Middletown, and the combination of river current and ebb tide can be strong, occasionally 3$\frac{1}{2}$ knots. The mean rise and fall of tides in the Connecticut varies from 3$\frac{1}{2}$ feet at Saybrook to 1$\frac{3}{4}$ feet at Hartford. The current turns at Portland about 3$\frac{3}{4}$ hours after the Race.

The entrance is clearly marked by Saybrook Light and a pair of stone jetties. The entire river is well marked by buoys, but reference to charts is essential, as the buoys are not always self-explanatory.

In entering between the jetties, watch for the sweep of the current across the entrance and note the shoals inside the jetties, particularly the one to starboard.

When Adrian Block first surveyed the "delightful banks" of the Connecticut River in 1614, he circumvented this timeless Saybrook Outer Bar, noting that the river here was "very shallow." Later on, lighthouses helped early captains negotiate the river's mouth when the outer Saybrook Light was erected in 1866 and the inner Lynde Point Lighthouse was built in 1839, replacing the original dating from 1803. But it wasn't until 1870 that the first federal dredging of the entrance was conducted by the U.S. Army Corps of Engineers. A channel of 8-foot depth and a width of 100 feet was then able to accommodate the growing number of steamboats running up to Essex, Goodspeed Landing, Middletown, and Hartford.

There has been a striking increase in the number of ports, marinas, and facilities along the Connecticut River in recent years. It is now possible to find overnight dockage or anchorage to suit almost any taste or need, from the clublike atmosphere of Hull Harbor One to the privacy of Selden Creek or Salmon Cove, from the active sailing community at Essex to the motorboat haven in landlocked Wethersfield Cove. In discussing the many ports and tie-ups along the river, we shall "cruise" northward from Long Island Sound. We should remind those proceeding upriver to give one prolonged blast followed by one short blast of the horn on approaching the railroad bridge if it is closed. The bridgemaster monitors VHF-13 and 16.

Although we have made every effort to spot the principal docks and marinas offering tie-ups or other facilities along the way, we won't guarantee that we have mentioned them all. In fact, we are sure that by the time you get there after reading this book, there will be some unmentioned new ones. But we think we have suggested enough possibilities to take care of any requirements. Most of the larger marinas monitor VHF-9 for reservations and all are open seven days a week.

A word of caution: Although the river is broad and inviting, there are many shoal areas. As always, it pays to have a chart close at hand and to keep track of where you are.

One final note: Due to the wake from heavy traffic along the lower Connecticut River, it is hazardous for masted vessels to lie alongside some of the higher wharves. Such a tie-up can roll your boat's spars right up against the pilings with unfortunate results.

1. Harbor One, Saybrook Point (west shore—12375). Located right below conspicuous Saybrook Point Marina, this marina is most convenient for those yachtsmen cruising Long Island Sound who wish to find an accessible haven closest to the Connecticut River entrance. There is 10 feet of water at the 84 slips, where gas, diesel fuel, water, electricity, ice, showers, a laundromat, crank-case service (in fifteen minutes), an emergency pump, and a reputable mechanic are all available. Two restaurants are within walking distance and a hotel is close by.

The grounds are spacious and manicured with the swimming pool a particular attraction. Paul Barton, the experienced owner, encouraged us to welcome all cruising craft, large or small, power or sail. Shelter from all winds, except perhaps strong easterlies coming across the river, is provided by a breakwater on the south side and outlying bulkheads. We have often enjoyed our visits here.

2. Saybrook Point Inn Marina, Saybrook Point (west shore— 12375). This operation, (203) 388-3862, has become larger and more elegant now, boasting 120 slips with a reported 18 feet MLW, an enlarged ship's store, and a 65-suite inn and conference center. It is located on the west bank opposite nun 10. Its restaurant is excellent.

Most deep-draft auxiliaries prefer to tie up at the outer dock. This is primarily a powerboat haven, and most yachts we have seen there belong to that class. However, it is convenient to any cruising boat whose crew wishes to gas up or stop for a meal at the Dock and Dine at Saybrook Point nearby.

The usual services include diesel fuel, gas, showers, a laundromat, ice, and supplies, plus cable TV. Ashore there is a swimming pool, tennis courts, and a marina pub. The marina's rules encourage your consideration for others staying here.

Within easy walking distance to the north is the Dock and Dine restaurant with good food and drink and space for six to ten boats to tie up.

North Cove and its channel, lying just northward, were first dredged in 1965 to provide a harbor of refuge for cruising yachtsmen. But beware: the 100-foot channel tends to silt up. The greatest amount of shoaling can occur between can 15 at the entrance and can 1, 400 yards to the west and on the southern edge of the channel. However, a Corps of Engineers dredging project should alleviate this problem for some years. Steer dead center as you run westward from can 15 through the middle of the narrow mouth of the cove between nun 2 and can 3. Be sure to compensate for the river's strong current abeam so as to avoid being swept up on the channel's shallow edges. The current dredging probably provides at least 8 feet MLW in the channel and eastern third of the cove and at least 6 feet in the remainder. Nevertheless, the stakes marking the rectangular dredged area must be observed carefully, because the remainder of this popular basin, especially along the northern and southwestern edges, is only a foot or so deep at low water. There is no space here for anchoring. We were warned by local residents to protect ourselves against the mosquitoes, which breed rather abundantly in the neighboring marshes.

The North Cove Yacht Club, founded in 1968, owns an attractive clubhouse, built in 1975, standing on the western shore of the cove. This is a friendly, active place offering reciprocal privileges to members of other recognized yacht clubs. The clubhouse is open all week. Although there is just one guest mooring, the club steward may assign you one vacated by a boat that is off cruising. He monitors VHF-68 and can provide you with ice, water, showers, and a booklet about Old Saybrook activities. At the dedication of the clubhouse, the fleet chaplain expressed this thoughtful wish: "May our burgee become a standard and hallmark for kindness and charity, for friendship and hospitality, for trust and thoughtfulness, and above all for good seamanship."

The town is a 1/4-mile walk up the road from the club. There you'll find sources for supplies and the Village Restaurant, serving good food at reasonable prices. North Cove is a fine protected spot where one can "get away from it all."

3. Ragged Rock Marine, Old Saybrook (west shore—12375). This marina lies in a dredged basin at the western end of a narrow charted creek whose entrance is just beyond the bascule railroad bridge near the location of the old ferry slip. Proceed up the middle of the creek, which is about 8 feet at MLW except right at the entrance where it is about 5 feet. There are 8 or 9 feet at the slips. The deep-water basin, nestled midst marshland, offers excellent security and practically no current. The marina's staff, including a mechanic, is on duty 7 days a week. Here you'll find marine supplies, slips with electricity, water, ice, and showers. We were assured by the management that the depths both in the creek and the mooring basin will be maintained. This is an interesting and very protected haven, and they monitor VHF-9.

4. Saybrook Marine Service, Old Saybrook (west shore—12375).
Just above Chimney Point and the railroad bridge, this long-established marina is owned by Marine Fashion, Inc., manufacturers of marine hardware. Most of the boats stored here for the winter are sailing craft, and they come in all sizes. There is 7^1/$_2$ feet at the dock at mean low water; water, ice, electric connections, and showers are available, and with an increased number of slips reportedly added, sufficient space for an overnight stay. Saybrook Marine owns a 30-ton travelift and a 2-ton derrick which can handle almost any hauling job and which have helped this place gain a good reputation for fast repair work.

5. River Landing Marina, Old Saybrook (west shore—12375).
Just beyond Saybrook and before reaching the fixed highway bridge, you will come upon one of the newer full-service marinas on the river. One glance at this manicured facility, with its concrete piers and modern-styled wooden buildings of many angular shapes, levels, and sizes, and you may understand why River Landing Marina likes to claim "the best dock facilities of the Connecticut River." Formerly the Black Swan Marina, River Landing has come under new management. Its inner basin, dredged to 12 feet at low water, offers complete protection. Report to the Texaco gas dock to be assigned one of the transient slips. River Landing's offerings run the gamut from business offices to specialty shops to showers, from a laundromat to a marine store. Transients have swimming pool privileges. VHF-9 is monitored for reservations, and free dockage is provided for patrons dining at the marina's Boater's Bar restaurant.

6. Oak Leaf Marina, Old Saybrook (west shore—12375). This is just beyond the fixed bridge. Here we have seen boats of all types, since, for total services, this is one of the best stopping places before one reaches Essex. At their dock, with variable depths, gas and diesel fuel are sold and there are slips with electrical outlets. Other services include a discount ship's store, showers, ice, and laundromat—all available seven days a week. Hauling and repair work are also undertaken, and a fine launching ramp is close by. Call channel 9 to see if they can fit you in.

7. Ferry Point Marina, Old Saybrook (west shore—12375). Unless you happen to be a native of the Connecticut or an avid reader of such cruising guides as this one, you might pass right by this marina, teeming with powerboats, tucked away in a secluded basin on the southwestern shore of Ferry Point. The narrow dredged channel, with 5 feet at MLW, runs south from a point just beyond some old stone piers located along the point's northern shore. On entering this channel, you will pass between some piles and note a sunken barge that marks its starboard edge. Gas, diesel fuel, water, showers, ice, a 25-ton travelift, and a ship's store are here, plus electricity at the slips, where 5 feet of water is reported at MLW. Food supplies are located about 3 miles away in Old Saybrook. Try the Saybrook Fish House just a stone's throw away should you be short of rations.

The basin is crowded deck-to-deck with sportfishermen, so don't be surprised by their crews' early risings or their boisterousness after a day's catch.

8. Old Lyme (east shore—12375). On approaching the first railroad bridge west of Old Lyme and finding it possibly closed, signal the bridgetender over VHF-13 for opening. Once through this bridge you will come upon the river's newest marina, The Old Lyme Dock Company, where there is no shortage of the patriotic spirit—for here flies quite the largest American flag we have ever seen hoisted at any marina or yacht club.

This tidy marina (monitors VHF-9) has much going for it. There is ample depth surrounding its finger piers where yachts up to 165 feet can tie up for gas, diesel fuel, ice, and electricity. For their crews there are spotless showers, marine supplies, and all types of transportation to laundromat, shopping centers and restaurants. We found it a bit more secluded and peaceful on this side of the river, and they claim the lowest fuel prices on the Connecticut.

Sheltered behind Calves Island and in attractive surroundings is one of the best ports on the river. Follow the channel behind Calves Island to a first-rate dock on the east shore of the channel, about halfway up to the point where the channel turns to the northwest. Nun RG is left well to port. The Old Lyme Marina, monitoring VHF-9, has 16 feet of water off the docks. Ice, water, electricity, showers, all types of professional repair work, and even taxi service are among the facilities here. The marine store is attractively furnished, and the whole place is kept "Bristol fashion," reflecting the proprietor's concern to offer the best in service. A shopping center with a good restaurant, a drug store, an A&P store, a bank, etc., are only five minutes away. Although they have 25 slips here, transient yachts often pick up one of the marina's 65 moorings set out in various depths and scattered throughout the channel to the north. No launch service is provided, and there is no space for anchoring, and even if there were, the current is quite strong.

When Old Lyme decided it needed a police boat for patrol and rescue, but the budget said "no," a group of concerned neighbors in the community, headed up by W. E. S. Griswold, Jr., and Len Abrahamsson, gave enthusiastic financial support to the project. Now when you happen to spot the powerboat *Friendship* patrolling the river, you'll be witness to a shining example of the spirit of Old Lyme.

For years we have read and heard about the glories of Lord Cove as a gunk hole, beautifully sheltered beneath the steeps of Lord Hill to the north. Morten Lund records in his book, *Eastward on Five Sounds,* that he reached Lord Creek way across the unmarked cove without mishap using power and depth sounder in a catamaran drawing $2^1/2$ feet. But we have been advised by Old Lyme natives that in a boat of any greater draft, it is unwise to venture beyond the cove's entrance between Goose Island and Quarry Hill. Use bow and stern anchors if you wish to lie to here.

Departing the marina by the same route you entered, you will pass into Calves Island Bar Channel where recent groundings have been sighted. These have occurred west of the island at nun 20 and flasher 22. So be sure to give these markers a wide berth and leave no wake along the entire passage between the fixed highway bridge and this flasher northwest of the island.

9. Essex (west shore—12375). Six miles above the entrance to the Connecticut River, this ancient town clambers up several hills above the valley and looks down on its three coves and one of the most active yachting scenes to be found on Long Island Sound. Few harbors are as popular as Essex among real cruising men, and few have as much to offer. Up to 1854, the town was called Potapaug.

Shallow-draft boats approaching Essex from the south may find secluded shelter in Middle Cove but no services. The latest chart shows two 3-foot spots along its narrow privately staked channel, and there is hardly any greater depth in the cove itself. This channel runs westward along the northern shore of Thatchbed Island.

Commodore Robert J. Shickel described the Essex Yacht Club in a letter:

Just to the starboard of the entrance to Middle Cove, along the western shore of the Connecticut River is Essex Yacht Club. The Club was originally established in 1933 by a hearty group and may be the only yacht club to have been established through the 'inspiration of frostbite dinghy sailing.' The Cruising Club of America has a station here with many of the moored yachts belonging to members of that famous organization. Essex Yacht Club is in commission year-round and overlooks the river and islands from its beautiful clubhouse. Yachts moored at the Club enjoy quiet evenings and beautiful mornings in this quaint New England harbor. The town of Essex, with its shops and restaurants, is a short stroll up Novelty Lane. EYC Club Manager Deb Zsigalov told us about the Club's services to cruising yachtsmen that include moorings, showers, a galley, bar, and a launch service. EYC monitors VHF-9 and can be reached at (203) 767-8121, phone and FAX. Credit cards are accepted.

The Essex Corinthian Yacht Club is located just to the north.

Close to the north of both clubs you can spot Brewers Chandlery East fuel dock with 8 feet at MLW. This marina and Essex Island Marina, located up in North Cove, are the only sources for fuel at Essex. Brewers offers moorings, launch service, showers, ice, marine supplies, and charts. Adjacent to it is the fenced-in Dauntless Yacht Club, said to be better known for its social activities than for its yachting. The Pettipaug Yacht Club is stationed upriver on the western shore facing Brockway Island. It is active in small-boat racing.

The cupola identified on the chart to the north marks the location of historic Steamboat Dock, recently restored by the Connecticut River Foundation. Few of us are aware of the role this property played in the history of the Connecticut River. During the eighteenth century more than 500 large commercial ships were built in this general location, and the present dock, built in the mid-nineteenth century, was a scheduled port of call for New York–to–Hartford passenger steamers. Now, through private donations and foundation membership, Steamboat Dock has become an impressive cultural center, including a museum, a library, a meeting place, and Wolcott Park, named in memory of Frank Wolcott, an avid yachtsman and conservationist. Alongside this property lies the Town Dock, permitting boats up to 40 feet to tie up for an hour or two, but note that there is only 3 feet here at low water. This is the only unrestricted land access available at Essex.

Northward, across the narrow channel leading to North Cove, is the attractive Colonial-style complex of the Essex Island Marina, where according to its slogan and our experience, "It's fun in the sun and cool in the pool." For transient boats of any size, this spot is "tops" in our book. Its management appears to have anticipated practically every visitor's need and whim—for his boat and for his crew. The brochure they'll hand you proves it. This is such a popular spot that placing reservations is suggested in advance by phoning (203) 767-1267. They also monitor VHF-9.

This marina is actually set on the southern tip of the island, so a ferry constantly runs guests across the 150-foot channel to the mainland. The ferry runs from April 15 to December 15, from 7:30 A.M. to 11:30 P.M. or to 1 A.M. on weekends. When it is not running, a floating bridge is put in place and blocks the channel. Numerous protective basins and floating docks frame the large administration building, swimming pool, repair shops, and The Galley Locker. The dockage fee includes use of all facilities and the various recreational activities for the family. They offer towing service and can "quick-haul" a boat as fast as any yard we've seen.

The Essex Boat Works, headed up by Stuart Ingersoll and Jeff Ridgeway, performs the repair work coming out of the Essex Island Marina. It is identified by a large red boat shed to port, just inside the entrance channel to North Cove. With a large crew on duty that will "do its best to accommodate you," this yard provides 7-day-a-week service and is especially equipped to handle emergency repairs. Although there are no slips here, a number of overnight moorings are rentable. Its workboat, named *Flora*, an oyster boat built in 1906, might look a bit old-fashioned, but the services here, including diesel engine repairs, are strictly up to date. Boat Works has an amazing facility for locating all types of hull fittings and engine parts quickly; they will even fly to get them.

Rather strong currents running through the North Cove channel often may give the helmsman a case of the jitters. One skipper, caught in a crosscurrent here, to the amusement of several bystanders, was heard to bellow, "I know all about the current, but I don't know what in hell to do about it!" Assuming, however, you handle this current like a Josh Slocum, you'll come up to the docks of the Dauntless Shipyard Marina, which runs yacht brokerages and accommodates mostly their own regular customers. What is impressive about Dauntless is its complex of facilities, all easy to reach. These include Connecticut Marine Instruments for electronics, Clark Sails for sail repair and manufacture, the publishers of *Soundings* magazine, the Dauntless Boathouse selling all kinds of marine gear and supplies, and a small restaurant named She Sells Sandwiches.

It is reported that there are normally eight hours of ebb current at Essex and four hours of flood. The special anchorage located near red flasher 26 and nun 28 is now all full of moorings with no room to anchor. There may be space by Nott Island out of the channel. Two anchors are advised, one upstream, the other downstream. We cannot close our report on Essex without mentioning the competence of Essex Machine Works in handling accident work, such as straightening prop shafts and reconditioning propellers.

The town of Essex is well worth a visit. "On Main Street, the interesting Griswold Inn, built in 1776, well preserves the flavor of an earlier day. Visitors are provided with the 'Rules of the Tavern,' which stipulate that bed and supper may be obtained for six pence, that no more than five may sleep in one bed, that boots may not be worn in bed, and organ-grinders must sleep in the washhouse, while razor-grinders and tinkers are not taken in at all."* We can recommend the drinks, food, and pictures at this fascinating inn, which is only a short walk from the waterfront.

If you are looking for a less expensive meal than that served at Griswold Inn, we might suggest the Black Seal, over on Main Street.

A rewarding experience is a walk up along shady Main Street lined with early-nineteenth-century houses, galleries and boutiques, spired churches, and specialty shops of all kinds. Larders can be stocked in town, about three blocks from the waterfront. The Connecticut River Museum is located at the foot of Main Street.

At Essex, in 1775, Uriah Hayden constructed the *Oliver Cromwell*, the first warship of the Continental Navy. A year later he built The Old Ship Tavern, a structure still in use as the headquarters of the Dauntless Yacht Club. On April 8, 1814, British marines landed near where the Steamboat Dock now stands and burned twenty-eight local ships.

A native of the river once described a visit to Essex as "coming home to the American self." More recently, marine architect Britton Chance put

---

*From *Where to Retire and How,* by Fessenden S. Blanchard (Dodd, Mead & Co., New York).

it another way in picturing this colorful old town. "It's become the center of gravity for yachting in the Northeast." After your visit, perhaps you will agree.

10. Hamburg Cove (east shore—12375). Half a mile above Essex, opposite Brockway's Island, is the entrance to Hamburg Cove, which is practically a fjord, 1^1/$_2$ miles long. The entrance is well marked with government buoys, and there is a depth of at least 6 feet, but the channel is narrow and buoys should be hugged, especially the nun at the mouth. It is also reported that these entrance buoys tend to shift from time to time, so enter the cove cautiously. We were told that the southern side of the entrance silts up more than the other so you should favor the northern side. All other markers are privately maintained by the Cove Landing Marina. Here you'll find a sheltered, idyllic anchorage but with poor holding ground and depths averaging 12 feet except at the edges. Only sky, glassy water dotted with moorings trees, and some houses are to be seen. Few who enter for the first time realize that a tiny channel, winding to the northeast, leads to a small, picturesque basin off the village of Hamburg. This channel is marked by beacons put out during the season by the Cove Landing Marina, located on the eastern shore of the basin, with 6 to 8 feet at its docks.

The Cove Landing Marina—(203) 434-5240—is the major marine facility in the cove, with 15 moorings, that have orange buoys marked CLM scattered around. They do not monitor VHF, so pick up a mooring and they will come out to see you. Ice, showers, heads, and a ship's store are available on the premises, and they have facilities for haulout, pumpout, and repairs.

The Hamburg Yacht Club is located just to the south, and Reynolds' Garage & Marine's docks can be found just to the north. Gary Reynolds told us that, although there is 2 to 3 feet of tide, he would not want to navigate a boat that draws more than 4 feet up to Hamburg. Gary's father also mentioned that the cove's water is cleaner now than it was fifty years ago when he was here as a young lad. Supplies are available at the Reynolds' store. Several good inns are at Old Lyme, about 5 miles away. The nearest railroad station is at Saybrook, about 8 miles away. If you have a chance, visit the state park 8 miles from the wharf. It is known as the Devil's Hop Yard.

The Outer Cove is the place to spend the night, in one of the most attractive and popular anchorages anywhere. Many of the ball-shaped moorings here are privately owned, but the orange ones marked CLM can be rented from the Cove Landing Marina. We were told that, although there is some space available for anchoring, the bottom was not good and it was not advisable. Shut in by wooded hills, the cove can be hot and noisy on weekends but, except in very warm weather, it is a delightful and beautiful spot.

11. Selden (or Shirley) Creek (east shore—12375, 12377). The entrance to Selden Creek is not impressive and does not reveal the attractiveness you discover farther up. You will find the opening on the east shore after passing the stone-walled Brockway's Landing. The entrance is in a flat, marshy area, flanked by the stumps of uprooted trees, and just upriver from a high rock cliff with two houses at its foot. Soundings by one of the authors in 1985 revealed at least 10 feet at low water in the center of the entrance, on a line running down the middle of the creek. A shoal makes out from the northern point and a smaller shoal from the south bank. There is plenty of deep water between these shoals, but it is advisable to proceed up the creek on a rising tide.

After you get inside, keep in the middle. The creek is only 50 feet wide in spots and continues for about 2 miles, with from 4 to 13 feet of water up to Selden Cove's entrance. The best anchorage for deep-draft vessels is under the first or second rock cliff, almost a mile up the creek along the starboard shore. Note a small iron ring set in the face of the second rock to be used for a possible tie-up. Carry a bow line to the shore and set out a stern anchor to prevent swinging across the channel here. Farther up, just below the cove, you will come to two forks in the channel. Stay out of the left or western fork since it leads to a dead end and has little water in it. The right fork, giving passage to the cove, carries about 3 feet at best at high water, but watch out for some boulders and tree stumps as you enter. If you are crafty enough to get into the cove at high water with a shallow-draft boat, don't anchor there for long or you'll get hung up. On one visit on an ebbing tide, many years ago, we were surprised to see a 30-foot auxiliary sloop on her beam's end in the middle of the cove. We hailed its crew, offering assistance, to which the skipper replied nonchalantly, "We're just sitting here waiting for that old tide to shift."

The current in the creek is not strong, but anchorage fore and aft is usually necessary. The upper passage directly from the cove to the river continues to shoal up and should be approached with caution on a rising tide.

Power Squadron Port Captain David Roberts writes: "As you are going north in Selden Creek, on your port side is Selden Island. The side facing the Connecticut River is the higher and dryer side. There are numerous campsites there, and a permit to use them is needed which can be obtained at Gillette Castle. They assign the site and you anchor your boat in front of the island. There are many trails and there are supposed to be some very cold and delicious fresh water springs."

During the Revolution, river shipping used to hide in Selden Creek to escape British raiding parties.

Farther upriver, along the west shore, facing Eustasia Island, you can spot the deep-water floating docks of the Deep River Marina, which probably attracts more sailing craft than any other facility north of Essex. There are reasons. Although diesel fuel and provisions are not available, Deep River does have gas, ice, water, electricity, moorings, outdoor grills, a marine store, and repair service; and housed within its large brown office building are some of the most splendid restrooms and showers to be seen at any marina. There's also something special here not easily found elsewhere—spacious manicured grounds, offering complete protection and solitude. Phone congenial and conservation-minded Doug or Karen Van Dyke at (203) 526-5560 for reservations.

About a mile north of Selden Cove is the Rhenish castle built by the actor William Gillette, who won fame for his portrayal of Sherlock Holmes. When he died in 1937, his will specified that he hoped the executors would see that the property did not get into "the possession of some blithering saphead who has no conception of where he is or with what surrounded." He need not have had any fear, for his estate is now the beautiful Gillette Castle State Park, commanding a superb view of the Connecticut River. If you want some exercise while moored in the creek, row across the cove and walk to the park, which is open from 11 A.M. to 5 P.M. every day from late May to October.

One can gain closer access to the castle by dinghy, having anchored off a small landing just above the Hadlyme ferry dock on the east shore, as shown on the chart. From here, it's a steep climb straight up the hill to meet the road leading to the castle grounds, about 400 yards to the north.

12. Connecticut River Marina, Chester (west shore—12377).

Across river from Selden Creek's northern exit lies the mouth of Chester Creek. Just south of the mouth is an open but sheltered rectangular basin in which is located the Connecticut River Marina—(203) 526-9076—

with about 5 feet of water at its approximately fifty slips. It shows clearly on the chart. This is a do-it-yourself marina with minimal facilities and in need of refurbishing, which is being planned. There is a travelift but no repair service. Most of the slips are rented by the season, but there are plans to make the marina more available to transients.

Just to the north of the basin a privately maintained buoy marks the entrance to sheltered Chester Creek. Crowded with local craft, this tiny creek is receptive to transient yachts.

Power Squadron Port Captain David Roberts writes:

There are two marinas on the west side of Chester Creek and two yacht clubs on the east side. They all are maintained very nicely.

Approaching from the green can 37, stay to the middle-right side of the creek, as there is a rock off the point on the port side about 10 feet off shore. On your starboard is a small rock jetty with a blinking red light. The middle of the creek has about 4 to 5 feet of water at low tide.

The creek is not very wide, but two boats can pass port to port. There are some good-size boats 36 feet to low 40 feet in the marinas or yacht clubs.

The first marina when you are coming up the creek on the westside is Chester Marina operated by Gil Bartlett. The facilities include a pool, ship's store, marine repair, restrooms with showers, ice, barbecue area, boat launch, and a 35-ton open-end travel lift, and water and electricity on docks. Transients are welcome; call on channel 9 or 16 or phone at 526-2227.

The next marina on the west side is Hays Haven operated by Jim Hays. Their facilities consist of gas, ice, ship's store, marine repair, restrooms with showers, boat launch, and a smaller open-end travel lift, and also water and electricity on docks.

The two yacht clubs, Pattaconk and Springfield, do not have enough slips to accommodate transients. Although Pattaconk does have moorage out in front of the beach and clubhouse, it is just north of the entrance to the creek. It is marked on the chart. They offer this and the facilities to other yacht club members.

If you have a dinghy, a nice pleasurable cruise up the creek can be taken. Once you get under the Essex Valley Railroad Bridge and Route 154, you enter a wildlife sanctuary. It goes up for about 3/4 mile.

There is another sanctuary reachable by dinghy; it is on the east side of the river. There is a day beacon across the river from Pattaconk, just south of Gillette Castle and the ferry landing. It is shoaled on the downriver side so stay close to the rock formation to port supporting the Day Beacon. It is advisable to head in at mid to high tide. There are many streams to venture up which are very pretty and peaceful. Watch out for depth and trees.

A short walk from this area, about ½ mile brings you into the town of Chester. It has quaint shops and several restaurants. You can also walk into Deep River, a little farther. There you have a full grocery store, hardware, liquor, and other stores.

A short distance north of Fort Hill as marked on the chart, a basin with floating docks appears, shaped like the end of a golf club. In reality, this basin, which is the home of Chrisholm Marina—(203) 526-5147, VHF-9—is much larger than the chart has depicted. Depths here have been recorded at 6 feet MLW. Named after its late founder, Chrisholm is a rather pleasant and very protected stopping place. Its services, for both power- and sailboats, include repair work, electrical outlets, marine supplies, ice, and fuel. Showers and a free pumpout facility are added conveniences.

13. Middletown Yacht Club (west shore—12377).

On the west bank opposite the lower end of Lord Island, the Middletown Yacht Club has its well-groomed headquarters. A dredged basin with bulkheads on three sides and rows of slips provides an efficient-looking modern layout. The clubhouse, which is located on high ground, overlooks the river and a large swimming pool, the center of activity. The inner dock records 4 feet while the outer dock shows 8 feet, all at MLW. Water, ice, electricity, and showers are provided but no gas, repairs, or moorings. Use of the pool is included in the dockage fee. Members of recognized yacht clubs would do well to stop at this fine, friendly club.

Slightly to the north and on the east bank is the entrance to Chapman Pond, which is owned by the Nature Conservancy. It is very shallow but can be entered by dinghy or canoe.

14. Goodspeed's Landing, East Haddam (east shore—12377).

A stopover here promises a rewarding experience for anyone who is interested in American theatrical history or who enjoys fine continental cuisine.

If you are a member of the Goodspeed Opera House, call Edward Blaschik at (203) 873-8664 to reserve space at their dock. Otherwise there is no longer any space here to tie up. A short walk will take you to the center of the charming old town, where all types of supplies may be purchased. Just north of the bridge on the west shore lies a marked channel leading to Andrews Marina catering to small powerboats. Don't attempt entering unless your boat draws under four feet. The bridge has a 24-foot clearance at low water.

In 1877, William Goodspeed, a shipbuilder, created the Goodspeed Opera House with its ornate, Victorian facade. It became a rousing success, but by the late 1950s it was forsaken and ready for demolition. This triggered widespread interest in Goodspeed's value to history, and the Goodspeed Opera House Foundation was formed to refurbish it. It now has an active season from mid-June to mid-September, offering the finest in Broadway drama and musicals, and is noted as the only theater in the United States dedicated to the heritage, preservation, and development of the American musical. The first production of *Man of La Mancha* was launched here. Performances begin at 8 P.M., with matinees on Wednesday at 2:30 P.M. and Sundays at 5 P.M. and showings on Saturdays at 5 and 9 P.M.

The Gelston House, next door, is a charming Victorian establishment where one can enjoy a view of the river's rustic landscape and some unusual culinary delights. It was closed for several years, but has reopened recently.

The New England Steamboat Lines runs its Camelot Cruises out of Haddam. A 500-passenger excursion boat leaves daily on the Greenport Cruise on Wednesdays through Saturdays. The cruise to Sag Harbor departs also at 9 A.M. every Sunday, Monday, and Tuesday. These boats are due back at Haddam at 6 P.M. To reach more distant ports, American Cruise Lines offers cruises from Haddam to places like Block Island, Martha's Vineyard, Nantucket, and Cape Cod.

The story goes that in earlier times a certain vociferous mate, who served aboard one of the steamers on the New York–to–Hartford run, would bellow out as his ship approached these neighboring river towns: "Hadlyme! Haddam! North Haddam! East Haddam! Middle Haddam! Wish that the devil had 'em!"

15. Salmon River (east shore—12377). Just above East Haddam is the entrance to Salmon River, where a good anchorage in deep water is to be found in the narrow part of the channel. But feel your way in carefully for the entrance is subject to shoaling and, as is frequently the case with tributaries leading into larger rivers, the upriver point has a fairly long shoal, to port as you go in. A good anchorage is just opposite the first tiny creek you will meet to starboard. The latest *Coast Pilot* reports that Salmon Cove "is navigable only by small craft at high tide. The entrance to the cove is subject to shoaling. Considerable grass in the channel and cove makes boat operation difficult." Based on a recent arduous exploration upstream, we can subscribe to the *Pilot's* last sentence. Depths recorded on the current chart are badly outdated. Fouling our propeller while stirring bottom mud was our experience in a boat of 2-foot draft. Beyond the aforementioned creek, the unmarked channel begins to shoal along much of its western edge to muddy, grassy depths of 2 to 3 feet with less water to starboard. It is risky indeed to venture beyond Cones Point. The land is marshy along these shores, but to the east the heights rise to 300 feet or more. It is intriguing to explore the Moodus River northward by dinghy or canoe, with Mount Tom rising 300 feet above you.

Almost due west from the Salmon River entrance and on the western shore you will approach Damar/Midway Marina—(203) 345-4330. It reports 8 feet at its slips supplied with water and electricity and provides ice, showers, a laundromat, a discount marine store with E & B pricing, and a full-service yard. Note the "Slow No Wake" buoys here; the place is pretty exposed.

You may witness as your cruise takes you on upriver a nostalgic scene from yesteryear: A venerable steam engine, rushing along the western shore, sounding its mournful whistle, and drawing along a string of 100-year-old coaches, wends its way across the fields and marshlands of the valley. This is the revived Connecticut Valley Railroad running excursions from Essex to Chester and connecting with the riverboats at Deep River.

The loveliest part of the Connecticut River lies between Salmon River and Middletown, especially the passage through The Straits just below Middletown.

16. Portland (east (north) shore—12377). The Portland Boat Works is a high-class yard catering to inboards, but we can't explain why they close down the first two weeks of August. Gas, water, electricity, hauling, engine repairs, pumpout facility, and a ship's store are all here, as well as possible overnight dockage in 6-foot depths. Just above on the same shore are the Yankee Boatyard (VHF-68) and the Riverside Marina. They both have electricity and water at the slips, ice, showers, store, gas, and repair facilities. Yankee Boatyard has diesel, moorings, rigging repair, and 12 feet MLW at the slips, while Riverside has 22 feet of water, but caters less to transients, featuring "affordable boating." On your approach to these yards leave nun 88 to starboard. We learned that the government buoys are not put in until the shad-fishing season is over around the end of May. We don't know when they are removed, but watch the chart carefully if you are an out-of-season boater.

Approximately 1/2 mile beyond them across on the southern shore note a prominent tan building which houses the America's Cup Restaurant, one of the few convenient dock and dine accommodations on the Connecticut.

Middletown, here, is the principal shopping center of Middlesex County and the home of Wesleyan University. It was once an important shipping port for the West Indies. Its name resulted from the fact that the city is about halfway between Saybrook and Hartford.

The river between Middletown and Hartford is less settled and also less beautiful than it is below, but it is nevertheless pleasant. Except in Wethersfield Cove, the only good anchorages are in the river itself—within the charted special anchorage areas for small craft along the northern and eastern shores between Bodkin Rock and Portland.

17. Rocky Hill (west shore—12377). Just above the ferry landing there is a fine launching ramp. Also, across the river on the bend above the east-side ferry landing can be found a possible anchorage in pretty surroundings. At Hales Landing runs our nation's oldest continuing operating ferry service. Its first trip across river between Rocky Hill and Glastonbury took place in 1655.

18. South Wethersfield (west shore—12377). The latest chart will show you that a gunk hole has been formed through the western shore of the river about 2 miles south of Wethersfield Cove. It is such a concealed place that it hasn't been given a proper name, so natives call it simply "No Name Cove."

This rectangular basin, 1,000 yards long and almost as wide, was dredged out in recent years to provide fill for the construction of nearby Highway 91. Its narrow entrance is difficult to spot but lies on the west shore at the foot of Crow Point, a mile beyond nun 126. This entrance is shallow, but if you are fortunate enough to enter, you'll probably find yourself alone with no marinas to mar the natural beauty of the still water surrounded by tiny beaches, lush trees, and bushes. The cove is incomparable. Although there is no one around to tell us, it may closely resemble the Wethersfield Cove of a century or more ago.

19. Wethersfield Cove (12377). This is a rather unusual, completely landlocked cove with a very narrow entrance, 60 feet wide and 1,500 feet long, subject to considerable shoaling. The shallowest point, $4^{1}/_{2}$ feet at MLW, is at the entrance of the channel between the green and red government-maintained and charted buoys. In 1986, however, the dredging by the Army Corps of Engineers restored this channel to its original dimensions—60 feet wide, 6 feet deep at low water—with this same depth being carried throughout most of the basin's southern sector. The tidal change is about $1^{1}/_{2}$ feet, so most motor cruisers have no trouble getting in. The fixed highway bridge over the channel allows a 38-foot vertical clearance at normal river levels. Keep in the middle of the entrance channel and then follow the buoys to the Wethersfield Cove Yacht Club dock on the southwest shore.

The club has gas and water, is accessible to stores nearby and to public transportation, and is most hospitable to visitors and to members of other yacht clubs. Moorings and slips are often available. The harbormaster at the Cove Park Anchorage on the southeastern shore may also be able to provide a mooring. The bottom is soft clay, so set your anchor well in a blow.

An excellent launching ramp is located on Cove Park's shore, and inland there are picnic tables and telephones. The old stone-and-wood building, The Cove Warehouse, built around 1700, is where traders stored their loads of fish and furs during the eighteenth century. On a recent visit, the well-rusted chain and padlock indicated that it is not opened very often. There are also several historic houses and museums open to the public within a long but easy walk.

Two events have taken place that have stripped this cove of much of its former appeal. Extreme water pollution, an increasing problem along the Connecticut, prohibits any swimming here. And the fixed highway bridge, arching over the channel, allows only a 38-foot vertical clearance and so prevents most sailing craft over 27 feet from entering.

If you are able to enter Wethersfield Cove, take a deep breath. You may sense a lingering scent of onions that were widely farmed through-out this area nearly two centuries ago. According to historical records, vast fields were covered with the pungent bulb and cultivated almost entirely by women and girls. "Samuel Peters, in his romancing history of Connecticut, in 1781 wrote, 'It is the rule with Wethersfield parents to buy annually a silk gown for each daughter above the age of seven till she is married. The young beauty is obliged in return to weed a patch of onions with her own hand.'"*

Olfactory matters aside, yachts would do well to make Wethersfield Cove the end of their upriver navigation. There are no good yacht facilities in Hartford, and above Hartford the river is usually too shoal for cruiser navigation except possibly by expert pilots with local knowledge.

"Connecticut River above Hartford," says the *Coast Pilot*, "is prac-tically unimproved, but is navigable about 30 miles to Holyoke for boats not exceeding 3-foot draft, when the river is not low. The channel is constantly shifting."

Niantic River, Connecticut (13211). Before you approach this river, note that a special anchorage area off the Niantic Bay Yacht Club on the western side of Niantic Bay has been assigned by the Coast Guard and appears on the latest charts. The club has guest moorings and slips, but its anchorage is also wide open to winds from the east and southeast. Its basin at Crescent Beach, however, is protected on the south and east by a breakwater. Another possible anchorage selected by the Bayreuther brothers is just northeast of Wigwam Rock off McCook Point, affording good protection from northerlies and westerlies.

Entry into the Niantic River requires going under a railroad bridge and then a road bridge and encountering currents there that are still swift enough so that a sailboat is well advised to make the passage at slack water. The channel is winding but well marked. As the chart shows, the area on either side of the channel is very shoal.

On approaching this passageway, you will see that with the support of the Coast Guard administration at Governor's Island, New York, the long war of the bridges is over and boaters along this river have appar-ently won. Gone is the slow, antiquated swing bridge, now replaced by a handsome bascule bridge whose tall concrete pylons support a 2,050-

*From *The Connecticut River* by Edwin M. Bacon (G. P. Putnam's Sons, New York, 1906).

foot-long span approaching the river and provide a draw with a vertical clearance of 50 feet at high water. This new structure promises to reduce the former traffic congestion here. The closed highway bridge has a vertical clearance of about 32 feet. The railroad bridge has a clearance of 11 feet, so many boats will require the opening of both bridges in order to pass through.

Although the first bridge may be open, unless a train is approaching, the second (highway) bridge is usually closed. Both bridges open on signal of one long blast and one short blast of horn or whistle. Acknowledgment from both bridges is the same as your own signal for them to open. When either draw cannot open or is open and must close at once, the bridgetenders will sound five blasts. In this event, back off and wait, while staying within the turning basins, which have been dredged on both sides of the bridge and marked with poles on which reflectors have been placed. Between the two bridges you may come to lie along the bulkheading there. Note, also, that from 7 to 8 A.M. and from 4 to 5 P.M., Monday through Friday except holidays, these draws need not open for vessels. The bridges monitor VHF-13.

Proceeding up the winding, marked channel bordered by mud shoals, you will note similar-looking marinas lined up in the following order: Niantic River Marina; Boats, Inc., catering primarily to powerboats and with the accent on fishing; Watermark Enterprises, with a marine railway; and Niantic Boatyard, also with a railway. The services here are rather complete and comparable, but water at their docks runs only about 4 feet.

Currently, day mark number 17 has an osprey nest on it with young ones aboard. Ospreys are making a good comeback with local help so they should become more prevalent.

About three-quarters of a mile above these facilities, the narrow 50-foot-wide channel will lead you to the entrance to landlocked Smith Cove on your port hand. But on the way there, be on the alert for several menacing shoal spots with depths at low water to only 4 feet. One is 100 feet downstream from red marker 14, and the others are in the vicinity of green markers 21 and 27. Privately maintained stakes, with appropriately marked red and green arrows, have been set out to line the $5^1/2$-foot-deep channel leading to Bayreuther Marina, whose slips offer 8-foot depths. To enter this channel, make sure to bear off to port just before reaching marker 27, located in the main channel. Also note the black daymarker with the sign "BBY—Keep to Port." Do this as you head for the first of the marina's markers leading to Smith Cove. Since most of the cove is 3 feet deep, with a mud bottom, a tie-up at Bayreuther is advised, although guest moorings are available for boats of under 3-foot draft.

The marina manager keeps his establishment "Bristol fashion" and obviously caters to transients. He has about everything to suit you and your boat's needs and fancy, including gas and diesel fuel, excellent repairmen on duty, electronic repair, a 30-ton travelift, a fine marine store, ice, polished restrooms and showers, and a snack bar which makes excellent sandwiches. Motels and a shopping center are nearby. A courtesy car is at your disposal. If you are in Niantic Bay and need help in getting to this marina, they will send you a pilot on call. VHF-9 is monitored. Yachtsmen who are between cruises often use Bayreuther as a layover preferable to New London.

The quiet cove, almost pondlike, presents the observer with a pleasant image. The water is clear, the swimming good, for boats putting in here are not permitted to pump their heads unless equipped with a retaining tank. Fish such as flounder, stripers, and mackerel abound here and along the river.

The channel farther up the river is apt to shift from time to time, but the marks are moved to conform to the changes. Niantic River is a beautiful spot, widens into a well-sheltered lake, and offers good holding ground in about 15 feet of water south of Sandy Point's bluff or along the upper reaches of the river's western fork.

Water activities here combine those of seacoast and inland lakes.

Excellent taxi service from Niantic can take you to good restaurants in the vicinity and in Old Lyme.

Millstone Point, Connecticut (13211). The Third Edition of this *Guide*, published in 1946, described Millstone Point Cove as "an intriguing little cove on the southwest side of Millstone Point (east side of Niantic Bay)—a quaint, secluded place, usually unfrequented by yachts." Regrettably, the passing years have not helped preserve its natural solitude, and another gunk hole has become a sacrifice, this time to our nuclear age.

Today, Millstone Cove is marked by a 389-foot-high, red-and-white-banded ventilation stack belonging to the Northeast Utilities' Millstone Nuclear Power Station. Since our federal government now requires very tight security around nuclear power plants, anyone entering Millstone

Cove would be questioned and probably asked to leave unless it was an emergency situation. From this standpoint, Millstone could be an ideal spot to summon help through the security guards on duty. For the cruising yachtsman, therefore, Millstone should be considered a harbor of refuge in emergencies only.

As for the other property at Millstone Point, including Fox Island and Bay Point beach, picnic area, and visitors' information center, the growth in construction has forced the closing of these areas to the public, according to Clifford Hill, nuclear information manager for Northeast Utilities.

The station's Environmental Laboratory occupies the big stone quarry, said to be one of the oldest in southern New England. Boats are not permitted to enter here through the opening to Twotree Island Channel.

New London, Connecticut (13213, 13212). This is one of the leading yacht centers on the Sound, and provides virtually every requirement the cruising yachtsman may seek, except possibly a snug anchorage. New London Harbor, formed by the Thames River, is large and seldom quiet. The last time we looked, there were a lot of lobster buoys west of the channel in the lower part of the harbor. But it is fairly well protected, and has all sorts of provisions for cruisers.

The best small-boat anchorage is within the charted area along the west side of the lower harbor just south of Greens Harbor, but the area is pretty full of moorings. Heavy repair work is done at the Thames Shipyard; small repairs can be handled by a mechanic at any one of the yacht stations we will mention.

Harbor conditions are generally good except in strong southerly winds, when it is advisable to anchor in the upper harbor, north of the United States Coast Guard docks on the west side. These docks are distinguishable at night by a red light at the outer end. Another good place to anchor is off the Coast Guard Academy just above the I-95 bridge.

Burr's Yacht Haven, (203) 443-8457, just below the Orient Point Ferry and about 1 mile from the entrance on the western shore in Greens Harbor, is an excellent place to leave a boat or to outfit for a trip. In entering this harbor, be absolutely sure to keep well inside (south) of both nuns 2 and 4 to avoid Hog Bank Rocks. Permanent moorings, in the shape of large blue-and-white ball buoys, are available with launch service, and good care and security will be provided any boat left with the management. During the week you can leave your car at Burr's parking lot, or on the weekend at the municipal lot one block away.

Moorings may be assigned and picked up after checking personally with the dockmaster. Many convenient slips with electrical connections have been built at the wharf for those who prefer to tie up there in 9 feet MLW. Here you'll find "complete one-stop service" for Burr's claims that, "if we haven't got it, we can get it." VHF-9 and 68 are monitored.

Gas, diesel fuel, ice, water, etc., are found at the dock, and up at the marine store, operated by Burr's owner, Raymond Bergamo, you can find an ample stock of hardware and charts. Complete engine/hull repair work is available. On the premises are showers, a laundromat, and highly recommended Chuck's Steak House, where informal dress is permissible.

One block west of Burr's straight up the hill is a road on which buses run to New London every thirty minutes. Also located here is a small grocery store called the Sea Breeze, where you can pick up supplies, or they'll deliver if you call 443-9696. Their hours on weekdays are 8 A.M. to 6:30 P.M., Saturdays 6 A.M. to 6 P.M., and Sundays 6 A.M. to 4 P.M. Taxis can be ordered quickly by phone to provide transportation to the New London railroad station, where most through-trains between Boston and New York stop. Ferries also run regularly to Fishers Island, Block Island, and Orient Point from docks located just northeast of Shaw Cove.

At the northern end of Greens Harbor is the A. W. Marina—(203) 443-6076—catering mostly to small powerboats. Just above that is the newest marina in the harbor, the Ferry Slip. It is a dockominium complex with yard, travelift, and very elegant facilities for people. We were told that when 60 percent of the dockominiums are sold, it will become a yacht club. They usually have ten or more slips available for transients depending on who is out cruising. They have no VHF facilities yet, but reservations can be made by calling (203) 443-9038. Repair facilities seem limited but are readily available nearby.

Just south of Burr's lies the new Thamesport Marina, (203) 442-1151, VHF-9, replacing the old Marsters Marine Service. New docks with 110 slips and classy electrical and water outlets are being built, and a building is being renovated for a clubhouse. The fuel dock is 150 feet long. Cocoanut Joe's and Fred's Shanty eating places are part of the operation. The Thames Yacht Club is located next door. On one of our visits here, the people couldn't have been nicer in rightfully showing off their fine clubhouse, including immaculate showers and snack bar. Visiting yachtsmen may make use of its sandy beach and perhaps a spare mooring or two, but they can obtain no gas or supplies. This active sailing club, open from 10 A.M. to 6 P.M., offers anchorage in the most attractive surroundings found on the Thames.

Now that landlocked Shaw Cove's hurricane bulkhead has been completed upriver, on the west side of the Thames, yachts can put into Crocker's Boatyard, with its vastly expanded facilities. Six feet can be carried in the channel leading to the cove. On the way, you will pass through a railroad swing bridge with a 6-foot clearance when closed. The draw opens on signal from 5 A.M. to 11 P.M. from April 1 to November 30. You can signal Crocker's on VHF-9 and 6 and (203) 443-6304.

The boatyard offers gas, ice, showers, complete repairs, marine supplies, and 10 feet of water at its floating docks and is accessible to restaurants. It has been run by five straight generations of Crockers.

There is some protection for shoal-draft craft off the Shennecossett Yacht Club behind Pine Island on the east side of the river entrance, but there are limited supplies—only gas, water, and ice. Anchoring here saves making the trip up the river, yet it is not recommended for an overnight anchorage unless you're desperate. A new breakwater has reduced the swells and wind from westerlies, but the noise from nearby Trumbull Airport precludes a tranquil sojourn. This small, crowded harbor is marked by a prominent watertower of the Coast Guard station on Avery Point. If you are still tempted to enter, make your approach through the western passage until you reach the yacht club's dock, with a reported 7-foot depth. Here you can find gas, ice, marine supplies, and perhaps a spare slip. Spicer's Marine just beyond the yacht club has gas, water, and ice with a nearby state launching ramp, but at this spot the water shoals rapidly to less than 3 feet at MLW.

Places of interest in New London include Connecticut College, the United States Submarine Base and the adjacent Nautilus Memorial, and the U.S. Coast Guard Academy where band concerts are held during summer weekends and a visit aboard the training ship *Eagle* promises a treat if she happens to be in port. All these are above the railroad and I-95 bridges.

It is interesting, from any of the tie-ups in New London, to see the sleek submarines glide by, to watch fine-looking yachts as they come and go, to share in the conversation and activities at one of the leading ports or rendezvous for boating people on the New England coast.

The Thames is also renowned as the scene of the traditional Harvard-Yale crew race each June. These have produced many tall tales over the years, few better than one told by Robert Sylvester in his article entitled "The Stonington Whalers."*

Of the other old Whalers whom I personally knew, one performed a feat of seamanship which, I have no doubt, is still remembered by various millionaire yachtsmen of the East as well as by me.

He was Cap'n Ben Chesebrough, descendent of Stonington's first settler and one of the great sailors of all time. When the whaling industry started to fade, Cap'n Ben took a job as captain of John E. Atwood's schooner yacht, *The Gazelle*.

Mr. Atwood, as was his custom, attended the Harvard-Yale boat races on the Thames River. Cap'n Ben sailed his boss right into the thick of traffic at the finish line. Atwood fretted a bit over this.

"It'll be hard getting out," he grouched.

"It'll be all right," opined Cap'n Ben.

The race over, Chesebrough eyed the masters of the packed craft who were tacking and hauling sail and going through other nerve-wracking maneuvers in the attempt to get their boats out of the jam and headed for the sea. Chesebrough ordered some tackle changed and then took the wheel.

Five minutes later the owners and navigators of the throng in the Thames stood aghast and watched *The Gazelle* calmly sailing out of the Thames *backwards*. There wasn't another navigator there who could tell how it was done, and Cap'n Ben preferred to keep his own navigation secrets.*

City Pier, beyond Shaw Cove, is the center of New London's revitalized waterfront. Overnight and transient day dockage areas are available. Throughout the summer, waterfront festivals, outdoor concerts, and arts and crafts shows take place on the pier and adjacent State Street. Bank Street, extending south and formerly the commercial center of New London, is now a renovated area of shops, restaurants, and boutiques. Nearby Whale Oil Row is lined with several historic sites.

*From *Yankees Under Sail*, edited by Richard Heckman (Yankee Inc.).

Special Note on Tides. The tide runs strongly off the southern end of Bartlett Reef, near New London, and the same is true of Black Point.

The tides are strongest at the easterly end of the Sound—especially east of Falkner Island. The tide is almost twice as strong outside Long Sand Shoal—near the Cornfield lighted buoy—as inside the shoal. A correspondent reports finding an ebb tide of from 1¹/₂ to 2 knots off Cornfield and making good time to New London from the Duck Island westerly breakwater by taking the slightly longer outside route. (See special government tide and current book on Long Island Sound tides or the current charts in the *Eldridge Tide and Pilot Book*.) Therefore, should you be riding a fair current along the 6-mile length of Long Sand Shoal and be heading up the Sound, stay to the south and gain the extra lift. Bucking the current, however, run north of the shoal, where the velocity is weaker.

Also note that in running from the east or from the west between Duck Island Roads and the Connecticut River, prepare to be set north on the flood and south on the ebb.

Norwich, Connecticut (12372). This harbor is being added to the *Guide* because of its newest marina. The Marina at American Wharf is an elegant 187-slip operation in the city of Norwich. Although it is about 11 miles up the Thames River from New London, it has become a destination for many cruisers because of its facilities and now, partly at least, its proximity to the new Foxwoods Casino operated by the Mash-antucket Pequot Indians. In fact, the casino and marina are doing some joint marketing and offer programs combining a stay at the marina with visits to the casino. Call Dockmaster/Manager Karen Staples at the marina on VHF 68 or (203) 887-1138 for particulars. The marina offers all the usual amenities plus cable TV at the slips, a swimming pool, picnic areas, a fine restaurant, snack bar, pumpout station, boutique, and ship's store, and many events during the season held under a large tent covering the "promenade." Norwich has some interesting historic landmarks.

Navigation is quite straightforward with a well-marked 11-foot-deep channel all the way up the Thames River to the large turning basin in front of the marina, where 30 feet is reported just off the slips. The only hazards shown on the chart and mentioned in the *Coast Pilot* are some dikes which are submerged at half-tide along both sides from Easter

Point to Norwich. The bascule railroad bridge at New London has a vertical clearance of 30 feet when closed. The nearby fixed highway bridge has a clearance of 135 feet, and another highway bridge about 7 miles farther upriver has a clearance of 75 feet. Anchoring is forbidden in the turning basin, but is possible just above the fixed bridges in the Shetucket River if you can manage the 13-foot clearance.

Chapter V

South Shore of Long Island Sound

Manhasset Bay to Montauk Point

Manhasset Bay and Port Washington, Long Island, New York (12366). Manhasset Bay, though large, is one of the best harbors on Long Island Sound. It has deep water everywhere and a good holding bottom, is easy to enter by day or night, and has plenty of good anchorage space with protection from wind or sea. There are practically no tidal currents except at the entrance, and the average rise of tide is about 6 feet.

Few, if any, harbors on the Atlantic Coast have as many services and facilities to offer yachtsmen as Manhasset Bay. There are so many yacht clubs—we have counted eight—that we can mention only several of the best known. Boatyards, marinas, marine supply shops, public and private docks, waterfront restaurants greet the mariner whichever way he looks.

One of the two oldest yacht clubs on Long Island Sound, the North Shore Yacht Club, housed in a small white building with red trim in Manorhaven on the north shore, has guest mooring with launch service. Organized as the New York Canoe Club in 1871, it has been going ever since and gives visitors a friendly reception, as we know from experience.

The Capri Marina & Yachting Center consists of two luxurious marinas, Capri Marina East, mostly for sailing craft, and Capri Marina West, which flank the yacht club. Both have about everything to offer including slips and moorings, 24-hour launch service, a pumpout station, complete dockside services, showers, laundromats, a 70-ton travelift, full repairs, and even a courtesy car. For many other accommodations, patrons can visit their concierge office. Both marinas monitor VHF-9 using a VHF-72 working channel and record 8 feet of water dockside. Capri West may reserve you a slip or mooring if you phone (516) 883-7802.

There are two excellent restaurants here. Capri West has The Barge, a floating establishment for dinner specializing in fine seafood dishes and preparing complete "to-go" menus on call. Then there's Latitudes open daily, serving modern lunch and dinner fare, and providing a splendid view of the bay. A source for all kinds of services and provisions is just a 5-minute walk away.

Behind Toms Point are several small marinas, but the real display of facilities is at Port Washington, along the eastern shore of Manhasset Bay. Here from north to south, are three large and well-known yacht clubs. The Knickerbocker Yacht Club (1874) was sponsor of the first Frostbite Regatta on January 2, 1932. The first prize, won by Colin Ratsey, was a suitably engraved gallon alcohol tin—empty. The Manhasset Bay Yacht Club (1891) began life on a scow with a piano and a bar and now has luxurious quarters full of yachting memorabilia, a swimming pool, a restaurant, and some guest moorings and has always been a leader in frostbite competition. It monitors VHF-68. The Port Washington Yacht Club, using VHF-74, lies farthest south marked by a modern clubhouse flanked by a pool with a long pier out in front. Having picked up a mooring here on direction of the launchman and registered at the main office, guests may use the club's facilities, restaurant, and swimming pool. These clubs supply no fuel but are hospitable to yachtsmen from other recognized clubs offering reciprocal privileges. All maintain launch services.

The Manhasset harbormaster advises that yachts should not try to anchor in the special anchorage area north of the yacht clubs and marked on the chart.

Among the leading boatyards and marine supply houses along the Port Washington shore, from north to south, is Cow Bay Marine Service which has marine supplies and performs all types of repairs on hull, engine, and rigging but offers no accommodations for transients. Next comes the Manhasset Bay Marina, identified by a prominent lighthouse and reportedly the top repair facility in the bay.

For supplies, one may be able to tie up temporarily at the North Hempstead Town Dock just north of Louie's Shore Restaurant, where you will find 4 feet at low water. Here you can stay only 20 minutes, but stores for provisions are just a block away. Patrons of Louie's can tie up in 5 feet MLW dockside for a dinner prepared by fourth-generation continued management. Next comes Northstar Marine, probably one of the most completely stocked ship's chandlers on Long Island, with a courtesy dock. The southernmost of all these facilities is Jimmy's Back Yard, a waterfront restaurant recommended to us.

There is little commercial traffic in Manhasset Bay, just swarms of yachts, large and small. The Coast Guard has estimated that there are now over 200,000 small craft plying Long Island Sound each summer, and at certain times one might imagine they have all gathered together in Manhasset Bay. Manhasset, at the southern end of the bay, has some interesting old houses, such as the Onderdonk House, considered a fine example of Greek Revival architecture. It also has an active shopping center.

Port Washington is a former seventeenth-century cow pasture that became a twentieth-century suburb. In 1643, 18 English families rowed across Long Island Sound from Stamford seeking religious freedom. After bartering with the natives, they bought what amounts to the western half of Nassau County from the Marsapeake, Merrick, and Rockaway Indians. Not surprisingly, the peninsula became known as Cow Neck and the bay on the west side—now Manhasset Bay—was called Cow Bay.

Glen Cove (Hempstead Harbor), Long Island, New York (12366).

"The old order changeth, yielding place to new." Gone is the glitter from the Glen Cove yachting scene. All that was left was a landmark replica of the famous Station 10 of the New York Yacht Club, once located just inside the breakwater on the east shore. Fire destroyed this small gray building with wide overhanging eaves in early 1981. The larger building, once the clubhouse where the "Four Hundred" of the yachting world were wont to gather, was rafted away in June 1949 to become a fixture on the grounds of the Marine Historical Association at Mystic Seaport. This was the end of an era at Glen Cove, when palatial yachts belonging to such men as J. Pierpont Morgan, Jr., and Cornelius Vanderbilt lay moored off Station 10.

Now the site is called Glen Cove Landing and the anchorage area is Hempstead Harbor. A new building houses the Glen Cove Yacht Club, an autonomous organization. Although there is no space allowed for a tie-up dockside, guest moorings are available for a fee with launch service provided over VHF-68. It is pretty isolated here, with added protection from the breakwater and good holding ground. But this is no place to be anchored in a nor'wester unless you are tucked in behind the breakwater.

Off the dock are many small sailboats and motor cruisers where once *Corsair* lay. The most suitable anchorage is along the east shore, just beyond the fleet. But the best shelter from northerly winds is still off the yacht club's dock behind the breakwater. It is also much cooler there on hot summer nights than it is at the landlocked Glen Cove Yacht Service docks, described later.

South of Glen Cove Landing, also on the east shore, just north of the entrance to Mosquito Cove, is the charming, shipshape Hempstead Harbor Club. We hope that the name of the cove is not suggestive, though there are marshes nearby. The dockmaster, who monitors VHF-68, says that there is 6 feet at low water at the club dock and that the club offers reciprocal privileges to members of other recognized yacht clubs. There are several guest moorings in deep water, but these are open to the northward for a considerable distance and under some conditions provide an uncomfortable anchorage. The club does not supply gas, but water and ice are obtainable. Another club, the Sea Cliff Yacht Club, is on the south side of the cove. From the channel, head almost due south in making your approach to the extending pier where there is 4 feet MLW. Not only is Sea Cliff, founded in 1892, an appealing-looking club, but its members are a spirited group. On our latest visit, Vice-Commodore Herman Neiges told us of his club's active junior sailing and interclub racing programs including such contributions as these that Sea Cliff has made to yachting. In 1961, it established and donated the International Catamaran Challenge Trophy and sponsored the first race. Known as the "Little America's Cup," it is one of the most prestigious yachting trophies in the world. And in 1977, the club helped initiate the first race of what has become an annual affair—the Around Long Island Regatta—and has been its cohost ever since. Sea Cliff rebuilt its clubhouse after a tragic fire took place on August 15, 1980.

Available for a fee to members of recognized yacht clubs are Sea Cliff's guest moorings with launch service daily over VHF-9 until 9 P.M., a fine restaurant with a delicious cuisine and splendid harbor view, a snack bar, showers, and a swimming pool.

The 6-foot-deep channel of Glen Cove Creek, leading from Mosquito Cove, is marked by buoys and continues to shoal up in spots. It is advisable to keep in dead center. The Brewer Yacht Yard at Glen Cove is the first facility you will come upon on your starboard hand. Located in a protected basin, this marina accommodates boats up to 50 feet with complete repair services, but it pumps no fuel. There are showers here with electricity and water at the slips, a pumpout facility, and towing services if they are hailed on VHF-71. The installation of a swimming pool was being planned at the time of writing. Many boat owners from local clubs store their yachts here with the help of Brewer's 30-ton lift.

In the second basin beyond, with a mean depth of 6 feet, one may find the largest full-service marina in Glen Cove—Glen Cove Yacht Service. It offers gas, diesel fuel, ice, water, marine supplies, slips with electricity, and a pumpout station. This place may well be your best bet for the deepest water in the creek, perhaps the most active dockage, and the most convenient location to stores and restaurants. In the summer you will find the creek not only extremely sociable but often quite hot.

At the end of the creek lies the Gulf gas and diesel dock of the Glen Cove Marina where 5 feet MLW has been recorded. Report here to be assigned a slip with ice, water, electricity, and showers on tap. This marina offers a full-time mechanic and sail repair, and on weekends the harbor patrol's office monitors VHF-16 in case of emergencies. The town of Sea Cliff is one-half mile up the hill.

At the south end of the harbor on the east shore opposite Bar Beach is the site of the old Fyfe Shipyard, which from its humble beginnings in 1905, came to be known as the "Tiffany" of boatyards. Here such majestic "gold-platers" as J. P. Morgan's *Corsair* and Marjorie Merriweather Post's *Sea Cloud* came to be fitted out in times gone past. Now it is out of business, perhaps having been too wedded to wood construction in the age of fiberglass. The Long Island Lighting Company has taken over the property.

A bit farther north on the eastern shore above Glenwood Landing is Tappen Marina and Beach, a municipal facility operated by the town of Oyster Bay. Until 3 P.M. daily, gas is supplied as well as pumpout service dockside where there is 5 feet MLW. There is an overnight dockage charge at the finger piers.

South of Bar Beach, the buoys have been removed in recent years, and the upper harbor is of interest only to gunkholers on a rising tide. The mean tidal range is 8.6 feet. In Mott's Cove, just south of the power plant, is the Burtis Boat Works, accessible only at high water.

Hempstead Harbor was first entered in 1640 by immigrants from Lynn, Massachusetts, and the first use of the necks of land now occupied by great estates and summer homes was for the common pasturage of cattle. Settlers worshipped on Sundays in stockades, assembling at the call of kettledrums from the ramparts.

The town of Glen Cove was called Musketo (or Musceta) Cove until 1834. This word really meant to the Indians "cove of grassy flats"; but because it was confused with "mosquito," the new name was wisely adopted.

The Long Island Lighting Company buildings dominate the upper harbor, which is less attractive than it is nearer the entrance. A small boat basin is located at Glenwood Landing.

Oyster Bay, Long Island, New York (12365). This is an attractive, well-protected bay with several good anchorages. One is off the Seawanhaka Corinthian Yacht Club in the cove west of Plum Point, Centre Island. This club, organized in 1871, is one of the two oldest yacht clubs still in business on Long Island Sound, the other being the North Shore Yacht Club of Port Washington. The surroundings are lovely, but supplies are unavailable, and the tide runs strongly.

Seawanhaka's services, including meals, are available only to yachts flying the burgee of a recognized yacht club. There are no designated guest moorings, but moorings of members whose yachts are away are made available to guests for a fee. There is no overnight dockage and no anchoring possible within the moored fleet although there may be an anchoring space south of the moorings. Launch service in season runs between the hours of 8 A.M. and 12 P.M. It operates from the westernmost dock where visiting yachts should first report to be assigned a mooring. This dock is used mainly for repairs, supplying fuel, ice, and water, and docking here is available only to club members. The middle pier is reserved for swimming, and the easternmost dock is used for dropping off personnel entering the clubhouse. They monitor channel 9.

"At the time of Seawanhaka's organization, the group who left the handling of their yachts to professional skippers and crews, the wealthier members, were in control of the New York Yacht Club. Some of the other group, the do-it-yourself exponents, who skippered and sailed their own boats, decided to form a new club in which the principles of amateur or 'Corinthian' racing would prevail."* Apparently, sailing with amateur crews had long been popular in England, but it was the founding fathers of this over-one-hundred-year-old club who are recognized as having introduced an entirely new trend in racing to American yachting.

The Cruising Club of America, which has held many a rendezvous in Oyster Bay, usually anchors off the southern tip of Centre Island and outside of the main channel or, preferably we think, in the large bight between Cove Neck and the wharf at Oyster Bay.

The former shoal area that ran along the southern shore of the harbor from the oyster dock west to the charted dredged canal has been removed, giving the various facilities approach and dockside depths of at least 18 feet MLW. The first marina you will reach is Oyster Bay Marine Center, run by young, hospitable John McGrane, who told us he can provide visiting yachts with gas, diesel fuel, water, ice, and showers. There is a charge for overnight moorings with launch service running from 7 A.M. to 11 P.M. Since the slips dockside are available by reservation only, phone ahead at (516) 922-6331. They monitor VHF-71, offer a good selection of marine hardware, and have an extensive repair and towing service.

Practically next door is the Sagamore Yacht Club, housed in an attractive shingled building, which we have often enjoyed visiting. There is 7-foot depth dockside with electricity, water, showers and a phone inside the clubhouse. VHF-78 is monitored for launch service, which runs 9 A.M. to 10 P.M. on weekdays and 8 A.M. to 12 A.M. on weekends. You may have to settle for a guest mooring if one is available, since slip space is hard to come by anywhere in the harbor. This very tidy club offers reciprocal guest privileges to members of other recognized yacht clubs. The town of Oyster Bay has further developed its Roosevelt Memorial Park Boat Basin, shown on the chart due south of Brickyard Point. Gas may be obtained here, but unfortunately the docking facilities are open only to local residents. Supplies can be obtained in the town nearby.

Jakobson's Shipyard, long known to many Long Island Sound yachtsmen, is located in the cove to the west of the flagpole. Having been acquired by a tugboat association, it no longer caters to transient boats.

Some possible anchorages can be found just south of Brickyard Point

*From *Long Island Sound,* by Fessenden S. Blanchard (D. Van Nostrand Co., Inc., Princeton, N.J.).

and Moses Point, as shown on the chart. Another good anchorage, with less current than the others and good swimming, is at the northerly end of West Harbor, west of Centre Island; but keep well away from Brick-yard (Soper) Point to avoid some outlying rocks. West Harbor is much like an inland lake surrounded by residential property with well-protected anchorages. Shoal-draft craft sometimes go through the draw-bridge into Mill Neck Creek and anchor there, but the current is strong at the bridge and the charted soundings are unreliable. If curiosity gets the better of you, go in on a rising tide but proceed with care.

New York State and the federal government are becoming concerned over the proximity of shellfish beds and anchored boats with overboard discharges, and there may soon be areas of no overnight anchoring and/or discharges.

Theodore Roosevelt's famous home, Sagamore Hill, is about 1½ miles from Oyster Bay Village. It is open seven days a week from 9:30 A.M. to 6 P.M., Memorial Day to Labor Day, and well worth a visit, especially by admirers of T. R. "After all," he once wrote, "fond as I am of the White House and much though I have appreciated these years in it, there isn't any place in the world like home—like Sagamore Hill. . . ."

Cold Spring Harbor, Long Island, New York (12365). A hundred and fifty years ago Cold Spring Harbor was a whaling port, with a main street on which so many languages were spoken that it was called Bedlam Street. Today, so far as we know, whatever bedlam there is in the vicinity is left behind in the Sand Hole at Lloyd Point, which you pass on your way to one of the prettiest and most foolproof harbors on the sound. Its clean waters, now being restocked and seeded with healthy clam beds, are providing a new resource for the local baymen, and it has been vastly improved through dredging at the southern end of its channel.

It is almost impossible to get into any trouble in Cold Spring Harbor, at least in your navigating. A conspicuous lighthouse shows you the way in; once you are past this, there are no obstacles to avoid if you keep a reasonable distance from shore. The waterfront is private, lovely, and unspoiled. The only place at which gas is available is concealed from the outer harbor behind the Cold Spring Beach peninsula at the southern end of the harbor. A narrow, unbuoyed deep-water channel with well over 10 feet at MLW has been dredged through the cut between the north end of the peninsula and an island, enabling yachts to tie up at

H & M Powle's Marina and obtain gas, diesel, and a snack at a dockside clam bar farther up on the eastern shore. As you enter this cut, favor the peninsula's shore and, once having passed through, hug the shoreline to port proceeding all the way upchannel. Near Powle's are the Old Whaler Inn and the Country Kitchen, both recommended eating spots.

Good water can be carried in the channel all the way to the delightful basin at the harbor's head. The Whaler's Cove Yacht Club to port offers only water, ice, and electricity at its slips and no showers, but has become a popular visiting place for boats no longer than 45 feet overall. As with many yacht clubs having reciprocal privilege arrangements, dock space is available provided a member's slip is open. The best water, 7 feet MLW, is to be found along the eastern shore. We were advised to rent an overnight mooring from Powle's and to stay within the perimeter marked by the mooring floats, since there are mud flats to the west.

The Cold Spring Harbor Beach Club, on the east shore near the head of the harbor, is a yacht club, as well as an attractive tennis and beach club. There is at least 9 feet at the dock. In summer, the small basin, protected by a hook of land and a jetty, is filled with small sailboats and dinghies. Here, where there's a fine fleet of Atlantics, we were first introduced to the Laser class years ago. Visitors from other recognized yacht clubs, we have been told, are given reciprocal privileges, and several guest moorings with launch service are usually available—but no gas or ice. The club has put in a swimming pool and runs a snack bar during the day. Anchorage Inn, about $1/2$ mile from the club, offers good accommodations.

Cold Spring Harbor's main street, a short walk from Powle's, is lined with fascinating shops offering you a chance to pick up supplies of all kinds. Also located here is the town's Whaling Museum Society, open daily during summer months from 11 A.M. to 5 P.M. It exhibits an interesting collection of whaling paraphernalia, including a whaleboat, old prints, scrimshaw, ship models, whaling irons, and logbooks.

The "Sand Hole" at Lloyd Point, Long Island, New York (12365). This popular weekend harbor is inadequately charted, so the description that follows may be helpful to the few people who haven't already been there.

The "Sand Hole," or "Sand Diggers" as it is often called by Long Islanders (its official name is Fairchild Basin), was dug out of the low-lying end of Lloyd Point and is not easy to recognize at a distance until

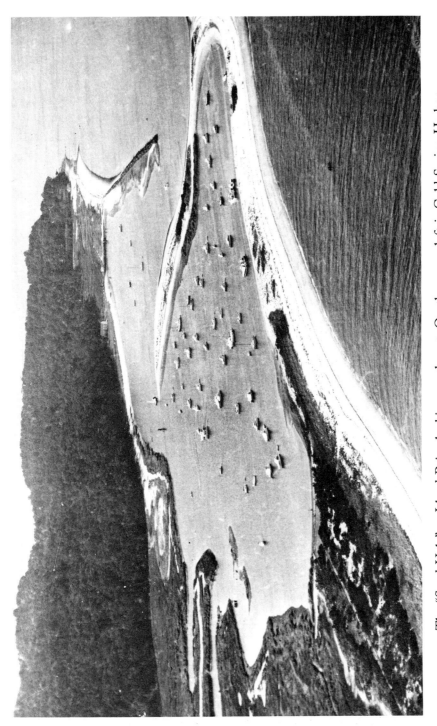

The "Sand Hole" at Lloyd Point looking southwest. On the upper left is Cold Spring Harbor and at the top right lies the entrance to Oyster Bay Harbor. *Skyviews Survey Inc.*

perhaps you see some tall spars apparently rising out of the sand. The high land south of the Sand Hole is visible for a long distance. Since there is an often submerged breakwater on your starboard hand, projecting northward at the harbor's mouth, as well as shoals building to port, don't enter too "carelesslike."

Head into the opening, giving the breakwater a fair berth but keeping clear of those shoals, which extend inward for several hundred feet from the north shore of the entrance. After that, follow the shore to port. This maneuver will involve curving north for a short stretch, as you run between parallel shoalings from each spit. It shelves off fairly steeply most of the way, but don't get too close. Follow the dark, deeper water to port as you make your final swing into the hole. Visiting yachts may come there to anchor no closer than 200 feet offshore, but their crews are not permitted to land. Make sure to avoid the shallow spots marked on the chart along the eastern shore as well as at the northern end of the hole. Rafting-up is forbidden. The holding ground is good.

The "Sand Hole" is popular among the weekend yachting fraternity of New York City and points east. During July and August, it is apt to be crowded with motorboats of every description bearing occupants of both sexes possessed of varying musical abilities and financial resources. If you plan to spend a night there, we'd suggest avoiding midsummer weekends. It is now under the control of the New York State Park Commission and recently became a part of the Caumsett State Park, a 1,426-acre tract in the center of Lloyd Neck.

No supplies or facilities of any kind are available nearer than Cold Spring Harbor. When it isn't too crowded, it is a pleasant place to anchor, though the presence of an untouchable beach can be frustrating.

Lloyd Harbor, Long Island, New York (12365). This excellent anchorage is on the southeast side of Lloyd Neck, just west of the entrance to Huntington Bay. The most popular anchorage is in the northeast corner of the harbor, in sticky mud, behind the sandspit. The holding ground here is good. Unfortunately, there are now many moorings in this area and anchoring is not permitted where so indicated by signs. Anchoring is still permitted in the southern part.

In a strong southwesterly, anchorage off the southwest shore of the harbor is to be preferred, though it is lined with private estates.

In a dinghy one can sail westward far up the harbor to the narrow strip of land that separates Lloyd Harbor from Oyster Bay to the west. This is one of the most isolated anchorages to be found within a similar distance of New York City. The shores are thickly wooded. There are no stores or facilities of any kind, but you can land on the east beach.

Yachtsmen who go ashore and roam over the sandspit will find genuine Texas cactus growing wild, a rarity in these latitudes.

Although many more deep-water cruising yachts are to be seen here than in the "Sand Hole," the chief "out" about Lloyd Harbor is its popularity, especially on weekends. But if you like to visit around or to watch some fine-looking yachts come and go, you will enjoy it there. And if you are from suburban New York, you'll undoubtedly see some of your friends. Many boats leave here after dark to return to Northport or Huntington.

Whereas under ordinary conditions this is a well-sheltered, landlocked harbor, in strong gales from the eastward at high tide the water from Huntington Bay may sweep in over the narrow point and make it extremely unpleasant. At times like these it is well to run up into Huntington Harbor close by. This is also the place to go for gas or supplies.

We recall the cooling breeze on hot summer evenings wafting down the long western channel that leads to Oyster Bay. Nor can we forget the sound of sailors singing to the crackling of a fire on a chilly autumn night, huddled around the ruins of the point's old light.

Huntington, Long Island, New York (12365). This is one of the most sheltered harbors on Long Island and the most convenient port for fuel and other supplies in the Huntington Bay area. Its major drawback is the ever-increasing congestion. The harbor is seemingly one vast fleet of wall-to-wall boats except for the narrow channel, marked by town-maintained buoys, resembling the exit lane of a modern shopping complex. Eight feet can be carried in the main channel where the speed limit is 5 mph.

Local residents of Huntington have formed a Lloyd Harbor Lighthouse fund-raising group to try to save the disintegrating structure you will see marking the entrance to Huntington and Lloyd Harbors. It will require about half a million dollars to restore the 75-year-old light.

In entering, be prepared to find a stiff current in the narrow cut off Wincoma Point. After passing this point, keep straight ahead until you have left the flashing green buoy to port. Follow the buoys southward and then east between hundreds of yachts moored on either side of the channel. A less-crowded anchorage, if you can find swinging space, may be found in the cove to starboard after having passed the lighted channel buoy inside the entrance. In here also are the 250 moorings of the Castle Cove Marina on the starboard shore. Call VHF-9 or (516) 421-3366 for rental information or launch service. They also have some repair facilities and a pumpout station. On the nearby hill stands a prominent red-roofed baronial building housing the Huntington Art Center and open to the public. Around the bend, also on the starboard shore of the harbor, is the Wyncote Yacht Club where gas, ice, and electricity are on tap and a spare slip is possibly available in 6 feet of water.

A good plan is to continue up the harbor to the hospitable Huntington Yacht Club, marked on the chart. This club, to port just beyond nun 12, has gas, diesel fuel, water, and ice, and offers its facilities to visiting yachtsmen. The clubhouse is a modern structure, with a full-service dining room and bar that has a magnificent view of the harbor. There is also an Olympic-size swimming pool with bath and shower facilities. The restaurant offers poolside service. From May through October, the club and restaurant are open seven days a week, and from November through April, five days a week. The modern docks provide electricity, water, and cable TV and can accommodate vessels up to 100 feet. Guest moorings are also available with launch service which monitors VHF-10. Advance reservations can be made by calling the dockmaster at (516) 427-4949. We thank Fleet Captain Mel Kantor for updating us on this club.

Beyond, on the east shore just north of the "Old Town Dock," is Knutson's Marina—(516) 673-0700, VHF-9—which hauls, stores, and repairs large yachts. It also has water, pumpout facility, showers, some overnight dockage space, and moorings for transients with launch service provided. Its mechanics are top-notch. Tom Knutson III is in charge here. For supplies we suggest that you tie up to the town dock for a maximum time limit of one hour while you visit the nearby delicatessen and 7-11 store. The harbormaster can usually be found in a white building close to the dock. Farther to the south lies the Ketewomoke Yacht Club. Coney's Marine—(516) 421-3366, VHF-9—is also on the eastern side with few shoreside facilities but with some 300 moorings for rent in the harbor and at associated Castle Cove Marina near C"9" in the channel. They provide launch service from 8 A.M. to 11 P.M. and have ice, heads, and showers shoreside. A King Kullen supermarket is within walking distance of the head of the harbor. Good restaurants include the Harbor Club, TK's Galley, CoCo's, and Tutto Pazzo. Around the corner north of the bridge is the sizable Willis Marine Center with slips and moorings and launch service provided from 7 A.M. up to 10 P.M. There's also electricity, gas, water, ice, showers, and a fine marine store.

Mill Dam Marina just to the west is used by local boaters. And West Shore Marina—(516) 427-3444, VHF-9—Huntington's newest facility, with 250 slips, is located in the southwest corner of the harbor. It is quite elegant, handling boats from 20 to 90 feet overall with 18 feet MLW of water at the slips, and serves the boating needs of many of the local residents. Knutson Marine, next to Willis Marine, offers a good supply at discount prices.

Beyond the bridge across the pond some fine concrete ramps and a nearby parking space offer encouragement to owners of trailer-borne outboards. The shores of the harbor are pretty and illustrate what a residential community can do with its waterfront. If you enjoy seeing a wide variety of boats and crowds of people of all ages having a mad whirl on the water, come to Huntington. The harbor is well protected from sea and wind, and transportation can be obtained to the town of Huntington, 2 or 3 miles away, where there are stores and a railroad station.

At Halesite in Huntington is a monument to Nathan Hale, the noted American spy, who landed there and was captured by the British in September 1776. On the monument are the famous words uttered by Captain Hale shortly before he died: "I only regret I have but one life to lose for my country."

Water quality here has improved, due to a combined program of environmental education, beach stabilization, wetland creation, and sewer and shorefront construction management. Portions of Huntington, Centerport, and Northport harbors, closed for years with badly polluted waters, have been reopened for clamming. These harbors were the first on Long Island to qualify under the state's water quality standards, and other areas of the Sound and outer bays are again harvesting clam beds.

The waters near Greenwich Point, Connecticut, have also improved to the extent that shellfishing is again legal after many years.

Special Note on Entrance to Northport Bay, Long Island, New York (12365). When entering from the west in fair weather, skirt along the row of nuns off Lloyd Neck. Then steer southward, heading just to the left of the nearest tall gray watertower that rises above the houses in the middle of the shore ahead and that is shown on the chart as located at Huntington Beach. The flashing buoy off the tip of West Beach marks the turn toward Price Bend, Northport, and Duck Island Harbor.

Price Bend, Long Island, New York (12365). This anchorage, open to the south for some distance, used to be a favorite rendezvous for the Cruising Club of America in May and October. The entrance between buoys along the shore to the south is easy to follow. In entering, leave can 3 to port and then swing your bow in a wide arc toward the north to avoid the charted shoals. The holding ground is rather poor, and in two October rendezvous a number of Cruising Club boats dragged their anchors. The area is no longer deserted, but there are no stores nearer than Northport. The shoreline is pleasant, with clean, coarse sand beaches left by dredging operations extending north and south. These are weed-free and offer good swimming and steep shores even at low tide. This popular sandspit, on which the foundations of an old sand-and-gravel company may still be seen, is now open to the public under the name of Hobart Beach, established for the town of Huntington. The north and east sides of Price's Bend are private and now all built up, including the entire shoreline between the northern end of the sandspit and the southern end of the Eaton's Neck cove.

Duck Island Harbor, Eaton's Neck, Long Island, New York (12365). This harbor should not be confused with Duck Island Roads, 45 miles to the east on the Connecticut shore. This is a remote, unspoiled, seldom visited, well-protected, but small and shallow anchorage on the north-east side of Northport Bay, open across the bay to the south and southwest. Note that off Winkle Point, Little Neck Point, and Duck Island Bluff, red stakes have been placed in 10 feet of water. Stay outside of these and you'll avoid grounding. In entering, go to a point about 75 feet west of the flashing red buoy off Duck Island Bluff. Then steer for the entrance, curving slightly to the west to avoid a 4-foot spot off the eastern shore. At low tide soundings are desirable.

There is 12 feet at the entrance and 8 feet a little way in, but the water shoals rapidly with a 7-foot tide range. Although the harbor is a haven for water-skiers, there is little other traffic, and hence one can safely lie in mid-channel just inside the entrance.

The chief disadvantages of the harbor are difficulty in making a landing at low tide and lack of supplies. Asharoken police boats hound these waters to prevent crews from venturing ashore. A local ordinance forbids rafting and refuse-throwing and rules that there must be at least a 150-foot berth between anchored vessels.

Duck Island is well suited to anyone desiring quiet and good protection.

Another popular anchorage offering shelter in northerlies is behind the bluff rimming the south shore of Duck Island. The water shoals rapidly northward here so anchor at least 300 yards offshore.

Northport, Long Island, New York (12365). Like all the ports on Huntington Bay, this harbor is attractive. Under most conditions the shelter is fairly good, though it can be very rough there in nor'westers. A place to go, if you are a member of a recognized yacht club and present your club's personal membership card, is to the refurbished Northport Yacht Club, formerly called the Edgewater Yacht Club. This is at the first large pier to which you come, on your port hand, after passing Bluff Point. There you can obtain gas, water, showers, ice, diesel fuel, and launch service to and from the guest moorings which lie across the channel. The launch runs from 8 A.M. to 10 P.M. on weekdays and from 8 A.M. to midnight on weekends. Check first with the dockmaster to be assigned a color-coded space alongside, where you can tie up for a thirty-minute limit. The gas docks marked in red offer only 4 feet at low water; there's an 8-foot rise and fall of tide here. Dockage is not available overnight and no advance reservations are accepted.

The Northport Yacht Club is a very active sailing center with about 60 youngsters in its junior racing program. We found the swimming pool and the restaurant with bar most appealing, enhanced by the view of a spectacular sunset for which the club is noted. The nearby Mariners Inn has unfortunately closed.

Farther south, on the same shore, is the Seymour Boat Shops with gas, ice, water, and marine supplies, but only one slip. Its repair work is said to be excellent; Centerport Yacht Club members are among Seymour's most loyal customers. Just beyond lies the public dock with an amber light and a two-hour tie-up limit. There may be space at this dock for a twenty-four-hour tie-up in 8 feet. Many restaurants and shops are nearby, but after 8 P.M. you'll be charged a flat rate for an overnight stay.

Looking to the southwest, you will note that along the port shore a winding channel, recently dredged to a MLW of 5 to 12 feet and marked with private buoys, leads to the protected basin shown due south on the chart. Keep in mid-channel close to these buoys as you make your approach to the most elaborate complex in the harbor, Britannia Yacht and Racquet Club—(516) 261-5600, VHF-9. There seems to be almost everything here including tennis, swimming pool, snack bar, workout facility, showers, sauna, 24-hour security, taxi service to town, full repair facility with mechanics on duty, Texaco fuel (diesel and 93- and 89-octane), and a ship's store.

Once called Cowharbor, this old seafaring town still clings to its waterfront life. Cowharbor Day, held annually in the second week of September, is one of the town's major attractions. Another is a special exhibit at the Northport Historical Museum which depicts the harbor's prosperous role in the nineteenth-century shipbuilding and fishing industries. The incorporated village of Northport has its own bay constable and harbormaster.

Across Northport Harbor, directly west of Seymour's and the Northport Village Dock, is the Centerport Yacht Club. The clubhouse is a lovely old mansion built around 1903 which offers a great view of the picturesque harbor and village. Members of recognized clubs may enjoy lunch and dinner outside on the porch or patio during warm weather or inside when it's not clement. The club floats offer a minimum of 6 feet at low water, with ice and water available. Guest moorings and launch service are available, but no slips. You can call ahead by phone—(516) 261-5440—or radio—channel 68—for reservations. Ashore are a restaurant, bar, showers, snack bar, and pool. The club has a fleet of over 200 vessels in its mooring field with many racers dry sailed. The junior program is very active with about 80 participants, mostly in Optimists, Blue Jays, and Lasers. Several recent Long Island Sound Junior Champions have come from CYC. We are indebted to Commodore Christopher Gross for this update.

The most interesting thing about the Northport-Centerport area is the Vanderbilt Museum—on the hills of Little Neck, part of the village of Centerport. Open to the public every day except Monday, and well worth the visit, it is located a short walk up the road from the Centerport Yacht Club. The estate had its own golf course, and oddly enough the tee for the first hole was on the roof of the main building. Seventeen thousand varieties of marine- and wildlife are housed here—animals, birds, fish, shells, shields, daggers, guns—collected from many parts of the world by the adventurous William K. Vanderbilt. There are also bathtubs of solid marble and gold plumbing fixtures, reminiscent of the good old days when millionaires were millionaires and expressed themselves grandly.

Once ships built in Northport sailed around the world. Now it is a deservedly popular and attractive center of yachting activities.

Eatons Neck Basin, Long Island, New York (12365). The very narrow entrance is clearly marked by buoys well south of the tip of the point; as you make your approach, note that the jetties on either side are under water from half to flood tide. A long, dangerous reef runs northward directly from the green lighted buoy. A Coast Guard officer at the Eatons Neck station claims that "People try to cut inside the buoy off the basin entrance and it can't be done. There is no shortcut into or out of the basin!" Unbelievably, at least thirty skippers judged otherwise several years ago and had to pay a pretty price. A depth of 8 feet MLW can be carried through the basin's entrance. The basin is known locally as Coast Guard Cove.

In the channel from the buoys up to an anchorage inside the western shore of the spit there is a range from 10 to 21 feet at low tide. The entrance buoys make access to this excellent harbor under power an easy matter. The swimming is as good as this section of the Sound affords. The water in the lagoon is, at least in early June, much warmer than on the outer beach.

On a recent visit we wanted to learn more about restrictions within the basin, so we visited Coast Guardsman Richard Rose up at his station to relay them on to our fellow yachtsmen: Don't anchor anywhere in the channel and note that the white can buoys at the head of the harbor are reserved for Coast Guard personnel only. The pumping of heads is forbidden unless they are chemically treated. Boats should anchor no closer than 150 feet apart, and no rafting is allowed. Since the land surrounding the basin is the private property of the trustees of the Henry Morgan estate, an Asharoken town ordinance rules that no one can venture ashore.

The most peaceful anchorage in mud bottom can be found up along the western shore, preferably in the northwestern section of the basin where the 10-foot spot appears on the chart. But once you are anchored, prepare for heavy wakes from mission-bound Coast Guard rescue craft, which often bolt from the basin like so many midget PT boats attacking at flank speed. On one of our visits here, a line squall, packing up to 50-knot winds, with stinging rain, came screaming across the basin, turning it into a seething caldron. But the fleet there rode it out safely in relative protection.

As a refuge during thick weather, however, this cove is impossible for rest and relaxation because of the proximity (only a few yards away) of the Eatons Neck Point fog signal. We were shown around the station and reminded that the following lighthouses, formerly operated by Eatons Neck Point by remote control, are now completely automated: Penfield Reef, Stratford Point, Stratford Shoal, Greens Ledge, and Great Captain's Island. Eatons Neck is reportedly the fourth-busiest Coast Guard station in the United States, behind only Miami; Cape May, New Jersey; and San Francisco. Looking backward, this station was opened in 1792 by order of President George Washington.

The official historian of the United States Coast Guard, Robert Scheina, estimates that about 1,000 lighthouses still stand along our nation's coasts. About 500 of these are still operated by the Coast Guard.

The future of these historic beacons, victims of efficiency and new technology, appears not totally bleak, however. During the past several years, almost 100 have reportedly been saved from destruction by concerned individuals, public agencies, and private corporations. With such support, many lighthouses will fortunately be preserved as examples of our maritime heritage for future generations.

As if to keep up with the Eatons Neck station, the 100-year-old Stratford Shoals Lighthouse, in the middle of the Sound about 5 miles north of Port Jefferson, has installed the nation's first solar cell-powered RAMOS weather station, reporting meteorological data leading to improved weather forecasts in an area heavily used by commercial and recreational shipping.

Northport Basin, Northport, Long Island, New York (12365). This small basin is nostalgically known as the Asharoken Beach Sand Hole, located at the eastern end of Asharoken Beach, which rims the easterly shore of Eatons Neck. It's identified as Northport Basin on the chart and is used only as a harbor of refuge.

The route to the basin is easily identified by a power plant with four 610-foot smokestacks. An elevated mooring platform, for off-loading oil, is out in the Sound about 1¹/₂ miles due north of the basin's entrance.

Mooring buoys with flashing lights mark each end of the platform. There is also a fog signal.

As you approach the entrance, there are large sand cliffs and private lighted and unlighted buoys. Jetties mark the eastern and western sides of the entry channel, which is about 12 feet deep. Run in parallel to the east jetty, avoiding the dangerous rock at the end of the west jetty to starboard. Once inside, be sure to keep away from the plant's concrete docks to port, where currents often swirl. Minimum depth throughout the area is 7 feet at MLW. Your best anchorage is in the small bight to starboard, well out of the narrow main channel. A fine launching ramp runs to the shore nearby.

It is still an intriguing place, much of its old charm lost by the installation of the power plant to meet the needs of an expanding population. The nearest source of supplies is at Northport, about 1½ miles away.

This harbor is the easternmost of a number of harbors on the North Shore of Long Island, from Manhasset Bay to the Asharoken Beach Sand Hole. Eastward, the shore is far less hospitable to cruising vessels, with Port Jefferson, Mount Sinai, and Mattituck Inlet the only available ports between this harbor of refuge and Greenport.

Port Jefferson, Long Island, New York (12362). Few yachtsmen who have cruised Long Island Sound have failed to visit "Port Jeff," and many of them have stopped there more than once. It is an ideal place for a yacht-club cruise to rendezvous. It is large and deep enough for a good-sized fleet; it is completely landlocked; all kinds of supplies are conveniently available; and it offers railway connections to New York, as well as ferry connections across the Sound to Bridgeport. And—another major point—except for Mount Sinai Harbor, where there are few supplies, it is the last port on the Long Island shore, as you head eastward, until Mattituck is reached 25 miles away. And Mattituck has its limitations, so that for some cruising yachts the nearest good Long Island harbor is at Greenport, 52 miles away. The chief trouble with Port Jeff is its size, making it far from snug when the wind blows from the wrong direction.

In approaching Port Jefferson from any direction, it is wise to keep offshore and watch the chart carefully, as there are outlying rocks and shoals. The entrance is narrow and there is apt to be a strong tidal current in or out. An experienced cruising man warns that:

Sometimes a really dangerous sea makes up outside and between the jetties on an ebb tide against strong northerly or northwesterly winds. Entering under such conditions is possible, provided proper care is taken, but leaving is attended by risk. I have seen many vessels trying to leave get completely out of control between the jetties in high seas, and strongly recommend that all vessels in harbor during a strong northwester not attempt to leave until the tide floods.

Another experienced cruiser feels that this is too strong a statement. Suffice it to say, treat it with respect.

For convenience to docks and supplies the best anchorage is along the eastern shore off the piers, where there is ample protection except in a hard northwester. In that eventuality one can run toward the "Sand Hole," often called Mount Misery Cove, just inside the harbor entrance to the east. This is protected perfectly on all sides, but is a long way from supplies. Fessenden Blanchard went in there many years ago on the brigantine *Yankee,* which drew 9 feet. To enter the Sand Hole, make southward for green flashing bell 5, leave it to port, and then head for the bluff rising from the entrance's starboard shore. Follow close along the piers south of the entrance while favoring the starboard shore until about one-third of the way in. Then you can bear off to port, anchoring in the northeastern sector of the hole under the steep sandbank there. One must be careful in the hole, however, for it is filling in and offers poor holding ground. The chart shows "spoils area" at the entrance and central part, so it may be filling in faster than one would otherwise expect. A sunken barge just below the surface at low water has been reported in the bight to the southeast. An alternative anchorage is in the lee of the outer beaches, and particularly at a spot about 500 yards east of the main channel just south of the sandspit. Swimming is not advised in the hole.

Although many boats like to anchor in the lee of Old Field Beach, it is wise to keep well offshore, avoiding the various shoal spots shown on the chart. The bottom here is mud. In southerlies and westerlies, a possible anchorage is off the northeast shore of Strongs Neck if one avoids the 5-foot shoal in the center of the bight. The *Coast Pilot* warns that strangers should not attempt to enter the narrow channel leading westward to Conscience Bay, for treacherous bars and rocks are there. But we are not the only ones who have enjoyed anchoring in the peaceful and pretty gunk hole just beyond the narrows. Favor the starboard shore going through until you approach a small sandy beach close to the 2-foot mark appearing on the chart. Then swing over to mid-channel and slightly favor the port shore going in. With lovely homes and marshes surrounding us, the only nautical neighbor we had was a 40-foot sloop, whose skipper must obviously know his way around these parts.

For those anchoring in the main harbor and wishing to go ashore for supplies or a good meal, the prominent pier farthest to the east is the dock of the Setauket Yacht Club, whose former floating clubhouse, the old ferryboat *Newport*, proved unsatisfactory. The club has 6 feet MLW dockside and a white dockhouse. There are guest moorings for transient yachts, and their launch, monitoring VHF-68, runs from 8 A.M. to 10 P.M. Established in 1959, this club has an active junior sailing program and has built an attractive new clubhouse overlooking the harbor. A work program was initiated in its early days requiring every member to put in ten hours of maintenance work or pay $40 dues.

The next pier to the west is called Bayles Dock Marina at Danfords Inn—(516) 928-5200 ext. 123, or VHF-9 and 71—catering solely to transients and with a 40-foot-tall white heron at the eastern end of the outlying dock. Check in with the dockmaster at the large center building dockside and pick up his "Welcome Packet." Bayles has gas, diesel fuel, ice, showers, a laundromat, and electricity. Danfords Inn Restaurant, specializing in seafood, is right on the waterside with its Take-Out Chandlery ready to prepare a variety of provisions for you to bring aboard. A free dinghy tie-up is available here for your convenience. The Danfords complex is one of the bright, new developments along the waterfront.

The next dock to the west belongs to the Bridgeport & Port Jefferson Steamboat Company, with ferries like the *Grand Republic* operating across the Sound several times a day during the summer season. This is the sixth in a line of ferries dating back to the 1880s when P. T. Barnum started the business. He wintered his circus animals in Port Jefferson and had to shuttle them across the Sound to and from Bridgeport.

At the next dock to the west are the yellow Port Jeff Launch Service boats, providing service to their many moorings in the harbor. Call (516) 331-2049 or VHF-68 to obtain a mooring or a launch. At the same dock and also painted a brilliant yellow are boats of the Port Jeff Marine Maintenance Company—(516) 473-6416, VHF-68. They do most of the repair work in the harbor by coming to your boat. They also have a shore facility a couple of miles inland and means for getting your boat there.

The location of the Port Jefferson Town Marina is identified on the chart and can also be sighted from seaward by lining up on two range lights—one on the outer dock and the other atop a small white observation tower inland. Here you can find gas, diesel fuel, a pumpout facility, and slips with electricity within the inner basins in approximately 7 feet low water. For reservations, phone (516) 331-3567.

That attractive brick building in the southwest corner of the harbor is the clubhouse of the Port Jefferson Yacht Club. It has moorings, launch service, a dock with 5-foot depth, a bar, showers, and several slips. The club can be reached on VHF-68. In coming up to its main dock, we add one note of caution to prevent possible stranding. Note the string of barges just to the northwest of the club. Since these mark the deepest water, be sure to keep them close aboard as you make your approach. White and orange buoys run outside the club's dock to prevent boats from anchoring beyond them and to keep a channel open for the barges. On our latest visit here, we were welcomed by former Commodores Ed Williams and Pierre Hahn who told us of their expansion plans. Other yachtsmen have reported equally warm receptions here.

Port Jefferson was widely known as a shipbuilding center in the nineteenth and early twentieth centuries, and somewhat less known as a bootlegging center during Prohibition. Formerly known as Drowned Meadow because of tidal flooding, Port Jefferson is rich in history. It has an abundance of interesting shops and restaurants and provides a variety of places to stay. All are within walking distance of the harbor.

For nautical needs, Gudzik's Marine is just across Route 25A from the Port Jefferson Yacht Club. They provide engine repair services and have a dock nearby with a hauling capability. Caraftis Marine, a block away, has fishing equipment and a selection of fiberglass and rubber dinghies.

Accommodations are available at: the Compass Rose, a bed and breakfast only a short walk west on 25A; the Harborside Inn, a motel adjacent to Gudzik's Marine; and the picturesque Danfords Inn & Restaurant, located directly on the harbor next to the ferry.

Most of the shops and restaurants are within a five-square-block area in Lower Port Jefferson Village. The shops are many and varied. On West Broadway we have the Yuppy Puppy, a pet store, while around the corner on Main Street is the Pindar Wine Shop, offering tastings and sales of their Long Island wines. Moore's Market, a gourmet takeout shop, and a specialty yogurt shop are not far away. Chocolate, cookies,

Italian ices, books, art, clocks, clothing, and antiques are among the other wares offered by the local stores.

The Mather House Museum on Prospect Street is home to the local historical society and offers a view of Port Jefferson's past.

Port Jefferson has many fine restaurants. Some, such as Port Wind, Lutzens, Danfords, The Steam Room, and Noodles, have harbor views. Most take advantage of the local abundance of seafood. Pasta may be had at many of the restaurants, but the Village Pasta Company and Pasta Pasta feature these popular dishes. The Printer's Devil has a pub-type atmosphere and is a good bet for a hamburger as well as steaks and seafood. Harrington's is a restaurant that features jazz every night—and for a taste of Spain, Costa de España. The diversity of the eating places is remarkable—and this is only a sample. Furthermore, if you continue up Main Street to the top of the hill, you arrive at Port Jefferson Station where the Long Island Railroad has a terminal. Here you can find Zorba, a Greek restaurant, and Hana, featuring Japanese cuisine.

Also on the heights overlooking the harbor you will find two primary-care, community-oriented hospitals, St. Charles and Mather.

As you depart from Port Jefferson, take a look at the steep bluffs along Old Field Point to the west. They are being eaten up by erosion at a critical rate. A study undertaken by scientists of the Marine Sciences Center of the State University of New York at Stony Brook reveals the areas in Suffolk County where the most rapid erosion is taking place: Old Field Point receding 5.2 feet a year, Crane Neck Point at 2.6 feet, and Miller Place and an area near Orient Point each with 2 feet receding per year. Widening the protective beaches along the foot of these bluffs is the best natural barrier to this alarming cliffside erosion.

Setauket, Port Jefferson, Long Island, New York (12362).

Picturesque Setauket Harbor may be reached by following a dredged 150-foot channel winding west from nun 2 between Tinkers Point and Strongs Neck. The latest *Coast Pilot* reports shoaling in this channel with "a depth of about $2^{1}/_{2}$ feet MLW in 1981 available in the channel all the way to the boatyard at Setauket." The entrance is easily identified from Port Jefferson Harbor by the high wooded bluff that marks the northeast point on Strongs Neck. Since the harbor is also quite shallow, boats of deep draft should not attempt to enter except at high tide and under power. There is a mean range of tide of about $6^{1}/_{2}$ feet, and it is wise to keep in mid-channel away from the mud flats extending from both shores.

Once well past the shoaling at Tinkers Point and heading due south, you will have good water for ¹/₂-mile length in mid-channel until you come abeam of the Setauket Harbor Boat Basin down on the port shore. This inner, very narrow channel is poorly marked by buoys or ranges, some of them uncharted and privately maintained. One often has to wend one's way among the congested boats at their private moorings, since they actually mark the deepest water. One may have difficulty in locating sufficient swinging room in which to drop the hook.

Since dredged channels have a way of filling, we'd advise caution and a flooding tide for yachts entering this harbor for the first time. If your boat doesn't draw too much, however, Setauket is worth trying.

Once you get into the deep area south of Strongs Neck, you will probably be glad you came. It is much snugger than Port Jeff, and

Mt. Sinai, looking toward Cedar Beach. *Aero Graphics Corp.*

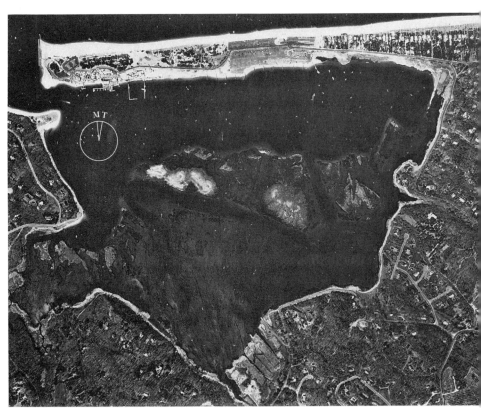

attractive. There is a small boatyard on the east shore of the shallow cove to the south, which can be reached only at high tide.

Mount Sinai, Long Island, New York (12362). This harbor, about $2^1/_2$ miles east of Port Jefferson, is recommended for those who like an evening "away from it all," especially if you have a sailing tender or one with an outboard motor for exploring the shallow inner harbor. The channel entrance can be spotted at the easternmost end of a long high bluff running along the northern shore of Mount Misery Point. Enter carefully midway between the short jetties, which are usually awash at high water. The one to the east normally has a flashing light on it. Attempting to negotiate this channel at night without this vital beacon lighting the way is risky business, as has been confirmed to us by Mount Sinai Yacht Club officers. A helpful guide to the helmsman during daylight, however, in making a center line approach between the jetties is the existence of a large red-and-white ball buoy situated approximately $^1/_4$ mile off the channel's entrance. This dredged channel, in which the current runs up to 2 knots, has a controlling depth of 8 feet. And the narrow inlet that used to run behind the sandspit to starboard has completely filled in.

Mount Sinai Harbor has undergone quite a change in recent years due to sizable dredging throughout the northern sector of the harbor. Dredging has been completed on a 10-foot-deep channel with a constant width of 1,200 feet running eastward all the way from the main entrance channel and passing south of Cedar Beach to the marshes bordering the harbor's eastern shore. Unlighted green buoys maintained by the town mark this channel, in which a speed limit of 5 mph is strictly enforced. A possible anchorage, therefore, is anywhere you can find swinging room along the southern side of this dredged trough, but most yachtsmen prefer to anchor along the prominent but small spit just southeast of the harbor's entrance.

In 1964 this harbor was blessed by the establishment of a new yacht club—the Mount Sinai Yacht Club, located on the southwestern point of Cedar Beach. The Mount Sinai Yacht Club has continued to grow through the efforts of its membership, which prides itself on the fact that most of the work is done during work parties. The clubhouse was created out of a retired barge which was hauled ashore by the membership and converted into a charming clubhouse with a dramatic view of the harbor. The clubhouse has a restaurant and bar within and a large deck outside.

The membership puts together many social events throughout the year, ranging from clambakes to cocktail parties and many events for children and young adults.

In 1991 the Mount Sinai Yacht Club opened up its new marina facility in front of the clubhouse, with 100 new floating slips and a new gas/diesel pumping facility. Visiting yachtsmen are always welcome to visit the club and will find the dockage rates to be very reasonable and the membership to be warm and friendly. Visitors should tie up and inquire within the clubhouse or contact the club on VHF-9. The Yacht Club lies between two boatyards, where repairs and parts can be obtained. Local restaurants and the quaint village of Port Jefferson are only a short taxi ride away.

Visiting yachtsmen will be welcomed by Commodore Ken Laucella and the officers and members, who will be happy to assist them in any way they can. We thank Past Commodore John Thompson for this update on his club.

Beyond to port lies the Mount Sinai Marina, which with its 8 floating docks, proves that powerboats have discovered Mount Sinai. This site is choked with local small craft, is brightly lighted at night, and is no source for supplies. For repair work, you can put into Old Man's Boatyard, located just beyond can 11 on the port shore.

The balance of the harbor is covered with shoal mud flats and marshes, which are often dry at low water. Despite these, Mount Sinai is crowded on weekends, for the place is picturesque and away from the lights and sounds of a town, and the swimming on Cedar Beach is excellent. The land to the west is high, wooded, with many private estates.

A delightful old fisherman with a personality as salty as his looks, who did not give us his name "less the police seek me out," warned us to avoid the uncharted rocks that lie 1/2 mile off Cedar Beach.

Mattituck Inlet, Long Island, New York (12358). During World War II, this harbor was so long neglected that by 1946 a bar with only 1 foot at low water had built up between the outer jetties. Since then, the federal government has often redredged the channel, designated as a port of refuge, and added further improvements to help make the harbor an outstanding one. It is the only available harbor on the north shore of Long Island between Port Jefferson or Mount Sinai and Greenport, making it particularly important to yachtsmen cruising Long Island Sound. More and more boats are visiting here, since it offers excellent

Mattituck Inlet, revealing its 1.8 mile length, ending in the turning basin at Mattituck.
Aero Graphics Co.

protection should sudden storms or foul weather arise. Once you get inside, the harbor provides absolute shelter and a chance to get supplies conveniently, and it is an interesting place withal.

The 1992 *Coast Pilot* reports that, "from a survey taken in 1987 in Mattituck, the controlling depth was 4 feet (6 feet at mid-channel) from the entrance for about 1.8 miles to the turning basin at Mattituck with 7 feet available in the basin." Privately maintained floats and stakes string along the entire channel marking the deepest water. The mean tide range is about 5 feet.

The entrance to Mattituck Inlet is not easy to identify from some distance away, as the breakwaters, though long, are low. The shore is a low point of white sand between fairly high hills and cliffs on both sides. A long break in the bluffs marks the inlet, further identified by a flashing beacon silhouetted against the prominent tanks of the Mattituck Petroleum Corporation. Entering is difficult should you have a northerly wind and the 3-knot tidal current running against you. Pick gong buoy 3A and then head for the tower on the starboard or west jetty, which has a flashing light. Can 1 facing this light should be held close to port coming in, for swirling currents have built up extensive shoals stretching out into the channel from the western breakwater. When you reach a point halfway up the entrance channel between the two jetties, keep an eye open for two red "lobster-pot" buoys. These mark some rocks located along the eastern side of the channel so be careful to keep them well to your port on entering. Also watch for shoals farther in to port, especially as you approach the first bend. Inside the inlet you will also see a sign that reads, "Non-resident boats must tie up at a Commercial Marina or anchor in the Federal Anchorage at the head of the creek." No anchorage is permitted elsewhere!

In coming up the creek, you may find some dock space but almost no "people" facilities at the Mattituck Fishing Station & Marina—(516) 298-8886, VHF-58—a short way up on the starboard side, or dock at the Old Mill Inn—(516) 298-8080, VHF-68—with 18 feet MLW and giving priority to diners. Mattituck Inlet Marina and Shipyard—(516) 298-4480, VHF-68—just above the bridge, has a swimming pool, gas, diesel fuel, ice, slips with electricity, repair work, and the most complete services in the harbor.

The MATT-A-MAR Marina—(516) 298-4739, VHF-68—is on the eastern shore at the head of the harbor, with 8 feet MLW at some of the slips, gas, diesel, ice, pool, a short walk to the village, the Touch of Venice restaurant with snack bar, and a tree-shaded, grassy picnic area. It's a really nice destination for a family with young children.

The Mattituck Park District Marina at the head of the channel has a landing dock, with 6 feet of water, only a short walk from the center of the village. The basin here lies in quite charming surroundings, with an atmosphere one could describe as homey. On a summer weekend, this spot attracts as many as fifty boats resting at anchor, with more at dockside, where the depths are 6 feet MLW. Although there is considerable seaweed in the basin, the holding ground is reported to be good, providing the anchor is well set in. Use plenty of scope; then take up on the rode. The harbormaster is stationed at this marina, where there's an opportunity for a shower, brief dockage, and a possible mooring. Nearby stores include Raynor & Suter, offering a complete line of nautical equipment, a bank, a pharmacy, a market, a deli, a U.S. post office, and what you will. For a meal you can phone nearby Villa D'oro or Coach Stoppe for transportation. The Coffee Pot is best for breakfast. Most of these places are open on Sundays.

Stuart MacMillan, a former harbormaster we met here years ago, sold Gideon Bibles very successfully in his free time. Perhaps that's why we listened so intently when he gave us a local fisherman's advice, which we couldn't resist putting into verse:

> When sailing by Long Island Shore,
> A storm approaching from the nor'
> A rising tide will drive away;
> If *falling* tide, make port and pray!

Less than twenty-four hours later, the weather gave us the chance to test its veracity. After being holed up safe and sound in Mount Sinai during a violent thunder squall, all we can say is that it works!

On your walk to town for any supplies you cannot obtain here, you will be surprised to come across something least expected—a tank museum whose owner must obviously be a tank and armored-vehicle buff. He has parked his ironclad "behemoths" in his private "armory" of regulation Army green where they may be seen by the curious on Sunday afternoons. Perhaps, after all, Mattituck does deserve the claim that it is "the village that has everything."

Plum Gut Harbor, Plum Island, New York (13209). This is a scooped-out puddle, nearly landlocked, with about 14 feet in the entrance and harbor, though some shoaling has occurred. Keep midway between the lighted jetties, equipped with a fog signal, and head for the wharves, where yachts seeking shelter usually lie. Plum Gut Harbor and the island itself are under the supervision of the U.S. Department of Agriculture, which maintains there its Animal Disease Laboratory, "the nation's only research center for the study of contagious foreign animal diseases." Shore visits are only by permission of the local representative of that department, as suggested in the following tactful reply to our inquiry: "Ferry or government boats use the wharf daily. Harbor would be sought by yachtsmen only as a harbor of refuge."

A correspondent, writing about Potter Cove in Narragansett Bay, says, "The mosquitoes are bad but not as bad as at Plum Island."

It is reported that Plum Island got its name from early explorers who were enchanted by the beach plums growing along the shore. In 1659 the ruling Indian chief of Long Island sold this island to the first European owner for a coat, a barrel of biscuits, and one hundred fishhooks.

Plum Gut is a vicious piece of water, where seven currents come together and form a tide rip that can run as high as 10 knots. Although larger vessels stay to the outside of Plum Island, smaller craft heading for Peconic Bay or the south shore of Long Island must traverse the Gut.

Plum Island Light, a beacon to mariners since 1897, is deactivated and now shows an automated flashing white light. The familiar stone house, dating back to 1869, stands 75 feet above sea level at the northwestern point of the 850-acre island. In 1989, the last five manned lighthouses in the First Coast Guard District became automated. These include the stations at Ambrose Light, Watch Hill, New London Ledge, Montauk Point, and Coney Island.

Meanwhile, Orient Point Light, or the "Coffee Pot," is now the primary navigational aid. Standing 65 feet above sea level, Orient Point Light shows a 5-second flashing white light with a range of 16 miles.

Whenever the going gets rough, the only visual bearings you can now expect bracketing the Gut are the Orient Point Light and, if you can pick them up, the two jetty lights at the entrance to Plum Gut Harbor.

Shelter Island and Shelter Island Sound, Long Island, New York (12358). Shelter Island is best known as a delightful summer resort of wooded hills, winding roads, and snug harbors, with a year-round population of about 2,000 and a summer population several times that number. It is a connecting link between the north and south flukes of

Shelter Island looking northwest. Counter clockwise from Mashomack Point in lower left lies Majors Harbor; Smith Cove and West Neck Harbor. At the top of the photograph Dering Harbor faces Greenport and on the right can be seen Coecles Harbor and its entrance. *Skyviews Survey Inc.*

eastern Long Island. With its five harbors, each providing its own special charm, the island has long been a popular rendezvous for Long Island Sound cruising people.

Though not settled by whites until 1652, Shelter Island, which the Indians called "Ahaquatawamock," had several English owners before then, from whom it successively acquired the names of "Mr. Farrett's Island" and "Mr. Goodyear's Island." In 1651, Mr. Goodyear sold the island for "1,600 pounds of good merchantable Muscavado sugar"— which has been calculated at a valuation of 1¢ an acre, based on the price of sugar at that time. Over 150 years ago, ships large enough to cross the ocean with a fair-sized cargo were built on Shelter Island, on a tributary of West Neck Creek.

The principal whaling ports on the Atlantic Coast were Province-town, Nantucket, New Bedford, Fairhaven, New London, and Sag Harbor. Many young men of Shelter Island sailed from the last of these harbors. Whales have been seen or caught between Shelter Island and Greenport.

Eventually Shelter Island became a summer resort, the new era beginning in 1871, when a group of Methodists began to hold annual camp meetings. A year later a hotel went up. Now sportfishing and summer visitors are leading industries.

Just before his death in 1929, Samuel H. Groser wrote a poem about Shelter Island, called "My Playland," in which (in the second verse) he expressed his "poignant longing":

> For the wonderful view from its headlands,
> For the clear, cool, starry nights,
> For the gorgeous hues of the sunsets,
> And the harbor with myriad lights;
> For the shady roads through the woodlands,
> For the green on the Dering side,
> For Ram Head, and White Hill, and the beaches,
> For the lap of the lazy tide.*

Although we found the tide anything but lazy, to the rest of these sentiments we would add a hearty assent.

---

*Historical data and verse from *History of Shelter Island*, by Ralph G. Duvall, with a supplement by Jean L. Schladermundt (Shelter Island Heights Association).

There are two ferry services to and from Shelter Island: one between Greenport and Dering Harbor on the northwest shore, and one from the south shore of the island at Smith Cove to North Haven Peninsula and Sag Harbor.

In discussing the harbors on, or across from, Shelter Island, we'll first go around Shelter Island via Shelter Island Sound in a counterclockwise direction. Those who want to go farther, into Great and Little Peconic Bays, will find the harbors on these bays covered in the Peconic Bays section.

1. Greenport, Long Island, New York (12358). This is the leading port in the Shelter Island Sound area from the point of view of boatyards, gas docks, marine hardware, and general facilities of all kinds. But it is by no means the most beautiful, and it is noted more as a fishing headquarters than as a rendezvous for yacht-club fleets.

As you approach the town in daylight, the white church spire near its northern end and the standpipe that shows up over the center are good landmarks; at night, the best reference is a television tower with a fixed red light, identified on the chart. The flashing red Greenport Harbor Light, on the end of the breakwater off Youngs Point, is the most obvious guide for those entering the harbor after dark.

Although many boats anchor southwest of the breakwater, this anchorage is frequently very uneasy, since the water is apt to be choppy along here and there is a considerable sweep from the southwest. The best place for the night by far is in Stirling Basin, which has been dredged to a depth of 8 feet at low water. Buoys mark the edges of the basin's shoal area. Since this harbor is tight for space and has considerable boating traffic, anchoring is not recommended. It is better to follow up the 100-foot-wide channel with 9-foot depth leading up to the head of the basin. In the western fork is situated the rather swanky Townsend Manor Marina, boasting an attractive Colonial-style hotel and restaurant and offering weary crews a dip into the swimming pool or into a cocktail. Use of the pool is included in the dockage fee. Their services also include gas, ice, water, showers, and fifty slips with electrical connections and a mechanic on call. This marina provides peaceful protection and the opportunity to visit the center of town, only a fifteen-minute walk away. They can be reached by telephone at (516) 477-2000 or on VHF-9. Just to the south along the basin's shore you'll pass Greg's Seafood, formerly Pell's Fish Market, an excellent source for the freshest of seafood.

The most impressive marina in Stirling Basin is the Stirling-By-The-Sea Marina, which claims to be one of the finest and most immaculate on the East Coast. It assures its visitors security and tranquility within a 10-acre parklike setting at the end of the eastern fork. The facilities are just too numerous to list here; these are just a few: complete dock service including gas, diesel fuel, and ice; showers; laundromat; pumpout facility; fixed docks and finger slips for yachts up to 85 feet with 10-foot depth alongside; a freshwater swimming pool; and the elegant Boathouse Restaurant, affording a panoramic view of the harbor. All types of repair work can be undertaken; there's even a bubbling system, for the marina is open all year round. Bike rentals and, nearby, a golf course, tennis courts, a riding stable, and picnic grounds all help make this a great spot for family fun. Slip reservations should be made at least twenty-four hours in advance of arrival by phoning (516) 477-0828. There are no supplies near here.

Also in the basin, just southeast of this marina, is a marked channel leading to Brewer Yacht Yard at Greenport. Here is one of the more recent additions to the Brewer family of yacht yards. With two 20-ton travelifts, Brewer's is fully capable of accommodating boats in excess of 40 feet with full-time, professional repair personnel on hand. Transient yachts are also welcomed here for overnight dockage.

There are several large shipyards along the Greenport waterfront between Stirling Basin and the ferry slip. Greenport Yacht and Shipbuilding in this area is well equipped to do all kinds of work. Along the bight west of the ferry slip can be bought gas and diesel fuel.

Nearby, the town, resembling a slice of New England, furnishes a wide variety of everything, including marine hardware, charts, and antiques and paintings in a fascinating store run by S. T. Preston & Son since 1888. The oldest family-owned restaurant in the United States, Claudio's Restaurant and Marina at the foot of Main Street, has a fine reputation among cruising yachtsmen, due in part to its succulent seafood and ocean-fresh lobster. To the west, Mitchell's Marina & Restaurant is a bit less expensive and formal but also provides dock space to its patrons. It's close to a fishing supply store and market. At both these places we were told that "you don't have to climb into any fancy dress to eat here." Such an open invitation reminded us of how a dedicated Greenport fisherman once admonished a roving reporter with these salty words: "You want cocktail parties, you head on over to the Southside. You wanna be yourself, you stay over here on the North Fork." So far as we know, there is no important yacht club on the Greenport waterfront; the nearest is across Shelter Island Sound at Dering Harbor.

Greenport has direct rail connection with New York City; Cross Sound Ferry Services, Inc., operates a ferry daily between Orient Point and New London. First called Stirling, then Greenhill, and finally named Greenport in the early nineteenth century, this is a splendid place to meet guests, fit out, leave the boat for a while, or enjoy the bustling, boaty atmosphere. It's one of the few places left on the East Coast where you can see commercial fishing trawlers unload their catch.

Northeast toward Orient Point lies Gull Pond, set between Youngs Point and Cleaves Point. It is a secure basin for craft drawing 3 feet or less; a launching ramp is at the entrance. Although the chart shows a depth of 6 feet in the 35-foot narrow entrance between the jetties, only about 4 feet can be carried over an outer bar at low water. Once inside, however, the controlling depth throughout most of the pond is 10 feet MLW. But be sure to stay at least 40 feet off the marshes running along the port shore. The private moorings should also be given wide berth when dropping anchor here. Part of this place's charm comes from its snugness, its lack of commercialism, and the attractive appearance of the private homes gathered along the eastern shore. Two creeks running north from the pond have been dredged to good depths for further gunkholing. The northwest channel leading to a smaller hole is preferable to the one that stretches more northward.

2. Dering Harbor, Shelter Island, New York (12358). If you want to see a fine-looking collection of sailing yachts, you will find them at Dering Harbor at almost any time during the summer months. They may be there for Off Soundings or Storm Trysail races, a Corinthian cruise, or perhaps an American Yacht Club rendezvous, or just a lot of handsome yachts following their own inclinations. The harbor is attractive, and the Shelter Island Yacht Club, on the point to starboard of the entrance, is most hospitable to members of other recognized yacht clubs. The clubhouse has a restaurant and bar accommodating 210 people.

The only objection to Dering Harbor is that it is very uncomfortable in northwesters. The Essex Station of the Cruising Club of America moved to Stirling Basin at Greenport for that reason. However, the protection is good with winds from all other directions, and we have stayed there many times in complete comfort, usually finding friends among the fleet, savoring the keen enjoyment that comes from watching yachts coming in to find anchorage while we were already well fixed for the night.

In entering, be sure to stay well off the northern tip of Shelter Island Heights, where shoaling to 4 feet has been reported. At night, the club can be sighted by the three vertical lights running up its flagpole and by a red light placed at the eastern end of its dock. Depths throughout the harbor are ample, though behind the yacht-club hook of land the chart shows 4 feet, and the area here is too small, anyway, to offer protection to many yachts in northwesters.

The Shelter Island Yacht Club, which celebrated its centennial in 1986, has always had its social side, but its chief emphasis has been continually on yachting and yacht racing. On July 14, 1886, it was incorporated with an active membership of 26 and an initiation fee and annual dues of $5 each.

The club offers guest moorings for a charge with launch service running from 8 A.M. to 8 P.M. on weekdays and from 8 A.M. to 10:30 P.M. on weekends. We have found the holding ground to be excellent.

Gas, diesel fuel, water, block ice, showers, a laundromat, a pumpout system, a shore meal, and supplies, including spirits, can all be obtained at the head of the harbor at Piccozzi's Dering Harbor Marina, located to the north of Chases Creek. This marina, monitoring VHF-9, has 25 slips, with 10 feet at its dock. Nearby are tennis courts and the Dory Restaurant, dishing up tasty seafood at moderate prices. For repairs, contact Coecles Harbor Marina and they will send you immediate help. Just to the east, the festive Dering Harbor Inn provides a pier where you can tie up for a meal. Boats can tie up at the town dock at two-hour intervals.

You can also stretch your sea legs by visiting historic Chequit Inn, enjoying the sights along the way. From the yacht club walk up Chequit Avenue and take a second left. You will pass by charming houses, quaint little shops, and The Cook, a popular restaurant featuring a continental menu.

Dering Harbor also provides easy access by ferry to Greenport. A short hike, again straight up Chequit Avenue, will bring you to the landing where a ferry departs every twenty minutes. The last trip returning to the island leaves Greenport at 12:30 P.M.

The harbor is named for Thomas Dering, a well-known Boston merchant, who married a Shelter Island woman named Mary Sylvester and took up residence there in 1760. He became a leading citizen, serving as supervisor of Shelter Island, and after the Revolution was instrumental in helping the islanders regain property occupied by the British.

3. Southold, Long Island, New York (12358). In Southold Bay, across from Jennings Point, are three marinas all in fairly shallow water. The most easterly one is the Brick Cove Marina (516) 477-0830— formerly Young's Boatyard and Marina, located in the inlet just to the east of Mill Creek and close by the charted stack on Conkling Point. A short distance to the west is the Mill Creek Inn Marina—(516) 765-1010—with restaurant, heads and showers, numerous slips, and $4^1/2$ feet of water. The name appears on the roof of the restaurant, and the entrance is right by the charted stack southeast of Hashamomuck Pond. Just to the west is the extensive Port of Egypt Marina—(516) 765-2445—with many slips, a large marine store, engine repair service 7 days a week, and Armando's Seafood Barge restaurant. Enter through the privately maintained buoys just west of those for the Mill Creek Inn, and swing to port around the sandy island to the marina. They report 5 feet MLW. The accent in all these marinas is on power, but there are some sailboats too.

In checking our latest charts at the time of writing, we noted that there was $6^1/2$ feet at MLW at the channel entrance to Southold, that Jockey Creek carried 6 feet for the most part down the middle, and that Town Creek showed about a foot more of depth all the way to its head. These depths are good for a width of about 75 feet except for the reported shoaling in Town Creek to $4^1/2$ feet at low water. The harbor entrance is marked not only by a prominent white tower inland to port and small red and green buoys but by bulkheads and sandy beaches to both port and starboard. Uncharted red and black vertical stakes clearly identify the channel, which is rimmed by extremely shoal water. Make your approach from due east and you will not run into trouble. At the docks, just inside to starboard, the depths are not greater than in the channel.

These docks on Founders Landing offer you the deepest water at any marina in Southold and belong to Goldsmith's Boat Shop, which provides gas, water, electricity, and telephone, besides repairs, hauling, and limited dockage. You will have plenty of neighbors and little privacy if tied up at the dock, and the surroundings of a boatyard are not usually ideal, but this place is well protected. A suitable anchorage may be found up Jockey Creek; or, as we did, run up to the head of Town Creek, which is not only a pleasant spot but extremely convenient to the Southold Town Dock.

The unpretentious Southold Yacht Club is on the northern tip of Paradise Point.

4. West Neck Harbor, Shelter Island, New York (12358). In approaching this harbor from the west and in passing red flasher 16, make sure to avoid the fish weir extending out from Gleason Point.

The entrance to this harbor is very misleading. When you are looking at the chart, it appears that the 4-second flasher R 2 is so close to the end of Shell Beach that there is little or no room at all to leave it to starboard upon entering. However, this channel is not nearly as difficult to negotiate as the chart implies.

In entering the harbor, it is best to take advantage of a rising tide, for the channel has a depth of only 4 feet at low water. The tidal range is about 2 feet. A green can is firmly planted in the sand on the very tip of Shell Beach. There is plenty of water on the channel side of this can, so it is best to favor this side of the channel. Thirty to fifty yards to the northeast lies the flashing 4-second nun, R 2. This nun marks the end of a sandbar that is constantly shifting, so stay far away from R 2 upon entering.

As soon as you pass through the channel, come immediately to port where you will find depths of 20 feet or more. Following along the contour of Shell Beach will keep you in plenty of water and will lead you directly into one of the finest anchorages on Shelter Island.

West Neck Harbor buoy 4, a nun buoy farther on, has also been set in 8 feet of water. Your chart may not reflect these changes. The tidal range is about 2 feet so one may wisely prefer to enter the channel on a rising tide.

After passing these red buoys, keeping them close to starboard, swing slowly to port and run parallel but not too close to Shell Beach. In this way, you will avoid the middle ground to starboard and observe the sign that says "Anchor no closer than 400 feet offshore." After you have run along two-thirds of the length of Shell Beach, swing northwest toward the neck marking the entrance to West Neck Creek. As you pass the neck, be sure to give it a wide berth while avoiding the 4-foot spot in mid-channel just beyond. The entrance can be further identified by a flagpole ahead on the port shore and by a large harbor sign, which should be left to starboard. Having passed all of this, keep generally in the middle. The channel into West Neck Bay has been shoaling in recent years, and latest soundings showed 6 feet at low water where 10 feet appear on the chart.

Those yachts wishing to spend the night at a slip can do so at the Island Boat Yard and Marina. Complete with forty transient slips, electricity, water, showers, pumpout facility, swimming pool, public phones, laundry, and a snack bar, this is West Neck Harbor's only public marina. To reach it, bear to port after passing around the tip of Shell Beach. This will keep you in plenty of deep water. Looking off to starboard, you will see nun 4; keep it off to starboard. Continuing past R 4 in a northwesterly direction will bring you into a well-marked, privately maintained channel with a depth of 6 feet MLW and, before long, The Island Boatyard and Marina located just at the mouth of Menantic Creek. For reservations and additional information, call them on VHF-9 or at (516) 749-3333.

Although in very hot weather it would probably be cooler in the wide part of the lower harbor or in West Neck Bay at the other end, the snuggest and prettiest anchorages are in West Neck Creek in one of the spots where it widens out. A very good place for dropping your hook is in the bight with 5-foot depth just before West Neck Creek turns to the west into West Neck Bay. Here there is a deeply shelving beach for easy landing and a road leading to a store only 3/4 mile away. Farther up on West Neck Bay, the best anchorages are either near the docks along the southeastern shore or on either side of the small point that juts out from the northern shore.

West Neck Harbor is one of the most attractive, unspoiled, and well-protected harbors in the entire Shelter Island–Peconic Bay area. It is unfortunate that the chart depths are so deceptive. With the prevailing tidal difference of about 21/2 feet, sailing yachts drawing no more than 5 feet should have no difficulty in entering, except at low tide. Most motor cruisers will have no trouble at any time if they stick to the channel.

5. Smith Cove, Shelter Island, New York (12358). On southern Shelter Island, this cove offers an attractive anchorage amidst quiet surroundings reminiscent of the coast of Maine. There is a nice beach under a fairly high bluff, and you will find that deep water runs surprisingly close to the shore. It is open to the southeast, but well protected in winds from other directions. A small marina named Shelter Island

Marina & Fishing Station is located on the west shore. Facilities here include: slips, ice, water, electricity, laundromat, and showers. No marine supplies are available, and the nearest grocery store is 2¹/₂ miles away.

For those boats anchoring in the harbor, no trespassing along private shorefront property is permitted. The ferry to North Haven Peninsula and Sag Harbor runs from Smith Cove.

6. Majors Harbor, Shelter Island, New York (12358). About a mile southeast of Smith Cove, Majors Harbor provides the same kind of protection in northerly winds and exposure to the south. On entering the harbor from the north, one should keep well to starboard of the rocks lying off Majors Point and shown on the chart. Spread out before you appears a sandy crescent-shaped beach bordered by a colorful tree line and tall grass. The clear, clean water and smooth bottom will tempt your crew to take a swim in perfect solitude; the romantic appearance of the land calls for a picnic or further adventures along the shore. We were tempted to do so until we noticed signs reading "Beware of dogs. No fishing, hunting or trespassing under penalty of the law." Notice also and keep clear of the long fish weir extending south from the inner shore of Majors Point.

7. Sag Harbor, Long Island, New York (12358). This harbor is well protected from all seas by the breakwater, on the western end of which stands a skeleton tower marked by a flashing green light. The only officially assigned anchorage spot is in the area of the second can near the breakwater at the harbor's entrance. Yachts coming in to anchor must give privately moored boats a wide berth, and no rafting is permitted. The Sag Harbor Yacht Club to the starboard—or west—of where the large oil tanks used to be has no launch service, but all yachtsmen are welcomed whether or not they are affiliated with any yacht club. There is 8 feet at the outer dock and 6 feet in the slips, where gas, water, diesel fuel, ice, and electricity are obtainable. There is a moderate charge for overnight dockage, and although there is no club restaurant, food and supplies may be purchased in the center of town nearby. An excellent launching ramp lies in the small inner basin. The club, founded in 1898, is housed in a trim little blue-and-white building, formerly a New York Yacht Club station on Shelter Island. It was slid over the ice to its new home one wintry day in 1920.

Yachts looking to pick up a mooring should contact the Sag Harbor harbormaster, Doug Beverly, on VHF-9. Mr. Beverly is also in charge of the Sag Harbor Marine Facility which has thirty slips and is located just past the yacht club. Included in this facility is a pretty little park, complete with barbecues. The facility also has electricity, water, and showers. Reservations can be made by phoning (516) 725-2368.

Directly next door to the Sag Harbor Marine Facility is the Waterfront Marina with seventy slips and 10 feet of water at low tide. They can accommodate vessels up to 200 feet in length. Electricity, showers, and ice are available here, but no fuel of any kind. For reservations contact Dockmaster Nancy Haynes on VHF-9 or at (516) 725-3886.

Those vessels requiring repair work should contact Ship Ashore Marina at (516) 725-3755 or the Sag Harbor Yacht Yard at (516) 725-3838. Both monitor VHF-9. Sag Harbor's Information Center, housed in an old windmill at the head of Long Wharf, is a good source of information on what to see and where to eat in this little piece of New England.

Do not attempt to go into Sag Harbor after dark; there are too many outlying shoals and unlighted buoys, especially off the eastern shore of North Haven Peninsula. A particularly dangerous spot is Little Gull Island, formed by a cluster of rocks just south of lighted buoy 13. In daylight, the entrance presents no difficulties. Bayard Hooper of Sag Harbor has written to tell us that when approaching from the east and after passing buoy 9, several people have mistaken the white-and-orange buoy just west of those rocks for a channel marker because in the setting sun they couldn't discern its color and so drove onto the rocks. To be safe, leave lighted buoy 11 to port before heading in to the end of the breakwater.

The channel up into Sag Harbor Cove just west of the main harbor has been dredged to a width of 75 feet and a depth of about 8 feet, and is marked by privately maintained buoys. If you can pass under the fixed bridge with its vertical clearance of 20 feet at mean high water, you will find first to port Whalers Marina, convenient to the center of town. Beyond and to port lies Baron's Cove Marina. There's 8 feet at low water at their outer dock and about 4 feet in the bulkheaded basin. They do have plans however, to increase the depth inside the basin to 6 feet by the summer of 1994. They offer gas (no diesel), water, ice, electricity, snack bar, laundromat, showers, and a swimming pool and can accommodate vessels up to 60 feet in length. Across the street is the Baron's Cove Inn and the Sag Harbor Inn. An IGA market for supplies, closed Sundays, is in a Colonial brick building nearby; a variety of stores and restaurants are grouped along Main Street just beyond. For reservations contact manager George Wunchel on VHF-9 or at (516) 725-3939.

You may wish to venture farther by following the buoyed channel to the west, leading you to Long Beach, where there is excellent swimming on the Noyack Bay side. Although it appears from the chart that 7 feet can be carried around Brush Neck, the deepest water has not been marked, and all we saw were a few small powerboats. Check at Baron's before taking this passage. The area up there is pleasantly surrounded by houses tucked along the shore.

The Indians called this area "Weg-Wag-O-Nock," meaning "foot of the hill." The center of the present village formed their settlement. About 1675, the Narragansett fishermen dug crude shelters out of the sand dunes to the east. From 1707 to 1730, substantial homes were built, and Sag Harbor began to take form. It is now a National Historic Site because it exhibits the second-largest collection of Colonial buildings in the United States.

It is a village of historic firsts. The first weekly newspaper, the first magazine, and the first daily newspaper were printed here on the first printing press on Long Island. The Sag Harbor Express is the oldest newspaper on Long Island, still being printed over on Main Street. The first customhouse in the United States established by an Act of Congress in 1789 is here for tourists to view, and the oldest fire department in New York is housed in a museum open to the public. The first American ship to enter the forbidden ports of Japan in 1845 was the *Manhattan* out of Sag Harbor.

That same year, this port boasted a fleet of sixty-three whaling vessels, ranking it second in size only to New Bedford. Its last whaler, the *Myra*, cleared the harbor in 1871, never to return. Actual relics from those days can now be seen as bluish-white curbstones lining the streets of the village. They provided ballast for the ships. Other tools of the whaling industry and one of the finest collections of scrimshaw to be seen in the country are exhibited at the stately and popular Whaling Museum on the corner of Main and Garden Streets. On our entering the museum, the doorkeeper suggested to us that we "pause for a moment and make a wish for you have just passed through the jawbones of a whale!" This reminded us of a verse from a sea chantey of a whaler who got at least part of his wish.

We've come home as clean as we started out
And we didn't get a whale
We didn't get a bar'l of oil
But we had a damn fine sail!

8. Coecles Harbor, Shelter Island, New York (12358). Recent storms have shifted and narrowed the entrance to the harbor, so extra care is required. Corrective dredging is planned soon. Coecles, pronounced like the word "cockles," is well marked by privately maintained tripods, beacons, and buoys. The best plan is to head in from a point nearly perpendicular to the eastern shore of Ram Island to reach lighted green can 1 about ¹/₂ mile due east of Reel Point. Keep in mid-channel while passing between the red flashing beacon set on the end of the spit to starboard and green can 5 to port. Once well beyond the entrance, steer dead ahead or make a broad swing to port according to where you want to go and the anchorage that provides the best protection from the prevailing wind. Coecles Harbor is large and unfavorable in northeast winds.

The most popular anchorages are as follows: (1) In the first large bight to the south of the entrance. This is very pretty and more "away from it all" than other anchorages. Be sure to clear can 5 before turning to enter this bight. (2) In the first bight to the north after entering. Here some yachts are moored and there are a number of private docks. (3) In the second and third bights to the north. Mooring in the eastern sector of this second bight will bring you, by dinghy and a short walk, to the Ram's Head Inn located on the western end of Big Ram Island. The inn, which permits informal attire, serves excellent food and, in overlooking the harbor, is considered Shelter Island's most beautifully located resort. (4) At the dock with 5¹/₂ feet MLW or on the moorings of the full-service Coecles Harbor Marina & Boatyard, located on the upper western shore of the harbor, just beyond a small island.

The marina provides most required services for boat and sailor. The dockmaster monitors VHF-9 from 8 A.M. to 6 P.M. They have hauling capabilities and full-time mechanics to handle practically any type of repair work. Gas, diesel fuel, water, ice, and electricity are available at the berths; ashore you can find showers, a laundromat, marine store, snack bar, picnic grounds, a swimming pool, and even bike rentals. For those who register here, transportation is provided at 10 A.M. and at 4 P.M.

daily to pick up supplies. Rides to the Ram's Head Inn and other places can also be arranged.

Coecles Harbor is pretty and unspoiled by commercial activities, though too large to be snug, like West Neck Creek, for example. There is comparatively little traffic in the harbor, and particularly in the southern bight just beyond the entrance you may have the place almost to yourself.

Along the neck that connects Ram Island with the rest of Shelter Island are some huge osprey nests, perched on the tops of telegraph poles.

It can be rough at the entrance of Coecles Harbor when the wind blows strongly from often turbulent Gardiners Bay, so use care in entering. Once inside, you can find protection from any wind by choosing the right bight.

Peconic Bays (Great and Little), Long Island, New York (12358). In discussing the harbors along the two Peconic Bays, we shall again follow a counterclockwise course, as we leave Shelter Island Sound and enter Little Peconic Bay, heading for Nassau Point. There are still no good harbors on the north shore until this point is rounded. However, those skippers whose boats are shallow-draft and who are dying to discover new gunk holes may want to poke into two dredged creeks located in the extreme northwestern end of Hog Neck Bay. There is about 6 feet of water in the channel leading into and connecting with a number of shorter finger channels inside of Corey Creek, which is shown on the chart as due east of Laughing Water. And just to the southwest, red privately maintained stakes mark the 7-foot channel running to the tip of Indian Neck and then westward into Richmond Creek. Through all these very narrow channels, you must proceed cautiously, while following the markers closely. You won't find any facilities, only enchanting surroundings. Should you decide to anchor for the night in one of the creeks, allow for the effects of current and run up your anchor light.

One of the authors will not soon forget a struggle he once had trying to bring his sloop around high and wooded Nassau Point from Hog Neck Bay, in the face of a rising easterly gale. There is a long and dangerous shoal, which we first had to weather. Never did a port look better to us than the tiny private lagoon, which we found in the lee of the point.

1. Cutchogue Harbor, Little Peconic Bay (12358). Across Cutchogue Harbor, which as a whole is fairly open to winds from southwest to southeast, there is a "barb" of what looks like a Nassau Point "spear." This forms a shelter (known as the Horseshoe) from southerly winds and is often used for this purpose by boats drawing 6 feet or less. There are no landing facilities except a sand beach and no supplies. A preferred anchorage is along the inner western shore of the barb.

Nassau Point is hilly and occupied by many attractive estates, several of which have their own lagoons. Channels have been privately dredged in East and Mud Creeks and Broadwater Cove, offering some dinghy sailing and gunkholing for shallow-draft boats. The vicinity is covered with shoaling creeks, but you never can tell where you might find a possible anchorage.

There is a 2-knot flow and a 6-foot depth through the main channel leading to East and Mud creeks running to the northwest and to Haywater and Broadwater Coves running to the east. Red and green private markers line the channel. Follow the middle of the channel. As you pass the sandspit to starboard, don't cut around it sharply to the east or you'll probably run aground in shallow Haywater Cove. Rather, maintain your original course as you detour around the east shore of the large grassy island located north of the entrance.

Here you'll find yourself in the middle of a waterway labyrinth, but it is an easy matter to run due north into Mud Creek, where we have sounded 7 feet. Follow the channel all the way up, noting the mud flats extending along both sides as the channel first widens. A prettier passage is promised by following the eastward channel into Broadwater Cove. Favor the port side of this channel to its head in the northwest quadrant of the cove. Steady depths of 6 feet can be carried up as far as a red-staked area where the channel turns to port and it shoals to less than 3 feet. There is complete seclusion here. Similar depths are found in the staked channel in East Creek, which unfortunately leads into a tiny barren mudhole. With the very limited traffic running through these marshy creeks, however, a yachtsman is fairly free to select the anchorage of his choice—one which will guarantee sufficient swinging room, water under the keel, and a view that's most pleasing to the eye. The depths given above are approximate because of silting problems.

If you do not draw over 5 feet with sail or power, you can make a delightful stop at fairly sizable, well-maintained Cutchogue Harbor Marina—(516) 734-6993, VHF-9—which has slips and general services with a mechanic on duty and is located off Marsh Point at the starboard entrance to Wickham Creek, recently dredged to 6 feet MLW.

A small town dock also permits two-hour docking. We might note here that there is bad shoaling off to port as you make your approach. The staked entrance channel is extremely narrow but deep along its middle. There's 6 feet off the marina's slips, which afford unusual peace, security, and a broad view of wetlands to the west. Ice, gas, marine supplies, and showers are on tap here. The creek has little room for an anchorage. Even the Southold Town Police can be found docking here.

2. New Suffolk, Little Peconic Bay (12358). On the point on the west side of the entrance of Cutchogue Harbor is an intriguing little lagoon. It is known as Schoolhouse Creek and shows on the chart as a tiny "slit" in the shore, just north of the streets of New Suffolk. Its entrance can be spotted about a half mile north of green flasher 3. The main channel, dredged to 5 feet MLW periodically, is marked. As you approach, shoaling can be seen off to starboard and also along the inner bulkhead to port with its projecting rocks. Don't try it under sail, but if you have power, keep in the middle. The channel frequently fills in and then gets dredged again, so check up on dredging operations. The tide rises about $3^{1}/_{2}$ feet.

Inside the entrance, the controlling depths remain at 5 feet, and you will find on both sides of two narrow forked channels rows of slips occupied by numerous motorboats, large and small—almost all equipped for taking out fishing parties. It gives perfect protection. George Moore, one of the local fishermen, rode out the 1938 hurricane here in complete security.

In May and June nearly every slip is taken by pleasure boats, for that is the big season for flounder and weakfish. Later there are a few vacant slips. New Suffolk Shipyard and Marina—(516) 734-6311, VHF-9—between the forks of the channel where the depth is reported at about 5 feet at its gas dock, has a few slips, is a handy source for supplies, and with its 15-ton travelift is equipped to repair boats up to 40 feet. Schoolhouse Creek has much of the atmosphere of a down east fishing village. Near this basin is the site of the first submarine base in America, where the U.S.S. *Holland*, the first submarine commissioned by the U.S. Navy, was based for trials between 1899 and 1905.

Just to the south of Schoolhouse Creek are two breakwaters. The one nearest to the end of the point, on the south, belongs to the town. Behind it lies as tiny a basin as you'll find anywhere, but it affords good protection and depth. Run out both bow and stern anchors. A launching ramp can be observed ashore. Between this breakwater and the creek is another small town basin, with more than 10 feet of water, enclosed by a partly submerged breakwater and piles. You can tie up here at Frank's Marine Service—(516) 734-4024, VHF-9—get supplies nearby, and be well protected except from strong easterlies. In the December 1992 nor'easter, they suffered severe damage to the breakwater, but repairs are underway although not yet completed. New Suffolk has good eating places and stores, with fishing-party signs and bait on all sides. Just one step away from Frank's marine the quaint Galley Ho Restaurant has often served us the very best food this side of Greenport.

3. Mattituck, Great Peconic Bay (12358). On a heading west toward Mattituck, you will pass through North Race, leaving flashing green buoy 3 to port and nun 4 to starboard to avoid the nasty bar running all the way from this nun northward to the mainland. Readers who are fascinated by the migratory habits of animals might be interested in learning of reports that deer have been spotted crossing North Race on their way to and from Robins Island. Their familiarity with the rules of the road has yet to be determined.

Although there is at present 5 feet at low water at the entrance to James Creek, there is a 3-foot rise in tide, making this inlet a possible harbor of refuge for a small craft caught in foul weather along the northern shore of Great Peconic Bay. The creek's entrance is just to the right of a long, concrete bulkhead running parallel to the shore. After having left the red-marked private stakes close to starboard outside the creek, favor the port side of the channel once you're past the breakwater. You will experience very little tide rip. When you swing past the first bend to starboard, you will spot Strong's Marine—(516) 298-4770, VHF-68—situated on grassy mud banks but surrounded by some attractive private estates. Mr. Strong, the manager, offered us gas and water and advised us that boats over 30 feet should not enter this inlet because of the lack of turning and anchorage space. The upper end of the narrow channel to the west has been dredged to 5 feet, where the red stakes must be kept close aboard. The best way to find a peaceful refuge here is to take a slip at the marina if one is vacant or, if you must, to anchor just beyond the marina where the channel opens up.

4. South Jamesport, Flanders Bay (12358). One-half mile northeast of Miamogue Point, a channel has been dredged through East

Creek running into a bulkheaded well-protected basin. A 6-foot depth can be carried all the way in. A lighted red piling stands well off the entrance to the southeast. On our most recent visit, we entered between the two prominent sandspits while following the red and green buoys. Stay in the middle and swing to starboard into the basin, giving the starboard shore fairly good berth. You can anchor here, tie up to the bulkheads surrounding the basin, or run in to the East Creek Marina—(516) 722-4842—on the eastern shore, where overnight slips are available. Gas, water, ice, electricity, and a small store and snack bar can be found here. This place is appealingly different and provides an excellent launching ramp. There's at least 6 feet of clear water in the basin. Everywhere you look there is sand, which has helped to form an unspoiled swimming beach to the east.

Half a mile west of Miamogue Point is the Great Peconic Bay Marina—(516) 722-3565—whose facilities make this one of the better havens to be found in the western part of Great Peconic Bay. The entrance is just west of Miamogue Point and can be detected at night by a flashing red light set out by the marina. It is further identified by a prominent bulkhead. Approach the opening from the south, passing between flashing red buoy 4 and green can 5 until you reach three prominent striped stakes, which should be left closely to port. The channel depth is 6 feet at low water, with a $3^1/_2$ foot rise and fall in tide. Soon you'll note the marina's basin dredged to a depth of about 6 feet and accommodating yachts up to 55 feet overall. You will find a 25-ton travelift, complete repair work, marine supplies, floating docks, gas, diesel, ice, showers, and a chance to take a stroll around the nearby summer colony.

5. Aquebogue, Flanders Bay (12358). Proceeding west from lighted buoy 9, near the entrance to the Peconic River, you can pick up the red and green private buoys marking the narrow channel leading into Meetinghouse Creek, reportedly shoaling to 5 feet MLW. Pass close to the light off the point, keeping it to starboard. Farther in on the starboard shore rests the modern, clean-looking Larry's Lighthouse Marina— (516) 722-3400. This is the finest overall marina to be found in Flanders Bay. Its manager, Larry Galasso, mentioned its services, which include gas, diesel fuel, water, ice, showers, electricity, a laundromat, slips, a 30-ton travelift with complete repair work, a well-stocked marine store specializing in a large stock of engine parts, and Meetinghouse Creek

Inn. This marina is open 7 days a week. Food supplies may be purchased at a general store located at the head of the creek. Whether you stay here or anchor in the northern end of the channel, Meetinghouse Creek as a port of call is to be preferred over less convenient Riverhead. Boats can even anchor in the dredged 5-foot channels off Terrys Creek to the west of Indian Island or up into Reeves Creek to the east, but do so with caution, since markers may not be there to guide you.

6. Riverhead, Flanders Bay (12358). On a cruise in Flanders Bay, we made a run in a power boat approximately 2^1/$_2$ miles from flashing green buoy 9 all the way up the dredged channel in the Peconic River to flashing buoy 17, which faces the new Peconic River Yacht Basin—(516) 727-8386. It would have been impossible for a sailing auxiliary to have done the same, due to the limiting 25-foot vertical clearance afforded by the fixed bridge crossing the river a mile above the channel's mouth. The Peconic River, which has a controlling depth of 4^1/$_2$ feet at the time of writing, is far less commercial looking than in the recent past, and the view of the lush wetlands bordering both shores is pleasing to the eye.

Privately maintained lights mark the narrow channel, but proceed carefully since some of these may be slightly off station.

We were impressed with the attractive layout of the Peconic River Yacht Basin when we arrived at its sheltered docks on the northern shore at the head of the channel. They are fully equipped to take care of transient yachts, mostly powerboats, but no diesel fuel is available. A fine swimming pool and a snack bar have been built, shops are just a few steps away, and the Rendez-vous Restaurant is well recommended.

Settled in about 1690 and once called "Occabog," Riverhead was formerly part of the town of Southold. The Suffolk County Historical Society and the Historical Museum are located in town and well worth a visit.

7. Flanders, Flanders Bay (12358). In the southern part of Reeves Bay is the small Gateway Marina—(516) 727-1028—with 3 feet MLW, heads and showers, and engine repairs in a pleasant spot. The entrance channel is dredged down the middle and may have some privately maintained buoys.

8. Red Creek Pond, Great Peconic Bay (12358). Red Creek Pond, lying to the east of Red Cedar Point, has been opened up to permit visits from boats of under 4-foot draft. Privately maintained buoys mark the narrow channel, in which we recorded a depth of about 5 feet at low water in 1985. Favor the lighted green pole on entering. The pond offers privacy, and except for a few attractive summer houses, it has kept its primordial charm. There are no markers within, so it is wise to anchor in or close to the end of the dredged channel halfway down along the eastern shore. We saw a few small auxiliary sloops anchored snugly in this area. The pond's bottom is said to be mud.

9. Shinnecock Canal Basin, Great Peconic Bay (12358). If you wish to find shelter for the night in the southern part of Great Peconic Bay and your boat doesn't draw over 10 feet, go into the basin at the northerly entrance of the Shinnecock Canal. It is just to port as you enter, and you can tie up at the bulkhead, but not for more than 7 days. One must obtain a permit for a longer stay. This basin, in which the Shinnecock Marina—(516) 854-4949—is located, belongs to Suffolk County, has a dockmaster, water, electricity, pumpout facilities, showers, and heads. Docking fees cover from midnight to midnight or any part thereof. No swirling from the canal's current is felt here. At the basin's outer edge you'll find a hand-operated rig to unstep your mast should you desire to proceed south through the canal. A fine swimming beach is located just to the north.

The mile-long canal has been dredged to a controlling depth of 5 feet above the locks and to a depth of $4^{1}/_{2}$ feet below them. The entrance channel leading from the Sound records a depth of at least 10 feet.

Hampton Harbor Marina—(516) 728-8200, VHF-68—formerly Corrigan's Yacht Yard, catering to sportfishermen and cruisers, is located on the west side north of the bridges. There is 8 to 14 feet of water off the slips. Gas, diesel fuel, water, electricity, ice, marine supplies, and complete repair service can be found here, and many facilities have been upgraded recently. Many of the marinas along the canal have courtesy cars for use in picking up supplies.

Beyond Hampton's and still north of the bridges lies Modern Yachts—(516) 728-2266—a full-service yard that welcomes transients. It boasts a 40-ton hoist and complete and elaborate facilities including swimming pool, picnic areas, and repair facilities for big boats.

If your craft is a powerboat with a mast height of under 20 feet and a draft of under $4^{1}/_{2}$ feet, you may go, preferably at high tide, through the Shinnecock Canal, explore the great bays along the outer Long Island shore, and poke your nose out into the Atlantic. We were told that there is some shoaling at the gates just below the first bridge, where the current runs about $1^1/2$ knots. When the gates are opened to permit the flow to set south through the canal, currents can build up to a nasty 5 knots. There is no difficulty in gaining passage through the gates if one observes their lights and signals properly.

The Indian Cove Marina—(516) 728-2800—with restaurant on the starboard shore below the second bridge, can guarantee the whole family a quiet night ashore in attractive surroundings. Patrons can tie up at the motel's docks in 4 feet of water. Just beyond is the Mariner's Cove Marina—(516) 728-0608—with barbecue facilities, volleyball, and badminton. Natives of Shinnecock recommended the Canal Restaurant near the second bridge and the Rip Tide as places to go for the best in meals.

Cold Spring Pond, whose entrance lies a mile east of the canal, is not recommended as a harbor for deep-draft cruising boats. Its approach has shoaled to 2 feet at MLW, the depth is not much greater in its channel, and there is an overhead power cable with a clearance of only 34 feet at the entrance to the pond. Skippers should not enter here without local knowledge.

10. Sebonac Creek, Southampton, Great Peconic Bay (12358). The low-lying entrance to this very appealing creek may be spotted just to the north of the famous National Golf Links of America Course, situated on rolling hills. A prominent flagpole in front of its clubhouse and the charted windmill just south of the entrance are the most visible references in helping you pick up the opening to the creek. Approach the channel entrance lined with red and green Styrofoam block buoys. The depth at the entrance is $4^1/2$ feet. A white range light rises off the sandy point to port, and shortly beyond stands a red-lighted range tower in midstream. Keep this to starboard as you wend your way up the marked creek, which has shoaled to a depth of 5 feet at low water all the way in.

One-half mile in on the port side, the strictly private Bull Head Yacht Club—(516) 283-4403—has a first-class dock, with $4^1/2$ feet at low tide, at the end of a road leading to the northeast shore of Bullhead Bay. It provides slips, moorings, freshwater, and electricity, as well as restrooms and showers housed in a fine clubhouse. All the docks have been built and maintained by the club's hard-working membership. The best anchorage for deep-draft boats is in 7 feet of water off the northeastern shore of Ram Island facing the club docks. The town dock next to the club has 5 feet at MLW, but watch out for a large submerged rock lying 100 feet off its outer end and further marked by a green-and-red buoy. Phone Sal's Market for food supplies.

This is one of the best ports in the Peconic Bay area, affording excellent protection in easterly winds, a 3-foot rise and fall in tide, and most scenic surroundings.

11. North Sea Harbor, Little Peconic Bay (12358). This is another harbor that looks impossible for all but craft with drafts of under 2 or 3 feet, and the *Coast Pilot* confirms that it is "an excellent harbor of refuge for boats with drafts not exceeding 3½ feet." Any greater draft should not attempt the channel since its depth throughout records only 4 feet at best. Enter the narrow channel between the light to starboard and can 1. Favor cans 3 and 5 farther upchannel but don't get too close to the port shore at the first bend for you may interfere with the casting of some fisherman. Your boat will face a rather fierce current should you try to enter this harbor at ebb tide.

There is a bulkhead inside which is part of the Conscience Point Marina and Restaurant—(516) 283-8295—where gas, diesel, pumpout, heads, and showers are also available. Don't go beyond here without local knowledge; there are some unmarked shoals. The small Dave Bofill Marina—(516) 283-4841—can be found on the southwestern shore of the harbor, but use caution in getting here, for there are few markers inside. The bottom is soft, with good holding ground and 3 feet MLW.

At present, this harbor is much less appealing to us than nearby Wooley Pond, which is to be preferred in almost all respects.

In 1640, colonists from Lynn, Massachusetts, landed on Conscience Point and founded Southampton, the first English settlement in New York State.

12. Wooley Pond, Little Peconic Bay (12358). This is a fascinating little place on the eastern shore of Little Peconic Bay, providing good protection even in northerly winds. A large and sturdy lighted black beacon and nun 2 show the well-concealed entrance through which the tide rushes fast, continually piling up sand dunes on both shores. Standing on a spit of land just south of the opening is a large, white angular building which can be used as a reference to help guide your approach. In recent years, the channel has been maintained to a depth of 6 feet MLW. Favor the nun on entering; then try to keep in the middle of the channel while avoiding the visible shoals on either hand, one to port which you reach first and one to starboard just inside. Once past the entrance and its Scylla and Charybdis, you swing sharply to starboard and follow a fairly straight channel into Wooley Pond, favoring the nuns all the way in.

The scenery is pleasant, but the pond is restrictive; don't anchor if you draw more than 3 feet. Proceed, instead, to the foot of the marked channel and tie up to starboard at the docks of the Peconic Marina—(516) 283-3799—in 5 feet of water. There are no moorings, but slips are available, as well as gas, diesel, water, ice, and supplies; a mechanic is on duty. An unpretentious bar and restaurant complete the facilities. Yachts will find this a snug haven providing they stay within the markers and use care in negotiating the challenging entrance with its swirling current.

13. Mill Creek, Noyack Bay (12358). While beating against a strong westerly on one of our cruises in Noyack Bay, we decided to make a run for protection to Mill Creek Harbor, located on its southern shore. It turned out to be a wise decision, for this well-sheltered harbor, not often used by cruising boats, continues to expand its facilities. A prominent pointed radio tower standing inland is almost due south and on a line with the 100-foot channel. There was 8 feet in the channel at the time of writing, with 6 feet available within the inner basin at low water, but shoaling there continues at the time of writing. First, pick up the lighted red stake as you make your approach. On entering, keep well to starboard of the can, which marks shoaling water along the built-up sandbar. Keep between the red and green buoys until you make your sharp swing to port outside of the green can and stake located off the end of the spit. After you have rounded the spit to reach the inner harbor, you will pick up ahead to starboard the large shed of the Noyac Marina—(516) 725-3333—nestled among a string of small private homes. The hospitable owners can supply you with gas, water, ice, and all types of fishing gear and marine equipment. This marina also specializes in servicing outboards. When we last visited, the place was relatively inactive and for sale, due to the death of one of the owners. You can tie up to the bulkhead in about 5 feet of water or pick up a possible overnight mooring nestled midst a crowded fleet of small craft.

Mill Creek is only 4 miles by car and 7 miles by boat from Sag Harbor. The Mill Creek Marina—(516) 725-1351—lies at the foot of the road along the southeastern shore of the creek. Floating docks, water, ice, gas, showers, electricity, a fish market, and the Inn at Mill Creek are all available here. This is a spot that will offer you delightful snugness in pleasant surroundings. Mill Creek is a small fishing center, and only 2 miles away lies Jessup Neck, reputed to be the finest fishing grounds in the area, where blues, weakfish, kings, and porgies abound. This neck is a federal preserve, open to landing parties for swimming and exploring. But the Department of the Interior's Fish and Wildlife Service advises that from April 1 to August 1 people will not be allowed near these 80 acres. The least tern and piping plover are now on the federal endangered species lists. The very presence of humans is enough to stop these birds from nesting at their favorite spot, this open beach.

14. Northwest Harbor, Long Island, New York (12358). Heading east to Three Mile Harbor from Sag Harbor, one passes along Northwest Harbor, whose southern shore is marked by a bluff on Barcelona Point. Just to the east of this point, a shallow, tricky channel for shoal-draft boats has been dredged southward through a sandbar into Northwest Creek, located to the south of Cedar Point. The mouth of the creek is difficult to spot from seaward since both shorelines appear to overlap, blinding the entrance. There are private markers here but a bow lookout must be posted. And as the mid-channel has a reported depth of only 3 feet at low water, be sure to stay in the middle and prepare to face a 2-knot current while avoiding the very shallow water stretching out from the sandspit to starboard. Once past this shoal, favor the starboard shore, and as you pass through the cut, keep off the shoreline to port. Then pass the three nuns close to starboard as you head for the dock front along the eastern shore. Don't expect to find any facilities here, just a few small cottages and outboards. There's at least 6 feet in the anchorage area, which is open to the south but otherwise well sheltered. This "secret" harbor has a quiet and natural charm. Its lovely sandy beach and wetland to the south merely help to "gild the lily."

15. Threemile Harbor, Gardiners Bay (13209). This is a first-class protected harbor, which is large and deep enough for a whole yacht club fleet. In approaching its entrance from the west, be sure to keep outside of can 1, which marks a rock ledge 1½ miles east of the light on Cedar Point. This ledge is known locally as Hedges Bank. The harbor is identified from seaward by a lighted Morse Code A buoy "TM" lying 800 yards due north of the channel's entrance.

Enter between the two privately maintained lights set at the end of each jetty, favoring the east side of the channel. Its centerline has been dredged to a 150-foot width and to a controlled depth of 8 feet. Now follow the line of buoys arranged to guide you in as you prepare to face a current of up to 3 knots. The harbor's tide range is $2^1/_2$ feet and the holding ground is good.

The first facility upchannel to port is the Harbor Marina, which has complete repair service, gas, diesel fuel, ice, showers, slips with electricity for boats up to 50 feet, a laundromat, and a gourmet restaurant. It caters primarily to powerboats.

The second facility, also on the port, is Maidstone Harbor—(516) 324-2651.) Its basin with 6 feet at mean low water is marked on the chart. Here you can find hot showers, electricity at the slips, and a laundromat. Bostwick's Restaurant, formerly The Sea Wolf Restaurant, is open for dinner.

Yachtsmen will especially appreciate the new East Hampton Point Marina located just past Maidstone Harbor—(516) 324-8400. A merger of the earlier Wings Point Yacht Club and the Maidstone Boat Yard, East Hampton Point is now under new ownership and managed by Lester Black. On making your approach, head due east directly toward the fuel dock where you'll find ample depth. Call the marina on VHF-9, and dockhands will assign you a slip behind the protected, 8-feet-deep basin.

East Hampton Point is a first-rate marina offering a full range of services, including fuel, electricity, water, ice, showers, marine supplies, laundry, and repair facilities. In addition, East Hampton Point has an indoor-outdoor restaurant, swimming pool, tennis courts, and most recently, extremely attractive vacation cottages. East Hampton Point is a beautiful waterfront resort.

A bad shoal lies well off and parallel to this marina's basin. Therefore, if you are leaving the marina and are headed for the mooring area, turn to port and continue southward until you are well beyond the marina. Only then can you turn to starboard out of the channel and into the anchorage area. Those yachts intending to pick up a mooring must contact the East Hampton harbormaster on VHF-9 or by telephone at (516) 329-3078. The harbormaster now has control of all moorings.

Yachts may also proceed up the channel in 7 feet at low water to put into several small marinas along the port shore. The Shagwong Marina basin, faced by a bulkhead, has thirty-three slips in $4^1/_2$ feet MLW. They have a few transient slips and can be reached on VHF-9 or by telephone at (516) 324-4830.

There is more water and space farther up at Threemile's oldest marina, Halsey's Marina—(516) 324-9894. The trimmed grass bordering the docks adds great appeal to this secluded spot.

There is 6 feet of water in the main channel leading finally to the cove at the southern head of the harbor, but watch out for the shoaling to port as you enter. Along the eastern fork of this cove lies a tiny basin in which is housed Gardiner's Marina, clean and attractive, offering slips and basic shipboard necessities including gas, diesel fuel, ice, electricity, and showers; this is the nearest facility to the village and ocean beach. Here you'll be "guests" of Robert Gardiner, owner of nearby Gardiner's Island. Moored sailing craft mark the deepest water in the basin; the town dock with a depth of 10 feet is just to the south, while beyond rests the deep-water dock of the Threemile Harbor Boatyard run by Sam Story, who has gained an excellent reputation for efficient service and for doing all types of repair work. This is about the only place in the harbor you can find block ice and a well-equipped ship's store. Although no anchoring is permitted in the cove, this is one of the few places in Threemile where you can pick up food supplies conveniently. The town park adjoining makes the surroundings pleasing to the eye but less private than the outer harbor.

If you happen to be moored in Threemile Harbor on the third weekend of July, you simply cannot miss the Grucci's fireworks display. People come from miles around to witness a dazzling aerial spectacle.

16. Acabonack Harbor, Gardiners Bay (13209). On our first visit here, many years ago, the late Captain H. R. Miller of the Devon Yacht Club gave us a guided tour of this harbor, opened up in 1959 for small shoal-draft boats. The southern tip of Cape Gardiner, forming a breakwater to the harbor, has been completely filled in to the mainland and a new channel cut through it due west of nun 8. The 75-foot channel, according to 1981 soundings, recorded a depth of $2^1/_2$ feet MLW, and this entrance with its swift currents tends to silt up, resulting in unpredictable depths. In late 1993, local authorities reported that this harbor was in critical need of dredging. Take careful soundings, therefore, as you head west from nun 8. The mean range of tide here is almost 2 feet. You will soon pass between small, privately maintained, lighted red and green markers. Note the reported submerged rock marked on the chart as being located on the channel's southern edge and keep this to port. Once you have passed between the two sandspits, it is advisable to follow the deepest but narrowest channel running southward and marked with five green buoys and three red markers. Four feet can be carried here, but avoid the shoal to port as you proceed. Farther beyond the public launching ramp to port lies the harbor's best anchorage area. Do not adventure up any other charted but unbuoyed channels without local knowledge. The harbor bottom is clay.

You will have to anchor here, as there are no facilities, but this adds to the place's natural charm. Captain Miller, as a former president of the East Hampton Baymen's Association, a conservationist group, was largely responsible for developing, yet not spoiling, this rustic area, which has few homes, picturesque marshes, and beaches lined with multicolored shells.

The Devon Yacht Club lies 2 miles to the southeast. It has long been identified by name on government charts, and its minute dredged basin, also designated, might serve as a possible place of refuge in an emergency. Reciprocal guest privileges are extended to members of other recognized yacht clubs.

From seaward, Devon's low-lying clubhouse is seen standing in front of a wide, white beach with the entrance to the basin just to the southeast. Check with the dockmaster on VHF-9 for clearance before entering. You should pass between two markers which indicate the short channel to the basin as well as an outer sandbar covered by only 4 feet at low water. It is therefore advised that boats come in here between one hour before high water and one hour after. Once inside, you may be assigned a slip in 6 feet of water and charged a flat rate for an overnight stay. This charge also covers the use of the restaurant and snack bar, showers, clubhouse, and beach area. Coats and ties are required at meals.

In recent years, Devon has hosted the New York Yacht Club fleet as well as the American Yacht Club and the Corinthians. Large fleets must anchor offshore where it is widely exposed. Even in moderate winds, the considerable current and poor holding ground made some of the Corinthian boats drag, so use plenty of scope. Although the club encourages such group visits, from our own observation it appears that Devon may much prefer hosting a yacht club fleet offshore to welcoming the single transient yacht to its marina. Perhaps this is understandable. With the presence of members' boats, space is very limited in the basin as well as along the club's 400-foot dock.

The Devon Yacht Club was founded in 1917, under the name of the Gardiner's Bay Boat Club, by a group of summer residents, largely from Cincinnati.

Little may one realize that Gardiner's Island, perched in the bay about 4 miles north of the Devon Yacht Club, boasts the longest ownership by a continued dynasty of any piece of land in the United States. Purchased in 1639 by Lion Gardiner from the Montauk Indians for a blanket, some trinkets, a very large dog, and a bottle of rum, it is now preserved as a naturalist's paradise by the sixteenth Lord of the Manor, Robert David Lion Gardiner. Deer and wild turkeys roam the island underbrush, hundreds of different bird species make it their home, and as many as 150 majestic ospreys nest here regularly from March to September. Equally impressive are the Gardiner mansion and the eighteenth-century windmill, both midway up the western side of the island in the deepest part of the island's curving shoreline that forms Cherry Harbor. It affords some protection for anchoring, but there are no real harbors here.

Such an intriguing place may tempt you to pay a visit ashore, but don't try unless you happen to be a Gardiner—just listen to an anecdote that Mitchel Levitas spun in *The New York Times*.

> Among the uninvited visitors shooed off a few years ago were several brothers Rockefeller. Jock Mackay, who has worked and lived on the island since he left Scotland in 1929, spotted the group disembarking from a boat. When he asked them to leave, recalls Mackay, the visitors identified themselves, adding that they were friends of the absent proprietor. Mackay was not moved. "I'm sorry," he said, "I don't care if you're Astorbilts, you'll have to go."

Approximately 3 miles east-northeast of Gardiner's Island, the U.S. Navy has established a restricted anchorage area for the exclusive use of its submarines operating out of New London. It is shown on the chart as a $^3/_4$- by 2-mile rectangle. Regulations state that no vessel or person may approach or remain within 500 yards of a U.S. Navy submarine anchored in this area.

17. Napeague Harbor (13209). Although Napeague Harbor is without doubt one of the prettiest harbors in or around Long Island, it has a number of strikes against it. To begin with, its entrance channels are narrow and unmarked and tend to silt. The harbor is shoal for the most part and too large to be snug. And, due to an effort to reseed the harbor with scallops, anchoring is strictly forbidden.

Those of you who are daring and wish to visit this quiet harbor should be aware that the entrance is both difficult to see and hard to negotiate. When making your approach, be sure that you are at least a good 1/4 mile southwest of nun 2 before turning out of the channel and heading for the harbor entrance. The privately maintained harbor channel is 30 feet wide and has a reported depth of 4 feet at low water. Tidal range within the harbor is 2 feet; this causes a strong current during the ebb and the flood. Once inside, turn directly to port where you will find plenty of water along the eastern shore. Be aware of the three rocks shown on the chart off to port.

Because we are hopeful that some day cruising vessels will once again be able to take advantage of this lovely spot, we leave Napeague Harbor with these words by Francis Fleetwood of the nearby Devon Yacht Club.

Napeague Harbor is my favorite anchorage north of the I.C.W. and I regularly anchor there. I draw 5 feet with my 38-foot sloop. It reminds me of the Exumas. The anchorage is surrounded by state park. On weekends there are a few fishermen at the entrance but during the week the place is empty. I have never seen more than two other boats on weekends. The best place to anchor is near the mouth of the northerly channel for there is no reason to go farther in. The swimming is good; the holding ground first-rate.

17. Montauk (Great Pond) (13209). This is primarily a great sportfishing port, which caters more to fisherman than to cruising yachtsmen. However, Montauk has much to offer and is an exciting port of call.

When you are approaching the harbor's entrance, the first buoy you will come to is Morse Alpha "M," which is now lighted. The two jetties marking the channel's entrance are marked by a green 4-second flasher and a red 5-second flasher with a horn. The controlling depth in the channel is 10^1/$_2$ feet MLW to the boat basin northwestward of Star Island, with a depth of 9 feet MLW in the basin itself. You can also carry 10^1/$_2$ feet in the east channel to the yacht basin east of Star Island.

"Montauk is not a good place to spend the night riding at anchor," says the commodore of a leading Long Island Sound yacht club. "The currents swirl all over the place, causing anchored yachts to swing every which way." This report is true, and with the advent of some outstanding marinas affording boats good protection dockside, many yachtsmen prefer to tie up, keeping their anchors stowed away. Montauk's mean range of tide is about 2 feet.

As you come in, most water is to the west, and as you get to the southerly end of the lighted jetties, swing away from the day beacon on your starboard hand and over slightly to port toward the channel center where there is ample water. Only a fairly small area off the docks to starboard has deep water, with about 10 feet, and this is near the channel through which the $2^{1}/_{2}$-knot tide sweeps. In the small bight on the western shore, facing the Coast Guard station, lies the Montauk Marine Basin with gas, diesel fuel, ice, water, showers, electricity, a laundromat, countless slips, and grocery supplies. The Gosman's Dock complex providing a variety of shops and restaurants is just a step away. The channel leading to the head of the basin is reported to have a depth now of 8 feet MLW. Traveling south from Gosman's, you will pass a number of docks belonging to or associated with restaurants. The first of these is Salivar Dock Restaurant—(516) 668-2555—followed by Christman's Dock and Johny Marlin's (formerly Tuma's Dock). The Viking Dock— (516) 668-5700—is home to the Viking Fleet, where ferry service, fishing charters, and whale-watching tours are all available during the summer months. The Uihlein Marina & Boat Rental—(516) 668-3799—has three transient berths for boats up to 36 feet. They offer a variety of repair services and can be reached on VHF-14. Montauk Marine Basin—(516) 668-5900—has fifty transient berths, can accommodate vessels in excess of 100 feet, offers cable television, phone jacks, showers, and a complete line of repair services. Still proceeding south, next you will come to Offshore Sports Marina—(516) 668-2406. They offer forty transient slips and can accommodate vessels up to 70 feet. They are reported to have 6 feet MLW at their dock and offer the usual services. Captain's Cove Marina is next, offering six transient berths and accommodating boats up to 17 feet in length. Dockside depth is reported to be 5 feet. Sportfishermen will find plenty of companionship and special services here. Gas, diesel, ice, water, showers, electricity, marine and fishing supplies, and a large variety of repair services are all here. They can be reached on VHF-19 or by phone at (516) 668-5600. If fishing is your passion and your vessel is too large for the Captain's Cove Marina, you will feel right at home at the West Lake Fishing Lodge located a short distance away. The West Lake Fishing Lodge offers thirty transient slips, 6 feet dockside depth, showers, marine and tackle shop, pumpout, ice, and motel. In addition, their restaurant, Fish Tails

Galley, serves breakfast, lunch, and dinner beginning at 4:30 A.M. Contact them on VHF-19 or by phone at (516) 668-5600. Lastly, at the end of the channel lies the Snug Harbor Motel and Marina offering twenty transient slips and similar services including a motel and swimming pool. Contact them on VHF-16 or by phone at (516) 668-2860.

Over on the less-crowded western shore of Star Island, next to the Coast Guard station, lies the Star Island Yacht Club & Marina, housed in a two-story tan building of modern design. Here is one of the more recently built public marinas in Montauk, with complete boatyard services seven days a week. With 9 feet MLW at its slips and fuel dock, it can accommodate boats up to 100 feet overall. And like so many of the newer marinas in the harbor, this one has something for everybody—a bar, supplies, a laundromat, a swimming pool, and a tennis court, with a restaurant nearby.

On the eastern shore of Star Island stretches one of the largest public resort-marinas to be found anywhere. It offers superb dock-space accommodations for visiting yachts, and the use of swimming pools and tennis courts surrounded by lovely landscaping. The first-class service provided here requires first-class rates. The Montauk Yacht Club Resort, the first marina you will come upon as you proceed south, was undergoing a complete change in ownership at the time of writing. Just beyond, you will see "the sort of place our forefathers must have had in mind when they invented money." This is the Montauk Yacht Club & Inn's own description of their resort. In promising to provide the "matchless service of a bygone era," it furnishes such niceties as dockside "room" service, box lunches, on-board telephones, a restaurant, MATV, and complimentary transportation to golf courses and shopping in the village. "All the services of the hotel are available to the yachtsman," and that would include indoor heated swimming, sauna, and Jacuzzi, not to mention billiards-room rights. Why, all this pampering might even make one balk at the very thought of ever returning to that self-reliant existence, the spartan cruising life. The sign showing "Montauk Yacht Club & Villas" marks the location of the club's marina operation. Check in here if you want to lay over for the night.

Should you decide to proceed on, however, you can reach the southern part of Lake Montauk by passing between the three sets of red and green privately maintained buoys which have been set out in 4 feet at low water. You may swing over to port into 8-foot depths only after having passed the last green can, number 7. A pier shown on the chart as jutting out from the shoreline southwest of Prospect Hill designates the location of the Montauk Lake Club. Behind its prominent control tower rises its headquarters, a beautiful Norman villa. Being quietly sheltered and away from it all once made this a choice spot for the cruising family. Unfortunately, it is now a private club and no longer open to the general public.

Montauk was once the home of the Montaukett Indians, a peaceful tribe that lived well off local game, the ocean, and the land. In 1614, the Dutch explorer Adrian Block came ashore and, according to historians, was the first white man to set foot in Suffolk County. By 1686, white settlers had bought all of Montauk's 10,000 acres for 100 pounds. Descendants of the Montauketts no longer live in the hamlet, but reside in East Hampton Village, just to the west of Montauk.

This seaport became one of America's first cattle- and sheep-ranching areas, then a whaling center, and finally a commercial fishing port near the turn of the century. Its year-round population is about 3,000, which rises to about 18,000 during the summer season. It is now very much on the move.

Montauk Manor, built in the 1920s, closed in 1964 but is now converted into condominium apartments. Gosman's Dock, located to starboard at the harbor's entrance, has bloomed into a clean, colorful, and charming group of boutiques and restaurants near the fishing docks. Much of Montauk's past is equally colorful.

Here was the scene of the final encampment of the Spanish-American War's Rough Riders, commanded by Theodore Roosevelt. Roosevelt brought 2,800 of his Rough Riders to the Deep Hollow Ranch when the unit was to be disbanded. In his diaries, Roosevelt recalls that "galloping over the open, rolling country through the cool fall evenings made us feel we were out on the great western plains." Today, Deep Hollow Ranch has been renamed Indian Field Ranch and is located near Captain's Marina. With horses to rent, there are special tours for would-be Rough Riders and secluded trails for the more-experienced equestrian.

The Star Island Casino, now the site of the Montauk Yacht Club Resort, housed illegal gambling throughout the 1920s, and well into the 1930s, when the law finally put it out of business. It was here that Mayor Jimmy Walker of New York was "pinched" in a police raid. He hung a white towel over his arm, posed briefly as a waiter, and finally fled barefoot down the dock to the sanctuary of the nearby yacht club.

One of the most tragic boating accidents off Montauk was the capsizing of the fishing boat *Pelican* on September 1, 1952. Of the sixty-four persons aboard, forty-five lost their lives.

Montauk is the last harbor to the eastward on Long Island and thus a good "jumping-off place" for Block Island, about 18 miles away, and points east. Its famous lighthouse, constructed in 1796 by order of President George Washington, is an octagonal stone tower 108 feet high, with the light 168 feet above sea level. Henry Baker was its keeper during the first quarter of the nineteenth century. His pay was $333.33 a year.

When Walt Whitman, Long Island's renowned "poet laureate," once visited Montauk, he strolled upon its golden shores, perhaps gazed seaward from these very bluffs, and put these inspiring words to paper:

I stand on some mighty eagle's beak,
Eastward the sea absorbing, viewing, (Nothing but sea and sky)
The tossing waves, the foam, the ships, in the distance
The wild unrest, the snowy, curling caps—that
Inbound urge and urge of waves,
Seeking the shore forever.

Chapter VI

Fishers Island to Buzzards Bay, Including Narragansett Bay

Special Note on Fishers Island Sound. All wise yachtsmen use the current whenever possible when going east or west along the shore. For that reason it is well to remember that the velocity of the currents through The Race is twice as great as through Fishers Island Sound. It may be preferable, therefore, in heading east or west, to work your way through Watch Hill Passage. Note here that in strong easterlies and westerlies cans 3 and 5 are often swept nearly underwater at times of maximum flow, although the currents in this passage run considerably weaker than at The Race. The government publication *Tidal Current Charts: Block Island Sound and Eastern Long Island Sound Including the Thames and Connecticut Rivers,* available at all National Ocean Survey sales agents or from the National Ocean Survey, Distribution Division (C44), Washington, DC 20235, shows the direction and strength of currents each hour. This portfolio is extremely useful in these waters. There have been many navigational-aid changes recently along this section of the coast, so it is necessary for yachtsmen to refer to the latest charts.

In most areas, you can guess what the currents are doing if you know the time of high tide. That is true here also in the harbors, but not out in the Sound. The current may be ebbing in the harbor but still flooding strongly in the Sound. This is because high tide moves westward through Long Island Sound over a period of 3 hours or more, so current is still flowing into the mouth long after high tide has passed. The same effect is present at other points in the Sound, but is greatest here at the mouth, and more important because the currents are stronger. The only way to know the status of tide and current here is to use the appropriate tables.

There are often fluky winds and "soft spots" off New London Harbor and west of Dumpling Island. There is an eddy on the flood, and little current, close under the west end of Fishers Island.

Several years ago, 3-acre North Dumpling Island was being sold for $2.5 million to any taker. This price included an eleven-room residence, a caretaker's cottage, a boathouse, and a right little, tight little island with a 360-degree view.

For those who like to gamble, there is a new incentive to visit this region: the Foxwoods Casino operated by the Mashantucket Pequot Indians in Ledyard. It is quite accessible by taxi from any of the harbors from New London to Watch Hill.

1. Silver Eel Cove, Fishers Island (13214). This tiny harbor on the extreme western tip of the island is not reserved solely for government use. Steamers from New London dock here, instead of in West Harbor as formerly, and use a dock on the west shore next to the Fishers Island Coast Guard Station. However, there may be room for a few yachts to tie up but not for an anchorage. Although the protection is very good, no gas or supplies were available when we last visited, and the place is uninviting, with government buildings all around and cars going to and from the steamers. The entrance between the lighted docks is not easy to negotiate in westerly winds, and one should be on the lookout for reported pilings that have washed into the channel. Silver Eel Cove is valuable chiefly as a convenient and safe harbor of refuge, or as a takeoff point for The Race.

2. Hay Harbor, Fishers Island (13214). This harbor makes a quiet mooring for shoal-draft powerboats. The channel is narrow and difficult without local knowledge and not recommended for keel boats. We poked in here in a boat drawing 3 feet and experienced little difficulty, having posted a bow watch. A local authority says that if one observes and follows local stakes, 4 feet can be taken inside, though how this is done at low water is not evident on the chart. Once inside, there is good water in the western part of the harbor and dock.

3. West Harbor, Fishers Island (13214). Among cruising people this is by far the most popular harbor on Fishers Island, and deservedly so. It is easy to enter, provided you watch the shoal to starboard. Well protected except from the northeast, it has good holding ground and is altogether delightful. Although the channel records a depth of 12 feet at the time of writing, we were told not to hug nun 14 too closely to starboard. And deep-draft boats should be especially wary of the 5-foot spot and rock just beyond this nun. The rock has a sign on it.

Steamers from New London no longer use West Harbor, though the steamer dock is still available for tying up. They now run between New London and Silver Eel Cove, as already pointed out. Gas, diesel fuel, water, and ice are available in West Harbor at the Mobil station's dock just beyond the old steamboat wharf. The Fishers Island Yacht Club, in a small white clubhouse beyond the gas dock to starboard, is hospitable to visiting yachtsmen from other recognized clubs. It has showers and launch service from 8 A.M. to 8 P.M. Dock space, so limited at Fishers, and two transient moorings can only be obtained through Fishers Island Marina—(516) 788-7245, VHF-9—located next to the yacht club. All former anchorage areas are now filled with moorings. Shoal-draft boats can obtain complete shelter from all winds in the coves at the south end of the harbor if they can find space.

A channel leading into these shallow inner coves has been dredged, primarily for local commercial use, to a controlled depth of 7 feet at low water. From this narrow buoyed channel's entrance, just southward of Goose Island, boats drawing less than 5 feet may proceed in a southeasterly direction. A pair of buoys northwest of Goose Island helps to point out this passage. Toward the end of this channel, along the port shore, lie the finger piers and marine railway of the Pirates Cove Marina—(516) 788-7528, VHF-9—but they have no facilities for transients and mostly handle only emergency repairs, because parts take a while to arrive. The two nearby basins, congested with local craft, are possible anchorage areas if you can find swinging space.

The Island Galley is a restaurant on the Mobil station's dock selling lobsters, cold drinks, and snacks. One can obtain supplies at the Village Market or at the Fishers Island Shopping Center. Unfortunately, the restaurant at the old Pequot Inn now has pool tables instead of dining tables, and no longer serves food and drink.

West Harbor is typically high-class residential, with many fine yachts permanently moored there in summer. There is plenty to do ashore, but as in other, similar communities, some things may be expensive. The swimming is very good.

Fishers Island has existed for most of a century as a summer playground for the wealthy, whose palatial estates provide the major reason for its being. Now rising taxes, high prices, and a changing life-style are reducing its population—from 508 year-round residents in 1960 to 462 in 1970 to 350 in 1986. The main industry of these people is the summer residents, who as "the working rich," have nowadays less vacation time on the island and thus less time to spend money here. Moreover, two-thirds of the island is privately owned by the summer people. As one native islander has said, "What we need is for more people to come out here right now." But as long as there is Fishers, he may have no fear of a shortage of enthusiastic and loyal boating people.

4. East Harbor, Fishers Island (13214). There is considerable foul ground in East Harbor, but it is well marked with buoys. A good guide on entering is the prominent former Coast Guard station near South Beach, which is now privately owned. The long-private Fishers Island Club pier is the first one you will see to starboard. We found shoal water right off both of these docks. An excellent 18-hole golf course borders on East Harbor. The harbor is exposed to winds from northeast to northwest, but the holding ground is fairly good.

Noank, Connecticut (13214). The Noank peninsula at the mouth of the Mystic River has water on three sides and was originally an Indian summer fishing encampment. It then became a center for building wooden ships and is now a fishing and residential village. For the cruiser, a special attraction is that fresh fruits and vegetables can be obtained within walking distance of all the marinas in Noank. The Universal Store in the center of the peninsula is a small supermarket carrying all the usual items, and a liquor store is alongside. Next door is the Noank Bakery. There are two good restaurants, the Seahorse at Spicer's Marina and the Fisherman at the bridge across the entrance to Palmer's Cove to the west. Also Abbott's Lobster in the Rough Restaurant on the shore of the river is famed throughout the region, and people come from miles around to eat outside and inside and to watch the boats in the nearby channel. New in 1994 is an outdoor seafood restaurant at the Noank Shipyard. The marinas along Noank's eastern shore are exposed to easterly winds and to the wash from the much-used Mystic River channel. See "Mystic Region" (below) for information on navigation and places to stay.

Mason Island, Connecticut (13214). Mason Island, named for John Mason, who led an attack on a Pequot Indian village and so secured the region for further development, is mostly a private residential community with a few marinas on it. It is connected to the mainland by a causeway.

On the east side of the island, with less luxury and more privacy, there is an anchorage between Mason and Dodges Islands off the flagstaff of the Mason Island Yacht Club, which has a pier on the east shore of Mason Island just north of Enders Island. Visiting yachtsmen from other recognized yacht clubs are welcomed at the this attractive club, located on the private property of the Mason Island Company.

Ten feet can be carried 100 yards north of the flagstaff. There is excellent holding ground and plenty of room to swing, but the place is not good in a blow, as it is open to the south and has a long sweep to the north also. On the way up to this secluded, attractive anchorage, be sure to leave nun 6 well to starboard to avoid the rocks northwest of the buoy.

In northerlies, better protection can be found by running around Enders Island into the bight between there and Mason Point. See "Mystic Region" for more information on navigation and places to stay.

Mystic, Connecticut (13214). Mystic is a village on both sides of the Mystic River, connected by a drawbridge. In addition to the usual tourist amenities and shops, there is an A&P store a few blocks east of the bridge, and also a very good market for fresh fruits and vegetables. The famed Mystic Seaport Museum is located above the bridge, and the Mystic Aquarium is a little east of the river and just south of Route I-95. Old Mystic Village, a collection of tourist shops, is just west of the aquarium. There is a bus line with trolley-shaped vehicles that travels a route around all the points of interest. See "Mystic Region" for information on navigation and places to stay.

Mystic Region, Connecticut (13214). In previous editions, Noank, Mystic, and Mason Island were treated separately, but they are really all part of Mystic Harbor so it seems easier and more meaningful to treat them mostly together. The Mystic region including the Mystic Seaport Museum and the Mystic Aquarium is now a very popular tourist desti-

View of the Mystic Seaport Museum at Mystic, Connecticut. Note the whaler, *Charles W. Morgan*, at lower right. *Claire White Peterson Photo.*

nation by land as well as by sea. The new Foxwoods Casino for gambling is a short distance to the north, and is adding to the attraction of the region for visitors.

Anchoring space is pretty limited except for the area between Noank and Groton Long Point. The area is wide open to the south, and most of the better-protected spots have moorings in them. There is some space along the north shore of Mason Island, in quite shallow water, but if you don't draw more than 3 or 4 feet, you might find a spot if you're careful. Another possibility is along the east shore of Mason Island in the special anchorage area shown on the chart. This is also open to the south, but the farther into these inlets you go, the more protected they are. They also become shallower, although some 30-foot sailboats are moored quite far into the cove along the east shore of Mason Island.

With about 20 marinas in the area there are many slips and moorings to rent. A very brief description of each follows, as you would meet them traveling from west to east and up the river. The Mystic River is a no-discharge zone. A few marinas have pumpout stations, and at least one boat now provides this service. Call on VHF-9 for Mystic River Pump-out Boat, and you will probably get a reply.

Spicers Noank Marina is located in West Cove. From the C"1" buoy, head for the forest of masts in the cove and pick up the first of the daymarkers just north of Mouse Island and follow them in. Call on VHF-68 or (203) 536-4978 for instructions. This marina has moorings with launch service and slips, and offers full service with fine floating concrete docks carrying water and electricity but no fuel. It has heads and showers, laundry, ice, the Seahorse Restaurant, good repair and haulout facilities including Schick's Marine Service for good engine work, and a pumpout station. The controlling depth in the channel is 7¹/₂ feet MLW, and about the same at the slips. This is also home for Golden Era Boats and our own Coastline Sailing School and Yacht Charters.

From C"1" follow the buoys into the Mystic River. Note that at the spindle you are meeting another entrance coming in from the east. If you decide to take this passage instead of continuing up the river, remember that you are now exiting and you no longer leave red markers to starboard. A friend lost the end of his finger here in the process of getting unstuck when he didn't realize this. Stay in the channel and don't get too close to the buoys and you'll have no trouble. The controlling depth in the channel all the way to Mystic Seaport is about 14 feet MLW. John Eginton, captain of the schooner *Mystic Clipper*, says to favor the outside of the curves, which is generally the green side except the red side is deeper where the channel swings around Sixpenny Island, and not go directly from buoy 14 to buoy 17 as there is a 9-foot region there.

Noank Shipyard with its fuel dock is the first marina you'll come to. This is a full-service marina with all the usual services plus Dockside Electronics which monitors channel 9 and will fix any electronic problems you may have. The marina also monitors VHF-9, or you can call them at (203) 536-9651 or just land at the fuel dock. A dockside restaurant is also here.

The Maxwell Boat Yard is next, a relatively small marina with minimum facilities. They can be reached at (203) 536-9076.

Abbott's Lobster in the Rough Restaurant is next with a dock and a few tie-up spaces for boaters who want to sample the fare; both tourists and locals come here to eat or to take out the good food. The gulls like the food too, so don't leave it unattended long at an outdoor table.

Next in line is Haring's Dock with fuel and Ford's Lobsters, where you can buy lobsters to cook aboard. Legend has it that Mrs. Haring used to keep an ax handy to cut the lines of anyone who smoked while getting fuel, and she used it a few times.

A little distance beyond is the Ram Island Yacht Club, with a flagpole on the pier. This modest-sized club has $4^{1}/_{2}$ feet at MLW and few services for transients, but may have a guest mooring available.

Next is the Noank Village Boatyard monitoring VHF-68 with phone number (203) 536-1770. This is a much-improved full-service yard that has slips and moorings with launch service. It has repair and haulout facilities and new buildings ashore.

Some of the moorings in this area are owned by the Beebe Cove Marina which is located in Beebe Cove. Their shore facilities are quite limited and must be accessed by taking a dinghy or launch under the railroad bridge. Their moorings are generally rented on a seasonal basis, but they might have one in a pinch. They can be called on (203) 536-0221.

All the marinas mentioned so far are in Noank and are within walking distance of grocery and liquor stores and restaurants, as mentioned earlier. From here, the channel turns east and then north around Sixpenny Island.

Soon thereafter on the starboard side you will come to the quite elegant Mystic River Marina located on the shore of Mason Island. This is a full-service marina with fuel dock, slips with 8 feet of water MLW, and electricity, water, cable TV, and telephone lines on the docks. The pool is a highlight, and also the restaurant, though at the time of writing it was not in action. Good repair and haulout facilities are available as well as a ship's store. The nearest supplies are in downtown Mystic, which is a little far for walking.

Near N"26" a privately maintained set of markers leads off to the east and comes first to the Mason Island Marina which monitors VHF-9 and can also be reached at (203) 536-2608. The controlling depth to here is 5 feet MLW, and the slips have about the same. They have floating docks with water and electricity, and ice, showers, haulout, repairs, and a store.

The privately maintained markers continue to the new Mystic Cove Marina located on the east side of Murphy Point. The controlling depth to the marina is 3 feet MLW, with 6 feet at the slips. They have ice, laundry, showers, a pumpout station, haulout and repair facilities, and a store. As you would guess from the depths, there is not a mast in sight at their slips, and they mostly have seasonal renters, but they do have occasional transients. Their phone number is (203) 536-4945. A plus here is that they are the closest marina to the Flood Tide Restaurant, our favorite spot for a special breakfast, just across the water on the hill beside Pequotsepos Brook. A small dinghy could get under the railroad and road bridges and take you right to the restaurant, but the road bridge is being reworked and that may no longer be possible.

On the way to the Mystic Cove Marina you can see off to starboard two small marinas accommodating mostly small powerboats near the causeway to Mason Island. If you are in a pinch for a tie-up, you might try calling Browers Cove Marina—(203) 536-8864—at the Mason Island end or Shaffers Boat Livery—(203) 536-8713—at the mainland end. You might also find space to anchor, but it's all pretty shallow so be careful.

Continuing on beyond N"26" in the channel on Willow Point to port is the full-service Mystic Shipyard, established in 1843. They monitor channels 9 and 68, and can also be reached at (203) 536-9436. They have ice, laundry, showers, a ship's store, extensive haulout and repair services, and water and electricity on the docks. There is 8 or 9 feet of depth at the slips. A fish market and a gourmet prepared-food market are a few blocks away. From here it is a reasonable walk to downtown Mystic, although grocery stores are across the river.

Tucked in a little cove just beyond is the very small Willow Point Marina—(203) 536-9873—with very few facilities.

Continuing upriver, one comes to the full-service Brewer Yacht Yard on Murphy Point, formerly the Whitmar Marina. They have showers, ice, laundry, pool, and haulout and repair services. They also have a Boaters World discount store, as do most Brewer yards now. They can be reached at (203) 536-2293. Brewer's is within walking distance of the Mystic Railroad Station, an A&P supermarket, and also Sandy's fruit and vegetable market.

Just above this is the Gwenmor Marina—(203) 536-0281—also full-service and near food supplies.

The next item of interest is the railroad swing bridge, which is usually open but closes when a train needs to pass. If it is closed, call the bridge keeper on VHF-13, and he will tell you about how long it will be before he can open it again.

Above the bridge on the port side are four smallish marinas fairly close together, which cater mostly to seasonal people but may have some space for transients. All are within easy walking distance of downtown Mystic and food stores.

The first is Fort Rachel Marina—(203) 536-6647, VHF-9—lying right along the railroad tracks. The name comes from the Revolutionary War era when a gun crew was stationed here near the then local red-light district to prevent British ships from coming farther up the river. It is improving its facilities and offers heads and showers, water and electricity on the docks, fiberglass and some engine repair facilities, and haulout capability. One of our boats spends winters there.

Next is the new Mystic Harbor Marine—(203) 536-1210—with only heads and showers, although the slips have water and electricity.

Then comes the Carija Boatworks—(203) 536-9440—with haulout and hull repair facilities, showers, and water and electricity at the slips.

Next is the Mystic Downtown Marina, (203) 572-5942, which used to be named the Mystic Marine Railway. It is in operation but is in transition and in need of refurbishing. It can sometimes handle transients.

On the east side of the river above the swing bridge is the extensive waterfront of Seaport Marine—(203) 536-9681. This is a combination of working yard, dockominiums, and seasonal renters. Their strength is in handling large boats. They have slips up to 85 feet and can haul out larger boats than any other facility on the Mystic River. Their workshops contain many old belt-driven machines, and old axes, adzes, and caulking mallets are on the walls, but the repair capability is first-rate. Personal facilities are limited to heads and showers, but they are practically in downtown Mystic where facilities of all kinds are available.

The next item of interest is the bascule drawbridge in the center of Mystic. From May 1 through October 31, and between the hours of 7:15 A.M. and 7:15 P.M., the bridge will open at quarter past the hour if there are boats waiting to pass. Currently the 12:15 P.M. opening is not being observed as an experiment; this will probably continue.

Above the bridge is the famed Mystic Seaport Museum, which should be toured by all who are interested in boats, and also by those interested in the shoreside activities of the late 1800s. They have docks for visitors, but advance reservations are generally needed. Reservations may be made by calling (203) 572-5391 and making a $25 deposit. Reservations are held until the 5:15 P.M. bridge opening unless a late arrival is prearranged. Changes must reach the dock office prior to 5 P.M. on the original reservation date or the space will be forfeited. Members get reduced rates and from October through April can dock free except on Saturdays, with a two-night maximum per visit. There are good facilities for people in the New York Yacht Club Station 10 Annex, and the

Seaman's Inn restaurant is close at hand, but there are no haulout or repair facilities. It's a great destination for boat people, and all the facilities and points of interest in downtown Mystic are within walking distance. The price of admission to the seaport is included in the dockage fee; people who are not docking must pay for admission.

Above the seaport, navigation becomes questionable, but for those boats that can handle depths of 30 inches MLW and can get under the 25-foot clearance of the I-95 bridge, the Mystic Basin Marina is a possibility. This is a nice small full-service marina located about ¹/₂ mile north of the bridge on the east side of the river. It is very protected and has a ship's store with some of the lowest prices around. It can be reached at (203) 536-4930 or on VHF-68. It is within walking distance of shops near I-95 and the Old Mystic Village collection of tourist shops to the south, and to the historic real village of Old Mystic to the north. There are privately maintained markers leading into it, but call first for instructions.

The exhibits to visit and the things to see at Mystic Seaport are almost endless. In 1985, the seaport opened an immense art gallery with the capacity to display a minimum of 100 large works at any given time. Further establishing itself as a leader in the marine art world, it recently purchased the Rosenfeld Collection, the most sizable single collection of maritime photographs in the world, containing more than one million images taken from 1880 to 1982.

Frankly, you, your family, and your guests will need at least one full day to see Mystic Seaport properly. Go aboard the tall ships for a keener flavor of their meaning, study the Mystic River Diorama to waft yourself back properly a hundred years to Mystic's formative days, and allow plenty of time to see the formal maritime exhibits and to observe the craft shops in action. Also share the pride and fun of the members of the Joseph Conrad summer camp. These young people are in residence training as part of the seaport-sponsored educational program based on the *Joseph Conrad,* a nineteenth-century, square-rigged training ship.

Other historic vessels to be boarded include the great whaling ship *Charles W. Morgan,* the Grand Banks fishing schooner *L. A. Dunton,* and the *Sabino,* the last active coal-fired steamer in the country, which allows visitors an opportunity to cruise aboard. Visitors can also enjoy a sail around the harbor in a 20-foot reproduction of a Crosby catboat or rent various small sailboats and rowboats. The 60-foot schooner *Brilliant,* formerly used as a yacht, regularly cruises southern New England waters with young and old participants.

The Seaport Planetarium offers several programs, including courses in celestial navigation. Of special interest is the Skywatcher's Guide on Wednesday evenings, when after the presentation in the planetarium, there is outdoor observation through telescopes, weather permitting.

So, by all means, head for Mystic Seaport, take heed of their cheery welcome aboard, and linger a while to relax and to absorb a host of exciting activities and memories.

Stonington, Connecticut (13214). Stonington makes an excellent stopping place. It is well protected, except during hurricane tides, by three breakwaters, the east one 2,000 feet long. In winds from south to northwest, or in no winds at all, the prettiest, quietest, and cleanest anchorage, though the least convenient for landing or supplies, is behind the second breakwater—the long one to port off the west shore. In northwesters you can carry 9 feet close to the west shore. In southwest

The inner breakwater at Stonington is shown on lower left. A boat may be seen rounding Sandy Point, heading through Little Narragansett Bay toward Watch Hill and the Pawcatuck River. *Aero Graphics Co.*

winds, anchorage in the angle of the breakwater is to be preferred. In northerly or easterly winds good shelter can be obtained either behind the small breakwater on the east shore or in the special anchorage area well up the harbor if there is space. This last anchorage is good under ordinary conditions. The only "out" about this area is its congestion and the noise from the passing trains on the main shore line of Amtrak.

In fog, a different sound reverberates across Stonington Harbor. Natives call it the "humidity horn" or, as one shellback snarled, "Everything you can lay a tongue to!" Yachtsmen, however, attempting to enter the harbor in poor visibility will probably bless the blast. It's the foghorn established at the Stonington outer breakwater light, sounding one blast every ten seconds.

The attractive Wadawanuck Yacht Club, on the northeast shore at the head of the harbor, is part of the larger Wadawanuck Club, which engages in athletic and social activities other than yachting. As such, this club is without the launch service, guest moorings, and dock space usually available at larger clubs. Its members, however, participate enthusiastically in the harbor's traditional Wednesday Night Dinghy Series, open to a variety of one-design classes. During one of these races, you can spot as many as seventy-five sailboats tacking to and fro behind the breakwaters.

Yachts visiting Stonington usually put into Dodson Boat Yard run by Robert Snyder and tucked away in the northeast "special anchorage area" shown on the chart. He continues to "improve on an already perfect situation" in serving what previous owner Johnny Dodson used to call "just salty boat-loving people." This is the one all-service facility in the harbor of prime attraction to sailing craft. Dockside, there is berth space for about thirty boats in 7 feet low water. Gas, diesel fuel, water, ice, and electricity are available. Overnight moorings (there are about one hundred) may be rented with launch service running from 8 A.M. to 10 P.M. and monitoring VHF-78. Repair work and hauling are performed, and a marine store, dinghy dock, showers, laundromat, and the Boatyard Cafe are all on hand. Although the holding ground is mud, it is choked with eel grass, which suggests mooring rather than anchoring, and anchoring space is almost nonexistent. Experience has taught us to phone Dodson's ahead of arrival, if possible, to be guaranteed an overnight reservation. Phone (203) 535-1507.

The Stonington Harbor Management Commission is bringing order to this port's increasing congestion. Bob Snyder reports that "there's a great deal of pressure to have more moorings at Stonington." Agreeing that there is a need for a practical harbor plan, Bob states, "It's vital to have a degree of order in the assignment and placement of moorings." As a partial solution to the problem, one of the commission's plans calls for dredging to provide additional mooring space in the northwest corner of the harbor.

Stonington Boat Works is no more. In 1980, this historic yard, which turned out fishing draggers in Stonington's heyday as a fishing village, was razed to make way for the waterfront condominiums visible today.

Stonington has all the facilities a yachtsman is apt to desire in the way of supplies, repairs, and communications. The shopping district on Water Street includes gifts, art galleries, antiques, grocery stores, gourmet foods, liquor, ladies' wear, and a dry cleaner. The Harbor View Restaurant, far down Water Street toward the point, is a must for anyone who dotes on French cuisine. A long pier of the Skipper's Dock and Harbor View juts out from the shore inside Stonington's inner breakwater. Skipper's Dock has complimentary dockage with the possibility of an overnight tie-up for a nominal fee and dishes up lobster, steamers, chowder, and what have you, for patrons to eat informally dockside or to spirit aboard. Noah's Restaurant just to the north is also very good, as is One South Cafe near Dodson's.

"The Village Fair" is a Stonington tradition held on the first Saturday in August for young and old. The annual "Blessing of the Fleet" in July is a festival for the last commercial fishing fleet in Connecticut. If you happen to run into this, be ready for parades, balloons, plenty of people, and excitement galore.

Stonington helped to make history and was once called a "nursery for seamen." Captain Edmund Fanning of Stonington served as a midshipman under John Paul Jones. When he was eighteen years old (July 15, 1798), he discovered the Fanning Islands, now an important air stop on the Pacific Ocean. During the Revolution and the War of 1812, the town was twice attacked by the British and twice successfully repelled the invaders. Some British cannonballs are now valued relics.* The town has that intangible quality called "atmosphere," and it's fun to wander through its streets, perhaps on the way to view relics of bygone days in the

---

*Historical data from *Connecticut*—American Guide Series (Houghton Mifflin Co., Boston).

museum of the Stonington Historical Society at the old granite light-house near Stonington Point.

Watch Hill, Rhode Island (13214). If you plan to bypass this harbor and negotiate Watch Hill Passage, we would like to alert the helmsman. You will note the sideways set of the strong current through this area—southward on the ebb, northward on the flood. If not aware of these conditions and the possibility of buoys' being towed under, you can inadvertently be swept toward the rocks and reefs bordering the passage.

As the chart clearly shows, the anchorage at Stonington is nearer the east-west course through Fishers Island Sound than is the anchorage at Watch Hill. To reach the latter, it is necessary to go a considerable distance to the north around Sandy Point and then southeast through a well-buoyed but narrow channel. For this reason, Watch Hill is a less frequent port of call for 'longshore cruisers than it deserves to be, as it has been an attractive seashore resort since 1840, when its lighthouse keeper, Captain Jonathan Nash, built the area's first beach hotel.

The 1992 *Coast Pilot* says that "in December 1989 the controlling depth was 4$^{1}/_{2}$ feet from the entrance to Little Narragansett Bay to the entrance to the Pawcatuck River." Stay close to the northern part of the channel near green flasher 3 north of Sandy Point because the shoal there is moving into the channel. Before the 1938 hurricane, Sandy Point was attached to Napatree Point, so it has a history of moving. The *Coast Pilot* recommends that strangers seek local knowledge because of rocks and shoals at the edges of the channel. Dredging is under consideration by the Army Corps of Engineers. After that, follow the entrance channel carefully, while avoiding a host of lobster pots floating about. Stick close to the green cans to port. Continue to follow the tight upper channel carefully as there are rocks and shoal spots in several places just off the channel. According to local yachtsmen, at least 8 feet can be carried at low water through the short channel leading into Watch Hill Cove.

There are several good docks for visiting yachts. The first to starboard that entering yachts will reach is the hospitable Watch Hill Yacht Club's, where the usual reciprocal privileges are given to members of other recognized yacht clubs. Launch service runs here, and you may be able to pick up a spare mooring in the 10-foot anchorage area by first checking with the club steward on VHF-10. They do not accept reservations. A possible anchorage may be found just west of the club's small-boat fleet outside the breakwater, or run up the cove to the large Watch Hill Docks, operated by Frank Hall Boat Yard—(401) 348-8005. Here one can find overnight dockage, water, ice on order, diesel fuel, and electricity, with a depth of 7 feet alongside and a dinghy dock for anchored boaters. Check for space with the dockmaster. This is such a popular spot for visiting yachts that he suggests you phone his office at (401) 596-7807 at least two weeks in advance of your arrival for a slip reservation. Even a deposit is required. No gas is available in the cove until you reach the Watch Hill Boat Yard. Stores are near at hand, and the Watch Hill Inn offers exceptional dining overlooking Little Narragansett Bay.

Donald Greene, commodore of the yacht club, advises that no lights are required within the inner anchorage and that no rafting is permitted in the inner harbor. He also suggests that Jim Long, who is at the Watch Hill Boat Yard up the Pawcatuck River, will service your boat at the yacht club; phone him at (401) 348-8148.

The only "out" about Watch Hill is that it usually takes a terrible licking in hurricanes, for the protecting Napatree Beach is low and hurricane-driven tides go right over it. Hurricane Carol (August 31, 1954) badly damaged the yacht club's house and docks. It is also vulnerable to winds coming in from the north to northwest. In a blow you can move above the mouth of the Pawcatuck River on the west side in reportedly good holding ground. There are three state moorings in Watch Hill Cove.

A recent correspondent writes that "more might be said about the pleasures of Napatree Point. It is most accessible by boat, offering a beautiful beach on the south side—fine for swimming and picnicking. The best anchorage is along the northern shore in the 7-foot charted area midway between the mainland and the point. There's not much protection and the tidal currents become stronger closer to the point. This spot is popular on the weekends because it also promises a pleasant walk on the beach and tempts the kids to explore the ruins of a mysterious old gun emplacement." Watch out for the poison ivy. These are part of the remains of Fort Mansfield, an abandoned coast artillery station built before World War I. There is an osprey nest fairly far out along the bay side, which should not be disturbed.

Westerly, Rhode Island (13214). Those who want better protection or who like to poke their way up rivers or creeks may find it interesting to go up the scenic Pawcatuck River for all or part of the way to Westerly. From Watch Hill Cove, a mid-channel depth of 7 feet MLW can be carried as far as nun 14 located off Certain Draw Point. On your way, you will first see to starboard the Watch Hill Boat Yard—(401) 348-8148, VHF-9—headquarters on Colonel Willie Cove. To reach there, make a heading, just before reaching nun 4, toward the marshy end of Graves Neck. Having passed this point fairly close aboard, swing to the southeast to pick up the yard's buoyed channel. Depths for this approach are 5 feet. They have tie-ups and moorings available, and there is some anchoring space in the cove. A little farther up on the east side is the Avondale Boat Yard—(401) 348-8187, VHF-16—with fuel, and just above that is the Frank Hall Boat Yard—(401) 348-8005, VHF-9—now run by his grandson John. All three of these marinas have slips with electricity and water and can do major repairs and haulouts and have marine stores. There is a small convenience store a short distance from the Frank Hall Boat Yard. The small Greenhaven Marina across the river has few facilities but might have a slip for a small boat in a pinch. The Lotteryville Marina—(401) 348-8064—just south of the Frank Hall Boat Yard seemed a little less active when we were there, but might be a possibility for a slip.

Still farther up, there is a tight anchorage to port just beyond nun 14, where the bottom is mud. The river narrows considerably at Pawcatuck Rock and nun 16, and then opens again. To starboard are the marina and clubhouse of the Westerly Yacht Club—(401) 596-7556, VHF-9—which has many slips with water and electricity and many powerboats tied up in $5^1/_2$ feet of water. Any available slips will be rented to members in good standing of other yacht clubs. Across the river is the new Stonington on the River dockominiums, which have some slips available to transients. Their docks sport cable TV and phone connections as well as water and electricity. A pool and "common room" with dry bar and TV are available for use.

The government buoys end by the yacht club, and the buoys farther up the river are privately maintained. Norwest Marine—(203) 599-2442, VHF-68—is located a mile or so farther up on the west side. They have slips, a store, fuel, and a group of outdoor grills and picnic tables for their customers. The channel is marked and passable for some deep keels, but the local word is that "you can't follow along the red line" and that a recent hurricane silted things in quite a bit. So stay clear of the east side of the channel. Farther up the river on the east side are three marinas predominantly oriented to powerboats and offering repair services. In order, they are: Pier 65 Marine Services—(401) 596-6530—with one head, one shower, and limited repair facilities; the Westerly Marina—

(401) 596-1727—with no apparent transient facilities; and the Viking Marina—(401) 348-0277—with heads and showers and the Dockside Restaurant on the premises. There were a few large sailboats up there, but it would be wise to call for local knowledge if you draw more than 3 or 4 feet. Still farther up river the beautiful scenery is replaced by old factory buildings. When you get as far up as the Route 1 bridge, you can tie up, but you need a ladder to get up to the land.

On our many visits here, we are always treated to an idyllic scene of countless swans and cygnets wending their way upstream. There must be several hundred of them at least—all feeding, as we were once told, on the green sea moss thriving so abundantly along the river coves.

Block Island, Rhode Island (13217, 13215). Although discovered by Giovanni da Verrazano in 1524, Block Island was named for Adriaen Block, who first arrived there, nearly ninety years later, on his way to Narragansett Bay. Verrazano found the hills of the island covered with trees, most of which have long since gone, though various types of wild flowers now help to fill the aesthetic gap. The Indians called it the Isle of Manisses or Little God's Island. The clay-formed Mohegan Bluffs, which remind one of the chalk cliffs of Dover, stretch along the island's southern shore, rising to more than 200 feet above sea level. They were so named when, centuries ago, the island's Manissean Indians drove a group of invading Mohegans across the moors and over these majestic bluffs to their deaths.

About 5 miles long and with an elevation of 211 feet, this is the first of the outlying islands encountered on the way east from Long Island Sound. Though not so attractive as Martha's Vineyard, Nantucket, and other islands farther east, it is an interesting place to visit and a convenient offshore stopping point on the way to Vineyard Sound.

There are two good harbors, one on the east and one on the west side of the island; the latter is the harbor usually preferred by yachtsmen, as the former is small and used mainly by commercial fishermen. There is a good deal of open water between Long Island, Block Island, and the mainland, so anyone who ventures to Block Island in a small boat must be prepared to go to sea. Fogs are frequent in Block Island Sound during July and August and the current information in *Eldridge* must be carefully determined. It has been estimated that 500,000 recreational craft frequent busy Block Island Sound and the east entrance to Long Island Sound each year.

In the vicinity of Montauk, on the ebb tide, there is a decided trend of the current to the eastward. If one is bound for Block Island, it is well to get away from the Long Island shore, so as to minimize the current and avoid the rips off Montauk. One correspondent writes: "I decided at the last moment, 5:30 P.M., to sail to Block Island in a light 4-knot wind at full ebb tide. The course was east by north. I sailed northeast, and hit Salt Pond Light on the nose at 10:15 P.M."

As one approaches "Block" from east or west in clear visibility, it resembles two islands, with the northern part hilly only along its eastern shore and the southern part mostly high ground, the tallest point of which is marked by a stone castle atop Beacon Hill at a 200-foot level. Coming from Point Judith, stay well clear of Block Island North Reef, which kicks up a vicious rip when the tidal current runs strong and especially when there is an opposing wind. Should you run round the island to New Harbor from the east or make for Old Harbor from the west be sure to stay north of 1 BI Bell. And if you are going around the south end of the island in heavy weather, watch out for breaking seas on Southwest Ledge. Southeast Light, housed in a 67-foot tower, with a radio beacon and fog signal, looms high on the southeast point of the island. Its fog signal is reported difficult to hear close to, but is quite audible several miles away.

1. Great Salt Pond, Block Island (13217).   Because of two jetty lights, the fog signal on this jetty to the southwest of the entrance, and the Block Island Coast Guard Station nearby—this harbor, whose southern part is called New Harbor, is quite easy to make. A new white beacon flashing red has been constructed on the end of the southwest jetty. In 1990, the 150-foot-wide channel recorded depths of 15 feet with shoaling to starboard on entering. As most of the bad weather at Block Island comes from the east, it is to be preferred to Old Harbor, though it is large and can be rough, particularly in a northeast gale. In proceeding upchannel, keep well off the submerged pipeline and cable area running parallel and off of most of the western shore as shown on the chart. Block Island is such a popular place, especially on weekends and holidays, that it is not uncommon to have upward of 1,500 boats anchored there during the summer months. There are at present ninety transient moorings that are managed by the town. These are lime-green in color and are available on a first-come, first-served basis. All are located in the southwestern part of the harbor. In 1994 the fee for a mooring was $30 per night and included free pumpout services. The harbormaster will come alongside to collect. The usual anchorage is near the southeast end, well off the ferry landing in 15 to 48 feet. Take extreme care to leave a fairway to the landing. It is often difficult to set an anchor, and dragging is fairly common.

Meanwhile, the New Shoreham Town Committee has approved a harbor plan. The plan calls for the formation of a restricted anchorage in the northeast corner of the pond. This will serve two purposes. It can be opened up temporarily as a harbor of refuge in case of severe storms and will provide a protected bed for the seeding of scallops and quahogs.

In a storm, go to the snug inner harbor, readily navigable and land-locked as noted on the chart north of Fort I. Proceed to the steamer dock and follow in closely along its eastern side. The 10-foot channel will lead you to an inlet known as the Hog Pen or Smuggler's Cove. Smuggler's Cove Marina, located there, has provisions for sale. Payne's Dock at the landing has good facilities, with dockage and electricity, gas, diesel fuel, ice, showers, groceries, charts, bicycles for rent, and local delicacies—clam cakes and chowder. This is a favorite marina to many people, and its lack of repair service is apparently no drawback. Payne's monitors VHF-68. Aldo's Bakery is well known, but tastier pastry can reportedly be found in a small shop on the corner of the Block Island Grocery. In 1994 a boat from Aldo's Bakery was selling wares through the mooring area in the morning.

Champlin's Marina, down on the western shore of the harbor, is the home base for Block Island Race Week, sponsored every other year since 1965 (non–Bermuda Race years) by the Storm Trysail Club. Among the facilities or supplies obtainable here are gas, diesel fuel, water, ice, marine supplies, charts, engine repairs, showers, a salt-water swimming pool, laundromat, bike and car rentals, boat charters, a restaurant, and basic food supplies in a shack dockside. Although Champlin's monitors VHF-68, we were advised to phone for a slip reservation: (401) 466-2641. Launch service, provided for a fee and operated by Oldport Marine Services and Champlin's, runs regularly to and from Block Island Boat Basin, Payne's, and Champlin's from 7:30 A.M. to 1 A.M. On a recent visit to this harbor, there were so many boats lined up at the fuel dock, we had to wait an hour for our turn at the pump. However, at midmorning in 1994, there was no problem.

Deadeye Dick's Restaurant, 200 yards up the road from the steamboat dock, is well recommended for its excellent service and food, particularly its swordfish and lobsters. Ballard's Inn, over at Old Harbor, has been renovated and offers room and board the year round. Champlin runs a jitney service to and from the center of town and to Ballard's every twenty minutes. Smuggler's Cove is a new restaurant next door to Deadeye Dick's, specializing in seafood dishes.

We have often been reminded by other yachtsmen that this harbor is deep and that the bottom close to shore, although quite shallow, shelves off steeply. Yachts setting their anchors must allow for plenty of scope and swinging room. And in case of a blow, they usually head for the southeast sector of the harbor for protection. How well we remember observing a Cruising Club fleet safely ride out a driving gale while anchored along the shore just to the northwest of Champlin's dock where the nearby bluffs afford shelter from winds out of the south and west.

Champlin has an attractive competitor lying just to the west of the ferry landing. Block Island Boat Basin has become a popular port of call of the Off Soundings fleet and appeals to family groups. It doesn't boast a swimming pool, but in other respects its services are comparable to Champlin's. In addition, it has a 25-ton lift, complete repair work, the well-stocked Windjammer Gift Store, the Oar Restaurant for cocktails and light meals, a marine store, and the Marina Deli, where food supplies may be purchased. There's even a diver on hand for underwater repair work. Depths at the floating docks are 10 feet MLW. This place is quiet at night, perhaps due to the no-rafting rule strictly enforced. Their free bus service over to Ballard's Inn is a wonderful convenience. The Boat Basin suggests you call (401) 466-2631 to reserve a slip.

For excellent surf bathing, take the dinghy to the shore east by north from Champlin's dock, $1/2$ to $3/4$ mile. Then cross the road and take the path through a break in the fence to the ocean. It is also a short distance by land from the marinas. Here is 2-mile Crescent Beach; once practically deserted, it now has a state bathhouse with free changing rooms and lockers, a snack bar, and lifeguards. It still remains one of the most beautiful beaches we know of along the New England coast.

The Interstate Navigation Co. (Point Judith, Rhode Island) operates steamers between Point Judith and Block Island, four times daily in summer and once a day (except Sundays) in winter. It also runs daily trips in summer from Providence and Newport, arriving and departing from Old Harbor. The Nelseco Navigation Co. (New London, Connecticut) operates between New London and Block Island once a day in summer. Sailing time from Point Judith is about one and one-quarter hours; from

New London, two and one-quarter hours. Get in touch with these companies if you want their latest schedules. Viking Airlines runs daily flights between Block Island and Providence, and Block Island and Westerly.

A sightseeing trip is one of the memorable pleasures a cruise to Block Island provides. Take a taxi or peddle a bike past miles of moors, rolling hills, and magnificent sand dunes and cliffs, without a tree in sight. There are hundreds of freshwater ponds, 365 to be exact. Head north from Old Harbor on Corn Neck Road leading to Sachem Pond and stop for a dip on Crescent Beach on the way. About 1 1/2 miles beyond lies The Maze, a labyrinth of over 10 miles of crisscrossing paths meandering through pine forests that emerge magnificently above the high cliffs at the northeast end of the island. Or head south following High Street (it turns into Pilot Hill Road after a while) to the Mohegan Trail, a dirt path that leads to the Bluffs.

Here, according to Dr. Gerald Abbott of the Block Island Historical Society, is "absolutely the most popular tourist attraction on Block Island. It's come to symbolize the island." This is Southeast Light, first lighted in 1875 with a range of 21 miles. Until very recently, the light perched just 86 feet away from an eroding cliff, but thanks to a valiant fund raising drive to save the Gothic Revival, Southeast Light has been successfully moved back to safer ground. We attended the re-lighting ceremony in 1994.

For quick trips around the Island, cabs are available at Champlin's or the ferry dock or from town. Mrs. Melvin Rose, better known as Maizie, who was one of our drivers several years ago, wrote a fine book about her island entitled *Block Island Scrap Book*. Another book we can heartily recommend is *Block Island Lore and Legends* by Mrs. Frederick N. Ritchie.

John P. Runyon, a Corinthian yachtsman, beautifully describes just one of the many spells that Block Island casts over us in this description of Block Island Race Week:

> It is a weeklong gathering of yachts from the entire Atlantic Sea-board from 64-footers to the MORCs. No one who has seen or participated in the morning parade of three hundred magnificent yachts down the channel out of Great Pond, sometimes in bright early-morning sunlight, often in swirling fog, can fail to be thrilled as this great fleet debouches into Block Island Sound, maneuvering

around the Committee Boat for the starts of the many classes. Or at the heart-stopping sight of the forest of masts with fluttering burgees and the gleaming hulls filling every available space in Champlin's and the Block Island Marina with the overflow moored so thickly that the New London ferry can barely get through to its slip. And there is the fun of joining in the variety of shore activities planned for the afternoons and one lay day—everything from kite flying, to trap shooting, to dancing, to the traditional band. There are the crowds waiting anxiously around the bulletin boards for the day's results to be posted, the lobster dinners ashore, the beer, the sociability, the excitement and the fun!

2. Block Island Harbor on East Harbor (13217). This artificial harbor on the eastern shore, shown on the chart as Old Harbor, is likely to be crowded in summer. In coming in from the east in a fog, watch for the dead spot under the cliffs; you may not hear the foghorn at Block Island Southeast Lighthouse. A member of the Cruising Club of America lost a boat here a few years ago. "Lots of others, too," writes a correspondent.

Since there is heavy traffic from the ferries from Point Judith and Providence in the inner harbor, no anchoring is permitted here. However, visiting boats may arrange with the harbormaster to tie up, if there is space, at the town dock. There's solid bulkheading along the eastern shore of this basin in front of Ballard's Inn; make sure to stay clear of the ferry dock to the west. Old Harbor Dock now has gas, diesel fuel, ice, water, and showers in the inn. In 1986, a devastating fire reduced Ballard's Inn to ashes but left the dock area untouched. An even larger Ballard's Inn has been built on the original site. Register at the dockmaster's office at the head of the harbor. At low water the depths are 14 feet in the inner harbor and 12 feet in the less-protected outer basin.

Old Harbor is closer to most of the "action" on the island with interesting shops, boutiques, hotels, night spots, and restaurants all within walking distance. There is an annotated map of the island published by the Chamber of Commerce that you can pick up at the ferry dock or at just about any of the gift shops. Stylish Manisses up the hill from the harbor is a restored Victorian building with a bustling restaurant. All kinds of provisions can be purchased here in New Shoreham at the largest market in town, Block Island Grocery. The Spring House, the largest and oldest hotel, built in 1852, is on a hill a short walk south of

Port Judith Harbor of Refuge and Point Judith Pond looking East.
Aero Graphics Corp.

town. Jackets are required in its dining room. Nearby, the 1661 Inn has a reported reputation for the best gourmet dining on the island, and Ernie's Old Harbor Restaurant caters to seafood gourmands. There's a rusticated movie theatre here, but if you want a picture of Block Island nightlife, try Smuggler's Cove or the Block Island Inn.

Block Island was never popular as a summer resort for the very well-to-do. There are no imposing "cottages" like those to be found in Newport and on Fishers Island. There was no adequate harbor at first, so the whaling vessels didn't put in. Perhaps that's why you don't see any imposing mansions with their "captain's walks," like those found on the Vineyard. But Block Island's heyday finally arrived during the latter half of the nineteenth century, when Victorian architecture was all the rage.

The famous Ocean View Hotel was erected in 1873 and stood on that prominent knoll above Old Harbor's entrance. It had two notable features: It had the longest bar in the world (287 feet long, with one hundred bar stools), and it was the summer White House of President

Grant. Whether there was any connection between these two facts, no one has discovered. All we know is that the bartenders wore roller skates to provide for their thirsty customers with unusual alacrity, and that this wonderful old homestead burned to the ground in 1966.

Point Judith Harbor of Refuge, Rhode Island (13219). If you are approaching Point Judith Light from the northeast, be careful to maintain a course 2 miles off of Point Judith Neck. These offshore waters are thriving with fish traps. "The Point appears like a Nag's Head and is pretty bold," comments the *American Coast Pilot* published in 1798.

Anchor in the southern end of the harbor—the angle of the main breakwater—in about 4 fathoms. This is almost the only good holding ground, and here the water is usually quietest. One should be aware of the heavy kelp at the bottom; a sandbar continues to build up inside the elbow of the breakwater and parallel along it to the north, so give it a good berth.

Care should be taken not to anchor too far southward in the V-shaped part of the breakwater. In sudden northwest squalls at night, several boats have gone ashore on the inside of the breakwater and been completely wrecked. While the water inside the breakwater is apparently calm, the surge of the sea penetrates through the rocks, making landing on all parts of the V-shaped breakwater difficult, except in the calmest weather. Note that East breakwater light 3 has been equipped with a flashing green light with a square-shaped green daymark, while West breakwater light 2 has a red reflector and a triangular red daymark.

Since this can often be an uneasy, godforsaken anchorage for a small yacht, most skippers wisely prefer to go north toward Point Judith Pond following the marked channel while avoiding the fish nets and lobster pots strung along its western edge. The only difficulty about Galilee is revealed by Bob Brow, superintendent of State Piers. "This port is basically commercial and we have very few transients in pleasure craft. The Block Island Ferry dock is here and the state piers, which offer no services, are all assigned to draggers, lobstermen, and sports fishing charterers." The alternative is to proceed up the main channel in the pond for 3 or 4 miles to the thriving city of Wakefield.

Galilee, Rhode Island (13219). There are now no sources for fuel or supplies along the east shore at Galilee or docks where visiting yachts can tie up conveniently. If you do find a spot, you can obtain any necessary information at the Coast Guard station on the waterfront or from the harbormaster, whose office is on the shore end of the state pier. Once ashore, you will find on the main road stores, restaurants, hot-dog joints, and what have you. Don't forget to visit George's Restaurant located at the foot of the main road. It's a mecca for seafood gourmands. You'll see a mixture of all kinds of people, from genuine fishermen to tourists in search of atmosphere or a good time. The noise pollution emitted here at dawn by fishermen, gulls, and engines shouldn't upset the early riser.

This port is a good place for shelter, but you will like it better on weekdays than on weekends unless you are very gregarious by nature. The tide is strong at times, and if you are at anchor, you may do some swinging. This is especially true if you attempt to anchor in the small dredged basin shown on the chart as directly south of Little Comfort Island and the Stonington Seafood docks. The best depth here, 6 feet MLW, is found right off the commercial docks. But this place, with its mud bottom and its almost imperceptible whirlpool action caused by the tidal currents, will have you swinging on your anchor and may even break it out.

To reach Snug Harbor on the west shore of Point Judith Pond just beyond Galilee, proceed northward, having left nun 2 to starboard. Anticipate heavy boat traffic pouring through the narrow main channel at nun 2A, which should be kept well to starboard due to a shoal encroaching from the east. First you'll come upon Snug Harbor Marina—(401) 783-7766—catering mostly to powerboats and offering slips, gas, diesel fuel, ice, groceries, a fish market, and a tackle shop, but no repair service. Next, Point Judith Marina—(401) 789-7189—near nun 4, identified by a large Texaco sign just beyond the defunct Rhode Island Marine Services, has 8 feet of water dockside and specializes in handling sailcraft. It reportedly has very competent and complete repair service and a 30-ton travelift. And, finally, you will reach Salt Pond Marine Railway, which handles mostly commercial vessels, but is also a full-service yard and provides showers and supplies. All of these monitor VHF-9 and are fine facilities, but once tied up at one of the slips, you are apt to get a good roll from the nearby channel traffic. Excellent quahauging is reported to be found in the pond.

Wakefield, Rhode Island (13219). If you have time and your boat draws under 4½ feet, you can follow, preferably at high water, the buoyed channel for 3 or 4 miles to the attractive city of Wakefield, where there are good shopping facilities, motels, eating places, etc. Note on the chart the comment that "improved channels shown by broken lines are subject to shoaling, particularly at the edges." Most experienced boating people also know that channels dredged out of shoal and marsh can silt up quickly, especially in a storm. The passage from Snug Harbor, beginning at can 7 and extending to nun 12 south of Plato Island, is a channel where it is beginning to be a problem, and there are no immediate plans for dredging.

Making this passage on a *flood* tide, during one of our visits, we tailed a Concordia yawl of 5'8" draft without incident. The mean range of tide is 3 feet. Consult your chart and favor the port side of the channel all the way up. Along the way, anchorage can be found in several places, one of which is Smelt Brook Cove in the northwestern part of Judith Pond just north of Crown Point. Stay fairly close to the port shore on entering, since a rock ledge lies along the northern mouth of the cove. Here you can lie at a quiet anchorage in about 5 feet of water lined with a gravel bottom. Another good anchorage, though exposed to the north and south, is between Gardner and Beach Islands. As you proceed northward between the channel's nun 16 and can 21, be sure to follow the buoys rather than what appears on the chart as the deeper water. A dangerous spot for strangers is what natives term "Bill's Island," a rock shelf to starboard between nuns 16 and 18. Move cautiously throughout this area, keeping both rock and nun at least 100 feet to starboard. Also farther up the very narrow channel lie charted rocks due south of nun 24. These can be avoided by giving this nun sufficient berth.

During our many visits to Wakefield, we became friendly with the late Bill Schmid of the Ram Point Marina—(401) 783-4535—now run by his son, Curt. We can still vouch for their very competent engine and hull repair work as well as for their genial hospitality. Their other services include gas, diesel fuel, laundry, pumpout, water, ice, showers, electricity, a 15-ton travelift, and slips with 5 feet MLW. Curt monitors VHF-9; his office is open from 8 A.M. to 8 P.M. We suggest you do not anchor here at Wakefield since the basin's mud bottom offers poor holding ground. Instead, hang on to one of the marina's moorings for a nominal overnight charge. This is such a popular spot that it might be wise to phone (401) 783-4535 or radio ahead for an advance reservation. Ram Point's facilities are quite adequate, but you'll have to go a mile to Wakefield for supplies. The marina's store is well stocked with charts, marine gear, and gifts.

Two small yacht clubs, the Point Judith Yacht Club and the University of Rhode Island Sailing Club, are perched farther up on the same shore. The yacht club, housed in a small shingled clubhouse, offers showers, ice, and a possible slip for the night. If you wish to dock and dine next door, try the South Shore Grill, formerly Long John's Restaurant and Marina, reportedly good but expensive. Stone Cove Marine at the head of the pond is a haven for powerboats and is crowded with local craft. Just south of Ram Point Marina is the Silver Spring Marina—(401) 783-0783—in somewhat shallow water with planned dredging, full service, a good store, and a family atmosphere. The following reputable restaurants can easily be reached by taxi: Larchwood Inn requires only casual dress and offers music and dancing; the Sweet Meadows Inn is located in a charming old mansion, caters to guests in more formal attire, and is quite expensive; and Open Hearth Steaks invites its customers to "come as you are."

Narragansett Bay, Rhode Island and Massachusetts (13223, 13224, 13221). A well-known manufacturer of small boats tells of a yachtsman who chartered a yacht from him in Narragansett Bay for a period of three weeks during World War II, and then discovered that he couldn't take the boat out of the bay. A submarine net barred his way.

"Don't keep her any longer than you want to and we'll fix the price accordingly," said the boat manufacturer.

Three weeks passed, with nothing heard from the fellow who did the chartering until the last day.

"I could have spent a month cruising in Narragansett Bay," was his enthusiastic comment.

This well-protected, well-buoyed, well-lighted bay of many good harbors affords some delightful sailing, despite the omnipresent United States Navy. The scenery is restful and pastoral, the water is generally smooth, and the wind is usually just right. At the foot of the bay is the famous yachting harbor of Newport, where the Bermuda racing fleet gathers every other June. At the head of the bay, 24 miles from the open sea, are two great cities: Providence and Fall River. In between is an almost bewildering collection of islands, peninsulas, bays, and passages, easy to navigate, lovely to sail.

As in Buzzards Bay, the prevailing summer winds are from the southwest, but they are usually less violent. A typical summer day is likely to include a light northerly in the early morning, then a calm until the early afternoon, when a moderate sou'wester will begin to stir up a few whitecaps. With evening, calm again descends upon the waters of the bay. The swimming is good in many parts of the lower bay—not so good near Providence and Fall River.

Although Narragansett Bay took severe beatings from the hurricanes of September 21, 1938, and August 31, 1954 (Hurricane Carol), and also damage from subsequent hurricanes, its yacht clubs and fleets have recovered, and the area is far better equipped than ever before to take another, if it comes. For instance, the Rhode Island Yacht Club, on the Providence River, which has had two clubhouses washed away, is now perched up in the air on "stilts."

There are at least thirty-five good harbors in Rhode Island waters, including Narragansett Bay (a small part of which is in Massachusetts), and we have counted twenty-eight yacht clubs. Boatyards and marinas are well spread out over the bay. At the time of writing there are seventeen state summer-guest moorings strategically placed in various harbors. These moorings are about 2 feet in diameter and are stenciled with the words "State of R.I. Guest Mooring Buoy." They are maintained by the Rhode Island Department of Natural Resources, are marked with the weights of the anchors, and are limited to 12-hour use. Yachtsmen are also advised to keep a sharp lookout, especially at night, for fish weirs or traps, which, as shown by the dotted lines on the charts, are strung out throughout the bay.

The increasing number of the most dangerous fish trap areas that run considerably offshore in Rhode Island waters are located along the east side of Point Judith Neck, east of Brenton Reef, south of Aquidneck Island, and around Sakonnet Point, and a single trap can usually be spotted near the entrance to Sakonnet Harbor. Our advice in avoiding these menacing weirs is as follows: Do not cross anywhere between the lines of the dark-colored floating drums, don't try to pass inshore of the trap areas, and don't cut between two traps that appear to be a pair. The best tactic to take is to bypass them, keeping well offshore of them at all times.

A word of caution: The Brenton Reef Tower has been taken down, and plans to replace it are unknown at time of writing. This long-familiar reference point, located about 1½ miles south of Beaver Neck on

Conanicut Island, along with its light and horn, is totally gone, so don't look for it or be confused when it doesn't appear.

The Rhode Island Yachting Association is active in sponsoring and stimulating racing, and the Twenty Hundred Club sponsors races by cruising craft to Cuttyhunk and elsewhere. Indeed it is a fine cruising area, as recognized by the Cruising Club of America, one of whose summer-cruise announcements contained these words: "Your Committee, having had so many wonderful reports of cruising in Narragansett Bay, has scheduled the next rendezvous at Bristol, Rhode Island."

There are three important passages running up the bay in a northerly direction: the *West Passage,* starting between the mainland on the west side of the bay and Conanicut Island; the *East Passage,* between Conanicut and Aquidneck Islands, with Newport as the usual takeoff point; and the *Sakonnet River,* with Sakonnet Harbor at its southern end. Newport and Sakonnet harbors are convenient ports of call for 'longshore cruisers, but we are not forgetting here that they are also starting points for cruising on Narragansett Bay.

In this book we shall follow each of the three above passages northward, stopping at each harbor on the way. The ports are all in Rhode Island, unless otherwise stated. As usual, we are giving the numbers of the largest-scale charts available. Chart 13221, however, covers very well the whole bay.

West Passage

1. Dutch Island Harbor (13223). Among many Rhode Island yachtsmen, this is the most popular harbor on the bay, not for its facilities, for there are almost none, but partly because of its lack of them. It is unspoiled, uncrowded even when a yacht-club fleet makes it a rendezvous; the swimming is fine, and except in blows from the north it is fairly well protected.

The blinking red beacon of Dutch Island Lighthouse, which has guided boats along the west passage of Narrangansett Bay since 1827, flashes no more. An official has stated that "since the Navy left Newport, vandals have had a field day," and apparently the high repair costs were instrumental in deciding to close the lighthouse down. The light has been replaced by a lighted gong buoy on the southern side of the passage to help the helmsman enter this harbor at night.

There are no important outlying obstacles at the harbor's entrance after you have left nun 2 to starboard. Dutch Harbor Shipyard, on the east shore just north of a prominent steel pier, has a deep-water dock with gas, diesel fuel, ice, and water on tap. It is a small working yard with limited "people" services, but with a pumpout station nearby. Although the dock can accommodate several boats, the approach to it must be kept clear. Brad Lorensen, who runs this marina, can be reached at (401) 423-0630 or VHF-68 to reserve one of his twenty-plus guest moorings with launch service provided. Yachts preferring to anchor (the harbor's bottom is silt providing good holding ground) must stay out of the permanent mooring area.

Supplies may be purchased within a pleasant 10-minute walk up the street from the marina to the first traffic light. Turn left at the light to come upon Cumberland Farms or turn right to reach a supermarket, laundromat, telephones, hardware store, pizza place, and post office.

The New York Yacht Club's fleet of over one hundred yachts made Dutch Island Harbor a port of call in 1985. This gives you an idea of its spaciousness. At the time of writing there are five state moorings here in summer. If none is available when you arrive, the best anchorage is between the wharf at the northerly end of Fox Hill and the eastern shore of the harbor or in the small bight on the southeast side of Dutch Island. Those trailers swarming on top of Fox Hill congregate in what is called the Fort Getty Recreation Area. An excellent launching ramp is at the foot of the hill.

2. Wickford (13223). In contrast to Dutch Island Harbor, Wickford has more facilities than any port on the bay. On approaching the harbor, pick up the church spire in Wickford or the prominent abandoned lighthouse on Poplar Point. Some may prefer to anchor behind the breakwaters in the outer harbor to obtain more privacy, perhaps using one of the three state moorings in that area, but most visitors go into Wickford Cove, where they have much to choose from.

Along the east shore, to port as one enters this cove, sits the large marina of Wickford Shipyard—(401) 294-3361. Besides many slips, gas, diesel fuel, water, electricity, telephones, ice, hauling and repair work, showers, and swimming pool, this marina has a fine marine supply store. The harbormaster may be found at the town dock, chiefly commercial, which lies across the shipyard at the cove's entrance. Only commercial craft can tie up there.

Proceeding up the channel, dredged to a controlling depth of 6 feet MLW, one finds to port another first-class establishment, the Brewer's Wickford Cove Marina, which caters to boats of all types up to 50 feet overall. It has slips plus some moorings and launch service, fuel, and laundry, and is a full-service marina monitoring VHF-9. For a variety of supplies, one can pass westward through the marked channel in Wickford Cove to a public dock located up on the west shore. Here you can tie up for a 2-hour limit, partake of a quick meal at the Harborside Grill or Wickford Diner, pick up supplies at nearby Ryan's Market (open Sundays), and stroll among the pleasant shops and quaint old streets of the town. But remember that everything closes down at 6 P.M. when they roll up the sidewalks. The prestigious Wickford Art Festival, always held on the weekend following the Fourth of July, is a traditional event not to be missed.

Since there is no first-class restaurant in town, we were interested to learn from another cruising man that the Carriage Inn in North Kingstown offers crews visiting Wickford Cove Marina shuttle service to and from the inn. One can contact this casual though favored restaurant by phoning 294-2727.

There are also two boatyards on Mill Cove, located to the north: Pleasant Street Wharf and Johnson's Boat Yard. Favor the starboard side of this cove's channel going in; its depth has been controlled to at least $6^{1}/_{2}$ feet MLW throughout. On one of our visits, we had a delightful chat with Ralph Vale, one of the founders and former commodores of the Wickford Yacht Club, situated on Pleasant Street Wharf at the entrance to Mill Cove. It is a "fun club," hosting an active sailing program. The clubhouse, which is an antique oyster house dating back to the seventeen hundreds, has been completely refurbished while maintaining much of its original charm. Wickford certainly welcomes visiting club yachtsmen, though it has limited facilities for them. If one of the club's five guest moorings, marked blue and white, is not available to you on inquiring at the club dock, go next door to the gas dock of the Pleasant Street Wharf to be assigned one of theirs in Mill Cove. Anchoring is not recommended in the congested cove where depths vary from 4 to 6 feet MLW.

Wickford traces its origins to 1640, when Richard Smith, an associate of Roger Williams, established an Indian trading post on nearby Cocumscussoc Brook. He named the general area Wickford, supposedly in honor of Elizabeth Winthrop, wife of the governor of Connecticut and a native of Wickford, England. Capitalizing on its harbor, the village first developed into a shipping center for wealthy Narragansett planters and after the Revolution became a maritime community, with its economy based on fishing, boatbuilding, and related industries.

Today, some leading yachtsmen put Wickford at the head of their list of appealing Narragansett Bay harbors, not only because of its perfect shelter and the many modern facilities and conveniences available but because it is a remarkably preserved post-Colonial town, crowded with lovely Georgian-period houses. As many as 850 pleasure craft have been counted here on a summer's day!

3. Allen Harbor (13223). This harbor lies on the western shore of the West Passage between Wickford and East Greenwich and is under the supervision of the North Kingstown harbormaster. The latest *Coast Pilot* says that it "is entered through a buoyed channel which has a depth of about 8 feet," and this is verified on examining the current chart. However, local authorities reported to us at the time of writing that boats of 5-foot draft have touched bottom in the channel at low water. Despite this, Allen Harbor offers excellent protection midst pleasant surroundings and is used extensively by the members of the Quonset Davisville Navy Yacht Club located on the southeastern shore. With all the moorings and dolphins private, none are to be picked up, and with no facilities here for transient yachts, one is forced to drop anchor in soft bottom in a good depth of 10 feet. Note that the government has placed a buoy well out from Calf Pasture, since shoaling has extended farther to the east than is indicated on the chart. Stay well offshore!

4. East Greenwich (13224). We are indebted to William Pearson of the East Greenwich Yacht Club for updating this section for us.

This harbor is attractive, and the shelter and facilities are good. Now that all of the grade crossings have been eliminated, Amtrak no longer blows the whistle all the way through town, so it is also rather quiet. At the north end of the cove, it can be a little choppy in a northeaster, but the rest of the cove is the best hurricane hole in the area.

The entrance is made by observing C-3 Middle Ground (which is due west from Warwick Light) to C-5 Sally Rock. You may see some boats cutting inside C-5, but it takes local knowledge to make it safely, so do not try it. Turn southwest to N-6 Chepiwanoxet, and be certain to keep it to starboard. To port is the beach at Goddard State Park. There are a couple of state moorings just off the beach, the holding ground is good, and the swimming is popular. Except for some chop caused by passing powerboats, it is a good place to overnight except in the worst of a northerly.

Continue straight past N-6 to C-7. At night, you can see the lights at Norton's Shipyard, but be absolutely certain to keep C-7 to port. A bad shoal extends nearly to the can from Long Point, and if you cut inside it, you will definitely run aground while everyone on shore is watching you. Once past C-7, you can go nearly anywhere in the cove except right up against the eastern shore. However, because of the large number of moorings in the cove, anchoring is generally not possible.

Norton's, which monitors VHF-9, has over 40 years of experience in handling all types of marine repairs on vessels up to 150 feet. They have slips and moorings available for transients along with fuel, water, ice, a ship's store, and a small restaurant.

The next facility to the south is the East Greenwich Yacht Club. Established in 1909, it is the largest yacht club on the bay. Its location is marked by a prominent flagpole flying the club's red and white burgee. The club will rent available slips and moorings, and transients are welcome to use the bar in the clubhouse and the showers and laundry in a separate facility across the street. Gas, diesel fuel, ice, and water are also available. During the summer, the club's launch services the moorings from 0800 to 2200. Due to the large number of yachting events that are sponsored by the club, it is advisable to make advanced reservations for specific dates. The Club monitors VHF-9, and the phone is (401) 884-7700.

South of the Yacht Club are three good restaurants that all have a limited number of guest slips, some of which are available only for the duration of dinner. The first is Twenty Water Street and its Milt's Marina, followed by the Inn Between, and finally, the Harbourside Lobstermania.

Two blocks up the hill from the waterfront is Main Street, which is a link in the Route 1 Post Road. You should be able to find whatever you need in the way of hardware, cameras, drug stores, and a supermarket. For good food try the Kent on Main Street or Pal's on Division Street. East Greenwich has a large number of early-American houses and one of Rhode Island's original state houses.

If you like shore exercise in pleasant surroundings, take a walk or play golf in Goddard State Park which forms the entire eastern shore of the cove and is actually in the adjacent city of Warwick. Hiking can be reached by a short row across the cove, but the golf course is at the far end of the park and will require a ride.

5. Apponaug Cove (13224). About 2 miles north of Greenwich Cove, tucked away in the northwest corner of Greenwich Bay, lies the entrance to this cove. It runs between Arnold Neck to the west and Cedar Tree Point to the east.

Before entering the channel, you will note the rather expansive Brewer's Marina—(401) 884-0544—located on the western shore just southwest of can 3. This place provides full marina and repair service with good water dockside, a restaurant, and a pool. Just beyond Brewer's is the Masthead Marina with comparable facilities including slips, gas, showers, ice, electricity, repair work, and access to supplies. The Chart House restaurant and Marina Club are there also. Both these places attract both sail- and powerboats, having constructed sizable breakwaters to provide greater protection in easterlies.

The cove, which forms the northwestern arm of Greenwich Bay, is navigable through its channel with a depth of 6 feet MLW. However, the channel is tending to shoal in spots, and boats drawing more than 4 feet are advised to proceed with caution at low water. There is a 4-foot tide range here.

The channel leading to the cove begins at nun 2 just off Cedar Tree Point and is reported to be 6 feet MLW all the way to the cove. On Arnold Neck to port, you can pick up a mooring or slip space at Apponaug Harbor Marina—(401) 739-5005—the home of the Apponaug Harbor Yacht Club, which has turned out some of the best racing skippers on the bay. Check in with the very obliging marina manager at the main dock, which has a depth of 6 feet. He'll assign you a slip or an overnight mooring for a fee. Ice, showers, and all types of repair work are on hand, but no fuel; the marina is popular with sailing craft, but one must go to Brewer's for diesel repairs and gas. Supplies can be picked up with taxi service to nearby Apponaug and the Theodore Francis Airport is only six minutes away. Moorings for deep-draft vessels are found outside the harbor, south of Arnold Neck. For a more protected but very tight anchorage in a strong southerly, you can venture farther into the cove through the channel, keeping to the east to avoid the sandbar extending from the west between cans 5 and 7. Anchor in the cove southwest of nun 8.

Ponaug Marina at the head of this cove has only 4 feet at its docks at low water, but its owner, Ray Chase, can take care of powerboats up to 40 feet. Here you will have the opportunity to take on supplies and gas and to enjoy a satisfying meal at the Boathouse Tavern only ³/₄ mile away. The surroundings are pleasant and quite peaceful, disturbed only by the airplane traffic and trains rumbling over the bridge to the west.

6. Warwick Cove (13224). A man who knows the bay says that this is a "nice harbor." With a 5-foot rise and fall of tide here the entrance is tricky, but at low water it has 5 or 6 feet both at the entrance and inside if you know where to go. The channel is "snaky" so you should follow it carefully. A local authority urged favoring the east shore in approaching the entrance. Farther in, watch out for a bad shoal, bare at low water, extending 150 yards westward from the west side of the channel between cans 5 and 7 to the southeast tip of Horse Neck. We have sounded 6 feet at MLW along much of the 150-foot-wide channel with slight shoaling recorded in the 300-yard stretch southwest of nun 10. Angel Marina is the first one to port, but it is mainly for commercial and local boats. Next to port is the Warwick Cove Marina—(401) 737-2446—which seems to have grown around existing buildings but has good capabilities. There are two mooring basins with 6-foot depths located alongside the channel halfway up. One is across from the Warwick Cove Marina and the other is just to the north along the western shore. See the marina manager, for advice on dockage and most any other service needed by cruising people. His slips providing a 10-foot depth are the deepest in the cove, and he offers gas, diesel fuel, ice, water, electricity, and a possible mooring for the night. A shopping center is located nearby.

Across the channel from this marina on the eastern shore is the Harbor Light Marina, with a protected basin dredged to 6 feet and a 60-ton travelift, but its "people facilities" are limited to one porta-john and a telephone. It was pumping no fuel when we visited. Extensive engine repair work is performed at C-Lark Marina—(401) 739-3871—teeming with powerboats farther up to port. Next is Carlson's Marina—(401) 738-4278—offering full service plus a pool and snack bar. Just beyond is the Wharf Marina—(401) 737-2446—specializing in servicing large sailing craft, having slips and moorings, and monitoring

VHF-9. Bay Marina—(401) 739-6435—with 6 feet at the end of its docks is at the head of the cove.

A yachtsman whose home port is Warwick Cove writes that "there are no fewer than seven restaurants within walking distance from any marina on the west shore and I recommend the Inn. It is a busy place but the food is ample in quality and quantity, service is excellent and the price very reasonable. A grocery store is handy and is open from 8 A.M. to 9 P.M. six days a week. Also Trident Marine is nearby for those who are looking for any marine hardware or supplies."

Apparently Narragansett Bay sailors zealously resist any navigational changes they feel might endanger their safety at sea. They went along with the automation of Warwick Neck Light, but the possible removal of its foghorn was simply too much for them to take. A brouhaha between boaters and the Coast Guard followed. Even the *Providence Journal-Bulletin* hooted, "A good healthy foghorn is as much a part of the Ocean State as clam cakes at Point Judith." Finally the Coast Guard backed down and the horn remains with the strength of its signal of every 15 seconds reduced to one-half mile, still sufficient to carry across the channel between Warwick Neck and Patience Island. The only drawback about Warwick Cove is that it has become a congested paradise for local craft, leaving little room for the transient yacht. Unattended boats should have ports and hatches locked here.

7. Bullock Cove, Providence River (east shore—13224). Here is a fine protected harbor whose main channel was dredged in 1990 to produce 8 feet in the channel to the mooring and turning basin and 6 feet throughout the basin. Follow the buoys carefully since they and the dolphins have been shifted to signal the best water. Inside, on the west shore, are the Narragansett Terrace Yacht Club and the Bullock Cove Marina; both places are congested with moored boats and have facilities for people. On the starboard side is Lavins Marina—(401) 246-1180—with 4 feet MLW at the slips and gas, ice, showers, water, and electricity. Farther up to starboard, just below the final basin, is the large Brewer's Cove Haven Marina—(401) 246-1600, VHF-9—which we have found to be most complete and cooperative. They can't provide provisions but do offer yachtsmen the opportunity to have cookouts near attractive Memorial Haines State Park. The Crescent Amusement Park, providing fun for the family, is fairly close at hand, and the marina can provide bicycles for a local 20-mile bike path. This marina, one of the most popular facilities on the east shore of Narragansett Bay, can accommodate boats of 11-foot draft at its floating slips. The row of dolphins mark the north and south channels to these slips. Here you will find ice, electricity, and water, and ashore a marine store, travelift, showers, and professional repairmen on duty. After all, they are the crew who refurbished the 125-foot gaff-topsail schooner *Bill of Rights* and claim to have hauled more America's Cup boats than any other yard in the world.

Bullock Neck is a nice residential area, and the harbor is one of the snuggest and most attractive on the bay, deep enough for most cruising yachts and marred only by unsightly floating algae occasionally brought to the surface after a summer storm. It's still a wise move to post a lookout, however, whenever negotiating this channel at low tide.

8. Pawtuxet Cove, Providence River (west shore—13224). The construction of a prominent 800-yard dike south of Pawtuxet Neck several years ago has made the southern end of this cove a sheltered and rather fascinating place. The dike runs from Rock Island northward to a point just south of the cove's entrance. Come between can 1 and nun 2 heading westward. Proceed up the middle of the 4½-foot dredged channel, pick up can 5, keeping it to port, and then make a wide turn around the end of the breakwater to enter into the 100-yard-wide south basin, whose depth is reported to be 4½ feet MLW at the time of writing. The dike helps make this place a safe anchorage but it is still open a bit to the south. A string of condominiums rise up along the shore behind.

In 1986, the narrow channel leading northward recorded only 2 feet MLW all the way to the turning basin at the head of Pawtuxet Cove. Harbormaster Richard Greenwood in the same year reported that there were no immediate plans to redredge the channel and advised all of us to consult local authorities concerning the very latest depths here. Meanwhile, boats of very shallow draft can take advantage of the services of the Frank Pettis Boat Yard—(401) 781-2340, VHF-65—up to port with 5½ feet MLW at the docks and the Pawtuxet Cove Marina farther on to starboard.

9. Edgewood, Cranston, Providence River (west shore—13224). Although this section of the Providence River above the Pawtuxet River is too wide and exposed to be called a harbor, the presence on this shore of two leading yacht clubs makes it a rewarding port of call for visiting yachts cruising on the bay. From south to north these are the Rhode Island Yacht Club, organized in 1875 and thus one of the oldest yacht clubs in the country, and the Edgewood Yacht Club, organized in 1889 and now sometimes called "the sailingest club on the bay."

The Rhode Island Yacht Club is on the north end of Washouset Point on Pawtuxet Neck and easily recognized as the "club on stilts," resting one story up on large steel-and-concrete pillars, high enough, it is hoped, to avoid the fate of its predecessors, swept away by hurricanes. Until recently, perhaps, this club stressed social rather than yachting activities, but now the pendulum has swung and there is increased boating activity here. They have 60 slips and 60-plus moorings with launch service. Overnight transient dock and shower facilities are available for guests and visitors with reciprocal privileges from other clubs. Ice and water are available at the docks, there are several restaurants within walking distance, and there is access to supplies.

The Edgewood Yacht Club, which though battered, has survived all hurricanes to date, is a short distance to the north. Here a very active sailing program is undertaken, with much stress on junior activities. It boasts the first sailing school on these waters and has won the Narragansett Bay Junior Racing Championships. The Victorian clubhouse is on the National Register of Historic Places. This busy club is most hospitable to visiting yachtsmen from other yacht clubs, as we know from our own experience; if a spare mooring is available, we feel sure a visitor would be accommodated. Make your approach directly to the club docks through the deepest water from a point in the channel midway between nun 6 and can 7. Ice and water are found at the floating slips in 5-foot depths, but no fuel or meals are served. The launch operates from 8:30 A.M. to 9 P.M., monitoring VHF-9.

Various intercollegiate yacht races have been hosted here, and from what we have seen, the club carries out well the simply stated objectives of its constitution: "To encourage the sport of yachting, to promote the science of seamanship and navigation, and to provide and maintain a suitable club house and anchorage for the recreation and use of its members."

On the same shore just north of the Edgewood Yacht Club and protected by a breakwater and Fields Point, lies Port Edgewood—(401) 941-2000—a marina identified by a large gray boat shed. This spot has gas, ice, a marine store with charts, and complete repair service; it

Newport, Rhode Island, looking north. Bull Point on Conanicut Island is at the left; Fort Adams is in the center and Goat Island is in the upper right. Mark the entrance. The Ida Lewis Yacht Club, with its prominent pier, is due south of Goat Island. *Aero Graphics Corp.*

remains largely a boat dealer but has room or moorings for transient yachts with 5 feet MLW at the docks.

Since yachtsmen when cruising will generally prefer to stay away from the heart of a big city, we shall end our voyage up the West Passage of Narragansett Bay here and go back to the entrance of the East Passage.

East Passage. In making your way up the East Passage, note the historic 107-year-old Rose Island Light House Station, just below the Newport suspension bridge, which was abandoned for many years. Lighted Bell R12, just off the southwest shore of the island, replaced it. Although the light is owned by the city of Newport, the private Rose Island Lighthouse Foundation worked to restore the light. The light has now been restored, and is in operation as a 6-second, flashing white light. It is open to the public from 10 A.M. to 4 P.M. for day use and has several rooms available for guests in turn-of-the-century style. Ferry service is available, and boaters can anchor south of the landing and come ashore by dinghy except during the nesting period from April 1 to July 15. Call (401) 847-4242 for information about a unique experience.

10. Newport, Aquidneck Island, Rhode Island (13223, 13221).
One of the principal summer resorts and yachting centers of the Atlantic Coast, Newport is not always a snug or quiet anchorage, although its inner harbor has undergone a dramatic restoration in recent years. To confuse the waters further, it is an important commercial center. But the two harbors (inner and outer), divided by Goat Island, are protected, well marked, and lighted, so that Newport is easy of access at all times. Newport is the most practical 'longshore harbor capable of holding a fleet of yachts between Stonington, Connecticut, and Padanaram in Buzzards Bay. Being near the entrance of Narragansett Bay, it is a convenient harbor for those cruising alongshore, as well as a good takeoff point for bay cruising.

During the summer season, Newport's harbormaster, Jake Farrell, is available from 0800 to 0200 seven days a week. If you have any questions, call him at (401) 848-6492 or on VHF-16. The city of Newport has seven 5-ton moorings that are available for larger yachts.

Much of the information on mooring and anchoring in this harbor has kindly been furnished by William Muessel, Newport's assistant harbormaster, and most of it has been checked for this edition by Jake Farrell:

Newport Harbor now has three designated mooring areas where anchoring is prohibited. These are so designated on Chart 13223 as 1, 2, and 3. Within these three areas, there are approximately 1,000 moorings which have now encroached on the former anchorage in Brenton Cove. Although not shown on the chart the *northern end of mooring area 1* is now an exclusive anchorage zone free of moorings. This zone forms a triangle bounded by Ida Lewis Rock (Ida Lewis Yacht Club clubhouse), Little Ida Lewis Rock (Red Day Marker on Rock), and the light at Fort Adams. The zone here will accommodate approximately 100 yachts, depending on size.

There is a minimum depth here of 15 feet with good holding ground (black muck). An electrical submarine cable carrying 23,000 volts to Jamestown follows along the northern boundary of this anchorage zone, and the chart designates this as a cable area to be avoided when anchoring. There are large cable crossing signs on the Newport and Fort Adams shores and large white steel balls with "Cable Crossing, Anchor to South Only" signs attached in marking the cable run on the surface. Any yachtsman having questions on anchoring should call the harbormaster on VHF-16, who cautions against anchoring south of Ida Lewis Rock, where there is little water.

Moorings are rented by Oldport Marine Services—(401) 847-9109, VHF-68—Newport Mooring Service—(401) 846-7535, VHF-9—or Long Wharf Mooring Marina—(401) 849-2210, VHF-9. Oldport also operates a launch and ferry service which makes hourly runs around the harbor from the Museum of Yachting, and will pick up crews on signal from boats both in the harbor and in Brenton Cove. They also provide repair service at your boat. Newport Launch—(401) 949-5126, VHF-68—provides launch service.

The Newport Harbor Patrol is now a professional group providing security by patrolling among yachts visiting Newport. Yet it is still advisable to leave your boat well secured, especially if it is riding offshore. Visiting yachtsmen are not to hang on to any of the private moorings without prior consent of the mooring's owner. Upon notification by a private mooring owner that an unauthorized boat is on his mooring, the harbormaster will remove said boat.

The Ida Lewis Yacht Club—(401) 846-1969, VHF-78A—is a favorite for many cruising people. It has guest moorings with launch service provided. Gas and dining facilities are not available. The club is located in the eastern part of Brenton Cove and occupies the lighthouse, kept at one time by Ida Lewis, where she made such a reputation for the rescue of seamen in distress that several rocks were named for her. The eighteen lives she saved are represented by the eighteen stars in the club's burgee. Her rescues, some of which are recorded on the wall of the clubhouse, were made between 1859 and 1906. The club, organized in 1928, has a 300-foot gangway to the shore. There is a landing float on the west side, and the club is hospitable to visiting yachtsmen from other recognized yacht clubs, as we have always found. This club is primarily interested in sailing, and the water is deep nearby. In June, during even-numbered years, Brenton Cove and vicinity is the rendezvous for the Bermuda Race fleet, and there, on the eve of the race, is to be seen one of the finest gatherings of cruising yachts to be witnessed anywhere in the United States. On odd-numbered years, the Annapolis-Newport Race now ends at Newport and the local Museum of Yachting sponsors its annual Classic Yacht Regatta. This is a race among antique sailing vessels competing over an 18-mile course around Conanicut Island. During all of these major events Newport is the hub of the yachting universe, and the Ida Lewis Yacht Club is in the middle of that hub.

New York Yacht Club's stately new Newport annex at Harbour Court has limited facilities for transient yachts and these are only available to the club's members and their invited guests. Its 550-foot frontage and French Renaissance–style château will be seen just west of the Ida Lewis Yacht Club; at night green-red-green lights atop Harbour Court's flagpole mark its location.

The Newport Yacht Club, organized in 1894 and now celebrating its 100th year of continuous operation, is located on the northeast corner of the harbor. The club has reserved slips, some guest moorings, and its own launch service. For those people renting slip space, there is ice, water, and the use of the showers and the clubhouse, but no fuel is available. Many of the area's finest restaurants are within walking distance of the yacht club. Advance slip reservations can be made by contacting the steward at (401) 846-9410 or on VHF-78. Slips or front pier dockage is available for yachts from 20 to 150 feet. We thank Vice-Commodore Cliff Mitchell for this update.

J. T.'s Ship Chandlery—(401) 846-7256—has moved to 364 Thames Street, claiming to have "everything for the yachtsman" and promising free delivery to the Newport Yachting Center. In the event this is your first extended visit to Newport, it's a short walk over to the Newport Gateway and Visitors Center at 10 America's Cup Avenue. Here you can pick up on any day in the week such useful guides as the *Best Read Guide—Newport* and *Newport This Week*.

The harbor's waterfront facing the Newport Yacht Club has undergone a dramatic, faithfully styled restoration, recapturing much of the Colonial charm of old Newport. Running from north to south, the following points of interest can be seen: Long Wharf Promenade with its many shops; The Brick Market on Upper Thames Street with many more shops; the Newport Harbor Hotel and Marina including a swimming pool and historic Bowen's Wharf, an eighteenth-century cobblestoned wharf, with its restaurants, taverns, and many charming shops.

The Newport Harbor Hotel and Marina makes some slips and over-night moorings along its waterfront available. This is a convenient location for a layover. The hotel's pool, showers, and sauna are available to its guests, but there is no fuel supply. Oldport Marine Services which runs a harbor launch out of Sayer's Wharf and Newport Yachting Center provides full-time mechanical and engine repair service.

As a matter of fact, to guarantee your boat a mooring or tie-up, we suggest that you phone or write in advance of your arrival to let any one of the following Newport marinas of your choice know your specific visit plans. These facilities, with their full range of services, run along the commercial waterfront on the east side of the harbor. Listed from north to south, here are their names and phone numbers:

First comes Newport Offshore—(401) 846-6000—located on Long Wharf just below the bridge to Goat Island. It has the most extensive repair and about the only haulout facilities in Newport and has some transient facilities. Next is the Newport Yacht Club, and then the Long Wharf Mooring Marina—(401) 849-2210, VHF-9 and 16—with shore facilities in the houseboat *Hurricane Gloria* (named for its predecessor which was destroyed). They have moorings and dock space, and guests have pool, sauna, etc., privileges at the Marriott Hotel, a short distance away. Next is the Newport Harbor Hotel and Marina—(401) 847-9000, VHF-9—with heads and showers and the Waverleys restaurant. Next is Bannister's Wharf—(401) 846-4500—with emergency repair service and two excellent eating places, the Cooke House and Black Pearl Tavern. The cup defender *Courageous* had its berth here. Next comes Newport Yachting Center—(401) 847-9047, VHF-9—a large many-slip, full-service marina, which is host to the Newport International Boat Show and other shows and events. They also have passes to the Marriott Hotel, several blocks away. The Moorings Restaurant still remains. Next is Christie's—(401) 848-7950, VHF-9—with dock space for yachts up to 150 feet, which is Newport's oldest waterfront restaurant, affording a spectacular view of the harbor. Then comes Newport Onshore—(401) 849-0480, VHF-9—which still takes some transients although they are 100 percent dockominiums. Showers, laundry, and ice are available. The last in line is the Newport Marina—(401) 849-2293, VHF-9—which was formerly named Williams and Manchester. They have showers, a laundromat, a small pool, and dockominiums. The Pier Restaurant is close at hand and has music nightly. All of these have signs at the ends of their docks so you can find them.

Tucked in just north of Newport Onshore and the Armory is the small Ann Street Pier for small boats and short stays.

If you are looking for charts of waters from all over the world or any special books to add to your ship's library, you will likely find them at The Armchair Sailor—a nautical treasure of a bookstore managed by Ron Barr. Located on Lower Thames Street near Wellington, it has become a popular Newport landmark. Those who go overboard for nautical literature will have fun browsing here.

Looking to the west, one can easily observe the result of Goat Island's face-lifting. The large brick building, resembling a fancy grain elevator, is the Double Tree Islander Newport—(401) 849-2600—not connected with the Goat Island Marina—(401) 849-5655—whose headquarters is housed in a prominent concrete building just to the south. This expansive marina offers sheltered dockage with 150 slips providing water and electricity. To be assigned a slip, put in at the gas dock facing the inner harbor, where fuel, ice, and a laundromat are available. Large power cruisers are usually tied up at the outer docks, and sailing craft are assigned dockage on the north side of the marina building. At the end of the bridge along the causeway a convenient shuttle bus to town may be picked up. Goat Island Marina is the host marina for the Single-Handed Transatlantic Race from Plymouth, England, every four years. Other events include the BOC Single-Handed Around the World Race and the Double-Handed Trans-Atlantic Race held every four years.

When the America's Cup was lost, Newport created a new organization called Sail Newport in order to bring in major yachting events. For detailed information on upcoming programs, call their office at (401) 846-1983.

One cannot write up Newport without noting her Colonial sloop-of-war *Providence.* Another spectacle is *Bill of Rights,* a replica of a 125-foot gaff-topsail schooner of the 1850s. She is now being used for commercially scheduled windjammer cruises in southern New England and Chesapeake Bay waters. Her builder, the late Harvey Gamage, is considered by his fellow natives down east to be the last of the great builders of wooden ships. Concerning *Bill of Rights,* he said, "The last time I see this ship is when it's put its tail to me and is disappearing down the harbor. I won't ever see it again, but I will know it is a good ship, because I built it." With frequent visits from the likes of *Shenandoah, Brilliant,* and other American sail-training vessels, one can admire more traditional ship designs here perhaps than anywhere, with the exception of Mystic Seaport.

Now another historic vessel, one of the last still existing, has been donated to Newport's Museum of Yachting in Fort Adams State Park. She is *Shamrock V,* Sir Thomas Lipton's last challenger for the Cup in 1930, which lost to *Enterprise* when the races first moved to Newport. One word describes her: massive. With a length of 126 feet, a mast of 160 feet in height, and a keel weighing 92 tons, she is three times the size of a "Twelve." This author's first introduction to the world of yachting took place at Newport Harbor in 1930 when, as a young lad, he came alongside this majestic work of art, resplendent in a shining coat of shamrock green, her deck and brightwork brighter than bright. Sir Thomas gave him a warm wave of welcome, and the boating fever took hold for life.

The Museum of Yachting also contains exhibits of wooden craft, yachting memorabilia, and a work area where visitors can watch craftsmen restore wooden boats. It is open 10 A.M. to 5 P.M. Tuesday to Sunday from May to October. At the time of writing, there are plans to move most of the exhibits to a downtown location on Thames Street, but to keep the restoration work at Fort Abams, and to sell the *Shamrock V* to help finance the move and expansion. There is considerable opposition to the sale.

There are plenty of other places to go and things to do in Newport, which boasts more Colonial-era houses, about four hundred, than any other city in the country. You may visit the Casino, which houses the Tennis Hall of Fame, go see the first synagogue in the Americas, or take a stroll along Cliff Walk, a path that runs 3$^1/_2$ miles between Easton's Beach and Bailey's Beach. Along the way, you can catch splendid views of the Atlantic and a backyard glimpse of some of Newport's great mansions.

Like Glen Cove, Long Island, Newport is reminiscent of the bygone days of great estates, when palatial steam yachts rode at anchor. Many of the estates have since been sold to schools or other institutions and, to understate the situation, yachts are smaller now.

11. Jamestown, Conanicut Island (13223, 13221). Although this is an open anchorage on the west side of the East Passage, the presence of the hospitable Conanicut Yacht Club, a short distance north of the old ferry dock and just south of Bryer Point, is an incentive to drop anchor off the club and hope for a reasonably calm night, since the holding ground is rather poor and the water comparatively shallow. This yacht club, founded in 1891 originally as the Jamestown Yacht Club, has a fine clubhouse, including a 220-foot pier with a 5-foot depth at its outer end. Visiting yachtsmen are welcomed provided they are members of other recognized and accredited yacht clubs. But to be a guest, you must first obtain a club member to act as your host. Once this is done, phone ahead to the club's steward at (401) 423-1424 to register. Conanicut's services are limited to five guest moorings with launch service running from 8 A.M. to 8 P.M., showers, ice, a bar, and a buffet served three times a week. In approaching Jamestown Harbor from the south, be sure to give The Dumplings a very wide berth as you swing gradually around to port heading in. This spot is a poor place to be in an easterly blow.

The Conanicut Marina—(401) 423-7157—just to the south of the yacht club, lies in a protected basin next to the old ferry dock and in front of the old Bay View Hotel. This full-service marina, managed by Bill Munger, monitors VHF-9 and 71 for reservations. Here you'll find gas, diesel fuel, ice, water, electricity, plentiful slips in 10 feet MLW, moorings, launch service from 8 A.M. to 9 P.M., marine supplies, showers, a laundromat, general repair work, and restaurants nearby. It is also accessible to a variety of stores for supplies. Regular bus service runs to Newport and to the Kingston railroad station. A one-way trip takes 20 minutes. A new ferry service has started from the old ferry dock to Bannister's Wharf in Newport every hour on the hour, carrying a maximum of six passengers, but it was not in action in 1994.

South of the old ferry dock on the eastern shore leading toward Bull Point and inside of the Dumpling Islands and outlying rocks is the pier of the Jamestown Boat Yard—(401) 423-0600, VHF-72—which caters to local craft and transients and specializes in high-quality repair work. Jono and Ruth Billings have taken over this yard, operated for many years by the late Charles Wharton. If you are stopping here, you can go on either side of the small island just in front of the yard's dock. The Dumpling Association has a private dock just south of the dock. To the north, Clark's Boat Yard—(401) 423-1545, VHF-6—has some moorings but no heads or showers. This used to be the Round House Shipyard.

Approaching the Jamestown Boat Yard, one can't help gaping up in awe at the strange-looking house perched like a giant osprey nest atop one of the rocky Dumpling Islands. Built in 1904, and christened Clingstone in true nautical tradition, it was the dream house of Joseph Wharton, a wealthy ship owner and father of Charles Wharton. The house was built with 12- by 14-inch white-oak ship timbers from Tennessee. The present owner claims, "It isn't just nailed, it is pinned and tenoned like a clipper ship." What's more, it's shingled both inside and out. Let us hope that such a spectacle will stand as permanently as the foundation upon which it is built.

To the west, between Southwest Point and Short Point, many boatmen—far too many, in fact—have found Mackerel Cove a most inviting place in which to venture. The entire rockbound shoreline is privately owned and unspoiled. A pebbly swimming beach stretches across the head of the cove, and although it is public, no one is permitted to build fires or to picnic there. Yachtsmen will find this harbor devoid of any facilities, a fact that adds to its charm, and they are advised to navigate slowly, reducing their boats' wash to a minimum. Although the holding ground is good, don't get caught here in a strong southerly.

While you are at Jamestown, get someone to drive you to the southern end of Conanicut Island at Beavertail Point, the site of the third-oldest lighthouse erected on the Atlantic Coast. The view looking down from the cliffs is impressive.

The Jamestown high-level bridge across the West Passage brings Conanicut Island and Jamestown in the line of traffic from the New York area to Newport and Cape Cod.

12. Coasters Harbor and Coddington Cove (13223, 13221). Just above Newport, these harbors are very much Navy, and visiting yachts are not encouraged to enter. Navy requirements have precedence. The Navy is also active in Melville.

However, there are two full-service marinas located within a basin just to the north of Melville. The basin is shown on the chart as an inlet due south of Coggeshall Point on the western shore of Rhode Island and northeast of Dyer Island. Little Harbor Marine—(401) 683-5700—part of Ted Hood's Marine Complex, is in the southern part of the basin, and the East Passage Yachting Center—(401) 683-4000—is in the northern part. Both monitor VHF-9 and both have many slips with full-service facilities, but Ted Hood's probably has more marine activities associated with it. The entrance, just north of a prominent steel pier, is marked by nun 10, which can be passed on either side. Pass between the red and green buoys keeping the dolphins to port. The very well-run Windsails Restaurant is nearby. The only drawback for those who want to be conveniently near Newport is that these marinas lie 5 miles away to the north. A convenient overland passage to Newport is provided, however, by a nearby railroad.

In 1993 plans were unveiled to add a 1,500-slip marina to the Ted Hood Complex just to the south in Weaver Cove.

13. Potter Cove, Prudence Island, Narragansett Bay (13224, 13221). Here is an excellent anchorage, protected from virtually all winds, on the northeasterly end of Prudence Island. Three nuns lead to the cove's mouth. Many yachtsmen confuse this harbor with the other Potter Cove located on the eastern shore of Conanicut Island. But there is no comparison. Our leading authority on this harbor was once a professional clam digger, who "hung out" there or in the cove on the other side of the island most of the time. Here is how he feels about it:

> One of the reasons Potter Cove is so well thought of is that there's absolutely nothing there but a landlocked anchorage. There is a well up at the farm that has good water. Don't fail to fill a jug or two while there. There is no "most convenient wharf for visiting yachtsmen." If you want to go ashore, you either row or swim. The "best place to obtain a meal" is in your own galley, and if you are looking for a hotel, crawl into your bunk and forget it. Never go to sleep on a strange craft.
>
> Follow the buoys in entering and anchor anywhere. It is crowded on weekends but restful and quiet through the week. There is good clam digging.

The state guest moorings are marked by ball floats painted white with a blue stripe and are located along the western shore of the cove. The nearest source of gas, supplies, and repairs is at Bristol, about 3 miles away by water. Potter Cove is worth visiting, but be sure your screens are working, and try not to pick a weekend. A visitor to this harbor has reported that "the mosquitoes had either departed by the time we got there or their numbers and hunger have been exaggerated." From our experience, we have learned that if the mosquitoes don't appear on the scene, the horseflies probably will; your insecticide is your best defense.

The north end of Prudence Island is part of the Narragansett Bay Island Park System. The park system also has control of the south end of the island, former U.S. Navy land, while the middle of the island is all private property. If the cove happens to be too chockablock for your liking, you might go over to the bight just inside the southeast corner of nearby Hog Island. It may be crowded here in the afternoon, but many of the boats depart before dark.

A delightful ditty repeated by generations of sailors of the bay runs, "Prudence, Patience, Hope, and Despair, and little Fox Island right over there." Where else but in New England waters would you find islands on any chart with names like these? Can you spot them?

14. Bristol (13224, 13221). If you are entering or leaving Mount Hope Bay, while passing under the Mount Hope Bridge, you may be curious about a modern-looking complex on Bristol Point to the north. This is the $7.5-million campus of Roger Williams College.

Bristol Harbor is large and exposed for some distance to the southwest and south. However, under the conditions usually prevailing in summer it is one of the most satisfactory ports on the bay for an overnight stop, and large enough to hold a club fleet without crowding. The hospitality of the Bristol Yacht Club, the facilities in the harbor, the Herreshoff Marine Museum on the site of the yard where Nathaniel and his sons conjured up their yacht-building wizardry, and the many fine old houses all combine to give Bristol a special appeal to cruising yachtsmen.

The Bristol Yacht Club moved in 1955 to its present commodious headquarters on Popasquash Neck along the west side of the harbor near its northern end. The club has come a long way since the days when dues were 5¢ a month and those in arrears for six months' dues were liable to expulsion.

On one of our visits here, former Fleet Captain Seth Paull filled us in on a bit of its history. His grandfather, Commodore William Trotter, founded the club in 1877 as The Neptune Boat Club of Bristol, with a fleet of six-oared shells. Its laudatory purpose was "for the encouragement of boating, other athletic exercises and social enjoyment, and for the promotion of physical and mental culture." The marine architect, Halsey Herreshoff, who operates his firm in Bristol, is at present one of the yacht club's most distinguished members.

It is now rated among the leading clubs on Narragansett Bay and, as such, has hosted the National Ensign Championship and the Atlantic Coast 110 Championship. It boasts an extremely active junior sailing program. We were most recently greeted by the club's steward, who reminded us that members of other recognized yacht clubs are made welcome. The clubhouse provides a barroom and showers. There are three state moorings at the extreme head of the harbor, but if these are not available, signal the launchman for a possibly vacant club mooring. Launch service runs from 8 A.M. to 9 P.M. while monitoring VHF-68. Water and ice can be drawn at the club dock where there is 6 feet at low water.

Two Bristol Harbor police boats, under the control of the harbormaster, patrol nightly the harbor and adjacent waters.

Southeast of the yacht club and on the east shore a state pier is located and appears on the chart. The harbormaster is located on the second floor of the Bristol Community Building, which was formerly an armory and looks like one and is on the waterfront near the state pier. He can be reached by calling the police department at (401) 253-6611. Contact him for a possible tie-up at one of the public moorings or at one of his slips. Here you'll find a launching ramp, parking area, and public telephone, and you'll be close to the center of town where all types of supplies may be purchased. Near the launching ramp and close to a prominent standpipe lies a small dinghy beach providing easy access to land. Toward the head of the harbor at 119 Hope Street, The Lobster Pot is a recommended waterside eating place. The S.S. Dion Restaurant allows casual attire and offers a broad menu. Very popular Balzano's Restaurant located in town specializes in delicious Italian food and seafood.

Bristol does it up red, white, and blue in celebrating the Fourth of July. Actually, the Fourth starts on the third—by early afternoon the demonstrative patriots are in the pubs and on the streets. All over town sharp explosions startle the poor townspeople and things get rowdier and louder as evening approaches. But the morning of the Fourth is another matter entirely. Responsible planning and precise organization produce such a glorious parade that the celebration annually draws up to 250,000 spectators, 25 bands, 34 floats, 5,000 marchers, and 300 state-police officers. A red, white, and blue stripe is painted down the center of the parade route, and it remains as a reminder until the next year. Hundreds more view the festivities from boats in the harbor, joined by various Navy ships. It should be a pretty good show. After all, it's the oldest annually run Fourth of July parade in our nation. The citizens of Bristol have been marching to the music of the Fourth since 1776.

South of the town on Ferry Road along the western shore of Bristol Point stand Blithewold Gardens and Arboretum, one of New England's most attractive landscape gardens. The 33-acre estate overlooking Narragansett Bay was the turn-of-the-century summer residence of Penn-sylvania coal magnate Augustus Van Wickle and his late daughter Marjorie Lyon. The grounds and mansion are open to the public from 10 A.M. to 4 P.M. every day but Mondays and holidays. If you want to escape to a garden wonderland, visit here.

Also south of the business center, about a half mile, the Herreshoff boatyard has been turned into an intimate, well-organized museum which still retains the feeling of a boat shop. In all the important races from 1890 to the time of Captain Nathanael Herreshoff's death in 1938, the boats he designed won more prizes than those of all the other yacht designers put together. The workshop, where Captain Nat lived, is open Monday through Friday from 1 to 4 P.M. and Saturday and Sunday from 11 A.M. to 4 P.M.. For further information, call (401) 253-5000. If you are lucky, his grandson, Halsey, will show you around this fascinating museum, which displays photographs and half-models of classic yachts built here, including such America's Cup defenders as *Vigilant* (1893) and *Rainbow* (1934).

You will also hear many amusing yarns about the legendary designer. One favorite concerns the owner of a respectable but rather beamy yacht, a centerboarder of 11-foot draft. This New York Yacht Club member, angry at constantly losing to the new Herreshoff one-design known as the Seventies, with a waterline length of 70 feet, which drew 15 feet, complained to Captain Nat: "Mr. Herreshoff, isn't there some condition when my yacht can beat the new Seventies?" To which Captain Nat replied, "Yes, when there is less than 15 feet of water." Obviously, he was a man of few words.

The museum can be seen from the water by detecting a prominent flagpole and several vintage boats set on cradles along the eastern shore of the harbor.

We were advised by a local authority to warn visiting yachts to keep well off the Castle Island light, as there are some uncharted rocks, with only 6 feet at low water over them, a short distance to the west of the light.

15. Warren and Barrington Rivers (13224, 13221). This anchorage, about 2 miles up the Warren River, is practically landlocked. The approach is narrow and tortuous, but well buoyed and easy to negotiate under power. Some yachts often find a pleasant anchorage in northerly and westerly winds in the middle of Smith Cove away from the river's current. Upriver to starboard, just before you turn into the Barrington River, is the late Bill Dyer's Anchorage, Inc., where the famous "Dyer dinks" are made. Be sure to pay this interesting place a visit, whether or not you are contemplating a new dinghy. Bill's grandson, Dyer Jones, is the owner here now. Next to Dyer's, you can tie up in good water at the dock of the Wharf Tavern. They'll give you a good meal and don't require formal attire. The Water Street Yacht Service is located near here with a good marine store and a consignment section which may have just what you want at an attractive price.

Most yachts continue into Barrington River to the attractive Barrington Yacht Club—(401) 245-1181—located below the bridge to Barrington on the west shore of Tyler Point. Just before reaching the club, you will pass the new Barrington Marina on the point's southern tip. This is the yacht club's facility, providing slip space for twenty-five boats belonging to members and transients. Red range markers on both ends of the clubhouse help you determine the limits of the dredged channel. There is 6 feet of water at the dock of this active club, and since a 3- to 4-knot current runs in the river, it is foolish to try to anchor but far wiser to pick up one of their moorings if available. On leaving the club dock, make sure to keep the marked obstruction buoy to port. Gas, diesel fuel, water, and ice are on tap at the dock. A clubhouse extension provides showers, snack bar, and assembly hall, all available to members of recognized clubs that offer reciprocal privileges. The launch runs from 8 A.M. to 9 P.M. and monitors VHF-68. All visitors are charged a fee for a mooring or a slip. Stanley's Boat Yard is nearby with very competent repair service and well-stocked marine supplies. The office of Thurston Sails is also near at hand. Supplies can be bought on Water Street in Warren across the bridge toward the east, or in Barrington.

One of the outstanding clubs on Narrangansett Bay, the Barrington Yacht Club is the headquarters of a fine-looking fleet of cruising yachts, as well as the home of many one-design racing boats. It boasts one of the larger Optimist and 420 fleets in the country. In 1976 it hosted the World Championship 420 Cup with 75 boats competing. It also has Capris.

We shall now go back to the entrance of the third passage up Narragansett Bay—the Sakonnet River and Mount Hope Bay.

The Sakonnet River and Mount Hope Bay. The Sakonnet River is the third and most easterly of the three passages leading northward up

Narragansett Bay. Some bay yachtsmen call it the most beautiful of the three, especially in the fall, when the leaves are turning color.

16. Sakonnet Harbor (13221). Sakonnet Harbor, located at the eastern edge of the river's mouth, also called Little Compton, is a good example of what humans have done to turn a rather poor harbor into a snug harbor of refuge. To attain this, the basin was dredged to 8 feet, a dangerous rock in the middle removed, and the breakwater extended to 800 feet in length, thus providing some protection from northwesterlies, which was sorely needed. It still has its drawbacks. You can practically walk across the harbor on boats in summer, it's so tight. The holding ground is found to be poor, especially along the inside of the breakwater. Shoaling to 3 feet at low water has occurred along the inner arm of the breakwater, and to 5 feet in the harbor's southeast corner. There is an average of 8 feet throughout most of the anchorage area. Special care is required in setting anchors, since the bottom is foul in spots. Joel Bengtson, a sailor out of Warwick Cove, concurs. He writes: "A word to the wise, beware of the bottom here. It is foul due to some ledge that was blasted away to expand the anchorage area and also to a large number of abandoned mooring devices. I helped one soul recover his #225 Danforth anchor only after we had succeeded in bending its components into spaghetti trying every trick in the book to break it out."

No wonder it is preferable to try and reserve the Sakonnet Yacht Club guest mooring by signaling the steward there or by phoning ahead at (401) 635-2681. The best alternative is to contact Phil Martin, the harbormaster, over VHF-6 or call him at (401) 635-2311. He controls all other moorings in the harbor.

The Sakonnet Yacht Club, organized by John Alden, Edward Brayton, and others, is near the head of the harbor and has a long pier on the east side with 6 feet at MLW at its outer end. A 6-foot-deep channel has been dredged from the middle of the harbor to the club's dock. Few facilities may be found here. The Sakonnet Point Marina run by Peter Sullivan is located near the end of Breakwater Point on the west side. Call (401) 635-4753 or over VHF-6 for a possible overnight slip where ice, electricity, and water are on tap. You will find 6 feet at low water dockside. The Stonehouse Club, which is a short walk away, serves good meals with a $5 surcharge for non-members. There is no fuel in the harbor.

In approaching Sakonnet Harbor, keep well off Sakonnet Point and watch out at the harbor's entrance for long lines of fish weirs, sometimes poorly marked. The best plan is to pick up whistle SR, head from there to red bell 2A, and from there make for the breakwater marked by a flashing light and a set of triangle markers at its outer end. Be sure to keep clear of the harbor's eastern shore.

Sakonnet Point Light, a half-mile southwest of Sakonnet Point, is about to be relit, but there is some technicality in the way at time of writing. Its designation is Fl W 4s, 8NM (red sector from 225 to 010 degrees). The century-old lighthouse has been restored and repainted through the fund-raising efforts of the Friends of Sakonnet Lighthouse, Inc., organized under the leadership of a local resident, Orson St. John. The 66-foot-tall structure, built of steel, has now been placed on the National Register of Historic Landmarks.

17. Sachuest Cove (13221). Behind (north of) Flint Point, on the western side of the entrance to the Sakonnet River, is an anchorage that is better than any to be found in Sakonnet Harbor from the point of view of providing accessibility, room, and a splendid swimming beach easily reached by dinghy. Recently it has become a paradise for windsurfers. Except in winds from north to east it offers good shelter and has been highly recommended by several yachtsmen for its excellent holding ground. There were some empty moorings off the Navy and Middle-town beaches when we last visited. We understand that they are all private moorings.

18. Fogland Harbor (13221). This is also easy of access and roomy. If you don't need supplies, you may prefer it to Sakonnet. It is open from northwest to north-northeast, but the holding ground is good.

A yachtsman advises: "In entering the harbor, follow the channel north in Sakonnet River until 100 yards past the point. Then turn and go straight into the middle of the bight. Swing south to a line between the point and two flat-topped modern bungalows on the east shore. There is 12 feet of water here at low tide. If you row ashore and phone from a nearby farmhouse, the garage at Tiverton will send down a taxi for the 4-mile trip to Tiverton."

19. Tiverton (13221). Between the old Stone Bridge, which used to connect Almy Point on Aquidneck Island with the mainland, and the Tiverton fixed bridge, is a section of the Sakonnet River that has become an active yachting center. The channel span of the Stone Bridge has been removed, and the tide rushes through. Go through this bridge and obtain an anchorage or dockage at Tiverton on the east shore. Above the new bridge, with a vertical clearance of 57 to 70 feet, access is given to Mount Hope Bay and the mill city of Fall River in Massachusetts.

The homey Tiverton Yacht Club has a dock on the eastern waterfront, though its clubhouse is across the main street, a three-story house with a cupola. The club is very active in small one-design class racing, in which older members, known as the "Dashing Daddies," also participate. As the house rules of the club state, "Privileges of the club will be extended to visiting yachtsmen at all times." They may be able to use the deep-water dock space if any is open; showers are in the clubhouse, as well as a snack bar.

The Stone Bridge Marina just above that bridge on the west shore has no transient facilities or fuel. The Standish Boat Yard—(401) 624-4075, VHF-16—identified by its white building and lettering in the roof, farther to the north on the east shore, does hauling, repair work on engines, hulls, sails, and electronic gear, supplies marine charts in a well-equipped store, and provides gas, diesel fuel, water, and ice at its main dock, recording 15 feet at low water. It has slips and moorings available but no showers. Taking a fifteen-minute walk south along the main road will lead you to a grocery, a bank, and a package store.

Gardiner Marine—(401) 624-6175, VHF-72—on the east side has moorings and dockage and full boat services with heads but no showers.

The Pirate Cove Marina—(401) 683-3030, VHF-9 and 65—directed by the appropriately named Donald Kidd, is across the river from Standish, protected behind a stone breakwater, its entrance indicated by a white marker at the breakwater's northern end near a small prominent bridge. You will lie away from the current here, and although the basin is often crowded with local craft, this marina is set up for transients, providing slips and moorings with a good 10-foot depth. One can pick up gas, diesel fuel, water, ice, and marine supplies, showers can be taken, and there's a courtesy car available for obtaining food supplies. For a meal we suggest Fifteen Point Road Restaurant, just a five-minute walk away, and The Sportsman, serving tempting food at reasonable prices to informally dressed patrons.

Brewer's Sakonnet Marina may also be found on the west shore, with its entrance at the foot of a large brown boat shed just southwest of can 17. By following this channel very slowly with its 10-foot depth, you will arrive at the fuel dock of what its owners call the "quintessential New England facility." It is nestled in a protected, picturesque basin offering almost all the services the transient boater could want. A swimming pool is on the property and a source for supplies, an inn, and even a golf course are nearby. This is our favorite marina on the Sakonnet River; we are probably not alone. Phoning ahead for a slip at (401) 683-3551 might be a wise move. The marina monitors VHF-9, and one office handles both north and south yards.

We do not suggest anchoring in Tiverton Harbor, for the river current runs from 4 to 5 knots at times between the bridges.

Tiverton, originally the home of the Pocasset Indians, is an interesting place for a visit, though too near Fall River, it would appear, for good swimming.

20. Kickamuit River, Mt. Hope Bay (13221). An attractive anchorage, though too large to be snug, lies in the river to the east of Bristol Neck. Keep close to the nuns in the narrow entrance channel of 6-foot depth, as outlying rocks line the shore. Your best shelter can be found along the shore beyond can 1 and just north of the little neck to port. The small community of Coggeshall on the point is residential. For facilities and supplies, one must go to Fall River, since none can be found here.

21. Cole River, Mass., Mount Hope Bay (13221). This anchorage is not snug, being wide open to the south until you get into the narrow part of the river, where it is marshy and too shallow for cruising boats. The modest Swansea Marina is on the east shore of the wide part of the river, at South Swansea on Gardners Neck. Gasoline, water, ice, electricity, repairs, showers, and a snack bar are available. There is a reported 6 feet of water at the pump. The yard has moorings, transient slips, and a travelift, and supplies are not far away. We found the best anchorage in the deep-water area southwest of the marina.

22. Fall River, Mass. (13221). A visit to Fall River can be a visit to a living museum. There is the Marine Museum and the Historical Society with an exhibit about Lizzie Borden and the world-famous ax murders in 1892. Ethnic restaurants and bakeries as well as factory outlet stores for bargain purchases are all to be explored.

But the most popular tourist attraction of all is Battleship Cove located on the eastern shore of the Taunton River just above the first fixed bridge, the Braga Bridge. Visitors anchor in the cove and dinghy ashore to board and tour the nation's largest collection of U.S. Navy vessels open to the public in one location, or to ride on the newly installed carousel. Here are berthed "Big Mamie," the battleship *Massachusetts*—the official war memorial of the state; the destroyer *Kennedy;* the submarine *Lionfish;* a landing craft; and *PT 765.* The replica of the H.M.S. *Bounty,* which was used in the movie *Mutiny on the Bounty,* has been given to the Fall River Chamber of Commerce Foundation and will be berthed in Battleship Cove. Just south of the bridge stands the Marine Museum containing a fascinating collection of ship models and memorabilia from the days of the old Fall River Day Line. Nowhere else can one see more vividly how our Navy men fought, on the sea and under it, during World War II. Exposition tours run daily during the year and from 9 A.M. to 7 P.M. during the summer. Christina's Marina—(508) 679-8158, VHF-9—in Battleship Cove or the Borden Light Marina—(508) 678-7547—a little to the south may have a slip available. They both have showers, ice, and a ship's store. Christina's has a cafe on the premises, and Borden Light has haulout, repair, and pumpout facilities.

With Fall River we end our cruise on the Sakonnet River and Mount Hope Bay and so on Narragansett Bay. We now go back to Sakonnet Point and head eastward from there toward Buzzards Bay.

Westport, Massachusetts (13228). Don't be confused by the two Westports, Westport Harbor at Acoaxet and Westport Point upriver. The yacht club and the facilities are at the latter Westport. The entrance is a bit tricky, and there is a 3- or 4-knot current. A local authority advises as follows: "Pick up bell 'WH' southeast of Twomile Rock and stand toward the Knubble (a conspicuous high rock) until Dogfish Ledge marked by can 3 is abeam to port. Then head for nun 4 off Halfmile Rock and leave it close to starboard." After that swing around the Knubble, marked by flashing light 5 and a day beacon, and follow the light to starboard. Don't attempt to enter in strong southerly winds, when the sea breaks on the bar at the entrance. This hidden entrance made Westport a perfect hideout for rumrunners during Prohibition days. Long before then, the illusion of an unbroken coastline from the open sea made Westport a haven for early smugglers and Revolutionists.

The best anchorages and docking facilities are off Westport Point, but if you prefer to anchor below despite the strong tide, pick a spot just above can 13 and about southwest of nun 14. Beware the Lion's Tongue shoal to the northwest which is reported to have come out a lot recently. But most cruising yachts go farther up the channel, which carries 8 feet MLW, all the way to F. L. Tripp & Sons Marina or to the nearby Westport Yacht Club on the south shore on Horseneck Point, south of can 23. If you do proceed upriver, Stephen E. Taylor, the grandson of the celebrated marine architect Starling Burgess, advised that the "channel between nun 14 and can 15 has shifted to the west by nearly a full width of the channel. The charted indication of 'under 3 feet reported' is to be taken quite literally in mid-channel; but if one holds well to the west side, even a little beyond the range between cans 15 and 17, one can get by at MLW drawing 5'6"."

The very reliable Tripp yard—(508) 636-4058—founded in 1930, is run by Carl Tripp. In producing the popular Compleat Angler, a line of trim 22-foot fiberglass fishing boats, they proudly claim to be "builders for those who care a little more." Transient slips and moorings are available here, and VHF-9 is monitored. Other services include gas, diesel fuel, water, ice, electricity, a marine store with charts, and showers, plus electronic, hull, and engine repair work. They also have a free pumpout station set up by the town of Westport to help keep the river clean.

On one of our visits, we picked up a deep-water mooring at the yacht club next door and came in on the launch to have a friendly chat with former Commodore Emile Durand. "Visitors love this place," he exclaimed enthusiastically, and from what we saw of the general area, we could understand the reasons for his remark. The Westport Yacht Club, offering reciprocal club privileges, has a snack bar, showers, and a nice sandy beach and runs a jitney service to town. It also has ample dock facilities with 8-foot depths. At Mr. Durand's suggestion, we have often enjoyed taking nature walks to the south, leading into the Cherry & Webb Conservation Area. Take a narrow path to the left of the parking lot across from the club to get there. Here you will find a secluded bird sanctuary, wonderfully shaped pieces of driftwood, and dunes presenting a fine panoramic view of the coast and harbor channel. The surfing and swimming along Horseneck Beach to the east are absolutely first-rate. The eastern half of this beach is state-owned and is open to the public for swimming daily from 8 A.M. to 6 P.M.

Farther upriver to starboard facing nun 26 lies an 8-foot channel leading to the dock of the Moby Dick Wharf Restaurant, which reopened in August 1993. The seafood is recommended here, and a limited number of overnight berths may be available. Dress in its Lobster Pot Lounge is informal. Moby Dick's Sandwich Shop across the road dishes out tasty quahaug chowder. Groceries used to be obtainable at the Westport Market, about ⅓ mile north of the bascule bridge, but at the time of writing it was closed.

The central village of Westport, some distance up the river and beyond its navigable part, is an old town, part of which was purchased in 1652 by Miles Standish from the Indians "for ten shillings and sundry commodities." Later on in the whaling era, during the first half of the nineteenth century, "Paquachuck," as the Indians called it, became an active whaling port. Prior to the Civil War, it aided many Southern slaves in their escapes northward by land and sea. Westport and its sister port, Eastport, Maine, were so named because they formed the early existing boundaries of the Massachusetts Bay Colony.

West of the Knubble lies the village of Acoaxet. For those of you who, like Professor Henry Higgins, are sticklers for precise enunciation, the natives here call it *A-cokes-et*.

Chapter VII

Buzzards Bay, the Elizabeth Islands, and the Cape Cod Canal

As a cruising ground, Buzzards Bay has much to recommend it. Calms are few, for the southwest wind blows up the bay nearly every afternoon, sometimes strongly enough to become a reefing breeze. Fogs are few, seldom as "choking thick" as the down-east specimens, and usually of short duration. The summer sun will usually burn off the fog before noon. Aids to navigation are frequent, large, and noisy. There is a lane of lighted buoys from Penikese to the Canal. There is plenty of company, for the bay is scoured daily by hundreds of yachts—outboards, Beetle Cats, power cruisers, and some of the largest, fastest, and handsomest ocean racers on the east coast. Add the possibility of meeting a square-rigged topsail schooner and a replica of a down-east coaster with a gaff topsail set from hoops aloft. Harbors here range from the busy fishing port of New Bedford to yachty Padanaram and picturesque Cuttyhunk. But no harbor in this area—within easy reach of Boston, New York, and Providence—is deserted.

A late-breaking piece of news is that the Buzzards Bay entrance light, marked "Buzzards" on the chart and about 2 miles west of the Sow and Pigs bell "SP" off of Cuttyhunk Island, will have a new tower. While it is being built, the light will operate at reduced intensity and a large lighted buoy has been located about 4,600 yards west of the tower to aid navigators.

Tidal Currents. An almost indispensable guide to tidal currents in Buzzards Bay, Nantucket and Vineyard Sounds, and the "holes" between the Elizabeth Islands is *Eldridge Tide and Pilot Book,* published by Marion Jewett White on Commercial Wharf in Boston. By means of a series of current diagrams, one for each hour of the tide, the book comes as close to predicting tidal conditions as the mind of man can do it. *The Tidal Current Charts, Narragansett Bay to Nantucket Sound* (consisting of two sets of charts) are very useful and may be obtained from National Ocean Survey sales agents or from the National Ocean Survey, Distribution Division (C44), Riverdale, Maryland 20840.

The problem centers around the difference in water level between Buzzards Bay and Vineyard Sound. Whenever the water is higher in the bay, the current will flow southeastward into the Sound, and vice versa. Because the times of high water are radically different in the bay, Vineyard Sound, and Nantucket Sound, the tidal currents, although predictable, are irregular.

Because the tidal currents run with inspiring velocity, particularly in the "holes," careful attention should be paid to their direction. Note that, if one must buck the tide, it is better to do so in Buzzards Bay than in Vineyard Sound.

Included annually in *Eldridge* is a letter the original publisher wrote to skippers and mates navigating Vineyard Sound, pointing out that vessels entering Vineyard Sound from the south will experience a strong set to the northwest on both flood and ebb, thus giving the shores of Cuttyhunk and Nashawena the title of "The Graveyard," because of the number of vessels wrecked there. The letter is interesting not only for its information but for the pleasant and personal touch it imparts to an otherwise arid volume of tables and factual information.

Around the Cape or Through the Canal? As he approaches the Texas Tower at the entrance to Buzzards Bay, the eastward-bound skipper must decide whether to sail up Buzzards Bay and pass through the Cape Cod Canal or to sail up Vineyard Sound, east through Nantucket Sound, and then up the outside of the Cape.

The route through the canal is shorter. On a voyage from Woods Hole to Gloucester, the canal saves 36 miles. There are several excellent harbors in Buzzards Bay and beyond the canal in Massachusetts Bay. The route is through protected waters all the way, and except between the eastern end of the canal and Plymouth, buoys are noisy and close together. The waters of Buzzards Bay and Cape Cod Bay are crowded with commercial craft, fishermen, fine yachts, and big steamers.

Should you decide on this course, see page 319 for specific advice on the canal.

The route through the sounds and around the Cape, however, is a good deal more challenging. Once committed to this route, one must be prepared to keep going. From West Chop to Pollock Rip the course lies among shoals and through tide rips. Then one faces open ocean and apparently endless beach, with no practical shelter whatever before Provincetown, 45 miles away.

But there is something about the long, seemingly endless dunes of the Cape that has a peculiar fascination to many yachtsmen. What appears to be a point, which you never seem to pass, keeps always ahead of you as you go on for mile after mile. The gradual convex curve of the Cape gives this illusion. Were it not for the famous lighthouses, Chatham, Nauset, and Cape Cod (or Highland), Race Point, Wood End, and Long Point, you might wonder if you were holding your own.

Until the Cape Cod Canal was opened in 1914, the route around the Cape was crowded with sailing vessels and steamers. Whalers, fishermen, and square-rigged cargo vessels ran down the line of lightships or lay at anchor in Vineyard Haven or Menemsha Bight awaiting a fair wind. Almost every winter gale caught several vessels on the dangerous shoals, parted their ground tackle, and drove them ashore. Coast Guardsmen at lifesaving stations manned surfboats to the rescue with courage, strength, and skill now legendary. The great five- and six-masted coal schooners of the first quarter of this century were the last; now only an occasional tanker or fisherman and an infrequent yacht make the passage. However, anyone who undertakes the lonely voyage can take a good deal of satisfaction in having made successfully a difficult passage.

Harbors on the Buzzards Bay Mainland, Massachusetts

Padanaram, South Dartmouth (13229). We are now back on the northwest shore of Buzzards Bay, opposite the Elizabeth Islands. Padanaram is the next good mainland harbor going east after Westport.

On the chart it is called Apponaganset Bay, the town is South Dartmouth, and yet to all yachtsmen and many others, it is known as Padanaram. The only recognition the chart gives to that name is at Padanaram Breakwater. Authorities differ as to how the name "Padanaram" came to be applied to the port. One explanation, told to an interested cruising man by a member of the New Bedford Yacht Club, is as follows:

A man named Laban once lived in South Dartmouth. He thought that if he ran water over a mill wheel he would get enough power to raise the water up again, with something left over for other purposes. He built a mill to test the idea, which was dubbed Laban's Folly. Then, as the Biblical Laban lived in Padanaram, the locality was unofficially given the name. The Biblical reference is Genesis 28:1, 2, which reads:

> And Isaac called Jacob, and blessed him, and charged him, and said unto him, Thou shalt not take a wife of the daughters of Canaan. Arise, go to Padan-aram, to the house of Bethuel thy mother's father; and take thee a wife from thence of the daughters of Laban thy mother's brother.

A student of local history discounts the story, placing the first use of the name for this community much earlier than Laban's Folly, and says that the term "Padanaram" was first applied to Howland's house, there almost a century before. Anyway, we'll join everybody else and call it Padanaram. Padan-aram was one of the original names of Mesopotamia, which lay between the Tigris and Euphrates Rivers in Assyria.

The harbormaster has designated the southwest corner of the harbor as a suitable anchorage area since there is good water and holding ground there. The New York Yacht Club fleet usually anchors off this shore on its summer cruise. Another excellent and lively anchorage in the Apponaganset River is off the South Dartmouth headquarters of the New Bedford Yacht Club, at the head of the harbor to starboard. Heading toward Padanaram from the south, your initial landfall will be a prominent radar installation on Round Hill Point, off of which rise Dumpling Rocks. Strangers approaching the harbor from the west should make the sandspit red flashing bell and then proceed to West Passage lighted buoy 9, which is in a northerly direction and is a lighted gong. They are then able to lay a course directly from there to the Padanaram breakwater off Ricketsons Point, although they will pass close to C"1", which should be left to port to avoid Hussey Rock in 4 feet of water. This gives an excellent entrance in either darkness or fog. It gives better than 18-foot draft right to the breakwater, eliminating all possibility of getting into any trouble with the numerous rocks in that part of the bay. The breakwater light has been equipped with four triangle-shaped red daymarks with red reflective borders.

A breakwater at Ricketsons Point, with a flashing red light on its western end, protects the anchorage from the east except in abnormally high tides. Only south and southeast gales and hurricanes cause any trouble at anchorage, and the breakwater breaks all but the worst of these seas. For a quiet spot, especially desirable for one entering after sundown, swerve in toward shore to starboard immediately after passing the breakwater and anchor just inside the breakwater. It is quiet and calm, and there is no disturbance from the town and automobiles, or from the numerous craft plying about in the large fleet usually anchored in the inner reaches of the harbor. Also the water is cleaner here, and an early-morning dip can be enjoyed.

There are, however, landing facilities at the New Bedford Yacht Club—(508) 997-0762, VHF-68—and it is more convenient. Depth at the main dock is 7 to 10 feet with 4 feet at its newer dock to the south. Visiting yachtsmen must register at the clubhouse to be granted recipro-cal guest privileges. Two club tenders run from 8 A.M. to 9 P.M. daily, monitoring VHF-68. It is often possible to obtain a mooring and slip space if available from the steward, who will issue you a guest card good for seventy-two hours. Gas, diesel fuel, and ice are available at the dock from 8 A.M. to 10 P.M. Showers can be found in the clubhouse, and stores, where all kinds of supplies may be purchased, are only a short walk away. The club serves lunch Tuesday through Friday, and dinner Wednesday through Sunday. A cab can take you to a laundromat located 3 miles away toward New Bedford.

The New Bedford Yacht Club, founded in 1877 and originally located on Popes Island in New Bedford Harbor, was hit hard by Hurricane Carol in 1954. The fine old clubhouse survived, and its shore property offers a protective bulkhead, a cement boat-launching ramp, and exten-sive dockage.

There is much yachting life in the harbor; the New Bedford Yacht Club races many boats each Wednesday in July and August. In the latter month, the club holds the three-day biennial Buzzards Bay Regatta. There are several dinner-dances held throughout the season at the clubhouse, at which all visiting yachtsmen are welcome. The New York Yacht Club has often paid Padanaram squadron visits during its annual cruise in late July or early August. New Bedford's racing tradition is epitomized in its Whaler's Race in the spring around the whistler off No Man's Land, thence either way around Block Island, and homeward to Padanaram.

The village boasts no hotel, but there are several bed-and-breakfast places, and there is no shortage of good eating places. Joy's Landing serves excellent seafood, and the Village Galley is recommended for breakfast and lunch. The Bridge Street Cafe has a varied menu served in an appealing setting.

Padanaram is only a short run by automobile or bus from New Bedford, and is much to be preferred to that port. There are two marine yards located on the Apponaganset River. One is the Concordia Company, which is famous for Concordia yawls and Beetle Cats and is located directly north on property adjoining the yacht club. Here you may obtain marine services. They also have a marine railway that can handle boats up to 50 feet in length. There is 6 or 7 feet of water at the ways at low tide. Mechanical service and riggers are available.

On adjoining property is a shop called The Packet, which has a fine supply of government charts, sports clothes, and many other things of interest to the boating set, including postal service. Norman Fortier, one of the country's leading marine photographers, occupies a fascinating studio next door. Many a skipper has arranged here to have Fortier "shoot" his or her vessel hard on the wind off Padanaram. Some even radio the marine operator for him to race out as far as Buzzards Bay to get a shot. Near his studio is Manchester Yacht Sails, Inc., a renowned sail loft. You will find them most obliging when it comes to repairs or a new set. Two doors away, a visit to the Village Bookshop to pick up a copy of the latest best-seller or to have a chat with the owner will prove rewarding.

Down the main street there's a package store right next to Village Market Place specializing in the sale of fresh meats and fish.

Davis and Tripp—(508) 993-9232, VHF-9—run by Jim Tripp and located close to the bridge, has gas and some dock space with electricity, water, depths ranging from 2 to 13 feet, and repair facilities. And up the river above the drawbridge lies Marshall Marine, famous for building Marshall Cats.

Yachts over 50 feet in length requiring yard facilities will find several in New Bedford and Fairhaven.

New Bedford and Fairhaven (13229). Once famous as a whaling port, New Bedford later became an important textile center. It also has managed over the years to get in the way of at least two devastating hurricanes, one in September 1944, which finished off the clubhouse of the New Bedford Yacht Club on the Fairhaven Bridge, and another, Hurricane Carol, on August 31, 1954, which badly damaged some of the harbor's boatyards and docks—to say nothing of its fleet.

Finally, New Bedford, Fairhaven, and the federal government decided to take action in preventing such future storm devastation, and in 1965 a huge $18 million hurricane dike was completed. This 4,600-foot barrier, located at the mouth of the Acushnet River, runs west from Fort Phoenix to the southern tip of Palmer Island, thence all the way to the western shore. At the location of the present channel, there are two gates, one on each side of a 150-foot opening. These massive hinged gates may be swung shut to close off the harbor in case of storms. In entering through these gates, we spotted a high green light to port and a red to starboard. The current through this opening reaches a maximum of 2.4 knots, and the tide has a tendency to set you to the east as you pass through. A diaphragm horn has been installed on the west gate, sounding one 2-second blast every 10 seconds. This beautifully constructed barrier, having a maximum clearance of only 2 inches between all its rocks, has now helped to make New Bedford a major harbor of refuge for cruising yachtsmen.

The former yacht club station on Popes Island is now a small marina, known as the Outdoorsman or Captain LeRoy's—(508) 979-1456— which specializes in fishing tackle, marine equipment, etc. They have docking facilities for cruising yachts and also supply gas, diesel fuel, water, ice, etc. There's just 5 feet dockside here, and no hauling or repair work is conducted.

Also on Popes Island is the new 198-slip Popes Island Marina—(508) 993-1770, VHF-8—developed by the state Department of Environmental Management to enhance tourism and attract cruising people. Electricity and water are at the concrete floating docks, and showers, laundry, and pumpout facilities are also available.

On the Fairhaven shore, just beyond nun 12, is Fairhaven Shipyard, equipped with sizable dockage and complete services such as gas, diesel fuel, water, ice, a marine store, showers, and a laundromat. Go up to the gas dock to be assigned a slip. This yard's main function is hauling, repairs, and storage, and it has been known to maintain yachts up to 150 feet in length and 15-foot draft. A market is only a 15-minute walk away, taxis are available on call, and there is access to air transportation. D. N.

Kelley & Son—(508) 999-6266, VHF-9—also has deep water at its yard farther north and duplicates most of the services found at Fairhaven Shipyard. From our experience, however, Kelley does not appear to be in the transient business. Stores and a restaurant are nearby, and it is only a short distance to town. Davy's Locker over on the western shore of the harbor has the best food around, and the prices are reasonable.

The new Seaport Inn and Marina just south of the Route 6 bridge has 86 slips with telephone and cable TV hookups at the floating docks, and the inn has two restaurants. Repair facilities are nearby.

Padanaram has taken the place of New Bedford as the important yachting center of the vicinity, and what was once a branch station of the New Bedford Yacht Club is now the headquarters of that outstanding club. There is no station in New Bedford.

C. E. Beckman—(508) 994-9674—still has its well-equipped marine hardware store in New Bedford.

In 1959, a plaque honoring Captain Joshua Slocum was dedicated at Fairhaven's Poverty Point. For it was here, on the bank of the Acushnet River, that Slocum had rebuilt and launched in 1894 his 36-foot cutter, *Spray,* in which he became the first man to circumnavigate the world alone. Recently the Whaling Museum completed a permanent Slocum exhibit.

New Bedford and Fairhaven have many attractions for yachtsmen, this center being the best for nautical supplies between Boston and Narragansett Bay. Cape Island Express—(508) 997-1688—runs steamers from New Bedford to Martha's Vineyard (Vineyard Haven); the trip takes $1^1/2$ hours each way.

Plans for dredging the harbor are being delayed because of concerns that PCBs in the bottom will be stirred up and will harm shellfish beds.

In 1924 there were only two of the old whaling vessels left: *Charles W. Morgan* and *Wanderer,* built in Mattapoisett in 1878. Today only the former remains, lovingly preserved by the Marine Historical Association, Inc., at Mystic Seaport, Mystic, Connecticut, a place that every lover of boats should visit. As for *Wanderer,* she set out from New Bedford in August 1924, on her last whaling voyage. On the night of the twenty-sixth she anchored in lower Buzzards Bay. That night the tail end of a West Indies hurricane came up the coast. While her captain was ashore, she dragged anchor, drifted across the lower bay, and was completely wrecked on the reef southwest of Cuttyhunk Island.

Mattapoisett (13229). Large and easy to enter, with few outlying obstacles, Mattapoisett Harbor serves as a popular rendezvous for club fleets, particularly for that of the New York Yacht Club, which meets there from time to time. Its disadvantage from a cruising man's viewpoint is its size and the fact that it is wide open to the southeast. Nevertheless, in ordinary summer weather it is usually satisfactory, but is becoming increasingly more crowded. Depths are about right for all concerned. Good anchorage is obtainable right up to the town wharf with the amber light. Even the *Shenandoah,* a beautiful 120-foot topsail-rigged schooner, makes Mattapoisett a regular port of call.

But the harbor has surprisingly limited dock space. Mattapoisett Boat Yard—(508) 758-6662, VHF-68—has a yard and short dock located not far beyond the lighthouse on the northeast shore just inside of Ned's Point Light. Moorings are provided for visiting yachts. There is 5 feet at their float at low tide, and the yard does engine servicing and repairs and has a 35-ton Acme lift. Gas, diesel fuel, and water are on tap, and there's a marine store, ice, and a launch which monitors VHF-16 and 68.

The Mattapoisett Yacht Club with its recently renovated clubhouse sits right next door. Small, most unpretentious, it is hospitable to visitors from other yacht clubs. Its founding in 1889, according to Lloyds Register, makes it the third-oldest yacht club on Buzzards Bay; only Beverly Yacht Club at Marion (1871) and New Bedford Yacht Club (1877) predate it. There are no slips here, but launch service is provided with a possible few guest moorings. We are requested by Commodore John Anderson to emphasize that overboard pumping should be kept to a minimum to prevent the closing of shellfish beds, and that all of Buzzards Bay is similarly under stress.

A small public dock offering a 4-foot depth at mean low water is located just above nun 8 at the northern end of the harbor, where gas and diesel fuel are available. On the east side of the long wharf, there is a large rock about 150 feet off of the short wharf in line with its eastern corner. Steve Mach, harbormaster and wharf commissioner, can usually be found in a small white building at the inland end of these wharves. He monitors VHF-9 and 16 and can tell you about the mobile pumpout system. The model of a swordfish on a pole rises above the gas pier with a sign bidding "Welcome to Mattapoisett." Here you can tie up for one hour. Five guest moorings lie off this pier, first come, first served. The town dock also has two good floats and a pumpout station.

A twenty-minute walk from the town dock will take you to a laundry, an A&P supermarket, a Cumberland Farms store, a pharmacy, a post office, a bakery, and banks. A variety of food may be found at the oriental Cathay Temple, Nick's Pizza, and the Mattapoisett Chowder House. A step away on the main street is a most accommodating liquor store also providing dairy products. If you want a fine view of the harbor while enjoying a first-class dinner with music, drop in at the rare old Mattapoisett Inn right across from Shipyard Park, where band concerts serenade on Wednesdays and square dances run on Saturdays. Cannon Street offers the sightseer a special opportunity to view a line of charming Colonial houses shaded by majestic, towering trees.

The local repair facilities, plentiful and excellent, can fill any boat's needs. Brownell Boat Works is a full-service yard located one mile from the town wharf and can render the simplest repair to the complete construction of a 52-foot sportfisherman. It has a hauling trailer with a 30-ton capacity. Other yards carry on the Mattapoisett tradition of master boatbuilding. Over on Aucoot Cove, about two miles to the northwest, Edey & Duff are famous for their quality yachts, the Stone Horse and Dovekie.

One of the favorite anchorages of Mary Brown, an owner of a Stone Horse sloop, is at Molly's Cove, not marked on the chart but seen as a small bight halfway up the harbor, on the western shore. She recalls that, "after going ashore to the Mattapoisett Inn for dinner or the liquor and health food stores at the head of the town dock, I haul anchor and go over to Molly's Cove for the night—quiet, scenic, and closer to the entrance for the next day's departure. It offers the best shelter in the harbor from the south. I anchor in 10 feet of water near the Concordia yawl *Verity* and a Doughdish usually moored there. At night, a private floodlight shines just south of the cove."

Mattapoisett, called by the Indians "Place of Rest," did not always build "a good honest boat." A native, Anne Stowell, has unearthed this account from earlier days:

The late Wilson Barstow, who lived to be over 90 and died in 1981, said in a communication to the press about 30 years ago that vessels were built here as early as 1740 or 1750, sloops and small schooners. There was no science; they were built by sight of the eye and good judgment! There were no models.

Queer results were sometimes produced by this method. "Mr. Hastings," says Wilson Barstow, "was put in a towering passion by being told that his starboard bow was all on one side, and one sloop was nicknamed

Sippican Harbor's crowded anchorage at Marion lies north of Ram Island, at the right. *James W. Sewall Co.*

Bowline because she was so crooked." The old whaler *Trident*, of 448 tons, built in 1828, was so much out of true that she carried 150 more barrels of oil on one side of the keel than on the other. Sailors said she was "sure logy on one tack, but sailed like the very mischief on the other."*

Today, an impressive-looking flagpole rises above Shipyard Park, the site of Jonathan Holmes' shipyard where whalers were once built. It is the original mizzenmast of the *Wanderer*, helping retain some of Mattapoisett's nautical heritage.

Marion (Sippican) (13236). Here is one of the best all-round harbors on the coast. To the east of the entrance is Bird Island Lighthouse. Totally dark for the past forty-three years, it was relit on July 9, 1976, after a community financial effort restored the light, but it was closed down again in 1987.

To the west is Blake Point, marked by Converse Point on the chart, occupied by summer homes and marked by a tall flagpole. This western shore should be given a wide berth, as there are many outlying rocks. The red Sippican Harbor lighted buoy 8, showing a flashing red light every

*From *Mattapoisett & Old Rochester* (Grafton Press, 1907).

four seconds, at the entrance off Ram Island, though close to the westerly shore, must be left to starboard, as its color indicates. In off-season, this light is replaced by a nun. The green can and the little island beyond are then left to port. At night it is important to note that there are no range lights in the harbor. Like Mattapoisett, Sippican can easily be entered under sail.

The harbor's popularity, especially on weekends, affords limited space for anchoring; permanent moorings are everywhere. One frustrated skipper reports that "there is now no room to anchor in this harbor and no more than three boats may raft on a mooring." If one looks about, however, a possible anchorage just might be spotted. An opening may appear to the north of Little Island (just west of can 9) in 9 feet. A more protected and preferable choice is to moor south of Ram Island in the deeper water there while making sure to keep well clear of those charted rocks. Other possible anchorages are in the good water to the south of Allens Point or farther to the north along this point's western shore. These two areas, however, are apt to be rough in strong southerlies.

It is more convenient, of course, off the Beverly Yacht Club or Barden's Boat Yard on the west shore beyond. This club used to have its clubhouse on Butler Point but lost it in the hurricane of 1938. A new clubhouse was erected at Barden's yard next to the town dock. The club is now well established in a clubhouse converted from a former residence and located just to the south of Barden's Boat Yard and the town dock, where there is 5 feet MLW. Do not come up alongside the yacht club float at the end of the pier; it's a busy place and the water is shallow. Members of other recognized yacht clubs granting reciprocal privileges are welcomed here. The launchman, once hailed, may be fortunate in spotting a vacant mooring for you. His service runs from 8 A.M. to 9:15 P.M. and he should be signaled with three blasts and a display of your T-flag or a call on VHF-68. Beverly has no gas or slips, but does provide showers and ice, as well as a bar and small grill, both of which are open from 11:30 A.M. to 5 P.M. Many yachts stop here before or after passing through the Cape Cod Canal, as Marion is neither too near nor too far from the canal entrance.

The Beverly Yacht Club, the oldest on Buzzards Bay and one of the oldest in the country, was organized, according to Lloyds Register, in 1871. However, as the *New Bedford Standard Times* reports, it was formally launched in February 1872, at a supper party held by Edward and Walter Burgess in their Boston home. This was the family, specifically Edward and subsequently W. Starling, who designed so many successful defenders of the America's Cup. The club name came from the fact that the founders had their summer residence in Beverly, on "The North Shore" of Massachusetts Bay, and the early activities took place there. According to James R. Fraser, the club historian: "Three things emerge from the history of the Beverly Yacht Club. The first is the interesting evolution of its present location, the second is its unsurpassed tradition in small-boat racing, and the third is a characteristic of family participation that has become stronger over the years." Following a trial race on August 3, 1912, land at the end of Butler Point was purchased, and the club finally moved to Marion.*

Fred Coulson runs Barden's Boat Yard—(508) 748-0250, VHF-9—just to the north of the yacht club. See him for a possible mooring, but be reminded that there are only three designated guest moorings in the entire harbor. We suggest that you reserve a mooring from him in advance by telephone. Water and ice are available at the stone pier, where there is 4 feet at MLW. Sperry Sails has a loft nearby. Fred Coulson and his men are unexcelled for prompt service and repairs, as we know from our own experience. Both Barden's and Burr Brothers close down tighter than a drum on Sunday afternoons at 4 P.M. The harbormaster may be seen patrolling the harbor in his Boston Whaler.

After Fessenden Blanchard's death in 1963, his friends wished to express their affection through an appropriate memorial. After contact with the officers of the Cruising Club of America, of which he was a member, it was decided to establish through voluntary contributions a "Blanchard Memorial Guest Mooring" for member yachtsmen putting into Marion Harbor. Therefore, in the spring of 1965, a 600-pound mushroom anchor was set out in 10 feet of water located well to the east of the Beverly Yacht Club, where we hope it will be for many years to come. It can be identified by the blue-and-white burgee of the Cruising Club. See the club's launchman for its use, remembering that Cruising Club members have mooring priority.

North of can 13, the winding channel is marked by privately maintained buoys all the way to Burr Brothers Boatyard. This channel records 5 feet to the Old Town Landing Wharf, then 4 feet at MLW to Burr's. Toward the northern end of this channel, favor the left side and note that

*From *Block Island to Nantucket*, by Fessenden S. Blanchard (D. Van Nostrand Co., Inc., Princeton, N.J.).

the black striped buoy is a mid-channel marker. Burr's has transient slips at finger piers in 5 feet at low water, moorings, gas, diesel fuel, ice, electricity, launch service to and from its moorings, and all types of repair work. Burr Brothers monitors VHF-68. They supply the only fuel in the harbor.

Marion is also a good supply port. Near the town dock you will find a restaurant named Harriet's with outside tables, open for lunch and dinner except on Mondays. The Marion General Store is almost next door, with a wide selection of supplies including liquor and baked goods. The post office is up the street. Other recommended restaurants nearby include L'Auberge and The Wave, which is accessible by cab on nearby Route 6.

There is little nightlife in Marion, but concerts are given occasionally at the bandstand next to Barden's. A visit to the Marion Art Center, housed in a converted church, and to the Sippican Historical Society is well worthwhile.

Here, too, is the home port of the lovely black-hulled two-master *Tabor Boy,* the training ship of Tabor Academy, whose red-roofed campus can be seen just above Barden's. Many homes of Boston summer residents are on wooded slopes on both shores. Some of the finest sailing on the coast is near at hand, and many of the best harbors are within a day's sail. The town has a large summer weekend population, as it is accessible from Boston or New York via New Bedford or Providence.

Hurricane Gloria hit Marion Harbor hard in September 1985. Fifty-nine beached boats lined its shores to the tune of several million dollars in damage, according to Chris Taft. On a Pearson 26, washed up high and dry ¼ mile from the harbor, the luckless owner hung a sign on the bow pulpit. It read, "Private Property. *Please!* Do Not Make A Sad Situation Worse!"* But, not to be defeated, and with true Yankee ingenuity, a group of other woebegone owners improved their situations miraculously. They banded together and hired a helicopter equipped with giant slings to airlift their stranded boats safely seaward. There was no serious damage from Hurricane Bob.

Marion was the home of Captain Benjamin S. Briggs, master of the doomed half-brig, *Mary Celeste,* whose crew's complete disappearance off the Azores in 1872 still remains the world's greatest sea mystery. The Sippican Historical Society maintains the Mary Celeste Museum in the

*Gail S. Sleeman, "Hurricane Gloria," *Offshore,* December 1985, p. 34.

center of Marion. It is open to visitors on Saturdays free of charge and displays memorabilia related to the ship and her master.

Though settled in 1679, Marion was named for a famous Revolutionary hero, Francis Marion, the "Swamp Fox," about whom the "Song of Marion's Men" was written.* On May 14, 1852, the town became officially Marion, though the harbor is still Sippican. Cruising yachtsmen, however, speak of it fondly as Marion Harbor.

Wareham (13236). Once a whaling and shipbuilding port, Wareham has become an important cranberry center, though on the Wareham River the number of boats being built is probably greater than ever before. These are the products of the Cape Cod Shipbuilding Company, well known for such small sailboats as Raven, Mercury, and Bullseye.

Wareham Harbor now has the distinction of being the first official federal no-discharge zone on the East Coast. This applies to treated as well as untreated sewage, and is probably just the first of many.

Although somewhat off the main track toward the Cape Cod Canal, Wareham River offers several possible anchorages or tie-ups for yachts drawing well under 6 feet. One of these is under the partial lee of Long Beach Point, and the other in the narrow part of the river off Wareham Neck below the bridge. The latter is convenient to the town of Wareham and supplies, but it takes quite a jaunt upriver to get there. Long Beach Point, much of which is underwater at high tide, is about 1 1/2 miles from nun 2 off Great Hill and an equal distance to the docks up at Wareham.

A conspicuous tall stack and an elevated tank in Wareham help identify the river's entrance. In 1986, the controlling depth in the crooked, twisting channel was 4 feet MLW with depths shoaling to 2 and 3 feet close to its edges. The mean range of tide is 4 feet, but the most difficult passage is at Quahaug Bar, at can 17, where depths cannot always be counted on. Going upchannel, note the charted rock just south of can 21, don't be lured into Broad Marsh River no matter how inviting it looks, and keep nun 32 well to starboard farther up. Warr's Marine— (508) 295-0022, VHF-9—located on the port shore just above nun 30, has 10 feet at its main dock at low water. Warr's has moorings, slips, electricity, gas, diesel fuel, water, showers, ice, pumpout, and all types of repair and marine supply service. Since a 3-knot current runs along this

*As reported in *Massachusetts,* American Guide Series (Houghton Mifflin Co., Boston).

upper part of the narrow channel, we were definitely advised not to attempt anchoring. The depth at Wareham's wharves is 9 feet according to the chart. The *Coast Pilot* advises strangers to obtain local information about channel depths before attempting to navigate the river.

Most of us today are too young to remember the days when women began to wear bloomers for bicycle riding. We therefore won't recall this story of a lady on a bicycle who was so dressed and was heading for Cape Cod:

"Is this the way to Ware-um?" she asked.

"I don't know," replied an old eccentric standing in the road. "I never seen 'em before."

Onset (13236). This popular harbor is a valuable asset to the cruising man who may want to make an early start through the canal or who, heading the other way, may find the going too rough on Buzzards Bay and would like to hang over awhile.

There are two anchorages here: (1) off the Onset Town Wharf at the end of the channel and (2) the special anchorage area off Point Independence, this latter place being larger and less noisy, with depths of 5 to 12 feet; riding lights are not required. Of the approaches to them, a local authority writes as follows:

> When approaching from the Cape Cod Canal or from Buzzards Bay, turn westerly into the 100-foot Onset Bay channel, keeping about 75 feet to the southwest of flashing green light 21 on a steel-pile dolphin. Expect to fight a violent crosscurrent going at 90 degrees to the channel entering Onset and often towing under the entrance buoys. The Onset Bay channel has a minimum depth of 12 to 15 feet to Wickets Island and thence 14 feet to the 200-foot Onset Town Wharf. There is 8 to 15 feet in this basin. The channel is well marked with eight green and seven red buoys. Coming into the inner harbor at night, use the high wide arc light on the town wharf as a range light, after making the turns at Wickets Island. Both the Onset and Point Independence anchorages are well sheltered, offering safe anchorage and excellent holding ground.

The small cove just north of Hog Neck looks inviting and has been suggested as a possible anchorage area. But it is no place for an overnight stop since it is exposed to turbulence, and the holding ground, choked with eel grass, is poor.

The proximity of the business district offers an unusual convenience for purchasing supplies of every kind and having repairs made by competent and experienced mechanics. Water is furnished pleasure craft without charge on application to the harbormaster, Bill Ellis, who is on duty all year round at his office near the town wharf. He has six slips and four moorings which can be reserved for overnight use by phoning (508) 295-8160 or calling him over VHF-9. To ensure greater comfort for all visiting yachts, speed regulations will be strictly enforced in the vicinity of both anchorage basins. There is 13 feet at MLW along the face of the wharf, where boats are permitted to tie up for one hour to stock up on provisions—but do not leave your boat completely unattended.

Craft drawing less than 7 feet can also use the Point Independence anchorage basin. Swing northeasterly after passing red buoy 10, giving both Onset Island to starboard and Wickets Island to port a good berth until off the large marine railway on the mainland. Then veer west to an anchorage.

The best anchorage in this basin is off the Point Independence Yacht Club dock. The club people are obliging and will supply gas, diesel fuel, and water, and order ice for you. The club has showers and usually guest moorings but only about 6 feet at its docks. Stores for supplies are a short walk to the west, but we understand that Onset Cash Market will deliver groceries to the club Monday through Saturday from 9 A.M. to 4:30 P.M. One of the best restaurants in Onset is the Onset Boat Club, specializing in Italian cuisine and seafood, all reasonably priced. It is just across the nearby bridge.

If you walk there, you will pass by Onset Bay Marina, a full-service yard that invites transient boaters to call them over VHF-9 for reservations. There are very few conveniences that they don't provide the visiting yachtsman and his vessel here.

In Colonial days, Onset was a part of the Plymouth Colony, furnishing the Wampanoag Indian tribe with productive summer fishing grounds.

Boating people are now being asked to cooperate to keep Onset Bay and adjacent waters free of pollution. Complete information of interest to all concerned can be obtained from the Onset Bay Chamber of Commerce.

Cape Cod Canal (13236). For a yacht under 65 feet in length, passage through the canal is easy and under ordinary circumstances involves no formality whatever. The most important consideration is a fair tide. A head tide running at something like 4 knots makes at best a tedious passage. At worst, it can delay the yacht's passage so much that the canal administration may require the yacht to take a tow from a canal tug and pay for it. Maximum time of passage through the land cut is 2¹/₂ hours. Consult the *Eldridge Tide and Pilot Book* for the time of current changes at the railroad bridge. One may wait out a foul tide at the East Boat Basin or at Onset or Monument Beach.

The following are the principal regulations applying to vessels under 65 feet. The complete regulations are published in *Coast Pilot 2*, section 207.

1) Vessels must proceed straight through the Canal. No anchoring, stopping or turning around is permitted except in emergency.

2) All vessels must use power; however, sail may be set to a fair wind to improve speed or maneuverability. Vessels without power must be towed.

3) Listen to channel 13 VHF for communications from the Canal office.

4) Traffic lights at Wings Neck and Sandwich do not apply to vessels under 65 feet and are supplementary to radio communication.

5) Vessels moving with the tide have right of way over those moving against it *except* that vessels under 65 feet shall not interfere with larger vessels.

6) Inland Rules of the Road, not COLREGS, apply in the Canal and Buzzards Bay, except as in 5 above.

7) Fishing from vessels is prohibited, but fishing from the bank is permitted.

8) Speed must be moderate with due regard to the effect of the vessel's wake.

9) The railroad bridge is kept raised except when it must be lowered for a train. When it is about to be lowered, the bridgetender will blow two blasts; when it is about to be raised, one blast. When the bridge is lowered in thick weather, he will blow four blasts every two minutes. The danger signal is five blasts.

10) No oil or refuse may be thrown into the Canal.

11) If an emergency situation seems to be developing, call the Canal office at once on channel 13.

Entering the canal from the west with a fair wind and tide seldom presents a problem. However, the westbound vessel emerging from the canal with a fair tide may find a strong southwest breeze blowing up Buzzards Bay and raising a very steep breaking chop. The best tactic is to slow down and let the tide do the work. As soon as possible after passing flashing bouy 10, set sail and stand off on the starboard tack over the flats. The sea will be much less and the foredeck may even dry off.

The East Boat Basin near the eastern end of the canal may be helpful, and is covered at the beginning of Chapter IX.

Pocasset (13236). This is the first harbor on the east side of Buzzards Bay available to one coming west through the canal, and for one bound east it is a good place in which to wait out an adverse tide.

Entrance from the canal is easy. Leave the dredged channel at flashing buoy 10, round the abandoned lighthouse on Wings Neck, and follow the shore into the harbor behind Bassetts Island, leaving nun 2 to starboard.

In approaching from the south, be wary of Southwest Ledge, marked by three nuns off Scraggy Neck. Either keep to the westward of all three or run inside the ledge. The most dangerous part of the ledge lies south of nun 2. To hit it, one would have to run close to nun 8, which is said to "move," and should be warned thereby. However, Parker's Boatyard reports having repaired a good many boats that have struck this rock each season. Indeed, on a hazy, blowy southwest day one of our writers confused nun 2 with nun 8 and only an all-standing gybe and the gods that look after the careless navigator saved him from losing his boat. The rock north of nun 10 reported in 1971 was said by a local authority in 1985 to have disappeared.

If you elect to go inside the ledge, look for flasher 1 on Seal Rocks. It is a small buoy and hard to find from down the bay, for Scraggy Neck blends deceptively with the land behind it. However, there is a large white house on the end of Nyes Neck, and the abandoned lighthouse on Wings Neck is prominent. Give the flasher a generous berth, round Scraggy Neck, and leave nun 2 off Bassetts Island to starboard.

There is usually room to anchor in the southern part of the cove out of the tide. There are several moorings here, most of them private. However, Parker's Boatyard in Red Brook Harbor may know of one which will be vacant over night. Call the yard on VHF-9.

This is a quiet anchorage, frequented principally by those in search of quiet. There is no public landing and very little reason to land. Both shores are privately owned and the north end of Bassetts Island is infested with poison ivy and wood ticks. There is a small yacht club, The Buzzards, in the cove to port just inside the entrance. It has no facilities for visitors although there is reported to be a public telephone on the wharf.

Some of the ladies of the club, it is said, objected to the name "The Buzzards" as undignified and sought to change it. They were heavily outvoted and the name persists.

One may wonder how Buzzards Bay, so far from the usual habitat of buzzards, acquired its name. In Colonial times the name "buzzard" was applied in England to any broad-winged, slow-flying hawk useless for falconry. Early settlers called the osprey, then common in these waters, a buzzard, and hence the name of the bay. The term as applied to birds is a pejorative one, and carried over to people, it is even more so. A buzzard is a stupid, lazy, shiftless person. So the ladies were right: a club of buzzards would be a sorry lot. But the name remains and like "wharf rat" has acquired a certain dignity, a sort of sneaker snobbery.

North of Pocasset Harbor is Phinney's Harbor at Bourne. It can be entered by leaving the canal channel just south of flashing red bell 18 and going southeast around Mashnee to the GR "C" buoy. The Bourne Marina—(508) 759-2512—may have dock space, and there is a reported 8 feet of depth off Monument Beach.

Red Brook Harbor (13236). This popular and well-protected harbor can be entered either through Pocasset Harbor or from the south. The northern channel by Cape Cod standards is deep and well buoyed. The channel is intricate, but the government buoys, supplemented by small local buoys constructed of conical highway markers on little rafts, make it perfectly clear. The southern entrance is shoal and very narrow but is well marked although the chart is not encouraging.

Those seeking peace and privacy can anchor off the east shore of Bassetts Island north of can 11. The southern end of the island is owned by the town and is open to the public.

The western part of Red Brook Harbor is heavily peppered with moorings maintained by the two boatyards, Kingman's and Parker's. Kingman's—(508) 563-7136, VHF 9 and 71—provides almost any service needed or desired by the cruising yachtsman. It has moorings, launch service, slips with water and electricity, showers, laun-

dromats, and a restaurant, bar, and gift shop. A stout travelift can haul
almost any boat which can get into Red Brook Harbor. Repairs to hull,
spars, sails, engines, and electronic gear can be made at the yard, or
arranged through the yard office. There is no store nearby, but the stores
can deliver.

Parker's yard—(508) 563-9366—just south of Kingman's, was established by Raz Parker and is operated by him and his son Bruce, who is in
sympathy with his father's ideas. Raz says, "Parker's yard is 95 percent
sailboats. Able work-type powerboats are welcome; all others keep to
hell out." This apparently inhospitable attitude, however, is belied by the
friendly and informal atmosphere of the yard. The yard maintains about
100 moorings, some of which are always available for cruising boats. The
moderate mooring fee includes launch service and the use of shower,
toilet, and sitting room in the yard-run Red Brook Harbor Yacht Club.
There is a telephone on the back of the yacht club building. The yard has
a lift and is equipped to make repairs on the kinds of boats which are
welcomed.

Mr. Parker has been assisted in recent years by several attractive
launch-drivers and dock people, at least two of whom have proved
themselves talented cooks. Carol Lee Mason and Kim Keeshan have
published *Parker's Boatyard Cookbook,* available at the yard office and
highly reliable.

Also at Parker's yard in 1985 was Elio Oliva, a craftsman in any
medium. He has finished out a number of Friendship sloop hulls in truly
elegant fashion and made small brass replicas of the *Constitution*'s guns
which make handsome saluting cannons. A visit to Parker's Boatyard,
"the boatyard with a yacht club atmosphere," is almost guaranteed to be
an interesting experience.

In the event of a heavy blow or a hurricane, Red Brook Harbor is as
well protected a harbor as Buzzards Bay affords. There are several other
anchorages in the region:

Barlows Landing. This cove provides good protection for shoal-
draft boats. No moorings are available here. There is a float at which one
can land, the nearest landing to a grocery store in the region.

Hospital Cove. This cove, north and east of Scraggy Neck, is
principally used by local boats but is a well-protected, quiet place to
anchor if a visitor can find swinging room.

Hen Cove. This shallow cove is for the shoal-draft gunkholer and is of little interest to most cruising boats.

Megansett (13236). In ordinary weather Megansett Harbor is entirely satisfactory, although large and subject to some motion from a sea running up the bay. There is better protection off the Megansett Yacht Club behind the jetty at the head of the harbor. The town wharf is used by the club, which maintains two guest moorings in the cove. There is no gas at the float, but it can be obtained at Fiddler's Cove. In a hard northwester the anchorage can be uncomfortable. One correspondent recommends following the dredged channel into Squeteague Harbor, but the 1992 *Coast Pilot* recommends local knowledge for the privately marked channel.

On the southern shore of Megansett Harbor is Rands Harbor, which looks like an inverted Y on the chart. A local resident writes: "The entrance is virtually impossible at low tide and features a large poorly marked rock in dead center. The rock is not on the chart."

Fiddler's Cove (13236). The dredged channel into Fiddler's Cove, marked by privately maintained buoys, has a depth of about 6 feet at low water. The basin inside is largely occupied by the new Fiddlers Cove Marina—(508) 564-6327, VHF-9—with finger piers. There is no room to anchor, but a slip may be available. Formerly labeled a "powerboathole," this basin is now occupied by auxiliaries as much as by powerboats. Of course there is no room to maneuver here under sail.

Gasoline, diesel fuel, water, cable TV, pumpout, and ice are available at the marina, and there is a laundromat ashore. There is a clubhouse with heads, showers, lounge area with pool table, kitchenette, and full repair services. A store is nearby. This is a secure and convenient refuge but rather too crowded for anyone who goes cruising to get away from the congestion of city life.

Silver Beach, Wild Harbor (13236). Wild Harbor is wide open to the usual southwest breeze and is of no value as a shelter except in northerly or easterly weather. From the head of Wild Harbor there is a narrow shoal channel leading into Silver Beach Harbor, but this basin is too shoal for almost any cruising boat. It supports a considerable population of small outboards and Beetle Cats.

West Falmouth. Anchorage may be made off the big houses to starboard, about 150 yards beyond the breakwater. *Colonial Gas Co., James W. Sewall Co.*

West Falmouth, Massachusetts (13230). This harbor, well marked by a lighted bell, a can, and a nun outside and protected by a breakwater, is easy to enter and is well protected for boats drawing 6 feet or less. Enter carefully and anchor at the edge of the channel about 150 yards inside the breakwater. The tide runs about 1 knot here but is not a serious problem. Shoal-draft vessels may continue up the channel, well buoyed with privately maintained cans and nuns on a miniature scale, to the basin where Chart 13230 shows 6 feet. There are no shoreside facilities for transients. From here it is a short walk to a well-equipped store.

This is a clean and quiet harbor with attractive estates on the shores and no commercial interests except the unobtrusive gasoline wharf at the

Quisset's inner harbor to the north is secure against all winds. *Colonial Gas Co., James W. Sewall Co.*

head of the inner harbor. The lovely summer morning the writer spent in West Falmouth was made lively by schooling mackerel, diving terns, and vigorous activity in Beetle Cats by the younger members of the Chappaquoit Yacht Club. One of our writers spent a summer here many years ago and sailed a 14-foot sailboat all around the harbor. At low tide he found it quite shallow in the southern part.

Quissett (Quamquissett), Massachusetts (13230). Quissett is a secure and convenient anchorage, perhaps less likely to be overcrowded than Hadley Harbor and easier of access than Woods Hole. A large standpipe on the hill behind the harbor and a bare rocky point on the north side of the entrance are the best landmarks for one approaching the harbor from the west. A small lighted buoy off the entrance is a good mark at night but is hard to distinguish against the shore behind it by day. The channel inside the flasher is well marked by cans and nuns.

In ordinary summer weather, anchorage in the outer harbor is entirely satisfactory. In the event of a smoky sou'wester, one can move under the

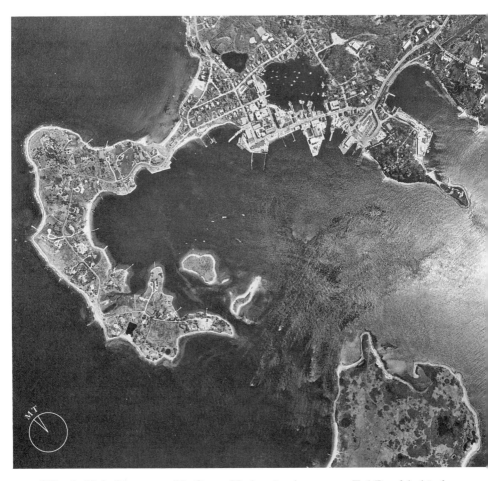

Woods Hole Passage, with Great Harbor in the center, Eel Pond behind its bridge, and Little Harbor to the right. *Colonial Gas Co., James W. Sewall Co.*

southern shore for excellent protection; but if the wind shifts to the northwest—a likely development—this berth might be uneasy.

The inner harbor is secure against all winds. In entering, favor the northern shore, respecting the privately maintained buoys, and carefully avoiding both the rock shown as a tiny island on Chart 13230 and a sandbar making out from the shore to port. Once inside, you will find no room to anchor, for the inner harbor is crowded with moorings. However, the boatyard at the head of the harbor maintains a few rental moorings for transients.

Land at the boatyard wharf, where ice and water are available but no fuel. Here there is a public telephone but no slips, no laundry machine, no stores, and none of the "attractions" of busier ports. Minor repairs can be handled or arranged for at the boatyard.

There used to be a large hotel on the point at the west end of the inner harbor. This has now been torn down although some of the lesser buildings remain. The entire point, formerly the property of the late Miss Cornelia Carey, was left by her to the Salt Pond Areas and Bird Sanctuaries, Inc. There is a pleasant walk around the point starting at the wharf in the northwest corner of the harbor. The Quissett Yacht Club has the use of this wharf, but the club owns no land or buildings and has no facilities for visitors.

Woods Hole, Massachusetts (13229). Before you enter Woods Hole, consult carefully the large-scale chart and be sure of the layout. Once you get into the tide, things are likely to appear confusing, and a great many vessels go aground because their skippers become disoriented.

Entering from the Buzzards Bay side, notice that the passage is buoyed on the basis of entering from the eastward. Therefore red buoys are to be left to port. It is not necessary for a small boat to go way out to the first entrance buoy. Make the red flasher 10, leave it to port, and continue by the two big nuns, leaving them to port. Between the second nun, 6, and the lighted beacon, 5, you must decide whether to follow the cans to starboard down Broadway and out into Vineyard Sound or to follow the nuns to port into Woods Hole Harbor. Both courses are clearly marked by big buoys. Nevertheless, at times when the tide is running hard, even these buoys are pulled under. Don't be confused if you see some of these buoys tilting against the current. Some are apparently attached to a point above their center of resistance instead of at the bottom as is normal.

It is of the greatest importance to keep a sharp eye astern as well as ahead in order to notice to what extent the vessel is being set sideways by meeting the current at an angle. The turn at can 3 is particularly dangerous, for one rounds the can and heads up Broadway, feeling that the worst is over, and finds himself set sideways onto Middle Ledge or onto the can itself.

The tide may reach 6 knots at its greatest strength and seldom runs less than 4 knots at full flood or ebb, so even though the distance through the Hole is short, it is worth planning the passage for slack water or a fair tide, particularly on one's first trip. However, in ordinary weather most yachts can make it against the tide. One of our writers negotiated the

Hole under sail, single reefed, against the tide, although he does not recommend the practice as a usual thing. We understand that fast displacement powerboats running against the current can throw wakes large enough to cause standing waves which are big enough to be a hazard to smaller boats. Be forewarned.

In making the passage from Vineyard Sound westward, be wary of Great Ledge. Pass between green flasher 1 and nun 2 or go all the way up to the flashing red bell 2. Note that the beacon inside nun 4 is very small and low. It barely shows its red triangle above high water.

The steamers running from Woods Hole to Martha's Vineyard normally use the southerly passage to the west of Great Ledge. In the writer's observation, their skippers are careful of yachts and are ready to give the right-of-way where they are required to do so. However, the cautious and considerate yachtsman will remember the note in the Inland Rules, which gives the right-of-way to a large vessel under power in a narrow channel. He will also remember that a steamer constructed on the lines of a warehouse must maintain considerable headway in order to keep control in strong winds and tides. Whether he has the right-of-way or not, the yachtsman will take clear and definite action to avoid these monsters in sufficient time to make his intentions clear to them. In thick weather, he will display his biggest radar reflector, blow his horn vigorously, and use the channel east of Great Ledge.

There are three anchorages in Woods Hole:

1. Great Harbor. Enter from Buzzards Bay by following the line of nuns around to port at flashing beacon 5. Leave flashing beacon 4 and nun 2 to port and then leave can 9 to *port.* The best anchorage is well up in the northwest part of the harbor, in about two fathoms.

In entering from Vineyard Sound, note that there is a range of green lights, the southerly one flashing, which lead in from red flashing bell 2.

The Woods Hole Yacht Club, whose landing and small building are below the northern range light, has one guest mooring, which is likely to be occupied. There may be an orange balloon labeled WHYC in the middle of the harbor. This is *not* a mooring but marks one end of the starting line for small boats that race in the harbor.

The steel ball labeled WHYC is a rugged guest mooring but a bit hard on topsides should the tide set you down on it. Do not trust the private moorings here as many of them are for small boats.

There are two floats at the Yacht Club. The west or inner stone dock with a depth of 4 feet is used for dinghies, and the outer timber pier with a depth of 8 feet is used by the sailing school and for cruising vessels for 30-minute tie-ups while loading or unloading. Water and power are available on request to the steward. There is a pay telephone in the clubhouse, which is open and in the charge of a steward from 8 A.M. to sunset. It is a pleasant walk up the road to the right from the club to town. The large wooden pier to the right is best left for commercial fishing boats.

2. Eel Pond. The entrance to this bottle-tight pond lies between the ships of the Oceanographic Institute and the steamer wharf. It is a narrow cut and looks rather perilous in a brisk southwester. Before approaching the entrance, call Buzz Harvey at Woods Hole Marine on VHF-9 and inquire for a mooring or slip inside. If one is available, ask also for the proper bridge signal. In the past it has been two long and two short, not the same as the one long and one short which alerts most bridgetenders. If the bridge does not open on signal, tie up alongside the entrance cut and inquire; during morning and evening rush hours the bridge does not open.

At Woods Hole Marine—(508) 540-2402—one can get gasoline, water, and ice. The head of the wharf is right on the main street handy to grocery stores, restaurants, bus station, and steamer wharf. The Sea Store has a small variety of rigging supplies.

The steamers for Martha's Vineyard leave from the wharf just east of the bridge and connect at the wharf with buses for Boston. The boat for Nantucket now leaves from Hyannis. Ferry passage to Nantucket is also available from the Vineyard, from about May 25 to about September 15.

3. Little Harbor. Formerly considered too exposed for an anchorage, Little Harbor now is home port for a considerable fleet of moored yachts, as well as a base for the Coast Guard. It would be an acceptable anchorage except in a strong southerly but, as it is exposed to the length of Vineyard Sound, would seldom be a quiet one. Large vessels sometimes occupy the Coast Guard moorings, so allow plenty of swinging room for them. There is a landing on the western shore. Under most circumstances Great Harbor is to be preferred.

Three famous institutions make Woods Hole a center for study of the ocean and marine life: Woods Hole Oceanographic Institute, Marine Biological Laboratory, and United States Fish and Wildlife Service. The latter maintains an aquarium and a number of exhibits of commercial fishing methods that are well worth a visit. The harbor is busy with Coast Guard vessels, steamers, and research vessels.

Hadley Harbor (13229). This is one of the best-protected and most attractive anchorages in the cruising ground south of Cape Cod. It is easy of access, and the dangers are clearly marked. The tide does not run hard by Cape Cod standards, and there is deep water right up to the shores of Nonamessett Island. Bull Island deserves a little more respect, but the half-tide rocks indicated are within 50 yards of high-water mark. Given a working breeze, there should be no great difficulty in entering under sail. Respect the buoys and keep your bowsprit out of the bushes.

Anchor clear of the channel which runs down the middle of the inner harbor. It should be kept open for the freight boat, which supplies the inhabitants of Naushon. There are no guest moorings.

Like most "unspoiled" places near centers of population, Hadley Harbor is invariably crowded in summer. If you come late, you may not be able to find swinging room. Rather than anchor on too short scope or bump your neighbors in the night, anchor either north of Bull Island or north of Goats Neck. Both these coves are shallow but are adequate for most small cruising boats in search of swinging room.

Naushon Island is owned by the Naushon Trust and has been in the Forbes family for a great many years. They have built on the island but have preserved most of it in its natural state. It is inhabited by deer, sheep, and many species of birds. In order to keep it unspoiled, the Trust asks that no visitors come ashore except on Bulls Island, where a float is provided in summer. Picnics, fires under careful control, and dogs are allowed here. Bring your own fuel. Because the island has been so carefully protected, one may sit in one's cockpit at sunset and watch deer come unafraid to the shore to browse.

Recently the deer have been found to carry a pinhead-sized tick which communicates to humans Lyme disease. This is a painful and debilitating affliction from which it may take weeks to recover. The ticks may be found in the bushes and grass wherever there are deer. This includes all of the Elizabeth Islands except perhaps Cuttyhunk and Penikese. Nantucket and the Vineyard are also infested.

Robinsons Hole (13230). This is the next passage south of Woods Hole between Buzzards Bay and Vineyard Sound. The tide does not run as hard here as it does through Woods Hole and presents no serious obstacle in ordinary circumstances to a yacht under power. It is buoyed on the basis of entering from Vineyard Sound. Red buoys should be left to *port* on entering from Buzzards Bay. It appears from the chart that a direct course from nun 6 to nun 8 runs right over a half-tide rock. However, one of our writers, proceeding with great caution against the tide, did not find this to be the case, since he did not actually see bottom. Can 1 is often pulled under by the tide.

There is no good anchorage here, as the shores are rocky and the tide runs hard. Both Naushon and Pasque are privately owned and off limits to visitors, in the interests of preserving them in their wild state. Both islands are regularly patrolled.

Quicks Hole (13230). This hole, between Nashawena and Pasque, is much more easily negotiated than Robinsons Hole. North Rock and South Rock are both prominent at all tides. Felix Ledge, with 16 feet of water, marked by a can, is of no concern to most yachts, and the ledge on the eastern side is marked by a flasher. The tide runs hard but presents no insuperable problem, although beating against it in a moderate breeze is quite a challenge. There is good anchorage in summer weather off the beach on the Nashawena side. This beach of fine white sand is very popular with visitors and, while seldom crowded by city standards, is likely to be well populated on weekends. However, the crowd melts away rapidly in the late afternoon, leaving the beach to the few who are willing to wait for it.

Landing on Pasque is prohibited. One can land on the Nashawena beach but should not venture inland and should not bring dogs ashore, as the island is inhabited mainly by sheep and is infested by ticks which carry Lyme disease.

Flounder have been caught on the sandy bottom off the beach, and striped bass are said to frequent the hole. Many eager fishermen patrol these waters, but the writer has dragged a lure from North Rock to South Rock many times with no response whatever from bass or bluefish. However, you will never catch a fish if you don't go fishing. It may be worth a try.

One should remember that all of the Elizabeth Islands except Cuttyhunk and Penikese are privately owned by people who are trying to keep them in their original wild state. With a few disgraceful exceptions, yachtsmen honor this public-spirited intention, confine their visits to the beaches, and help to save for all of us a few small islands of solitude untrampled by the feet of megalopolis.

Canapitsit Channel (13230). Despite a grim write-up in the *Coast Pilot,* Canapitsit Channel is passable for shoal-draft boats. Local knowledge at Cuttyhunk declared there was "plenty of water," but declined to express the idea in feet or fathoms. It is "shallow on the edges" and the first can, 5, should be given a good berth. Strangers are urged to try it for the first time on an incoming tide. It should be avoided entirely if a heavy sea is running.

Penikese Island, Massachusetts (13230). The waters around this island are shoal and tide-scoured. Any approach must be made with an attentive eye to the chart and the depth sounder.

Penikese was the site of one of the first marine biology laboratories in the world. Louis Agassiz worked on the island for a number of years. Later it became a leper colony and then was abandoned to the gulls and the terns. In 1973 George Cadwalader established the Penikese Island School, an institution which he describes in his own words:

Penikese Island School is a non-profit Massachusetts corporation founded in 1973 to provide a program of character-building activities and vocational training for troubled 14- to 18-year-old boys. The school teaches the skills and attitudes needed to live in a remote, self-sufficient community. Staff and students, working together, have built all the school buildings; raise and cook much of their own food; and operate the boat which provides the island's only link to the mainland. Penikese tries to be a place where honesty, cooperation, and loyalty contribute visibly to the happiness of the community and where students can learn the pride in workmanship, tolerance to frustration, and ability to accept criticism they must have to compete effectively on the job market.

The island is a state-owned wildlife sanctuary, with the school serving as caretaker for the Massachusetts Division of Fisheries and Wildlife. Visitors are asked to check in with the staff at the main house where they can usually find a hot cup of coffee. Penikese is best approached by steering north from the Cuttyhunk bell, leaving the Gull Island Shoal well to starboard, and heading for the saltbox

Cuttyhunk Harbor. The dredged areas are clearly shown, leading in a narrow path to the inner fish pier and to starboard beyond the entrance. *James W. Sewall Co.*

building while keeping a good eye on the fathometer. There is about 5 feet of water at the end of the jetty at high tide. Eelgrass can be thick in late summer, making anchoring with a Danforth difficult. Penikese is wide open to the southeast and should be avoided when the wind is in that quarter.

Cuttyhunk (13230). Situated as it is within a half-day's sail of many yacht anchorages, Cuttyhunk is a fragile place, easily destroyed by its admirers. It has a remote island quality composed of simplicity, bleakness, and independence, of its moors, wild roses, ducks, rabbits, and the surrounding sea. Its inhabitants and its visitors sense this fragility and for the most part treat it with the respect accorded a museum piece.

If you plan to visit the island, try to get in early. Buzzards Bay overnighters as well as a large number of Connecticut and Rhode Island cruising people are likely to crowd the anchorage and the marina, especially on summer weekends.

The huge three-bladed wind machine that used to be a landmark on the summit of the island is now gone, so don't look for it.

Beware of the shoals around Penikese. Although very few of them show on a calm day, they are really there. Several cans and nuns will lead you in from the northwest. From the northeast it is a clear course from bell CH. Nun 2E will keep you off the Gull Island shoals, even if you cannot see Gull Island, which is little more than a sandbar. The shore of Nashawena, studded with half-tide rocks, drops off within 200 yards of the beach. A scale-up is likely here in the fog.

In entering the dredged channel into Cuttyhunk Pond, leave the lighted beacon on the end of the north jetty to starboard. The beacon on the south jetty has been replaced with a can, which must be left generously to port. The south jetty is submerged at high tide and picks up several boats each year. Keep in the middle of the dredged channel.

The dredged mooring basin inside the pond is more or less square. The entrance channel runs along the southern side. Keep outside, north of a line between the first two wharves and the marina. The dredged channel continues to the fish dock beyond the marina, leaving a prominent pile to starboard. The pile is identified with a triangular red-and-yellow sign. The western side of the dredged area runs from this pile toward a brown, flat-roofed house on the northern shore. In moving from the fish dock into the anchorage, be sure to leave this pile to port. The north side of the anchorage lies more or less on a range established by an old wharf and a little gray house more than halfway up the hill to the west. The east side lines up roughly with the Coast Guard wharf.

In the southern part of the dredged area the town of Gosnold has established about 46 rental moorings. These are available on a first-come basis. Just pick one up. Be prepared to supply your own line to the buoy. Someone will shortly appear to collect the rental fee. If the moorings are all taken by the time you get in, you may be fortunate enough to find a generous skipper with whom you can raft up. The number of boats on a single mooring is limited to three. If you draw little water, you may find room to anchor along the north side of the basin. Be sure to back down hard and set your anchor firmly, as the bottom is foul with weed. You can tie up to one of the pilings on the west side. If you like to lie in a slip, call the wharfinger (dockmaster) at (508) 990-7578 or on VHF-9. About 50 slips are available for transients. A correspondent notes that the anchorage is closed to shellfishing because of pollution and advises against swimming there. There is no fuel available on the island and there are no pumpout facilities. Solid waste should be sorted for recycling if you bring it ashore.

If none of these alternatives is available, you will have to lie outside. Jim Barry maintains about 25 stout 4,000-pound moorings in the outer harbor from July 1 until Labor Day. Call him on channel 72 at Frog Pond Marine. The fee for the mooring includes launch service. From Frog Pond Marine you can order, delivered to your boat, ice, newspapers, and breakfast muffins. Other moorings available outside belong to the Jenkins family.

Mel Door maintains two guest moorings marked with cone-shaped buoys northeast of the jetties. Call "Canapitsit" on channel 9 before picking one up. Or call "Cuttyhunk Fuel" on channel 9 for a mooring.

And of course one may lie to his own anchor in the outer harbor. On a quiet night or with the wind to the southward, the outer harbor is well protected, cool, and clean. However, a vigorous northeast or northwest wind may make it virtually untenable.

About cocktail time you will probably be visited by a floating "raw bar" operated by Seth Garfield and offering oysters, littleneck clams, and cherrystones from West End Pond, or you can call on VHF-72. The clams are "wild," but he cultivates the oysters. His family has summered on Cuttyhunk for generations, and after he and his wife Dorothy graduated in marine biology from the University of Rhode Island, they conceived the idea of an oyster farm. West End Pond seemed ideal. It is well protected, yet has an outlet to the sea through which the tide runs vigorously. The water is unpolluted and predators are few. In the event of an oil spill outside, the Coast Guard booms off the inlet.

In 1980 they experimented with different species and in 1981 planted 100,000 European Belon oysters. These flourished, so they increased their planting to 600,000 in 1985. The Garfields buy the seed oysters from Maine—West Southport, Damariscotta, and Blue Hill. After two or three months in floating boxes, they are transferred to "Japanese lanterns," perforated cylinders with shelves inside. After fifteen to thirty months they are harvested. In the summer, they are sold locally. In the winter they are harvested four days per week and packed in seaweed, which is wet enough and cold enough to keep them alive. Mr. Garfield takes them to New Bedford whence they are shipped all over the country. The oyster bar in Grand Central Station, New York, is one of his principal customers.

There is a water hose on the fish dock, but as this wharf is much used, do not plan to lie alongside more than a few minutes. Here also is the office of the wharfinger, an officer of the town of Gosnold and a most authoritative and helpful gentleman.

Near the wharf are several public telephones. About 100 yards up the hill to the right is a general store carrying basic groceries and a surprisingly varied assortment of other merchandise. The store closes at 6 P.M. Nearby is The Bakery supplying freshly baked goods and delicatessen. The Bakery is open 7 A.M. to 2 P.M. for breakfast and lunch. Unfortunately, the Allen House has closed down. Note that Gosnold is a dry town.

If you must return to the States, you can take the mail boat *Alert* from the ferry wharf at 3 P.M. or call Gid Fisher who operates the Island Shuttle. He can land you in New Bedford in ten minutes or in Boston in half an hour.

Continue up the hill for a magnificent view of the island, Gay Head, Vineyard Sound, and Buzzards Bay. On a clear day you can see from the bridges at the canal to the beaches below Westport and from Noman's Land north to the south shore of the Cape. Looking down on the peaceful anchorage, it is hard to believe that winter gales sometimes drive seas right over the narrow beach protecting its western side. The road to the summit, lined with well-constructed stone walls, appears rather surprising on a bleak hill. It was built by the late William M. Wood of the American Woolen Company as the approach to a projected mansion on top of the island. The mansion never materialized.

Bushwhacking across lots on Cuttyhunk is out. The land is all privately owned, and the owners look on trespassers without enthusiasm. There is a path around the southern shore, to which anyone will direct you, and a road out the spit toward Canapitsit Channel. Otherwise, visitors should keep to paved roads and the beaches.

Weather permitting, Roman Catholic services are held in the Cuttyhunk church on Sunday mornings, and Protestant services on Sunday evenings. Aside from informal socializing around the telephone booths, the fish dock, and the marina and aboard yachts, there is no nightlife on Cuttyhunk, and early in the evening the anchorage usually quiets down.

An interesting reminder of old times is the remains of a railway across the sand spit on the starboard hand as you enter the anchorage. Before the pond was dredged and the channel cut, there was enough water in the pond for the big catboats used by Cuttyhunk fishermen, but not enough water in the channel. Ordinarily the boats lay outside, but in threatening weather they were floated onto a cradle mounted on a car, and hauled over the spit to a safe berth in the pond.

It is a pleasant 45-minute walk to the west end of the island, where one is likely to see deer grazing at morning and evening.

On the island in West End Pond rises a tower in memory of Bartholomew Gosnold, who tried to establish a trading colony on Cuttyhunk in 1602. His biography, entitled *Bartholomew Gosnold: Discoverer and Planter,* was written by Warner F. Gookin, completed after Gookin's death by Philip L. Barbour, and published in 1963 by Archon Books, Hamden, Connecticut. It traces, in detail fascinating to the modern navigator, Gosnold's exploration from his landfall near Cape Neddick to Cape Cod Bay and at last to Cuttyhunk. Gosnold, embayed by Cape Cod, climbed a hill near Barnstable, saw Nantucket Sound, and got the lay of the land. Then he rounded the Cape, entered Nantucket Sound through Muskeget Channel, and explored Martha's Vineyard, the Elizabeth Islands, and Buzzards Bay. The first he named after his daughter, and the second name he applied to Cuttyhunk and Nashawena, then one island, in honor of his sister. Gosnold built a house on an island in the pond on Cuttyhunk, established contact with local Indians, and made a good beginning at a trade in fur and "copper," a name given loosely to metal in general. However, the half of his crew who had agreed to stay in America with him changed their minds. Disappointed, he loaded his ship principally with sassafras and cedar, realizing enough for a break-even voyage, and returned to England. He never returned to Cuttyhunk, but was a leader in the Jamestown colony in 1607, and died in Virginia on August 22, 1607, a serious loss to that colony.

Mr. Gookin's enthusiasm for Gosnold is unmeasured and he romanticizes both Gosnold and the Indians. The claim that Gosnold was the first Englishman to see Cape Cod and the waters of Nantucket Sound and Buzzards Bay is debatable. The first Indians whom he met after his landfall in Maine came out to his ship in a boat, not a canoe, and were wearing European clothes. However, Gosnold well deserves his monument.

Chapter VIII

Vineyard and Nantucket Sounds and the Voyage around Cape Cod

General Conditions. Vineyard Sound presents few difficulties. Its entrance from the west is clearly marked by the Buzzards Bay tower (see page 302), a lighted whistle off Sow and Pigs, a lighted gong on Devils Bridge, and Gay Head light. The only obstruction to a yacht is Middle Ground Shoal, clearly marked on its western end by a flashing bell. There are excellent harbors at Menemsha Pond, Quicks Hole, Woods Hole, and Vineyard Haven. Overnight anchorage in quiet weather can be found in Menemsha Bight and Tarpaulin Cove, shelters once frequented by coasting schooners waiting out a foul tide.

Pay particular attention to George W. Eldridge's letter to skippers and mates in the *Eldridge Tide and Pilot Book*. The gist of it is that the first of the flood tide, instead of setting northeast up the Sound, sets north toward the shores of Nashawena and Pasque. A vessel bucking an ebb tide running southwest out of the Sound is set heavily to the north, especially on the starboard tack. Consequently in thick weather keep a sharp eye on the fathometer and tack to the south in a depth of less than 10 fathoms. In the event of a head tide, it might be better to lie over in Menemsha, Quicks Hole, or Tarpaulin Cove and enjoy those picturesque anchorages than to buck the tide up the Sound.

With an ebb tide running against a hard southwest wind, Vineyard Sound can be a lumpy spot, particularly off West Chop, where the current often reaches 3 or 4 knots.

The voyage through Nantucket Sound presents no serious problems by day or night in clear weather with good visibility. It is only about 30 miles from West Chop to Monomoy, and with a 1- or 2-knot tide running under you, it should be no more than a half-day's sail. The land on both sides is so low that it soon drops out of sight from the deck of a small yacht, leaving watertowers peering over the horizon at odd intervals. One runs compass courses from bell to whistle to gong, surrounded by unseen shoals and moved by unpredictable currents. It is a weird sensation for the navigator unaccustomed to it. In the event of a head tide, light airs, or poor visibility, there are a number of picturesque little harbors on the south side of the Cape for shoal-draft yachts. Woods Hole, Falmouth, Hyannis, and Stage Harbor are deep-water harbors, as the term is understood on the Cape. The harbors on Martha's Vineyard and Nantucket are good stopping places as well as worthwhile objectives in themselves.

The wise skipper will be alert for the many other yachts and for the larger commercial vessels which traverse these waters. While many steamers now use the Cape Cod Canal, big fishermen, excursion boats, ferries to Martha's Vineyard and Nantucket, and occasional tugs will be found following the well-buoyed channels. A large radar reflector and a sharp lookout are sensible precautions at all times. The small yacht will always avoid even the appearance of confrontation with a much bigger vessel, regardless of the Rules of the Road.

If you must navigate this channel in thick weather, do so with extreme caution. The following account of the loss of a well-found yawl under the command of an experienced skipper should emphasize the possible dangers. Read it with Chart 13244 before you, and bear in mind that it was written in the thirties, when Handkerchief Shoal and Stone Horse Shoal were marked by lightships with powerful horns. Recently the buoyage has been changed, but the shoals are still there.

The yawl left Nantucket on a clear day with clear weather reported ahead. The Handkerchief Lightship south of Handkerchief Shoal to the southwest of Monomoy was picked up without difficulty in clear weather. From there the course is NE by E $1/2$ E to the Stone Horse Lightship with its diaphone, 5 miles away and about $5/8$ mile off the Monomoy beach. The wind was light southwest, almost dead astern.

According to the current tables there would be slack water on that day (August 5, 1938) at the time when the yawl might expect to arrive at

Stone Horse. Then a flood tide would have carried her on her way. To allow for a possible set toward the shore during the last of the ebb, the skipper headed half a point to the eastward of the course to Stone Horse, toward the flashing white bell 9. This buoy is nearly 1 mile off Monomoy and more than 1/2 mile outside nun 12, which marks the edge of the shoal southeast of Monomoy. So it seemed as if the margin of safety were sufficient, especially with slack water supposed to be due.

After a mile or two of the 5-mile course had been completed, the fog came in thick, and from then on the lead was in constant use. The sound of the horn on Handkerchief continued to come down clearly on the following wind. But still no sound was heard either of the diaphone on Stone Horse to leeward or of the bell. In fact, neither the diaphone nor the bell ever was heard, even from less than a mile away.

When the log indicated that the bell should have been picked up or Stone Horse heard, the skipper decided to anchor until he could determine his position.

As the vessel swung toward the shore for heading into the wind, she struck. All efforts to get her off failed, for, despite the prediction of the current table, a strong northwesterly ebb continued for two hours to drive the yawl more firmly into the sand. Being a keel boat, she heeled far over on her side. Waves and current combined to fill her gradually with sand and water.

A rift in the fog soon disclosed the fact that the boat had struck on the shoal off Monomoy Point near nun 12. Despite the efforts of the nearby Coast Guard, the yawl, embedded in the sand, could not be hauled off and was a total loss.

The Coast Guard reported that fishing craft had gone ashore almost every day for a week at the same place and for the same reasons.

What are the lessons to be drawn for cruising men from this experience? The opinions expressed by the skipper of the lost yawl can be summed up as follows:

1. Off Monomoy, the direction, velocity, and time of change of the current are unpredictable. This is confirmed by the experience of the Coast Guard. In this case, the tide continued to ebb two hours after predicted slack water. Instead of ebbing in a westerly direction as expected, the current had a rotary motion, swinging

around Monomoy in a clockwise direction, being northwesterly off the point.

(*Note:* The *Coast Pilot* reports that the average velocity of the current at Stone Horse Shoal Lightship at strength of flood is about 2 knots, and at strength of ebb $1^3/_4$ knots. The greatest observed velocity was 3.6 knots. Flood current there sets about NE $^1/_2$ E and ebb about SW by W $^1/_2$ W. Such a direction would not have set the yawl on Monomoy Point, but a northwesterly current with the strength indicated above might and evidently did.)

2. Don't rely on hearing fog signals against the wind.

3. Don't sail through this area in thick weather on a dead-reckoning basis, though you may have no trouble even in a fog with an accurate radio direction finder, fathometer, and other modern improvements (such as loran, radar, or GPS).

To the above, the authors would like to add this warning: If you want to go through what are considered by many the most dangerous waters on the New England coast, pick your weather. If caught off Monomoy in fog, anchor and await favorable conditions.

Cruising men have contributed several other suggestions about the navigation of Nantucket Sound.

Fog is much more frequent in Nantucket Sound than it is at Race Point or even outside Pollock Rip. Southerly breezes are likely to bring it in, and although it may burn off in the middle of a hot day, only a change of wind to a northerly quadrant will dry it up.

Winds are subject to sudden changes in direction and velocity. A strong breeze kicks up a short, sharp chop, not very high, but enough to swamp a tender or soak down the sunbathers in short order. When the breeze drops, however, the sea subsides quickly.

In warm summer weather the southwest breeze may continue day and night, but outside Pollock Rip it usually dies away in the late afternoon. Yachts often sail right out of the wind in coming out of Pollock Rip.

There is an intricate shortcut between Handkerchief Shoal and Monomoy that may save a small boat many miles in a passage from one of the south shore harbors. It is to be attempted only on a clear day with a moderate breeze or with local knowledge, as it is not well marked.

The water in Nantucket Sound is warm enough for pleasant swimming. The fishing is usually good. There are many yachts traversing

342 The Cruising Guide to the New England Coast

these waters, from the humblest of backyard boats to the most elegant schooners, ocean-racing yawls, and motor yachts.

The smaller ports are often picturesque—sometimes pointedly so—and in spite of the crowds of people that press in upon places like Hyannis, there are secluded backwaters, coves, and tidal rivers inhabited by birds, fish, and muskrats.

Occasionally, however, Nantucket Sound gets a bit gritty. A hard easterly with a flood tide, for example, can raise a short, violent sea against which few auxiliaries can make progress. If one is set onto a shoal under these conditions, he is in serious trouble.

Although traveling the main ship channel bound either east or west is easy, use extreme caution in crossing the shoals from north to south. The buoyage is not calculated to make navigation easy. Cans and nuns become of the greatest significance, so clear weather is a necessity. The tide will be running across your course rather than with you or against you. Landmarks are of very little help for, in the hardest part of the trip, low-lying land is below the horizon, and one water tank looks much like another to the stranger.

Menemsha, Massachusetts (13233). This is the first shelter one comes to on entering Vineyard Sound from the south and west. Although coasting schooners used to anchor in Menemsha Bight awaiting a fair tide, it is really too rolly to be considered a comfortable anchorage. There are, however, five moorings available in the bight for $15 per night.

Menemsha Basin to port as you enter between the jetties is usually crowded with sportfisherman and party boats in the finger piers and stacked three deep along the wharf. There is no room to anchor, but there are two moorings where you will be rafted with two, three, or even possibly four other boats. The charge per boat is $15 per night. For information about the moorings, contact the harbormaster on VHF-9 or by telephone at (508) 645-2846.

Gasoline, diesel fuel, water, ice, marine supplies, and fishing gear are available on the wharf at Dutcher Dock. There is a grocery store a short walk up the road, and buses run in the summer to Vineyard Haven.

Menemsha Basin awakes early as fishermen "rev up" for the grounds to the south and east.

The channel to Menemsha Pond is frequently dredged but quickly shoals up. The worst place is on the east side near can 5. One should be

Menemsha Basin, Martha's Vineyard, Mass. Menemsha Basin and the entrance to the constantly shoaling Menemsha Pond. *Martha's Vineyard Commission, James W. Sewall Co.*

able to carry 4 feet up the channel, cautiously, at half-tide, and vessels drawing 6 feet have made it. The pond is much more peaceful and attractive than the busy basin. The best anchorage is in the eastern part. Use of a head with overboard discharge is forbidden as the pond is a shellfish farming area.

A visit to the cliffs at Gay Head light will provide you with a fantastic view of the surrounding area.

Tarpaulin Cove, Massachusetts (13230). This delightful anchorage on the eastern side of Naushon Island is much frequented by picnic parties on weekends, but during the week there seems to be plenty of room. The best place to anchor is off the southwest end of the beach under the light. Chart and lead are safe guides, as the water shoals gradually.

The beach is of fine, soft sand, delightful for swimming, although there is little shelter from the sun on a hot day. Late in the afternoon, however, many of the visitors depart, and on a quiet evening the beach and anchorage are peaceful and sometimes almost deserted. A correspondent suggests: "Repeated nights spent at Tarpaulin Cove have taught me that the stern anchor, enabling one to lie with the swell regardless of the wind, makes life much more pleasant when the steamer wash swells come in, as they always do during the night."

Fires and camping ashore are forbidden.

Naushon abounds in sheep, deer, and ducks, which the owners are trying to preserve. Therefore, no dogs or guns should be brought ashore, and visitors are asked not to venture inland from the beach. The island is infested with ticks which carry Lyme disease. The trustees maintain a mounted patrol.

A correspondent adds:

> I adventured along the entire rim of the cove to enjoy one of the most pleasant moments of our cruise—outstaring a beautiful fawn nestled in a grove of beech trees and at only a 30-foot distance.

Lake Tashmoo, Martha's Vineyard, Massachusetts (13233). This is a landlocked and attractive anchorage. According to the Tashmoo Boatyard, the entrance channel has just recently been dredged to a depth of 7 feet at low water. However, the bottom is prone to shifting and silting, so it is wise to enter the harbor on a rising tide. Inside there is a depth of 10 feet in the anchorage.

Upon entering the channel, favor the east jetty sharply. The shoalest place is between the can and nun inside the entrance; make it by here and you're home free.

For updated information or local knowledge, contact the Tashmoo Boatyard on VHF-9 or call them at (508) 693-9311. They are located on the east side of the pond and provide moorings to visiting yachtsmen.

Vineyard Haven, Massachusetts (13233). Formerly known as Holmes' Hole and a popular place for coasters waiting for a "chance along" through Nantucket Sound or Vineyard Sound, this is a well-sheltered and convenient harbor for the modern cruising yacht.

Enter between East Chop and West Chop. The name "chop" refers neither to the state of the sea nor to a cut of meat but is an eighteenth-century English word meaning jaw or cheek.

The tide runs very hard around this corner of the island, harder than anywhere else in Nantucket Sound, reaching $4^1/2$ knots at times. This is comparable to a Bay of Fundy tide and is not worth bucking, even under power. Better to lie over a few hours and enjoy attractions ashore.

Entrance is easy with the few dangers clearly marked. As you enter, call the harbormaster on VHF-9 for a mooring behind the breakwater. The

Lake Tashmoo, Martha's Vineyard, Mass. Make it through the shoaling sands at the entrance to Lake Tashmoo and you're home free. *Martha's Vineyard Commission, James W. Sewall Co.*

basin is crowded with local boats and moorings, leaving no room to anchor. If no mooring is available, try for a slip at the marina to the left of the steamer wharf on your port bow as you enter. Gasoline, diesel fuel, water, and ice are available here, and electric current is provided in the slips.

If neither mooring nor slip is available, anchor outside the breakwater. A berth here is cleaner and cooler than one inside and except in heavy northerly weather is well protected. Frequent steamer wakes may be a little disturbing.

In a dinghy, land at the town wharf north of the steamer wharf or on the beach near it. Turn left on Water Street for an A&P supermarket, a Cumberland Farms store open in the evening, an outdoor telephone, the post office, and the marina. On the wharf here is the justly famous Black Dog Tavern. It does not take reservations, so come early for dinner. The tavern is open for breakfast at 6:30 and also runs a bakery behind it. The Black Dog now sells lots of nonfood items and has a mail order catalog. A correspondent notes: "A certain amount of cachet attaches to each year's Black Dog T-shirt."

Nearby is the Chamber of Commerce information booth and the bus station from which buses run frequently to other parts of Martha's Vineyard in season.

Repairs to engines can be arranged through the marina.

The Martha's Vineyard Shipyard—(508) 693-0400—on the southeast shore of the inner harbor has several marine railways and docks and is well equipped to make repairs. They also have a first-class store for marine supplies and gadgets. This yard has a fine reputation. Nearby is the Vinyard Haven Marina—(508) 693-0720—which specializes in "concierge service" and provides transients with about all the personal services you can think of. Another boatyard, which is much smaller but also does first-class work, is located at the end of the short westerly arm of Lagoon Pond. It is known as Maciel Marine, Ltd.—(508) 693-4174, VHF-9—and is run by Robert E. Maciel. The yard repairs outboards, inboards, and diesel engines, has a towboat, and does salvage work anywhere on Martha's Vineyard. The yard also mans the bridge into the lagoon. Hours are 8:15–8:45, 10:15–11:00, 3:15–4:00, 5:00–5:45, and 7:30–8:00. To have the bridge opened, call on channel 9, "Vineyard Haven Bridge Tender." Maciel Marine can supply gasoline and has 42 slips for boats under 25 feet.

Also in Vineyard Haven is the well-known Gannon and Benjamin Marine Railway yard (693-4658) which designs, builds, and repairs wooden boats. It offers moorings to transients, though only in the outer harbor.

Vineyard Haven is a good spot from which to visit the northwestern part of the island. Automobiles and bicycles can be rented in the village. The Vineyard Haven Yacht Club well north (outside) of the breakwater is an active racing organization and has a small pier and station but no regular launch service.

Vineyard Haven was famous for a long time as the home of Captain George W. ("Yours for a Fair Tide") Eldridge, son of the Captain George Eldridge of Chatham, who made the first accurate large-scale charts of important fishing grounds.

The story goes that in the early seventies the elder George was publishing a book well known to mariners of that time, the *Compass Test.* *Eldridge Tide and Pilot Book* continues the story:

> He told his son, George W., who was at the time in poor health, that if he would go to Vineyard Haven and take charge of selling the

book there he might have the gross receipts. This offer was accepted and George began his work. As the ships came into the harbor he would go out to them in his sailboat and offer his book for sale. While engaged in this work he was constantly being asked by mariners as to what time the tide TURNED to run east or west in the Sound. This set him to thinking whether or not some sort of a table might be prepared which would give mariners this important information. So with this in mind he began making observations, and one day, while in the famous ship chandlery store of Charles Holmes, he picked up one of the Holmes business cards and on the back of it made the first rough draft of a current table. This was in August of 1874. Shortly after, with the help of his father, he worked out the tables for the places, other than Vineyard Sound, which were of the most importance, and in 1875 the first Tide Book was published. It did not take long for mariners to realize the help that this sort of work could be to them, and it soon became an almost indispensable book to all who sailed the Atlantic Coast from New York East. From time to time the captain added important infor-mation for seamen, one of the most important things being the explanation of the action of the currents, which caused so many vessels to founder in the "Graveyard." The book has even been referred to as the Mariner's Bible, so constantly is it used and so helpful has it been in making navigation safer.

One Saturday night in July one of the writers beat up Vineyard Haven Harbor and anchored in the southerly part of the harbor long after dark. Sunday morning he was startled to find himself lying close under the quarter of a nineteenth-century topsail schooner, Captain Robert S. Douglas' *Shenandoah*. Built by Harvey Gamage in 1964 in South Bristol, Maine, for the passenger trade, she had some difficulty weathering the Coast Guard regulations. Since then she has been a great addition to waters formerly crowded with coasting schooners, fishermen, whalers, and naval vessels, all under sail.

Oak Bluffs, Martha's Vineyard, Massachusetts (13238). The well-protected harbor at Oak Bluffs, 4 miles eastward of Vineyard Haven, is formed by Lake Anthony, entered by a cut in the beach. Two jetties, with a light on the northerly one, protect the entrance. The entrance is somewhat narrow for craft without a motor, but it is possible to approach

Edgartown, Martha's Vineyard, Mass. Note Middle Flats to starboard of Edgartown's entrance, and Chappaquiddick to port. *Martha's Vineyard Commission, James W. Sewall Co.*

the jetties closely on either side. There is a depth of 7 or 8 feet in the pond, which is usually crowded in July and August.

The small "made" harbor is so crowded that anchoring is forbidden. Ask for a mooring at the harbormaster's office at the steamer wharf slip. If none is available, local rule and custom sanction tying alongside another moored boat with as many as three boats permitted on one mooring. Three hundred boats can be accommodated.

The usual supplies of gasoline, diesel oil, water, and ice are available at the wharves. The main street borders the anchorage, whence groceries are easily obtained. There are no repair facilities.

Oak Bluffs in the nineteenth century was famous as a camp-meeting center for religious groups. The old Methodist campground with its gingerbread cottages and main building with a prominent cupola is but a short distance from the harbor. The town is now heavily crowded with campers, craftsmen, artists, and musicians. Supplemented by literally hundreds of day visitors disgorged by the frequent steamers, these people provide a lively and noisy atmosphere. Weekends are said to be "something else again!"

In 1984 a correspondent wrote: "You might mention the carousel—one of the oldest in the country—and the fine self-guided walking tour of the Methodist Camp, a *must* for lovers of Victoriana."

Edgartown, Massachusetts (13238). This is a lively and picturesque town in which all kinds of supplies and repairs are available. In the busy anchorage you will be surrounded by some of the most elegant yachts of the Atlantic Coast.

Entrance is easy in clear weather. The Squash Meadow and Middle Flats are clearly marked, although the can at the west end of the Squash Meadow is too small to look as menacing as it should. If you can make bell 2 on Middle Flats, even in thick weather, you can make your way into the harbor by following the line of the bell, the nun, and the flasher on the east edge of the shoal.

Many yachts enter Edgartown under sail. The shores are quite steep, and the wind is usually brisk as it comes off the warm land in summer. However, make due allowance for a strong run of tide and watch for the ferry carrying cars from Edgartown to Chappaquiddick. It crosses at the sharp bend inside the lighthouse.

Anchoring in Edgartown is chancy. The harbor is crowded with moorings, the bottom is gravel, and the tide runs hard.

Moorings are now being operated by the town. Edgartown Marine, which used to operate moorings, launches, fuel, and shore facilities has closed down in a dispute with the town, and the whole situation is in a state of flux. Edgartown Marine was the only marina in the harbor, so facilities are greatly reduced.

Our understanding in October 1994 is that moorings with yellow balls can be reserved by calling the harbormaster's office at (508) 627-4746; moorings with light blue balls are available on a first-come, first-served basis; gasoline is available from an onshore tank, and diesel fuel from a tank truck; launch service is available from Old Port Marine, a Newport-based company under contract to the town, probably by calling on channel 68; a mechanic is available 5 days a week; showers are available at the Edgartown Community Center; there is a free pumpout station on Memorial Wharf; and Edgartown Marine is probably for sale. This is obviously a temporary, jury-rigged arrangement, which will probably be changed soon. If you are planning a visit, we suggest a call to the harbormaster's office to get the latest information.

The Edgartown Yacht Club, whose dignified nineteenth-century clubhouse stands on the starboard hand as you come up the channel, finds itself not quite up to coping with the twentieth-century yachting scene. The club is hospitable by inclination and would like to welcome cruising people, but there are just too many of them. Club facilities are open on a cash- and space-available basis to members of yacht clubs belonging to the United States Sailing Association and to those cruising people introduced by a member of the Edgartown Yacht Club. The club maintains a bar and serves lunch and dinner by reservation every day from late June until the weekend after Labor Day. The snack bar is open daily from early June through Columbus Day weekend.

The club does not provide guest moorings, dockage, or a launch service. Registered visitors may use the dinghy float on the southeast face of the club wharf, but space here is limited. In season, the club monitors channel 9.

An A&P and an excellent fish market, Edgartown Seafood, are a long twenty-minute walk to the west on the tar road. The walk alone is worth the trip, for the first part is through shady streets lined with the eighteenth- and nineteenth-century mansions of Edgartown whalers, traders, privateers, and shipbuilders. The second half of the trip reflects the income tax, the automobile civilization, and the twentieth-century influence of suburbia.

Old buildings and narrow streets give Edgartown an antique flavor somewhat modified by boutiques, gift shops, and modern restaurants. The summer population has a heavy accent on youth, some quite picturesquely dressed and adorned, but, to the casual visitor at least, very pleasantly disposed. Their grandparents, living in the antebellum yachting tradition, are almost equally evident.

Cape Poge Bay has nice swimming but is shallow and difficult to get into.

First settled in 1642, the town, when incorporated in 1671, was named for Edgar, the son of James II. In the eighteenth and nineteenth centuries, Edgartown was a successful whaling port. Men ashore were active in refining whale oil and making candles, while the women turned out socks, mittens, and wigs. In the Edgartown Cemetery there are headstones dating as far back as 1670, many with curious epitaphs.

Cruising people not in need of supplies or the services of a boatyard sometimes prefer to go through Edgartown Harbor and anchor in Katama Bay. Under ordinary circumstances this is a quiet, clean, and protected anchorage with less scour of tide than Edgartown Harbor.

Nantucket, Massachusetts (13242), (13241). Nantucket Island, objective of many a Cape Cod cruise, is well worth a visit of several days. The island is far enough offshore to have an atmosphere of its own despite frequent visits of large steamers bearing heavy cargoes of tourists. Its history, dating from the Vikings' visit about A.D. 1000 (if we accept Pohl's deduction) to the decline of its whaling industry at the time of the Civil War, is a romantic and exciting one. Populated by what Herman Melville calls "fighting Quakers," it was the home port of a hardy, enterprising, audacious people who sailed wherever there was water to float their square-ended vessels. Many a South Sea Island native knew of Nantucket before he ever heard of Boston, New York, or London. Names of Nantucket skippers and vessels still cling to Pacific islands.

The approach to Nantucket from the west is clearly marked by a row of lighted buoys ending with the horn buoy on Cross Rip. Note that the buoy does not groan like a whistle buoy but bleats like a sheep. That is, the pitch is constant and does not go from low to high as does a whistle.

On the run from East Chop with a flood tide, one seems to be set to the south of the course, especially in the last two hours of the flood.

In clear weather, one can cut Cross Rip, pass between can 5 and nun 4, leave can 3 to port, and turn around the end of Tuckernuck Shoal. The flood tide sets to the south on this course. Keep the bell bearing about southeast as you approach it. Local yachts treat Tuckernuck Shoal rather lightly and are seen sailing about in what the writer considered rather perilous circumstances. The answer to his query on the matter was, "There is plenty of water there. Quite big boats go right across it." Still, soundings in single-digit numbers 4 miles offshore are worthy of some attention.

Your first sign of land on a clear day will be a tower well to the west of the town. Then the gilded dome of a church and the tops of other buildings in the town will appear. You will not see land from the deck of a yacht until well inside bell 1.

In approaching Nantucket, be prepared for a change in the weather. In 1971 the writer passed can 5 with a pleasant, gentle northwest breeze and charged past Brant Point shortly afterward single-reefed, soaking wet, with the peapod half full of water. In 1977 a pleasant southwest breeze off can 5 expired completely and only the tide, errant zephyrs, and constitutional indolence saved him from use of the iron topsail. In 1985 a northerly breeze died without leaving even an errant zephyr, and we motored in ignominiously.

Once by Tuckernuck, run down to the red-and-white bell off the entrance and follow the buoys in. The tide follows the channel generally and runs with considerable velocity. If you are bucking it, you can easily be set to one side. The writer saw a large ketch on the flats to the east of the channel, all sail set, well heeled over, and motionless. Note too that steamers from Woods Hole and Hyannis use this channel as if it were their own. They do keep a good lookout and are as careful about yachts as they can be. However, not long ago a schooner, presuming on her privilege as a sailing vessel, was run down and sunk by a steamer. Fortunately, an amateur photographer caught the whole incident on film. The skipper of the steamer was exonerated, as he should have been. The Rules of the Road, both Inland and International, state, "A vessel of less than 20 meters or a sailing vessel shall not impede the passage of a vessel which can navigate safely only within a narrow channel or fairway."

There is a light on the end of the east jetty, and this jetty shows above high water for most of its length. The end of the west jetty is marked only by a nun and is often submerged at high water. Farther in, closer to the end of the jetty, is a white can with an orange diamond and the legend "DANGER SUBMERGED JETTY."

Brant Point Light and the range lights can be of help at night. A low-powered radio-direction-finder station is situated at the head of the channel. Its characteristic is BP (– · · ·   · – – ·).

Nantucket is one of the few harbors west of Portland, Maine, where there is sometimes room to anchor. The anchorage area is delineated by white buoys which carefully exclude the steamer channel and turning area. The area shoreward of a line between Great Point and Esther's Island is now a no-discharge zone. There are six pumpout stations on the island to relieve the situation. Dennis Metcalf rents moorings and monitors channel 68. To get ashore, you can call Nantucket Launch on channel 68 or use your own dinghy. Land at the float on the south side of the town wharf, the next one south of the Boat Basin.

If you wish to lie in the Boat Basin, it is well to make a reservation several days in advance by calling (508) 228-1333 or VHF-9. As you enter the harbor, call on channel 16 for a slip assignment and approach the south side of the stockade. Your slip assignment with a plan of the marina will be passed to you clipped to the end of a pole.

Inside, you will find 208 slips, each with connections for electricity, telephone, and television, including cable TV. On the wharf you will find a number of laundry machines, showers, and toilets. Crews are required to use the toilets on the wharf, and the management reserves the right to seal heads as a health measure, although such drastic action is seldom necessary. The basin maintains an efficient fire-extinguishing system and adequate security.

Gasoline, diesel fuel, ice, water, and some marine supplies are available on the south side of the basin wharf. Here also is the dockmaster's office.

If you need the assistance of a mechanic, electronic technician, or sailmaker, consult the dockmaster at (508) 228-7260. He is a reliable source of information on Nantucket and can arrange for almost any kind of help.

At the southern end of the harbor is the Nantucket Shipyard—(508) 228-0263. The yard is approached by a channel dredged to 9 feet at *high water.* In 1985 the best water favored the port side of the channel. There is a small turning basin off the yard. The channel and turning basin will be dredged again, we were told, when the main channel shoals up enough so the steamers bump. This happens every few years. The yard has a 20-ton lift which can accommodate vessels up to 9 feet in beam. Arrangements can be made for repairs to hull, engines, rigging, sails, and electronics, and yachts may be left in the yard's care. There is a marine supply store at the yard.

The Nantucket Yacht Club is located in the northwesterly corner of the harbor. Tremendous pressure from its own increased membership has forced it to suspend use of its facilities and services to cruising people. It maintains a limited launch service for its members only; and the club, while not inhospitable, is so busy with its own programs and so crowded with its own members that visitors cannot be encouraged.

An experienced explorer of the shoal and sandy channels south of Cape Cod contributes the following directions for getting to Head of the Harbor and Wauwinet:

I have taken the liberty of including a transparency of the Nantucket buoyage system I wrote you of. This is a delightful sail. I think that I've got all of the buoys straight, but continued refinement over a few years may still leave a few degrees in error in my locations. (You know small boats!) Here is a set of directions to the "Head of the Harbor," Nantucket—a good number of boats of decent size (up to 5-foot draft) do this trip and it is delightful and the mark of an adventuresome spirit. If you make it to Wauwinet (and you've a sailboat!), everyone in that small resort community will know that you have arrived and will happily greet you.

As you leave the general anchorage, look for the black-and-white cylinder just off First Point. Observe it well, as you'll be hunting for the next half-dozen. They are unnumbered—the numbers are only for my chart reference. Typically you skirt the shore finding the deepest water. The points are confusing and similar, so here are a few uncharted landmarks: There's a broken-down wooden pier off Second Point. The "Sherbourne Yacht Club," a grounded large red barge (belonging to some friends), is located at X next to Third Point. Buoy 5 has been difficult to locate recently and is perhaps intended only as a guide to the entrance of Polpis Harbor (which has its own red-and-black crosstick floats). So I have given course directions from 4 directly to 6—aiming directly for the middle of the very tall Pocono bluff. The hairiest negotiation comes at 7

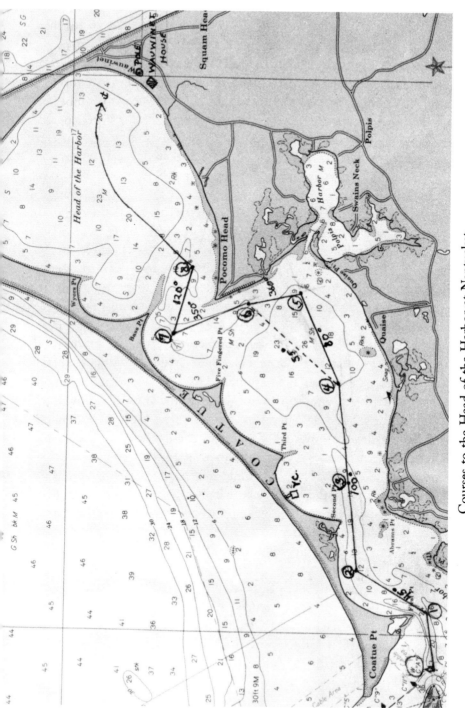

Courses to the Head of the Harbor at Nantucket

where one turns some 130 degrees to get around the shoal off Pocono sharply enough not to hit Bass Point. (Prepare to touch bottom!) Finally, after coming to buoy 8 (and these are all vertical-striped center-of-the-channel), head for the middle of the Head. A number of boats stop at many places along the way. The current can run up to 1 knot near buoys 1 through 3, but is less nearer the Head, I believe.

If you get this far and feel like a land-based meal, Wauwinet House can include you for dinner. The atmosphere is one of relaxed gentility.

In the 1890s, there used to be a sailing ferry that made the run from Wauwinet to Nantucket for the hotel guests.

Nantucket offers something for almost every taste. There are, of course, the usual food, clothing, and hardware stores. Then there are a great many little shops purveying all manner of craftwork and souvenirs. There are many excellent restaurants, among the best being The Chanticleer and Jared's.

Steamers run regularly in the summer to Vineyard Haven and throughout the year to Hyannis. There are frequent flights from the nearby airport to Boston and Hyannis.

The waterfront from the steamer wharf to the Boat Basin has been "restored." Low buildings, all finished in weathered shingles with white trim, crowd the narrow, cobbled streets. Even the A&P follows the pattern with small panes in its show windows. Inside, however, it is like any supermarket. Gift shops abound. There is a marine supply store close to the head of the Boat Basin wharf.

The Whaling Museum, to which anyone can direct you, is worth several hours for anyone interested in American maritime history. In the basement are excellent representations of the different trades involved in fitting out for a whaling voyage. Tools actually used by riggers, coopers, shipwrights, and sailmakers and samples of their workmanship are displayed. Upstairs there is a whaleboat completely fitted out and ready to lower. Pictures, charts, and whaling gear are attractively displayed with excellent explanatory placards. The writer and his crew found this museum in itself worth the whole trip.

Parts of the town retain the variety and individuality of old Nantucket. The mansions built by Coffins, Macys, and Starbucks still stand among shingled cottages and brick houses.

Nantucket beyond the town bears its own characteristic atmosphere. Rent a bicycle at one of the many waterfront shops and ride over to Surf Side. Outside the town, on the moors, you feel the bleak offshore quality of the place, despite the cars whizzing by your left ear. Scrubby pines, waving grass, thickets of bayberry and beach plum remind you that this is no continent but an island, which, if not actually afloat, at least stands up to ocean winds and ocean seas. The great South Beach confirms this. A steep sandy beach faces you with savage shoals offshore and a blank horizon. There is a refreshment stand, a lifeguard's tower, and perhaps a throng of bathers, but walk a half mile east or west along the beach and you are at sea.

Continue eastward to Siasconset, an attractive town of gray cottages and roses, on to Sankaty Head, and return to town by the back road.

It is wise to avoid the bushwhacking on Nantucket as the island is infested with ticks which may carry Lyme disease afflicting humans. The deer carry the disease and pass it on from generation to generation of ticks.

Lengthy as this account is, the writer cannot forbear to include the following extract from the *Sailor's Magazine* of November 1848. The article is entitled "A Cruise Along Shore in the Seventeenth Century":

I shall never forget that homeward passage. It was late in November, and we judged ourselves seven leagues southeast of Nantucket. The old man was below, on his beam ends, with a cruel rheumatism, when the wind, which had been blowing hard from the north, hauled to the east. The mate, whose name was Salter, had no thought of running under circumstances so unfavorable, and went below.

"Captain Phillips," said he, "the wind has canted to the eastward, but it is awful foggy—so thick that you can't see across the deck."

"Sound!" said the old man, "and pass the lead below."

They did so, and after a glance at it, he turned to the mate, and said, "Shake out all the reefs, keep her northwest two hours, then sound again, and let me see the lead."

"Yes sir," said the mate, and he passed up the companion-way, not particularly pleased with the prospect.

In two hours, soundings were again had, and the lead passed to the skipper.

"Five fathoms, with sand, and a cracking breeze," said Salter.

"Don't you mean seven fathoms, Mr. Salter?" asked the old man scraping the sand with the nail of his right forefinger.

"There might have been *about* seven sir," said the mate, "I allowed pretty largely for the drift: but it is best to be on the safe side."

"Right, Mr. Salter, right. I am glad to find you so particular. We are close in with the land, and can't be too careful. You may keep her northwest, half west; I don't expect you can *see* much, but if you don't *hear* anything in the course of fifteen minutes, let me know it.—An open ear for breakers, Mr. Salter! We must be cautious— very cautious, sir."

The mate, although a fellow of considerable grit, was somewhat staggered at the last orders. He, however, nodded a respectful assent, and made his way to the forward part of the vessel. The wind had freshened, and the *Little Mary* (as the schooner was called) was doing her prettiest. Salter leaned over the larboard bow, and was pondering upon the folly of running before a gale of wind through a fog, to make the land, with no other guide than a few particles of gray sand, in which he had no more confidence than he would have had in a piece of drift seaweed.

Eight or nine minutes only had passed, when the roar of breakers struck the ear of the mate. "Luff, luff, and shake her!" cried he. The schooner was brought to the wind in an instant. The foam from the receding waves was visible under her lee; but in a moment the dark line of Seconset head, in the southwest, told the mate that everything was right.

"We are clear of the scrape, so far," growled Salter, "but I don't think a handful of sand is a thing to run by in a time like this. I'll *know* if there *is* any difference between the bottom here, and the last we had. Sam, heave the lead, while I keep her steady."

The lead came up, and the mate declared not only the bottom, but the depth of the water to be the same. "I think," continued he, "all the sand within forty miles of this spot is alike. Sam, pass me some of that which the cook brought on board to clean his things with, while we were lying in Seconset. There," said he, comparing the two, "there is no difference, even in this, except what the water makes"; and he proceeded to prove his position by putting fresh tallow on the lead, and covering it with the sand which had been brought from the uplands of Seconset.

"Sam," said Salter, "you may wet that lead. I'll try it on the old man."

The lead was washed in the sea for a moment, and the mate took it below chuckling at the thought of snaring the old veteran.

"Captain Phillips," said he, with counterfeit anxiety, "the fifteen minutes are gone—it blows spitefully in flaws, and spits thick."

"Mr. Salter," returned the old man, raising himself in his berth to take the lead, "north west, half west, should have brought you within ear-shot of the breakers some minutes ago. I am afraid you have not kept her straight."

He raised the lead, and the first glance at the soundings seemed to shake his very soul—but the flush on his high, pale forehead passed away in an instant. Ordering the skylight to be removed, he placed the lead in a better position, and riveted his clear blue eye upon it for a full minute, when he turned to the mate, with the utmost coolness, and said, "Mr. Salter, I am glad to say that there has been no fault in your steering; the schooner *has* run north west, half west, as straight as a gun-barrel; at the same time I am very sorry to tell you that Nantucket is sunk, and that we are just over Seconset ridge!"

The South Shore of Cape Cod—Falmouth to Chatham

A shoal-draft boat which can ground out more or less on her bottom can well spend a week cruising in this area where running ashore means simply pushing off with an oar, getting overboard in warm waist-deep water, or at worst, taking out an anchor and waiting for the tide.

The shores are low and often marshy. Although the beaches are in many places heavily built up, the inlets between Falmouth and Point Gammon extend far enough inland to keep the main highway back from the shore. Hence the shallow inlets, marshy around the edges, are often quite clean and wild. The entrances to some of these have been dredged enough to give access to small boats. These channels tend to silt up so they should be entered cautiously and avoided in rough weather. Falmouth, Osterville, and Hyannis are kept dredged to more than 6 feet.

Outside the beach in Nantucket Sound the shoals run, in general, east and west with buoys on their ends and navigable water between them. It is perfectly possible to sail north of L'Hommedieu Shoal and even inside Succonnesset Shoal in order to approach the inlets on the shore. While shoal-draft local boats appear to treat these shoals lightly and to sail cheerfully across places where the chart shows depths in single digits, the stranger will want to be more cautious, following the chart and paying careful attention to the current charts in the *Eldridge Tide and Pilot Book.*

Beyond Point Gammon the inlets are fewer, do not extend far inland, and offer little to explore. Harwichport, Wychmere, and Saquatucket are pleasant and secure harbors but little more, although Stage Harbor is a worthwhile end in itself.

The tidal current floods to the east and ebbs to the west along this shore. The flood at Pollock Rip starts about 4 hours after high water at Boston and begins to run east along the south shore of the Cape about 2 to 2½ hours after that. Thus anyone bound east should be able to go through Woods Hole with a fair tide, starting at the time of low water at Boston, and carry a fair tide for 5 or 6 hours along the shore. Conversely, anyone bound west should leave Chatham at about the time of high water at Boston. The tide goes slack and turns somewhat earlier in the eastern part of Nantucket Sound than it does off Woods Hole.

All this, of course, is based on general averages. The phase of the moon, the state of the wind, and doubtless other less obvious forces make the precise times, directions, and velocities of the current more or less unpredictable. Nevertheless, the tide runs hard enough, 1 to 3 knots at strength, to make it worth planning for a fair tide.

Although in the summer the sea inside the shoals is usually smooth, small-boat sailors will avoid a situation where the tide is running hard against a strong wind, for in these shoal waters a steep and even dangerous sea can build quickly.

Falmouth, Massachusetts (13230). Falmouth is the place to go for anyone in need of supplies or repairs but it is not to be sought out as a picturesque anchorage.

Enter between the jetties, the western one with a flashing green light and a high-intensity beam to the southward. The entrance and the harbor have a depth of 7 feet MLW, and although the edges may shoal up some, most yachts may count on what Cape Cod authorities call "plenty of water." Call the harbormaster on channel 9 for a mooring. He has an office at the town marina north of the Flying Bridge restaurant on the west side of the harbor. MacDougall's Cape Cod Marine Service—(508) 548-1106—maintains moorings and slips for transients. Some of the moorings are rigged with long floating polypropylene pennants which are easily wound up in the propellers of the unwary. There is no place to anchor in Falmouth. The Falmouth Harbor Marina—(508) 457-7000—operated by the town, has been improved recently with bulkhead, pier, and piling work and a new office which has heads and showers for visitors. There are 70 slips with electricity and water, and those for season renters also have telephone and cable-TV hookups.

MacDougall's, located halfway up the east side of the harbor, is one of the best-known and most efficient yards on the Cape. Not only does this yard have capable carpenters, riggers, mechanics, and electronic technicians, but it has a complete sail loft capable of building you a new sail if the old one is too far gone to repair. Although small and maybe crowded on weekends, it is quiet and attractive. There is a marine store at the yard carrying the usual assortment of hardware, both the necessities and the frills. Falmouth Marine provides many of the same facilities and has a sound reputation. Gasoline, diesel oil, ice, and water are available at the boatyards and marinas. At the head of the harbor is Pier 37—(508) 540-0123, VHF-9—where boats up to 30 feet long and up to 6,500 pounds are stored on racks or stands and launched on demand. Repair services for powerboats are available as well as a restaurant. There is an A&P supermarket a healthy walk from the shore near the head of the harbor. The Flying Bridge restaurant on the west side is well spoken of and commands an interesting view of harbor traffic.

With steamers coming and going to Martha's Vineyard and a number of yachts coming into the boatyards seeking remedies for their ills "right away yesterday," Falmouth is a busy harbor. Again, it is a good place to get into when you need help or want to change crews or to lie over during a gale of wind, but it is also a great place to get out of in quest of quieter and more picturesque anchorages to the eastward.

Green Pond, Massachusetts (13229). This small harbor located $1^{1}/_{2}$ miles east of Falmouth has a narrow jettied entrance with a controlling depth in 1990 of about 6 feet up to the town landing. The Green Pond Marina—(508) 548-2635—with water, electricity, and telephone hookups at its 60 slips is about $^{1}/_{4}$ mile from the entrance and has about 5 feet at the slips. It also has gas, diesel, heads and showers, some moorings, and repair facilities.

Waquoit Bay, Massachusetts (13229 114 SC). This large shallow bay is what a shoal-draft boat is built for. Its upper reaches are secluded and quiet. There are several channels leading into it and communicating with other backwaters. A correspondent notes that a good anchorage can be found about 600 feet inside the jetties to port, just before the first nun. If you get close to shore, you will be out of the current and protected from the seas, but not from the wind coming over the dunes.

Entrance from Nantucket Sound is marked by flashing red bell 2 and a light on the east jetty. A beacon marks the west jetty. The jetties are hard to find from offshore, so first find the flashing red bell buoy R"2" about 1 mile southwest.

The most recent local report on this channel is that a number of boats of 5^1/$_2$- to 6-foot draft are home-ported in the bay and the current is not extreme.

The beaches on both sides of the entrance are clean and pleasant places to swim. Inside, the channel is marked by a series of cans, each marking the end of a sand spit. Local reports in 1994 gave depths of 5 feet all the way to the head of the bay and the Waquoit Yacht Club. The eastern part of the lower bay is popular with water-skiers but there is quieter anchorage on the west side above the prominent spit south of the Seapit River. There are no landing facilities here. Above the mouth of the Seapit River is a town landing, and above this is the Waquoit Yacht Club, with a fleet of small boats and occasionally a mooring to be had. There is not water enough at the float for a cruising boat. About a mile to the west, on the main road, is a store, but there are better and more convenient sources of supplies than Waquoit.

It is possible to follow the local buoys through the Seapit River and up the Childs River to the Edwards Boat Yard—(508) 548-2216—operated by Charley Swain. For this trip count on no more than 4 feet at low water. With local knowledge it is also possible to enter from the Sound through Eel Pond. The yard has facilities for repair of any boat that can reach it, and can provide gasoline, diesel oil, ice, and water. There is also a well-stocked marine store. Yachts lie in slips here, as the river is narrow. Charley claims there are more vessels in the Childs River than in any other single place on the south shore. This is the head of navigation on the Childs River for masted vessels, as a highway crosses the river just above the yard. Canoes can be rented for further exploration.

Great River and Little River join and flow together into the east side of Waquoit Bay. Each of these flows out of a large pond with islands and coves worth exploring in a sailing dinghy or rowboat. There are local buoys to guide you, and there is said to be a small boatyard on the west shore of the pond. Local yachtsmen declared Great River to be not navigable in 1977.

The fishing at the entrance to the bay is said to be sporty with bass and bluefish but beware of charted shoals.

Eel Pond (13229). This pond, with a cut through the beach, will be of little use to cruising boats until it is dredged out. In 1985 there was a depth of only 2 feet in the very narrow channel at the entrance, and the tide runs very swiftly across the bar. The latest edition of the *Coast Pilot* says: "The channel is subject to shoaling; extreme caution and local knowledge is advised."

Popponesset Bay (13229). This is a very shallow bay, with depths of as little as 2 feet reported in the entrance. However, the *Coast Pilot* reports a small marina on Daniels Island, so the bay must be navigable for small boats.

Osterville, Massachusetts (13229). The entrance to Osterville is reported to be about 7 feet, opening up a lovely area of protected water. One can carry 5 or 6 feet through the bridge to Little Island and up into North Bay. Shoal-draft boats can continue around Osterville Grand Island into Cotuit Bay and work back through the Seapuit River. The channel from Cotuit Bay out to Nantucket Sound has a depth of about 4 feet MLW and is clearly marked, but most boats use the Seapuit River entrance. For latest information on depths here, call the harbormaster's office at (508) 790-6273.

In approaching Osterville from the west, pass either inside or outside of Succonnesset Shoal and Wreck Shoal. Strangers will probably prefer the outside passage. Mr. Chester Crosby, who has sailed these waters for many years, described the bar west of the flasher on the west end of Succonnesset Shoal as "a cardiac arrest area." From the east, simply keep outside the line of buoys from Bishop and Clerks to flasher 1. Leave can 3 to port. The channel into West Bay then runs between a small, privately maintained red flashing buoy and a large green ball. If these are hard to find, note that the breakwater at the entrance lies close to the left of a line of cottages on the shore and to the right of a long space where there are none. This is an Audubon Bird Sanctuary. "Take only photographs; leave only footprints." Leave the breakwater close to starboard. The channel inside is well marked.

Just inside the breakwater the Seapuit River makes off to the westward, leading behind the beach into Cotuit Bay. It is shoal but pretty. Boats over 26 feet are forbidden to anchor in the river.

North of the Seapuit River on the west side of the channel is "Dupont's Creek," named after the owner of the estate on the point south of its entrance. It provides secure anchorage for a shoal-draft boat.

Just south of the bridge to Little Island a considerable cove makes in to the east. This is crowded with private moorings and cannot be regarded as a possible anchorage. The signal for the bridge is a long blast and a short one.

Osterville combines a lovely area for anchorage with a wide variety of supplies, services, and repair areas. Three marinas, each with an interesting history, line up along the inner harbor beyond the bridge.

Crosby Yacht Yard, Inc.—(508) 428-6958, VHF-9—run by Richard Egan and his family, builds fiberglass vessels of some repute, including the 26-foot gaff-rigged daysailer *Wianno Sr.* and the Crosby Tug, often used as a yacht club launch. They build and care for almost everything and can be counted on for any work. They maintain slips and moorings for transients in Osterville and Cotuit Bay.

Nauticus Marina—(508) 428-4537, VHF-9—home to Bill Koch's America 3 Team, is run by Carl Lessard. There are transient slips with at least 8 feet at low tide, but no other services.

Oyster Harbor Marine—VHF-79A—is a full-service marina with transient slips but is in the business of long-term slip lease.

In 1987, Chester A. Crosby, Jr., sold the yard and went to Vermont to breed cattle. Several of the Crosby clan are still employed by Egan at the original Crosby yard and are craftsmen of superior quality and dependability.

For more information on the area, visit the Osterville Historical Society, a short, pleasant walk up the street from the marina, open 1:30 to 4:30 P.M.

Anchoring is comfortable in North Bay, and exploration of the coves and islands here can be fun by sailing dinghy or canoe.

Hyannis, Massachusetts (13229). Hyannis is a busy summer resort town—hot, crowded with automobiles, and redolent of all that we go cruising to avoid. However, it is one of the few deep-water harbors on the south shore of the Cape and has facilities for repairs of all sorts. Communication with Boston and New York by bus and air is easily arranged. Steamers run to Martha's Vineyard and Nantucket.

If you contemplate running before a brisk southwest breeze for the entrance to Hyannis, you are likely to have no trouble avoiding the well-marked dangers. Note that Hurricane Bob destroyed the day marker on Southwest Rock, and it has been replaced temporarily by a red nun marked 2SR. Stay well eastward of it. We are advised that the areas around Southwest Rock and Collier Ledge are both nasty and have collected a lot of bottom paint. Visitors should give them a wide berth. However, as you get into the shoal water and fast tidal current west of Point Gammon, you may encounter a short steep chop, which could swamp your dinghy and soak you down and which would be dangerous in a small open boat. Once inside the breakwater at Hyannis Port, you should have no trouble making the flashing buoy at the entrance to the dredged channel. Thence follow the buoys into Hyannis.

The inner harbor is crowded with moorings and agitated by the steamers running to Nantucket so there is no room to anchor. You will probably have to lie in a slip at the Lewis Bay Marina or at Hyannis Marina, both on the east side of the entrance.

Hyannis Marina—(508) 775-5662, VHF-9—has slips with electric power, telephone, and cable-TV hookups, some of which are reserved for transients. Gasoline, diesel fuel, and ice are sold on the end of the wharf. At the head of the wharf is a well-equipped marine store with everything from the necessities like foul weather gear and charts to "gifts" and nautical knick-knacks. In the yard nearby are showers, a restaurant, a game room, a swimming pool, laundry machines, a sail loft, and an engine parts shop. An open-end, 35-ton lift can haul almost any yacht in Cape Cod waters, and the yard has staff and facilities for repairs of all kinds. Less than a mile away is a small convenience store. The closest supermarket is near the western end of the town's main street, a long, hot walk from the yard, but the marina does have some courtesy cars available. Hospital, bus depot, and airport are within easy reach by taxi.

The Lewis Bay Marina—VHF-68—has slips for transients and sells gasoline, diesel oil, and ice. It would be well to call ahead as slips are much in demand. Yachts up to 125 feet long drawing up to 10 feet can be

A view of Lewis Bay and at upper right the inner harbor at Hyannis. Egg Island constricts the entrance to the Bay. Easy anchorage may be made off the prominent jetty north of Dunbar Point if you wish to avoid crowded Hyannis. *Colonial Gas Co., James W. Sewall Co.*

accommodated in slips provided with electric current of 20 or 30 amps at 125 volts or 50 amps at 220 volts. Hookups for cable TV are also available. There are showers and laundry machines at the marina, and nearby is the Dockside Inn serving three meals daily with cocktails. The inn pool is available for transient guests. For those seeking less formal dining, there is a barbecue pit. The marina has a small marine store and, although it has no means of hauling boats, can see to in-the-water repairs. Also the marina can arrange transportation to bus station or airport.

Up the street from the marinas is the town of Hyannis. It consists principally of one long, long main street, lined with smart clothing stores, a Howard Johnson restaurant, various notion and pottery establishments, and indeed, everything but a grocery store. After a long trek to the westward, the hungry mariner will find an enormous brick-and-glass supermarket, providing for all his needs. On his journey along this hot, cement-paved sidewalk, he will see every type of summer costume, every kind of vacation-bound automobile, every aspect of the summer trade on Cape Cod. It is a far cry from a down-east general store, with its confused aroma of oilclothes, codline, and cheese.

About a mile out of town is a great shopping center with every conceivable type of store from Sears and Filene's to a boutique and a restaurant. Hyannis, indeed, has much to recommend it.

If you do not require the services of a metropolis, there are pleasanter places to spend the night than in Hyannis. The first is behind the breakwater at Hyannis Port. Seek the best lee you can find. The anchorage is seldom so crowded as to limit your choice. There is a small yacht club at which you can land if you want to, but unless you want to swim on the beach, there is little to land for. There is no store nearby, no facilities whatever for repair, and no public transportation. Ashore you will find large estates in unbroken rows along streets as suburban as Chestnut Hill and Wellesley. One of these, to the northeast of the clubhouse, is inhabited by the Kennedy family.

Another anchorage much favored by cruising men is under Harbor Bluff to the west of the channel. The headquarters of the Hyannis Yacht Club is here, and there may be a vacant mooring. Inquire of the steward.

One can anchor anywhere in Lewis Bay on a quiet night. Usually the wind dies with the sun, and of course no roll from outside can penetrate here. If you seek snugger anchorage, follow the directions generously contributed by an explorer willing to share his discoveries:

> Proceed up the channel to lighted buoy 18 and run 150 degrees magnetic, thus avoiding Egg Island. Now you might ask why a small boat would go all the way to #18 instead of turning to starboard at, say, #14. I've been aground so many times on the various flats, Egg Island, etc., at night that it seems better to go up to more protected waters and a known point before heading out of the channel. Keep an eye out for Fiddle Head Rock beacon and buoy off to starboard. You will have 5 feet of water all the way. This will bring you to a small stone jetty on the starboard side of a small cut. This cut is to the left of some tall trees. Beware of a shoal off the jetty and of one to the left of the cut. Go right down the middle of the cut. There is deep water right up to the beach at the right, but no place to stay overnight because of the current. Proceed around to port and anchor anywhere in the small bay. You'll be the only boat there on *any* night. If you proceed farther to the head of the harbor, you will find deeper anchorage and occasional company.

I have also had occasion to explore Uncle Roberts Cove. This one is *tough!* Egg Island is lined with poles at the south end, so that one can skirt along it and turn to port at the appropriate point. The rock labeled X on the accompanying chart is usually marked by a Clorox bottle. Proceed dead slow. The two rocks marked on the chart appear to be another small jetty, and one should pass fairly close to it. I sailed in, sailed off in the dinghy for an hour or two, leaving two students on board. The wind shifted and I returned to find them high and drying. (They hadn't noticed.) To make a long story short, the natives were *most* hospitable. A nice cove, but harder to get into than the first because of the nasty rocks all around.

Parkers River, South Yarmouth, Massachusetts (13229). There is a marina here providing the usual services, but no fuel. The entrance is very shoal and ever changing. The big movie screen that used to be a landmark is gone, but there is a new, large, mushroom-shaped water tower near the river. We understand the channel is marked "as well as it can be."

Bass River, Massachusetts (13229). This river, like Parkers River, has silted up in recent years, but local authorities claim $3^1/_2$ to 4 feet at low water. The entrance is well marked by local buoys.

Inside, on the west shore, is Ship Shops—(508) 398-2256, VHF-9 and 73—a marina with slips and full service.

Above the highway bridge, which has a vertical clearance reported to be 15 feet, is the Bass River Marina—(508) 394-8341, VHF-9. Gas, water, and ice, but no diesel fuel, are available, and there is the usual marine store. A public telephone, showers, and a head are near the wharf. The marina provides "in and out" storage and has slips for visitors. There is a mechanic in attendance for engine repair and the marina can send out for repairs to electronic equipment. There is a grocery store and a laundromat in town, close to the bridge.

Although the lower part of Bass River is not particularly attractive to the long-legged deep-water cruising boat, it is interesting because of the controversy over Leif Ericson's alleged visit.

A schoolteacher-become-archaeologist named Frederick J. Pohl believed that Follins Pond, 6 miles upriver, was the site of the Vinland of Leif Ericson and of his Viking encampment in A.D. 1003. Descriptions in ancient Norse sagas seemed to point to the south of the Cape, with Bass River as a likely possibility. But how was Dr. Pohl to find evidence in support of his theory?

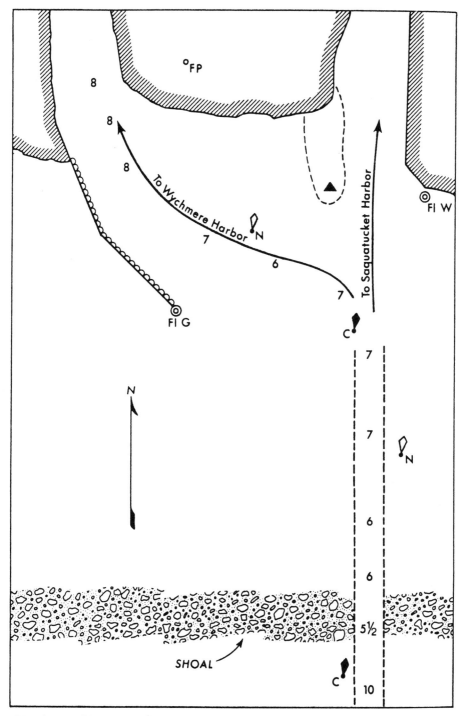

Wychmere Harbor.

He and his wife went to Bass River, and, first near the shore of Follins Pond and later at points on the river, they discovered mooring holes, of the type used by the Vikings, drilled in several rocks. The Vikings used to put spikes in such holes at an angle that would enable them to tie ropes around the spikes to hold their craft without danger of the ropes' slipping off. Dr. Pohl became convinced that these holes were not the drill holes used for blasting, but could be nothing else but holes drilled by the Vikings. He told his story to Morton Hunt. Hunt wrote an article and started a controversy. Some archaeologists raised objections to Pohl's theory, while others came to his support.

One of the criticisms pointed to the shoal water. How could a Viking ship have got that far? But Dr. Pohl adduced evidence to show that the sea level 1,000 years ago was 2 or 3 feet higher than it is today. In 1952 Dr. Pohl wrote *The Lost Discovery,* in which he traced in detail the travels of the Vikings in North America, backing his conclusions with most convincing evidence. Unlike many historians, Dr. Pohl took the trouble to visit the places he described.

Admiral Morison, in his scholarly and colorful *European Discovery of America: Northern Voyages* (1971), locates the Viking colony at L'Anse aux Meadows on the northeast peninsula of Newfoundland. He scorns all efforts to locate it in New England. He writes:

> These [mooring holes] were made by the English natives of New England to receive iron eye-bolts through which to reeve a line to a boat mooring or fish trap. I could have shown him some made for me! It is true that Scandinavians then, as now, liked to moor fore and aft, both to an anchor and to a ring-bolt or tree ashore. But in New England there were plenty of stout trees near shore and no need to drill holes in granite rocks.

Allen Harbor, Harwich Port, Massachusetts (13229). This is a bottle-tight dredged harbor but so crowded with local boats as to be of little use to the casual cruising yacht. In 1993 there was 4 feet of water in the entrance channel at low water. We were told that the last time the channel was dredged, the IRS was chasing the dredging company which left with 200 feet at the entrance still to go. Allen Harbor Marine Service—(508) 432-0353, VHF-9—on the westerly side of the harbor, may possibly have a slip available with electric power, telephone, water, and TV connections. Gasoline, diesel fuel, water, and ice are available here, and the yard can make repairs to electrical equipment as well as to inboard and outboard engines. There is a nautical gift shop. There is also a town wharf and a yacht club at which there might be room to tie up. There is no room to anchor.

For current information on Allen Harbor, call the Harwich Port harbormaster, Tom Leach, at Saquatucket on channel 9 or 68.

Wychmere Harbor, Harwich Port, Massachusetts (13225). Entrance to this tight little harbor is made clear by the drawing on page 000. After passing nun 2 and junction buoy W, turn to port, leaving inner nun 2 to starboard, and follow the line of nuns to the very narrow cut between Thompson's Clam Bar and the boatyard. There is about 5 feet at low water in the entrance. Favor the port side. The Stone Horse Yacht Club—(508) 432-0868—has guest moorings marked by posts with white tops. Call the Harwich Port Boat Works—(508) 432-1322, VHF-9—for a slip or mooring. It is possible to tie up briefly at the town pier on the easterly side of the harbor. There are moorings and an anchorage area inside the westerly jetty and also inside, southeast, of the line of nuns at the entrance.

The Boat Works can supply gasoline, diesel fuel, ice, and water and can make repairs to hulls of any material as well as to sails, rigging, electronics, and motors.

For current information on Wychmere, call Harbormaster Tom Leach at Saquatucket on channel 9 or 68.

Saquatucket, Harwich Port, Massachusetts (13229). The entrance to Saquatucket is perfectly clear and straightaway. The channel was dredged by the Army Corps of Engineers in August 1993. Inside there is no room to anchor and there are no moorings. The whole harbor is, however, filled with slips, frequently available for transients. Call ahead to Harbormaster Tom Leach or his assistant, Trevor Peterson, on VHF-9 or 68. If there are no slips in Saquatucket, Messrs. Leach and Peterson also oversee the activity of Wychmere and Allen Harbor and could direct you to a slip or mooring close by. Saquatucket has 110-volt current at 20 and 30 amps as well as gas, diesel fuel, and water at the fuel wharf at the east end of the harbor. Showers, laundry facilities, telephones, and the office of the harbormaster are located in the small house overlooking the usually quiet cove. There is a restaurant, Brax Landing, on the west end of the harbor as well as a small market, and a pizza and ice cream parlor within a tall gentleman's sight of the landing.

Many areas on the south shore of the Cape allow parking overnight for trailers and cars. Saquatucket does not. Launching is permitted at the boat marinas.

There is a great deal of windsurfing here.

Mr. Leach is most efficient and helpful and is distinguished for having designed the "Frosty," a 6-foot sailing pram built in considerable numbers and raced summer and winter in the area. It is light, easy to build, and fun to sail.

Stage Harbor, Chatham, Massachusetts (13229). Chatham is less submerged by the flood of summer visitors than most ports on the south shore of the Cape. There are still commercial fishing vessels based here. They are reminiscent of the husky catboats used in the days of sail—

Chatham, Mass. The entrance to Chatham, with Stage Harbor in the distance. Note the many dangerous, frequently shifting shoals. *Kelsey-Kennard.*

broad, shallow, with square stern and stubby bow. They are heavily powered and employed in dragging scallops as well as trap (weir) fishing. In the outer harbor there is a fish wharf and a small boatyard. The yacht club is not dominant. Such yachting as is based here is largely day sailing in small boats, although there is an increasing number of cruising yachts based here, but nothing like the pressure that builds up at Cuttyhunk or Hadley Harbor on a summer weekend.

Chatham is off the path of cruising yachts "doing" Nantucket Sound, most of whom find it far to leeward when bound either for Nantucket or Woods Hole, and to get out through Pollock Rip calls for a 12-mile beat around Handkerchief Shoal against the prevailing southwest wind. There is a channel between Handkerchief Shoal and Monomoy, which a local authority regards as perfectly practicable. In this author's opinion, a stranger should view it with great caution.

The entrance to Stage Harbor is clearly marked by a red-and-white Mo(A) bell "SH," a green flasher at the beginning of the dredged channel, and a red flasher opposite a small stone groin. Although the channel was dredged in the summer of 1993 to a depth of 10 feet, obtaining local knowledge is crucial for the exploration of any other area surrounding Chatham. Harbormaster Peter Ford monitors VHF-9 or can be reached by phone at (508) 945-5185. Hurricane Bob, which pounded the south shore in the late summer of 1991, opened up some of the northwestern corner, but this region is constantly in flux, and any travel through it is to be made only with the understanding that the local salvage companies are kept in business by unwary yachtsmen.

On a southwest breeze, a steep, confused chop is likely to build up outside the small groin because the south shore of the Cape and the shoals off Monomoy act like the sides of a funnel. This may surprise and distress the sailor running before it, particularly with an outgoing current, but it can be downright frightening to the skipper beating out against it. The worst section is near the channel entrance. By the time one gets a mile offshore, the sea becomes less agitated.

Stage Harbor is not the place to go in search of services. In the outer harbor there is a fish wharf, catering to a variety of oceangoing fishermen, but neither gas nor supplies are available. In summer, Stage Harbor Yacht Club provides races for children and seniors but is not equipped to satisfy the needs of cruising folk. Anchoring is only permitted in the area south of the dredged channel, west of nun 8. The best water is SSE of nun 6 in what used to be the entrance channel. Stage Harbor Marine rents moorings and can be reached on VHF-9 and (508) 945-1860. Monomoy Yacht Club also has a few which might be available for transients. There is no one in the clubhouse on a regular basis, but more information is available from Dick Bray at (508) 945-1580. No major repairs are done in Stage Harbor anymore, and Harbormaster Ford recommends Land and Sea in Harwich as a fine establishment for those in need.

With the lack of service in mind, it is understandable that Chatham is off the beaten path of most Nantucket Sound cruising yachts and could be a welcome change from the frazzle of the "full-service yard" crowd. Yachts which can pass beneath the 8-foot bridge at the head of the harbor will find a quiet, clean anchorage in the Mill Pond. The bridge opens with one hour's notice during the season; call the Chatham Police Department at (508) 945-1213. By dinghy, or cautious hand, one can also reach Little Mill Pond, where there is a town wharf. From there, the town shops are not far.

There is a great deal to see and do in Chatham. There are the well-known Chatham Murals, painted by Carol Wright and now housed in a barn at the Attwood House, as well as a fine railroad museum in the no-longer-used railroad station. There are frequent concerts and plays in town. The Chamber of Commerce, located at a booth next to the Town Hall or reachable at (508) 945-5199, has full information on all the aforementioned activities and many more.

Monomoy and Beyond

Cape Cod is the most conspicuous outpost of the mainland on the New England coast of the United States. It is a narrow glacial peninsula, constantly being modified through the action of wind and sea, but based on a rock-and-preglacial-clay foundation that is called by geologists one of the ancient drainage divides of the country. Much of it is terminal moraine, with its few large rocks brought by the glacier from far to the north and scattered around the Cape, conspicuous in the sandy soil.

The first part of the Cape to be seen by the early voyagers from overseas was its Great Beach, running from Provincetown on the north to the southern tip—a long and narrow spit of sand and marsh known as Monomoy Island. Between Monomoy and Nantucket and beyond to the southward are some of the most dangerous waters on our Atlantic

Coast—with shoals, variable currents, and frequent fogs that have challenged the courage and seamanship of cruising men since the days of Bartholomew Gosnold and Samuel de Champlain. As we have seen, these shoals affected the whole history of the Yankee coast.

Although Bartholomew Gosnold, the English explorer, gave the Cape its present name in 1602, there is little doubt that other Europeans had sighted the Cape in the preceding century.

From then until now, the sea has continued to take its toll, and the timbers of thousands of wrecks lie buried in the sands of the Outer Beach.

One of the Cape's occupations that has passed is "moon-cussing": cursing at the moon when it came out from behind a bank of clouds in time to show the beach to a ship that had sailed too close to the shore. According to a story related by Dr. Morison, a certain Reverend Mr. Lewis of Wellfleet saw through the window of his church a vessel going ashore. The congregation was nearer to the door, but apparently had their backs turned to the sea. Stopping his sermon, the pastor descended the pulpit stairs and with a shout of "Start fair!" led his congregation pell-mell out of the meetinghouse door.

Ralph Waldo Emerson wrote in 1854: "Went to Orleans Monday, to Nauset Light on the back of Cape Cod. The keeper Collins told us that he found obstinate resistance on the Cape to the project of building a lighthouse on this coast as it would injure the wrecking business."

Sometimes lifesaving and the plundering of wrecks were combined. But, compared to the splendid record of heroism of Cape Codders in saving shipwrecked men and women, the unsavory cases of moon-cussing were few indeed.

Edward Rowe Snow, author of *Romance of Boston Bay: Storms and Shipwrecks of New England* and other books, was taking a crowd of schoolchildren through an old house on Outer Brewster. There he found an old book, as it happened, a rare first edition. He took it to the Boston Public Library and there someone noticed certain letters were pricked with a pin. She listed the letters pricked, cracked the code, and got a lot of bearings on Nauset Beach.

Snow rushed down and dug here and there without success and gave up. His brother, a radar expert, rigged up a device like a mine detector to detect the presence of metal in the ground. They tried it, got a click, dug 8 feet down, and pulled out an iron box of gold coins worth $2,700. The whole place is now sanded over several feet deep again. Alton Hall Blackington told the yarn at a lecture in Concord, Massachusetts, and showed movies of the whole business.

This may suggest an addition to your cruising equipment.

On Nauset Beach in April 1717 pirate Samuel Bellamy's vessel *Whydah* was wrecked in a heavy spring gale. Only two of her crew survived to tell the world that she was heavily laden with treasure stolen in the Caribbean. The governor of Massachusetts sent Captain Cyprian Southack to investigate, but he returned empty handed.

On July 19, 1984, Barry Clifford, a professional salvor from Martha's Vineyard, having spent years in detective work on the story of the wreck and months in searching with a magnetometer, found the wreck about 1,500 feet off shore and, fortunately, a television crew was aboard that day to record the find. During the next year, Clifford and his crew brought up coins, gold bars, jewels, cannons, muskets, navigational instruments, even a leather shoe with a white stocking, in all 7,310 artifacts—and eventually, a bronze bell inscribed "THE WHYDAH GALLY 1716".

The dramatic story is told in *The Pirate Prince* by Barry Clifford with Peter Turchi (Simon & Schuster, New York, 1993) and is summarized in the April 1993 *Readers Digest*.

Before attempting Pollock Rip Channel, consult the *Eldridge Tide and Pilot Book* on the time of the fair current and plan to have it in your favor. If bound east, especially if there is a sea running outside, prepare for a rough passage, for a strong current meeting the sea roll can produce a rough and even dangerous rip. One can anchor and await slack water if the situation looks too dangerous to proceed, but once committed to the channel with a fair tide, to retreat can be difficult.

Beyond Monomoy, the navigator faces 35 miles of practically un-broken beach to Peaked Hill Bar at the tip of the Cape, and another long 10 miles to the first shelter at Provincetown. In an easterly storm, this beach can be a dangerous lee shore, but on an ordinary summer day, the trip is a pleasant sail. The bottom shoals gradually toward the shore, so that a sounding determines one's distance from the beach, a very hard thing to judge by eye. The beach is deserted for the most part—an occasional dune buggy breaking the monotony. At intervals, roads penetrate the dunes from towns on the other side, and there will be a flowering of beach umbrellas and a few bathers, but these are soon left astern. Progress is marked by an occasional tower, tank, or flagpole, by the light at Nauset, and by the great tower and radio mast at Highland Light. Offshore, beyond the 20-fathom curve, is a line of lighted whistles. Approaching darkness poses no great problem, for with the radio-direction station, the powerful beam at Highland Light, and the whistle off Peaked Hill Bar, one's position off the tip of the Cape is easily determined. From here, one can take off for Cape Ann, the Maine coast, or points east, or one can work around to Provincetown.

The approach to Provincetown can be long and slow, for the tide runs hard—up to 2 knots—and there can be an unpleasant rip off Race Point where the flood runs south, swinging around to the southeast between Race Point and Wood End. The ebb runs in the opposite direction.

Beware of Peaked Hill Bar and of Shank Painter Bar. The tendency is to close with the beach in anticipation of the next point, and it is almost impossible to judge accurately one's distance from a featureless beach. Rely on soundings and the line of buoys offshore.

There is considerable activity by draggers out of Provincetown. Some of them are very big, and they proceed with speed and determination.

Steamers bound in and out of Boston are no problem for a yacht bound for Provincetown, but anyone heading north of Race Point should display a radar reflector and keep a sharp lookout, particularly at night. These vessels travel at high speeds and are unwieldy to steer. Under conditions of limited visibility one can be run down with very little time to maneuver. The route around the Cape is interesting in its length and loneliness, especially when one remembers the *Mayflower* turning back from Pollock Rip's "shoals and roaring breakers." Along this beach moved the homeward-bound clippers and whalers in the 1850s, and later in the century racing fishermen and the fleets of four-, five-, and six-masted coal schooners, winged out and heavily loaded, bound east and beating westward in ballast through the shoals. The beaches, then patrolled by Coast Guardsmen, battered wrecks into the sand, from which they occasionally emerge. If one has never made this trip, it is worth doing at least once.

Chapter IX

Cape Cod Canal, Massachusetts, to Cape Elizabeth, Maine

East Boat Basin, Sandwich, Massachusetts (13246). This small basin lies inside the eastern end of the canal on the south side, about three-quarters of a mile from the end of the canal breakwater. This is a useful if not very attractive place for the westbound vessel to wait for a fair tide. An eastbound vessel may find it a good place to spend the night following a late-afternoon passage through the Canal. If one comes from the eastward, the entrance is easy to find in clear weather. The 300-foot stack on the power plant can be seen from Provincetown and it is distinguished by brightly flashing strobe lights which work day and night. From closer in, the jetties and the light on the northern one are easily picked out. In thick weather a radio beacon and fog signal make entrance easy, especially as the fog is likely to scale up along the south shore of Cape Cod Bay.

If one is beating down Cape Cod Bay against the southwest wind and chop, a good tactic is to stay on the starboard tack until well in under the Cape shore. Then on the other tack one can romp to the Canal with a good breeze and smooth water.

Important changes have been made here. The entire basin has now been converted to slips for the Sandwich Marina—(508) 833-0808—and there is no space for anchoring. It is no longer designated as a harbor of refuge.

A hard-top launching ramp for trailer craft is at the head of the cove.

Gasoline, ice, water, and diesel fuel are available at a float east of the marina, and there is a public telephone at the head of the wharf.

Less than a half mile from the shore is a large supermarket, the Purity Supreme. Head west along the road from the gasoline wharf, cross the parking lot and the railroad track, take the first road to the right, and you will see it immediately. There is a laundromat, a restaurant, and a bus station in Sandwich, three-quarters of a mile away. The bus trip to Boston takes an hour and a half.

Barnstable, Massachusetts (13251). This is a shallow estuary, the first harbor to the east of the Cape Cod Canal. It is obstructed by a bar, occasionally dredged. At high water on a smooth day it should be passable, but with any weight of wind from the north, especially with an ebb tide, it should not be approached. Don't even contemplate entering Barnstable under such conditions.

The channel inside is marked by government buoys, private buoys, and brush stakes. For a shoal-draft boat under oars or sail the narrow channels, sandy islands, and salt marshes can be fascinating.

Maraspin Creek itself, the commercial part of Barnstable, is not very attractive, especially at low water. There are several marinas here where gasoline, diesel fuel, and water are obtainable and a boatyard with a lift, a small marine store, and possibly a vacant slip. There is no room to anchor in the creek itself. A restaurant on the east shore offers free tie-up for customers.

Note that the range of the tide north of the Cape is about 9 feet while south of the Cape it is only 1 or 2 feet.

Sesuit, Massachusetts (13250). This is a small shoal harbor of no great scenic attractiveness, but a busy base for local boats. There is a bar at the entrance which shifts and is dredged at intervals. Call North Side Marina on channel 9 for the latest information. However, with the usual summer breeze from the southwest, there is no sea on the bar and with 8 to 10 feet of tide in Cape Cod Bay, there should be no difficulty in entering under ordinary conditions. The shoalest part is outside the west jetty. Favor the east jetty and then jog back to the middle of the channel.

A yawl drawing about 5 feet stood on a cradle in the parking lot. Her owner, engaged in putting a new counter on her, pronounced Sesuit the best harbor on the north side of the Cape, said that there was 5 feet on the bar, and declared that he never had any trouble coming or going.

There is no room to anchor. Inquire for a slip on the western shore. Gasoline, diesel fuel, water, and ice are available here. There is also a 15-ton travelift at the yard with facilities for ordinary repairs. The yard store sells marine supplies, charts, and fishing gear. There is a dive shop near the yard. A restaurant and a grocery store are in the village about three-quarters of a mile away.

Wellfleet, Massachusetts (13250). This is the only protection for a deep-draft yacht between the Canal and Provincetown. Barnstable, Rock Harbor, and Sesuit are small, shoal, and obstructed by bars which break in easterly weather. Entrance is clear from the chart, but the marks must be carefully followed, leaving bell 1 to port and the grounded target ship to starboard. The channel and harbor were dredged in 1985. The controlling depth was reported to be 8 feet in 1993.

There are 20 moorings for transients in the basin inside the breakwater. They are marked with blue-and-white buoys. Call the harbormaster, Glenn Shields, on channel 16. He assigns transients alternately to moorings owned by Bay Sails and to moorings owned by Wellfleet Marine. The charge is the same for each, but Wellfleet Marine maintains free launch service from 8 A.M. to 7 P.M. for those on its moorings.

There are slips for very shoal-draft boats behind the mole at the head of the harbor, the channel to which is marked by local buoys. As the range of tide is about 10 feet, larger yachts can get to the gasoline and diesel pumps behind the mole at high water. The harbormaster's office is on the mole close by.

Both Wellfleet Marine and Bay Sails have marine stores and can make repairs. Bay Sails is located on the main road back from the shore but has a Brownell trailer which can haul a yacht and transport it to their shop. Wellfleet Marine has a similar trailer, and its yard and marine store are adjacent to the wharf where commercial fishermen tie up.

There are several restaurants along the shore behind Wellfleet Marine, and there is a grocery store uptown. The lower spar of the town flagpole used to be the main boom of the Boston fishing schooner *Quannapowitt*, wrecked on the outside of the Cape in November 1913. It is an impressive stick.

If one must lay over in Wellfleet, there are a number of interesting places to visit. Wellfleet Marine or Harbormaster Shields can supply brochures and suggestions.

A 1985 visitor reported: "Ashore the town is a scenic delight; excellent restaurants nearby and a half-mile walk to a lovely, tree-shaded, and quite complete town center."

Provincetown (13249). In *Mourt's Relation* we read of the Pilgrims' arrival in New England: "After many difficulties in boisterous storms, at length, by God's providence upon the 9th of November, we espied land, which we deemed to be Cape Cod, and so afterward it proved. Upon the 11th of November we came to anchor in the bay, which is a good harbor and pleasant bay, circled round except in the entrance, which is about four miles over from land to land, compassed about to the very sea with oaks, pines, juniper, sassafras, and other sweet wood. It is a harbor wherein a thousand sail of ships may safely ride. There we relieved ourselves with wood and water and refreshed our people, while our shallop was fitted to coast the bay, to search for an habitation." Today the sweet woods are all gone and the harbor has been improved by a breakwater, but Provincetown is still a good shelter.

Provincetown is well worth a visit with its historical associations, its unique offshore atmosphere, vigorous commercial and sportfishing activity, and "counterculture" ashore. Just to get to Provincetown involves something of an offshore experience with the good chance of seeing whales, tuna, and offshore birds.

The most prominent landmark from any direction is the Pilgrim Monument, 348 feet above high water and visible all the way from Plymouth on a clear day. As one approaches the hook of the Cape from the west and north, a large water tank rises over the horizon and then Race Point Light, the abandoned Coast Guard station, and finally the yellow dunes. At night the airplane beacon at the airport east of Race Point is visible, and Highland Light can sometimes be seen over the land.

In clear weather one may cut Race Point bell and bell 1 off Wood End but must still keep well offshore to avoid Shank Painter Bar. The depth finder gives little warning as the bar rises steeply from over 100 feet to less than 20 feet and extends in some places over half a mile offshore. Distance from the featureless beach is hard to judge without a house, a car, or a man to give scale to the scene.

Long Point Light is conspicuous and the harbor entrance is further marked by a bell outside the light. Thence run for the light on the west end of the breakwater.

There are two marinas in Provincetown. On the westerly wharf, Fishermen's Wharf, is Provincetown Marina, and on the easterly wharf is Provincetown Yacht and Marine. Both have rental moorings and limited dock space. Call the dockmaster at either on channel 9. Do not anchor within 50 yards of a line from bell 3 to the west end of the breakwater. Also be aware that large excursion vessels come during the day to anchor outside the breakwater and shuttle passengers ashore. The harbormaster, whose office is on the easterly wharf, monitors channel 16 but is not concerned with renting moorings. Both marinas offer water, ice, showers, laundry machines, and the usual services. Provincetown Marina on the westerly wharf has fuel.

The moorings southwest of the wharves are entirely satisfactory in ordinary summer weather, but in the event of a really heavy blow, seek a mooring behind the breakwater. You will need permission from the owner and from the harbormaster to use one. Do not anchor behind the breakwater as the bottom is foul and there is scant room to swing. The alternative is to find a lee under whatever shore is to windward, but avoid the shellfish grant areas marked with yellow lights northeast of the breakwater.

Launch service in the mooring area is available at a modest fee. The long wharf farthest west is the Coast Guard base. There are two boatyards west of the wharves: Flyer's and Taves Corporation. Both have repair services to meet most emergencies.

The easterly wharf is used by big commercial fishermen, many of whom, now that cod and haddock are scarce, fish for "underutilized species": dogfish, skates, and squid. There is a market abroad for these and a developing market in this country, but commercial fishing is a shaky business at best with both fish supplies and market prices uncertain.

Here too are berths for several sailing excursion boats and a number of sportfishermen and charter boats. These search the waters of Cape Cod Bay and Stellwagen Bank for tuna. On calm days they troll to and fro, lookouts aloft watching for fins. At other times they anchor in a likely spot and fish near the bottom. The writer sailed through a fleet of about 30 anchored out of sight of land off Race Point. These are serious fishermen. Not only is tuna fishing great sport, but any fish brought in is quickly bought. Many are shipped fresh or frozen to Japan. A large tuna will bring several thousand dollars.

The only place to land from a dinghy is at a small float between the two wharves. From the gangway you step at once into a huge parking lot. There is a telephone on the far side of it and just beyond lies the narrow main street of Provincetown.

In the evenings, this is a sociological exhibit. The participants are of all ages, mostly young. They are clad in a wide range of fashions from almost nothing to the most exotic. Language overheard bears little relation to schoolroom English. Beer, soda, and foot-long hot dogs seem to be the principal sustenance. Rock rhythms assail the ear. The crowd mills and surges in and out of small shops which sell paintings, T-shirts with picturesque legends, brass, pewter, leather goods, and a variety of "gifts." It should be added that nearby are more conventional restaurants serving conventional meals in more formal surroundings. Also, Provincetown is the summer base for a number of serious artists.

In the morning, however, the streets are occupied by the ordinary residents of the town. There is a supermarket on the first street back from the shore, to which anyone will direct the visitor. The writer was told it was up a high hill and down the other side. This slight incline and decline was what passed for a high hill on the Cape.

There is a hardware store, Lands End, on the main street north of the wharves with a well-equipped marine department selling both commercial and yacht hardware and another, Marine Specialties, east of it.

It is worthwhile to spend a little time in Provincetown, once you arrive. The Pilgrim Monument, built in 1910 to commemorate the first landing of the Pilgrims in America, affords a magnificent view of the harbor, the town, the hook of the Cape, and the back shore. The cliffs across at Plymouth are often visible, and on a clear day the Blue Hills in Milton and the tall buildings of Boston show on the horizon. The monument is open from nine to five at a nominal cost.

At the foot of the tower is a museum with a number of relics of the town's history, most of it built around the fishing industry.

One can walk across to the dunes or ride a rented bicycle on a paved bicycle path or, for a price, join a tour in a "beach buggy." The dunes are ecologically very fragile, for they are held down by sparse tough beach grass and a scattering of scrubby bushes. If these are damaged, even over a small area, the dune will begin to move as the wind drifts sand up one side and down another, thus uprooting more grass. Be careful to walk where directed.

The back shore is largely controlled and preserved by the Cape Cod National Seashore. The view is stark and bleak, even on a pleasant summer day. A long, long beach backed by dunes stretches out of sight. Even on a quiet day, the sea lumps up and often breaks quite far out. In a storm with the air full of rain, sand, and flying spray, the sea boiling white, the steep confused waves breaking far up the beach, it is a daunting experience. The following account of a visit to the dunes comes from W. S. Carter's classic account of a cruise in a chartered fishing sloop in 1858.

As the Professor desired to examine a beach four or five miles distant, on which the Atlantic rolls its waves unchecked by any land nearer than the "far-off bright azores," we hired a wagon, a span of horses, and a queer little urchin of a driver, to conduct us thither over the sand-hills. In a few minutes we had left behind us the single street of the village and merged into a desert of white sand, that looked as if it had been rolled into high waves by a raging tempest, and then suddenly arrested and fixed before it had time to subside to a level. Here and there in the dells and hollows were patches of vegetation, alders, huckleberry-bushes, low pitch-pines, scrub-oaks, and clumps of wild roses, glowing with the brilliant hues which the sea air gives to flowers. But outside of the village there were no houses, fences, paths, or any traces whatever of man or beast. It was a wilderness, as it was when it first met the eyes of the Mayflower pilgrims. The horses that tugged us onward had the muscles of their rumps unusually developed from working always fetlock deep in sand.

At length we gained the shore and stood by the sea. A prodigious multitude of terns flew up at our approach, and wheeled around in the air clanging their wild and piercing cries. No other signs of life were visible, save a few white sails far away on the horizon. Signs of death were around us in the shape of fragments of wrecks thrown high on the beach by storms. I picked up a piece of bamboo which perhaps had floated from some vessel returning from India or China, or the isles of the East.

Provincetown is a good place from which to take a departure for the Maine coast or Nova Scotia or for the voyage around the Cape. It provides an interesting variation in a cruise east from the Canal. Bound west for the Canal against the southwest wind, you may be tempted to reach across to Provincetown from Cape Ann, but if the wind continues southwest, you will face a dead beat of many miles to the Canal. The shoal waters of Cape Cod Bay can kick up a violent short sea, which makes for a most unpleasant passage. It is preferable to hug the western shore of Cape Cod Bay, where the wind draws off the land and the water is likely to be smooth.

Plymouth, Massachusetts (13253). Plymouth is the only shelter available to a cruising yacht between Scituate and the Cape Cod Canal. With a considerable local fleet of its own, Plymouth is a crowded harbor during the summer months, but it is one of the most interesting in Massachusetts.

On coming from the Canal, one will easily pick out the conspicuous light on the Gurnet by day or night. There is a red sector to the south covering Mary Ann Rocks.

Note: **All of Plymouth Bay is a "no-discharge zone."**

The westward-bound skipper will find it a long way from Farnham Rock to the Gurnet, especially with a flood tide of $1/2$ knot against him. The nun on High Pine Ledge is hard to find in the afternoon sun, but there is a clump of pine trees on the shore about abreast of it, from which perhaps the rock is named.

In taking bearings on the high monuments back of the shore, note that the highest and most northerly one is on Captain's Hill in South Duxbury and is not to be confused with the monument in Plymouth. A signal strength anomaly has been reported by loran users 1 to 3 miles east of the Manomet nuclear power plant on the Seneca, New York, station, making loran fixes here unreliable. Fortunately the area of the anomaly is small.

The channel from the outer bell to Duxbury Pier Light is well buoyed. Brown's Bank on the southern side of the channel is usually submerged and often invisible. Treat flasher 3 respectfully.

At Duxbury Pier Light, locally known as Bug Light, the channels to Plymouth, Duxbury, and Kingston divide. One in search merely of shelter on a quiet night can avoid the 2-mile trip into Plymouth by anchoring behind Clark Island, an anchorage used by the Pilgrims' reconnaissance party in a northeasterly snowstorm in December 1620. However, the dredged channel into Plymouth is well buoyed and easily followed. At the elbow south of lighted beacon 12 and north of can 13 is a protected anchorage for those who do not seek port facilities. It is occasionally disturbed by the wakes of party boats and big commercial fishermen but is generally clean and quiet.

The channel is well lighted at night. A direct course can be followed from bell 9 to lighted beacon 12 and thence to lighted beacon 17, which may be difficult to distinguish from the shore lights behind it. From this beacon there are two ranges marked by red lights on the shore. Follow the southerly one until the northerly range lines up, and then follow that to the breakwater. The *Coast Pilot* reports that these ranges are difficult to identify by day.

As you approach the breakwater, call the Plymouth Yacht Club on channel 68 for a mooring. The mooring fee includes launch service and use of the club. There is 6 feet of water on the front of the yacht club float where gasoline, water, and ice are available, but no diesel fuel. Ask directions for coming alongside from the launch operators to avoid shoal spots. Showers are provided for cruising people. A cocktail lounge is open Thursday through Sunday nights. The stewards at the club are most accommodating and can supply accurate local information.

If you must anchor, call the harbormaster on channel 16.

North of the yacht club is Brewer's Plymouth Marine. Call on channel 9. There is 7 feet of water at their floats where gasoline, diesel fuel, ice, and water are available. They have facilities to haul any yacht which can approach their lift and can arrange for repairs to hull, rigging, engines, electronics, or refrigeration machinery. Showers and laundry facilities are on the wharf. There is a restaurant, Nanina, at the yard affording both casual and more formal dining and a chandlery offering clothing and marine accessories as well as the usual line of indispensable marine hardware. A slip for overnight is usually available. It is well to call ahead. Diesel fuel is available at the town wharf.

The town of Plymouth offers restaurants, grocery stores, liquor stores, gift shops, bus transportation to Boston and Cape Cod, and almost any service the cruising person could desire. The yacht club publishes a map showing locations of facilities in the town. The visitor planning to tour Plymouth would do well to rent a bicycle.

Prominent on the west shore of the harbor is *Mayflower II,* a replica of a seventeenth-century vessel of the same type as that on which the Pilgrims crossed the Atlantic in the fall of 1620. If she looks a bit high and cranky, it is because her 'tween decks were raised up a foot so tourists would not bump their heads on the deck beams. She was designed by George Baker, after extensive research into seventeenth-century ship-building practices, and built in England in 1957. She was sailed across the Atlantic in the summer of that year by Captain Alan Villiers in fifty-three days. The *National Geographic* magazine for November 1957 carried the story of the voyage. Exhibits and wax figures aboard help you to imagine what life was like in 1620 with 102 passengers and about 25 seamen on a winter crossing of the Atlantic. Alongside lies a reproduction of the shallop used to explore the coast of the Cape in search of a place to settle. A visit to the *Mayflower II* is well worth the modest price of a ticket.

In Plymouth there are other museums and exhibits of Colonial life, the most elaborate being Plimoth Plantation, a reconstruction of the Pilgrim settlement as it was in 1627. Guides costumed as Pilgrims explain the tools and household equipment of the early inhabitants and go on to discuss the customs, laws, religion, and economy of the village. It is well worth a half-day's thoughtful attention.

Duxbury, Massachusetts (13253). Follow the same course as though going to Plymouth as far as Duxbury Pier Light, where the dredged channel to Duxbury turns northward.

Although the anchorage may be crowded during July and August, the hospitable Duxbury Yacht Club often can provide moorings for visitors. Duxbury Marine Railway, Bayside Marine, and Long Point Marine provide some tie-up facilities and fuel, ice, and water. Winsor's offers meals and accommodations. There is a well-equipped grocery store in town.

The channel has shoaled up since last dredged and now has less than 4 feet in some places at low water and is nearly bare in others. Every northeast gale changes it. There are plans to dredge again in 1994 or 1995, but the soil is polluted and must be dumped far off shore by seagoing barges and tugs so it will be very expensive. Also, a gale in 1992 broke through the beach and caused serious erosion so there is agitation to save the beach at the expense of dredging the channel. The cautious skipper of a yacht drawing more than 4 feet will approach Duxbury only on the top half of a rising tide.

For a mooring, call Harbormaster Don Beers on channel 16. There is no room to anchor although Two Rock Channel east of the town is a possibility. The Duxbury Yacht Club, active since before 1904, affords showers and launch service from June 1 to Labor Day on a reciprocal basis. Or call the *E-Z Rider* launch.

A short distance from the yacht club is Millbrook Market and a constellation of pizza, ice cream, and sub shops. The Winsor House restaurant is less than a mile away, and it is about 2 miles to a supermarket and liquor store.

The Duxbury Yacht Club has a very active interclub racing program in the Optimist class and is making sailors of 8-year-olds.

The *Coast Pilot* promises fuel and tie-ups at marinas.

Green Harbor, Massachusetts (13253). This is a small and crowded inlet behind Brant Rock. The entrance channel is frequently dredged but is changed by every winter storm. Read the *Coast Pilot* for reported shoals outside the entrance. Avoid Green Harbor at low water or with any considerable sea running. Green Harbor Marina on the west side offers slips, gasoline, and a marine store. Taylor Marine on the east side offers moorings, slips, gasoline and diesel fuel, and the Taylor Marina Diner. There is no room to anchor. The Compass Rose offers fine dining.

A tuna tournament is held in August. A Japanese firm maintains a tuna-processing plant and ships the fish to Japan by air.

Green Harbor is a no-discharge zone.

This is not a particularly attractive harbor for a cruising boat, but unless there is a heavy sea running, it is an acceptable shelter. Plymouth or Scituate is to be preferred.

New Inlet, Massachusetts (13267). New Inlet is so called because the great storm of November 1898 broke through the beach between Third Cliff and Fourth Cliff about 2 miles south of Scituate, making a new mouth for the North River, which used to come out about 3 miles farther south near Rexham. The inlet gives access from Cape Cod Bay to the Herring River, the North River, and the South River.

The entrance is now a rather shoal estuary, marked by a white bell and a series of five nuns. If there is much of any sea running, especially on an ebb tide, do not attempt the entrance. However, on a reasonably smooth summer day, with the wind out to the southward or southwest, one should have no trouble.

Hug the nuns closely, as there are said to be boulders on the southern side of the channel, and keep the fathometer going. After a summer northeaster in 1977 nun 4 went adrift. A sportfisherman heading out rounded nun 6 and got onto the shoal to the north. He ran into two heavy breaking seas, was stove up, swamped, and sunk in a very short time. The crew was rescued.

The Herring River. After passing nun 10, go close to the sand spit and the shore to starboard. Here begins a series of black cans and bank markers leading up the Herring River. Despite several 3-foot soundings shown on the chart, one can carry a draft of 4 feet at low water up to James Landing. Favor the northerly shore and, in general, keep to the outside of the bends.

After a straight stretch of about half a mile, you will find the remains of the bulkhead and wharf of the Boston Sand and Gravel Co. Go in close to the bulkhead, follow close to the southeastern side of the wharf, turn sharply around the nun off the end of the wharf, proceed to the next nun, and continue more or less in the middle of the very narrow channel to the turning basin at the marina-boatyard.

Here are slips for ninety yachts, a travelift with a capacity of 25 tons, a crane to set spars, complete repair facilities for wooden and fiberglass hulls and for spars, rigging, and electronic gear. Mechanics skilled in working on both inboard and outboard motors are on duty. Gasoline, diesel oil, water, and ice can be purchased at the float. A marine store is near the head of the float. If you need groceries, it is likely that a man from the yard can give you a ride to Angelo's Market about half a mile up the road. The yard is open seven days a week from 8 A.M. to 6 P.M. in the summer.

If you do not care to push up the Herring River, anchor behind the sand spit by the first can and explore in the outboard. The tide does not run heavily in the Herring River but is quite swift at the turn between nuns 8 and 10.

The North River. One can go up the North River as far as the markers on the sides of the channel. Those to starboard are maintained by Scituate, those to port by Marshfield. Proceed with caution, as the channel is intricate and in some places quite shoal. Furthermore, ice sometimes carries markers away. A visitor to the North River writes:

> The salt meadows bordering the North River from New Inlet to the first highway drawbridge have yielded little of their beauty to civilization and from the first drawbridge to Hanover present delightful vistas of salt meadows against occasional groves of vener-able pine trees and the square white mansions built by the early inhabitants who converted the virgin forest into ships. At one time twenty-three shipyards operated on the river, eleven of them visible from the Hanover bridge, all seven or eight miles from the sea. Plaques along the riverbank tell where some of the principal yards

were located. How those builders launched their ships into the shallow river and got them downstream and over the bar is one of the many interesting corners of New England history.

Over 1,000 vessels were built on the North River between 1640 and 1872. One of these, the 83-foot ship *Columbia*, built in 1773, was the first United States vessel around Cape Horn, discovered the Columbia River on the Northwest Coast, opened the fur trade in Nootka Sound, crossed the Pacific to Canton, and returned around the world, the first United States vessel to do so.

The drawbridges can be opened, according to the *Coast Pilot*, with four hours notice during the summertime, but an inspection in 1985 showed no evidence that the draws had been used recently, and they did not appear to be in operating condition. Just above the first bridge is Mary's Boat Livery, a source of fuel, water, and local information.

The South River. South River is also narrow and shoal but it, too, is marked by stakes and local buoys. There is said to be good anchorage just south of its mouth, where the channel turns abruptly to the east.

With care, one can continue all the way to Humarock, where there is a considerable settlement with slips, moorings, landing floats, fuel, and the stores, restaurants, and snack shops incident to the summer trade. Also here is the South River Yacht Yard and Simms Brothers Marina—Boat Hauling, Storage and Transportation with fuel, water, and ice.

New Inlet, with its tributaries, is used principally by local fishermen, both amateur and professional, and by them it is navigated with confidence. The stranger with a taste for the unusual will find the salt meadows and quiet streams abundant with the life of the marshes a pleasant change from Cape Cod Bay.

Scituate, Massachusetts (13269). Scituate is the best shelter in the long stretch of shore from Minot's Light to Plymouth and is much used by yachts and fishermen. The abandoned lighthouse at the entrance is conspicuous from far offshore. The next mark is a red-and-white lighted gong buoy, from which a buoyed channel leads south of the flashing red light on the breakwater and into the harbor.

Scituate Harbor Yacht Club is prominent on the point to the northwest on entering. Cruising yacht club members will find water, showers, and directions to a mooring from their floats. Next to it is the Scituate

Harbor Marina. Just beyond on the northwest rim of the harbor is the smaller but salty Satuit Boat Club with a fine dock carrying 6 feet at low water and offering water, showers, and a couple of guest moorings. The SHYC launch runs daily in July and August, answering to three blasts, and the SBC responds to two blasts. If neither of these appears, call *E-Z Rider* on channel 9.

Farther to the west, beyond the public launching ramp, is O'Neil's Marina and the Pier 44 Restaurant, providing ice, water, a few transient slips, and Texaco gasoline and diesel fuel. Farther around the western rim is the large Scituate town pier, where the fishing fleet ties up. Ashore, in a compact half mile starting at the town pier, is a complete shopping area along Front Street. At the southern end of the block is a large super-market open seven days a week, and all along the street are scattered a laundromat, specialty shops, a twin cinema, package stores, a marine hardware store, and several fine restaurants.

Beyond the town pier a buoyed channel leads to the inner harbor. There is said to be 6 feet in the channel, but local knowledge advises favoring the cans, the east side of the channel, to avoid "speed bumps" northeast of the town pier. Severe storms of the last two years have silted in across the mud flats on both shores inside Lighthouse Point and on both sides of the Coast Guard station so that the soundings shown on the chart are perhaps too generous. Stay in the channel or where you see other boats moored. After the Mill Wharf Restaurant comes the Coastal Exxon fuel float, supplying gasoline, diesel fuel, and water. Approach this float from the south and sheer off sharply when leaving. Just north of the float several big timbers slant into the water, over which boats have bounced at low water. Also from here the public launch *E-Z Rider* (channel 9) can assign moorings and shuttle passengers to and from yachts. Beyond Mill Wharf is the modern harbormaster facility where Elmer Pooler and his competent crew are based. They oversee the Scituate Town Marina, where there are usually a few transient slips for hire with showers and 24-hour security. The inner harbor opens back to the east from the town marina, ending at Young's Boatyard where haulout and repairs are available.

Anchoring is not permitted in Scituate's harbor, nor is there any room for it. However, between Harbormaster Pooler, the two yacht club launches, *E-Z Rider,* and three marinas, the cruising yachtsman is rarely left unaccommodated.

Scituate is a complete supply port, affords a constant 6 to 8 feet at low water, is well managed and patrolled, and should satisfy every cruising need. However, in a strong September easterly Scituate can be uncomfortable, especially in the area outside the yacht club. The pilot of *E-Z Rider* observed, "In an easterly, waves comes in like freight trains. Nothing stops them till they hit the beach."

The town was attacked in the War of 1812 by the British. The story of how the attack was repulsed was told to the late Farnham Smith in 1879 by the two old ladies who as girls had been the heroines of the affair. *The Boston Evening Transcript* printed Mr. Smith's account, as follows:

> Rebecca . . . proceeds to tell us how happily their childhood was passed down by the lighthouse; that they all had to help work in those days, and when the war came they had hard work to make both ends meet; food, especially, was so high, and a meal was only got by long hard work; how mad the people got when they heard of vessels being burned by the British, especially if the vessels had grain or flour on board. That here in Scituate the men formed themselves into a guard to look out for the British ships, warn the people of their approach, and if possible protect their property; how one day when two of our ships were laden with precious flour, two British ships appeared, and the guard, not knowing they were then off the coast, had gone inland to help harvest grain, or something, she forgot just what. Rebecca looked out from the window and saw the boats being lowered to come into the harbor, and knew their object was to set fire to the American ships. What could she do to save them? Something *must* be done, so she called Abby and asked her advice. There was no time to lose. Couldn't they make believe the guard were coming— how? "Why, by playing on the fife and drum behind the barn out of sight of the 'Britishers.'" Fortunately both girls—in their teens then—were able to play, and fife and drum were in the house, and with a determination to do their duty they began; Rebecca played the fife, Abby beat the drum, the men in the boats heard the sound, looked about, stopped rowing, fearful of running into danger; then to the joy and relief of the girls, they saw the signal hoisted for the boats to return to the vessel. Tired as they were they gave the "Britishers" a parting tune, "Yankee Doodle."

Then there is the story of the salvage of the *Etrusco.* On the evening of March 16, 1956, in a howling northeast snowstorm, the 7,000-ton

Etrusco, trying to make Boston Harbor, ran ashore on Cedar Point outside Scituate. She had neither cargo nor ballast so could not be lightened.

Unable to get her off, her owners sold her to Global Shipping Co. of Panama for a reported $125,000, a fraction of her value. Global obtained the services of Admiral Curtis, USN, retired, who had been responsible for much of the salvage work at Pearl Harbor.

The admiral found *Etrusco* hard aground, sitting on her bottom on a stony beach only 100 yards from the high-water mark. The insurance companies declared her a "total loss." Everyone who knew anything about it said she would stay there until she rusted away. However, the admiral employed dynamite and bulldozers to dig a channel around her and astern to deep water. He ran heavy anchors out astern with their cables led to *Etrusco's* winches. A few days after Thanksgiving a high run of tides was expected, and a great effort was to be made with tugs and kedges to get her off.

On the day before Thanksgiving, with an easterly breeze piling the water on the South Shore, *Etrusco* began to move in her berth. Hastily, tugs were called, steam got on the winches, pumps started, and just before high water the vessel ground over the boulders, lifted and bumped a bit, and floated into the channel Admiral Curtis had prepared for her. She was carefully maneuvered into deep water and towed safely to Boston. A pile of scrap became a ship again, a challenge met and mastered.

Cohasset, Massachusetts (13269). Cohasset is the first shelter outside Boston Harbor for the westbound mariner. A sailing vessel hard on the usual southwester from a North Shore harbor is likely to see Minot's Light from a distance and to be attracted to Cohasset behind it, postponing the long beat down the shore to Scituate. However, Cohasset is crowded to the doorsill with local boats and has shoaled up so that the controlling depth at low water in 1993 was about 5 feet. If you are contemplating a visit to Cohasset, call the harbormaster on channel 16, 9, or 11 for an assessment of the current situation. If you get no response, persevere, for he is not always at his headquarters.

The Cohasset Yacht Club on your starboard side as you enter has a float but is likely to be crowded with its own members. There is a town landing off a pillared roof. There is a float at The Chart House Restaurant at the head of the harbor for the convenience of patrons, and there is a fuel float with water at the Olde Salt House, but there are no slips or moorings reserved for transients.

There are three approaches to Cohasset, none of them practical in heavy weather or fog. The eastern entrance is the easiest. From Davis Ledge gong proceed westward to the can on West Willies Ledge, leaving Minot's Light to starboard, thence leaving Jack Rock can to port, nun 4 to starboard, and the skeleton tower on which stands Sutton Hole Light to starboard, and thence up the dredged channel. Success on this eastern approach is absolutely dependent on finding several very silent buoys. It would be hazardous in the fog.

The middle channel into Cohasset is from Davis Ledge gong westward, leaving Minot's Light to port, to green flashing bell 1 off Hogshead Rock. Leave the bell close to port to avoid a 10-foot spot about west-southwest of the buoy and run for nun 4. Leave the nun to starboard and run for Sutton Hole, a white 4-second flasher on a skeleton tower. From Sutton Hole, follow the series of red flashers up the harbor.

The western course is found by leaving can 1 on Chittenden Rock to port and nun 4 on Buckthorn Rock to starboard. Pass either side of Barrel Rock beacon, but note that a 6-foot shoal extends to the south and east of the ledge. Leave nun 6 to starboard and leave Sutton Hole Light to starboard.

One can land at a float off a hot-topped wharf east of a boatyard on the south side bearing the sign "Mill River." The harbormaster operates from a little white building with windowboxes and radio antennas on the knoll above the landing. He can advise you on where to tie up for the night.

The boatyard can take care of repair work of all kinds.

A small but interesting maritime museum in the village, about $1/4$ mile from the harbor, is open 1:30 to 4:30 P.M. except Mondays with exhibits related to Minot's Light and lifesaving history.

On the high land behind the harbormaster's office are two circular granite platforms, which served as the test assembly platforms in the construction of Minot's Light many years ago. The original watch room of Minot's Light was replaced in 1987–88 and is on display here with a replica of the copper lantern room. At the easterly corner of the "island" is the headquarters of a sailing-instruction school for children who do their sailing in 10-foot Sprites.

Cohasset has many beautiful estates and an attractive year-round colony, many of whose members commute to Boston. On half a dozen weekend nights during the summer, the Cohasset Yacht Club holds dances for members and guests. There is a first-class golf club between Cohasset and Hingham. Minot's Light is now unwatched, so you probably cannot climb it. But try to imagine what it is like when great waves break on the 114-foot tower and shoot up above the light. This has actually happened. If you want local color and anecdotes, read Edward Rowe Snow's *History of Minot's Light.* A romantic significance is attached locally to the flashes of this light—one-four-three meaning "I love you."

Boston Harbor, Massachusetts (13270). Although vigorous efforts have been made in recent years to render Boston Harbor more attractive as a recreation area, and although the improvement is dramatic, there are more attractive places for the cruising yachtsman. The harbor is traversed by big vessels, particularly by tankers. These obviously must be avoided by yachts, as such big vessels cannot maneuver smartly. The powerful tugs in attendance on the steamers are busy and pay no heed to yachts. Fishing vessels, numerous party boats bound for Provincetown and the Boston Harbor islands, Coast Guard vessels, and innumerable small motorboats keep the waters agitated.

Nevertheless, a great deal of sailing is done right up in the inner harbor, and there are anchorages and marinas for small craft. If you want to visit a historic harbor, sail under the guns of U.S.S. *Constitution,* see steamers, tugs, and pilot boats in action, and lie more or less in the shadow of city buildings, a sail up the harbor is worthwhile. Following are notes on some of the anchorages:

Hull. This harbor, like all the others in Hingham Bay and Hull Bay, must be approached through either Hull Gut east of Peddocks Island or West Gut at the other end of the island. Hull Gut is the worst, but the tide rushes through both these narrow passages at an inspiring rate. When it sets against a heavy southwesterly or northeasterly wind, the passages can be dangerous for small craft. The harbor at Hull is a rather open bight, desirable principally for its convenience. It is a short walk to Telegraph Hill and Fort Revere, which has been converted to a park and from which a dramatic view of Boston Harbor extends from the Blue Hills and the tall buildings in the city all the way to Cape Ann, although the view westward is obscured by trees. There is an active Coast Guard station at Hull, which keeps a careful eye on Boston Harbor traffic.

Allerton. Hog Island in 1985 became Spinnaker Island, named by the developers of an impressive condominium layout. Its marina, on the west side of the causeway, is filled by slip owners. The Hull Yacht Club, east of the island, with deep water at low tide on only one side of the float, extends "reciprocal" member privileges. Sunset Marina nearby provides moorings, launch service, fuel, water, showers, washer and dryer, restaurant, and a crane lift. Call on channel 7.

Worlds End. East of Worlds End and Planters Hill and west of an extensive mudbank in the Weir River is a favorite anchorage. A few moorings lie along the edge of the channel, on which quantities of yachts raft up on weekends. Worlds End is a pleasant place to go ashore. It is a privately owned 250-acre property of the Trustees of Reservations, a Massachusetts non-profit corporation. Go ashore without picnic or bonfire and leave only your footprints. Bluefishing can be good west of the peninsula. Minimal shore facilities at the back of Nantasket Beach are at the head of navigation following the removal of Paragon Park and the roller coaster in 1985.

Hingham. One who threads the shoals of Hingham Bay will find the Hingham Yacht Club on the end of Crow Point. The club would like to be hospitable to all cruising men, but it is overwhelmed by weight of numbers, numbers of its own members as well as of visitors. Members of other yacht clubs should hail the float and inquire about moorings. The club fleet is moored not only in the dredged area south of Crow Point but even outside to the north and west of the point; the owners evidently think that the horrors of being confined ashore without a boat are less than the perils of a northeast storm. Gasoline and water, but no diesel fuel, were reported to be available at the yacht club. Call on channel 68.

For supplies, follow the buoyed channel into Hingham Harbor passing between Langley and Sarah islands. The late Mr. Blanchard, a former coauthor of this *Guide* and a summer resident of Hingham, claimed that the three islands just inside Crow Point were named for a Hingham girl known as "Ragged Sarah Langley." She later became Madame Derby, founder of Derby Academy. Dredging in 1986 made considerable improvement in the scope of the harbor.

Just east of an equestrian war memorial statue, known irreverently as the iron horse, is Kehoe's Ships' Chandlery. Here are floats with 5 feet of water or less alongside at low water, and a marine store with an extensive inventory. Kehoe's has moorings and launch service. East of Kehoe's is First Quality Marine with a number of moorings. Gasoline, ice, and water are available at both places. West of Kehoe's is the town landing. Across the highway is the Fruit Center, a well-supplied fruit and grocery store. Three restaurants are nearby. Diesel oil is available at the Sunoco station across the street.

Weymouth Back River is narrow and crowded but has two affiliated marinas, Hewitt's Cove Marina and Tern Marina, built on the site of the Bethlehem-Hingham Shipyard where over 250 ships were built in World War II. Tern Marina has 125 moorings and innumerable slips with electricity and water. The usual amenities—showers, toilets, laundry, ice, marine store—are only the beginning. It offers repairs of all kinds, a 35-ton travelift, security guards, restaurant, picnic tables, . . . To complete the list would be tedious. There are provision stores close at hand and commuter boats to Boston where anything can be obtained. It is a good place from which to start a cruise in search of peace and beauty.

Weymouth, Quincy, and Dorchester Bay afford adequate protection, but are crowded and not very attractive to cruising boats. Many small local craft, both sail and power, moor in these places and swarm out during late afternoons and weekends, somewhat to the dismay of those used to less-crowded waters. The Kennedy Library on the south point of Dorchester Bay west of Thompson Island is well worth a visit.

Boston Inner Harbor. A cruising man exploring Boston's inner harbor may be surprised by the large number of yachts now based at its wharves and sailing in the shadow of its skyscrapers. Although there is, of course, considerable traffic in large steamers, tugs, barges, and big fishermen, all intent on their own affairs, there is no great problem in keeping clear of them. It is rather interesting to sail up the harbor, skirting the wharves and sailing by the U.S.S. *Constitution*, the Coast Guard base, and the Nantucket Lightship, now tied up at a Boston wharf. Those who have not yet visited Boston by land may find its shops, theaters, and museums worth some of their cruising time.

Of course there is no place to anchor in Boston's inner harbor, but two marinas usually have space for cruising boats. They are both in Charlestown beyond and across from the Coast Guard wharf at the entrance to the Charles River. The first, Shipyard Quarters Marina, is east of the Navy Yard and the *Constitution* on Piers 6, 7, and 8. The office is on Pier 8, the easterly one. Call on channels 16, 68, or 71 for a slip. Besides the usual water and electrical hookups, one can plug into the cable TV and telephone systems. Ashore there are toilets and showers, laundry facilities, pumpout service, 24-hour security, and a nearby water shuttle to Boston running two or three times an hour. Also on hand are a restaurant and bar, limousine service, and a parking garage.

Constitution Marina, west of the *Constitution* close to the Charlestown bridge, has similar services. Call on channel 9 or 69. If Constitution Marina has no slip, the accommodating management will find you one somewhere else. There is a liquor store and a grocery store close by in Charlestown. The neighborhood outside the marina is not especially attractive, but it is said to be safe.

Repairs of all kinds can be arranged through either marina. Fuel is available at neither. The Boston Boat Yard on an East Boston pier displays a large Citgo sign. Turn in by a barge labeled "Cashman." Tirrell by the fish pier in South Boston supplies fuel for the fishing fleet.

Do not miss a visit to U.S.S. *Constitution,* built in 1797. She could outfight any frigate her size and outrun any vessel she could not fight. She was the pocket battleship of her time. She has been rebuilt several times and restored to her original rig. Guided tours which give one interested in maritime history an insight into life aboard a sailing warship are conducted through her and the nearby museum.

East of *Constitution* lies U.S.S. *Cassin Young,* a World War II destroyer built in the Charlestown Navy Yard. Inquire about visiting her. She is being preserved by the National Park Service.

Vessels with rigs less than 26 feet above the water can enter the Charles River through a lock above Constitution Marina and, having due regard for racing shells, canoes, and small sailboats with student skippers, can go all the way to Watertown. Some of the bridges farther up have clearances less than the 26 feet at the entrance. The Charles River and its adjacent shores are controlled by the Metropolitan District Commission, which operates a patrol boat and is quite particular about slow speed and no wake.

Tankers and freighters use the Mystic River to approach the warehouses and tank farms above the Mystic Bridge. There is little up here to attract yachtsmen.

Of course all Boston is easily accessible from the harbor. Transportation by air, rail, bus, or rental car is easily arranged. The Science Museum and the Aquarium where the water shuttle lands are only two of Boston's many museums. Everything else from ball games to exotic dining to the Quincy Market is within minutes from either marina.

Boston Harbor Islands. A number of islands in Boston Harbor have landing facilities and either slips or anchorages for visitors. These include Georges, Gallops, Lovell, Bumpkin, Peddocks, Great Brewster, and Grape. Most of these provide picnic places, pleasant trails, and good views, and some of them provide for overnight camping. Most are accessible to local residents by excursion boats.

Castle Island, now connected to South Boston by filled land, is notable for a monument to Donald McKay, designer and builder of American clipper ships, and for Fort Independence, where Edgar Allan Poe served as a soldier in the coast artillery. A skeleton found in the walled-up end of a corridor prompted him to write "The Cask of Amontillado." Georges Island, Lovell Island, the Brewsters, and Peddocks Island also have forts built to protect the harbor in early wars. One can land on Little Brewster and see Boston Light, one of the first lighthouses built in the United States. Great Brewster and Outer Brewster still bear signs of military occupation. The emplacements for 16-inch coast defense guns remain on Great Brewster, and the barracks used by those who tended antisubmarine nets stand on Outer Brewster.

While it is conceivable that a cruising man will enter Boston Harbor with eager curiosity, it is certain that he will leave the North Channel, bound east, with enthusiasm.

Marblehead, Massachusetts (13276). This harbor is described as the "yachting capital of the world." Of course, this is an overstatement, but few indeed are the harbors with a longer history of yachting, a more distinguished roster of famous yachts, and a more crowded calendar of present-day racing.

This harbor is wide open to the northeast. Though summer months rarely produce heavy seas and storms from that direction, it is quite another story during the late fall, winter, and early spring. A summer approach to the harbor is truly impressive due to the close-packed spars of the racing fleet, from small day sailers to the most elegant ocean racing yachts. To assist the visitor through the 1,800 moorings in the harbor, a marked channel with unnumbered private aids extends along the western shore from the entrance off Fort Sewall to the public landing at State Street in the heart of "Old Town" Marblehead. Water depth is ample up to the shore in most places.

Boston Yacht Club on the western shore of the harbor and Northern Ocean Marine next to the State Street landing have gasoline and diesel fuel. There are also facilities for haulout, and there is no shortage of marine-related services or products in Marblehead.

The harbormaster monitors channel 16 and can be reached by telephone at (617) 631-2386. There are three major yacht clubs in the harbor. Boston Yacht Club monitors channel 68 and its telephone number is (617) 631-3100. Over on the east side of the harbor, Corinthian Yacht Club near the lighthouse monitors channel 69 and CB-13; its telephone number is (617) 631-0005. Eastern Yacht Club a little farther down the east side monitors channel 69; its telephone number is (617) 631-1400. Marblehead and Dolfin Yacht Clubs on the west side of the harbor above Boston Yacht Club both monitor CB-13. West Shore Marine on the Salem side of Marblehead monitors channel 71.

Visitors should stop at the harbormaster's office on the Cliff Street landing for up-to-date information.

The harbormaster has placed five moorings at the entrance to the harbor. These are free, but they must be reserved in advance. They are suitable for large yachts, but small boats may find them too exposed. Moorings in calmer waters may be arranged through the dockmasters at the several yacht clubs. The charge for guest moorings usually covers launch service. Moorings are available to visitors on most nights except those before the Marblehead-Halifax Race in June and the PHRF New England Championship Regatta on the last weekend in August. If you cannot find a mooring, call West Shore Marine on the Salem side. They operate a launch service to the West Shore Town landing and a unique floating restaurant. The Salem side is shallower, better protected, and attractive, but move cautiously at low water for mooring blocks and mushroom anchors in shoal water can be perilous.

It is a short and pleasant walk to the main street through narrow byways, past small shingled houses and elegant mansions lined with fragrant rose gardens. On the main street are several grocery stores, clothing stores, gift shops, and almost any other kind of emporium you might seek. Pay special attention to Fred Wood's shop at the head of State Street, where such hard-to-find items as wicks and chimneys for various sizes of kerosene cabin lamps, three-arm protractors, yacht club burgees, charts, books, and navigational instruments are found.

Restaurants in various degrees of elegance abound both in Marblehead and in nearby Swampscott and Salem.

There are lovely Colonial and Georgian mansions at Bank and Washington Squares and elsewhere throughout the town, with the Lee Mansion (Marblehead Historical Society) and the King Hooper Mansion (Marblehead Arts Association) the most famous, and open to the public for a small fee. There are many less pretentious, dating from the time when this town was one of America's leading fishing and overseas trading ports. Josiah Cressy, master of the famous clipper *Flying Cloud*, was a Marblehead native, as were General John Glover, who commanded the amphibious regiment that rowed Washington across the Delaware; Elbridge Gerry, a signer of the Declaration of Independence and Vice-President of the United States under President Madison; Captain James Mugford, Revolutionary War hero; and Captain Nicholas Broughton, who commanded the first American naval vessel, the schooner *Hannah*.

The town lays claim to being the birthplace of the American Navy as *Hannah* was indeed commissioned for federal service while lying in Marblehead. The original of the famous painting *The Spirit of '76* hangs in Abbot Hall, where the town offices are located, and whose red-brick tower may be seen for many miles at sea. The old Town House at the lower center of town (head of State Street); St. Michael's Church, oldest Episcopal edifice in New England; the Old North Church, with a Bulfinch tower; the Eagle House, locale of the best-seller *The Hearth and the Eagle;* and Burial Hill, one of several cemeteries containing stones with quaint epitaphs, are other interesting sights.

Flanking the entrance of Marblehead Harbor, which was the home port of the America's Cup defenders *Mayflower, Puritan, Volunteer, Nefertiti,* and *Heritage* and many other historic racing yachts, are two interesting parks. On the starboard hand entering the port is old Fort Sewall, now a town park, whose guns saved U.S.S. *Constitution* during the War of 1812, when Old Ironsides was pursued by a superior British force. At Lighthouse Point is Chandler Hovey Park, given by a former commodore of the Eastern Yacht Club, which provides a superb yachting grandstand during the yachting season, and especially during Marblehead Race Week.

No discussion of Marblehead would be complete without mention of Race Week, once again called Marblehead Mid-Summer One-Design Regatta as it was prior to 1927, and usually held the third week in July. By day, astronomical numbers of boats race in many classes and over many courses. At night, they all moor in Marblehead somehow or dry-sail at clubs and yards surrounding the harbor. The evenings are spent in socializing. It is one of the biggest assemblies of sailing craft to be met with anywhere, and no place for the casual cruising man hoping for an unscheduled opportunity to obtain a mooring.

In 1965, and again in 1966, the federal government offered to build a breakwater at Marblehead to protect the harbor from northeasters. The town was to put up $357,000 and the government $2.6 million. However, the town meeting turned down the proposition in several successive votes. The principal argument against the breakwater was that it would make possible and profitable the construction of marinas at which hundreds of powerboats could berth. Not only would the concentration of power cruisers, with their noisome fumes and irritating wakes, be increased, but it would also narrow the entrance, increase the tidal current, and interfere with race courses which have been traditional for generations.

The Marblehead Town Meeting voted a resounding *No*.

Salem, Massachusetts (13276). Salem Harbor, though shoal, is well sheltered from all except northeast gales, and if you go up the dredged canal to Pickering Wharf, you will be sheltered from every wind.

Follow the buoyed channel around the northeast end of Marblehead and across toward the five stacks on the Salem shore. Two are nearly 500 feet tall, are day/night obstruction lighted, and can be seen for miles offshore. Once in the harbor, you will find moorings on both sides of the channel. There are two full-service marinas in Salem. To the right of the channel is the Hawthorne Cove Marina located in a northerly direction from day beacon 2. Call on channel 9 or follow their private aids. If possible, make a reservation by telephone, at (508) 744-9890.

Another full-service marina is Pickering Wharf Marina up the channel by Derby Wharf just before the bridge over South River. If you would prefer lying on a mooring to tying up in a slip with a city ambience, call Pickering on channel 9 and they can assign you a mooring in the harbor. Pickering's slips are provided with water and electricity and are close to grocery and marine hardware stores, restaurants, and Salem's maritime heritage.

To the left of the channel to Pickering Wharf is a buoyed channel to Palmer Cove Yacht Club, where a slip may be available to members of other yacht clubs.

If repairs are a problem, visit the Fred J. Dion Yacht Yard south of Palmer Point where there is a travelift, a railway, a crane, carpentry, rigging and machine shops, and a sail loft.

No fuel was available in Salem in 1994 unless enough was required to warrant calling a tank truck. Yachts bought fuel in Marblehead or lugged it in cans.

The principal reason for visiting Salem is its history, centered on the Peabody & Essex Museum in East India Square, which has been restored in the early-nineteenth-century tradition with cobbled streets and period buildings. The museum itself could hold a maritime historian for days. Here are models and half-models of sailing vessels from every period of American history, a model of a nineteenth-century shipyard, a fully equipped, full-size Banks fishing dory, and literally hundreds of navigational instruments, tools, paintings, documents, logbooks, and weapons. The exhibits of Chinese, Japanese, and East Indian arts and artifacts are almost unrivaled.

Another historical site is Derby Wharf, now in the process of restoration. Shortly, the construction of a full-size nineteenth-century trading vessel will be started, such a vessel as established Salem as the nation's principal importer of China and East India goods in the early nineteenth century.

There is an award-winning memorial to the victims of Salem's witch-hunting frenzy in the seventeenth century, an incident in New England history best put behind us.

Nathaniel Hawthorne, nineteenth-century novelist, was born in Salem, served as surveyor in the Salem Custom House from 1846 to 1849, and wrote in Salem *The House of the Seven Gables*. That house still stands in its original condition and is open to the public.

Nathaniel Bowditch was a distinguished native of Salem, famous for his *American Practical Navigator*. His correction of previously inaccurate navigational tables and his development of a simplified method for determining longitude by lunar observation led to American supremacy at sea, especially in the China trade. It enabled American shipmasters who knew the method to beat down the China Sea against the monsoon while others waited for a fair wind. He proved the precision of his navigation when he brought his ship *Putnam* into Salem Harbor in a northeast snowstorm on Christmas Eve, 1803. He was homeward bound with a cargo of pepper from Sumatra, had had no observation for two days, had seen no land, and had only several soundings on Georges Bank to establish his position. He saw the loom of Bakers Island and the next thing he saw was Derby Wharf.

Manchester, Massachusetts (13275). This is the pleasantest and most secure harbor on the south side of Cape Ann and consequently is heavily crowded. Permits for 750 moorings have been issued. Although there is no room to anchor, it is usually possible to find a vacant mooring or a place to lie alongside one of the boatyard wharves or floats.

Vessels over 45 feet long belonging to residents must moor outside can 5 in Manchester Bay. However, boatyards can usually accomodate visitors over 45 feet on rental moorings or alongside wharves. The outer anchorage is fair enough protection except in a heavy southwester. Reasonable protection except from an easterly can be found in the cove on the north side of Great Misery. Both Misery Islands belong to the Trustees of Public Reservations and provide excellent picnic spots.

Entrance to the inner harbor is well buoyed and is dredged from time to time. A depth of 7 feet at low water can be carried all the way to the railroad bridge although some shoaling between can 5 and can 7 has reduced the width of the channel. Stay close to can 5 as a bar builds to the eastward of it beyond the channel. After can 7, the throng of moored boats will keep you in the channel. Do not be tempted to anchor in the vacant spot of the constellation of moorings just above the yacht club between nuns 10 and 12. It is occupied by a solid piece of real estate.

Entering Manchester late on a summer afternoon is a little like driving up the Southeast Expressway. You will take your place in a parade of yachts moving single file up a narrow channel at the stately pace of the slowest. Occasionally a small powerboat will swing out of line and tear past like a motorcycle. Call Manchester Marine on channel 72, the harbormaster on channel 12 or 16, the yacht club on channel 78 for a mooring.

Manchester Marine near the head of the harbor can minister to whatever needs you may have. Gasoline, diesel fuel, ice, water, and a pumpout facility are available at the float. On the wharf are showers, telephones, and a well-appointed marine store. The yard has either present or on call seven days a week mechanics, electronics experts, carpenters, sailmakers, and plumbers. If you are in distress outside, the yard can tow you in in response to a radio call. Whatever your problem, consult Rob Hoyle, the manager.

Hooper's Market will deliver an order to the yard on request.

Next to Manchester Marine is the yard of Sam Crocker, grandson of the late S. S. Crocker, designer of many fast and comfortable yachts, many of which were built by his son, the current Sam's father, Sturgis. The yard builds, hauls, stores, and maintains yachts and can attend to almost any emergency.

Visiting yachtsmen may land at Morse Pier in the northeast corner of the harbor, at Reed's Park float opposite Morse Pier, or at the float of Manchester Harbor Boat Club. There is a one-hour tie-up limit at the town floats. Stores and two ice machines are a short walk away. The Historical Society is well worth a visit. The town, while graced with many buildings in the best style of late-Colonial and Federal architecture, strikes a suburban note. It is something of a surprise to step into the suburbs from the salt water.

The harbor is surrounded by handsome houses and well-kept shores, and one of its most attractive features is the multitude of fine yachts. A leisurely dinghy trip through the anchorage is an education in elegance. However, when a real northeaster is forecast and the fleet comes over from Marblehead and Salem to lie three-deep along floats and wharves, one can view as fine an assemblage of yachts as is gathered anywhere on the East Coast.

Beverly, Massachusetts (13276). The next harbor after Salem is Beverly. The harbor is deep and offers good protection in all but a roaring northeaster. Gas, water, and ice are available at the Jubilee Yacht Club floats located to starboard as you enter. The floats have plenty of water with 6 feet the minimum at dead low water. Anchoring is impossible due to the congestion, but moorings are generally available from the dockmaster or launch operators for yachts up to 40 feet. The club is hospitable and offers its launch, showers, and club privileges to members of other clubs.

Entering the harbor is straightforward. Just follow the channel buoys and resist the urge to cut across Monument Bar. Leave the granite monument to port when entering.

Gloucester, Massachusetts (13281). This is a well-protected harbor and easy of access at any time, with lights on Eastern Point breakwater and Ten Pound Island. In heavy weather, enter west of Round Rock. Notice on the western shore a bell on Norman's Woe, where Henry Wadsworth Longfellow wrecked the schooner *Hesperus* in verse. The wreck the poem describes was actually on the ledges off Cape Ann, but the romance of the name Norman's Woe was irresistible to the poet.

Gloucester is interesting as the scene of some of the earliest settlements on this coast. English fishermen were operating successfully from here before the Pilgrims landed at Plymouth. Here were drying stages and camps ashore for the crews who cured the fish. As there was always a rush in the spring for the best sites, it is probable that at an early date fishermen wintered here. Later, recognizing the economic possibilities of the salt-fish trade, Gloucester became one of the leading Massachusetts ports and the headquarters of the Atlantic fishery. With the growth of railroads, Boston became the center for the fresh-fish market, but through the early part of the century, the long main booms of Gloucester schooners swung past Eastern Point to fish on the Grand Banks. *Captains Courageous* took place on one of these vessels.

The Gloucester fishing schooner as developed in the early years of this century, like the clipper ship, the downeaster, and the great coal schooner, was one of the climaxes of the art of sailing ship design. She was well adapted to her intended use, fast, able, and overwhelmingly good-looking. She became the prototype for many successful yachts before modern materials and ultra-light design brought significant changes. To get some idea of what Gloucester schooners were like, read Albert Cook Church's *American Fishermen* and Joseph E. Garland's *Down to the Sea*. Howard Chapelle's *The American Fishing Schooner* is a technical and less colorful volume but is the ultimate authority on the subject. For a view of modern Gloucester fishermen, read Kim Bartlett's *The Finest Kind*.

As a memorial to the fishermen who have been lost from Gloucester, there has been erected, on the boulevard on the west side of the harbor, a stirring bronze statue of a fisherman at the wheel of a schooner. It is well worth seeing.

Although the fishing industry is nothing like what it used to be, Gloucester is still a busy fishing port. At the same time, it is making conscious efforts to be attractive to visitors both by land and by sea. There are several possible anchorages in Gloucester.

Eastern Point. Just inside the breakwater is Eastern Point Yacht Club, which maintains a number of guest moorings. This anchorage is sometimes rolly as seas bend around the end of the breakwater and is occasionally agitated by the wakes of big fishermen. In a heavy north-wester, it can be rough. However, it is quiet and cool, and unless one is in need of supplies or repairs, it is a most convenient stopping place.

One can land at the yacht club float where there is 8 feet alongside, but beware of a rock with only 3 feet over it south of the float. There is a water pipe, but no fuel is available.

The club has a bar and a dining room in very attractive surroundings. It serves meals to visitors, but reservations are recommended on Satur-day nights.

There is no store nearby.

One correspondent who cruises in a shoal-draft boat recommends Lighthouse Cove just north of the Eastern Point anchorage as a quieter spot but suggests anchoring bow and stern to face any incoming surge.

Smith Cove. Farther up the harbor on the east side behind Rocky Neck is the best protection in Gloucester. It is, therefore, densely crowded. Call the Gloucester police boat on channel 16 for the pos-sibility of a vacant mooring. At the head of the cove is Bickford's marina with a float selling fuel and providing fresh water. There may be an open slip here. The marina has a crane and a railway and can arrange repairs to hull and engine. Beacon Marine on the east side of the cove near its mouth can haul and repair the largest yachts. The wharves on the west side of Smith Cove are bases for party fishing and whale-watching boats, and some provide tie-ups for customers of waterfront restaurants. Rocky Neck is an active artist colony abounding in studio-galleries and small esoteric shops, yet with a large commercial marine railway at its northern end.

On the west side of the cove most easily reached from Bickford's is a small but adequate grocery.

Gloucester Inner Harbor. Behind the red-and-green flasher where the channels to the inner harbor divide, there may be a vacant mooring or room to anchor. Call the police boat on channel 16 for guidance. Although this is a secure enough anchorage in ordinary weather, it is wide open to the south and could not be described as peaceful or attractive. The ambience is urban. However, it is convenient to stores and restaurants and to Brown's Yacht Yard on the east shore, which can take care of almost any need a yacht may have. At the head of the northern channel of the inner harbor is Three Lanterns, one of the most complete marine supply stores in New England. Here, too, is a rigging loft which can supply, invent, or fabricate whatever any yacht or commercial vessel might require. To walk through it is an education.

Grocery stores are a short bus or taxi ride away.

Harbor Cove. The *Coast Pilot* declares that there is an anchorage off the Coast Guard base on the northerly point of Harbor Cove, but it appears to be a troubled berth. There is a town landing near the head of the cove on the west side where one can tie a dinghy and be right in town. In the event of a heavy northwest breeze, one might anchor in Western Harbor west of the entrance to the Annisquam Canal, but the shore is foul and the berth in any other breeze would be exposed.

Many yachts visit Gloucester for the annual Schooner Festival on the Labor Day weekend. It is a gala event with a fish fry ashore and races for traditional craft like catboats and Friendship sloops. The big attraction is the Mayor's Race for big schooners like *Spirit of Massachusetts* and *Adventure* of the type Gloucester fishermen used a century ago.

Annisquam River and Blynman Canal (13281). This is one of the busiest stretches of water in New England, constantly agitated by commercial fishermen, party boats, fast motorboats, and cruising yachts, both sail and power. One should not even approach the passage without Chart 13281 and an effective horn. The motor must be in reliable condition, especially as regards the reverse gear, for the tide, flooding in from both ends and meeting more or less in the middle, runs 4 knots at times under the bridges near the Gloucester end. If a bridgetender is slow or if a train is coming so the railroad bridge must be closed, it may take all the reverse that a low-powered auxiliary can muster to hold back against the current. There is scant room to turn, and no sailing vessel maneuvers well when going backward. This problem may arise unexpectedly if you are bound north, for the flood tide can set you down very hard on the first bridge as you enter from Gloucester Harbor and vessels bound south seem to have the right of way.

When a bridge does open, proceed cautiously. Heedless motorboats, familiar with the canal, sometimes come through at excessive speeds and with little concern for the cautious. Yet note that the bridges are narrow and the current is often swift, so that to maintain positive control of your vessel, considerable speed may be necessary.

The buoyage seemed reliable in 1992, but the channel is dredged through sand and mud, so bars build up and points make out. In general, favor the outside of a curve. Move carefully at low water.

Heronway Marina, Rust Island.   On a creek just south of the high fixed bridge carrying Route 128 is the Heronway Marina. The channel to it has a depth of 3 feet at low water. Fuel and minor supplies are available but it is primarily a facility for small boats.

Cape Ann Marina.   Between the railroad and Blynman bridges is the Cape Ann Marina, which has an enormous complex with literally hundreds of slips and every service the yachtsman could ask for except peace and quiet. There is little of that commodity on Cape Ann and none on the Annisquam River.

Gasoline, diesel oil, water, and ice are available on the outer float, where a brief tie-up is permitted. From June to September the float is manned from 7 A.M. to 7 P.M., on Friday and Saturday nights until 10 P.M. Hours are shorter during off seasons. Slips with water, electricity, and 24-hour security are available for transients. Showers, toilets, and laundry machines are located at the head of the wharf. A restaurant open from 5 A.M. until 11 P.M. is adjacent.

Close to the head of the wharf is a small store carrying a few simple groceries and various nautical novelties, such as T-shirts emblazoned with clever remarks, and the usual array of gifts. If you need more substantial supplies, call a cab.

Motel accommodations are available for those who prefer to sleep ashore.

On the same site is a 20-ton lift, which can be opened to take a masted vessel. They also have a 30-ton Brownell trailer. Your boat can be set up on a cradle in the yard where you can get at her or relaunched at once if all you need to do is change a wheel or slap on a coat of copper paint. For extensive repairs, Enos Marine has carpenters and mechanics. Damaged sails can be repaired in Gloucester or Marblehead. Behind the extensive parking lot is a well-appointed marine store selling paint, hardware, and many difficult-to-replace accessories, which are so easily broken or lost overboard.

A charter fishing fleet is based at the Cape Ann Marina to complete the services at a "complete service" establishment. Except that the surrounding marshes provide no very inspiring views, the constant traffic on the Canal and the bridges is disturbing, and the whole idea of 300 yachts crowded together is just not what we had in mind, the Cape Ann Marina is one of the best stopping places on Cape Ann.

South of the 128 bridge, one enters the Blynman Canal, a cut through the neck of Cape Ann to Gloucester Harbor. Bridgetenders can be reached on channel 13. The first bridge is a railroad bridge on a sharp turn in the channel. Approach cautiously, blow the horn vigorously, and keep far to the port side of the channel. Trains have the right of way. If the bridge does not open, you can probably turn around in the channel and stem the tide until it does. When the bridge opens, proceed with caution, and continue to sound the horn until you can see around the corner. There really is not room for two vessels to pass in the draw.

There is no sharp turn at the highway bridge but the current runs harder. If traffic is heavy, the bridge does not always open as rapidly as one in a boat might hope. The bridge was under repair in early 1993 and opened only on the hour. No one would state when repairs would be completed. Beyond the bridge in Gloucester Harbor there is shoal water and rocky bottom on both sides of the dredged channel. Run out to the red-and-white buoy and proceed from there.

On approaching the highway bridge from the south with a flood tide, beware of a brisk current running north through the draw. It will affect you at the red-and-white buoy, and with increasing force as you approach the bridge. Bridge operators monitor channel 13.

The well-known monument to Gloucester fishermen lost at sea faces Gloucester Harbor from the parkway east of the Canal. It is a stirring sculpture of a fisherman at the wheel of a schooner, well worth a visit if you have time ashore, and certainly worth a respectful glance through binoculars as you pass.

Annisquam, Massachusetts (13281). In ordinary summer weather the eastward-bound mariner will do well to motor through the Annisquam Canal and spend the night off the Annisquam Yacht Club, especially with an ebb tide in the morning. From Gloucester he would have to fight the tide all the way from Eastern Point to Thachers Island. From Annisquam, once he is clear of the river, the tide is negligible and he can head directly for Portsmouth, the Isles of Shoals, or Seguin. Also, the southwest breeze often draws pleasantly off the high land of Cape Ann before it strikes in off shore. Sometimes it can be more vigorous than merely pleasant.

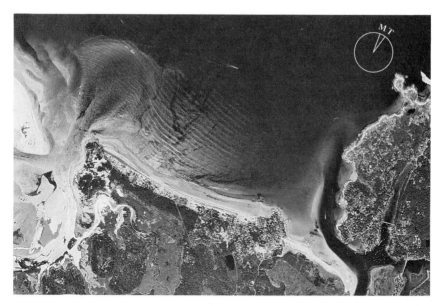

Castle Neck, the mouth of the Ipswich River, and the mouth of the Annisquam River. Notice the bar and the shoals along the channel in the Annisquam River. *Courtesy James W. Sewall Co.*

The westward-bound cruiser, after an offshore passage, may be happy to stop in Annisquam rather than motor through the Canal and roll in the anchorage under the Gloucester breakwater.

Entering from the north presents little difficulty for yachts of moderate draft in smooth weather. Three lighted bells and Annisquam Light cover the entrance with considerable margin for error. Even when fog is thick offshore, there is likely to be a good scale-up to leeward of Cape Ann off the entrance to the river. Make bell 2 off the channel dredged through the bar and follow the buoys up the river. Move a little cautiously, for the channel shifts and silts up between dredgings. If you are coming in at the end of the day, especially on a summer weekend, you will be assailed by a throng of high-powered outboard motorboats and sportfishermen, who have been lashing the waters of Ipswich Bay in quest of bluefish. They are all in a hurry, and only a few seem to have any concern for a low-powered auxiliary.

Either call the Annisquam Yacht Club on channel 68 or hail their float behind can 13 for a mooring. If there is no response, pick one up and await the club launch. Their moorings are white and orange. Beware of a $4^1/_2$-foot spot southeast of can 13 abreast the beacon to port. Leave can

13 to port and hug the line of small sailboats up to the float. Consult the manager, Bobby Marsolais. Dinner is served at the yacht club by reservation. There is a formal dining room where coat and tie are expected in addition to a snack bar where sailing clothes are fine.

If you cannot get a yacht-club mooring at the mouth of Lobster Cove, call Lobster Cove Market on channel 9. The market and its associated marina maintains several moorings and has some dock space near the head of the cove on the northern side. Gasoline, water, and ice are available at the marina float, where there is 8 feet of water at low tide. The market provides a variety of groceries, meats, seafoods, beer, and wine. There is a small restaurant and tables on the wharf where lunches and simple meals are served. From the head of the bridge above the market buses run to Gloucester where all kinds of marine supplies are available.

It is possible to anchor off the beach across the river from the entrance to Lobster Cove, but the holding ground is doubtful, the tide runs hard, the constant traffic is disturbing, and the area is crowded with moorings.

There is no boatyard in Lobster Cove, but Wheeler's Point Boat Yard about ½ mile up the Canal on the eastern side monitors channel 68, can tow you off the mud, and has an excellent mechanic.

Keep away from Annisquam in heavy weather, especially with the wind to the north and east. The seas break on the bar all across the entrance, and even the dredged channel is too shoal to be negotiated in heavy seas. In December 1975, *Aquarius,* a stout Nova Scotia fishing vessel converted to a yacht, was lost on Wingaersheek Beach. The skipper with an able crew left Portsmouth for Boston and had an easy run to Annisquam. When he found that the drawbridge could not be opened and a northeaster was forecast, he decided to go back to Portsmouth late in the afternoon. In the dark and snow, he missed the buoys off the mouth of the Piscataqua River and decided to ride out the gale at sea. In the morning he saw a flashing bell to leeward and ran in to identify it. He got into shoal water; breaking seas stove in his windshield, flooded the cockpit, and drowned out the engine. He tried to anchor, but the anchor dragged in the sandy bottom under the attack of the short, steep seas. He ordered the life raft inflated, burned flares, and had each person wear two life jackets. The boat filled and capsized, trapping two people under her. The skipper and two others fought their way ashore through the surf. One made his way to a cottage, whose inhabitants rescued the other two on the beach. Three others were lost. *Aquarius* drifted ashore on the beach and before noon was completely stripped by the local inhabitants.

Cape Ann, Massachusetts (13278, 13279). Rounding Cape Ann at night can be confusing. Thachers Island, an excellent mark by day with its twin towers, shows a red light with a 5-second flash at night, almost the same characteristic as Eastern Point; and each has a green flash to the northwestward of it. One navigator, admittedly very tired and confused, lost a schooner on Straitsmouth Island, thinking he was in Gloucester Harbor.

Clearing Thachers is no guarantee of safety, for Milk Island, the Londoner, and the Salvages are low, are not easily seen in fog or darkness, and extend far out under water. Furthermore, there is a submerged breakwater at the entrance to Sandy Bay. It was intended to provide a secure and accessible harbor of refuge for the Navy, but it was never finished and is now a menace. The area is well buoyed, however. Both ends of the breakwater are marked with lighted buoys, and there is a string of bells and whistles outside of all dangers. There is a radio direction finder station on Eastern Point, but the skipper is warned to be suspicious of radio bearings taken over high land.

Do not enter Sandy Bay between Straitsmouth Island and Gap Head.

It was on the ledges off Cape Ann that Longfellow's *Hesperus* was wrecked. The poem is an imaginative account of an actual incident. The skipper who wishes to impress his crew with the perils of a winter northeaster can read the poem aloud. However, in ordinary summer weather and with ordinary seamanlike caution, Cape Ann presents no great danger.

Rockport, Massachusetts (13279). Unless the visitor has friends here who can arrange with the harbormaster for a mooring or a chance to lie alongside one of the few wharves, Rockport is too crowded for the cruising man. It may be a foreshadowing of what we are coming to elsewhere. Yachts are moored fore and aft; an air view looks a little like a freshly opened sardine can. With boats rafted alongside those moored, it is almost literally possible to walk across the harbor. A channel is kept open for party boats and fishermen, most of whom have moorings in the inner harbor.

In an effort to discourage visitors, a town ordinance prohibits the sale of gasoline and diesel oil from the wharves. Fishermen lug fuel in cans, and the party boats fuel from tank trucks, which come down early in the morning. Water and ice are available at the yacht club, but you will not be allowed to lie at the float. Tie up alongside the pilings on the end of the wharf.

Rockport is not inhospitable, just crowded.

On a quiet night, yachts lie north of the breakwater off the beach. The holding ground is said to be good, and there is usually ample room to swing. A marina maintains several moorings. Call the Rockport harbor-master on channel 9 or 16. Land at the marina or row up to the yacht club. If there is any likelihood of the wind's coming off to the east, keep away from Sandy Bay. Gloucester is the nearest safe refuge.

Ashore, Rockport is unusual. It is an old fishing town which has been so "appreciated" that the appreciators and those who feed on them have submerged the town they came to appreciate. Bearskin Neck, which extends to the base of the breakwater on the north side of the harbor, used to support a nondescript collection of fish houses and camps. Some of the fish houses are still there, and replicas fill the spaces of those that have fallen down. Each is now the site of a gift shop, an artist's studio, or a craft shop. The street is crowded with sightseers and shoppers, most of whom will not be there tomorrow. The main street has a number of restaurants and coffee shops. Back from the shore a discreet three-quarters of a mile is a shopping center where the usual groceries are available. A bus runs to Gloucester and Annisquam.

A quaint town of old houses and winding streets, Rockport has a year-round population of 3,500. Settled in the late 1600s, it was a part of Gloucester until 1840. During the War of 1812, a British man-of-war bombarded the settlement, lobbing one cannonball into the steeple of the Congregational church, where it still remains. In the latter half of the 1800s, Rockport was famous for its granite quarries, and the stone for many a public building and the paving blocks of streets in many an Eastern city came from Rockport—hewn out of the quarries by Finnish, Swedish, and Irish quarrymen.

Just west of T-wharf is an old stone pier surmounted by a red fish-house. Paintings and drawings of it have appeared in countless exhibitions, and it is known to artists as Rockport's Motif Number One. It was destroyed in the great gale of February 1978. What remains today is a mock-up.

In the summer Rockport attracts busloads and carloads of visitors. Dressed in the most unconventional attire, they crowd the sidewalks and stores. They spill out into the streets. One frustrated resident writes in a letter that a helicopter is necessary to get from one place to another. To the yachtsman, Rockport is a good shelter, but it is a crowded harbor and a very busy town.

Granite Company Cove, Pigeon Cove, Lane's Cove, and Hodgkin's Cove are marginal shelters at best. With rocky bottom, small room to swing, few if any shore facilities, and a pervasive roll when there is any sea running outside, they are in general to be passed by. Anchorage north of the Rockport breakwater is to be preferred if no berth is available in Rockport Harbor.

Note on Leaving Cape Ann Bound East

As he passes the bell outside Annisquam or Thacher Island and the hills of Cape Ann drop astern, the eastward-bound skipper finds himself suddenly alone at sea and on his own. Ahead lie 65 miles of beach, stretching to Cape Elizabeth and the coves of Casco Bay. The only harbors suitable for deep-draft boats in any kind of a sea are Isles of Shoals, Portsmouth, York, and Cape Porpoise. All the others are shoal and have bars at the entrances. Even the harbors mentioned are not easy for the stranger in the fog, and on a foggy night to approach the shore anywhere along here would be foolhardy.

On a hazy day, the landmarks on the shore are difficult for the stranger to pick out. One cupola, water tower, or spire marked on the chart looks much like another. Lights and buoys are far apart. To add to the confusion, fishermen and big vessels making for Gloucester, Portsmouth, and Portland traverse these waters at high speed. Their whirling radar antennae are reassuring, but one wonders whether anyone is looking at the screen.

Finally, in the event of an easterly gale, the whole coast becomes a dangerous lee shore.

Nevertheless, if you are to enjoy the bays and islands of Maine, you have to cross this stretch. There are many things in your favor. White Island and Boon Island are prominent landmarks by day and night, the latter marked by a whistle buoy, as well as by a lighthouse and fog signal. There are large whistle buoys off York, Cape Porpoise, and Wood Island. At Whaleback, the Nubble, Goat Island, and Wood Island are lighthouses recognizable by day and prominent at night. The big light on

Cape Elizabeth and the bright quick flash on the Large Navigational Buoy (LNB) at Portland provide leading marks. To the skipper who has been this way before, the big hotel at Little Boars Head, the great white Wentworth Hotel at Portsmouth, Mount Agamenticus, Bald Head Cliff, and the watertowers at Cape Porpoise and Fortune's Rocks will be familiar landmarks. Gales are rare in summer and are usually well advertised. There isn't much to hit if you keep well clear of the land, Isles of Shoals, and Boon Island, and you will probably have a fair wind. Be sure of your compass. Lash a big radar reflector in the rigging, and strike out for Maine. You will probably have a lovely sail down east before a summer southwester and see the sun set behind the White Mountains.

Many navigators prefer to head directly for Seguin or Monhegan, making an overnight run of it. It seems that often, when there is a flat calm under the land, the southwesterly breeze airs along offshore at about 10 knots, often working considerably to the west during the night. One yachtsman who has made this run "scores of times" speaks of an easterly set. Between Isles of Shoals and the Portland LNB, both inside and outside Boon Island, the writer has found a northwesterly set both on flood and ebb. The navigator will do well to check his position frequently. The RDF on Monhegan is very powerful. That line, crossed with bearings on the Portland LNB and Halfway Rock, can be reassuring.

Of this run an experienced cruising man writes:

> In almost all cases we make the run on a tight schedule and always with a very experienced crew of four or five. In spite of having everything with us, I've run into more bad going in the Cape Ann to Casco Bay stretch than anywhere else, including east of Schoodic, Nova Scotia, or New Brunswick. The notes that follow are not intended to scare the cruising fraternity but I believe the real dangers in this specific 75-mile run should be pointed out.
>
> 1. There is frequently a major weather change along the route. Very often it is fine from Squam to York, but miserable beyond. Two years ago a nice SE breeze turned into a green-water-in-the-cockpit event, beginning at Wood Island. It was so bad that we had to put into the uninhabited islands of Saco Bay for overnight protection.
>
> 2. Really only two harbors on the whole route can be safely entered in a blow, particularly with poor visibility. The most frequently recommended, Cape Porpoise, is probably the worst. In

spite of the offshore whistle, inner bell, and Goat Island Light, you need only come on the land some 50 yards off course and you are in serious trouble on the ledges. Number-one choice by far is Wood Island. Its two approaches always provide a good lee; whether entering from east or west, the light is prominent and on a bold shore. Buoyage is excellent, regardless of the approach. The only precaution one need take is: avoid a southerly-sector approach to avoid the ledges off Fletchers Neck. The second reasonably easy entrance is Portsmouth, for obvious reasons. I cannot emphasize too strongly that Newburyport, York, Kennebunkport, Cape Porpoise, and Richmond Island are to be avoided, except under good sailing conditions.

3. When crossing even small bays along this route the going can be extremely rough even in NW breezes, when you would believe fair protection would be likely. Also, Portland Harbor entrance, including Cape Elizabeth, can be bad. This locale has been consistently the worst we have encountered along this stretch and this includes the Kennebec inside of Seguin.

4. The on-shore tide set from Portsmouth onward is a major navigation hazard. In spite of the fact that we make a major compensation for this effect we almost always fall inside of the anticipated landfall, particularly at the Cape Porpoise or Wood Island sea buoys.

Lest you believe I'm being overly pessimistic, I want to re-emphasize that I'm talking about making long hauls during the early summer and fall, when poor visibility is the rule. It is also true that we push along in spite of poor going, which would probably discourage the cruising man with time to spare. The point is that weather conditions can change quickly and the casual afternoon sail turns into a situation that makes it necessary to seek shelter in a hurry. Add some fog and darkness and a real party can result.

Essex, Massachusetts (13279). The approach to Essex is marked by a flashing green bell on the edge of the 3-fathom curve. In rough weather, keep well outside it and have nothing to do with any of the harbors in Ipswich Bay. Inside the bell are buoys marking the deepest water over a shallow bar. Local knowledge advises entering only on a calm day with a rising tide. Don't trust the buoys. The privately maintained orange and white buoys are said to be more reliable than the government buoys.

Inside the bar the depths drop off dramatically. In Essex Bay there is a good anchorage just behind Castle Neck, but it is apt to be crowded and noisy on weekends. Dredging the river to a depth of 4 feet all the way into town is planned for the fall of 1993. If one follows closely the well-marked channel, it is possible to travel through the beautiful marshes all the way up to the Route 133 bridge over the Essex Causeway.

There are three marinas. Essex Marina is just for storage and small engine repairs. Pike Marine has gas and does engine repair. Perkins Marine Inc. has full facilities: a travelift, boat transport, ice, gas, a launching ramp, and possibly slips if one calls ahead at (508) 768-7145. By calling Ed Perkins ahead, you may also be able to tie up temporarily to get supplies or visit the small but excellent Essex Shipbuilding Museum.

Essex has been a shipbuilding town since before 1668 when the town landing, just at the bridge on the causeway, was set aside for the purpose. Her white-oak and pine forests and her protected marshes were ideal for the industry. Over the centuries more than 4,000 ships were built in the yards which lined the river. Chebacco boats originated here, as did pinkies. Essex is most famous, however, for her beautiful fishing schooners, still being built in the early part of the twentieth century, including the *Columbia, Mayflower, Esperanto, Puritan,* and *Henry Ford.* Two small wooden-boat operations continue this tradition. Anyone interested in the history and craft of wooden shipbuilding should seek out Dana Story's *The Building of a Wooden Ship, Frame Up!,* and *Hail Columbia.* Albert Cook Church's *American Fishermen* is a remarkably complete photographic study of the building and operation of the Gloucester schooners, and Howard Chapelle's *American Fishing Schooners* is a thorough and detailed technical study of the vessels.

The Shipbuilding Museum contains boat-building tools, fully rigged models, and original builders' half-models from the Smithsonian Watercraft collection, plans, documents, photographs, hands-on exhibits for children, videos of boatbuilding in progress, and a full-scale replica of the frames for the schooner *Rob Roy* on the ways. Its largest exhibit, 91-foot fishing schooner *Evelina M. Goulart* built in 1927, is on display at the town landing.

Along the causeway are Colonial homes, old churches, antique shops, lodgings, and restaurants. Tom Shea's Restaurant has tie-up facilities while you dine or shop.

Essex is also famous for its clam industry. Woodman's has been frying clams at the same location since 1916. There are also two grocery stores and a drug store within walking distance.

Plum Island Sound, Massachusetts (13282). For the shoal-draft cruiser, this is an ideal place to explore. Most of the shore is salt marsh or sand dune, and much of it, including almost all of Plum Island and some of the western shore, is maintained by the U.S. Fish and Wildlife Service as a refuge. Water birds, particularly, are abundant. Many different species breed here or visit the island on their migrations.

No very satisfactory directions for entering Plum Island Sound can be given, because the bar is constantly changing and the buoys are moved in an effort to keep pace. One local authority states flatly that if you follow the buoys, you are sure to go aground. Another adds that at half-tide or better you can cross the bar anywhere, even where the buoys are. You have to go by the color of the water and the way the seas lump up over the shoal spots. The bottom is all sand, except for one ledge off the end of Plum Island.

Several rivers run into the Sound. The Ipswich River is said to be staked out; but as there is almost no water in it at low water, outboard skiffs are about the only traffic on it. Fox Creek is now silted up so as to be virtually no longer navigable.

The mouth of the Parker River is obstructed by a sandbar which shifts from time to time, but the channel above is deeper and at half-tide or better the river could be described as navigable. The wooded shores and salt marshes are pretty and abound with bird life. At the first bridge is Fernald Marine with a landing, a marine store, and a good mechanic. They do not sell gasoline, but just above the bridge is Riverfront Marine, which sells gasoline but not diesel fuel. They have a store, a small railway, a travelift, and extensive floats.

Behind Fernald's and a bit east of it is the shop of the Pert Lowell Company run by Mr. Lowell's son-in-law, Ralph Johnson. Years ago Mr. Lowell adapted the traditional Swampscott dory to sail and originated the popular Town Class. The shop is still building these as well as other small wooden boats and is almost the only place where one can buy mast hoops for gaff-rigged boats, wooden fairleads, deadeyes, and lizards.

There is a passage spanned by a narrow drawbridge from the northern end of Plum Island Sound into the Merrimac River. Unless it has been recently dredged, a tall man with a good pair of boots could walk up what channel remains at low water. However, with 8 feet of tide a shoal-draft boat could get through. It is more of an adventure than a navigable passage.

The channel, such as it is, turns sharply west to the north of the bridge and skirts the eastern side of Woodbridge Island. Beware of a ruined breakwater abreast the northern part of the island.

The northern part of Plum Island is thickly settled, mostly with summer beach cottages. The southern part is included in the Parker River Wildlife Refuge and is populated mostly by muskrats, foxes, ducks, geese, and a wealth of other birds. The eastern side is all beach, backed by sand dunes overgrown with coarse grass, beach plum, and wild rosebushes. There is a rough road down the western side on the edge of the marsh, which is a little easier walking than the soft sand of the beach. The Puritan judge Samuel Sewall reflected on the natural wealth and beauty of Plum Island about 1650:

> And as long as Plum Island shall faithfully keep the commanded post, notwithstanding all the hectoring words and hard blows of the proud and boisterous ocean; as long as any salmon or sturgeon shall swim in the streams of Merrimac, or any perch or pickerel in Crane Pond; as long as the sea-fowl shall know the time of their coming, and not neglect seasonably to visit the places of their acquaintance; as long as any cattle shall be fed with the grass growing in the meadows which do humbly bow down themselves before Turkey Hill; as long as any sheep shall walk down upon the river Parker and the fruitful marshes lying beneath; as long as any free and harmless doves shall find a white oak or other tree within the township to perch or feed or build a careless nest upon, and shall voluntarily present themselves to perform the office of gleaners after barley harvest; as long as nature shall not grow old and dote, but shall constantly remember to give the rows of Indian corn their education by pairs: so long shall Christians be born there, and being first made meet, shall from thence be translated, to be made partakers of the Inheritance of the saints in light.

Newburyport, Massachusetts (13282). Newburyport is well worth a visit, and the city is doing all it can to make the visit easy and interesting. However, the navigation of the Merrimac River demands careful attention. This river drains most of eastern and central New

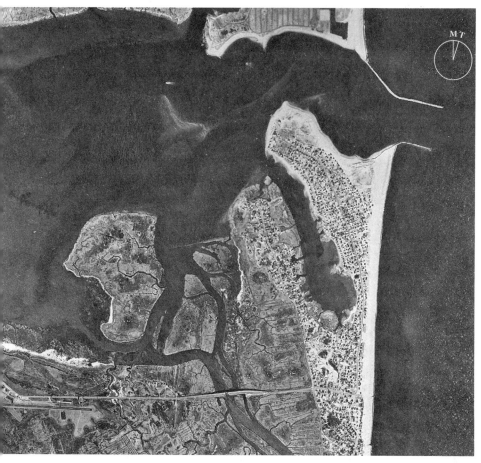

Entrance to the Merrimac River. The "cross" shown on the chart is the dark spot between Plum Island beach and the inlet. The shoals in the river and the tortuous channel inside Plum Island are clearly shown. *Courtesy James W. Sewall Co.*

Hampshire, bringing down not only a great rush of fresh water but considerable sand, mud, and silt. This torrent rushes out through a channel varying from 150 yards wide at can 17 to 350 yards between the jetties. When it meets the sea, the sand, mud, and silt drop out and form a bar outside the jetties. However, the flood tide twice a day stems this current and provides slack water at every turn of the tide and a fair current on which to enter. Also the channel through the bar is kept dredged to about 8 feet at low water. Yachts, fishing vessels, and party boats regularly cross the bar by day and night. Only in a vigorous easterly is the bar dangerous, a rare occurrence in the summer. The usual summer southwester blows off the Plum Island shore and builds up little sea.

As one approaches from offshore, the most obvious landmark is the dome of the Seabrook power station. This is not shown on the chart now current but is located in the town of Seabrook west of Hampton Harbor. In trying to distinguish tank from standpipe on this more or less featureless shore, remember that a tank stands on legs and a standpipe is like a great beer can standing on the ground. The two most obvious and useful tanks are the ones at Great Boars Head and Salisbury Beach. As you get closer, more landmarks appear.

Coming from Cape Ann or offshore, make the red-and-white MR whistle about a mile southeast of the jetties. The cross on the chart surmounts a cupola on a church, the largest building on Plum Island, but the cross itself is difficult to see. A flashing light with a red daymark on the northern shore shows a red sector over the shoals south of the channel and a white sector over the channel through the bar. It is obscured elsewhere. The ends of the jetties are unmarked, but there is a flashing red bell (6 seconds) inside the north jetty to be left close to starboard and a can off the south jetty. The next mark is a flashing green buoy to be left to port, and then another red flasher (4 seconds). There are three lights on the point to port. The most obvious and most useful is an occulting green light on a white conical tower. Then there is a violent quick-flashing strobe light on the roof of the Coast Guard station which, when it is activated, shouts "DANGER ROUGH BAR." It is intended to warn people coming out of the river and does not show well to seaward. It is activated, says the *Coast Pilot*, when seas on the bar exceed 2 feet. The writer, after spending several days in Newburyport during which vessels came and went over the bar frequently, concluded that it flashed on almost every ebb tide. If it is flashing, the bar is not necessarily dangerous; if it is extinguished, the bar is not necessarily safe. In approaching the entrance, remember that breaking seas seen from seaward look less dangerous than they are and from landward, more dangerous. The third light is a low-powered $2^{1}/_{2}$-second light marking the east side of the channel leading south to the west of the Coast Guard station. This inlet is usually crowded with small shoal-draft craft.

Coming from the eastward, one need not go out to the whistle. Make red bell 2 and round the north jetty.

Once inside, there is no difficulty following the channel up the river. Just be sure the current doesn't set you sideways onto the flats. On the ebb tide, do not round can 17 closely and turn in toward the American Yacht Club but go well by the can. This very hospitable club may be able to provide a mooring and a water hose. However, there is much to be said for pressing on up the river and calling the harbormaster on channel 9 for a berth alongside the city floats on the south side. Here you can lie alongside over night and visit the attractions of Newburyport conveniently. If you prefer a mooring, the harbormaster can direct you to one. You will lie to the tide, perhaps at times stern to the wind. Anything you drop overboard is gone. Rowing ashore can be quite an exercise, possibly landing you a considerable distance below your destination.

Fuel is available at Hilton's yard just below the bridge. The yard has a 100-ton lift and is equipped to make all kinds of repairs. Hudson's, just below Hilton's, has a good marine store, and nearby Rowe's sells and services electronic equipment.

Newburyport was a thriving trading and shipbuilding town in 1811 when its waterfront was wiped out by fire. The entire business district was soon rebuilt of brick to Federal standards of taste and construction and served the city well until Boston dominated Massachusetts trade with vessels too deep to cross the Merrimac River bar. Business fell off, the buildings were neglected or abandoned, and the wooden roofs leaked and fell in. In the 1970s when the city underwent an urban renewal program, the old buildings, still structurally sound, were restored to their original appearance and now present a gracious nineteenth-century air of stability, prosperity, and a certain elegance. Especially worth visiting is the old granite Custom House, now housing a maritime museum.

There is a White Hen Pantry nearby which carries sufficient provision to stave off starvation. Consult the harbormaster in his office next to the floats for a ride to the supermarket and for showers and laundry facilities. The Captain's Quarters behind Hilton's yard and The Starboard Galley east of the floats are attractive restaurants near the shore.

Buses run regularly to Boston and Portland.

In the event of really heavy weather such as a hurricane, proceed up the river through the bridge. Call on channel 16 and shift to 13 between 6 A.M. and 10 P.M. in the summer. There are several boatyards above the bridge with rental moorings in well-protected waters.

There are several eighteenth- and nineteenth-century houses that have been preserved as museums, among others, the Cushing House Museum owned by the Historical Society of Old Newbury. From the Custom House, walk up Fair Street and Fruit Street to High Street. The museum is on the corner to your right. You can get directions here to other historic sites, particularly to the house of Lord Timothy Dexter, merchant, author, and self-styled nobleman, who flourished in Newburyport's prosperous trading center days. One of those men who couldn't fail at anything, he shipped a load of warming pans to the West Indies. Contrary to the gloomy predictions of the more conservative merchants of Newburyport, he made a handsome profit. The warming pans were in great demand to dip molasses out of vats into hogsheads. A load of fur mittens in the same port netted a handsome profit when his ship encountered a Russian making up a cargo for home, with iron and flax to trade.

This eccentric gentleman wanted to be called "Lord" Timothy Dexter in defiance of the Constitution, and he offered to pave the main street of Newburyport in return for the handle to his name. Newburyport turned him down, but Danvers said that at that price he could call himself anything he wanted, and he moved to that town.

In his declining years he published a book, *A Pickle for the Knowing Ones.* The spelling and punctuation in the first edition were so unusual that he was much criticized. The second edition appeared with several pages of assorted punctuation and the advice, "Reader may pepper and salt to taste."

Almost any citizen of Newburyport can direct you to Timothy Dexter's house and add more legends to the sample above. The late John P. Marquand, himself a citizen of Newburyport, wrote a delightful book on his unusual fellow citizen.

Another authority is quoted as having said, "The story of Timothy Dexter is the story of Newburyport rum inside a fool."

Hampton, New Hampshire (13278). This harbor is of almost no use to the cruising yacht. There was a reported 4.7 feet on the bar at the entrance in 1986, and even at high water it would be impassable with any sea running. The bridge is manned at half-tide or better. Check by calling on VHF-16, 68, or 13.

The first wharves are reserved primarily for party boats and fishermen. A visiting yacht should bear around to starboard, following the channel, which is marked by local buoys if at all, to Hampton Beach Marina. The marina is crowded with local boats but will find room for transients if possible. There are no moorings available and anchorage space is severely limited. However, gasoline, diesel oil, water, ice, and marine supplies are available. A forklift and a launching ramp are located at the marina. Showers, laundry machines, and toilets are available.

As a refuge in bad weather Hampton is useless because of the shoal and difficult entrance. In good weather, there are better places.

The town is jammed into a narrow space between marsh and beach, traversed by Route 1A. It supports the usual grocery stores, a large number of restaurants, and a great many summer cottages, built upon the sand as close to high water as winter gales permit. Hampton, Rye, and Portsmouth harbors were dredged to project depth in 1987.

Rye Harbor, New Hampshire (13283). While small, Rye is the first harbor north of Cape Ann without a bar at its entrance. It is marked by a red-and-white "MoA" whistle about three-quarters of a mile outside the entrance, by a green can on a 5-foot rock off the south jetty and by a red flashing light on the north jetty with a high-intensity beam to seaward.

The harbor was dredged in 1990 and is reported to have 10 feet in the channel and 8 feet in the mooring area. It is a small and crowded harbor, but a mooring may be available if you call the harbormaster, preferably in advance, by telephone at (603) 431-1779 or on channel 9. There are two state piers, the northerly one for yachts, with water, electricity, and room for a few vessels to lie alongside. Gasoline and diesel fuel are available during the summer at unspecified hours. The harbor is home to several party boats, whale watchers, and fishermen. There is a small snack shop behind the wharf and a shore dinner restaurant on the south side.

There is a grocery store about half a mile south, on the state road. Ray's Restaurant, Saunders Restaurant, and The Pilot House, about a quarter of a mile south, are said to be excellent. Rye has attractive white sand beaches both north and south of the harbor.

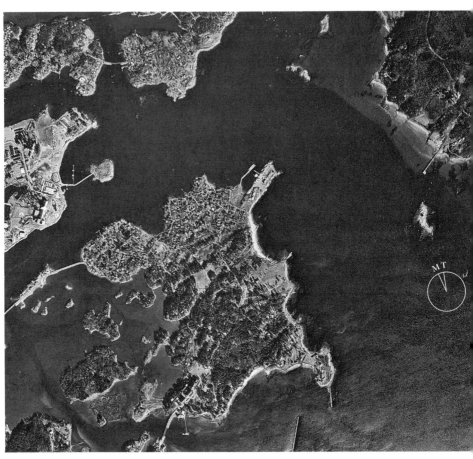

Portsmouth and Kittery Harbors. Little Harbor is in the lower part with the marina and the Wentworth Hotel. Notice the rock on the north side of the entrance. Pepperell Cove is at the top right and the entrance to Back Channel at the top left with Dion's boatyard. The Portsmouth Yacht Club wharf appears on the south side of the main channel. *Courtesy James W. Sewall Co.*

Portsmouth, New Hampshire (13283). Portsmouth, easy of entrance in almost any weather, is well marked by a lighted bell on Gunboat Shoal and a lighted whistle on Kitts Rocks. Inside is the powerful light and fog signal on Whaleback. Two range lights, the northerly one fixed red, the southerly one flashing red, are located on the Kittery shore behind Pepperrell Cove so as to lead one up the middle of the deep channel off the Coast Guard base. Here the green range lights on Pierces Island lead on up the river.

Portsmouth is a busy commercial harbor. Large vessels carrying gypsum, wire, oil, and liquefied natural gas (LNG) move in and out frequently. The Navy maintains a repair base for submarines on Seavey Island, and there is a Coast Guard base at Fort Constitution on the northeast point of Newcastle Island. Therefore, the yachtsman will do well to hang up a large radar reflector, keep a sharp lookout, and keep well clear of large vessels.

If you want to check the accuracy of your compass, note that the range lights for the entrance to the river lie on a course of 189°–009° magnetic and the face of the Coast Guard wharf lies due east-west magnetic. It is best to run these ranges at slack water, because the tide runs hard and makes staying on a range very difficult. Note that the ebb tide sweeps down the river past Pepperell Cove and then swings almost southwest, setting a vessel in on the shore near Little Harbor.

There are five possible anchorages at Portsmouth:

Little Harbor. This is the most convenient overnight stopping place for a yacht bound east or west along the shore as it avoids going up into the Piscataqua River, a slow business against the tide. Little Harbor is well enough sheltered in anything short of a heavy easterly. There is a nun and a can outside and a flashing red light on the end of the breakwater, but the principal mark for the entrance is the large, white Wentworth Hotel near the head of the harbor. This is no longer an active hotel but the site of a 220-slip marina. A 12-foot channel was dredged to the marina in 1994, but both the channel and mooring area have silted in some places, so it is best to stay close to the channel. Call Wentworth Marina on channel 16 or 71. A launch will appear to guide you to a slip or advise on a mooring. The marina sells gasoline, diesel fuel, and water but no groceries and has all the facilities and amenities of the luxury hotel it once was, including Ponte Vecchia restaurant with an Italian menu.

If you have any choice in moorings, choose one on the edge of the channel where you will lie to the tide, either bow or stern to the roll which makes in. If you try to avoid the tide, you will lie to the southwest wind, broadside to the roll.

One can, by observing great caution, circumnavigate Newcastle Island and come out in the river opposite Seavey Island, but this involves passing under a fixed bridge with only a 7-foot clearance, a good trip in a motorized dinghy.

Pepperrell Cove. This is an open bight in the northeast corner of the harbor, opposite Fort Constitution. There is ample depth here, but the cove is crowded with moorings and a roll makes in from outside. Edge up to the float and search out Frank Frisbee at the store or the harbormaster, either of whom may know of a vacant mooring. Do not lie on the front of the float except in very quiet weather. The roll is devastating. Lie on the west end with your bow to the southward. There is water enough to allow you to swing around and come alongside.

The Pepperrell Cove Yacht Club with headquarters on the wharf below the restaurant is primarily a cruising club and welcomes visitors for showers and whatever facilities it can provide. It is open weekends from Friday noon to Monday noon with launch service at a nominal charge. There are two guest moorings; call the launch driver on channel 68.

Frisbee's Store on the street up from the pier is an excellent small market and sells ice as well as groceries. It runs the gasoline and diesel pumps on the wharf. It is not open Sunday afternoons, but water is always available on the float. The town requests that visitors lie alongside only as long as is absolutely necessary since it is a busy place. The Frisbees run a good small restaurant, Captain Simeon's, very popular on weekends, just above the dock. It is closed on Tuesdays. There are other excellent eating places within a short taxi ride. Warren's Lobster House on the Kittery end of the first bridge has an excellent reputation.

Portsmouth Yacht Club. This hospitable yacht club is located just west of Salamander Point. The shoal water drops off steeply into the tide-scoured channel, making anchoring impossible. However, the club maintains four guest moorings and may have room to lie alongside. Gasoline, diesel oil, ice, and water are available from 8 A.M. to 8 P.M. until Labor Day, then 8 A.M. to 4 P.M. until October 12.

The modest mooring fee includes launch service when the club is open and use of the club's facilities including showers. Transients on yacht club

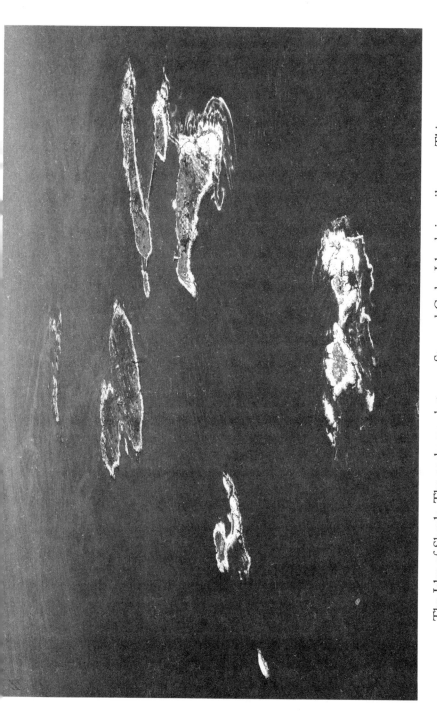

The Isles of Shoals. The anchorage between Star and Cedar Islands is easily seen. This photograph was taken before the Cornell Laboratory was established on Appledore Island. *Laurence Lowry.*

moorings or floats are welcome at the popular Wednesday night dinners if space is available. The club monitors channel 9 and is open from mid-May until October 20. Obviously hours at the beginning and end of the season are shorter than in midsummer.

Kittery Point Yacht Club. This club is not at Kittery Point but has a new clubhouse on Goat Island, Newcastle, with a float and six moorings, usually occupied by members' boats. The club is open weekends with launch service available, and provides showers and ice. A call to the club or the launch operator on channel 68 will elicit information on moorings.

Back Channel. This passage north of Seavey Island provides the best protection in Portsmouth, although it is quite a way from open water. In any kind of bad weather it is much to be preferred.

Pass Pepperrell Cove and the high land west of it. Leave nun 6 and the beacon on Hicks Rocks to starboard and cans 1 and 3 to port. Bear around to port. Dion's yard will be right ahead. Stop here and inquire for a mooring or a slip. This is a fully equipped yacht yard capable of doing repairs of any kind. It has a marine railway with a capacity of 100 tons and two Brownell over-the-road trailers. There is 22 feet of water at the dock. Moorings may be available. Call on channel 9 or 68. Showers and toilets are available during normal business hours. Dion's also maintains a brokerage facility. Take seriously the red-and-green can marking a 5-foot spot west of Dion's.

There are numerous private moorings up the back channel to which a local resident may be able to direct you. There is scant room to anchor.

Prescott Park. Just east of the first bridge, Memorial Bridge, is a small complex of piers and floats owned by the city of Portsmouth. There is ample depth here and room for about 25 yachts to lie overnight at a charge posted on the wharf. In 1993, the first two nights were free. The Boston-Portland bus stops opposite the church spire shown on the chart of Portsmouth. There are several good restaurants nearby, and Portsmouth shops are within easy reach. The nearby Portsmouth Fisherman's Co-op sells ice and diesel fuel.

Near Prescott Park and below the first bridge is Strawbery Banke. Note that "Strawbery" is spelled with one "r" in the second syllable. This is a developing preservation and restoration project and a museum showing Portsmouth as it was in the early days of the nineteenth century when the city was a center for shipbuilding, overseas trade, and inland distribution. A lagoon, then known as Puddle Dock, permitted vessels to lie out of the tide. Various trades flourished around the wharves. Old buildings have been rehabilitated, and in them people again practice these trades in the traditional way. In one shop a boatbuilder and a group of apprentices build small boats, some of them to order, particularly Swampscot dories and the like. Guided tours are available from May 1 to October 31. The project is well worth a visit and the yachtsman's support.

It is a short walk to U.S.S. *Albacore,* the country's second nuclear submarine, now open to visitors.

Above Prescott Park there are three bridges in Portsmouth: The first is the Memorial Bridge. The second is the Interstate Bridge, also a drawbridge with a lift span, and named long before I-95 was built. About 150 yards northeastward of the main span is a draw in the railroad bridge which, when open, affords a clearance of 34 feet under the fixed highway span. This draw is kept open except when a train is approaching. The third bridge is the I-95 highway bridge, a fixed bridge with a clearance of 165 feet. The specific instructions for signaling the Memorial Bridge and the Interstate Bridge are given in Chapter 2 of the *Coast Pilot.* However, the bridgetenders report that sound signals are unreliable because of the traffic noise on the bridges and because few yachts have loud enough horns anyway. The bridgetenders keep a sharp eye on river traffic and listen to channel 13 VHF. Bridges open only briefly on the hour and half-hour for yachts.

Kittery Landing. This establishment just below the first bridge on the Kittery side has floating docks out of the worst of the tide in the river. It has 30 slips which can accommodate yachts up to 75 feet and welcomes cruising boats. Call on channel 9 for the latest information. Shore power, water, showers, and toilets are available, but no fuel. This marina is within easy walking distance of Portsmouth shopping, which includes restaurants, groceries, and a laundromat. The Portsmouth Arts Festival, offering Broadway shows among its many attractions, provides free entertainment all summer, and is within walking distance as well. On long weekends or other busy days, call ahead for reservations at (207) 439-0577 any time.

Gosport Harbor, New Hampshire. Star, Cedar, Smuttynose, Malaga and Appledore Islands in a strong northwest breeze. Notice the boats moored in the smooth water between Cedar and Star Islands and east of the breakwater between Cedar and Smuttynose. *Courtesy James W. Sewall Co.*

Above the bridges, there is no difficulty about proceeding to Great Bay where there are two bridges with a vertical clearance of 46 feet.

Patten's Yacht Yard, formerly on Badgers Island, has moved to Eliot about 1¹/₂ miles above the I-95 bridge. It is a full-service yard offering accommodations and repair facilities to those bound to or from the attractive Great Bay cruising grounds.

Great Bay Marine is just inside the General Sullivan Bridge between Newington and Dover Point. It is a full-service marina with travelift and repair facilities of all kinds. Gasoline, diesel fuel, moorings, and slips are available. Call on channel 9 or 16.

Great Bay and the rivers that run into it are inhabited by many kinds of birds and surrounded by pleasant New Hampshire countryside.

Isles of Shoals, New Hampshire and Maine (13283). The state line runs between Star and Cedar Islands.

Don't miss the Isles of Shoals. Not only is it a convenient stopping place bound east or west, but the islands have an austere offshore quality found only in island harbors. Anchored in Gosport Harbor, you are sharing a long and colorful history beginning with the visit of Captain John Smith in 1614 after his rescue by Pochahontas in Virginia.

Gosport Harbor. Formed by Star, Cedar, Smuttynose, Malaga, and Appledore Islands, this is a satisfactory anchorage in ordinary summer weather although there is always a little motion—just enough to let you know you are at sea.

From the south, run for White Island with its powerful light and fog signal and leave it close to port. Leave the nun off Halfway Rocks to starboard and run into the harbor. The shores are bold and the water is deep.

Approach from the eastward, especially in thick weather, is more difficult because there is no bell, whistle, or horn north of the islands. If you have a quarter mile visibility, from York Ledge whistle 24YL run for the northwest side of Duck Island. When your depth finder shows less than 10 fathoms, you should hear the surf and see the loom of the island. Follow around the west side and look for nun 2, off Appledore. Thence follow the Appledore shore into the harbor. If it is very thick or likely to become so, the easiest and safest course is to run from York Ledge whistle to Kitts Rocks whistle 2KR outside Portsmouth Harbor and thence for red-and-white bell 15 in the entrance to Gosport Harbor.

There are many moorings in the harbor, some belonging to yachtsmen, some to mainland yacht clubs, and a few to local fishermen. Summer weekends are crowded, but if you come early or late in the season or in midweek, you can take any convenient mooring without a skiff on it, gambling that it is stout enough to hold you and that the owner will not return. Should he do so, of course it is incumbent on you to move at once and with a good grace. The best protection is in the cove between Star and Cedar Islands. If you have to anchor, get as far into this cove as possible and land your anchor on a mud bottom. Outside the mud, the bottom is smooth ledge and you might as well be anchored over a parking lot. Your anchor will drag until you fetch up on Appledore. The alternative is to rig a trip line and anchor close to the north shore of Star Island. The bottom is rocky and overgrown with kelp. Avoid anchoring to leeward of the incinerator.

In ordinary summer weather the harbor affords good protection, but in a heavy northwester it can become untenable. Your choices then are to go around Star Island and anchor in the lee of the breakwater between Smuttynose and Cedar Islands or to "reef your fores'l and scud for 'Squam [Annisquam]," in the words of an eighteenth-century inhabitant.

The harbor is protected by three breakwaters. The oldest, between Malaga and Smuttynose, was built about 1820 by Captain Sam Haley. Under a flat rock on Smuttynose he is said to have found four silver bars, which he used to finance the project. The other two breakwaters were built by the United States government. The one between Smuttynose and Cedar was built in 1821 and rebuilt in 1901 from stone quarried on Smuttynose. The one between Cedar and Star was built in 1904 and badly damaged in a gale in the winter of 1971–72. The government at first refused to rebuild it on the grounds that no vessels were registered in Gosport Harbor and that with powerful engines and improved navigational instruments, a harbor of refuge was unnecessary. Public pressure, however, changed the bureaucratic mind.

Star Island is dominated by the Star Island Conference Center where religious and educational conferences extend end to end and week to week from early June to late September. These conferences are, for the most part, concentrated fare with time carefully planned. Visitors are a distraction and an interruption but may land on the island between 9 A.M. and dusk except between 10:30 and 3:30 Saturdays, Sundays, and July 4 from mid-June until Labor Day. There is a store in the main building, the Oceanic, where gifts and books relating to the history of the island may be purchased. The island and the conference center are owned by the Star Island Corporation composed of Unitarian Universalists and members of the United Church of Christ and are dedicated "to the glory of God and the well-being of Man; to the brotherhood of all earnest souls; to the untrammelled study and utterance of the truth; to the promotion of pure religion," in the 1916 phraseology. These serious purposes do not seem to prevent the conferees from having a very good time.

There are no facilities ashore for yachtsmen at all. Do not plan to leave your trash ashore; the island has enough of a problem dealing with its own. There is no provision store and no public telephone.

Cedar Island is inhabited by lobstermen during the summer. They, too, are busy people.

Smuttynose is well worth a visit. Land on the beach between Malaga and Smuttynose, protected by Captain Haley's breakwater and pier. You will probably find there a pamphlet prepared by Laurence Throckmorton Bussey leading you about the island from one point of interest to another. The wreck of the Spanish brig *Conception* and the death by exposure of her crew in 1813, the gory ax murder of two women by Louis Wagner in 1873, and "Aunt Rozie's House" built by Rosamond Thaxter, granddaughter of the poet and painter Celia Thaxter are fully described. The island is still owned by their family.

Appledore, the largest island, has too long and colorful a history to deal with here. Like the other islands, it was settled early in the seventeenth century by fishermen and became a prosperous and somewhat undisciplined community. Later most of the inhabitants moved to Star Island. In 1847, Thomas Laighton, keeper of White Island Light, retired from that service and built a large summer hotel on Appledore. This soon became a popular summer center for artists, writers, musicians, and statesmen attracted by the high quality of the hotel, by each other, and by Laighton's daughter Celia, an attractive and accomplished poet. She eventually married her tutor and her father's partner, Levi Thaxter. Celia

York Harbor, Maine. The shoals off Stage Neck and Bragdon Island show
clearly. *Courtesy of York Harbormaster.*

planted a lovely flower garden, now re-established with the same plants. The hotel burned in 1914. The Navy occupied Appledore during World War II and built the observation tower on the summit.

The island is now almost entirely owned by the Star Island Corporation but leased to the Shoals Marine Laboratory, run jointly by Cornell University and the University of New Hampshire for the study and teaching of oceanography and marine biology. The laboratory was started by Professor John M. Kingsbury of Cornell, one of the most imaginative, resourceful, and energetic men to wear both work shoes and an academic gown. It is now under the leadership of John B. Heiser, Ph.D., of Cornell and Professor Arthur C. Borror of the University of New Hampshire. The faculty and students here are, like those on Star Island, busy people but are glad of interested visitors. Land at their wharf on the western side of the island, sign their book on a post near the wharf, and pick up a guided tour of the island.

The Shoals Marine Laboratory maintains no guest moorings. Do not take one of theirs. Some are for outboards too light to hold a cruising boat, and all are in constant and unpredictable use.

The Maine Isles of Shoals are a Registered National Historic Site. A large part of Appledore has been designated by the state of Maine a "critical natural area" as an intertidal region of exceptional richness and as a heron rookery. Bird species nesting on the islands, besides thousands of gulls, include black-crowned night herons, little blue herons, snowy egrets, and glossy ibis. Black guillemots and eider ducks nest on other islands of the Shoals. For several of these species, this represents the extremes of their range in America.

In the last year of her life, Celia Thaxter wrote a book about the garden in front of her cottage on Appledore, which had become nearly as famous as her salon within. With the help of the Rye Beach–Little Boar's Head Garden Club, the Shoals Marine Laboratory, and Cornell Plantations, students have reconstructed Celia's 1893 garden on the same spot, with the same botanical materials. Each year it is recreated by faithful volunteers with University of New Hampshire greenhouse assistance. A picnic table and descriptive historical information are provided near the garden for visitors.

The vegetation of Appledore, despite the centuries of human occupation, has now reverted to approximately what Captain John Smith described in 1614. Publications on the flora of Appledore, a checklist of the flora and fauna, a history of the breeding birds prepared by personnel of the Shoals Marine Laboratory, and a reprinted edition of Celia Thaxter's *An Island Garden* with color illustrations by Childe Hassam are available in the bookstore on Star Island or by writing The Shoals Marine Laboratory, G-14 Stimson Hall, Cornell University, Ithaca, New York 14853.

Lunging Island, or Londoners. On this island, west of Star Island, formerly owned by Oscar Laighton, the late Reverend Frank B. Crandall of Salem, Massachusetts, maintained a summer home. The cottage was kept supplied with food and clothing throughout the year for the relief of people marooned or shipwrecked on the island.

Mr. Crandall, one of the individual owners of a part of the Shoals, generously contributed the following:

The Isles of Shoals, as an abode of white men, is older than Plymouth. From 1615 on, it was a fishing base of British companies. My island was the base of the London Company. The word *Lunging* is said to be a sailor's corruption of "London." The other name, "Londoners," confirms this tradition. So my island has this bit of historic interest; it is the first "London" in the New World. The venerable Oscar Laighton used to tell me that the first general store at the Isles of Shoals was located on my island, as it was one place where a landing was possible in almost any weather. The old foundations still remain. My island also happens to be the location of the somewhat famous Honeymoon Cottage, so named because various notables in the past, such as Professor Forbes of Harvard, had their honeymoons in this secluded and idyllic spot.

The year before I was called to the colors as an Army chaplain in World War II, we discovered the evidence of a considerable excavation at the dead-low water line, when we arrived in late May to do some gardening work. The excavation was nearly filled in with sand, but a ring of boulders around the edge indicated that it was not the result of a sea action or tide force.

Later I learned that a company of divers, equipped with some really scientific metal finders, working on the radar principle, had come out to explore for bronze or treasure in our waters. Their report was that they located a quantity of bronze in the deep mud of Gosport harbor, probably bronze cannon from some of the old pirate craft sunk in the harbor. In two places they located a cache of gold, buried cleverly in the sand at a point somewhat below low water. One of these was at the spot where they dug on my beach within the harbor but were frustrated by finding that so much sand had washed in that, 11 feet down, the sea water pushed in through the sand faster than their pumps could take it out. They gave up the quest for the bronze also because of the accumulation of mud on the bottom. They were not equipped to go through this depth. In both cases they realized that it was an engineering operation and were not inclined to make the necessary investment.

York Harbor, Maine (13283). This is a secure harbor and one easily entered at night or, with due caution, in the fog. Although there is not a bar at the mouth of the York River, an ebb tide and an easterly wind build up a very steep breaking chop in the entrance. Twenty knots of easterly can raise a formidable sea.

From the south, the outer mark is York Ledge whistle 24YL. A direct course from the whistle to the bell YH off York Harbor leads you right across York Ledge, marked by a red-and-green nun. Leave it generously to port, but note that there is a 6-foot rock 0.3 mile northeast of the buoy. What the chart calls a "submerged pile" may still be visible on the shoalest part of the ledge. If this is visible or if the ledge is breaking, one could leave it generously to starboard.

From the north, pass the Nubble at Cape Neddick and run for the red-and-white bell YH off East Point.

The course in from the bell is well marked and there is a flashing red light on Stage Neck with a high-intensity beam over the channel. Keep to the starboard side of the channel close to nun 10, to prevent being swept across the channel by the swift tide onto the rock marked by a beacon on the port side. The western side of Stage Neck is a steep gravel beach which must be treated with respect at high water.

The tide runs very hard through the harbor on both the flood and ebb, and anchoring is practically impossible. Call the harbormaster, Peter Bradley, on channel 9 for a mooring, or Fred Muehl at York Harbor Marine Service for a mooring or a slip. Do not pick up a mooring at random, for it may be too light to hold your boat against the heavy tidal current.

In the middle of the cove off York Harbor Marine Service is a mud bar with about 4^1/$_2$ feet at low water. Do not try to approach the float at low water unless you can clear this bar. Gasoline, diesel fuel, ice, and water are available at the float, and there is a well-appointed marine store at the head of the wharf. Showers and laundry facilities are available here, and the yard is well equipped to make all kinds of repairs.

Up the bank from the yard is a restaurant with a pleasant view of the harbor, and beyond that is a big farmhouse, Dockside Guest Quarters, run by the family of David and Hariette Lusty, original entrepreneurs of the establishment on Harris Island. Here are accommodations ashore and a source of reliable local information.

Near the head of the harbor is Donnell's marina, with dockside accommodation for yachts of almost any length and up to 10-foot draft. Up the road a step from Donnell's is a small convenience store which can hold off starvation and thirst, but there is no other grocery store within easy walking distance of the harbor.

Cape Neddick Harbor, Maine (13283). Described in the 1950 *Coast Pilot* as a "foul bight," Cape Neddick Harbor has not changed significantly although later editions are more charitable. On a quiet summer night it is an acceptable anchorage. Late in the afternoon with a dying breeze, the 4 miles to York may look like a long beat in a sloppy sea. In anything easterly, Cape Neddick Harbor is a trap.

The conspicuous mark for the entrance is The Nubble, a high rock with a lighthouse close to Cape Neddick. The entrance is a mile north of The Nubble and is buoyed. Inside, however, one must move cautiously and examine the area where the yacht may swing at anchor for there are numerous boulders. One visitor grounded at midnight and could find no safe anchorage in the western part of the harbor at that hour.

There are no facilities at Cape Neddick. It would be used only as an overnight stop.

Perkins Cove, Maine (13286). This little hole in the wall about a mile north of the prominent hotel on Bald Head Cliff is marked by a red-and-white bell outside and by a nun and can close to the rocky shore marking the harbor entrance channel. The channel is narrow and shoal—about 6 feet at low water—and is spanned by a footbridge with a draw. The bridge is operated by the harbormaster or whoever happens to be nearby when you blow your horn. If no one responds, land someone on the float on the east side of the channel to raise the bridge.

Inside, the harbor is crowded with lobster boats, leaving no room to swing at anchor. A sign over the bridge warns, "Mooring in emergency only $20 per night."

As a refuge in rough weather, Perkins Cove is impossible as the sea would break all across the entrance. A boat with engine trouble in calm weather might sail and tow into the cove for help, but the skipper might prefer to stay at sea rather than to face the narrow channel and the bridge. If you must enter, call the harbormaster on channel 9 for advice and help.

The peninsula east of the harbor is crowded with shore dinner restaurants and gift shops, rather like Bearskin Neck at Rockport in small compass. There is no grocery store near the shore, but there is an outdoor telephone.

Wells, Maine (13286). This gap in the beach is no place for a cruising boat. In spite of repeated efforts to dredge it and to keep it dredged, the seas even in moderate weather break across the entrance and inside there is water enough at low tide for only very shoal-draft boats.

Inside the jetties, the channel bends sharply to the south and is obstructed by a middle ground which bares at low water. There is a wharf on the west side of the harbor.

Kennebunkport, Maine (13286). Kennebunkport is perfectly protected, easy to enter by day or night in ordinary weather, and affords most of the facilities a yacht may require.

Approaching from the east, make Cape Porpoise whistle and run directly to the flashing bell off the entrance to the Kennebunk River. From the west on a clear day you will see the white Colony Hotel east of the entrance from as far away as Bald Head Cliff. A long, low white bathhouse west of the entrance is prominent from the bell. Less obvious is a cable-TV tower with a flashing red light, marked "TR" on the chart, which is located behind Kennebunk Beach.

From the bell, it may be difficult to see can 3, but head 005 deg. mag. for 0.8 NM and you will find it. Enter between the breakwaters, leaving can 5 to port. Yachts drawing over 4 feet will do well to avoid the entrance at low water if a considerable sea is running.

The river has silted in considerably in recent years, and depths at low water can be as much as 2 feet less than those shown on the chart. After passing through the breakwaters, for deepest water stay close to nun 6 and then head directly for the first wharf visible on the eastern shore, keeping well clear of can 7 and the beach on the eastern side. Thereafter, stay close to the string of fishing boats and yachts moored along the western side of the channel.

On the eastern shore, the next building after the first wharf is the Kennebunk River Club. Its floats are protected by a massive stone jetty which lurks under the surface at high water but is marked by pylons at each end. The club maintains no facilities for visitors.

After the River Club, 150 yards beyond nun 8, the Coast Guard has recently installed a small nun to mark the sandbar which extends out from the eastern shore.

The banks of the Kennebunk River are a study in contrasts. To the east is a typical resort, lined with attractive houses, condominiums, motels, and restaurants. Most of the west bank, however, is taken up by the wooded preserve of a Franciscan monastery. The river itself is very crowded, with little or no room to anchor. Call one of the marinas listed below for slip space or a mooring.

Above can 13 is Chick's Marina, now owned and operated by the Katz family. Chick's has very few moorings, but has considerable space alongside with water, fuel, electricity, and cable-TV connections. At the head of the wharf are toilets, showers, a laundry machine, and an outdoor telephone. Chick's includes a marine store carrying charts, hardware, and a large assortment of necessities and gadgetry. Although Chick's has no repair facilities, they have a heavy-duty hydraulic trailer which can haul your boat and take it anywhere over the road. They can summon a tank truck for pumpout if necessary.

Next above Chick's is the Kennebunkport Yacht Club, which offers limited marina facilities. Immediately to the north is the Yachtsman Motor Inn and Marina, also with slips, offering the usual facilities but no haulout or repair. The motel attached to the marina can provide accommodations ashore.

Farther up the river on the east shore is the hospitable Arundel Yacht Club in a long low building that was built as a rope walk. The club has no moorings, but rents slips with the usual amenities but no fuel. To inquire, call them on channel 9.

Above the yacht club, the river becomes further constricted by wharves. Over on the west bank, in front of the long gray-shingled Shipyard Shopping Mall, is the Harborview Marina which can often accommodate transients. On the second deck of the mall is Federal Jack's

Pub, which boasts its own micro-brewery, and offers live entertainment on most summer evenings.

Just below the bridge, for practical purposes at the head of navigation, is the Performance Marine Boatyard. Although sometimes cramped and crowded, the yard has a travelift and a marine store and is capable of meeting most emergencies.

Surrounding the bridge and the river lies the town of Kennebunkport, well supplied with specialty and gift shops, and with more than a dozen restaurants of all types within a short distance of the river. A short walk west of the bridge is Meserve's, a good market with a large wine department and, in the summer, a selection of hard liquor. In response to a telephone call at (207) 967-5762, Meserve's will deliver an order of $50 or more to your yacht.

The novelist Booth Tarkington used to live on a schooner grounded out in the Kennebunk River. Besides writing the Penrod books, he wrote *Mary's Neck,* a story of Kennebunkport in Prohibition days. One of Tarkington's protégés was Kenneth Roberts, who used Kennebunkport as the setting for *Arundel, Rabble in Arms, Lively Lady,* and a number of his other historical novels. His descriptions of the country as it used to be and his accounts of historic campaigns of the American Revolution and of the War of 1812 are vivid and historically accurate.

After the violent winter storms of 1984, the remains of the vessel *Industry* came to light on Kennebunk Beach. She was built at St. George in 1770 and sailed in November with 13 people aboard. She was never heard of again, although she was uncovered briefly in a 1960 storm.

Anyone leaving Kennebunkport bound east can see the home of former President George Bush on the peninsula east of Cape Arundel.

Cape Porpoise, Maine (13286). The mark for Cape Porpoise is a whistle offshore and a prominent water tank of a flattened spherical shape. The church spire shown on the chart is not obvious from outside. From the whistle, make Old Prince bell and follow the buoyed channel.

Although there is not a bar at the entrance as there is at Newburyport and York, a strong easterly can kick up enough of a sea on the shoal spots in the entrance channel to give the entering skipper serious concern. In ordinary weather, however, his chief problem will be to avoid the astronomical number of lobster traps. After considerable legal conflict over the lobsterman's right to set his traps where the lobsters congregate and the mariner's right to a clear passage, the lobstermen—at least some of them—agreed to leave a clear channel among the traps. It is the mariner's business to find it. The best solution is to enter and leave under sail, which, fortunately, is easy in the prevailing southwest wind.

Entrance in the fog requires care and a dash of luck, for between Goat Island's fog signal and the channel lie numerous ledges. The two day beacons are very quiet indeed and cannot be approached closely.

Once inside, be careful to stay in the dredged area where the lobster boats moor. The flats are extensive and dry out well before low water. One visitor reported a lobsterman tending traps from a wheelbarrow!

You might as well anchor just inside the harbor entrance where there is ample room and good holding ground, for Cape Porpoise has no yacht club, no marina, no boatyard, and no rental moorings. It is a lobsterman's town. The boats are for the most part big, able, and fast. Their skippers have a day's work to do hauling as many as 500 traps and have little time for yachtsmen. The town wharf, the first on the east side, smells of bait and is a busy interface between business afloat and business ashore. The manager will sell gasoline or diesel fuel to yachtsmen if the transaction does not interfere with fishermen's needs.

If you do elect to buy fuel here, LOOK UP as you come alongside, for two steel I beams project over the water for lowering bait barrels and hauling up lobster crates. These fixtures could seriously damage a yacht's rigging.

The only public landing is at a float on the north side of the town wharf. It is crowded two-deep with dinghies, skiffs, half-dories, punts, inflatables, and even a canoe, living proof that there is no perfect tender. There is a public telephone on the south side of the building on the wharf and limited marine supplies are available at the small store within. A step away is a snack shop, The Lively Lobster, which serves seafood on a takeout basis but provides a deck with tables and benches, a pleasant place to lunch.

Fronting on the parking area is Seascapes, a prize-winning restaurant run by Angela and Arthur LeBlanc. When two rather scruffy-looking sailors off a small yacht paused in the door, nonplused by tablecloths, fluted wineglasses, and uniformed waitresses, and asked hesitantly if their dress was appropriate, Ms. LeBlanc replied, "Come on. I'll hide you!" and led them to a pleasant table with an inspiring view.

The village is a 3/4-mile walk up the road from the wharf, an agreeable change from the suburban atmosphere of harbors to the westward. At the four-corners are Bradbury's well-stocked market *cum* post office and

FAX machine, two restaurants, a hardware store, and various gift shops. Bradbury's carries a full range of groceries, fine wines, excellent meats, and gourmet items, and provides a ride to and from the pier if you call 967-3939. Starting in the summer of 1993, Visa and Mastercard will be accepted and cash advances can be secured. The Wayfarer Restaurant serves three hearty meals daily, and no-frills seafood and lobster dishes are the specialties of The Captain's and The Lobster Hut. Also at the corners are a hardware store/gas station, various gift shops, and a family practice physician's office, but the walk itself makes the trip worthwhile.

Although there is no boatyard at Cape Porpoise, in an emergency consult the manager on the town wharf. Help can be summoned from Kennebunkport if the problem cannot be solved by local ingenuity.

Cape Porpoise lobstermen seem to have acquired a reputation among some yachtsmen for being hostile. The writer, windbound for a day, found this not to be the case at all—quite the contrary. However, it's possible to see how a difference of opinion might arise between a lobsterman busy about a long day's work and a frustrated yachtsman trying to unwind a pot warp from around his propeller shaft with a boat hook. So if a lobsterman shatters the still dawn with the scream of his high-speed diesel and a violent wake to the distress of a sleeping yachtsman, he may not be harboring any ill will. It is just his way of telling the sleeper that working seamen are up and about their day's work.

Note on Tides. Between Cape Porpoise and Cape Elizabeth, indeed all along this shore, there seems to be a current setting to the northwest on both flood and ebb. The following note, received from a correspondent many years ago, seems significant, for the tides change little over the years:

Too much attention cannot be used when proceeding from Cape Porpoise to Portland Harbor in a fog, especially during spring tides with an easterly wind. Last summer, when lying at Wood Island waiting for a fog to clear, we saw a large schooner under a competent skipper almost bring up dead on Wood Island. The schooner had left Portland Harbor and laid out a course for Boon Island. The following day, when proceeding from Wood Island to Casco Bay, we saw a schooner high and dry on Shooting Rocks. It had come up in the fog the day before from Cape Porpoise and was putting into

Portland Harbor. When these courses are laid out on the chart, it is hard to believe that such things can happen, but unfortunately these are facts of incidents that occurred in August 1936.

The writer, as late as 1985, experienced the same set and has felt it nearly every time he has passed this way. Another correspondent, quoted on pages 414–415, reports the same effect. This current seems to be significant even well outside the Boon Island whistle and, on the run from Cape Porpoise to the buoys off Cape Elizabeth, it is often quite strong.

Wood Island, Biddeford Pool, Maine (13286). In anything but a heavy easterly, Biddeford Pool is easy of access. However, in really heavy weather, seas may break across the bar west of Wood Island, and the channel southeast of Wood Island would be impossible.

From far offshore, the tall water tank with the peaked top at Fortunes Rocks is an excellent mark for Fletcher Neck. It is shown on the chart inconspicuously as "tank."

The entrance to Biddeford Pool is well marked by a powerful light and fog signal on Wood Island and a whistle about 2 miles eastward. From the whistle, make the red-and-white bell northwestward of Wood Island and follow the buoys in. From the westward, if it isn't too rough and the visibility is acceptable, leave the nun on Danbury Reef to starboard and pass between Wood Island and Gooseberry Island and between nun 6 and can 7. From can 7 all the way into the Pool there is a dredged channel 10 feet deep at low water and 100 feet wide. Favor the western side of the channel as the shoals on Negro Island extend far out. The tide runs vigorously through this channel in and out of Biddeford Pool. Because the Pool is crowded, many yachts are moored outside in what the chart calls Wood Island Harbor. This is perfectly acceptable with a southerly or westerly wind.

The second wharf on the easterly side of the gut is the Biddeford Pool Yacht Club supervised by Janet and Helmut Kohl. They run a very busy program all summer but are eager to be helpful to visitors. Ask them about moorings, supplies, repairs, or emergencies in general. You may be able to raise them on channel 9 as you approach. Be very careful in coming alongside their float as the ebb tide rushing through the narrow gut can set you heavily against the float. Gasoline and diesel fuel are available in limited quantities.

One can land in a dinghy at the yacht club float inside the Pool. Ashore there is a well-supplied grocery store open until mid-September and two lobster shops which also sell ice. A short walk to the eastward on the road to the right as you leave the parking lot is Hattie's Deli selling light lunches and excellent homemade pie as well as a few selected necessities and luxuries for the galley.

In case of emergency of any kind, consult the Kohls. Help is at hand from Biddeford.

Saco River, Maine (13287). This is a shallow river with a swift current, swifter on the ebb than on the flood when the salt water flows upstream under the fresh water. The controlling depth to Biddeford is about 5 feet at low water, although there are deeper places for anchoring. There is a bar at the mouth of the river between the jetties, dangerous in an easterly wind on an ebb tide. Do not consider entering under these conditions.

The principal marine center on the river is at Camp Ellis just inside the jetties on the north side. Here is a large wharf, a dredged basin, occasional moorings, fuel from a stationary truck, considerable lobstering, and some yachting activity. There is a boatyard, Rumery's, in Biddeford on the south side of the river above Cow Island. Gasoline, diesel fuel, water, ice, and repairs are available. The following notes on the river were contributed by a visitor cruising in a shoal-draft catboat.

There is a very swift current from can 11 out through the breakwaters on the ebb.

South of Chase Point there is a launching ramp, a marina of sorts, and a few moorings—probably too close for anchoring.

Just east of can 15 there is 5 or 6 feet of water—plenty for a cat boat—and out of the swift current. Although we did not anchor, I would certainly give it a try for overnight.

Up the river from can 15, on the north shore, is a large string of floats with both power- and sailboats up to 30 feet. This Riverside Marina has about 40 or 50 boats.

The cruise up the river is pretty with rolling farmland and no evidence of industry until we reached Garden Point. With a fair wind it was a delightful sail down from Biddeford—a pleasant change from open water sailing.

Before entering the river, read the notes in the *Coast Pilot* warning of the dangers of the bar in an easterly breeze with an ebb tide.

Prouts Neck, Maine (13287). Unless he has a particular reason for visiting Prouts Neck, the cruising man will probably pass it by. Located behind a small breakwater on the west side of the neck, it is open to a wash from Saco Bay. The yacht club is said to have a powerful mooring and to be hospitable to visitors.

Up the road a good ¹/₂ mile is the elegant Black Point Inn, where he who remembered to make a reservation and to wear coat and tie can dine in style.

A considerable walk beyond the inn is a small store and post office.

There is a path around the neck called the Marginal Way, from which Winslow Homer painted a number of his well-known pictures. His studio is open from ten to four in the summer and is well worth a visit to one who admires his work.

Richmond Island Harbor, Maine (13287 231). This is a rather uneasy shelter west of the breakwater from Richmond Island to the shore. Because the breakwater is partly submerged at high water and because a wash works in around Richmond Island, there is usually some motion here. The best place to lie is close to the island and west of the breakwater.

Although local boats are moored on both sides of the breakwater, one can use Seal Cove to the east of the breakwater in northerly and easterly weather, but the holding ground is said to be poor. A correspondent writes: "Moderate to good holding ground if you tuck in close to the beach near the breakwater . . . Don't be misled by the view of the harbor from southwest. Continue northeast and it gets better-looking."

Richmond Island is privately owned, was a trading and fishing station in the earliest years of the seventeenth century, and because of the profusion of wild grapes was named Isle de Bacchus by Champlain and Pierre du Guast in 1605.

Chapter X

Portland to Rockland

From gray sea fog, from icy drift,
　From peril and from pain
The home-bound fisher greets thy lights
　O hundred-harbored Maine!

General Conditions. At Cape Elizabeth, the nature of the coast changes radically. You find yourself steering east and a little north, even east and a little south, instead of northerly. The beaches of Wells and Old Orchard give way to a succession of long, rocky peninsulas, which run out underwater for miles, showing themselves again as rocky islands and breaking ledges or just as shallower readings on the depth sounder.

The deep bays thus formed are peppered with ledges and studded with islands, most of them heavily wooded and some of them uninhabited. The North Atlantic breaks heavily on the outer islands, but the inner ones form many protected harbors. In Casco, Muscongus, and Penobscot Bays, most of the mainland harbors are inhabited in the winter by lobstermen and overlaid in the summer by a heavy population of vacationists, many of them transient but many, too, who own cottages scattered along the shore. Most of these small towns have a town wharf, a lobster car, a gas pump, and diesel oil. Don't plan to leave your boat alongside a lobster car any longer than necessary to fill your tank, for you will be interfering with those who come to sell lobsters, buy bait, and gas up.

449

In the last five years many of the small local grocery stores have closed. Local people are shopping at supermarkets often several miles from the shore. Plan, then, to be independent of stores for several days between major sources of supply like Portland, Boothbay Harbor, Camden, and Mount Desert. Most grocery stores, even the smallest, carry beer and wine. Hard liquor is sold only in state liquor stores and in a few Agency stores licensed by the state. Larger towns are likely to have hardware stores and drug stores, and the yachtier places may have a store selling marine hardware.

The blight of suburban yachting is spreading up the coast, but thus far you will find few marinas with acres of finger piers, few places to lie alongside and plug in your 120-volt system and your water hose. The farther east you go, the fewer of these you will find. Yacht clubs decrease in number and have simpler facilities. Rental moorings are scarcer. Land transportation is more difficult as the highways cross bridges far up the rivers and skirt the heads of the bays.

Boatyards are less frequent and major repair facilities are scattered rather thinly. However, unless you are in very serious trouble indeed, you can get help in a hurry almost anywhere between Portland and Rockland. Many lobstermen and many of the mechanics in small garages are excellent engine doctors.

The principal dangers in this area are well buoyed, and the offshore marks are big and loud. However, the less-frequented coves and reaches have many unmarked shoals, and the navigator must keep constant run of his position on a large-scale chart.

Fog is more frequent as one goes eastward, developing as saturated air from offshore is cooled when it meets the colder tidal waters near the coast. It may last a week or more, but often there will be a scale-up during the middle of the day, especially up the bays and behind the islands. Appendix E deals with fog in detail. The sections in Chapter II on weather and tides are particularly relevant to the Maine coast east of Portland. Rather than repeat them here, we urge the reader to review them before squaring away for Seguin.

The uninhabited islands of Maine all belong to someone. Some are the property of the Nature Conservancy or the Audubon Society or the Friends of Nature, but except for such as are in Acadia National Park or state owned, none are public property. Therefore, they must be treated with respect. If the owner is not present, and if there are no threatening "Keep Off" signs, it is probably all right to land on an island. However,

Portland Harbor, Maine. The four marinas and the anchorages at the Centerboard Yacht Club can be picked out. There are four big vessels at wharves or drydock and one more coming in, suggesting a great deal of traffic. The dredged channel to Marineast north of the first bridge is clear. *Courtesy of James W. Sewall Co.*

do not smoke ashore or build a fire. Of course, you will leave no trash around and will not disturb such local inhabitants as ospreys, herons, eider ducks, or terns.

Sometimes fishermen camp on islands in the summer to be near the lobstering. Do not judge them by the state of the camp, for these are temporary shelters only. It is well to introduce yourself when you come ashore and to make clear your intentions, for sometimes such an island is invaded by unpleasant and even destructive parties, so that the inhabitants become quite surly toward visitors.

On the whole, the local residents you meet will be pleasant and helpful people and they will keep an eye on you. Just look around carefully on any clear day and see how many lobster boats you can see. They see you and they communicate with each other by radio. If you need help suddenly, burn a flare and call "any vessel" on the radio.

Portland, Maine (13292). Portland is a large commercial harbor, agitated by island ferries and commercial fishermen and occasionally by big tankers and the ferry to Yarmouth, Nova Scotia. Nevertheless, in recent years Portland has been developed as a yachting center under the increasing pressure for mooring space.

Portland is reasonably well protected in anything short of an easterly gale and provides repair facilities of all kinds. It has good stores and is a convenient place to change crews as it has air and bus service and is soon to have train service. If one must lay over for a day or two, Portland provides much to do and see ashore with an art museum, old houses open to the public, a good library, the Maine Historical Society, and the Old Port Exchange, a part of the city restored to its nineteenth-century ambience with numerous small restaurants and specialty shops. However, it is in no sense the picturesque Maine the cruising man has come so far to see.

Portland is an easy harbor to make under almost any conditions. The Large Navigational Buoy with a brilliant flash and a horn is the outer mark. However, few yachts need to keep that far offshore. Coming from the west, make either the whistle on Old Anthony or bell 1, off Richmond Island. Thence make for the galaxy of lighted buoys between Cape Elizabeth and Portland and follow them up the harbor. With an ebb tide and the wind anywhere in the easterly or southerly quadrant, it can be quite rough off Portland Head.

From the east, the leading marks are Halfway Rock and Witch Rock whistle. The tall tower of Ram Island Ledge Light is very helpful. If the visibility is reasonably good, one can pass north of Ram Island and Cushing Island through Whitehead Passage. Whitehead, a prominent white cliff on the northeast corner of Cushing Island, is a good mark.

The principal hazard on entering Portland is the presence of big vessels. Review the whistle signals, keep the radio tuned to channel 13, do not hesitate to communicate with the pilothouse of tug or tanker to ask their intentions, and hoist the radar reflector high.

There are four large marinas in Portland. Spring Point Marina lies on the south side of the entrance to the harbor between Spring Point Light and the long wharf where tankers pump out cargo. This marina is the site of what was the East Yard in World War II. Here thirty 10,000-ton Ocean-class freighters and 132 Liberty ships were built in basins protected by a coffer dam. The finished ship was launched simply by flooding the basin. The ship was towed to the fitting-out pier, the dam closed, the basin pumped out, and a new keel laid the same day. The basin, now protected by a floating "breakwater" of 12,000 truck tires, provides slips for many local craft and reserves space for transients. Call on channel 9 and switch to 79.

Enter on the east, left, end of the breakwater; turn sharply to starboard to follow the inside of the breakwater and then to port. Tie up alongside the wharf and make arrangements for a slip.

Almost anything you could imagine a yacht might need is available here. Gasoline and diesel fuel, water, and ice are available at the fuel wharf, and a pumpout station is handy. Showers and laundry machines are at the head of the wharf. A very well-equipped marine hardware store and a small restaurant are close by. Facilities for the hauling and repair of wooden and fiberglass hulls, a sail and rigging loft, electronics shop, and engine repair shop are in buildings near the head of the wharf. Also here is a convenience store selling a few groceries and beer, wine, and soda. A bus runs to Portland for those with more complicated needs, and a taxi can be quickly summoned.

East of the marina is the Spring Point Museum, where the bow of the clipper ship *Snow Squall* is preserved. She was built at Cape Elizabeth in 1851. In 1864 she ran ashore in the Strait of Le Maire and limped into Port Stanley in the Falkland Islands where she was abandoned as a total loss. In 1987 Peter Throckmorton, Nicholas Dean, and others brought her bow back to South Portland.

On the east side of the harbor, inside the big oil storage tanks, is

Channel Crossing Marina, with all necessary services. Call on channel 9 or 68. Land at the outer float and move to a slip as directed. Fuel, water, and ice are provided at the shore end of the long float on the north side. There is a good restaurant at the head of the wharf: snacks on the deck, full service in the dining room. A small chandlery, showers, and laundry machines are opposite, and a short walk inland brings you to a satisfactory little grocery store. A fence and gate assure security. Repairs can be arranged through the dockmaster.

Above Channel Crossing are the moorings of the Centerboard Yacht Club, marked with flags. Call the Yacht Club on channel 68.

On the west side of the harbor is DiMillo's, which usually has a slip available for a transient. Call on channel 71. It has the advantage of being right in downtown Portland, close to a good grocery store a few steps southward at the head of Union Wharf and to Chase-Leavitt's excellent marine supply store on Dana Street, which starts two blocks south of DiMillo's. DiMillo's has a floating restaurant and bar, washing machines, showers, and toilets. The slips offer free power connections and water hoses on the wharf. At the outer float, gasoline, diesel fuel, ice, and water are available. There is a small marine-supply store and gift shop on the wharf. Security is provided by a fence and gate, to which you are given the combination when you register. Wakes of passing vessels disturb some berths during the day. In the event of a heavy northeasterly, DiMillo's might be an uneasy spot.

Farther up the harbor, beyond the Coast Guard wharf on the east side, is Marineast, reached by following privately maintained buoys marking a narrow dredged channel. The can and nun mark the channel to the Coast Guard wharf. Leave both to port. This is the smallest of the four marinas, the best protected, and the least stirred by wakes. There are the usual facilities including a marine supply store and a good restaurant, The Snow Squall. The marina also has a lift which can step a mast or haul a small boat. Although the marina does not make repairs, Ron Maguire, the proprietor, can readily find a carpenter, a mechanic, or a sailmaker in the area.

All kinds of repairs can be made in Portland. Consult Chase-Leavitt, either at their store on Dana Street or at their shop on the north side of Union Wharf.

In May 1775 British Captain Mowatt entered Portland to convoy a Captain Coulson, who was to load masts for shipment to England for the British Navy. A Brunswick company of the Sons of Liberty marched to Portland, where they ambushed and captured Mowatt. He gave his parole that if released, he would come ashore the next morning. He broke his parole and departed without the masts.

In October, Mowatt, under orders from Admiral Graves in Boston, returned to Portland to "execute a just punishment," as he said, and gave the citizens two hours "to remove the Human Species out of the said Town." The next morning he bombarded the town and sent a party ashore to set fires, which burned two-thirds of the town. He reported to Graves that by 6 P.M. "Falmouth with the Blockhouse and battery, the principal wharves and storehouses with eleven sail of vessels was all laid into ashes including a fine distillery." The raid, however, backfired, for outraged patriots used the atrocity to rally forces against the British.

In June 1863 Captain Moffit of the Confederate raider *Florida* sent Lieutenant Charles W. Read on a commerce-destroying mission. After considerable success, Read captured the fishing schooner *Archer* of Southport, transferred his crew to her, captured the sloop *Village* off Damariscove, impressed its crew of two as pilots, and sailed into Portland Harbor. He planned to seize the steamer *Chesapeake* and the revenue cutter *Caleb Cushing* and then return and destroy the shipping in the harbor and on the stocks. However, he needed an assistant engineer, whom he did not have, in order to handle the engines of *Chesapeake*, so Read seized the *Cushing*. However, the wind was light and the tide foul. The mayor of Portland and the collector of customs commandeered *Chesapeake* and two other steamers, armed them with field guns from the armory, and overhauled *Archer* and *Caleb Cushing*. The schooner was captured and Read blew up the *Cushing*. The result of this raid was far-reaching, leading to the hasty completion of Fort Popham on the Kennebec and the expensive fortification of many Maine harbors.

Falmouth Foreside, Maine (13290). On the mainland west of Clapboard Island and north of "S.E. GAB" on Chart 13290 is the yard of Handy Boat Service and the headquarters of the Portland Yacht Club. One may approach either from the south by Portland Head and up the buoyed channel west of Great Diamond and Little Diamond Islands, or through Hussey Sound. The latter is easier in the fog or at night. With an adverse tide, hug the Long Island shore. Respect the buoys, especially the nun south of Clapboard Island. At night, resist the temptation to run in for the lights in the anchorage as soon as Clapboard Island is cleared. One must first locate the can and beacon on York Ledge.

The anchorage is not very well protected in the usual afternoon southwesterly, but the chop dies with the wind at sunset. An easterly gets quite a rake from Clapboard Island, but one can shift to an anchorage close behind the island if it gets too uncomfortable.

Call Handy's on channel 9 for a mooring. If none is available, anchor so as not to obstruct the channels to Handy's and to the yacht club float.

It is best to use Handy's launch service to go ashore as there is scant room to tie a dinghy. Handy's can provide almost anything a cruising yacht may require. At the float one can get fuel, water, and ice, exchange CNG tanks, and pump out the holding tank. In the building behind the wharf is The Chandlery with a wide selection of marine hardware, clothes, books, charts, and "gifts." Below is The Galley offering snacks and full meals. The yard is equipped to haul vessels up to 35 tons and to repair either wood or fiberglass hulls and engines. Serious electronic repairs can be sent out. Richard Hallett Canvas and Sails can repair a sail or build a new one in short order.

Don't try to walk from Handy's to the yacht club. The way is steep and a real bushwhack. Rowing is easier.

The Portland Yacht Club welcomes cruising people. Call the steward on channel 68 for a vacant mooring. The club provides launch service and showers and serves meals by reservation. There is a bar which supplies the fixings, but bring your own bottle.

The club supports a busy summer program, the most popular event being the Monhegan Race held the second week in August. The casual cruising man does well to avoid the scene at that time as it is crowded with the high-speed racing fraternity. However, if you like to see the latest in modern yacht design or if you want to observe the sociology of the highly competitive, Maine offers no better opportunity. The race usually starts east of Clapboard Island on Saturday morning and runs to Cape Porpoise whistle, Manana whistle, Witch Rock bell, and back to the start. Smaller boats sail a shorter course. The race usually takes anywhere from 24 to 36 hours; but if the fleet strikes a soft spot, it may take days.

There is a small grocery store a short distance north on the main road. By taxi all the facilities of Portland are available including bus and airplane service. The owner with only a short time at his disposal can leave his boat under the eye of Handy's and can make quick connections to Boston, New York, or Washington.

In the event of really severe weather, it is well to leave Falmouth

Foreside for a more protected anchorage like South Freeport. After Hurricane Carol, a considerable part of the anchored fleet lay stranded along the shore.

Yarmouth, Maine (13290). It is a pleasant trip up the Royal River to a basin just below the Route 88 bridge.

Approaching from the bay, leave Mosiers Island to starboard and pick up the green flasher. Steer about 310 degrees to pick up a series of stakes, nuns, and cans which will take you around a sandbar at the mouth of the Royal River. The channel is well marked, though in poor light, markers are hard to see. We have found that the best time to go up the river is at $3/4$-tide with the tide rising. The *Coast Pilot* reports that above nun 16 the channel was bare at low water in 1990. As you leave the narrow part of the river, the channel takes a swing to starboard close to the Royal River Boat Yard. This is a full-service yard with power, water, ice, and diesel fuel. The river now opens up, and you can see the buildings of Yarmouth. Follow the buoys straight up the river into the basin which is a secure hurricane hole. There is a depth of about 6 feet in the basin.

You will pass Yankee Marina to port, which has floats with water, ice, and power. Yankee is a full-service yard with travelift and chandlery. The large blue building on your port is the old sardine factory and now serves as inside winter storage for Yankee Marina.

At the northerly end of the basin is Yarmouth Boat Yard which is also a full-service yard with chandlery. Usually float space at these marinas is filled, so either call ahead or plan to anchor in the basin. The town of Yarmouth with shopping facilities, banks, and restaurants is a $1/2$-mile walk. The anchorage, being near the highways, is a little noisy.

Between the two yards on the south bank is Lower Falls Landing, a gray-painted complex formerly a sardine factory. Here is one of the best bookstores on the coast, Harbour Books, with an outstanding marine section. In the same complex is a sailmaker, Shore Sails, a marine store, and an excellent restaurant as well as other shops.

Jewell Island, Maine (13290). This snug anchorage is the nearest in Casco Bay to the direct route alongshore, and hence much favored by cruising people. However, within half an hour by powerboat from the city of Portland and moorings of 5,000 yachts with home ports in Casco Bay, the cruising yacht will find little solitude here. On weekends, Cocktail Cove, as it has come to be called, is filled to capacity and the shores are crowded with campers. In midweek the visitor will find it less crowded, but the island is still pretty well trampled down. The island is owned by the Maine Bureau of Parks and Recreation and is supervised by volunteers, many of whom are members of the Maine Island Trail Association. These people watch for fires, provide outhouses for the many visitors, and pick up the leavings of the few irresponsibles who never learned in kindergarten to pick up their own messes.

From the west, make bell 2JR off Cliff Island and follow the shore of Jewell Island, giving it berth enough to avoid the dilapidated wharf and the ledges south of it. Leave nun 4 to starboard, round it, and favor the west side of the cove. There is about 7 feet at low water in the middle of the cove opposite the house on the little island. It shoals up rapidly toward the shores, and the head of the cove is dry at low water. The bottom is soft mud. There are several moorings, but to deal with impatient fishermen in the small hours can be distressing and the owners of other moorings are likely to want them in the late afternoon.

From the east, pass between Halfway Rock and Drunker's Ledge, keeping far enough to the north to see the southeast corner of Cliff Island. In thick weather, make bell BS. Pass south of West Brown Cow, which is prominent and always exposed. The rock southeast of it is a good mark but should be treated with respect. This detour to the north is taken to avoid the very extensive ledges east of Jewell Island, on which the writer has left red paint in years past. Round the northern end of Jewell Island, giving it a generous berth, and proceed up the cove, favoring the west side as before.

From the anchorage at Jewell Island, walk across the northern point to the Punchbowl. At low tide the water is trapped here and tempered somewhat by the sun. There is a nice beach, too. From the southern end of this cove runs a well-defined trail, once a jeep road, to the lookout towers at the southern end of the island. From the concrete towers on a clear day one can see all of Casco Bay, a view well worth the walk and climb. These towers were built during World War II as part of a coast defense battery to protect Portland. Bring a flashlight and explore the tunnels in the gun positions beyond the towers, but beware of open manholes.

The southern end of the island is steep, and in some places there are caves and cliffs of rather loose, rotten rock. It is overgrown with juniper, wild roses, raspberry bushes, and other prickly vegetation, so don't try it in short pants.

Mr. W. S. Carter and several friends visited Jewell Island in a fishing sloop in 1858. He wrote:

As cooked by the Pilot, we pronounced the haddock excellent; and after dinner we raised the anchor, hoisted sail, and cruised idly among the islands till near sunset, when we put into a delicious little cove—narrow, deep and shady—on Jewell's Island. As we glided in, an old fisherman who resided on the island came alongside in his dory to have a little chat, and gave us a magnificent lobster, which went immediately into the pot for supper. After coming to anchor, we all went ashore in our boat, except the Pilot, who was detained on board by his duties as cook, to explore the island, witness the sunset, and get milk, eggs, and butter from a farmhouse near our landing-place.

The island, which lies about ten miles east of Portland, seemed to be fertile and well cultivated. The farmhouse was built on elevated ground and the view of the sunset and of the island-studded bay was superb. Fresh and sweet were the eggs and milk and butter with which we returned to our sloop and very jolly the supper we had in the little cabin. The evening was pleasantly cool, and the Assyrian, remarking that boiled lobster was not wholesome unless well qualified with something acid, availed himself of the Pilot's steaming teakettle and brewed a pitcher of hot lemonade with a strong infusion of whiskey which he administered to each of us in proper doses, as a sure preventive against any ill effects from our supper.

By way of contrast, a twentieth-century visitor contributes the following:

Having been there many years ago I remembered it as a quiet and dramatic, unspoiled island. I suspect what I saw could be a case study in how an offshore island within an hour by outboard of a big city can become overpopulated in a hurry. We arrived at 3:30 on a hot Saturday afternoon. More than 30 assorted yachts were anchored in the cove. Many of them were rafted and on long scope so they continually drifted and fouled each other as the afternoon wore on. The cove was filled with small rubber outboards with children under ten orbiting the mother craft while mother took polaroid pictures, threw the film backing overboard, and shouted for Honey to mix another daiquiri. By five-thirty the small outboards were leaving, only to be replaced by the migration and nesting of large 30- to 40-foot power boats that came out and rafted up for a supper sail. I think this means power out from Portland at 15 knots for thirty minutes, raft up, and keep the power going to supply ice and light so they don't have to drink in the dark while they spew exhaust and banana daiquiris into the night air. It was by far the most unpleasant and insensitive group of people I met in any place along the coast. I am sure many of the people there were as disgusted as I was by the license a few took with what should have been a quiet and secluded refuge. Never was it more true that no man is an island.

I suspect much of what we found was because we were there on a weekend during hot weather. It may be much better at midweek. I will go back again in the hope that in the future we will have better luck on this trip. It is a lovely island and if respected can be enjoyed by us all. End of sermon.

South Freeport, Maine (13290). This quite large and perfectly protected harbor lies nearly at the head of Casco Bay. It is the center for considerable summer activity on the mainland and on nearby Bustins Island and Mosier Island. The chief landmark for the harbor is an imitation of a medieval castle tower on the shore to the west of the harbor. Casco Castle was part of a summer hotel built in 1908 by Amos F. Gerald, a trolley-car magnate, as an inducement for people to ride his trolley line from Portland. He had built and promoted a dozen such railways in Maine and was known as "the Electric Railroad King." In 1914 the wooden hotel burned, leaving only the tower.

There is a strong tide at the narrow entrance to the harbor. Follow the buoys carefully, favoring the left side. More than 300 boats are anchored here in the summer. As you head into the harbor, favor the west side as flats make out from the east side. The Harraseeket Yacht Club floats are on your port hand. Water is available at the floats and a telephone at the clubhouse. Inquire of the sailing instructor for an available mooring. The club has two guest moorings and an absent member's mooring may be available. Do not anchor. The tide and wind will play games with you. Don't plan to spend much time at the floats as an active sailing program is in progress most of the time.

As you proceed farther up the harbor, you will pass Strout's Point Marine, the town wharf, and South Freeport Marine. Both marinas offer full service with travelifts, fuel, power, water, chandlery, and rental moorings. South Freeport Marine, which listens to channel 9, is now run by John Brewer and is one of a "chain" of Brewer's Marinas. In addition to fuel, water, ice, and electric power for yachts berthed in slips, South Freeport Marine offers showers, laundromat, telephone, launch service, pumpout, and repair service for wood and fiberglass hulls, engines, and electronics. Rigging and sail repair can be arranged. The town wharf is crowded with commercial traffic. Harraseeket Lunch close by the wharf is a good place to eat a seafood snack or more. A short walk up the road behind South Freeport Marine and to the left on the main road is a small convenience store with the necessaries to support life aboard as well as milk, soda, beer, and wine.

A call to L. L. Bean will arrange a "courtesy" lift to their emporium in Freeport which is open 24 hours a day, selling equipment for hunting, fishing, canoeing, and other outdoor activities. Lately, satellite outlet stores have sprung up around Bean's. These might be of interest to those weathered in who enjoy shopping.

Mere Point, Maine (13290). This is a well-protected harbor northeast of Upper and Lower Goose Islands. The yacht club does not offer traditional yacht club services but does sponsor occasional racing. The marina is run by John Marsh. There is 3 to 4 feet at the floats at low water. Gasoline, diesel, ice, water, and moorings are available. Transportation is also available. The boatyard which is operated by Win Smith has a marine railway and can offer limited repair service.

Great Chebeague Island (13290). One fairly good anchorage in southerly weather is off Lobster Beach on the northeastern end of the island. A path leads southeast to the island's main road. One can land at the stone wharf in the cove on the northern part of the island and walk to a store in the middle of the island. A water taxi, *Islander*, runs from the stone wharf to Cousins Island, which is connected by a causeway to the mainland and thence to I-95 and megalopolis. Up the hill from the stone wharf is the Hillcrest Hotel and a golf course.

The Casco Bay Lines steamer lands at a wharf in Chandler Cove on the south end of the island connecting with Portland several times a day during the summer. This anchorage is acceptable on a quiet night or in northwesterly weather. Push well up into the cove. An easterly can raise a steep chop in the entrance to Chandler Cove.

On the east side of the island behind Crow Island is a small boatyard, its wharf bare at low water. At half-tide or better one can get alongside for gasoline and minor repairs.

Potts Harbor, South Harpswell, Maine (13290). This is a large harbor with plenty of room to anchor, and on a quiet summer night it is a peaceful spot. Although the harbor looks rather open and unprotected, when the tide ebbs, the ledges to the south break up any dangerous sea. However, if the afternoon breeze continues into the evening, it can be rolly.

From the west, enter between Horse Island and Upper Flag Island. From the east, follow the buoyed channel from Merriconeag Sound. It is not nearly as difficult as the chart suggests.

On the west shore of the harbor is Dolphin Marina, operated by Mal Saxton. The marina hauls and stores boats and can arrange for minor repairs. There are a number of rental moorings. The tide runs quite briskly through the anchorage. Gasoline and diesel fuel are available at the float where there is a depth of 15 feet at low water. There is a telephone on the wharf and a grocery store about a mile and a half up the road. Near the marina is a restaurant overlooking Casco Bay which makes a specialty of lobster stew, fish chowder, and homemade desserts. It is open from 8 A.M. until 8 P.M. year-round.

Eagle Island (13290). This island was given to Admiral Peary in recognition of his discovery of the North Pole. It is now a state park open from Memorial Day weekend until Labor Day. There are several guest moorings and an interesting museum displaying Peary memorabilia. On a quiet night this may be better than a crowded berth in Jewells Island.

Harpswell Harbor, West Harpswell, Maine (13290). This is probably the best-protected and quietest harbor in this part of Casco Bay in the usual southerly weather, although it would be uncomfortable in anything northeasterly. Notice the 1-foot sounding westerly of can 5. There are several private landings here but no facilities for visitors. The small town of West Harpswell is at the head of the harbor.

Mackerel Cove, Bailey Island, Maine (13290). This is a comparatively easy harbor to make at night, with lights on Halfway Rock and Little

Mark Island, a lighted gong on Turnip Ledge, and a flasher in the harbor mouth. Watch for the two peaks of Drunkers Ledges, one marked by a beacon and the other by a nun. In clear weather the most useful mark for the entrance is a pair of Coast Artillery observation towers. These are shown on Chart 13288 but not on 13290. However, they are close behind the house, which is shown on the latter chart. The harbor is open to the southwest and any southerly tends to make the anchorage uneasy. The farther in you go, the less swell you feel. But the anchorage is crowded, especially at the time of the Annual Bailey Island Tuna Tournament, held the last full week in July. The holding ground is good.

On the west side of the harbor is the Mackerel Cove Marina. Gasoline, diesel fuel, water, and ice are available at the float. It is possible that the manager would know of an available mooring. Call on channel 9.

There is also a coffee shop and a restaurant on the wharf serving lunch and dinner.

Skillings Boat Yard across the sandy spit west of the harbor can make repairs to hull, rigging, or engines.

At the north end of the island is a very small and well-protected cove on the west side of the bridge over Will's Gut. There are several moorings there and limited slip space.

Long Cove at the north end of Orrs Island on the west side of the bridge is sometimes used by local boats as a hurricane hole. Enter cautiously as the entrance is starred with half-tide rocks.

Quahog Bay, Maine (13290). This is a lovely spot to spend a day, especially if you have children aboard. On weekends, however, you may have a good deal of company. The swimming has none of the numbing, breathless quality of the offshore islands. There may be flounder to be caught, and there are beautiful protected coves to explore with an outboard or a sailing dinghy.

Enter from the south, preferably west of Pole Island. The ledges north and south of Pole Island and those on the shore of Pole Island itself seem to extend much farther to the east and west than the chart indicates. Shoal-draft boats can enter, carefully, from Ridley Cove north of Yarmouth Island.

Anchorage is good anywhere inside the bay although there is some kelp and weed on the bottom. One can push up behind the ledges and islets east of Snow Island for a really snug berth. There is an uncharted rock about where the chart shows 9 feet south of Ben Island.

There are now two wharves on the east side of the bay. The larger is Webber's Boatyard with heavy hauling equipment. Great Island Boat Yard in Orr's Cove sells fuel and marine supplies.

Cundy's Harbor, Maine (13290). This small harbor is well protected in anything but a heavy easterly. There are no guest moorings but there is room to anchor. Although there are now several local yachts moored here, the harbor is principally occupied by lobster boats and small draggers. Gasoline and diesel fuel are available on the northern wharf.

There are two stores. The one on the southerly wharf, Holbrook's, has basic grocery supplies. Watson's on the northerly wharf has some groceries, some marine supplies, some hardware, and lives up to the legend over the door, "General Store." It was established many years ago by the great-grandfather of the present owner. He was bound for Boothbay to establish a store there, was driven into Cundy's Harbor by stress of weather, and established his store here.

There is a small restaurant, The Block and Tackle, up the road a short distance to the north. There is also a snack bar, famous locally for blueberry cobbler in season.

Cundy's Harbor has a strong nineteenth-century coastal Maine atmosphere. The houses, most of them built in the last century, crowd the narrow neck of land between the harbor and Ridley Cove. Summer cottages and modern year-round retirement homes, built farther back and along the shores, cannot be seen from the anchorage and leave the harbor with an old-time ambience.

The Basin, Maine (13290). This is an attractive anchorage off the eastern side of the New Meadows River, a favorite with many. A frequent visitor warns that one should keep to the *outside* of the bends on entering, where the tide scours the channel. Also he warns of a rock almost in the middle of the anchorage. Although this is shown on the chart, it has picked up yachts in the past.

A visitor to The Basin contributes the following description of the rock in the entrance:

On entering The Basin from the New Meadows River, I found that the rock which is marked on the chart was above water, in fact had a seagull on it. This seemed to offer an opportunity to look it over for future reference. About 75 feet north of the rock the bottom came up rather suddenly and I decorated the granite with red bottom paint and a bit of lead. The rock, which is marked with a single asterisk is, I would estimate, over 100 feet long, extending roughly north-south. It appears to be a continuation of the two nearest points of land. Later the tide went down farther and a second part of the rock, about 40–50 feet north of the one which appeared first, also showed above water, in fact, a couple of seals indicated its location before it broke the surface.

Another rock has been reported off the northwest corner of Denny Point southwest of the 20-foot sounding. Weed shows above it at half-tide.

Sebasco, Maine (13290). Here is a good anchorage behind Harbor Island and its outlying ledges, although in a heavy southerly it might be uncomfortable. In entering, keep in the middle. Both shores are studded with ledges, the ones on Harbor Island making out *much* farther than one might expect from looking at the chart.

Sebasco Lodge, the prominent hotel on the eastern shore, maintains twenty guest moorings. The ones in front of the float on the west side are convenient, but if there is any chop running in the harbor, you can be more secure and comfortable on one of the western moorings. They are 2- to 7-ton granite blocks. A harbormaster is on duty from 8 A.M. to 5 P.M. daily between the last weekend in June and Labor Day.

Although Sebasco is far from the direct course across Casco Bay, one who takes the time to run up the bay will find a float with 6 feet at mean low water and with gasoline, water, and ice available. Just up the shore from the float is a snack bar open daily from midmorning to 5:30 P.M. You can normally make arrangements with the office for reservations in the main dining room. Adjacent to the snack bar is a lounge, with telephone, laundromat, restrooms, and showers opening off it.

Ashore there is a swimming pool, nine-hole golf course, tennis courts, bowling alleys, and a variety of family-style entertainment every evening, ranging from Bingo to dances. If space is available, sailors are welcome.

Buddy Brewer has a boat shop near Sebasco Village and can take care of ordinary repairs. H & H Boat Works has a heavy trailer which can haul a yacht. They do some repair work. Diesel fuel and provisions are available at West Point.

Small Point Harbor, Maine. Goose Rock is at the very top of the picture and the shoals east of it show as dim clouds in the channel. The lobster wharf and the Small Point Yacht Club wharf are evident and there are several boats in the anchorage. They are moored close together, indicating that the channel between the mud banks is very narrow here. At the left are Wood Island and Little Wood Island. *Courtesy James W. Sewall Co.*

If possible, leave Sebasco on the first of the ebb, keep to the eastern shore down to Cape Small, and get a fine lift to windward from the tide. It runs briskly down the New Meadows River and still faster out of the Kennebec. (See page 465 on the entrance to the Kennebec.) Across Sheepscot Bay the ebb tide sets to the south or southeast and is less important to the eastward-bound yacht.

Attractive as Sebasco is in moderate weather, in a strong southerly it is likely to be rough. Although you are probably safe enough on one of the big moorings, you will be much more comfortable in The Basin, Cundy's Harbor, or the pond at Small Point.

Small Point Harbor, Maine (13290). This harbor is the first shelter in Casco Bay for the westward-bound mariner and requires giving up very little distance to windward. Entrance from Cape Small is easy, but it is well to follow the buoys, leaving nun 2 on Gooseberry Ledge, the red-and-green nun on Middle Ledge, and nun 4 on Pitchpine Ledges to starboard. In thick weather, make red bell 4 off Wood Island and leave to starboard the red-and-green nun next to it. Then follow the bold shores of Wood Island and Little Wood Island and hunt for nun 4.

What is called Small Point Harbor on the chart may be good shelter for a coasting schooner, but a yachtsman might well consider it a roll hole. The least objectionable place to anchor is off the beach northeast of Goose Rock. The best move, however, is to move up into the pond behind Hermit Island. The tide runs hard in the channel and it would be very difficult under sail.

Enter north and east of Goose Rock. The rock is high and bare but not easy to distinguish from the land behind it. It lies south of the sandy beach on the mainland and is distinguished by several bright-white ledges. Round the northern end and proceed southerly up the narrow channel between moored racing boats. At low water there is a small beach on the eastern shore with a sandy shoal extending a short distance westward into the channel. About abreast the last white rocks on Goose Rock a steep mussel bar almost blocks the channel. Turn sharply eastward. The end of the bar is marked in summer by a small red spar placed by the Small Point Yacht Club, but it was not there in mid-September 1992. A dead windblown pine tree in a patch of bushes north of a white house was a good mark to head for in 1992.

Continue up the channel favoring the east side as there are ledges and mussel bars to the west. Pass a commercial wharf to starboard and the

Small Point Yacht Club to port and anchor among the yachts in the pool above. The anchorage is narrow and its sides are steep. The flats are extensive. What looks like an inland lake at high water becomes an eel rut. You may need a stern anchor to prevent swinging ashore.

There is no satisfactory place to land and little inducement. There is no store. The yacht club consists of a float with no facilities for cruisers, and there are no facilities at the commercial wharf either. It serves as a base for local lobstermen and could perhaps provide fuel in an emergency.

Mosquitoes resident in the extensive swamps behind Cape Small are said to be fierce.

The Kennebec River (13293). Inside or outside Seguin: When the eastward-bound mariner passes Cape Small and leaves Casco Bay, he must decide whether to go inside Fuller Rock, along the Cape Small shore, across the mouth of the Kennebec, and eastward through the passage between the Sisters and the Black Rocks, or outside Fuller Rock, outside Mile Ledge and Seguin, and across to the Cuckolds. The decision must be made largely on the basis of local conditions.

The inside route is shorter, and one is likely to find smoother water and more wind under the land. Under ordinary conditions, the inside route is preferable. However, if a strong ebb tide is running and the usual gentle southwester has worked itself up into a real breeze of wind, the tremendous rush of water pouring out of the river against the wind and sea can raise a short, high chop between Jackknife Ledge and the Sisters, which can be dangerous to a small yacht. It would be wise to go well outside Seguin under these conditions.

Also, if the weather is thick, there is a good deal to be said for keeping offshore. There is a magnetic disturbance for a mile or so around Ellingwood Rock, just north of Seguin, a disturbance which may not be evident at all, but which may set the compass off as much as a point (11°). The tide in the mouth of the river runs hard enough to set a yacht running for the lighted bell right down on Seguin Ledges. The flood tide could set one up on Whaleback or the Black Rocks. Allowance for the tide is guesswork at best. It is much easier and safer to make Fuller Rock and run for Mile Ledge bell, with the horn on Seguin for a guide, and then to square away for the Cuckolds. Its horn is not much good to windward, but there is a radio beacon on the light, which is very helpful, and a bell outside the light. Tom Rock is the only obstruction, and except on a very heavy flood tide and light air, it should cause no trouble. The

The mouth of the Kennebec River with Fort Popham in the upper left and the Etnier house on Long Island opposite.

writer once passed north of the Sisters and between Ellingwood Rock and Seguin in a breeze in which he should have been reefed. Even with a strong ebb tide, the situation was manageable. However, another yachtsman in similar circumstances twisted off his rudder post, went ashore on Whaleback, and lost his boat in a smoky sou'wester.

The following account from Carter's *Coast of New England* describes a squall off Seguin in 1858:

We made sail at once in the direction of Boothbay, but in the course of a couple of hours the wind rose to a gale. The sea grew very rough, and almost every minute a wave would break over our vessel and, sweeping along the deck, deluge the cockpit with water. We closed the cabin to keep it dry, and, gathering at the stern, watched the sea, not without anxiety. The air was so thick with mist that we could see nothing but the raging waves around us, and could not tell where we were going, though the sloop was plunging along at a fearful rate, her bows almost continually under water and her mast opening wide cracks at every tug of the sails. There was considerable danger of the mast's going overboard. In that case we should have been completely at the mercy of the waves, on a coast every inch of which was rockbound, so that, if our vessel struck, she would be pounded to pieces in ten minutes.

We drove madly along, the grim old Pilot at the helm, and the anxious Skipper, arrayed in oilskin to shed the wet, clinging to the mast and keeping a sharp lookout ahead. Suddenly the mist rose and rolled away before a sweeping blast, and then we saw Seguin lighthouse, and knew where we were. It was a superb and terrible sight—these wild reefs with the waves foaming and flashing over them, directly in our course. It was growing late, and the gale was on the increase. The sea was white with foam on the surface, but the great waves, as they came leaping and roaring at us, had a black and angry look not pleasant to behold. Our aged Pilot, as he sat clutching the helm, his hat drawn tightly over his brows to keep it from blowing off, glanced uneasily from time to time at the laboring and groaning mast, whose wide seams were alternately opening and shutting, but he said nothing. He had weathered many a harder gale, though never in so poor a craft. The Assyrian, clinging to the cover of the cabin for support, and with strong symptoms of seasickness in his face, at length broke out as a whooping billow swept over us, soaking him from head to foot:

"I say, Skipper, this is coming in rather strong. Can't we put in somewhere?"

The Skipper had been for some minutes watching a large schooner about a mile ahead of us, and, coming aft, said that it was hardly possible to weather Cape Newagin in such a storm, even if our mast held, about which he had great doubts. The schooner ahead of us was running for shelter into Sheepscut Bay, where there was an excellent harbor, and we could easily follow her in. The Pilot, after an emphatic reference to "that damned old stick," as he called the mast, assented to this opinion, and our course was accordingly changed to the northward.

Following the lead of the schooner for several miles, we reached about nightfall a beautiful and perfectly sheltered harbor, which the Skipper called sometimes Southport and sometimes Abenacook.

For a lighter view of this desperate passage, we add the following yarn (the source is unknown to the writer):

An old gentleman, who had been fishing all his life and who had wrung more water out of the cuffs of his pants than most of us have ever sailed over, made a little money in the summer taking summer boarders sailing in his sloop.

One day it breezed up southwest near Seguin and got pretty choppy. Spray was flying and she began to take water into the cockpit. The passengers were frightened, and finally one said, "Cap'n, we think you ought to offer prayer for our safety."

"I don't b'lieve that'll be necessary," answered the skipper, easing her over a sea.

"Well, we feel that it is your duty as captain of this boat to ask for Divine help and guidance in this emergency."

"All right," answered the skipper, "I'll do what I can if it'll ease you any." So with both hands on the tiller and the passengers kneeling around him, the captain prayed,

"Lord, I never have interfered in your affairs and you have always used me right. But these people have asked me to speak with you. Now I know we'll get in all right, but if you would like to make these people feel a lot better, you can go ahead and calm the waters. But just remember, Lord, this isn't the Sea of Galilee. This is the North Atlantic Ocean."

Our considered advice to those passing Seguin is to go inside unless a considerable sea is running or visibility is bad.

Seguin Island, Maine (13293). Seguin is one of the principal landfall lights on the coast and the outer mark for the Kennebec River. The light is now automated, personnel have been taken off, and all weather instruments removed. No longer is it possible to climb the tower. Nevertheless, Seguin is a dramatic island and well worth a lunch stop.

In approaching the cove on the eastern side, give the eastern point a generous berth on all sides and note that the eastern shore of this point is not at all bold. In 1992, there was a heavy Coast Guard mooring in the cove. If this has been removed, you will have to anchor. The water is deep and the bottom rocky and foul with kelp. You will probably find it easier to land on the beach than on the boathouse skids, which were made for Coast Guard peapods. Climb the tramway to the top of the island for a view extending from Monhegan to Cape Elizabeth. The White Mountains stand up grandly from here on a clear day. Gulls nest on the cliffs on the west side and on the northern ridge. From this grassy knoll the poet, the painter, the philosopher can perhaps take a sane and objective view of what otherwise seems a mad planet.

Fort Popham. Although it is possible to enter the river west of Pond Island and the aerial photograph makes this course appear logical, the better passage is east of the island. Practically speaking, you must have either a fair wind or a fair tide to get into the river under sail. With both, you will be hurried by Popham Beach, the fort, and the abandoned Coast Guard station. The grim-looking fort was built during the Civil War to protect the river, Bath in particular, from attack by the South. It has been called facetiously Maine's greatest compliment to the Confederate Navy.

However, it should be remembered that a Confederate naval vessel seized several vessels off the Maine coast, and in one of them a crew slipped into Portland Harbor and cut out the fast revenue cutter *Caleb Cushing.* After a spectacular chase, the Confederates were at length defeated, but there certainly was reason to be concerned about Confederate forces at one time.

The Sabino peninsula appears in the early history of our country several times.

In 1605, Champlain visited Sabino twice, once ascending the Kennebec and descending the Sasanoa and Sheepscot. He named Seguin "La Tortue" because of its resemblance to a tortoise. (Incidentally, the Abenaki word "Siguenoc" means tortoise.)

In 1606 Martin Pring visited the coast and wrote what must have been a glowing account of the Kennebec. Unfortunately Pring's account is lost, but we know that it caused Gorges and Popham of the Plymouth Company to send to Sabino, in the spring of 1607, two ships and 120 men, led by Ralegh Gilbert, Sir Humphrey's son, and old George Popham, who was nearly eighty years old.

The colony was well equipped and provisioned. It was going to a site well known. The natives were friendly and anxious to trade. The economic basis of the colony—salt cod, furs, and spar timber—was sound. The expedition was well financed, well manned, and well led. During the summer a number of houses were built and the *Virginia,* the first vessel built in New England, was launched and sent out to explore Penobscot and Casco Bays. The winter was hard, but far from intolerable, in spite of the loss by fire of a storehouse. Old George Popham died, to be sure, but young in heart as he was, it is not surprising, in view of his age. Even in Maine a man of seventy-six can succumb. In the spring a vessel arrived from England with more men and supplies, but with the sad news that Ralegh Gilbert's half-brother had died. Gilbert decided to return to England to take care of his inheritance. Popham was dead. Without leadership the colony disintegrated, some returning to England and others going south to Jamestown in the *Virginia.* It seems ironic that the English colony with the best chance of survival did not last, whereas Jamestown, badly led, badly manned, starved and diseased, and with no strong economic resources, survived and eventually prospered.

Apparently the Maine colony was not a complete failure, however, for Humphrey Damerill, one of the colonists, soon after established a store and fishing station at Damariscove. To Damariscove came the distressed Pilgrims in 1621, and there they received open-handed help. The story is told in greater detail in *Coastal Maine, a Maritime History.*

The best anchorage at Fort Popham is behind the fort in the mouth of Atkins Bay. Get in behind the hook just enough to get out of the tide. The place has silted up badly, so proceed with caution. Land on the beach. On the ebb tide the swimming is good on Popham Beach below the fort. Bluefish can sometimes be caught off the beach.

The River to Bath. Once by the turbulent narrows of Fort Popham, the Kennebec opens out into a smooth and pleasant stream. To sail up this river with a fair tide on a pleasant summer afternoon is one of the greatest pleasures Maine affords. The few dangers are clearly marked, and the current, though insistent, is not disturbing.

The big white house on Gilbert Head, the southern end of Long Island, was once inhabited by the Etniers, Stephen the painter and Elizabeth the author.

Above the high land of Parker Head is Parkers Flats where schooners and square-rigged vessels once anchored to await a fair tide and a tow up or down the river. The town of Phippsburg, marked by a white church steeple, was once a busy shipbuilding center. Wooden vessels were built all along the banks of the river, principally at Phippsburg, Bath, and Richmond but occasionally as far up as Gardiner.

Below Fiddler Reach on the west shore is Morse's Cove where Benedict Arnold's fleet anchored in 1775. The soldiers were landed at Pittston and marched up the Kennebec and down the Chaudière to attack Quebec on Christmas Eve in a snowstorm. Kenneth Roberts' *Arundel* gives a vivid account of the expedition.

Just above Fiddler Reach is the old Percy & Small shipyard, now owned by the Maine Maritime Museum and well worth a day's layover. Off the museum wharf are guest moorings, and lying in the river or alongside the wharf are several historic vessels. Most prominent is the Grand Banks schooner *Sherman Zwicker* built in Nova Scotia and for years an active fisherman. Her hold has been fitted with exhibits, a slide show with taped narration, and film clips showing the actual details of dory fishing. The Friendship sloop *Chance* is moored alongside, and the pinkie *Maine* built by the Apprenticeshop will be there unless she is off cruising.

Ashore is a fine new building finished in 1989 with a coordinated series of exhibits on Maine's maritime history. There are also exhibits of other artifacts, models, paintings, and dioramas showing what Bath was like when shipyards lined the shores building schooners, barges, steamers, naval vessels, and the great square-rigged downeasters in both wood and steel. Here was launched in 1909 the six-masted schooner *Wyoming*, 3,730 tons, the largest wooden sailing vessel to fly the American flag. Carrying 5,000 tons of coal, she was lost off Pollock Rip in March 1924.

Part of the Maine Maritime Museum is the Apprenticeshop, where apprentices learn to build small boats on the principle that anyone who can build a small boat can build anything and will develop the ability to use tools, planning skills, and patience, not all of which can be learned in conventional schools.

The museum gift shop sets a high standard. Its books and prints are sound historically and attractive artistically; its other merchandise is well worth careful inspection. The museum library is also a valuable resource.

Bath, Maine (13293). There is no landing place at Bath below the bridge. It opens for yachts from June 1 to September 30 *only* at 10 A.M. and 2 P.M. The bridgetenders listen to channels 13 and 16. It would be well to call them well in advance. This is the only bridge below Richmond and carries heavy traffic all summer. The roadway is only two lanes wide and, even without opening for shipping, it often backs up Route 1 traffic literally for miles.

Longreach Marina on the west side of the river above the bridge has several moorings and some slip space. Fuel and marine supplies are available here and the stores of Bath are close to the landing. There is a hospital in Bath.

Below the bridge is the Bath Iron Works, now building naval vessels and well-known during World War II for the high quality of its destroyers. One day during the war when the yard was operating at capacity with a dozen destroyers on the ways and lying alongside fitting-out wharves, a naval expediter stood on a crane tower with the yard superintendent, much impressed with the busy scene.

"And how many men are working here today?" he asked.

"About half of them," answered the dour downeaster.

Besides naval vessels, Bath Iron Works has built yachts, among them J. P. Morgan's *Corsair* and Harold Vanderbilt's Cup defender *Ranger,* last of the great J-boats. They have also launched container ships, fishing vessels, and passenger steamers. If one is fortunate enough to arrive on the day of a launching, stand on the bridge to see one of the most impressive marine shows of the century.

On the hill overlooking the river are many elegant homes built in the last century by wealthy shipbuilders, sea captains, and merchants.

Above Bath the river runs rapidly between high banks. There is a narrow place at Thorne Head where the tide is really inspiring. There are several anchorages among the little islands below Lines Island where one can get out of the tide to some extent. However, above The Chops, the tide becomes much less, the banks become lower, and the river widens out into the broad and shallow Merrymeeting Bay formed by the confluence of the Kennebec and the Androscoggin. This bay is inhabited by ducks and geese of many species. In the fall, when the migrants from farther north come through, the bay and the marshes are positively crowded. It is a delightful place.

Above the bay, behind Pork Point, is another possible anchorage in lovely surroundings, and there is another behind Carney Point on the east side. The preferred passage lies east of Swan Island. This large and lovely island is a game preserve. Deer can frequently be seen as one penetrates farther and farther into rural Maine.

At the head of Swan Island is an anchorage at the town of Richmond, just below the bridge. The town is a quiet spot, even in the summertime. There is a landing and the usual supplies are available.

If you are not planning to stop here and the bridge does not open on the usual signal, land at Richmond and look up the bridgetender. You will find it an interesting experience.

At Pittston, on the east bank just below South Gardiner, is a landing and a red house high on the hill overlooking it. This is Colburn's yard, the place where Arnold's soldiers were put ashore, where they picked up bateaux, and whence they plunged into the wilderness in the fall of 1775. The house on the hill is the headquarters of the Arnold Expedition Historical Society. The house is becoming a good museum and the people in charge are well worth visiting.

The river winds on past Gardiner and Farmingdale to Augusta, the head of navigation. If you feel that you are a long way from salt water here, take the first of the ebb and, with a northerly breeze or a modest engine, you can be off Seguin or the Cuckolds in six hours.

Harmon Harbor, Maine (13295, 13293). This is a pleasantly neglected cove on the west shore of the Sheepscot above Griffith Head, sufficiently protected from anything short of a determined smoky sou'wester. The narrow entrance lies between a nun to starboard and a bare rock to port. There is a wharf and float in shoal waters on the west shore belonging to Grey Havens Inn, the prominent hotel on the hill. This inn serves dinners Tuesdays through Fridays, and the Eberhart family which runs it is helpful to cruising people. There is no store at Harmon's Harbor and no fuel. It is a short walk to the store at Five Islands.

Five Islands, Maine (13293, 13295). This is a snug little harbor on the west shore of the Sheepscot River handy for the skipper who doesn't want to go all the way to Boothbay late in the day. On the usual southerly breeze it is a fair wind from The Sisters up the river, and one can fetch the Cuckolds from Five Islands in the morning. The usual entrance is north of Malden Island, the highest, and close to a nun in the middle of the harbor. The nun is said to mark an 11-foot rock, but the writer has never seen bottom there. The *Coast Pilot* recommends passing close to the north of it. The Five Islands Yacht Club maintains two guest moorings marked by red balloons and a float on Malden Island, but there are no shore facilities whatever.

One can enter from the north, but watch the chart carefully and stay close to the day beacon.

Ashore at the head of the town wharf is a small store and snack bar. On the wharf Ronnie and Diane Pinkham sell live and boiled lobsters and clams to be eaten on the wharf or taken aboard. The Sheepscot Bay Boat Company owned by Bill Plummer sells gasoline, diesel oil, and marine supplies. The yard maintains several rental moorings, has a 10-ton lift, and can make ordinary repairs to hull or engine. Plummer specializes in outboard motors, but adds, "If it makes smoke, we can fix it." He monitors channel 16. Behind the Sheepscot Bay Boat Company, Plummer's son has a shop where he builds and finishes fiberglass boats. He can make repairs to fiberglass hulls.

Many older cruising men will remember Five Islands as the home of the big Friendship sloop *Sky Pilot* owned by the late Reverend Nehemiah Boynton and his family. She was built in 1909 by Eugene McLain on Bremen Long Island as *Myrtle E.* and sold to Dr. Boynton the next year. She was decked over and finished up as a yacht although she still carried her original tall gaff-topsail rig. She served the Boynton family well until during World War II she sank at her winter mooring due to a neglected sea cock. Frank Sample, Jr., of Boothbay Harbor bought her, raised her, ballasted her with 9,000 ax heads, and sold her to Richard Swanson of Rockport, Massachusetts. She was the flagship of the Friendship Sloop Society under Swanson and was sold in 1967 to William Johnson of Florida. She was neglected and sank in the Dania River. When the government tried to remove her with a crane, she fell apart. A piece of her now lies in the Friendship Museum.

As the following incident took place off the Sheepscot River, this is an appropriate place for it. It was told over 50 years ago by Al Gould of the sloop *Curlew* to Reverend Edward Boynton, told by him to Robert F. Duncan the original author of this *Guide,* and overheard by the present writer as a small boy.

"There was a summer fellow up at Rockport who bought a beautiful lot of land on the shore a few years ago. Down in Phippsburg he saw an old colonial house which he thought would look well on his place on Beauchamp Point in Rockport. So he went to Captain John Snow, who is in the towage and lighterage business in Rockland and an expert in salvage and all maritime affairs, and asked him to go and look at the house and see whether he thought he could move it around for him.

"John went and looked at it, and thought he could. 'How much will it be to move it?' the man asked John. 'Well,' replied the captain, 'for a long time I have wanted one of those car floats they have in New York Harbor for my business down here. I know where there is one, secondhand, which can be bought cheap. I'll go and get it; move the house; set it up down to Rockport. When I've got it set up, you come down and look at it. If the job is satisfactory, you pay for the float and it belongs to me; and if you don't like the job, you can keep the car float and we'll forget all about any charge.' So the deal was made. John got the float, skidded the house in Phippsburg down onto it, towed it around outside and up Penobscot Bay, and skidded it ashore and into place. Then the owner came down to look at it. The job was perfect. Not even a crack in the plaster.

"One day in Rockport I met John," Al continued, "and asked him about it. John did not have much to say, as he is a very modest man. 'Wasn't there any particularly interesting thing on the way down?' I asked. 'Well,' said John, 'there was one. The fog shut in thick when we got out by Popham. I had the tug out ahead, and she was blowing one long and two short. And to make sure, I had a man up in the cupola of the house with a fish horn, and he was blowing one long and two short too. When we got about off Seguin and were about to make the turn, I heard a jangle of engine bells close aboard to starboard through the fog. A moment afterward the white hull of a steam yacht broke out of the fog. She had her engines going full speed astern with a jingle. You see, her skipper had got a glint in the fog and saw the house looming up dead ahead and thought he was right in on the beach, though there was not less than forty fathoms all around.'"

Note on the Inside Passage from Boothbay Harbor to Bath. Strangers with no more than 8 feet draft can, with the aid of Chart 13296, continue through Townsend Gut and Goose Rock Passage to the Kennebec River and Bath. This entire inside passage from Boothbay Harbor to Bath, though narrow, crooked, and with strong tidal currents, is one of the most delightful trips on the coast. The route is about 11 miles long, and it is well worth the time required, especially if the weather at sea is uncomfortable. Larger yachts should take a pilot, procurable at either end.

The Sasanoa River, leading from the Sheepscot River to the Kennebec River north of Georgetown and Arrowsic Islands, can be made under sail with a breeze from east around to southwest, and is more fun that way than under power. But one would do well to use the top half of the flood tide, when the current is not quite so swift. Note that at the strength of the current, in the narrow places the buoys are often run under for short periods.

The tide is not easily predictable in this passage, but works on the following general principle:

Hockamock Bay is a large body of water, so the flooding tide cannot fill it by the time of high water at Boothbay Harbor. Consequently, for nearly three hours after high water, the tide continues to run up the Sasanoa River from the Sheepscot River and down the Sasanoa River from the Kennebec River, of course with diminishing force, depending on the wind, the height of the tide, and doubtless many more obscure forces. When the level of water in Hockamock Bay approximates that in the Kennebec and Sheepscot Rivers, there is a brief period of slack water. Then the tide begins to run out of Hockamock Bay and so continues until about three hours after low water on the coast.

The Sasanoa River is not a pipeline and there is a lot of friction delaying the flow of water, particularly at Boiler Rock and the two Hell Gates. Consequently, the time of slack water at any spot on the river is difficult to estimate. However, the best move is to start from Boothbay

Harbor about *two hours before high water.* This would give something like slack water approaching Hockamock Bay and a fair current to the Kennebec River and down to Fort Popham.

Particular warning should be given of the two Hell Gates, particularly of the ledge above the Lower Hell Gate. An auxiliary may not be able to buck the tide through here, although a motor cruiser probably could do it. Coming down with the tide, one might think one was entering Niagara Gorge, but keep the power going and the clear channel will appear as you get closer. It is not a difficult place to negotiate, but is awesome, especially for the first time. The late Captain Wade of the *Balmy Days* said that this is a really dangerous place for a small boat.

The chart appears ambiguous about the island in the Upper Hell Gate. The usual channel is north of it, but there is plenty of water on either side.

Aside from being a handy passage to the Kennebec River, this is a beautiful trip. There are dozens of secluded anchorages in the ragged shores. The water is ideal for swimming. Clamming and fishing are possible in some places. But rig your mosquito defenses early.

Robinhood, Maine (13293, 13296). This quiet cove in the Sasanoa River is just below Knubble Bay. The entrance is clear from the chart, but is complicated by a powerful tidal current at Boiler Rock. The buoy is often towed under, and entrance against the tide is almost impossible without power. The tide at Goose Rock Passage looks worse than it is. Favor the bold southern shore on approaching the cove and take advantage of back eddies under the shore.

Once in out of the tide, the skipper will find a large, well-protected harbor off a good marina. Robinhood is a small Maine village still largely "undeveloped" by summer interests.

The Robinhood Marine Center on the western shore has rental moorings and dock space for transients. Ashore, the visitor will find showers, laundry facilities, and a stock room connected with the yard which carries many essential marine items. The nearest grocery store is 4 miles away in Georgetown, but there is a restaurant, the Osprey, close to the yard. The yard has a 35-ton travelift, open-ended so that a masted vessel can be easily hauled. The yard can make repairs to hull, spars, rigging, and engine.

Up the cove, above the yard, is a beautiful and secluded anchorage. Mosquito defenses are essential, however.

An atomic power plant, Maine Yankee, has been built on Back River just below Cowseagan Narrows. To increase the flow of water by the plant, the old Westport bridge and causeway were removed and a new bridge with a clearance of 100 feet was built across to Westport Island. It is now possible once again to circumnavigate Westport Island in a masted vessel, and one can approach Wiscasset either up the Sheepscot or from the Sasanoa River up Montsweag Bay and the Back River. The Back River is a most attractive and secluded spot, but the tide runs hard through the narrow channel.

MacMahan Island, Maine (13296). In approaching the island, beware of Bull Ledge, a half-tide rock well out in the river. It is marked by a red-and-green nun, but the nun is a considerable distance from the ledge.

One can enter between Turnip Island and Georgetown Island at the south end of MacMahan Island or from the north through Goose Rock Passage. The former passage is clear of dangers but the tide runs hard. After the narrow part, as the passage begins to open out, there is a rock on each side. The one to starboard is marked by a nun, and the other usually shows.

The entrance via Goose Rock Passage is marked by a beacon off Northeast Point and a can off the northwest point of the island. There are several small and peaceful coves along the northern shore of the island, but the land is privately owned and there is no public landing.

Wiscasset, Maine (13293). It is a pleasant and pretty sail up the Sheepscot River to Wiscasset, best done with a fair tide. There are no serious navigational hazards and there are several attractive anchorages out of the tide on the shore of Westport Island and up the Cross River and the Back River behind Barters Island. Schooners used to load ice from Knickerbocker Pond in the Back River. They were towed out backward as there was not room to turn them around.

At the tight turn below Wiscasset is a restoration of Fort Edgecomb built to protect Wiscasset when it was a busy commercial and shipbuilding center. On the north end of Westport Island is Sheepscot Marine where there are repair facilities, several moorings, and limited dock space, but no fuel. In the cove called The Eddy on Chart 13293 east of the fort is Eddy Marine, the marine center for Wiscasset. Here are moorings and dock space with water and electricity. Gasoline and diesel fuel are available as well as ice, showers, and a marine store. A mechanic is on call at short notice. A good restaurant, The Muddy Rudder, is at the east end of the bridge, a good walk up a pleasant road. There is no grocery store nearer than Wiscasset.

Anchorage at Wiscasset is off the yacht club south of the town. There are a few guest moorings. Water is available at the yacht club. Yachts may lie briefly at the town landing south of the derelict schooners. Supplies are available in the town and there are two well-supplied hardware stores. Two good places to eat ashore are Le Garage on the shore road behind the rotting schooners and Bailey House at the top of the hill on the main street. On summer weekends, reservations are advised. Buses ran through Wiscasset to Portland, Boston, and Rockland in 1993, but one should check on the service before relying on it.

The Old Jail has historical exhibits, and artists should not miss the Maine Art Gallery. The Central Maine Power Company operates a power plant just below the town. When it was supplied by water, Captain Eliot Winslow, a pilot from Boothbay, used to bring big vessels up the river. It was breathtaking to see him manuever a loaded tanker around the bend at Clough Point. It had to be done at the top of the tide, so a grounding would have been disastrous.

In addition to its lovely old residences and beautifully shaded streets, Wiscasset is notable for the hulks of two four-masted schooners rotting slowly away on the shore just south of Route 1. They are the *Hesper* and the *Luther P. Little*. Dick Vennerbeck tells their story in the *Maine Coast Fisherman* of July 1950:

> With their appearance of great age it is surprising to learn that they were built not so very long ago at the time of the First World War. For some time during and after the war they sailed out of Boston in the coastal trade; but about 1930, their usefulness diminished, they became the property of the Federal Government, and were tied up in Portland. At that time they were sold to a Mr. Winter at the U.S. Marshal's sale. How the *Hesper* and the *Luther P. Little* came to rest in Wiscasset is involved with the story of the old Wiscasset narrow-gauge railroad, since it was to serve this railroad that they were brought from Portland by Mr. Winter.
>
> As early as 1836 it was proposed that a rail line be built from Wiscasset to Canada in order to make Wiscasset the winter port of the St. Lawrence. Had this plan been successful, Wiscasset might well have become one of the East's most important seaports, ship-

ping Canadian timber and food. Misfortune dogged the plan for many years, however, until finally in 1892 a two-foot gauge railroad was begun. The line was to have been extended only as far as the Canadian border, but even this modified plan proved too difficult for the owners. The track was extended only as far as Albion, near Waterville, Maine. The railroad had varying fortunes during the 40 years of its existence, but its revenue steadily decreased. In the latter years of its operation the road was owned by Mr. Frank W. Winter, who bought the *Hesper* and the *Luther P. Little.*

Mr. Winter's plan was to use the two schooners as coal carriers for his railroad. When the vessels were towed to Wiscasset one did actually carry a load of coal, but not long afterwards, due to increased competition from other transportation systems, the narrow-gauge at Wiscasset was forced to close. With no job to do, and having no prospective buyers, the two schooners were scuttled and left at the wharf where they rest today.

So ended the active careers of the *Hesper* and the *Luther P. Little* and the life of a gallant little railroad. Its right of way and rotting piles may still be seen near the northern end of the Maine Central Railroad station platform.

Cozy Harbor, Maine (13293). This little harbor on the west side of Southport Island south of Hendrick's Head is so cozy that it is with difficulty one can get in. Unless you are confident of finding a mooring, go on to Ebenecook Harbor.

In entering Cozy Harbor, leave the red beacon a good 20 yards to starboard and pass close south of the can and about 10 yards south of the diminutive inner beacon. There is no room to anchor. Do not go north of the yacht club flagpole, as the harbor shoals up rapidly toward the head.

Mr. E. W. Pratt runs a snack bar, bowling alley, and small store on the east side. He is a reliable source of local information if not run ragged by persistent young members of the yacht club.

If more extensive supplies are needed, turn left at the head of the road leading up the hill. It is a short walk to Southport Island Market, a well-equipped general store.

The story is told of a lady, for many years a summer resident, who had had her cottage insulated and planned to spend the winter on Southport.

She announced her plan enthusiastically to the storekeeper and added, "But there are a lot of funny people around here, aren't there."

"Yes," replied the storekeeper, "there are. But they'll all be gone by Labor Day."

It was off Hendrick's Head during the last century that a vessel was wrecked in a heavy southeast snowstorm. The lightkeeper tried to launch a dory to rescue the crew but the sea was running too high. He built a big fire on the beach to let the people know that they were seen, but there was little he could do. Soon a light bundle came scudding down the gale. The keeper waded into the breakers and gaffed it ashore. It proved to be two feather beds tied together. Inside was a box and in the box a baby girl with a note from her mother commending her to the care of God. The vessel soon broke up and all the crew were lost, but the lightkeeper and his wife raised the baby girl. This story was printed in the *Boothbay Register* in October 1985, taken from *Lighthouses of New England* by Edward Rowe Snow.

Ebenecook Harbor, Maine (13246). This is a large and well-protected harbor, easy of access and with ample room to anchor. The easiest entrance is between Dogfish Point and the Green Islands. If the weather is thick, just follow the bold shore of Southport Island until you see the octagonal cottage on Dogfish Point. One can also enter north of the Green Islands, north of Boston Island, or either side of the Isle of Springs. From the eastward one enters through Townsend Gut. A large vessel can anchor anywhere in the harbor, but a small yacht will want to tuck into one of the coves. The most westerly cove is occupied by Boothbay Region Boatyard. Leave nun 2 to *port.* It is a mark for entering Ebenecook Harbor, not for the boatyard cove. Here are moorings for transients and ample facilities for hauling and repair. The marine store on the wharf is well supplied and can quickly obtain items from Portland which are not in stock. Charts and government publications are sold here. Gasoline, diesel fuel, ice, and water are provided at the floats. Southport Island Market is less than a mile away. Follow the road out of the yard to the main road and turn right.

The next cove to the eastward is shallow and one cannot push in very far, but it is quiet and well sheltered. Love's Cove, the most easterly of the three, is deep enough, well protected, pretty, and, comparatively speaking, secluded. The cable indicated on the chart runs across near the mouth of the cove and is no problem. Another pleasant berth is between the Green Islands. The chart will suggest others. Almost anywhere out of the tide is good.

Townsend Gut, Maine (13296). This is the passage from Ebenecook Harbor to Boothbay Harbor. It is spanned by a swing bridge and at the southern end is too narrow to beat through against the tide. With a fair wind, however, it can be easily negotiated under sail.

In approaching the Gut from Ebenecook Harbor, you will see nun 4 and will experience a strong inclination to leave it to starboard, for it appears to lie very close to the western shore. Do not do so! *Leave it to port!* A ledge runs from the buoy northward to the end of Indiantown Island, a ledge on which someone lands about once a week in the summertime.

Keep clear of the ledge to starboard at the edge of the cove above Cameron's Point and continue up the middle of the channel. Hodgdon Cove is a well-protected anchorage, although shoal near the shores and noisy in the daytime from the traffic in the Gut.

Blow a long blast and a short one for the bridge as you approach, or call Southport Bridge on channel 9. The bridgetenders are alert and open the bridge promptly. As you pass through, you will be asked the name of the yacht and her owner. This is said to be the result of an incident that occurred just after the bridge was built. Some people were skylarking about, going back and forth through the draw for the fun of seeing the machinery in action. However, their foolishness stalled a fire engine at a critical moment and a house was lost on Southport.

Dekker Cove, just south of the bridge, is another good anchorage. There is a seafood store and restaurant here. An excellent inn, Lawn-meer, is a short walk to the west on the main road.

South of Dekker Cove is the narrowest part of the passage. Favor the west shore. It is very steep beyond the point where a picturesque oak tree grows. There is a ledge on the east side that makes out just north of Juniper Point. It looks dangerous with the tide running madly over it. Nun 2 should also be left to port. Now head for the white church in Boothbay Harbor and run across.

If these narrow places make you chew your gum fast or smoke cigarettes in quick succession or shout at your crew, it may calm you to know that Captain Boyd Guild sailed the coaster *Alice Wentworth* through the Gut, and more recently he has sailed the three-masted schooner *Victory Chimes* through.

Newagen, Maine (13293). This small harbor is a blessing to the westward-bound mariner because it is right on his route. The alternatives—Boothbay Harbor, Five Islands, and Ebenecook—each require a long beat the following morning. On a quiet night, Newagen is a safe and comfortable anchorage. However, should it come on to blow hard from the south, it can be rolly for two hours either side of high water.

The eastward-bound skipper will see the houses at the head of the harbor from bell 2SR in the middle of the Sheepscot River. Head somewhat north of them to be sure to leave nun 2 to starboard. The direct course from nun 2 to the beacon in the harbor mouth will lead you across a kelp ledge which often breaks at low water. To avoid it, head for the white cottage on the point to port until you are nearly up to Hunting Island. Then pass halfway between the red beacon and the steep shore to port. A ledge bare at half-tide extends from the beacon to Hunting Island.

From the east, the obvious course is to round the bell off the Cuckolds. Then steer northwest, about for the building marked "Colonial Ho." on Chart 13293, until nun 2 shows to the eastward of Lower Mark Island. This will take you clear of the long ledge making out to the southwest of the Cuckolds. Then run for the nun.

An alternative is to pass inside the Cuckolds, a preferable course if the wind is light. It saves a tedious beat down to the bell, and there is likely to be a helpful draft under the Cuckolds on a quiet afternoon. Work up close to the mooring buoy north of the lighthouse, give the western island a fair berth, and beware of two ledges off the southern side of Cape Island. One is quite close under the shore and presents no serious problem. The other is a big flat rock extending perhaps 100 yards from the shore at low water. If there is any sea running, it will break at low water. Give the ledge running from Hunting Island to the nun a good berth. It extends out to the south of a direct line from the nun to the island and may still bear some of the writer's red paint.

Once inside the harbor, hail the first float to port and inquire for a vacant mooring. This float belongs to the Newagen Inn and may be occupied only by inn guests who do not know about moorings. In that case, pick up one of the blue buoys labeled "NI." It is unwise to pick up any other mooring in the harbor as some of them are intended for very small boats. The harbor is crowded with lobster boats and local yachts. There is almost no room to anchor.

There is a narrow channel navigable at half-tide for boats drawing up to 5 feet between the shore of Southport and the islet south of it at the eastern end of the harbor. Sound this out for yourself in the dinghy as the directions are complex. The passage is much used by local boats and saves the trip around Cape Island or the Cuckolds.

The town landing on the north side of the harbor, near its head has only 3 or 4 feet at low tide. However, there is little there to attract the cruising man. There is no fuel and no water on the wharf, and the road leads to a small village where there is a post office but no store.

On Cape Island is a private landing and the summer home of the late Margaret Hamilton, who acted the part of the Wicked Witch of the West in *The Wizard of Oz*.

The Newagen Inn, which stands on the hill north of the harbor entrance, offers a bar and pleasant dining room. On a rock beside the road leading up from the inn wharf is a bronze tablet reading:

NEWAGEN

The Earliest Locality
Visited and Named by
English Explorers
In the Boothbay Region

Here
Capt. Christopher Levett
And the Indian Sagamores
Menawarmet, Samoset
and Cogawesco
Met for Four Days in
December, 1623

Although Damariscove had been settled as early as 1606 if not before, Christopher Levett did indeed meet with the men listed and initiated a regular trade in furs. He spent a winter on House Island off Portland and ranged the coast from Boston at least as far east as Newagen.

That the land and waters of the Sheepscot have changed little in 200 years is clear from the following account of a cruise written by Jacob Bailey in *The Frontier Missionary*, edited by William S. Bartlett (Boston, 1853).

Boothbay Harbor, Maine. The inner harbor is at the upper right. Taken early in June, this gives no idea of how crowded the harbor becomes later in the season. Mill Cove is at the top center and the West Harbor with the yacht club southwest of it. The Gut with the drawbridge runs up the left side of the photograph. The tip of Squirrel Island shows at the bottom. *Courtesy James W. Sewall Co.*

June 9, 1779. About nine we got underway with a gentle breeze from the south-west, and fell down between Parker's island and Jeremisquam into Sheepscot River. The country hereabouts made a romantic appearance; fine groves of trees, shrubby evergreens, craggy rocks, cultivated fields and human habitations, alternately presented themselves to view, and yielded a profusion of pleasure to the imagination.

As night approached it grew perfectly calm, and we were obliged to anchor in Cape Newaggen harbour, a little to the west of Booth Bay. This is an excellent station for small shipping. The land rises with an easy slope from the water's edge on the north and partly on the east, while the remainder is surrounded with islands on which were erected fishermen's huts. Between these islands you pass into the harbour through very small inlets.

The origin of the name Newagen is obscure, but earliest references call it Capmanweggan, an Indian word, later corrupted to Cape Manwegan and then Cape Newagen.

Boothbay Harbor, Maine (13296, 13293). This is a large harbor, easy of access and well protected. It offers all the facilities necessary to a cruising yacht. It is a port we are always glad to get into and delighted to leave.

To enter from the west, simply round the bell off the Cuckolds, leave the red flasher north of Squirrel Island to starboard, the light on Burnt Island to port, the red flasher off Tumbler Island to starboard, and continue into either the West Harbor behind McKown Point or the inner harbor off the prominent white church to the northeast. Note that at night Burnt Island Light shows white sectors to the south and to the southeast to cover the entrance channels. The powerful horn on the Cuckolds is a great help in thick weather, although one cannot depend on hearing it far to windward. The short-range radio beacon is helpful although homing on it from the westward must be done cautiously, for ledges make out to the westward of the Cuckolds.

From the east, make the bell off the Hypocrites, leave Ram Island Light to port, run for Burnt Island Light, staying in the white sector, and then run up the harbor. The nuns and cans in Fisherman Island Passage, except for nun 8 on Card Ledge, need not be taken seriously by yachts drawing less than 6 feet unless there is a considerable sea running. Card

Ledge is a 2-foot rock which often breaks at low water. Under sail, especially late in the day, it is best to keep up close to Fisherman Island and Ram Island where there is usually smooth water and a good little breeze. A considerable dead spot lies off Ocean Point.

One might wonder at the name Hypocrites for the prominent ledge east of Fisherman Island. In early-Colonial days fishermen from England lived or camped on Damariscove, Outer Heron Island, and Fisherman Island. With the salt which they imported from Spain came large rations of hippocras wine, for salting fish is a thirsty business. The two islands now named Fisherman Island became known as the Hippocris Islands. Later, the name was dropped, retained only for the ledge. The name was corrupted from Hippocris to Hypocrites by a later age which knew more of hypocrisy than it did of hippocras.

Ram Island Light is now automated, and the bridge to the keeper's house has been torn down. The island belongs to the Coast Guard, which leases it to the Schooner Museum, Inc. This non-profit institution maintains it as a public facility. One is welcome to take the mooring and to land and picnic on the island, being careful not to set it afire or to alarm the goats in residence.

Boothbay Harbor has so much to offer that it is difficult to catalog it all. If you need fuel, the easiest and least expensive source is Coastal Marine Fuel, which has a fuel boat, *Service,* stationed at a float on the first mooring you come to on entering, the outer mooring off Sample's Shipyard. If you need 100 gallons or more, *Service* will come to your mooring or marina slip. Call Coastal Marine Service on channel 9. The only easy alternative for a yacht is Carousel Marina.

If you are in need of repairs to hull, engine, sails, spars, or electronics, call Sample's Shipyard on channel 9. Sample's has a marine railway capable of hauling any yacht on the coast as well as mechanics, carpenters, riggers, and electricians. Nathaniel Wilson, Sailmaker, is nearby in East Boothbay. The yard is not a marina—essentially a repair, storage, and maintenance yard. Do not obstruct the float or tie your dinghy there unless you have business with the yard. They have a number of rental moorings labeled "B," but there are more protected ones in the inner harbor or in the West Harbor.

In the inner harbor are several marinas all providing moorings and a variety of amenities. Tugboat Marina's moorings are red balls labeled "C" and numbered 3 to 24. Call on channel 9 or pick one up. At their wharf, the first on the northwest side, are slips with electricity, water, and cable

TV. At hand are showers, laundry machines, and a restaurant well spoken of and with frequent live entertainment.

Pier 1 at the head of the harbor on the same side offers moorings and slip space with electricity, water, and ice. In 1993 Pier 1 charged 25¢/foot/hour to tie up, and there was even a charge to tie your dinghy. There is a shower on the wharf. The principal advantage here is close proximity to stores.

On the east side, Marine Supply has moorings, a dinghy float, a pleasant restaurant, and a marine supply store. A launching ramp and an extended float is planned for 1994. Call on channel 9.

Captain Bob Fish, entrepreneur extraordinaire, owner of many of Boothbay Harbor's excursion boats, has a marina south of Marine Supply offering moorings, dock space with electric power, water, and ice. Up the hill behind the wharf is a snack shop serving breakfast, and a restaurant and motel. Again, call on channel 9. Next to the south is the town wharf, leased to fish and lobster companies, and then the Fishermen's Co-op, which has very little to do with yachts but sells lobsters, live or boiled, to take out or eat on the wharf. Next to the south is Brown Brothers Marina, again with moorings; dock space offering electricity, water, and cable TV, and with an excellent restaurant and motel. Last comes Carousel Marina, named after the movie version of the musical drama produced here in 1955. Again, they provide moorings and dock space with water and electricity, and Carousel also sells gasoline and diesel fuel. Ashore are showers, laundry machines, a breakfast buffet, and a restaurant. Their telephone is in a private room, not out in the rain, and they have a "courtesy car" you can borrow to do an errand. A launching ramp is at the edge of the parking space. There is a quite complete marine store with "discount prices," and a "yacht club" where you can relax on a layover day.

On the main street behind Pier 1 is Market Place, another excellent grocery store carrying meats, produce, and delicatessen items. They are proud of their selection of beer and wine, imported and domestic, and of their baked goods, personally baked by "the management." She is worth talking to. The store is now an agency liquor store. Gourmet coffees, snacks, pizza, and sandwiches custom-built to order are provided. The store will deliver dockside and can be called on channel 9.

If you follow the main street north, past the hardware store, up the hill, and by the prominent white church, you will find a shopping plaza with a supermarket on the left and a bank, laundromat, restaurant, and other emporia on the right.

No bus runs out of Boothbay Harbor, but a taxi is available which will take you to the bus in Wiscasset or the airport in Portland. In 1994 there was no scheduled air service to Wiscasset Airport, but charter flights were available.

When your necessities have been met in the inner harbor, you may want to withdraw to the somewhat less agitated West Harbor, home of the Boothbay Harbor Yacht Club. The club maintains a number of guest moorings, the fee for which includes launch service. The club offers showers, a laundry machine, and the privileges of its tennis courts, bar, and dining room to those on their moorings. There is a telephone at the club but no fuel and no supplies. The Coast Guard has a station on McKown Point and here too is The Bigelow Laboratory, engaged in marine biological and oceanographic research. There are often interesting exhibits here to which the public is welcome.

At the end of the last century, Boothbay Harbor was one of the busiest commercial towns on the coast. There were two fish-packing plants, a freezer which sold ice and frozen bait to the fishing fleet, several factories for trying out pogy (menhaden) oil, and a fertilizer plant combining the refuse from the pogy factories, bones from Argentina, and phosphate rock from Florida. There were icehouses from which ice was shipped in schooners to Southern and West Indian ports, a shipyard with all the trades connected with it, and a growing summer business. Steamers from Bath, Portland, and Rockland called daily, and smaller vessels communicated with harbors in Muscongus and Casco Bays. One of the town's leading entrepreneurs was Luther Maddocks. He developed, among other projects, several stores, two pogy factories, a dogfish business, and the town's water system. He engineered the laying of the water pipe to Squirrel Island and projected a railroad to Boothbay to join the Maine Central at Edgecomb. Characteristic of his energy and ingenuity is his exhibition of the whale.

In the 1890s the Grand Army of the Republic planned an encampment for Civil War veterans in Portland. Maddocks thought a whale would be a great attraction and a profitable venture although most of Boothbay held a contrary view. Nevertheless, he hired a 70-foot wooden barge from Bath and built a house over it, leaving one end open. He then loaded it with rocks, pulled the plugs, and sank it so the top of the house showed at high water. A whale was killed off Monhegan, towed in, eviscerated, and pulled into the house at high water, tail first. At low water the plugs were replaced, the rocks were thrown out, a sign 60 feet long was erected on the house, and the whole concern was towed to Portland. Although the mayor of Portland was reluctant to allow the barge within city limits, Luther, through his Portland business connections, overcame the mayor's objections with the promise that he would remove the whale if it became objectionable.

On the day of the opening parade, he hired a platoon of boys, outfitted them in elegant uniforms, and included them in the parade carrying a huge banner, "Go and See the Whale." He charged 10¢ admission and 8,000 people accepted his invitation. After several days the whale ripened, but he filled the carcass with salt, ice, and carbolic acid. On the last day of the encampment, visitors were permitted to cut off souvenirs.

Maddocks towed the barge and whale back to his pogy factory in Linekin Bay and tried out $150.00 worth of oil from it. Then he loaded the carcass with rocks, took it offshore, and sank it. However, as it decayed, it came to the surface. He then lashed it to the outer side of White Island, but it broke loose in a storm and disappeared.

Eventually it drifted ashore on Old Orchard Beach. Another entrepreneur put a tent over it and advertised it as a sea serpent. Hundreds came to see it. The Boston & Maine ran special trains from Boston. A professor from Chicago identified it as a whale. He took possession of it, cleaned up the skeleton, and shipped it to a Chicago museum where it is on display. Maddocks in his autobiography concludes the account: "It would appear that this whale made more history than any other whale of modern times, and it was outdone only by the whale that swallowed Jonah."

Linekin Bay (13293). This bay east of Spruce Point offers quieter anchorage than Boothbay Harbor except in southerly gales. On the west shore there is good anchorage in Lobster Cove. There is also a cove at the eastern corner at the head of the bay where the bay almost connects with the Damariscotta River. Here are the yards of J. Ervin Jones and Tim Hodgdon, builders of wooden boats. There is a paved launching ramp here and a town wharf. It is a short walk east on the road to the East Boothbay General Store, which provides the necessities as well as coffee, homemade doughnuts, and light lunches. Perch Cove on the east side of the bay is a pleasant spot. The writer of this section of the *Guide* lives a mile farther south, next to the yard of Paul E. Luke Inc. Mr. Luke built elegant wooden yachts, before fiberglass, for clients of such designers as Alden, Sparkman & Stephens, Murray Peterson, and K. Aage Nielsen.

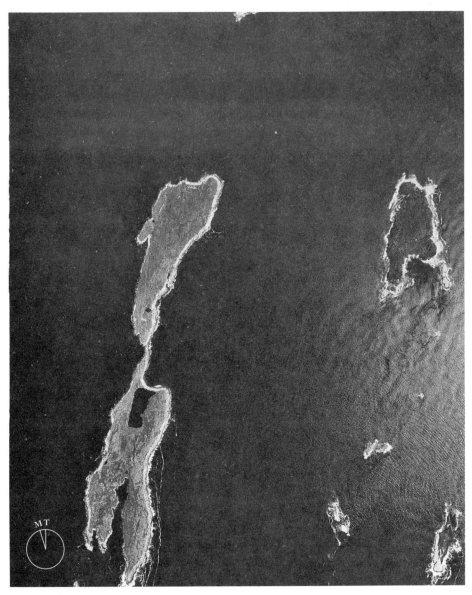

Damariscove, Maine. Damariscove Harbor shows clearly at the bottom of the picture, but the rock in the entrance is not distinguishable. Nevertheless, it is there. At the right is Pumpkin Island and Pumpkin Ledges. Outer Heron Island is at the right center and the tip of Fishermans Island is at the top. *Courtesy James W. Sewall Co.*

When wooden boats became prohibitively expensive, Luke turned to aluminum, building on his experience in steel at the old Rice Brothers yard in East Boothbay and mastering the techniques of handling aluminum from western, southern, and European yards. He has built a number of very successful aluminum yachts, beautifully finished. With the recent scarcity of contracts for luxury aluminum yachts in this country, the yard has turned to feathering propellers, three-piece Luke anchors, custom-built stoves, and storage and repair. There are several moorings off the yard and a marine railway, but no fuel at the float. Coastal Marine Electronics at the yard sells, installs, services, and repairs all kinds of electronic gear. The yard is now managed by Paul Luke's son, Frank, a real help in time of trouble.

A step north of the yard on the tar road is North Atlantic Industries run by John P. Luke. He builds aluminum boats of all sizes for many purposes and can fabricate in metal whatever special gadget is required. He is an ingenious, skillful, and most accommodating entrepreneur.

Between Negro Island and Ocean Point is a cove rather open to the south but acceptable on a quiet night. Off the pleasant Ocean Point Inn there is a town landing. In approaching this float, however, be wary of a large ledge to the south of it. Come in through the moorings and come cautiously. No supplies are available at Ocean Point.

There is a passage north of Negro Island marked by a privately maintained beacon. Excursion boats use it regularly, but it is strictly a local-knowledge job.

Damariscove, Maine (13293). This is the first of the Maine island harbors with an offshore atmosphere, a suggestion of what lies farther east. Entrance requires care and courage, but nothing extraordinary. From the west, round the gong on the Motions. Notice that the buoy is somewhat east of the ledge so that anyone coming from the north or bound toward Boothbay from the buoy is carried very close to the ledge. Round the buoy, go far enough east to open up the entrance, and run in. Favor the western side to avoid a flat ledge extending halfway across the entrance. It is shown on the chart as a half-tide rock and often breaks at low water. When you get abreast dry land on the west side, swing back to the middle. It looks narrow, but for over 350 years small vessels have beat out. Anchor in the wide part opposite the abandoned Coast Guard boathouse on firm sandy bottom in about 2 fathoms.

During the day, picnic parties from the Boothbay region visit the island in considerable numbers, but as the sun gets low, you will probably find yourself alone or with a like-minded soul.

The island is now owned by the Nature Conservancy and is occupied in summer by their caretakers. If you are careful to observe their rules and not to disturb any of the wildlife, you are welcome to explore the pond, the cliffs on the eastern shore, and the heath. A low tower on the eastern side is a reconstruction of a listening post built during World War II. German submarines waiting to attack convoys from East Coast ports to Halifax would lie on the bottom during the day and rise to charge batteries at night. Listeners could hear the diesel engines and call in planes from the Naval Air Station in Brunswick.

Land at the float near the head of the cove and sign the visitors' book. Here are booklets describing the island and the rules for visitors. The Nature Conservancy stewards live near by and are eager to be helpful.

The late Captain Edward A. McFarland of New Harbor used to tell of meeting Joshua Slocum and his fifteen-year-old son aboard the *Spray* in Damariscove after the sloop had returned from her round-the-world cruise. The *Spray* went ashore on the ledges in the entrance, but all hands turned to and got her off without serious damage.

This island, inhabited by white men for well over 350 years, was at last abandoned in 1959 when the Coast Guard moved to manned moorings in Boothbay Harbor. Late in the sixteenth or early in the seventeenth century English fishermen who came in the summer to fish offshore and dry their catch on the island must have built camps to live in and buildings substantial enough in which to store gear that they did not wish to take home and carry back again. Because the first vessels to arrive in the spring would appropriate the best sites, it seems likely that small parties would remain all winter to protect property and to fish. It is not surprising that we read little of this in published accounts, for most of these men were illiterate; and furthermore, no fisherman, having discovered a good place to fish, is eager to advertise it to others.

In 1608, a Captain Dameril, who was a member of the Gorges and Popham colony at the mouth of the Kennebec, established a store at Damariscove, which became known as Damerill's Isle. The Pilgrims at Plymouth, in distress for food in the spring of 1621, sent Edward Winslow to Damariscove for help. He was generously assisted. Of the settlement Charles K. Bolton writes in *The Real Founders of New England:*

It is not too much to affirm that Damariscove was, from 1608, let us say, to about 1625, the chief maritime port of New England. Here was the rendezvous for English, French and Dutch ships crossing the Atlantic, and for trade between Damariscove and New Netherland as well as Virginia to the south. Here men bartered with one another and with Indians, drank, gambled, quarreled, and sold indentured servants. In other words, the harbor which a Captain Damerill is assumed to have picked out years before had by the year 1622 become a typical commercial seaport on a miniature scale. In that year thirty ships rode in the harbor during the fishing season.

Little River, Maine (13293). This is a snug little cove on the west shore of the Damariscotta River, a good overnight stop for the westward-bound mariner who does not want to go any farther to leeward than necessary for shelter. It is also a good hurricane hole in the event of really severe weather. However, one must get in before the gale builds up, for a heavy sea breaks all across the mouth of the harbor.

Make the green-and-red gong off the south end of Reeds Island, leaving it close to starboard. Pass between the nun and the can. Pass closer to the white day beacon than you really want to, leaving it about 20 yards to port. Then head for the house on a black ledge on the western shore, run in close to it and head up the bold shore between it and the ledge to the east. The lobster traps make a good guide. Pick your way through them. Continue beyond the island with a house and landing to starboard and inquire at a wharf on the eastern shore for a vacant mooring. There is scant room to anchor. Here lobsters are bought from local fishermen and are sold nearby, live or boiled, at a small restaurant called Little River Lobster. There is a small marina, Spar Shed, on the western shore, but no store here. It is about a 45-minute walk to the East Boothbay General Store in East Boothbay.

Christmas Cove, Maine (13293). This picturesque and landlocked harbor has long been a favorite with cruising men. The origin of its name is confused. Some claim that John Smith lay here on Christmas Day, but the only year he was on the coast was 1614, and his was a summer trip.

The entrance is easy enough from the west. Pass between the nun north of Inner Heron Island and the tiny can off Foster Point. Former visitors will miss the big white pyramidal beacon, which used to stand on the ledge in the middle of the entrance. It has been replaced by a miserable iron spindle with a little red dayboard, quite invisible against the shore behind it from a distance of $1/4$ mile. However, you will see it before you hit the ledge and the shores are bold. Leave it to starboard and the spindle inside it to port.

From the east, round Thrumcap and run up the river, favoring the eastern shore so as to avoid the Washbowl, a shelving ledge to the east of Inner Heron. It always breaks. Shoal water extends far to the south and east. Continue up the river and enter as above.

Or come through the Thread of Life, less perilous than the name suggests. The entrance is buoyed. The southwest wind blows steadily through it, often quite freshly. The shores are bold, and the middle of the passage is deep. In general, tack when you have two or three pot buoys between you and the shore. Be sure to go *south* of Turnip Island. The writer's entire yachting career was nearly ignominiously ended before it began when his father, sailing the new family sloop on her maiden voyage from East Boothbay to New Harbor, neglected this precaution and saw boulders racing by very close to the keel. The old *Dorothy* was always a lucky vessel.

There are several guest moorings in Christmas Cove. Either hail the float at Coveside Marina on the north shore or pick one up and row ashore to consult with Mr. Mike Mitchell. He is a most helpful and hospitable gentleman, who exercises a great deal of authority over activities in Christmas Cove because his is the only gasoline pump on the shore. Hence rowdy people who speed about and disturb the peace of this pleasant anchorage soon run out of fuel—permanently.

Mr. Mitchell is the proprietor of the Coveside Inn, Motel, Marina, Restaurant, and Gift Shop. In former editions of this *Guide,* the author reflected his pleasant visits to the restaurant in extravagant terms. In one week in 1973 he received two letters from cruising people. One thanked him in enthusiastic language for recommending Coveside and the other reported profound dissatisfaction. Returning to check several times in recent years, the writer votes heavily in favor of Coveside's quality in bar, restaurant, and bakery. Don't miss the homemade pies.

Gasoline, diesel fuel, water, and ice are available at the float. There is a grocery store, Island Grocery and Lunch, about a mile away in South Bristol. You can call in your order (644-8552) and have it delivered to Coveside. If you have special problems, consult with Mr. Mitchell.

There is an active yacht club on the southern side of the harbor that runs small boat races and maintains an active social program.

If you have to anchor in Christmas Cove, beware of what looks like a good open place north of the casino wharf. It is a bare smooth ledge over which your anchor will bounce along until it fetches up in the mud beyond the ledge.

The short walk to the top of the ridge overlooking the harbor and Johns Bay is well worthwhile. Look over the Thread of Life, across Johns Bay to the fort at Pemaquid Harbor and the light on Pemaquid Point. Far offshore lies Monhegan Island.

Minor repairs can be made by Pete McFarland, who has a small yard up the northern cove. Anything he cannot handle can be done by the Gamage yard in South Bristol. Now that wooden vessels have become practically obsolete, the Gamage yard has turned to maintenance, storage, and repair work. They can repair both wood and fiberglass boats and can haul, either with travelift or railway, almost any yacht. They also have rental moorings and dock space alongside. Hail the float or go alongside and inquire.

South Bristol, Maine (13293). The harbor at South Bristol is a passage separating Rutherford's Island from the mainland. It is spanned at its narrowest point by a drawbridge. The western side of the bridge is fairly well sheltered and is dominated by the yard established and formerly owned by the late Harvey Gamage. Large wooden fishing vessels, oceanographic research vessels, yachts, and cruise schooners have been built here, among them *Bill of Rights* and *Shenandoah,* well known in Cape Cod waters. The Hudson River sloop *Clearwater,* the *Harvey Gamage,* and the schooner *Appledore,* which made a successful circumnavigation under Herbert Smith, were also launched here.

The channel under the drawbridge has a depth of 5 feet at low water and is spanned by a cable with a stated clearance of 55 feet at high water. There is no great ceremony involved in going through.

Blow the horn vigorously and early and approach slowly. The bridge is tended in the summer and usually opens promptly, but there is little room to turn as you get close and the tide runs vigorously. It is best not to go up to the beacon to port until the span begins to open. Then blow the horn again as you enter the narrow part, for anyone approaching from the east cannot be seen around the corner.

The basin on the east side is tight as a bottle, a perfect hurricane hole.

There are moorings here but little room to anchor. Fuel is available at a float and lobster car, at Eugley's wharf, and at the Fishermen's Co-op on the north side of the channel just east of the bridge.

Up the hill south of the bridge and a step to the right is the Island Grocery and Lunch, a well-stocked grocery and delicatessen with fruit, vegetables, and wine and beer, the only such store south of Damariscotta. The store will deliver an order to the shore in response to a telephone call (644-8552).

A deep, pretty, and easily negotiated channel leads down to McFarlands Cove and out into Johns Bay.

A story is told of how Harvey Gamage was hauling out a leaky sloop on his railway for a very agitated minister. As the sloop came dripping up the rails, the minister was running from one side of her to the other, noticing where water seemed to be coming out and talking constantly. Mr. Gamage, who had a well-deserved reputation for taciturnity, stood to one side with his foreman, suggesting a loose butt here and some recaulking there. The minister saw him, paused, and asked,

"How can you understand the problem when you haven't even looked at her?"

"I don't have to understand everything I know," answered Mr. Gamage.

East Boothbay, Maine (13293). There are three prominent establishments here. The most southerly, a big blue shed, is the yard of Washburn & Doughty building large steel vessels—fishermen, ferries, or whatever is needed. The yard is not much concerned with yacht work.

Next is Goudy & Stevens, a firm of long standing in East Boothbay, builders of wood and steel yachts, fishermen, research vessels, and oil skimmers. They may be best known for their replica of *America,* the schooner that won the Cup. They are now inactive.

The northerly establishment, formerly Hodgdon Brothers, is now the C & B Marina, named for Charles and Barbara Jenness, proprietors. This is a full-service marina which could become the principal yachting center of the Damariscotta River region. Call on channel 9 or 16 and ask for what you need. There are a number of moorings off the yard. Choose an inner one to get out of the tide. There is also slip space with water and electricity. At the fuel dock is gasoline, diesel fuel, and ice. Showers, a laundry machine, and a snack shop open 5 A.M. to 2 P.M. are behind the marine store on the wharf. There is a pay telephone in the hallway under the arched entrance behind the store.

If you are in need of repairs, C & B has a travelift which can haul masted vessels up to about 45 feet and a Brownell trailer which can move your boat anywhere. A launching ramp is planned for 1995. Craftsmen to repair wood or fiberglass boats are available, and a competent mechanic can treat an ailing engine. Coastal Marine Electronics at Luke's yard nearby can service or install electronic equipment. Overlooking the yard is the loft of Nathaniel Wilson, Sailmaker. He can repair or build a sail of either the most modern or traditional material. He learned his trade aboard the Coast Guard bark *Eagle* and has made sails for *Pride of Baltimore, Clearwater,* and *Joseph Conrad* as well as for modern racing yachts. He is an expert rigger.

To the left is the post office, and up the hill to the left is the East Boothbay General Store, selling the necessaries of life as well as dairy products, wine and beer, soda, homemade doughnuts, and custom-built sandwiches.

Up the road to the right is Andersen's Ceramics, where many original and creative figures are for sale. Beyond Andersen's is the studio of Earle Barlow, a marine artist of wide reputation. His paintings and models are not only artistically attractive but unfailingly accurate. Every line goes to the right pin. He has a small gallery where some of his work is exhibited and where prints of some of his outstanding paintings are sold.

A taxi can be called from Boothbay Harbor to connect with the bus at Wiscasset or with air transport at Portland, Augusta, or Rockland.

A good seafood restaurant, Lobsterman's Wharf, is between C & B and Goudy & Stevens, with a deck from which on a pleasant day one can supervise the busy shipyard scene.

Although some distance from the usual 'longshore route, East Boothbay can be a useful base from which to explore the Boothbay–Muscongus Bay area.

Damariscotta River, Maine (13293). The following account of the river and its attractions was provided by Edward A. Myers, for many years a resident of Lincoln County, founder of Saltwater Farm, and now retired, active in the cultivation of molluscs in his home cove.

A person with an occasional liking for quiet water and poking about could do worse than spend some time on the Damariscotta River, a 15-mile estuary which can accommodate 25 feet of draft for the first 13 miles and 10 feet at low water the rest of the way to the head of navigation at the bridge connecting the towns of Newcastle and

Damariscotta. Anyone with Chart 13293 can do it handily. There are supplies, a town landing abutting a small marina, an available mooring or two, and six eating places all within a quarter-mile of the town anchorage at Damariscotta.

Today's sailor is about a century too late to see the Damariscotta River in its heyday of ice companies, brick kilns, pogy factories, and feldspar quarries, all of which caused everything from scows to four-masters to be built locally to carry away the native produce. The developers, alas, have discovered the lands on both banks, but the land trusts of both Boothbay and the Damariscotta River Association are offsetting unplanned growth nicely with a number of preserves on the shores as you go up the river.

If fogged in in Christmas Cove or Little River, creep out to the west shore of the Damariscotta River, which is bold enough to let you see surf well before running out of water, and follow it north with a "fisherman-clear" offing up to Farnham Point. It can just as likely be a lovely summer's day a mile or so upriver, and there's a pleasant day's sail ahead of you in the bights and coves.

Above East Boothbay and South Bristol (described above) there is an anchorage at least every mile, and scarcely any spot where a fresh breeze can get enough fetch to bother your night's sleep.

1. Meadow Cove. About ¹/₂ mile above the boatyards of East Boothbay, anchor near the charted 27-foot spot, but work your way inshore a bit so as to need less scope and find some good mud. A decade ago, Meadow Cove was one of a number of spots along the Damariscotta chosen as the place to unload a million or more bucks' worth of marijuana. The narcs staked out all of them, far as we know, and the river has been no haven for substance abuse since.

2. The Back Narrows. Run right up the middle between can 11 and the Boothbay shore. (The overhead cable used to have a clearance of 46 feet, but maybe it's stretched over the years.) If you can get under comfortably, continue to the 13-foot sounding and favor the mainland shore when rounding up.

Both Meadow Cove and the Back Narrows are good places to await a fair tide through the regular narrows. No need to go down around Western Ledge, as there is good water to the north of it, on a line between the "W" of Western Ledge on the chart and the nun. Give nun

12 a modest berth if the tide is running hard. On the flood you will be set to the east as you pass the nun anyway. On spring tides at full ebb, the nun can be pulled under and has been timed as out of sight for three or four seconds. There isn't enough room on the chart to tell you this, but the two-foot sounding marked by the nun is about 50 yards southeast of it; east of that, there is a clear passage right up the east shore, where on repeated runs soundings have never been less than 14 feet. This is the route used by the locals if they need to get up through the narrows on the ebb. It's a nice back eddy, but as you clear the point on the east side, you will be set smartly to the west on the ebb, which keeps you away from that 4-foot spot and still gives you time to be out of the fast water before reaching Fort Island. This island was purchased by the state of Maine and is now a park.

3. Seal Cove. More than a mile in length, this deep cove is a secluded spot in which to spend the night or to explore with the dinghy. Coming upriver, head right up the middle between the islands. The island on your starboard hand, shown on the chart as Hodgsons Island, has been locally renamed Stratton Island. The gift of the Stratton family, the island is now a preserve of the Damariscotta River Association and has well-delineated nature trails. A good anchorage is at the 20-foot sounding. You may continue into the passage between the two bits of mainland which form the upper end of Seal Cove and find good anchorage at the 14-foot spot. When uncovered, the ledges around the 14-foot spot well in are generally covered with seals, young and mature. They are always fun to watch as they slither overboard at your approach. When the ledges are covered, the seals can be found out in the river, usually on the ledges west of Stratton Island.

4. High Head is ⁵/₈ mile to the north on the east shore opposite Carlisle Island. It is not identified on the chart, but one can get in a snuggery behind the head in 5 or 6 feet. The shore is bold except for the head of the cove. The lovely east shore has been purchased by a single owner who has covenanted it for one house and one dock. One or both may exist when you get there. It is a delight to report that the granite profile of Richard Nixon, something that might startle you as you approach from the southwest, has been worked over by the scouring ice and no longer looks like him.

5. Carlisle Island is a $^1/_2$ mile west of High Head on the Boothbay side, and uninhabited. If you stop there, be sure to have a trip line on the anchor, as the bottom is rocky and the tide busy.

On your way up, watch out for that three-foot sounding on the mainland about $^1/_4$ mile south of Carlisle. The print on the chart is tucked under the shore, but the shoal itself is nearly 100 yards out. It's rock and it's big, qualities a number of yachts have had to confirm at five or six hours of leisure. It is usually surrounded by pot buoys in the summer.

6. Pleasant Cove is around Carlisle Point to the west. As the chart indicates, favor the southerly shore on entering, after first giving the point itself a good berth. Land on the north shore near the road, an access now being used by clam diggers. If you can creep around the corner to the 8-foot sounding, "there you may lie safe from all winds," but you needn't go in that far for a safe anchorage.

7. Clark Cove lies on the east side of the river, about 1 mile northeast of the Pleasant Cove anchorage. This was once an extremely active spot, with a brickyard, a weir, and the wharf of the American Ice Company. Less than a century ago, vessels cleared from the wharf directly for London, South America, and such thirsty spots as Savannah, Charleston, and New Orleans. The kitchen of one of the houses is floored with South Carolina hard pine, swapped for bricks wanted by the Charleston-born mate of one of the ice schooners. The few pilings that marked the old ice wharf have been taken by the ice, which snapped them off well under low water.

There are two floats on the wharf, each with about 5 feet at mean low water. This is the aquaculture leasehold of Abandoned Farm, which is raising mussels, and has experimental plantings of quahaugs, oysters, and scallops as well. The owner requests that you do not disturb the laboratory. There are usually a couple of unoccupied moorings, but inquire ashore first, lest you pick up a buoy supporting a scallop line leading only to a cinder block on the bottom.

On clear northwest days it is possible to see Mount Washington from the South Bristol Town House on the hilltop, ten minutes' walk from the cove. The New Hampshire mountain makes quite a sight as it rears up 90 miles away.

8. Wadsworth Cove is a cozy spot, although big enough to hold a Cruising Club rendezvous some years ago. That can buoy is marking a long and unforgiving ledge running southwesterly all the way to the north shore of Pleasant Cove. When rounding the can to enter Wadsworth, hold on to the westward for a bit to be sure that you're clear of the ledge.

9. Poole's Landing, which once enjoyed a steamboat wharf over which feldspar and bricks were loaded, is a good little anchorage except in an easterly, rare there in the summer. The 11-foot sounding covers a couple of hundred yards, giving plenty of room for a yacht or two.

10. Salt Marsh Cove drains out to mud flats, but there is plenty of water and good bottom at the entrance; creep in a bit to get protection from the southerly.

11. Lowes Cove, across the river from Wadsworth, now has four or more moorings at its entrance; they hold the various research craft of the University of Maine's Marine Station. The cove drains out, but at high water it's worth a dinghy exploration to its very head if you'd like to observe the spectrum of spring, brook, marsh, wetland, mud-flat, shingle, and granite transition from the land to navigable water. Two-thirds of the way in, there is an abandoned brickyard, one of eighteen that flourished on the river in the days when Back Bay Boston needed Maine brick. Interesting to conjure how the old-timers worked brick scows in and out of such a bight.

Lowes Cove's north shore is formed by Wentworth Point, a gift of 130 acres to the University of Maine from the late Ira C. Darling. The property has well over a mile of shoreline. The faculty at the Darling Center now numbers nine, and the summer population, with students, graduate assistants, and staff is usually over fifty. Research is currently being conducted in the areas of benthic processes, seaweed biology and ecology, physiological ecology, fish diseases, trace metals in seawater and sediments, biochemical genetics and systematics, and marine-organisms culture, by which 27 species have been successfully raised since the completion of the aquaculture building in 1972.

There is a substantial steel and concrete pier with float and runway on the north side. Landing by dinghy is recommended. The center monitors channels 9 and 69 so it's possible to reserve a mooring if one is available.

There are guided tours from 1 to 4 P.M. during the summer on Sundays and Wednesdays with volunteer leaders from the Gulf of Maine Foundation. The aquaculture building, enlarged in 1991, with an extra field-staging building, is at the head of the pier. It's a pleasant 1/2-mile stroll by unpaved road to the center's headquarters in various structures which once served as a dairy farm. Picnicking, camping, and hunting are understandably prohibited.

12. Dodge Lower Cove. Follow the chart and notice the red spindle on Glidden Ledge is not at the westernmost edge. After coming up with the spindle, hold to the channel along the westerly shore until the ledges are abeam to starboard; then lay your course for can 17. (This amendment is suggested because two men, both of Damariscotta, came up through at night, held to the westerly shore, and found a ledge. The fact that it was well above the ledges and actually part of the shore just shows how careful you have to be in the writing.)

On the northerly shore of the cove, about between the 9- and 12-foot soundings, is the float for Dodge Point, a substantial tract acquired by the Damariscotta River Association and then conveyed to the state for a park. From the float there are nature trails which go to Dodge Upper Cove and include a brickyard, a beaver pond, and a couple of pocket beaches.

13. Mears Cove, just below the Glidden Ledges, has obviously been scoured out by the ebbing tides along its south shore. I noticed a 36-foot ketch tied right up to the shore at about where the "M" in Mears appears on the chart. There is a Dodge Cove Oyster Company leasehold in the middle of the cove. The oysters are planted on the bottom, so it's a good idea not to anchor inside the quadrangle of marker buoys. The south side of Mears Cove is laid out for 34 houses, a few of which are already built. The development has a common dock and float from which leads a 1/2-mile road to the main drag and the Wawenock Golf Club.

14. Hunters Landing on the east side of the river directly opposite Dodge Point is scheduled to be a public landing for uptown South Bristol. Less than a half-mile walk up from the landing is the Walpole Meeting House built in 1772 and well preserved. Hunter's Landing is just north of Wiley Point, the landing place of a punitive expedition sent from Boston by Governor Andros of Massachusetts around the turn of the eighteenth century. The splenetic governor sent the task force to punish the wrong Indians, in this case the peaceful Wawenocks. The latter rose to the occasion, however, and massacred most of the force in what is now a suburban development of Damariscotta.

15. Prentiss Cove, 1 mile above Wiley Point, is a good place to stop for a swim on a hot August day, but you're getting into the developers' area, and it's probably necessary to wear a swimsuit nowadays.

One should have the current (1993) Chart 13293, for the beacons and buoys in the upper part of the river have been renumbered. Unless it is the top of the tide, run the buoys carefully from Prentiss Cove to the head of navigation. Be sure to locate can 17 and head for it as it always appears to the east of where the chart says it is. You cannot sail a course from nun 20 to can 21 unless your boat is amphibious. Favor the west shore a bit, give the long Goose Rocks a berth, and when you are well up to Hall Point, lay for can 21. Between can 23 and nun 24 opposite the Riverside Boat Yard there are a number of moorings set out by the yard and by local yachtsmen. There are generally no lobster or crab pots this far upriver so the small buoys you see are probably moorings, most of them on fairly long pennants because of the tide. *Caveat,* powerboats.

16. Damariscotta and Newcastle. After passing nun 24, favor the Newcastle side of the river until up with the small boat anchorage north of Jacks Point, then cross the river toward the many-floated Damariscotta Town Landing. What's left of the old wharves on the Newcastle side are not in good repair or suitable for landing. The tide floods from east to west across the end of the Schooner Landing restaurant and marina on the Damariscotta side, and some allowance should be made for it. It would be possible by a combination of carelessness and bad luck to be carried up under the bridge by the flood (which overruns the tide book by about an hour), the last such mishap being a steamboat in 1918. Nick Chasse's Marina, a mile or more away on Route 1 (207) 563-5983, maintains a couple of moorings on the Damariscotta side, so you can arrange for one by telephone. The Damariscotta Information Bureau is at the head of the main street; just opposite is the Chapman-Hall House, restored as a museum of local and county history. Striped bass and bluefish are to be caught in the river, either from the boat or from the bridge, if your presence coincides with the fishes' circadian rhythms (which may be ten or twenty years apart). Bob Gilliam's fresh-fish market is a hundred yards from the town landing, off the bow of the ancient coaster *Lois M. Candage,* almost rotted away by now.

Riverside Boat Company (563-3398), Paul Bryant, Proprietor and Harbormaster, is an accommodating yard for repairs and storage. The yard's float is available to dinghies for two hours on each side of high water. If the tide is right, the float is handy to The Newcastle Inn (563-5685), where a full-course *prix fixe* dinner is served nightly; if the tide isn't right, it's a 15-minute walk from the Damariscotta Town Landing to the inn.

Anchorage, in the event there are no moorings available, is in the channel in good mud bottom. If you are lucky with a patent anchor, you may bring up a bit of brain coral dumped there by sailing vessels returning in ballast from alewife voyages to the West Indies. Hang a bucket over the stern to help lying with the tide, but don't forget to take it in in the morning.

Below the red brick Congregational Church on the Newcastle side are the bedding logs of a shipyard where the *Wild Rover* was constructed over a century ago. This ship rescued a Japanese castaway from the China coast, returned him to Boston, and sponsored his religious education at Amherst. He returned to his home country to establish the first Christian college in Japan. The great-grandson of *Wild Rover*'s owner attended the centenary of Doshisha University and found a bas-relief of the ship over the doorway of the college's oldest building.

A mile north of the Twin Villages, on both sides of the river are enormous mounds of American oyster shells left by feasting Indians many centuries ago. One estimate places the Newcastle shell heap at twelve million bushels. They are indicated on Chart 13293 at Glidden Point. Go up in the dinghy to be there at slack water, at that point about 85 minutes after the book tide at Portland. (Here Mr. Myers' account ends.)

On your way down the river, look over your taffrail for the ghost of the clipper ship *Flying Scud,* launched in 1853 by Metcalf and Norris in Damariscotta. She has a claim to being the fastest clipper ever built. So fast was her passage down the river that her skipper believed her chronometer was out of order. On her first voyage, from New York to Melbourne, she ran 446 nautical miles in one day. Her log book for that voyage has been lost, so the record is disputed, but there seems no reason to doubt her master's word or his arithmetic. He is believed when he reported that on the same voyage the vessel, loaded with iron, was struck

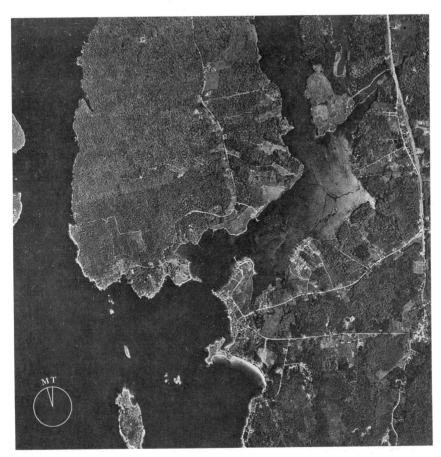

Pemaquid Harbor, Maine. The outer anchorage is in the center with the channel to the inner basin off the Co-op eastward of it. McFarland Point and Witch Island appear on the left with the entrance to the Johns River above them. *Courtesy James W. Sewall Co.*

by lightning. The iron was magnetized and so affected the compass that in order to show an accurate course, it had to be lashed to a plank projected over the port side. Even so, overloaded and trimmed 2 feet down by the head, she made the voyage in 76 days.

McFarland's Cove, Maine (13293). This is a delightful secluded anchorage on the west side of Johns Bay northward and northwestward of Witch Island. It can be approached either from Johns Bay or through the South Bristol Gut. A steep hill 150 feet high rises from its western shore. Anchor about halfway between Witch Island and the shore to the westward in 3 or 4 fathoms. Watch out for the rock awash at low water 200 feet off the northwest point of Davis Point.

There are no supplies here, the nearest being at South Bristol less than a mile to the southwest.

Pemaquid Harbor, Maine (13293). From the south, enter close to the east shore of Johns Island. The ledge to starboard, Knowles Rocks, is really a small island and always shows. Swing to the east and pass halfway between the wharf in front of the restored stone tower of Old Fort William Henry and the islet opposite. Anchor east of the islet out of the tide. This cove shoals up quite far out from the shore but affords good anchorage. However, if you find it rolly here, and you probably will, go up the Pemaquid River beyond the shore dinner wharf, cross the bar, and anchor in a perfectly protected basin behind the ledges. There is about $4^1/_2$ feet at the float at low water.

The bar has a depth of about 3 feet at low water and is certainly negotiable for most yachts at half-tide or better. Pause at the Pemaquid Pier on the south side for up-to-date information about the channel, but lacking that, pass within about 75 yards of the northern rock, which shows except at the top of the tide. The lobster buoys, seldom set in less than 6 feet, are helpful, and the airplane picture should help. Above the bar there is ample room to anchor, but one must allow for about 8 to 10 feet of tide.

Gasoline and diesel fuel are available at the Fishermen's Co-op on the north side of the inner harbor where there is about 3 feet at low water.

This harbor was one of the first places on the coast occupied by white men, and before that, it was one of the principal Indian settlements. In 1605 Waymouth found a large Indian town here. He kidnapped two of its leaders, Nahanada, who was returned by Martin Pring in 1606, and Skidwarres, who was returned in 1607 by Gilbert on his expedition to establish a colony at the mouth of Kennebec. Samoset, a friend of Squanto, was a resident of Pemaquid Harbor and New Harbor in the first quarter of the seventeenth century. He spoke English, welcomed the Pilgrims to Plymouth, and did a great deal to encourage trade and friendly relations between the races.

The English established themselves at Pemaquid early in the seventeenth century, about the same time the French occupied Castine. Raids and counterraids succeeded each other through that century, interrupted by Indian attacks and by pirates. Until the French finally abandoned their ambitions in Maine in the middle of the eighteenth century, Pemaquid was the British outpost.

On the night of September 4, 1813, the British brig *Boxer* lay off the fort and sailed out to be defeated by the American *Enterprise* the next day.

Inside the tower of the old fort is an interesting exhibit of artifacts recovered from the harbor and the site of the old fort. In the summer of 1965, Mrs. Helen Blakemore Camp commenced archaeological exploration of the area west of the old clam factory and shore dinner wharf. There is now a state museum near the restaurant displaying many of the relics uncovered, and the work is still in progress. There are restrooms and a telephone there.

Lobsters, clams, and soft drinks are available at the second wharf in from the harbor entrance on the south side. The Chart House Restaurant at the head of the wharf serves seafood dinners either inside or on the wharf. The nearest store is in New Harbor, a mile eastward.

Minor repairs can be made at Konitsky Boat Works outside the park entrance.

There are two beaches close to this anchorage, a rarity on this rocky coast. The larger is south of the village facing south to Johns Bay and the open sea. The breakers can be big enough here to tumble a swimmer about, but seldom is swimming dangerous. The other beach faces west toward Johns Island. It is well protected and the water is warmer than at the larger beach.

Pemaquid Point, Maine (13293). Pemaquid Point is forked with a wide-open rocky cove between the two parts. The eastern promontory is a high ledge of dark rock with a conspicuous dike of white granite running its length. There is an automatic light on the top of this dike and a state park nearby. The rocks are likely to be black with tourists watching the spectacular surf. The western point is longer than the eastern one and of low shelving rock. From it a ledge runs off more than a mile to a red-and-green can buoy. In really heavy weather, such as occurs after a hurricane or a prolonged northeast gale, the sea breaks all the way from the point to a rock outside the can. In ordinary summer weather, however, it is perfectly safe to leave the unlighted gong off the point close to port bound east.

On an ordinary summer day the wind is quite likely to be soft between the gong and the light and for some little distance east. It is often quicker and more comfortable, particularly if bound west under sail, to stand well offshore.

The breeze seems to pick up along the east shore of the point once you are well by the light, so anyone bound up Muscongus Bay from the west can weigh the advantages of slopping through the soft spot to pick up the fresher breeze under the shore. On a rough day, beware of Pumpkin Cove Ledge, an unmarked rock with about 20 feet of water a mile northeast of the light.

Mackerel and bluefish often are plentiful off Pemaquid Point.

Pemaquid Point has had its tragedies. In the storm of September 16 and 17, 1903, the coaster *Sadie and Lillie* and the fishing schooner *George F. Edmunds* were lost. The crew of one of these was saved when a man swam ashore through the breakers with a lead line and hauled the others through the surf one by one. Vessels were sometimes lost if a skipper neglected the western point and turned the corner after passing the light.

Muscongus Bay, Maine (13301). Many yachtsmen in their enthusiasm to "get somewhere" sail from Pemaquid Point directly across Muscongus Bay to Old Man whistle or to the bell on Eastern Egg Rock, thence up Davis Strait to Port Clyde. However, there is much to be said for a leisurely exploration of the small communities in the bay, such as New Harbor, Round Pond, and Friendship. Also, there are numerous good harbors on islands in the bay like Georges Harbor, Harbor Island, and Otter Island. Between the islands and ledges the water is deep and in general, the shores are bold.

A century ago Muscongus Bay was a very busy place. There were brick works, granite quarries, sawmills, gristmills, and pogy factories where now there are quiet coves with occasional summer cottages. At Waldoboro in 1888 was launched the world's first five-masted schooner, *Gov. Ames*, followed by five more between 1900 and 1909. Today one may wonder how such big vessels were launched into such eel ruts as the Medomak River. Of course the river has silted up some since those days, and they surely picked a high tide for the launching. The big schooners were towed down to Round Pond and fitted out there. But the towns in Muscongus Bay were essentially fishing and boatbuilding communities. With the establishment of daily steamer service to Portland about 1900, the fresh-fish market of Boston was opened to Maine fishermen. This led to the development of the able Friendship sloops on Bremen Long

Island and later in Friendship and the building of fishing boats all along the shore.

Today one can sail up Muscongus Sound, through the Lower Narrows, around Bremen Long Island, and through Friendship Harbor by shores which appear almost uninhabited.

The outer islands like Harbor, Allen, Benner, and Haddock are rougher, especially on their seaward side, and are principally inhabited by herons, eiders, terns, cormorants, and the ubiquitous herring gull. On Eastern Egg Rock the Audubon Society has made an effort to re-establish a nesting colony of puffins. They brought in chicks from New Brunswick, fed them on frozen smelts and vitamins, and established them in burrows on the rock. They did this every year for five years, and then at last the puffins began to return, often bringing friends. There is now a breeding colony of some size on Eastern Egg Rock. Although landing is forbidden, you can often see puffins as you sail by early in the summer.

One can often catch mackerel by trailing a line astern, and the occasional bluefish or striped bass can be challenging.

Muscongus Bay is just too good to miss.

Muscongus Bay to Tenants Harbor and Whitehead (13301). The usual route is from Pemaquid Point to Eastern Egg Rock bell, through Davis Strait to Marshall Point, Mosquito Island bell, and across to Whitehead. There are several interesting variations to this route.

One can follow the eastern shore of Pemaquid Neck up to New Harbor. Although there is often a soft spot off Pemaquid Point, once by the light, one will often find a good breeze up the shore. From New Harbor one can cross Muscongus Bay south of Haddock Island and north of Franklin Island. Three ugly rocks, entirely unmarked except for encircling lobster traps, lie close to the north of this course: The Devil's Back, The Devil's Limb, and The Devil's Elbow. The Back almost always breaks and often stands up above the water prominently. The Elbow breaks at low water and in heavy weather and is difficult to find, especially for one heading west in the late afternoon. Leave Gangway Ledge on either side, generously, and pass through the rock-studded gut between Barter Island and Thompson Island. Hang very close to the southwest side of the Barter Island shore. Don't cut out into the middle. When almost through, head for Gig Rock bell, pass south of Old Horse Ledge and Hooper Rock, and join the other course.

Another alternative is to go outside from Pemaquid Point to Old Man Ledge off Allen Island, thence to the bell off Old Cilley Ledge, to Mosquito whistle, and on to Whitehead or Two Bush. This is an easy course to navigate in the fog with large noisy marks, but it is a route favored by large commercial vessels bound up Penobscot Bay. On a clear day, it is a lovely offshore run. The wreck indicated on Old Cilley Ledge was that of the 3,500-ton concrete steamer *Polias*, which went ashore there in February 1920. She was launched in February 1919 at Long Island City, New York, in the rush to build ships for World War I. Nothing is left of her now.

The third alternative is to run up Muscongus Sound, through the Lower Narrows or across Muscongus Bar, through Cow Island Narrows, Friendship Harbor, Morse's Bay, and Seavey Island Passage north of McGee Island. This much longer, slower, and more intricate route is highly recommended.

New Harbor, Maine (13301). This harbor is a convenient, if crowded, stopping place close to the route alongshore and easy of access. In considering an initial visit to New Harbor, the cruising sailor should bear two facts in mind: first, that it is small, crowded, and devoted primarily to commercial fishing, and has been for the better part of three centuries, and second, that a glance at the chart before entering is well worthwhile for the skipper of any boat drawing more than a foot or two.

Notice that there is a considerable ledge running across the entrance of the harbor from the north. It is marked by a small nun well over on the southern shore. Leave this nun to *starboard*. Furthermore, in recent years the nun has often been out of position and sometimes winds itself up in its own mooring chain and disappears entirely. The wise skipper will stay well over on the southern shore of the harbor before swinging into mid-channel to leave the green beacon to port.

The Gosnold Arms, an inn and restaurant on the north shore, maintains two guest moorings off the first granite wharf. There are several big fishermen's moorings farther in, but as these are occupied often by big seiners that come and go at night in pursuit of herring, a visitor should not take one without inquiring at the Fishermen's Co-op, clearly labeled on the north shore.

Anchorage for a shoal-draft boat may be found near the head of the harbor, above the mooring area, and shelter for one or two yachts may be

New Harbor.

found in the mouth of Back Cove to port on entering. Because Back Cove is narrow and crowded, it is best to lay out a stern anchor.

No berth in New Harbor is comfortable in a heavy easterly.

New Harbor is an active fishing town, its harbor crowded with fishing vessels, some over 80 feet long, leaving no room for a yacht to anchor inside the wharves. Lobstermen with a long day's work ahead leave early in the morning, perhaps disturbing a yachtsman's slumber.

Gasoline, diesel fuel, and water are available at the co-op and at Shaw's, the wharf next to it. Both wharves have restaurants specializing in shore dinners. People come from far and near, by land and sea to dine here, and the public address system announcing that number 163 is now ready may be disturbing in the early evening.

The nearest grocery store is Reilly's in the village on the hill. From the town landing on the gravel beach at the head of the harbor, it is a short uphill walk.

A pleasant outing ashore can be had by walking west on the north-side road to the junction of Routes 32 and 130 and turning right for a few hundred yards to the Samoset. Food there is inexpensive and good, and it is a favorite gathering place for local people. Total distance from the shore is no more than a generous mile.

Two preserves owned by the Nature Conservancy offer other chances to stretch one's legs. Both are reached by walking east on the north-side road. Salt Pond, a half-acre tidal pool once frequented by Rachel Carson, is a short stroll from the harbor and offers a fine view up Muscongus Bay. The LaVerna Preserve, a rocky shoreline backed by spruce forest, is about a mile and a half farther along. The entrance road is perhaps a mile above Salt Pond and is marked with a signpost. Great scenery and much wildlife, including nesting ospreys, make a visit worth the effort.

There are many other attractions nearby. The view from Pemaquid Point, comprising the whole coast from Monhegan to Seguin, is the culmination of a pleasant walk. If there has been a heavy southerly or southeasterly, the surf there is a thrilling sight.

There are two good beaches. One is Pemaquid Beach, about a mile to the west of the hill. Leave the garage to port and bear left on entering Pemaquid Beach, a village about a mile west of New Harbor on Johns Bay. Or walk about a mile east from the harbor on the road that runs along the north side to Long Cove. Here is a sand spit, bare at low tide. Although small, it is an attractive little beach and nearer than Pemaquid.

At low tide, after a southerly breeze, the water is warmer here than anywhere else.

One John Brown was a landowner in New Harbor in 1625, and as of that date increased his estate by the purchase of Muscongus Island. He must have been pretty well established by that time. A stone marker to the west on the road along the north side of the harbor relates the story of his deed to the property.

The late Mr. Harold Castner of Damriscotta, an authority on local history, wrote of this transaction:

> John Brown and his son-in-law John Pierce bought the entire John Brown Tract in 1625 for 50 beaver skins and the very first deed in America was executed, which is recorded in Wiscasset even now. . . . Because of the phraseology of that deed it has been used ever since in America; and Abraham Shurt, the chief magistrate who did it, has been called "The Father of American Conveyances."

One could not close an account of New Harbor without relating an incident that occurred many years ago at Penniman's Store on the hill.

A local workman, well known for his conservative approach to financial matters, drove up to the gasoline pump at the store. The proprietor's son, a youngster of some fourteen summers, promptly appeared and grasped the pump hose.

"Shall I fill her up?" piped the boy.

"No, no, just one gallon," quickly replied the owner of the car.

"What you tryin' to do, Gilbert, wean 'er?" was the prompt and fitting rejoinder.

The *Enterprise* and the *Boxer*

Because the surrender in this famous battle was at a point some 4 or 5 miles east from Pemaquid Point, 4 miles southwest of Eastern Egg Rock at the mouth of the Georges River, and about 7 miles west northwest of Monhegan, it is appropriate to mention it here.

The full story of the action between the British *Boxer* and the American *Enterprise* off Pemaquid Point on September 5, 1813, is a commentary on the economic, political, and military background of both nations at that confusing juncture in their histories.

In the spring of 1813, a Mr. Tappan of Portland headed a syndicate to buy woolen cloth for the American Army. The army desperately needed the cloth for uniforms and blankets, so was not overly particular about where it came from. Tappan found a supply in Saint John, New Brunswick, part of the British dominions with which his country was at war. Nevertheless, it was cloth and was available if the syndicate would see to its delivery at Bath. So the Tappan syndicate chartered the neutral Swedish brig *Margaretta* and sent her to Saint John for the cloth. The British were willing to sell the cloth to anyone, even their enemies, because they were badly impoverished by the heavy expenses of the Napoleonic Wars and wanted money more than they wanted the American Army to go without blankets. Consequently, *Margaretta* loaded British cloth in Saint John for Bath, while H.M.S. *Boxer* was fitting out in the same harbor to cruise against U.S.S. *Enterprise* and American privateers.

As *Margaretta* and *Boxer* were ready to leave at about the same time, Tappan suggested to Captain Blyth of *Boxer* that, in exchange for a draft of £100 on a London bank, he convoy *Margaretta* to Bath, as loaded with British goods and bound for an American port, she was susceptible to capture by privateers from either country. Blyth accepted and left Saint John in company with the neutral Swedish brig, under charter to his enemy, loaded with British cloth to warm his enemy's army!

Off West Quoddy Head in the fog he even took *Margaretta* in tow.

The comic-opera quality of the whole incident is emphasized by a capture *Boxer* had made off Campobello on an earlier voyage, a small boat with a picnic party led by the wife of the American commanding officer at Eastport. Blyth released the ladies, and the American officer wrote him a gracious letter of appreciation through the press.

On September 4, early in the morning, *Boxer* and *Margaretta* were off Monhegan. A small boat came off to her asking for medical help, as a fisherman on the island had been hurt. *Boxer*'s surgeon went ashore with the fisherman, accompanied by two midshipmen and a British Army lieutenant, who was taking the cruise on *Boxer* for his health. They carried fowling pieces with the intention of shooting pigeons.

At eleven o'clock that morning, *Enterprise*, under Lieutenant Burrows, was sweeping out of Portland in a flat calm. A light southerly air came in during the afternoon. As *Boxer* and *Margaretta* parted company near Seguin about three o'clock that afternoon, Blyth fired a few guns after his convoy, "should any idle folks be looking on."

Enterprise, slowly crossing Casco Bay, heard the firing but in the haze could see nothing. *Boxer* turned east and lay that night behind Johns Island in Pemaquid Harbor. *Enterprise,* almost becalmed, jogged eastward during the night. Dawn found her off Pumpkin Rock with a light northerly air.

Burrows saw *Boxer*'s spars over Johns Island, recognized her, and hauled on the wind. About seven o'clock *Boxer* made sail and stood down Johns Bay, firing three guns as a signal to the party ashore on Monhegan. About eight-thirty, off Pemaquid Point, *Boxer* broke out her colors and fired a gun. Burrows, to leeward in the light northerly air, was advised by a local pilot that the wind would come southerly later in the day and kept offshore.

At eleven, both vessels lay becalmed about 5 miles west of Monhegan. The pigeon-shooting party appeared in a rowboat, heading for *Boxer.* The breeze came in SSW, however; both brigs stood off to the southeast on the starboard tack, and the rowboat returned to Monhegan.

Burrows was now to windward and found that his vessel was faster than *Boxer* on any point of sailing. Accordingly, at three o'clock, he put his helm up, ran down to *Boxer,* and, broadside to broadside, both vessels fired away. Captain Blyth was killed at the first broadside. Burrows was mortally wounded by a musket ball very soon after but lay propped up on deck and encouraged his officers. Lieutenant McCall took command.

Enterprise's main braces were shot away and the sails on her mainmast swung aback. But McCall set foresail and jib, ranged ahead of *Boxer,* and swung across her bow, coming so close that both vessels prepared to board. However, they did not strike. As *Enterprise* crossed *Boxer*'s bow, McCall himself sighted a long nine that had been moved aft to the port quarter and struck *Boxer*'s main topmast just above the cap of the lower mast. Her main topmast and topgallant carried away and dragged overside to leeward.

McCall then took in foresail and jib, luffed across *Boxer*'s bows, and raked her with four broadsides.

Enterprise ceased fire and called, "Have you struck?"

Boxer replied, "We will never strike to any damned shingle jack!"

Enterprise repeated the question and received an affirmative answer.

"Then haul down your colors," hailed *Enterprise.*

"We can't. They're nailed aloft," was the answer.

Enterprise withheld her fire while the colors were lowered.

Both vessels returned to Portland. Before the funerals of the two captains were held, a Mr. Kinsman, representing Mr. Tappan, asked

McCall for permission to examine Captain Blyth's effects. McCall refused, and Kinsman explained the "deal" Tappan had had with Blyth. McCall, realizing the embarrassment to Tappan and to Blyth's family, not to mention the confused international repercussions, found the draft for £100 in Blyth's pocket, signed by Tappan, and permitted Kinsman to exchange it for $500 in specie.

An armed sloop was sent to capture the party on Monhegan, and a magnificent funeral was conducted for both captains in Portland.

As evidence of the good sportsmanship with which the whole affair was conducted, I quote a paragraph from Captain Sherwood Picking's *Sea Fight off Monhegan:*

> —the two crews fought with equal bravery. James, historian of the British Navy, who rarely has a good word to say of Americans, is forced to the damaging admission that "—upon the whole, the action of the *Boxer* and the *Enterprise* was a very creditable affair to the Americans." On the American part this equality of courage was freely admitted. At a naval dinner given in New York shortly after the battle, one of the toasts offered was, "to the crew of the *Boxer:* enemies by law, but by gallantry, brothers."

Many a yacht race is fought with more acerbity than was this important naval engagement.

The ensign of the *Boxer* is among the trophies of the Naval Academy at Annapolis, and the tattered folds of the *Enterprise* are close by those of the *Bonhomme Richard* in the National Museum, Washington, D.C.

The sternboard of the *Boxer,* about 10 feet long, beautifully painted, hangs on the south wall of the George B. Wendell Collection in Mystic Seaport, Mystic, Connecticut. There is a local tradition about Boothbay that a long spar buried in the grass at the north end of Damariscove Island was the *Boxer's* maintopmast. Rumor has it that the spar floated ashore at Damariscove and was erected at the north end of the island as a flagpole, where it stood for many years toward the end of the last century.

The source for this very circumstantial account is Captain Sherwood Picking's *Sea Fight off Monhegan,* published in 1941 by the Marchigonne Press in Portland. Captain Picking, a Portland man himself, was a naval officer, a seaman, and a yachtsman. He had access not only to McCall's report of the battle and to the British Admiralty's minutes of the court-martial conducted later but to letters and memoirs of many of the participants. The account is admirably documented and most interestingly written. Captain Picking was, unfortunately, killed in an airplane crash in 1941, while on his way to England to serve as a liaison officer with the British Navy.

Round Pond, Maine (13301). Round Pond is almost certainly the snuggest anchorage between the Boothbay area and Tenants Harbor. Accordingly, yachting activity has proliferated dramatically within the past ten years. A large fleet of cruising and racing craft is permanently moored here. There is considerable racing during many of the weekends in the summer. The Padebco yard stores, builds, and maintains both yachts and fishing boats. Almost every night during the cruising season the harbor is crowded with cruising yachts, leaving little or no room to anchor. The Padebco yard maintains a few rental moorings, clearly marked.

Access is easy, shelter is almost total, and the holding ground is excellent. There is plenty of water in most of the harbor, but the shores make well out in the northern and southern ends. All floats and wharves, with one exception, have only 2 or 3 feet at low water and must therefore be approached on the tide. Two of these wharves belong to lobster buyers, one to the Padebco yard, and one to the town of Bristol. This public facility, which includes two launching ramps, is maintained by the Village Improvement Association and can be reached during the lower stages of the tide by shallow-draft boats following a somewhat vague channel constructed to line up with the town wharf itself.

No water is available, but gasoline may be had from the lobster buyers. The Padebco yard can handle most repairs to mast, rigging, hull, or engine and diesel parts may be obtained from the Di Pietro Kay company about five minutes away by car. There is a shoreside restaurant, a combination gift shop and ice cream parlor, and a well-stocked market on the hill overlooking the harbor. The Padebco yard has several moorings for rent. Midcoast Marine, with a Brownell trailer in nearby Bristol Mills uses the town ramps for a hauling and overland delivery service and also stores boats for the winter.

The Cabadetis Boat Club (no clubhouse, no launch service, no uniforms, no steward) runs a lively and popular racing schedule under PHRF rules, and participation is urged on any visiting yacht which is in port on any of the race weekends and possesses a valid PHRF certificate. There is a guest entry fee of $5 per mast. Interested skippers should get

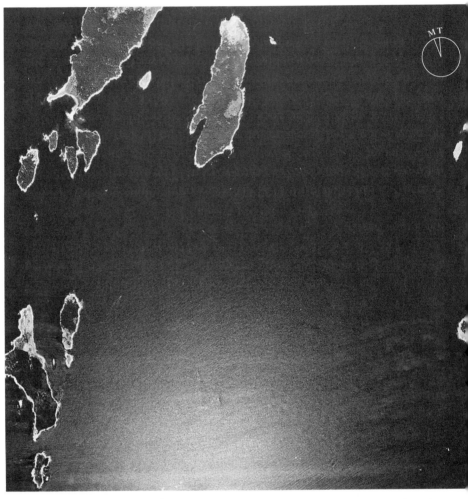

Muscongus Bay, Hall Island, and Harbor Island are at the lower left with Black, Cranberry and Otter Island in the upper left. The cove on Otter Island shows clearly. McGee and Thompson Islands are at the right. The tip of Franklin Island is at the bottom with the end of Long Ledge to the right of it. Gangway Ledge and The Kegs can be discerned with a glass. *Courtesy James W. Sewall Co.*

in touch with Commodore Paul Cunningham (who is also harbormaster) at the Padebco yard.

During the last century, Round Pond was a busy commercial port, building boats and vessels, shipping fish and granite, and engaging in overseas trade. Captain Joshua Slocum put in here in *Spray* after leaving Gloucester on his famous trip alone around the world.

Muscongus Bar, Maine (13301). This boulder-strewn bar between Louds Island and Hog Island can be crossed at half-tide or better with a draft of 4 or 5 feet by crossing close north of a bush stake on the southern part of the bar. This is the shoalest place, but there are no boulders here. If no bush is visible, cross one-third of the way from Louds Island to Hog Island. At this place there is about a foot of water at a "low dreen" tide, so half-tide would provide better than 4 feet. This crossing can save considerable time for one bound east from Round Pond.

For a picnic ashore and a swim, try the beach on the north end of Louds Island, but anchor well off, at least 100 yards, as the beach shelves very gradually and there are boulders near the southern end.

Muscongus, Maine (13301). This is a shallow bight in the west shore of Muscongus Sound above Round Pond. There is often a mooring available and one is unlikely to encounter other cruising yachts here. There is a wharf and float where one might land, but no fuel or water and little reason to go ashore. There is no store closer than Round Pond. For major repairs one must look to Paul Cunningham's Padebco yard in Round Pond.

Harbor Island, Maine (13301). This is a well-protected harbor, occasionally crowded with yachts. The dangers are unmarked but not difficult to avoid.

The north ends of both Harbor and Hall Islands are shoal. If entering from the west, keep far enough off the Harbor Island point to see the south end of Davis Island (grassy) over the north end of Hall Island. When Franklin Island Light shows over the grassy southern end of Hall, run up for it until well by the first trees on Hall Island. From there, follow the Hall Island shore. You can go as far up as the fishermen's camps on Hall Island and anchor in 4 fathoms with mud bottom.

A Muscongus Bay resident comments: "Use the entering ranges mentioned in the *Guide,* but do so with caution, as they bring you close to

Muscongus Sound, Maine. Muscongus Bar, between Hog Island at the upper right and Louds Island below it, shows clearly. Fortunately a boat was crossing it as the picture was taken. Round Pond, now much more crowded, is at the lower left with Muscongus Harbor at the top center. *Courtesy James W. Sewall Co.*

shoal areas. These areas are well delineated by the pot buoys, however, and water unoccupied by these is probably quite safe."

If entering from the east, give the north point of Hall Island a very good berth at high water and a generous berth at low water. Continue across the harbor to pick up the Franklin Island range, as noted above.

Do not go above the first wharf on Hall Island as the cove above that is foul and the flats make out. There is a rock that has tripped many a yacht just off the second wharf on Hall Island. Pass north of the private red-and-black buoy.

There is no permanent settlement here. Fishermen camp on Hall Island in the summer for the lobstering. There is an old stone house on Harbor Island, now used as a summer home. Ask the owner's permission to explore the cliffs and caves on the island's west shore.

Eider ducks nest on the grassy northern end of the island. It would be well to avoid invading the nursery in July and early August.

Harbor Island is clean, quiet, well sheltered, and right on the direct course from Port Clyde to New Harbor, Pemaquid, and the west, via the Thompson-Barter Passage. Also, it is a good base from which to explore the beautiful islands of Muscongus Bay.

Medomak River, Maine (13301). This river runs into the head of Muscongus Bay and is most pleasantly neglected by high-pressure cruising people. The islands and shores are mostly wooded, inhabited by herons, ducks, cormorants, the ubiquitous gull, summer cottagers, and a few farmers and clam diggers.

There are three passages from Muscongus Bay into the upper river. Whichever you choose should be taken on the flood tide. The most intricate and the least settled is Back River Passage east of Hungry Island. There is a possible anchorage in the mouth of Goose River. The middle channel, Flying Passage, lies between Hungry Island and the cliffy bold shore of Bremen Long Island. It is deep, well marked, and not intricate. The westerly one, Hockomock Channel, lies between Bremen Long Island and Keene's Neck. It takes you from Muscongus Sound through the Lower Narrows and by the Audubon Nature Camp. Favor the northern, Keene's Neck, side and give the big rock on the mussel bar off the north end of Hog Island a good berth, for the bar extends beyond the rock. You cannot run directly from can 7A to nun 6. You will see the abandoned five-masted schooner *Cora F. Cressy*, once a coal schooner, then a floating restaurant, then an unsuccessful lobster pound, and finally a breakwater. On your starboard side is the indented shore of Bremen Long Island, once an active year-round community of fishermen and boatbuilders. Here what we now call the Friendship sloop was developed in the 1890s. In 1900 twenty sloops were under construction on the island, most of them along this western shore. The village of Medomak is on the port side. The tide will hustle you up to the mouth of Broad Cove and Dutch Neck, so named because in the eighteenth century Samuel Waldo brought German farmers from the Rhineland to colonize his semi-feudal domain on the shores of the Medomak. Names on the modern chart remind us of these sturdy immigrants: Bremen, Havener Point, Waltz Point, and finally Waldoboro. A new marina run by Blair Payne opened in 1994 on Dutch Neck.

Few yachtsmen will care to go above Havener Point with a deep-draft boat, but if you do, plan to anchor bow and stern to keep from swinging over the flats at high water. The tide runs very hard through the narrows north of Locust Island, often pulling the buoys under.

As you come down on the tide, consider that in December 1888 the Storer yard in Waldoboro launched the *Gov. Ames,* the first five-masted schooner built on the Atlantic Coast. She was 245 feet long and registered 1,778 tons. She was towed down the narrow channel between the flats on two successive high-water slack tides and fitted out at Muscongus. Between 1900 and 1904 six more five-masters were built in Waldoboro for the Palmer line.

A more thorough treatment of the Medomak River may be found in an article by J. Malcolm Barter in the May 1985 issue of *Down East.*

Friendship, Maine (13301). This harbor, near the head of Muscongus Bay, is well protected in anything short of a southwest gale of wind and is an interesting place to visit. Entrance from the west is easy. Simply follow the bold shores of Harbor, Black, and Friendship Islands, running short courses from point to point in thick weather. You will probably get a scale-up as you approach the harbor.

From the east, make nun 2 off the western point of Gay Island and run up the middle of Morse Bay, favoring the bold western shore. The tide runs hard through here, and there is a string of ledges up the eastern shore, with one half-tide rock well out in the middle. You cannot run a direct course from nun 2 to the can off the northern end of Morse Island without hitting this ledge. You will find the can much farther around to the east than you expect.

Friendship with Morse's Bay and the St. George River. Pleasant Point Gut is just to the left of the center in the upper part of the picture.

From the can, run down to the two nuns and through the passage west of Garrison Island into Friendship Harbor. Respect the can at the north end of this passage. A bar runs from it to the south and forms the west side of the channel. The writer saw a husky schooner high and dry on this bar. She struck on a falling tide and lay right down on her side.

Do not ignore the 5-foot sounding on the north side of the harbor off a prominent shell heap. A rock is really there and yachts have found it.

Anchor east of the beacon with the square dayboard, as close to the Friendship Long Island shore as draft permits.

Friendship, like Cape Porpoise, New Harbor, and Vinalhaven, is almost wholly devoted to lobstering and is concerned very little with yachting. There is practically no tourist industry in town and only a few summer people. The wharves are very busy with fishermen coming and going at all daylight hours. Yachts are not encouraged to come alongside. Gasoline and diesel oil are available at the town wharf, clearly labeled farther up the harbor, but there is little depth of water alongside so it is available only at half-tide or better.

There is no store at the shore, but it is a pleasant 20-minute walk to the town where there are two grocery stores and a hardware store.

Repairs to hull, spars, or engine can be handled by the Lash Brothers Boat Yard in Hatchet Cove.

Should one have compass problems, two ranges might prove useful. To steer magnetic north, line up the red beacon on the north side of the harbor with the inner edge of the outer stone pier on a wharf behind it. To head west magnetic, line up the beacon with the tallest tree on Ram Island about three-quarters the length of the island from south to north.

Friendship Sloops and the Friendship Sloop Society

During the 19th century local fishermen evolved the Muscongus Bay sloop, a small centerboard boat for spring, summer, and fall fishing and lobstering. Seldom if ever did they fish in the winter. The fish were salted and dried, the lobsters sold to local canneries. However, with the establishment of a steamship line running daily to Portland and connecting with trains for Boston, the Boston fresh-fish and live-lobster market was opened to Muscongus Bay fishermen, and this required their fishing right around the calendar.

For winter fishing, something stouter than a Muscongus Bay sloop

A Friendship sloop photographed in her working rig in the early years of the century. *The Friendship Museum.*

was needed. Following the lead of the Gloucester fishing schooners, which developed from Collins and Lawlor's *Harry L. Belden* and from Edward Burgess's *Fredonia* model, the builders on Bremen Long Island developed what we now call the Friendship sloop. It is likely that they were influenced by George M. McLain, a Bremen man who skippered and designed Gloucester schooners. Both types of boats had the same clipper bows, sharp entrance, easy turn to the bilge amidships, and flat run. Both had an elegance and a power built into the design which made them not only efficient as fishermen but pleasing to the eye. A Friendship sloop sits on the water with the lightness of a tern. The sweep of her sheer from clipper bow to tucked-up counter gives her grace, and the size of her mainsail spells power.

One Bremen Long Island builder, Wilbur A. Morse, moved to Friendship and built sloops on something like an assembly-line basis. With five or six sloops building at the same time, he might launch one as often as every month or six weeks. He defined a Friendship sloop as a sloop built in Friendship by Wilbur Morse, and he sold so many up and down the coast that all "sloop boats" of this general model became known as Friendship sloops regardless of who built them or where they were built.

They were used for seining, handlining, and trawling, and the smaller ones were used for lobstering among the ledges. The bigger ones, up to nearly 50 feet, fished offshore or carried freight.

Friendship sloops were admirably adapted to their use. The high, sharp bow knifed through a chop, throwing the water for the most part out and down. The low freeboard amidships made it easy to lift lobster traps and fish over the side. The broad beam gave the boat stiffness, and provided a wide, steady working platform; and the flat run left the water astern with scarcely a bubble. She was ballasted with beach rocks at first although later sloops had iron keels and iron ballast inside. With a boom as long as the boat's waterline, she swung a powerful mainsail and usually carried two headsails. In the summer, many sloops set main and jib topsails for speed in light airs. Anyone who has seen a Friendship sloop with anything like her original rig slashing through the afternoon chop will not soon forget her.

With the advent of the gasoline engine about 1914, fishing under sail became obsolete. Sloops were abandoned or sold to summer people as yachts. They were popular with some, but the long boom and huge mainsail were too much for many yachtsmen so they cut off the mainsail

Eastward, a modern Friendship sloop. *Rubican Photo.*

at the first reef band and then complained that the boat was slow, heavy, a dog. Few new sloops were built, and most of the old ones rotted away. By 1960 a Friendship sloop was a rare sight.

The Friendship Sloop Society. In the fall of 1960, Bernard Mac-Kenzie entered his old cut-down Morse-built Friendship sloop *Voyager* in the Boston Power Squadron's Bang-and-Go-Back race. The idea was that all boats would start together. When the first one reached the outer mark, a gun would be fired and all boats would tack and head for the finish line, thus each establishing her own handicap. *Voyager,* perhaps a bit logy on the outward trip in the gentle breeze, stood up to it like a lady as the wind increased on the way home and crossed the finish line in the smoke of the gun.

MacKenzie was so pleased with his vessel that he traveled to Friendship and enlisted the enthusiastic support of Herald Jones, the Lash brothers, Carlton Simmons, the Robertses, and John Gould. With publicity in the *Boston Globe,* through Earl Banner, the Friendship Sloop Society was started to preserve and perpetuate the type. With this purpose in mind, about fifteen sloops gathered at Friendship in 1961 to hold a regatta. Since then a considerable number of new sloops have been built, some by the Lash Brothers in Friendship and some by other builders up and down the coast.

Since 1969, five fiberglass models have been built. Bruno & Stillman in Newfields, New Hampshire, built several 30-foot sloops designed as yachts. Their topsides were raised up, their rig shortened, and the open cockpit replaced by a cabin. Jarvis Newman in Southwest Harbor, Maine, used *Old Baldy,* a wooden 25-foot Friendship, as a plug and produced a thoroughly authentic hull which has been very successful. He followed this with a 31-foot model using the restored McLain-built *Dictator* as a plug. Passamaquoddy Yachts built a wooden 22-foot sloop, used it as a plug, and produced several hulls. The shop burned, and Ahern used one of Passamaquoddy's fiberglass hulls as a mold for several more. Finally a 19-foot fiberglass Friendship sloop was built by Ahern from a Bolger design and five hulls taken from that mold.

For many years Friendship sloops from as far away as Connecticut, New York, and New Jersey gathered at Friendship every July for three days of racing and conviviality. In 1984 the races were moved to Boothbay during the week before the last full weekend in July. After the races, the sloops sail to Friendship and on Saturday participate in

Friendship Day, usually opening the festivities with a parade of sloops in the harbor.

Almost the only point on which the members of the society fail to find friendly agreement is a definition of a Friendship sloop. From their recent book, *Enduring Friendships,* we quote:

> A Friendship Sloop is a gaff-rigged sloop with a fisherman look about her. A Friendship Sloop is a beautiful fusion of form and function. A Friendship Sloop is a state of mind composed of independence, tradition, resourcefulness, and a most fortuitous combination of geography and language in the name Friendship.

The Friendship Museum. Under the leadership of Mrs. Betty Roberts, the Friendship Museum has been incorporated to preserve records and relics of the old days in Friendship. The town gave the museum the old brick schoolhouse, and generous people have contributed tools, pictures, artifacts, and records.

An extensive study of the origin and development of the Friendship sloop will be found in *Friendship Sloops* by Roger F. Duncan (International Marine Publishing Co., Camden, Me., 1985).

Georges Harbor, Maine (13301). This convenient and little-used anchorage lies between Allen and Benner Islands on the south and Davis Island on the north. The snuggest anchorage is between Allen and Benner Islands. In entering from the south, hug the Allen Island shore to avoid a ledge in mid-channel making off the Benner Island shore. Anchor wherever you can find swinging room. One correspondent writes: "There really is a wire (as indicated on the chart) on the bottom—somewhat off a shack on the west shore—wire runs east and west."

If the tide sets against the wind, you may lie broadside and roll uncomfortably. A line to a tree ashore will straighten you out.

The writer once saw a little two-masted coaster moored to trees ashore loading pulpwood through a chute.

A quieter berth is off the cove in the north end of Allen Island. Work in as close as your draft will permit and anchor off the stony beach. The ragged ledges make out quite far, so move cautiously.

Mrs. James Wyeth bought Allen Island in 1978 to save it from a developer with a vision of golf courses, marinas, and condominiums. The Island Institute, interested in using the resources of the island construc-

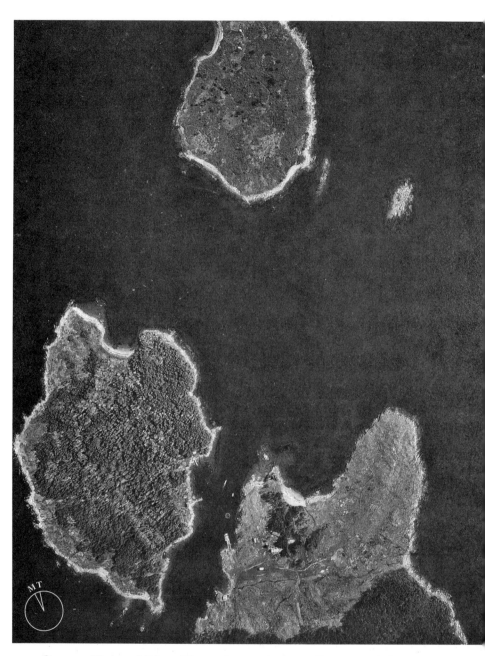

Georges Harbor, Maine. The anchorage between Benner and Allen Island is evident with bold water on the Allen Island shore. The circle is a salmon pen. The ledges in the cove north of Allen Island demonstrate the need for a cautious approach. Woods on the east shore of Benner Island have now been cut down. *Courtesy James W. Sewall Co.*

tively, worked with Mrs. Wyeth; they built a wharf and cleared off the spruce and birch growth on the north end of the island for firewood and pulp. They made a road to the south end of the island where grows what is as close to virgin forest as can be found on a Maine island, and they cut from elsewhere on the island some spruce lumber. Part of this was used to restore a house which had been floated over from Metinic, part was used to build a new building, and part was sold ashore. To keep the north end cleared after it was cut, a flock of 20 sheep was set ashore. These at once disappeared into the woods but reappear on occasion. The Island Institute plans to moor several salmon pens north of the gut between Allen and Benner Islands and will continue to develop the resources of Allen Island responsibly.

Mrs. Wyeth has built a substantial wharf and house on Benner Island and moved to the island several small houses. Cruising people will watch this development with confidence that the ecology and beauty of the island will be enhanced.

Rosier and Waymouth Visit Allen Island in 1605

The granite cross on the shore of Allen Island overlooking the harbor was dedicated in 1905 to celebrate the 300th anniversary of George Waymouth's visit. The following account is abridged from *Coastal Maine: A Maritime History* (W. W. Norton & Co., New York, 1992).

In 1605, George Waymouth sailed in *Archangel* from Plymouth, England, sent by Sir Thomas Arundel and the Earl of Southampton to find a site for a colony in New England as a refuge for English Catholics.

Waymouth's Maine landfall was Monhegan. Like other visitors before and after, he found plenty of codfish, wood, water, and wild roses, but a wretched anchorage. From the anchorage, writes James Rosier, historian of the expedition,

> We might discern the mainland from the west-southwest to the east-northeast, and a great way (as it then seemed and we afterward found it) up into the main we might discern very high mountains, though the main seemed but low land. . . .

These mountains were the Camden Hills. Proponents of the White Mountains do not realize how dimly the White Mountains are visible on the clearest days and how boldly the Camden Hills stand up on any but the haziest days.

Finding Monhegan to be as uneasy an anchorage as it is to this day,

> We weighed anchor about twelve o'clock, and came to the other islands more adjoining to the main, and in the road directly with the mountains, about three leagues from the island where we had anchored.

North of Allen Island, possibly in the same spot where Champlain had spent a night in 1604,

> We found a convenient harbor; which it pleased God to send us far beyond our expectation, in a most safe berth defended from all winds, in an excellent depth of water for ships of any burthen in six, seven, eight, nine, and ten fathoms, upon a clay ooze, very tough.

The new anchorage was unquestionably Georges Harbor north of Allen Island and protected by Burnt, Davis, Allen, and Benner Islands. Waymouth named it Pentecost Harbor. Rosier describes the scene in delightful and delighted language. He describes scenes of aboriginal picnics and mentions the "cranes" we see today, called great blue herons by the ornithologists, but still "blue cranes" by the fishermen.

The crew, led by Captain Waymouth, turned to energetically to put together a small boat they had brought with them, the boat later referred to as the "light horseman." They dug a well and sank a barrel in it, sent a boat's crew fishing for cod, haddock, and "thorneback" (which may be dogfish), explored the islands, cut firewood, and made several spare spars. They picked up great blue mussels with pearls in them and marveled at "the shells all glittering with mother of Pearle." Meanwhile, they lived like kings on lobsters, flounders, lumpfish, and strawberries. Of American strawberries one of England's noted doctors of the time wrote, "God could have made, but never did make a better Berry." They found even the spruce gum as sweet as frankincense. What an Eden it was that they had found! And Rosier describes it with the ecstasy of one set down in Paradise.

Then natives appeared with brilliantly painted faces, dressed in skins. Of course they had seen Europeans before, and friendly relations were at once established. Knives, rings, tobacco pipes, and peacock feathers were offered, and the Indians responded with beaver skins. One afternoon, all hands had a lobster bake on the shore and lay around afterward smoking tobacco through the broken large claws of lobsters. Rosier writes of his Indian friends:

> They all seemed very civil and merry: shewing tokens of much thankfulness, for those things which we gave them. We found them then (as after) a people of exceeding good invention, quick understanding, and ready capacity.

He admired their women and little children:

> They [the women] were very well favored in proportion of countenance, though colored black, low of stature, and fat, bareheaded as the men, wearing their hair long; they had two little male children of a year and a half old as we judged, very fat and of good countenances, which they love tenderly.

The savages had good table manners, he records, and showed proper respect for Christian services:

> They behaved themselves very civilly, neither laughing nor talking all the time, and at supper fed not like men of rude education, neither would they eat or drink more than seemed to content nature; they desired peas to carry ashore to their women, which we gave them with fish and bread, and lent them pewter dishes which they carefully brought again.

On June 3 they visited the Indian camp at New Harbor, going in their "light horseman," surrounded by a fleet of canoes. Although they feared treachery at first, the trip turned out to be a great success, with trading and feasting. But the worm at the bud of this rose shows in a sentence of Rosier's: "Thus because we found the place answerable to the intent of our discovery, namely, fit for any nation to inhabit, we used the people with as great kindness as we could devise, or found them capable of."

One day, five or six Englishmen jumped two Indians with whom they were sitting around ashore eating peas. They had a hard time subduing the Indians, but they did it at last and tied them up below with three others. Rosier shows little regret and no guilt at this betrayal of trust. He writes:

We would have been very loth to have done them any hurt, which of necessity we would have been constrained to have done if we had attempted them in a multitude, which we must and would, rather than have wanted them, being a matter of great importance for the full accomplishment of our voyage.

Having seized five Indians and two canoes and having set up a cross on the shore, Waymouth left Pentecost Harbor behind, explored the St. George River, and headed for home.

After pausing on Cashes Ledge to catch some more codfish, they returned to England to report their success and prepare a new expedition.

The captured Indians soon regained their good dispositions. They shared everything they had with one another, were friendly and merry. When they had acquired some command of English, they described with appropriate gesture and enthusiasm their method of killing, cutting up, and eating whales. Rosier lists their names as Tahanedo, Amoret, Skicowaros, Maneddo, and Saffacomoit.

When Waymouth arrived in England, his backers applied for a charter, but the discovery of Guy Fawkes and the Gunpowder Plot in November 1605 put Catholics in no position to seek favors from the King. Sir Ferdinando Gorges and Sir John Popham with others set up the Plymouth Company, received a charter, "adopted" the Indians, and prepared to establish a colony at the mouth of the Kennebec. The Indians were well treated, questioned, and found to be truthful, friendly, intelligent, and naturally enthusiastic about their country. These, of course, have always been characteristics of Maine men.

We know that Tahanedo, alias Nahanada, was taken back to Pemaquid by Pring in 1606, and that Skicowaros, or Skidwarres, returned in *Mary and John* in 1607 as a guide for the Plymouth Company's Kennebec expedition. Maneddo probably died in Spain, for there is no record of his return to England after his capture by the Spanish with Challons in 1606. Saffacomit, returned from Spain after Challons' disastrous voyage, was sent home by Gorges in 1614 with Captain Hobson and apparently died soon after. The remaining Indian, called by Rosier "Amoret," was really Tisquantum, as this is the name Gorges gives him. He was sent home by Captain John Smith in 1614 when Smith visited Monhegan and then coasted south to Cape Cod. Tisquantum was left on the Cape, as his home had been at Plymouth. But before he could get to Plymouth, a

Captain Hunt, who had been left in Maine by Smith to complete a cargo, stopped at the Cape. Tisquantum, who had been well treated by Smith's party, came aboard Hunt's vessel with sixteen other Indians. They were at once clapped under hatches; and Hunt sailed for Málaga, where he sold them as slaves. However, the Spanish recognized that they would not make good slaves, and they were released and taken care of by some monks near Málaga. An English vessel, loading wine at Málaga for thirsty Newfoundland fishermen, took Tisquantum to Newfoundland, where he met Captain Mason, the governor. He introduced him to Captain Dermer, who was much interested in New England and wanted to start a colony. He took Tisquantum back to England to talk with Gorges again, and then to Monhegan and south to the Cape. Here at last Tisquantum was free to go home. He returned to Plymouth in the fall of 1620 just ahead of the Pilgrims, to find his village wiped out by disease. He spent the winter with the Wampanoags on the Cape and in the spring stepped out of the woods with his friend Samoset to greet the Pilgrims with his famous words, "Welcome, Englishmen"—the only man in the world acquainted with Indian ways and English people, the only man in the world who could have saved the Plymouth plantation.

Other Anchorages in Muscongus Bay

For the information of the leisurely cruiser, there are a number of attractive out-of-the-way anchorages in Muscongus Bay, some of them of no value as shelter in a storm and most of them inaccessible from the mainland and without supplies.

Marsh Harbor. This lies between Louds Island and Marsh Island. The anchorage is at the northeast end of the passage close to Marsh Island and off a small beach that faces south. It is good shelter on a quiet night. However, the island is privately owned, and one should not invade the owner's privacy without permission. There is a house and landing on the north end of the island.

Greenland Cove. This lies at the north end of Muscongus Sound and is completely sheltered. Anchor under the lee of Ram Island in a southerly.

Louds Island East Cove. Here is a sweet anchorage off a beach, where Chart 13301 shows 9 feet at the northeast corner of the island, but it is rather open to the southeast. Enter cautiously. For shoal-draft boats only.

Louds Island. The cove northwest of Marsh Island affords good shelter in anything but a heavy southeaster. However, the head of the cove dries out at low water, so proceed cautiously. The island no longer has a year-round community but in the summer is occupied by a few lobstermen and a number of vacationers. There is no store, no fuel wharf, and no facilities whatever for yachts. It is a most attractive island.

One of its most interesting features is its unique political history. It was formerly known as Muscongus Island or Samoset's Island. Samoset is said to have lived and died here and to be buried in an Indian cemetery on the north end of the island. The first white settler was William Gould in 1650. Louds, Carters, and Polands followed.

At the time of Lincoln's first election, the islanders voted as part of Bristol, but in that election their vote was thrown out due to a controversy. In protest, the islanders refused to pay taxes to Bristol, which had done little for them anyway as they supported their own schools by the sale of fishing rights. They were willing to support the United States, but not Bristol. When the Civil War draft was made, the island was included with Bristol and an unfair proportion assigned to the islanders. They refused to honor the draft, made what they felt was a fair apportionment, and bought substitutes.

Since then they have continued to pay taxes to the United States and to the state of Maine but not to Bristol.

Hog Island. North of Muscongus Island lies Hog Island, "330 acres of untouched wilderness," probably the only mature and unspoiled forest the cruising man will find. The story of the establishment of this island as a sanctuary begins in 1908, when Mabel Loomis Todd, on a cruise in Muscongus Bay, learned of the imminent destruction of Hog Island's forest by a lumber company. She bought the island at once, except for the peninsula at the north end, where a hotel stood, and it was untouched for decades.

Then, in 1935, Dr. James Todd, no relation to Mabel Loomis Todd, bought the peninsula on the north end and gave it to the National Audubon Society. In 1936, a summer camp was started here to interpret to adults the local ecosystem through trips dealing with marine life, bird life, plant and animal life, geology, soil, water, and weather. Over half the participants are teachers and youth leaders, although every other profession and interest group is represented. Fifty-five campers participate in each of the four 2-week sessions each summer. An average of thirty-three states, two Canadian provinces, and one foreign country are represented each year. In 1960, Mrs. Walter V. Bingham, the owner of Mabel Loomis Todd's part of the island, gave her part to the Audubon Society. Henceforth, the entire island will be maintained as the Todd Wildlife Sanctuary.

If not occupied by the camp boats, two moorings are available for overnight use. They are located in the cove at the north end of the island off the floats and are identified by N.A.S. on each. If you anchor, be certain you are south enough to get out of the tide, but move cautiously, as the cove shoals up rapidly. Beware of the mussel bar, bare at low water, which connects Hog Island with a big rock in the middle of the Narrows. Give the rock a berth. The bar extends a short distance beyond it. And stay well south of the white "Cable Crossing" signs. The camp's electric and water supply crosses from the mainland at this point. A Visitor Center with a small natural history bookstore and exhibit area is located on the mainland opposite the camp in the left-hand red barn. It is open from 10 A.M. to 5 P.M. daily from June 30 to August 20 each year. There is a self-guided nature trail starting at the Visitor Center and leading half a mile through the fields and spruce woods of Hockamock Point. To anyone with a serious interest in natural history, especially ornithology, the island is well worth a visit. For more information, write Education Department, National Audubon Society, 950 Third Avenue, New York, NY 10022.

No supplies are available here although there is a lobster pound to which gasoline is piped behind the beached schooner *Cora F. Cressy*. This schooner was once in the coasting trade. She was bought by Levaggi, the famous restauranteur of Boston, and tied up to a Boston pier as a floating nightclub. This proved unprofitable so she was sold to Mr. Zahn of Medomak and towed here about 1936. He started to drill holes in her to use her as a floating lobster pound, but she was so heavily constructed that he could not drill enough holes to provide circulation for the lobsters. She now serves as a breakwater and provides one side of his pound. She seems unlikely ever to move from her present berth.

Otter Island. There is a deep, narrow cove in the southern end of this heavily wooded island that makes a good anchorage on an ordinary summer night. The west shore of the cove is very bold. There is room for a handy sloop to round to and anchor. The owners live in a house at the north end and request that visitors stay along the shore and light no fires. No camping is permitted.

Cranberry Island. There is a good summer anchorage in the northeast cove between Cranberry and Friendship Islands. Anchor among the lobster boats or just outside. There are no supplies, but there is a small settlement of fishermen who come in the summer for the lobstering.

Oar Island. There is an anchorage north of the island off the Lusty Lobster plant. Gasoline and, of course, lobsters are available here and also at the lobster pound behind Oar Island, where the hulk of the five-master *Cora F. Cressy* lies. There are launching ramps at Waldoboro and Dutch Neck. There is a store at Medomak.

Burnt Island. This large and heavily wooded island has now been abandoned by the Coast Guard. However, the substantial wharf on the west side still stands. One can anchor off the wharf, although it is rather an uneasy berth. The cable area on Chart 13301 appears to fill the entire area, but the old cable, if it is still there, actually comes ashore on the south side of the cove south of the wharf. Look sharp and you will probably see it and can avoid anchoring on top of it. If you do hook it with an anchor, you can probably haul it up enough with a winch to get clear, and of course it is no longer in use.

An alternate anchorage is in the cove north of the bar between Burnt and Little Burnt. This is ordinarily a quieter anchorage. On his way to establish the colony at the mouth of the Kennebec, Raleigh Gilbert lay here in 1607 for one night but soon moved over to Georges Harbor, a procedure that the writer heartily recommends. In mid-July Little Burnt is a good place to pick raspberries.

The island is now occupied by an outpost of Outward Bound School, which is further described under Hurricane Island in Penobscot Bay. One can land at the wharf or on the beach and walk to the top of the island or follow as much of the path around the island as is still visible.

Monhegan Island, Maine (13301). This is a foreign country to the cruising man bound east from Falmouth Foreside, Sebasco, Boothbay

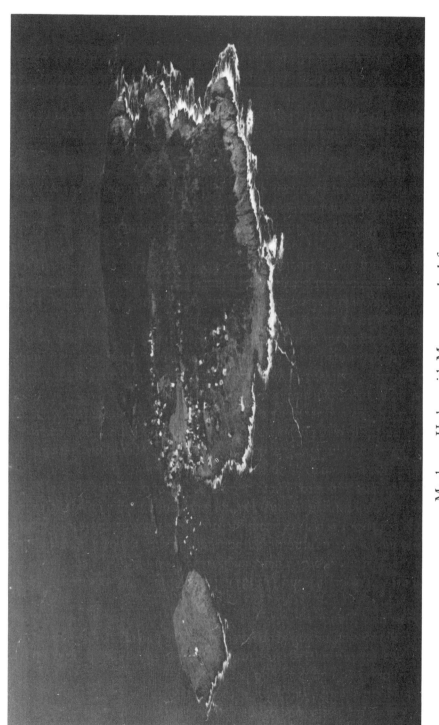

Monhegan Harbor with Manana on the left.

Harbor, and "civilized" mainland ports. High, rocky, unprotected, and alone, Monhegan lies 9 miles to the south and east of Pemaquid in an atmosphere all its own.

In approaching from the west, make for the middle of the island until the light-green shape of Manana is distinguishable from the dark green of Monhegan. Run in to the north of Manana, being respectful of a can marking a half-tide rock northwest of Manana. Leave this can to *starboard;* that is, go to the *north* of it. The shores of Manana, Smuttynose, and Monhegan are quite bold and the water is very clear.

The northeast corner of Smuttynose, the black islet between Monhegan and Manana, makes out a little. The writer stubbed his toe on this ledge pretty hard. Enter between Smuttynose and Monhegan.

It is possible, of course, to pass south of Manana and run down into the harbor. Favor the Manana shore. A shoal makes out from the Monhegan side on which for many years a breakwater has been projected. If there is much wind and sea, this route can be exciting, especially as there is scant room to round to among the moorings. One yachtsman caught in this predicament had to run right out the northern entrance and round to outside. If there is little wind, it is likely to be soft to the south and southwest of Manana. The breeze draws nicely through the harbor and up the Monhegan shore, so the northern entrance is preferable. One can spend a most uncomfortable half-hour slopping around in the tide and chop to the south. In thick weather the horn and radio beacon on Manana make approach from the west simple enough. From the east one loses the horn near the cliffs, but there are several bells, gongs, and whistles.

The tide runs quite hard in and out of the St. George River and will set you north on the flood and south on the ebb. Two wrecks on the southern end of Monhegan are reminders of this.

Hail the wharf for the harbormaster. If he is not there, land at the southernmost beach north of the little breakwater and ask at the first fish house or up the bank at the store. If you still cannot find him, take a mooring with no skiff on it, leave a responsible person aboard, and go ashore and find him.

If there is no mooring without a skiff, you will have to anchor, a messy business at Monhegan. The bottom in the harbor is sandy and is encumbered with chains. One can anchor south of the moorings but the bottom is rocky. A better alternative is north of Smuttynose between Nigh Duck Rock and the shore. The water is deep here and the bottom rocky and it is quite a pull to the wharf. Wherever you anchor, be sure to use a trip line. There are several moorings east of Nigh Duck used by big fishermen and the excursion boat *Balmy Days* from Boothbay. She will be using it from about eleven to three. With permission, you can move to it after she leaves.

A yacht can lie alongside the wharf at Monhegan, but this has disadvantages. The tide runs hard by the front of the wharf and is likely to set one off to the westward. Unless there is someone on the wharf to catch a line—and there often is—making fast to a piling calls for an agile hand on the foredeck. And once made fast, you will soon have to move for the mail boat from Port Clyde or for the *Balmy Days.* One can slide in on the north side of the wharf and tie up with long lines to allow for the tide. The only "out" about this is that others do the same and tramp back and forth across one's boat, scrub off topside paint, and bump interminably alongside.

Few yachts spend the night at Monhegan, so you can probably get a mooring for the night, but it is a miserable place to lie, for the ebb tide running out of the St. George River swings you broadside to the swell and you roll to the jingle and clink of every spare shackle in every locker aboard. One would do well to run for New Harbor, Christmas Cove, Georges Harbor, or Port Clyde.

Overlooking the harbor is the Island Inn, an old-fashioned resort hotel with wide veranda, long steps, and a fancy cupola. Rooms and meals are obtainable here. The Trailing Yew serves meals in less formal style.

Climb the steep little dirt road by the Island Inn and look back over the harbor. The bleak, treeless bulk of Manana, the restless harbor, the fish houses at your feet suggest Newfoundland, Labrador, or the islands west and north of Scotland.

At the crossroads beyond the inn, turn left and climb the hill to the lighthouse, one of the principal landfall lights on the coast. It is now unwatched but supervised by the crew from the radio beacon and fog signal station on Manana. In the house formerly occupied by the keeper of Monhegan Light is a small museum, neat as a pin and very helpful in understanding some of the history of Monhegan and the details of the fishing and lobstering business.

There is a path north and east of the light leading through the woods to the east side of the island. Ledges jab through the thin soil, and old twisty trees cling to the rocky ridge of the island; even down in the valley where the woods are tall and quiet, you can hear the surf on the shore. In a few minutes you will come out on the 120-foot cliff at Whitehead, from which, on a clear day, you can see Matinicus Rock, Isle au Haut, the Camden Hills, and the islands at the entrance to Penobscot Bay.

Don't climb down the cliffs. It is perfectly possible, but the rock is "rotten" and a chunk of it may break off in your hand or under your foot. There have been a number of tragic accidents here in recent years in which someone has fallen overboard and others have drowned attempting a rescue. The water off the cliffs is deep and there is always a sea running here. The "suds" around the rocks consist of so much air and so little water that it is too thin to support a swimmer but too wet to breathe.

Continue around the island to the south. Notice the dead trees behind Burnt Head, killed one winter when an easterly gale piled *solid green water* over the cliff.

On the southern end of the island lie two wrecks. The larger is that of the tug *D. T. Sheridan,* which went ashore in heavy snow early one February morning in 1950. She was bound east, towing a barge, and in due course made Manana whistle. She laid a course to clear the south end of Monhegan and was running on the fathometer. A strong flood tide set her so far to the north that she struck the Washerwoman, a rock on the southern extremity of the island. The shore was so steep that the fathometer gave no warning. The barge was cast off and later picked up. Efforts to get the tug off failed, and a gale broke her in two and scattered her all over the southern end of the island. Even now the wreckage is impressive. The other wreck is a little white yawl that struck in the same place under almost identical circumstances on a foggy morning in June 1956. Little is left of her now but her iron keel.

After leaving the wrecks, follow the path up the hill, by several quaint cottages with carefully tended gardens, and continue down the road by the Monhegan House and the Trailing Yew to the Monhegan Store. Here is a generous variety of canned goods, meat, fruit, and frozen foods. There is a pay phone here and another on the porch of the Monhegan House. The post office is on the road just before you turn left up the hill.

Many of the summer inhabitants of Monhegan are artists, which perhaps accounts for the unusual costumes, hats, beards, and footgear as well as for splashes of paint on the rocks in unexpected places. A well-known artist who lived on Monhegan was Rockwell Kent. His painting of Manana in winter hangs in the Metropolitan Museum of Art in New

York. James Wyeth has a summer home on the island. Some of his pictures may be seen in the Farnsworth Museum in Rockland, among other distinguished places.

You may be fortunate enough to meet one of the year-round Monhegan residents. They are rugged and sensible people. On or about January 1, subject to fish-house consensus, is Trap Day, the day on which the lobstermen set out traps. They lobster all winter in the deep water around the island in their fast, able, and well-equipped powerboats. Fog, snow, heavy winter winds, and those biting, numbing northwesters they endure to haul and bait and set and haul again, dipping their woolen mittens overboard so their hands won't freeze. But the lobsters are plentiful and hard in winter and the price is high. On June 1 they take up their traps as the lobsters begin to move inshore to warmer, shallower waters to shed. During the summer, Monhegan lobstermen overhaul their gear and go seining or trawling or take jobs ashore.

Go ashore on Manana and visit the fog-signal station and radio beacon. Perhaps one of the crew will show you the Viking runes carved in a ledge in a gully. These marks have been the subject of much controversy, some claiming them to be runes, and disbelievers challenging the believers to translate them. Recently Professor Barry Fell, in his book *America B.C.* (Quadrangle Books, New York, 1976), makes an interesting case for the inscription's being Ogam, a Bronze Age language, of which he has found many other examples in America and from which he deduces a considerable European presence on this continent long before historic times. He translates the inscription "Ships from Phoenicia, Cargo platform," a reference to Manana as a place to exchange cargoes.

Monhegan is historic ground, as a plaque near the schoolhouse will testify. From about 1610 on, it was the base for English fishermen on the coast. In 1614, Captain John Smith of Pocahontas fame tried to organize an expedition to New England. As there seemed to be no prospect of loot, gold mines, or a northwest passage, he got no backers. However, when he began to hint at the possibility of an Eldorado in Maine, and when he guaranteed to bring home a load of fish in case the gold was not easy to get at, he was swamped with investors.

He arrived in May 1614, set his crew to fishing at once, and built a small boat. In this he and a few chosen friends explored the coast from the Penobscot River to Cape Cod, making an excellent chart. They returned to Monhegan to find one ship loaded with cod and the other nearly so. Smith sailed for Spain with the loaded vessel, sold the codfish there to a population who had had enough of herring and sardines, and returned to England with a very handsome profit.

The next year Smith sailed with a fleet of seventeen sail, intending to plant a permanent colony in Maine; but storms, privateers, and pirates broke up the expedition.

One winter night in recent years with a heavy southerly blowing and a frightful sea running up the harbor, two Coast Guardsmen from Manana started across to Monhegan in an outboard. Before they got halfway, their motor was drowned and the boat went ashore on Smuttynose. They scrambled up the rock through the surf and, cold, wet, and alone in the black night, awaited rescue. Death from hypothermia was an imminent possibility. After futile attempts by other Coast Guardsmen to launch another outboard from Manana, two fishermen on Monhegan launched a dory, rowed up to the lee side of the ledge, and took the men off safely.

Note on Approaching the Coast from Nova Scotia. The navigator should head for Matinicus Rock rather than for Monhegan. Manana's fog signal is on the west side of the island. The high cliffs on Monhegan make it more or less inaudible to the eastward, whereas the horn on Matinicus Rock is unobstructed and usually audible for miles to the south and east.

Approaching Monhegan from the east in thick weather, you can pass well south of the island and head for Manana whistle southwest of Monhegan. As you pass south of the cliffs, you will open up the horn on Manana. Or pass north of the island where you will probably get a scale-up. As you pass the cliffs, you will hear the surf, the horn on Manana, and the gong off Eastern Duck Rock.

Pleasant Point Gut, Maine (13301). This gut forms a bottle-tight anchorage between Gay Island and the mainland. Entrance is easy. In running up the river, be very generous to the half-tide ledge to the west of Hupper Island. It extends far out into the river. Favor the western shore. The lobster traps around it are very helpful. Leave the can outside the gut to *starboard*. It is placed for vessels entering the river. Favor the northern shore. Ledges make out far northward and northeastward from Flea Island at high water, but at low water almost everything is exposed. Once inside, continue close to the mainland shore among the anchored lobster boats. There is an extensive mud flat behind Flea Island, on which the writer spent an ignominious hour or two. Deep-draft boats can anchor in the bight of the northern shore just inside Flea Island. Those of shoal draft can go on up the harbor. Just south of the westernmost wharf is a half-tide rock. The rest of the harbor is soft bottom.

At half-tide or better a boat drawing 4 feet can easily go through behind Gay Island into Davis Cove and Friendship Harbor, but the channel is tortuous. Directions for it are picturesque but confusing. Take a local pilot for best results. The harbormaster is a good one to ask.

On the night of August 24, 1981, the 85-foot motor yacht *Bull Moose* dragged her anchor in this harbor when the wind shifted to the east and went ashore on the northern shore. Her stern caught on a rock at high water. As the tide ebbed, her bow dropped under water and she filled through ventilators and hatches. After two days of working with big pumps and a floating crane, she was floated; but all her machinery, electronics, and interior appointments were ruined by diesel oil and salt water. She had to be entirely rebuilt below.

There is a wharf with a gas pump and a lobster car on the north shore where fish and lobsters are shipped by truck. At the head of the wharf is a small store selling fisherman's supplies, candy, and tobacco, but no food. The nearest grocery store is 4 miles up the road. Next to the wharf is a lobster pound, now abandoned, because the lobsters somehow found a way out unknown to the owner.

Pleasant Point Gut is a good place to hide in the event of really heavy weather.

Turkey Cove and Maplejuice Cove, Maine (13301). These are quiet and unfrequented anchorages with nothing much to offer but peace and scenery. One cannot easily land at either, as the flats make out. Maplejuice Cove borders on the farm where Andrew Wyeth did much of his best work. There was a plan to restore the place and to collect here a museum of Wyeth memorabilia. However, even before the project got under way, so many visitors thronged into town that the roads were torn up, parking became a problem, and all the difficulties connected with crowds of people proved too much for the town to handle. The project has been abandoned, at least temporarily.

St. George River, Maine (13301). This broad and beautiful river was selected by Waymouth and Rosier in 1605 as the best place at which to establish a permanent English colony in Maine. Rosier wrote:

"I will not prefer it before our river Thames, because it is England's richest treasure," and then added that he wished that the Thames had all the desirable features of the St. George. He left for England with this sentence of regret: ". . . the river . . . did so ravish us with all variety of pleasantness, as we could not tell what to commend, but only admired . . . and we all concluded . . . that we should never see the like river in every degree equal until it pleased God we beheld the same again."

The river is remarkably free of navigational hazards, the most dangerous being an unmarked ledge west of Hupper Island in the mouth of the river. Keep well on the western side of the river to avoid this. Other dangers are marked.

There are several attractive coves along the shores. All are well charted and none have public landings or any facilities whatever. There are said to be striped bass in the river in a good year.

The trip up the river is relatively easy if you just follow the buoys and never let your depth finder read below 18 feet at low water as that means you are drifting out of the channel. When you reach Thomaston and the last red nun before the monument, steer for the left (westerly) side of the railroad bridge which will keep you on a wide swing around the monument (around 25 to 30 yards). After swinging around the monument, hug the docks closely as that is the best water.

The first floats you will come to are those of Lyman-Morse Boatbuilding Co. Feel free to tie up overnight, and if a longer stay is contemplated, contact them for arrangements as they also maintain moorings in the river and in Maplejuice Cove. They will come down to help you in Maplejuice Cove if necessary. If you need substantial quantities of fuel, a truck can be called to the wharf.

The next dock is the town landing which also accepts boats for limited amounts of time (overnight if necessary). The next wharf, behind Harbor View Tavern, has fuel pumps, but its future was uncertain in 1993. Jeff's Marine near the bridge also welcomes visitors and services outboards and small boats but has no fuel.

Lyman Yacht Services has expanded and has opened up with full-service facilities that can handle any repairs, including hauling and storage.

A short walk up Knox Street and left on Main will take you to the well-stocked Thomaston Market and also to a five-and-dime store and a

The back entrance to Port Clyde from the St. George River. Leave the round wooded island and the tiny islet in front of it to starboard in entering from the river.

hardware store. A laundromat, three banks, a coffee shop, a drug store, a newsstand, and two good bookstores all make this an excellent and convenient place to have work done or obtain supplies before or after cruising Penobscot Bay.

Thomaston is one and a half hours from the Portland airport and five minutes from the Owls Head airport where you can get regular air service on Bar Harbor Airlines or rent an Avis or Hertz car. In 1994 a bus ran through Thomaston to Portland and Boston.

If you want a pleasant walk, Thomaston is loaded with sailing history as it used to be a major building center for coastal schooners and large sailing barques. The town is full of lovely old captains' houses and it is a short taxi ride or a reasonable walk to General Knox's mansion.

Port Clyde, Maine (13301). Port Clyde, formerly known as Herring Gut, lies between Hupper Island and Marshall Point. Easy of access, right on the east-west course alongshore, and fairly well protected, Port Clyde was much used by coasting schooners waiting for a "chance along."

From the west it is usually approached through Davis Strait. From the nun in Davis Strait a course for Marshall Point Light will lead you to Gig Rock bell, the Sisters can, and Allen Ledge. The can on Allen Ledge must be left to starboard. It is a mark for the passage alongshore and not for the entrance to Port Clyde. However, the two nuns inside are to be left to starboard, and can 1 to port.

From the east, a course from Mosquito bell to Marshall Point Light will lead to can 1 off Gunning Rocks. Unless there is a big sea running, most yachts could continue to Marshall Point without rounding nun 4 on Marshall Ledge.

There are several moorings in the middle of the harbor off the store, some of which may be rental moorings. Others are heavy winter moorings, awkward and dirty to handle on deck but secure. Call the Port Clyde General Store on channel 16 or 9 to inquire.

If there is any considerable breeze on the ebb tide, the anchorage may be rolly. A berth close under Hupper Island may be quieter. An alternative is to go through the gut between Raspberry Island and the mainland and anchor north of Hupper Island. The passage looks more difficult than it is. Entering from the south, favor the east shore by the old fish-packing wharf to avoid the kelp ledge in mid-channel. Keep to the starboard side, the outside of the bend, by a dammed-up cove and several wharves. Just west of the cove is a rock close under the shore marked with an iron spike now partly hidden by a wharf. Swing into the middle of the channel and anchor under Hupper Island as much out of the tide as possible. From the west, favor the rock with the spike to avoid two ledges making off from Raspberry Island.

The southerly of the two wharves on the eastern shore of the harbor is used by the Monhegan mail boat, *Laura B.* Land at the northerly wharf, owned by the store. Here are gasoline, diesel fuel, and water. There is 10 feet alongside at low water.

The store at the head of the wharf is making a determined effort to attract yachtsmen. It provides a good selection of meats, groceries, beer, and wine as well as a stock of clothing, "gifts," marine hardware, and charts. Propane gas tanks can be refilled at the store. There is a shower; bring your own towels and soap. There are tables on the wharf where one can eat lobsters or light lunches. The store is open from 8 A.M. to 8 P.M. daily and from 9 to 6:30 on Sunday. There is a public pay telephone outside.

The nearest place for major repairs is Tenants Harbor, but the store can recommend a local mechanic or carpenter.

Up the hill from the store are two restaurants, the Ocean House (dry) and the Black Harpoon (damp). There is also a variety store, an art gallery, a post office, and a garage. A considerable walk to the south is Marshall Point Light with a small museum.

Mosquito Island. In running from the can on Gunning Rocks to Mosquito bell, you will cross a 14-foot spot on Barter Shoal, seldom a matter for concern. However, in heavy weather the sea will hump up menacingly here and it is well to keep away from it.

There is usually a good draft of breeze from Davis Strait by Port Clyde and out almost to Mosquito bell, but as soon as one rounds the bell and squares away for Whitehead, the wind dies out and the going gets sloppy. One answer is to cut Mosquito bell as much as possible and follow the eastern shore of Mosquito Island and Hart Neck almost up to Tenants Harbor, and then go across to Whitehead. There is usually a good breeze under the shore and the course from Tenants Harbor across to White-head will bring the usual southwest breeze comfortably on the quarter. This course is but little longer and is usually appreciably faster.

Another alternative is to pass inside of Mosquito Island, thus sailing a shorter course in calm water with a good breeze. A yachtsman who made the passage bound west in a Bermuda 40 drawing 4 feet at less than half-tide reported no depths less than 12 feet. His notes follow:

> Go to the north side of the channel, very close to the shore of Mosquito Head. Watch for a rock off to the west of Mosquito Harbor. Give nun 2 a good berth.
>
> Presumably, staying close to the northern shore and the rock off Mosquito Harbor will keep you clear of the two big ledges west of Mosquito Island.

Tenants Harbor, Maine (13301). In anything but an easterly gale, Tenants Harbor affords a quiet anchorage. Marked by the conspicuous abandoned white lighthouse on Southern Island and by a lighted bell, Tenants Harbor is easy of access at any time. Keep more or less in the middle; if anything, favoring the northern shore. Anchor where draft and inclination dictate. There is usually plenty of room.

The first two wharves on the north side of the harbor are Witham's and Art's Lobster. They are commercial fishing operations and clearly prefer yachts to land farther up at Cod End. If only a mooring is desired, hail Mark Asplund at Art's Lobster, but do not land alongside. He has at least eight moorings and does emergency diving.

Lehtinen's boatyard, now owned by James Wyeth, is on the next wharf and, although small, is an efficient and active operation. The yard rents moorings, can haul boats up to 40 feet, can make repairs in both wood and fiberglass, and has a mechanic available.

The next wharf is Cod End operated by Susan and Anne Miller. This is the hub for yacht service at Tenants Harbor. They rent moorings marked with buoys labeled "COD END RENTAL." At their float, *which has only 4 feet at low water,* they sell gasoline, diesel fuel, and ice. Water is available too. In the shop at the head of the wharf are charts, fresh fish, some marine hardware, and a good seafood restaurant, which may be crowded. One can call Cod End on channel 9 to see how crowded, but they do not take reservations and serve on a first-come basis.

At the head of the driveway is the East Wind Hotel. They serve dinner from five to eight in the evening but their other facilities are for their own guests.

There are several other restaurants to the left on the main road. To the right is a well-stocked general store open from 8 A.M. until 8 P.M. daily and until 6 P.M. on Sundays. The only readily available public telephone is in front of the store. Also a short distance to the right is a laundromat with showers.

If one is not in need of supplies and seeks peace and quiet, he would be well advised to try Long Cove to the north of the entrance to Tenants Harbor. There is good shelter behind Spectacle Island.

Alternate Courses:
Muscle Ridge Channel or Two-Bush Channel

The navigator may be in doubt whether to work his way through the islands and ledges of the Muscle Ridges or to take the longer and easier course outside.

Bound East. In most cases, especially if the tide is fair, the best course is inside. The run from Mosquito Island to Whitehead is less than 6 miles, a good deal shorter than the run to Two-Bush. If you change your mind on the way, Tenants Harbor is close to leeward. From Whitehead you can run on up the channel if the tide is fair or wait out a foul tide in Seal Harbor. If the weather is thick, you may have some trouble making Whitehead, because the sound of the fog signal does not seem to carry well against the wind. However, before you can get into any trouble, you will be able to hear it. There is a bell on Southeast Breaker and a good horn on Two-Bush.

The course up the channel is easy, even in thick weather. However, on most days there will be a scale-up in the channel. The islands to the south seem to dry up the fog and stimulate the wind. The tide runs hard but pretty much along the course. One can usually get an echo with the horn off the high land at Sprucehead. The fathometer provides a safe way to prevent wandering to either side of the channel. There are several shelters easily available should the tide turn. Best of all, perhaps, the sea is smooth and the traffic is not likely to be dangerous.

Outside, the breeze may be lighter, the sea rougher, the runs between buoys longer, and the traffic perilous indeed. A 100,000-ton tanker cannot maneuver with agility. The tide seems to run to the west with greater strength and for a longer time than it runs east. The only possible shelter on the outside course is Home Harbor, and that is difficult in the fog.

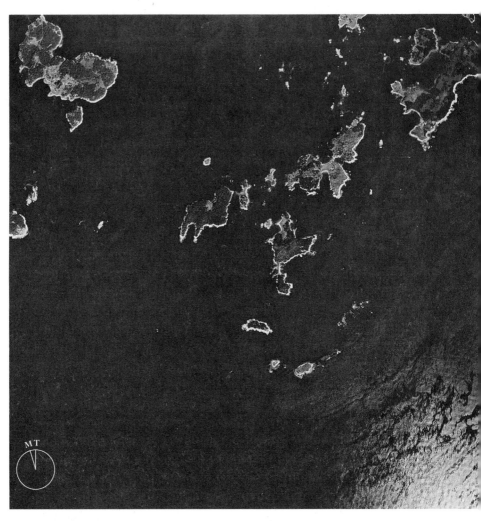

Muscle Ridge Channel, Maine. This excellent photograph was taken in 1957, but the islands and ledges haven't moved much. Two Bush Island is the farthest south. North of it is Pleasant Island and Home Harbor. The passage west of Flag Island is clear. Yellow Ledge east of Hewett Island stands out sharply. Whitehead is on the western border with Seal Harbor north of it. There is now a causeway between Sprucehead Island and Burnt Island. *Courtesy James W. Sewall Co.*

Bound West. With the wind northwest, particularly if it is early in the day, the inside passage is much to be preferred, for it keeps one to windward, and the northerly is likely to hold longer and blow harder under the land than it does offshore. However, if it gets to be midmorning, the outside course may be a good gamble, for the wind may very well shift southerly within a few hours, and distance down the bay becomes distance to windward. If the northwester holds long enough to get you by the Two-Bush gong, you can probably fetch right into Port Clyde on the southerly. If the wind does not shift, Monhegan or Georges Harbor is a realistic shelter.

If the wind is southerly, the beat down the Muscle Ridges with a fair tide is pretty and provides an active day for all hands on sheets and backstays. The wind will be fresher under the islands than it will outside. However, the beat down the bay has its pleasures, too, and one who likes being to windward can be happy off Two-Bush, where he can fetch a long way to the westward. The beat from Whitehead around Mosquito bell can be a long pull.

If it is thick and calm, you might as well motor outside, where the buoys are loud and the navigation easy. Be sure to hang up a radar reflector.

At night, the outside route is to be preferred, for the lighted buoys are a great help. The only drawback is the occasional presence of supertankers, which must be treated with the greatest respect.

Whitehead Island. There is a cove behind the lighthouse, formerly used by the Coast Guard; unfortunately their big moorings have now been removed. The holding ground is good, but a trip line on the anchor is not amiss here as the bottom is rocky. A wash works in around the point of the island, but on a quiet night is not unpleasant. In a southerly blow it would roll a small boat around uncomfortably but would probably not be dangerous.

It is a pleasant walk down around the old Coast Guard station and the light. An inventive lightkeeper developed a scheme for compressing air for the fog signal by the action of the waves. It was reported to be quite successful until it was carried away in a gale. You may be able to find the irons in the rock where the floats were attached.

Seal Harbor. This harbor was once much used by coasters waiting out a foul tide but is little used by anyone today except lobstermen out of

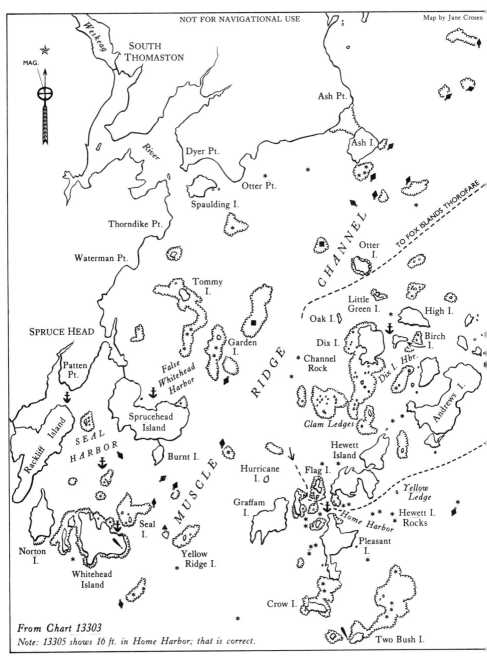

Map by Jane Crosen

MAG.

Weskeag

SOUTH
THOMASTON

Ash Pt.

River

Dyer Pt.

Ash I.

Otter Pt.

Spaulding I.

Thorndike Pt.

Waterman Pt.

CHANNEL

TO FOX ISLANDS THOROFARE

Otter
I.

Tommy
I.

Little
Green I.

High I.

Oak I.

SPRUCE HEAD

Dix I.

Birch
I.

Garden
I.

RIDGE

Channel
Rock

Dix I. Hbr.

Patten
Pt.

*False
Whitehead
Harbor*

Andrews I.

Sprucehead
Island

*SEAL
HARBOR*

Rackliff Island

Clam Ledges

Burnt I.

MUSCLE

Hewett
Island

Hurricane
I.

Flag I.

*Yellow
Ledge*

Graffam
I.

Hewett I.
Rocks

Home Harbor

Norton
I.

Seal
I.

Pleasant
I.

Whitehead
Island

Yellow
Ridge I.

Crow I.

From Chart 13303
Note: *13305 shows 16 ft. in Home Harbor; that is correct.*

Two Bush I.

Anchorages in Muscle Ridge Channel, Maine. *Map drawn by Jane Crosen.*

Sprucehead. You will not be crowded here as you might be at Tenants Harbor.

Enter between the red-and-green can and can 1. Run up the harbor, keeping the lobster boats in the *far* anchorage fine on the starboard bow. Keep well off the 2-foot spot inside of nun 4.

The anchorage behind the jetty is safe enough, but rolly. Unless you need supplies, continue up the harbor, keeping an eye open for the ledge off Slins Island to the west. The ledge is exposed one hour after high water but makes out to the northeast. The end of it was and may still be marked with an iron spike and a yellow cylinder.

When the lobster wharf on the northeast side of Sprucehead is about 150 yards abeam to starboard, turn sharply to port and run up the line of moorings for the fishing boats south of Patton Point. The channel is *narrow,* but it will take 8 feet at any tide. Do not go beyond the small beach east of the wharf on Patton Point and stay close to the moorings. The channel shoals up to mussel beds very quickly on both sides. There is good holding ground here.

One can anchor north of Long Ledge to avoid going all the way in to the anchorage described above, but the bottom, once stiff mud, is reported to be foul with kelp and eel grass.

Dix Island. The place labeled Dix Island Harbor is a secure anchorage, though not a snug one. Entrance is among unmarked ledges, but most of them show at high water, and all of them are evident at low water. A preferable anchorage for a small yacht is in the cove between Dix Island and Birch Island north of the bar. Enter either side of Oak Island, follow the north shore of Dix Island, and anchor northwest of the tip of Birch Island.

Dix Island is now owned by an association, whose intention it is to allow visitors on the island but not to encourage them. The president of the association writes:

Dix Island was once the site of a big quarry operation, with schooners and barges loading at the dock and gangs of stonecutters living ashore. The island is now owned by the members of the Dix Island Association, who have an interest in the preservation of the rich natural beauty, the historic significance, and a simple primitive life-style. Visitors may enjoy the shores; however, no fires or camping are allowed. The interior of the island is restricted to the private use of owners.

False Whitehead Harbor. This is a quiet cove. There is no problem in entering. It is not a long walk to the store at Sprucehead.

Home Harbor. This is a handy little place to know about, as it is well to windward in the prevailing southwester. It is between Pleasant and Hewett Islands just inside Two-Bush Island. From Home Harbor it is easy to get around Two-Bush and then fetch well down the coast. It is also a good place from which to take off for Matinicus. There are no supplies or facilities of any kind, but in past years there has been a settlement of fishermen who come out with their families from Rockland for the summer lobstering.

To enter from the east, go either side of Yellow Ledge, which is high, bold, and really yellow. Be sure to pick up Hewett Island Rocks and then follow the Hewett Island shore, giving the Pleasant Island shore a good berth off the high bluff. Anchor north of the fishing boats near the weir, where Chart 13305 shows 16 feet. To get out of the tide, creep with the lead as far south as possible. There is some scour of tide, but it is not uncomfortable.

To enter from Muscle Ridge Channel, run for Flag Island until you lose Whitehead Light. Then go right up the middle of a hole west of Flag Island. Keep in the middle and look out for a cross-tide. You will see bottom, but the writer has carried 5 feet through at low water. When you are through the narrow passage, follow the shore around to the east until well clear of ledges on the south. The east side of Flag Island looks good on the chart, but a visitor in 1985 found it studded with boulders. Fishermen use the west side consistently.

The cove in the south side of Hewett Island is a pleasant place to picnic or spend the night in anything but a persistent southerly.

Rockland, Maine (13305). With a light and fog signal on Owls Head and another on the breakwater, Rockland is easy to make in any weather, and for one in need of supplies or repairs or seeking to make a crew change, it is a most convenient port.

There are three anchorages. In easterly weather, especially if there is any real weight in the wind, the best place is in the northwest angle of the breakwater close to the shore. There are private moorings here for local boats, but there is plenty of room to anchor with adequate scope.

In strong southerly or southwesterly weather, follow the buoyed channel to starboard around the prominent Marine Colloids plant to the basin in Lermonds Cove. Here are moorings and a few slips maintained by Knight's Marine. Call on channel 9. Knight's has facilities for almost any repair work including a 35-ton travelift and an expert mechanic. Sail and electronics repair can be arranged by the sympathetic and helpful staff. Fuel, water, ice, showers, and laundromat are available. Across the street is an IGA supermarket, and a state liquor store is not far away.

From Lermonds Cove terminal the state ferries go to North Haven, Vinalhaven, and occasionally to Matinicus. From here and from the North End Shipyard on the northern side of the cove sail a number of coasting schooners known as "windjammers," carrying passengers on week-long excursions. On Monday mornings when they leave more or less together, they offer a romantic view of the past.

The third anchorage, perfectly acceptable on most summer nights, is found by following the buoys to port, close by the Coast Guard base, to a dredged mooring area. There are a great many moorings here, at least 25 labeled "City of Rockland." Call the Rockland harbormaster or the Chamber of Commerce on channel 9 for guidance. Launch service is available at a price by calling on channel 71, but there is usually room to tie a dinghy at the Chamber of Commerce float on the south side of the most southerly wharf off the city. Here the Chamber maintains showers, toilets, washers and dryers, a small office at the head of the wharf, and a pumpout station on the wharf.

Next north of the city wharf is the Black Pearl, a well-established restaurant with a long float for party boats and restaurant customers.

North of the Black Pearl is Rockland Landings Marina with moorings and dock space. Call on channel 16 and shift to a working channel. Fuel, water, and ice are available here with deep water off the face of the float. Rockland Landing is growing rapidly and expects soon to have more slips and dock space. They now have a mechanic and a diver on call, a restaurant and lounge, launch service, showers, and a laundry machine.

Next northward is Bitter End, another marina to which commercial party boats often tie up. Fuel and water are available here. Next northerly is the commercial fish pier, and beyond that is the Coast Guard wharf.

Repair services of all kinds are available at Rockland, through either Knight's Marine, the Chamber of Commerce, or Rockland Landings.

There are restaurants close to all the landings mentioned, and stores of all kinds lie along the main street. Bus service westward to Portland and Boston and eastward to Bangor is being restored. If one must lie over a day in Rockland, the Farnsworth Museum, with exhibits by Jamie Wyeth and Winslow Homer as well as other special exhibits, is an excellent resource. The Shore Village Museum a short walk from the shore has many artifacts from the old Lighthouse Service. A round trip on the state ferry through the islands west of Vinalhaven to Carvers Harbor affords a quick view of Maine at its best.

Rockland has many attractions but lacks the picturesque atmosphere of harbors to the eastward. The outward-bound mariner will leave with more anticipation than regret.

Chapter XI

Rockland to Schoodic Point

General Conditions. This region is the goal of many cruising men. The bays are broken up by hundreds of islands and inlets. The shores are usually bold and clean pink or yellowish granite. The islands are overgrown with dark spruce trees interspersed with fields of grass and raspberry bushes. Among the rocks are smooth, sandy beaches.

The harbors are many and vary from "live" yachting centers like Camden to uninhabited coves like Buckle Harbor. The local people are friendly and willing to help the stranger.

The weather is variable and interesting. It may be thick fog all day with nothing to be seen but an occasional buoy and the loom of spruce trees. Or it may "scale up" into a smoky sou'wester with a chop running up the bays and even the nearby shores a hazy blue-green. The next day it may come off a slashing northwester with the puffs off the hills and islands turning the water green and white and with every tree standing out clearly. On such a day the mountains of Mount Desert, Blue Hill, or Camden are sharp cut against the horizon. Whatever the weather, there is always a sheltered harbor to run for at night.

Fog. Don't worry about it. The frequency of fog and its dangers are vastly overrated. No one likes it. Dangerous situations can arise quickly. Carelessness brings its punishment swiftly. But for generations people have navigated Penobscot Bay in the fog and never before with such good equipment as we have today.

Appendix E in this volume deals with fog at some length.

Islands. The old man remembers that when you owned a boat, you owned all the islands. No longer is this the case. Now every island is someone's, and the owner is not unlikely to have built a house or camp on his island, to regard it as his kingdom, and to resent the intrusion of a stranger with a clam hoe or a bucket of lobsters to cook. If you decide to land on an island with a house on it, the only decent course is to identify yourself to the owners and ask permission to stretch your legs ashore. Thus approached, many owners will be hospitable.

Some islands are owned by conservation groups such as the Nature Conservancy, the National or Maine Audubon Society, or the Friends of Nature. Many of these islands harbor nesting seabird colonies: gulls, terns, herons, eiders, shags, or the more secretive, burrowing petrels. If so, the island is likely to be posted with signs identifying it as a bird nesting area and asking you not to land during the nesting season. Please respect these signs. Especially on smaller, treeless islands, even landing a boat on the shore in early summer can cause such disturbance to the nesting eiders or terns that they may abandon their young—or lose them to the black-backed gulls always waiting nearby.

However, as you sail by the island, you can observe a lot of domestic activity without disturbing the birds. In early spring you won't likely see the eiders who stay tucked low in the dense grass while brooding their eggs, but by mid-June you may see mothers and aunts with strings of young chicks paddling behind close to the shore among the floating seaweed. If there are terns nesting, there will be a constant traffic of comings and goings as they bring small fish to their mates and to their young. If you visit after nesting season (usually around August 1), you can safely explore the island and find the odd pedestal nests of cormorants or bits of down, the original insulation from an eider nest, and try to guess the island's erstwhile residents by the feathers and eggshell fragments you find.

If you see no bird sanctuary signs, you are welcome ashore to explore the island at any season. Some islands are inhabited by sheep left to pasture there for the milder months. The sheep won't mind your presence but they may panic and hurt themselves on the rocky terrain if you bring your dog. In any case, it is courteous to keep your pet on a leash when visiting any island.

Fire is a constant danger on islands. Open fires, above or below high-water mark, are illegal without a permit from the town in which the island lies, and all the organizations concerned with islands such as the Island Institute and the Maine Island Trail Association oppose fires. Do your smoking and cooking aboard.

There are still a few uninhabited islands. If you are fortunate enough to find one of these, anchor off the lee side and explore the shore in the dinghy. You will probably find a little beach to land on. You may startle some crows off the seaweed as you land. The rocks are usually steep, clean granite, and the water so clear that you can see bottom in 2 fathoms. Take a swim, or put on a mask and explore the ledges close to the shore. Inland you will find thick spruce brush. The blowdowns are usually grown up to raspberry or blackberry bushes. In mid-July or late August the sun-warmed berries are food for the gods—but don't go berrying in short pants!

On the seaward end of the island, if it is seldom visited, you may find the messy nests of gulls and shags with eggs or young birds in early July. Eiders and terns are less common but they do nest on Maine islands. Work back along the shore. You may find a lobster buoy or net float among the debris at high-water mark—or a bait box or a watch; you never know. A blue heron may fly up as you round a point.

In some islands there are caves and cliffs, great smooth ledges, or rough beaches. Ospreys often nest in trees near the shore. Climbing the tree is doubtful procedure. The birds resent your intrusion, the trees are often dead and the branches brittle, and the nest is so big and rough that you can't climb out around the edge anyway. Better not molest the local residents.

Leave nothing whatever behind you to show that you have been there. Whether you return aboard loaded with plunder or not, your trip ashore will be one of the pleasantest parts of the cruise to remember during a long, dreary February.

The Island Institute and the Maine Island Trail Association. From Hurricane Island Outward Bound School's interest in ecology developed the Island Institute, founded in 1983 and to a large extent powered by the contagious enthusiasm and dedication of Philip W. Conkling, author of *Islands in Time.* The mission of the institute "recognizes [that] the resources of Maine islands . . . are fragile, finite, and if lost, irreplaceable." Its mission is to encourage "wise use of resources by placing ourselves at the difficult and painful boundaries between competing interests and by advocating solutions that balance the needs of the coast's human and natural communities." It is no club of knee-jerk do-gooders but a practical organization that takes an active part in island life.

Since 1983 the institute has made notable progress. It has helped islanders to work together to support their schools, knowing that when the school is lost, the island community withers. It has encouraged teachers, parents, and students to understand that their communities are unique and valuable and has given substance to its words by providing financial aid to island scholars.

The institute has helped to encourage island economies. When aquaculture projects failed at Swans Island and Frenchboro, the institute took an active part in arranging refinancing under local control to save jobs and island income.

The *Island Journal* is the institute's annual publication, a prize winner. The *Working Waterfront* comes out more frequently with news and features on the economic aspects of island life, and the *InterIsland News* keeps up communications among island communities and those ashore who are interested in them. The institute's headquarters is at 60 Ocean Street, Rockland.

The Institute has recently agreed to take over from the Coast Guard many abondoned lighthouse properties and see that they are allocated to institutions which will preserve and maintain them.

From the institute sprang the Maine Island Trail Association, under the leadership of David Getchell, Sr., now carried on by Cate Cronin. The association has arranged with island owners, the state, and conservation groups a series of islands from Portland to Machias Bay where kayakers, canoeists, and small-boat sailors can explore and camp with the important condition that each leave the island better, or at least no worse, than he found it. Concern for birds, seals, and animals is paramount. Cleanliness and beauty follow close. The enthusiasm with which the Trail Association was founded has fired its members. The results of their care can be seen from Jewell Island eastward. The headquarters is at 41A Union Wharf, Portland.

Lobstering. You will see lobster buoys wherever the water is shoal and the bottom rocky. In the summer, when the water is warm, the lobsters are active, eat more, and seek the shallow rocky bottom to shed their shells and hide until their new shells harden up. If your lobster's shell feels like damp cardboard, it is a "shedder," with less meat for its size than a hard lobster.

In the summer, traps are set in from one to ten fathoms, often on the rocky slopes of underwater hills. The buoys serve as a warning to the navigator that he may be approaching shoal water and as an indication of the speed and direction of the tidal current.

The laws governing lobstering are comparatively few and loose. It is illegal to dive or drag for lobsters or to take them in any other way than in conventional traps. The lobsterman must have a license issued by the state, and only a licensed person may touch lobster gear. He must have the number of his license on each trap and buoy. His buoys must be painted in a characteristic pattern, and he must display a buoy prominently on his boat to ensure that he pulls only his own traps. Each trap must have an escape hatch to let out small lobsters and other creatures and must have a biodegradable panel to prevent a lost trap's fishing indefinitely. Legally, a lobsterman may set his traps anywhere he wants to, but he is supposed to leave a navigable channel. He may not keep any lobster less than $3^{1}/_{4}$ inches or over 5 inches from the eye socket to the back of the shell. He may not haul at night or from noon Saturday until dawn Monday in the summer. Then there are unwritten rules governing lobstering that must be observed. Each town or community has certain areas where its people may and may not fish. Communities of lobstermen are likely to resent newcomers to the area and "ragpickers," who set ten or a dozen traps and foul the gear of serious lobstermen. To violate unwritten rules brings a quick response, sometimes culminating in cutting off buoys or worse.

A lobsterman is an independent entrepreneur with a great deal of money tied up in his business. A trap with line and buoy costs about $50, and he may have upward of 500 traps. A boat capable of fishing offshore in winter, such as those you see at Monhegan or Matinicus, with a reliable engine, radio, radar, loran, depth finder, trap hauler, and whatever else he may need will cost well over $50,000. He must have a place to land and store bait, a pickup truck, and a shop or fish house in which to repair gear. He is likely to have invested over $100,000 and to have had to borrow some of it. He must buy bait and fuel daily, and one heavy gale may wipe him out. With lobsters between $2 and $3 a pound, the lobsterman is a very busy man on the water.

Yachtsmen have been heard to joke about hauling lobster traps. Everything is against it. Not only is it a form of stealing akin to shoplifting, but it is almost impossible to do it without being seen by someone ashore or afloat. Hauling a trap by hand is heavy, wet, dirty work. The trap will bang up the side of your boat and dirty the deck with bait drainings. And your chances of profiting from this dishonesty are no better than one in three. Joke about it if you must—it is about as funny as joking about bombs in an airport—but don't do it.

The line from a trap usually comes up to a bottle, called a toggle, and then to the buoy. The toggle is there to help float the line and to prevent the buoy from being pulled under by debris or tidal current. The chances of fouling a trap under sail are minimal, for there is considerable slack in the line and the boat just pushes the buoy aside. Under power, however, avoid passing between the buoy and the toggle, for the line may lie near the surface and be sucked in by the propeller. A nylon pot warp wound tightly around the shaft usually calls for a quick trip overboard and a sharp knife. Try to save the buoy and tie it to the line again. Your effort will be appreciated.

Lobstermen keep in touch with each other by radio, watch each other, and help each other. They watch you too and usually will be quick to help if you are in trouble. Respect them and keep out of their way.

You can best repay their help by giving of your friendship in return. A drink in your cockpit and a carton of cigarettes will be much appreciated. Anything else you care to do will probably be appreciated too. These men are not "quaint characters" but are often well-informed, intelligent, and independent businessmen engaged in a hazardous occupation that sometimes demands all the courage, endurance, and intelligence a person can call upon. Many of them have wrung more water out of their socks than most summer sailors ever see.

Supplies and Repairs. As you sail farther east, you are increasingly on your own. Although some towns have convenience stores or small grocery stores near the shore, many local people are now driving miles to supermarkets and the small stores near the shore are folding up. We will try to mention existing ones in descriptions of individual harbors. However, the cruising person should plan to be independent of stores for several days.

Most grocery stores carry wine and beer, but hard liquor is a state monopoly and is sold through Agency stores licensed by the state. Many of the larger markets are Agency stores.

Major repairs can be made at Rockland, Camden, Stonington, and Southwest Harbor. Many other harbors have small yards which can do good work, and almost every town has someone who can charm a gasoline or diesel engine into life. Sail repair is only a little more difficult. Bohndell's Sail Loft in Rockport, Robin Lincoln in Sedgewick, and Donald Hale in Sargentville are all reliable sailmakers.

Suggested Courses

Eggemoggin Reach. This is a pretty and usually unexciting sail through protected waters and is to be chosen if the fog is thick offshore. Eastbound, you will have a fair wind up West Penobscot Bay past the dramatic hill of Great Sprucehead, where Eliot Porter took the photographs for the Sierra Club's *Summer Island,* and among the smaller and equally beautiful islands of the upper bay. Bucks Harbor at the west end of the Reach is a good anchorage. Thence the course is about southeast down the Reach between Deer Isle and the shore, a pleasant sail with the wind abeam in an ordinary southwester. You are unlikely to encounter fog in the Reach, as the mass of Deer Isle dries it up. The wind often dies off the mouth of the Benjamin River but, after a short drift, it comes in again. In general, favor the southerly side of the passage for a fresher breeze.

Once out by the bell at Devils Head, cross Jericho Bay, pass through Casco Passage, and head for Bass Harbor Head on Mount Desert.

Westbound, the Reach is a pleasant relief from beating, but of course you will pay for it on the western end, for unless you can arrange a northwester or a dry easterly, you will have a long dead beat down Penobscot Bay. Still, it may be preferable to navigating the Thorofares in the fog.

The Thorofares. This route crosses West Penobscot Bay to Stand-in Point and passes through Fox Islands Thorofare between North Haven Island and Vinalhaven and past the village of North Haven. It then crosses East Penobscot Bay, leaving Mark Island to starboard bound east and through the well-buoyed passage between Deer Isle and the islands south of it. From here the course passes north of Eastern Mark Island, across Jericho Bay to York Narrows, and on to Mount Desert.

This course is more difficult in the fog than the course through Eggemoggin Reach, but as the tide runs pretty much along your course through the Thorofares, it does not set you off to either side in the tricky parts. The runs across the bays have noisy marks to run for.

This course keeps you to windward bound west. With luck and a close-winded boat, you can fetch the course with only a hitch to windward now and then. Certainly there is greater variety in the scenery.

A variation on this course is to sail from the eastern end of Fox Islands Thorofare to the whistle on the Brown Cow and then thread your way through the islands of Merchants Row, coming out either side of Saddleback Island and running across to York Narrows. This is by far the most interesting course although, for the stranger who would not recognize the islands, it can be a horror show in the fog. Still, on a sunny day you are likely to get a scale-up under Isle au Haut.

Outside. Another alternative is to go south of Vinalhaven, through the broken country to the southeast, past Otter and Brimstone Islands, south of Saddleback Ledge and Roaring Bull, south of Long Island, and then up the Western Way. Or you can go through Burnt Coat Harbor, pass west of Long Island, and run up the Western Way by Black Island. A very attractive feature of the outside passage is the approach to the Mount Desert hills on a fair afternoon, with the shadows changing as the sun swings west. In the fog, one misses this feature and must navigate among the offshore islands and ledges south of Vinalhaven and Swans Island, where the tide runs hard and there are few buoys. Those, for the most part, are rather silent. It is no place to be lost in the fog.

Rockport, Maine (13305). This harbor is easy of access in clear weather. Porterfield Ledge is a big cube of granite blocks with a daymark on top, and the abandoned lighthouse on Indian Island is prominent. At night the lighted beacon on Lowell Rock is a good guide. In the fog, simply make the bell buoy "RO," cross to the bold western shore, and follow it in.

The inner part of the harbor is peppered with moorings, some of which are reserved for cruising boats. Inquire at the float of Rockport Marine at the head of the harbor. There is at least 8 feet at low water here. Rockport Marine has a 35-ton travelift and repair facilities for hull, spars, and engines. The yard specializes in the storage, maintenance, and repair of wooden boats. Bob Chase at Bohndell's Sail Loft nearby can repair damage to sails and rigging. Fuel and water are piped to the float, and the yard maintains showers for visitors.

West of the yard is the Rockport Boat Club, a low-key club, friendly and hospitable, but with no facilities for visitors.

The nearest grocery store is a supermarket on Route 1—rather far to walk.

There is an excellent restaurant, the Sail Loft, up the hill from the yard.

Cruise schooners often lie in Rockport on Friday nights before their scheduled Saturday arrival in Camden or Rockland. They are picturesque if sometimes noisy neighbors.

On the west shore of the harbor is the Artisan's School, a college-level school which uses boatbuilding as a means of teaching not only the skillful use of tools but aesthetics, design, ecology, and small-business practices. The student also learns by experience the necessity of using his own skills in harmony with the skills of others to achieve a goal which none could reach alone. Supplemented by courses in English, history, mathematics, and science, the program leads to an Associate in Science degree. The shop is worth a visit if only to admire the elegant wooden boats under construction.

Rockport was well known during the nineteenth century for its lime. The ruins of the old kilns are still visible on the west shore. Many small schooners brought cords of wood to fire the kilns, and others took the lime off in barrels. A schooner had to be tight to carry lime, for if the lime got wet, it swelled, heated, and could set the vessel afire or burst her sides.

Much ice was shipped in schooners from Rockport to United States cities and to the West Indies before the days of mechanical refrigeration. The ice was so clear that it was said one could read a book through it.

From 1844 until 1892 the firm of Carleton, Norwood & Co. built 62 brigs, barks, ships, and schooners on the shores of Rockport Harbor. The biggest was the second four-masted ship built in the United States, *Frederick Billings*, built in 1885, 282 feet long. In 1895 she was set afire by her crew when loaded with nitrate. She exploded and sank in 20 minutes. All hands were saved.

Although Rockport was considered a good harbor by coaster skippers, with a chop running up the bay from the south, the yachtsman might find it a rolly anchorage, especially on the ebb tide.

Camden, Maine (13307, 13305). There are many reasons to visit Camden. It is easy of access under almost any conditions, with a light on the Graves and a bell outside it. Curtis Island shows a light and its shore is bold. A lighted beacon is on the ledge at the eastern entrance.

Camden, Maine. This picture was taken in early October, but even then the inner harbor was crowded. Notice the shoals off Curtis Island and in the northeast entrance. *Courtesy James W. Sewall Co.*

It has good stores, and a first-class boatyard, which can repair any damage to hull, spars, or engine. An excellent sailmaker lives nearby. Camden's stores can supply whatever you need, from charts and books to groceries and marine hardware. The Rockland airport is a taxi ride away. The town, back from the shore, has a quiet and dignified nineteenth-century air. The cruise schooner fleet sails from Camden on Monday mornings and returns Saturday noons, providing a great deal of picturesque activity. Finally, there are the Camden Hills, providing trails for a good walk ashore. As a place to change crews, stock up, or effect repairs, Camden is one of the best on the coast.

However, as a quiet place to spend the night, it is a dead loss. There is no room to anchor in the inner harbor and very little chance of getting a mooring there. The outer harbor, in spite of the protection offered by Curtis Island and Northeast Ledge, is a rolly berth for a yacht. It is so crowded with moorings that there is no room to anchor.

As you approach the harbor in search of a mooring, you have four alternatives: You can call Wayfarer Marine on channel 71. Their launch will likely be patrolling the harbor and can lead you to a mooring. If you use one of their moorings, launch service is free in response to a call on 71. Or you can call the harbormaster on channel 9. He too may be on the water and can establish you on a town mooring. Another alternative is to call the Camden Yacht Club on channel 68. They maintain several guest moorings and may know of a mooring belonging to an absent member. If you get no radio response, approach their float and inquire. There is a 20-minute limit on tie-up there, but that should be sufficient. A final alternative is to go alongside the float at Willey Wharf on the west side—clearly marked—and inquire for a mooring or a chance to tie up to one of their floats moored out in the harbor.

On the east side of the harbor is the headquarters of Wayfarer Marine. Equipped with a Brownell trailer, a travelift, and a mobile crane, they can haul almost any yacht on the coast and can repair hull, spars, or engine. Shore Sails at Wayfarer or Bob Chase at Bohndell's Sail Loft can take care of sails and rigging. Wayfarer sells, installs, and repairs electronic equipment as well. There is a fuel pump on the outer end of the Wayfarer wharf, but it is well to call in on the radio to see when it is likely to be available. At some times, yachts line up three deep. Wayfarer also provides pumpout service, water, and ice, and in their shop on the wharf they carry a wide selection of marine supplies.

During the cruising season, Wayfarer is a busy place with people on short vacations wanting everything yesterday. It will help both you and the yard to call ahead if you have a considerable problem.

North of Wayfarer is Harbor Head Marina, specializing in smaller boats and outboard engines.

On the west side of the harbor farthest to the south is the elegant Camden Yacht Club mentioned above, built during the last century by Cyrus H. K. Curtis. You can land at the club float in a dinghy, but check with the steward about where to tie up. North of the yacht club is Harbor Provisions, a market and delicatessen. Besides a wide selection of meats and groceries, the store provides ice, sandwiches, snacks, beer, wine, and in the summer, hard liquor. Furthermore, in response to a call on channel 71, they will deliver an order to your yacht.

The next wharf available to yachts is Willey Wharf providing fuel, ice, water, propane, and CNG as well as moorings and a float out in the harbor mentioned above. Still farther up the harbor is the town wharf with three floats, the most convenient place to land on the west side. The harbormaster keeps his aluminum launch here.

The town of Camden, a step back from the wharves, affords several good restaurants, grocery stores, a hardware store, a post office, a bank, and a fish market.

The literary side of life is well served at Camden. On the street along the shore is the Owl and Turtle Book Shop, so named because it is halfway between Owls Head at Rockland and Turtle Head on the north end of Islesboro. *Down East* magazine is on Route 1 between Rockport and Rockland. The office of International Marine Publishing Company is nearby on Route 1. It maintains a bookstore selling a wide range of nautical books, both its own publications and those of others, and sells by mail order as well as retail.

One project originating in Camden is the marine equivalent of the Western dude ranch: the schooner cruise. In 1936 Captain Frank Swift chartered the little coaster *Mabel* and fitted her out to carry passengers under rather Spartan conditions. He had a mate and a cook, and the passengers did all the work.

The idea caught on, so he bought a number of other ancient vessels, including *Annie K. Kimball, Lois M. Candage, Eva S. Cullison, Mattie, Mercantile, Stephen Taber,* and the newer *Endeavor* and *Enterprise.* No doubt there were others, and before long there was an impressive fleet. As the vessels got older and the Coast Guard regulations grew more stringent, many of the old vessels were squeezed out. However, others were found and several new ones built for the trade. Captain Jim Sharp found the Gloucester dory trawler *Adventure* and added her to the fleet. The three-masted schooner *Victory Chimes*, maintained by the late Captain Boyd Guild in spit-and-polish condition, was the largest boat in the fleet for many years. She was sold to a Lake Superior owner in 1985 but is now back on the coast. *Timberwind* and *Roseway*, former pilot schooners, joined the fleet, and *Sylvina Beal*, formerly a sardine carrier, was rerigged as a schooner. Havilah Hawkins had *Mary Day* built by Harvey Gamage in South Bristol especially for the business of carrying passengers, and the Lee brothers built *Heritage* and *Dayspring*, the latter unfortunately lost on a voyage north from the Caribbean in 1985. Also a number of yachts have joined the fleet.

The generic term "windjammer," originally applied scornfully by steamboat men to all sailing vessels, has now been applied specifically to cruise schooners. On the coast, these and none other are called windjammers. They are also known by less lovely names. All of these vessels operate under sail alone, except for such help as they get in calm weather from a yawl boat with a powerful diesel engine lashed under the stern of the schooner. Were it not for these vessels and for the others sailing out of Rockport and Rockland, there would be no sailing vessels on the coast to remind us of what the old-timers were like.

From Camden to Upper Penobscot Bay

Vessels bound for Eggemoggin Reach and the islands up the bay need not go around the whistle on Robinson Rock. Many yachts of moderate draft cross Job Island Bar between Job Island and Lime Island. Cross on a southeast course about 600 yards north of Little Bermuda, the grassy island on the bar. You will be nearer Little Bermuda than you are to Job Island, for you will notice that a long ledge makes out from the southern point of Job Island. The stranger making the passage for the first time would do well to choose a rising tide and to move cautiously.

A slightly longer but easier course is to run south of Lasell Island and then northward between Lime Island and Mouse Island. When leaving Camden, head for the high northern part of Lasell Island, a course that will carry you well clear of East Goose Rock. This rock is said to be inhabited by seals, but if you are close enough to see them, you will soon have more than seals to think about. Note that two unmarked half-tide rocks lie to the northeast of East Goose Rock.

The south end of Lasell Island is bold and picturesque. Follow it around and run up the east side. If you are bound for Pulpit Harbor, pass close north of Goose Island and leave can 1A to starboard. The rock west of can 1A always shows. Those bound up the bay will give can 3 off Mouse Island a good berth to starboard.

In navigating the waters between Islesboro and the mainland west of it, be alert for big vessels. They make bell 9 off Spruce Head on their way to oil and potato wharves at Searsport and Stockton. Keep the VHF radio tuned to channel 16. As they come up the bay, they often announce their positions and courses, prefixed by "Security." One can communicate with them on channel 13.

Gilkey Harbor, Islesboro, Maine (13309) (13305). This is a large but protected harbor, affording access to several summer communities and with impressive views of the Camden Hills. There are several small coves in which snug anchorage can be found for small boats. This was once a very fashionable summer community, but it has become somewhat less formal in the latter half of the century.

The easiest entrance, negotiable in almost any weather, is between Job Island and Seven Hundred Acre Island. A lighted bell marks the southern end of the latter island, and a nun marks the only outlying danger in the channel. The northern entrance between Grindle Point and Warren Island is also marked by a lighted bell and by a small flashing light on the ferry wharf at Grindle Point, where the ferry from Lincolnville Beach lands several times a day. There is another entrance from the south and east through Bracketts Channel between Islesboro on the east and Job, Middle, and Minots Islands and Tumbledown Dick on the west. It is a tortuous channel marked with local buoys. In 1992 they were yellow posts with black tops and were to be left close to port on entering. Early or late in the season they might not be on station, but Bracketts Channel saves a long trip around Job or Lasell Island.

Ames Cove is crowded with local moorings and can be rough in a brisk southwesterly. The Tarratine Yacht Club float has about 3 feet at low water. There is no store within walking distance although just up from the yacht club is the Blue Heron Restaurant with a reputation for excellent food. It is open for dinner only, and reservations are strongly recommended. About three-quarters of a mile away in Dark Harbor is

Oliver's, a restaurant and lounge. The famous Islesboro Inn is now a private residence. There is a boatyard in Ames Cove accessible at high water only.

Cradle Cove on Seven Hundred Acre Island is much better protected than Ames Cove. In entering, beware of the long ledge protecting the east side of the anchorage. Its northerly end is marked with a yellow keg, which should be left to port and given a generous berth. The anchorage is dominated by the Dark Harbor Boat Yard, which maintains several guest moorings. Pick one up and go ashore to negotiate or call on channel 9. If you arrive after hours, pick one up and settle up in the morning. There is 6 feet at the float at low water. Gasoline, diesel fuel, water, and ice are available Monday to Friday between 7 A.M. and 3:30 P.M. and on Saturdays and Sundays in July and August between 8 A.M. and 4 P.M. A marine hardware store and gift shop keep the same hours as the boatyard. Toilets, showers, laundry machines, and a soda machine are available at all times. The yard does welding, and is equipped to repair wood and fiberglass boats and marine engines both inboard and outboard and also rigging and small electronics.

The cove between Warren and Spruce Islands, across from Grindle Point, is a snug spot, perhaps less frequented than Cradle Cove. Warren Island is a state park, with shelters and fireplaces. The state maintains a wharf here and three guest moorings. In entering, favor the Warren Island shore and do not go in beyond the moorings, for the cove shoals up to flats. Parties from cruise schooners occasionally land here for cookouts, but the vessels anchor far enough to the north to cause little disturbance. Spruce Island is undeveloped.

There are several other coves around the shore of Islesboro, each well protected from one direction or another and none very heavily used. The skipper will select the one best suited for the day's conditions.

The sail up the Western Bay on a clear day is delightful, with the Camden Hills providing a backdrop to the west. The southwest wind usually draws briskly up this bay. However, there are few attractive harbors on the way.

Lincolnville Beach, Maine (13309). There is an anchorage here, rather exposed to easterly and northeasterly weather but quite good on an ordinary summer night. There is a guest mooring. The *Margaret Chase Smith* runs frequently from here to Grindle Point on Islesboro. The town wharf and float are on the north side of the ferry wharf. It is a busy place, but one can tie a dinghy here while visiting ashore. The Lincolnville Lobster Pound and Hemingway's Lobster Pound are well-recommended shore dinner places. There is a small village with a garage and the usual antique and variety stores. Route One goes right through the town and adds nothing to the sense of seclusion. There is a beach, best at high water. In any significant southerly or easterly breeze, it is an uncomfortable anchorage, but a good place to stop for a shore dinner.

Continuing up the bay, you come to Spruce Head and Great Spruce Head (not to be confused with Spruce Head Island in the Muscle Ridges, or again with Great Spruce Head Island, which is not more than 7 miles distant in West Penobscot Bay). Lighted bell 9 is a buoy that is religiously made by all commercial traffic passing up and down Penobscot Bay. You may avoid an unpleasant rendezvous with a supertanker by hugging the shore, which is bold here. From bell 9, it is nearly a straight run to Fort Point or Searsport, and a straight line leads southerly from bell 9 to Owls Head.

A correspondent, in a 25-footer in a dense fog, mistook the bow wave of a Spanish freighter, bound down the bay, for breakers on the shore, and in avoiding the supposed breakers passed actually under the bow of the freighter.

Saturday Cove (13309). This is a small bight about a mile north of Great Spruce Head and affords a picturesque anchorage on a quiet night. Proceed slowly and with an eye on the depth sounder, for much of the cove dries out at low water. There is a float at which one can land should one wish to visit the four corners, which is Northport.

The Battle of Saturday Cove was fought on September 23, 1814. A British naval vessel had captured two fishermen and tried to persuade them to pilot the vessel up Penobscot Bay. The fishermen refused and the British set them ashore. The men alerted the militia companies along the west shore of the bay as the vessel stood to the north and the next day anchored off Saturday Cove. Two barges manned by marines started ashore. Zachariah Lawrence, having heard nothing of the foregoing events, recognized the hostile intentions of the visitors and fired his musket at the barges. Hastily reloading, he ran from tree to wall to boulder, blazing away as fast as he could. The British retired for reinforcements, and Lawrence was joined by three armed neighbors. When the British returned with a third barge of marines and a swivel gun, the four did the best they could and retired in good order. The British landed, looted Shaws's store, ate Captain Amos Pendleton's breakfast as the captain left by the window, and stole his watch, among other valuables. Outraged, Captain Pendleton later went to Castine, the British base, protested the robbery, and got his watch back. After pillaging several other houses and arousing the ire of Mrs. Crowell, who resented the intrusion "in true womanly style," the British learned that a large force of Americans was approaching—the militia alerted the day before. The British retreated before the spirited fire of the militia, pursued to the last by Major Wilson of Camden, who waded waist deep into the waters of Saturday Cove and bade the British hit him if they could.

Bayside, Maine (13309). If you follow the mainland shore northward from Saturday Cove, you will come to the popular summer colony of Bayside. Here is located the Northport Yacht Club, a good wharf and a float with 6 feet at low water. A guest mooring is available, for the use of which you should see Mr. Al Keith, who lives near the wharf and is the most accommodating type of ingenious Yankee. He is, among other things, the harbormaster. There is a very well-organized and popular summer sailing program here for the young people.

The anchorage looks exposed, and it is to the east, but the usual summer southwester blows over the land, making a fine lee, and you will imagine yourself moored off the shore of a large lake, because there is no ground swell. Unless the wind is dead on shore, Bayside is a most attractive place.

Belfast, Maine (13309). Although still not one of the most picturesque ports on the coast, Belfast is now a pleasant place to visit.

Entrance is easy, as the harbor is wide open to the east and southeast, and the only obstruction, Steels Ledge, is clearly marked with a lighted beacon and a bell. There is a city boat landing and marina on the west shore just inside the stone wharf. There is 12 feet of water at the float, where gasoline, diesel fuel, ice, water, and marine hardware are available. There are several guest moorings and slips. Call the harbormaster on channel 16 or visit his office on the town wharf for mooring or slip.

Weathervane and Dockside Restaurants near the landing are said to be good shore dinner places.

Above the towboat wharf is Alex Turner's Belfast Boatyard with a Brownell trailer which can haul boats up to about 40 feet in length at the town launching ramp. The yard does major and minor repairs in wood or fiberglass, and gasoline and diesel engine repair. Here is a marine railway with 25-ton capacity, 8 slips, and 10 moorings.

Belfast is an official customs and immigration port of entry.

Searsport, Maine (13309). This is a pleasant anchorage on a summer night, although it would be rolly if the afternoon southerly persisted into the evening. It is wide open to the south and east. The town and the Penobscot Marine Museum both have guest moorings. The town mooring is rated for a 40-foot vessel or less, and the museum's mooring is rated for the schooner fleet (10 tons). Contact Hamilton Marine regarding use of the museum's mooring #58. The call letters are WHG 982—channels 16, 9, and 10.

There is a wharf at Searsport with about 10 feet of water on its outside face, alongside which cruise schooners often spend the night. Inside the wharf is a float and launching ramp with about 4 feet of water at low tide. No fuel is available; however, one of the finest marine hardware stores in Maine, Hamilton Marine, is located on Route 1.

Up the hill from the harbor, in the town of Searsport, is the Penobscot Marine Museum, which includes seven buildings, three of which are former sea captains' homes. This quaint museum tells the story of the Searsport sea captain's life at sea and at home with the aid of the original homes, and artifacts collected from the belongings of a long line of Searsport seafaring descendants.

At Macks Point is a large commercial wharf used by tankers. Their oil is piped to Montreal from here, but the pipeline is now much less used as supplies from the west and from Saint John, New Brunswick, are coming into Canada. Vessels also load potatoes from Aroostook here during the fall and early winter. The *Coast Pilot* lists cargoes of fertilizer, paper, scrap iron, bauxite, sulfur, and salt as well. It is said to be Maine's second-most important seaport.

Stockton Harbor, Maine (13309). This is a well-protected anchorage, little used by yachts. An old wharf is in ruins and is something of a menace, but there is a new wharf on the northeast corner of the cove and a marina is planned. However, Stockton affords by far the best protection of any harbor at the head of the bay west of the Penobscot River.

A port for container ships is planned on Sears Island. Whether this develops or not, Mack's Point will be frequented by big vessels which can be serious perils for yachts in thick weather or at night. Most of them move carefully and with some regard for small boats, but they are not very maneuverable. Listen to VHF-13.

The Penobscot River, Maine (13309). The sail up the Penobscot River is a pleasant variation in a coastal cruise, especially if the fog lies thick down the bay. The shores are high, mountainous in places, for the most part wooded and picturesque. Dangers are few and are well marked. Except for the occasional oil barge there is little traffic.

It is best to go up on the flood and return on the ebb. The Penobscot drains a vast area of central Maine, and all of that fresh water rushes down a narrow valley between high rocky banks. Consequently, the ebb tide is something no one wants to buck. Even on the flood, the fresh water sometimes continues to flow downstream on top of the heavier salt water flowing up and makes it appear on the surface that the ebb is more persistent than the flood. Nevertheless, the flood eventually asserts itself, and with a fair wind, a fair tide, and smooth water, passage up the river is easy.

Should it be necessary to anchor in the river, other than in a mooring area, try to get out of the tide and out of the buoyed channel. Hang up a radar reflector and a brilliant anchor light, for oil barges bound to or from Bangor traverse the river day and night.

Bucksport, Maine (13309). As one might expect, the tide runs hard by Fort Point. Above it one sees the graceful span of the Waldo-Hancock bridge, sweeping from Mount Waldo to Verona Island. Behind Verona Island is Bucksport. It has a municipal wharf but no facilities whatever for yachtsmen, except for the usual stores in town. There is a launching ramp on the northeast corner of Verona Island. The channel east of Verona Island is narrow and shoal. The clearance under the bridge from Verona Island to the eastern shore is only 17 feet and there is an overhead power cable east of the bridge with a clearance of 42 feet.

Winterport. There is no harbor here, but above a barge made fast to the shore for loading big vessels is Winterport Marine. At the float, where there is 14 feet at low water, gasoline, diesel fuel, and water are available. An extension of the dock planned for 1993 will provide electrical hookups. There is a travelift, and repairs of all kinds can be made. Several moorings marked with orange balls are maintained in the anchorage where launch service and towage are available. Provisions are available in the nearby town and marine supplies at the Winterport marine store. The owner, Peter Downey welcomes cruising people and will do whatever he can to assist. Call 223-8885.

Hampden. On the western shore of the river about a mile above nun 24 is a public marina owned by the town of Hampden with a landing wharf, two launching ramps, and ample parking space.

Up a buoyed channel dredged to a depth of 8 feet is Turtle Head Marina with limited dock space, 30 moorings, and a float where gasoline, diesel fuel, water, and ice are available. A restaurant is close by and a marine store is planned. Repairs of all kinds can be arranged. Boats up to 50 feet can be hauled on a Brownell hydraulic trailer.

Bangor. The Bangor waterfront has been vigorously developed and much improved in recent years. On the west shore below the first low bridge there is a landing wharf with water and power, a pumpout station, four guest moorings marked "CITY," restrooms, showers, and a harbormaster's office. The moorings are free for the first night with a nominal fee for subsequent nights. Dock space as available can be rented for up to three nights. No fuel was available at the landing in 1992. Restaurants and stores are within easy walking distance, and the airport is only a short taxi ride away. Express buses run from Bangor to Portland and Boston and there was bus service east of Bangor in 1992 to Calais and Saint John but not to Machias.

The waterfront at Bangor is still being improved and should be even more attractive in future seasons. Call the harbormaster for the latest information on channel 16 or by telephone at (207) 947-0341. Owners of lofty vessels should note that a new highway bridge is being built about a mile below the landing with a clearance of 70 feet.

The fixed bridge above the landing with a clearance of only 22 feet will stop most masted vessels, but the river is navigable for small powerboats as far as the waterworks dam via a tortuous channel. Just below the dam is the Bangor Salmon Pool, one of the few places where Atlantic salmon can still be caught. The first fish caught each year is sent to the President of the United States.

Bangor was once the world's greatest lumber port. Long logs, mostly white pine, were cut in the north woods, run down the river in the spring, sawed in mills at Bangor, and shipped out in barges and schooners. In one year 3,500 vessels cleared from Bangor, an impressive figure when one remembers that the river is frozen for four or five months in the winter. Schooners lay one alongside another at the wharves so, it was said, that one could cross the river stepping from deck to deck. The bottom of the river was so encumbered with sawdust and waterlogged waste from the sawmills that anchoring was impossible. Tugs towed schooners down the river, half a dozen rafted together. The schooners laid over a foul tide if necessary and set sail below Fort Point to beat down the bay in such numbers as we who rush to photograph one passing cruise schooner can hardly imagine. Wasson and Colcord's *Sailing Days on the Penobscot* gives a good picture of those stirring times.

Castine, Maine (13309). In spite of strong tides in the Bagaduce River, Castine is an easy harbor to make with bold shores north and south of it, a bell in the entrance, and a light on Dice Head. The light is down close to the water on a low skeleton tower, but the abandoned lighthouse high on the Head is visible far down the bay.

Push up the Bagaduce River past the restored earthworks of the early forts flying the French, Dutch, and British flags of their builders, past the *State of Maine,* vessel of the Maine Maritime Academy, and past several commercial wharves to the prominent Castine Yacht Club. Here are three moorings, a float at which one can lie temporarily, a telephone, showers, and a friendly welcome.

For gasoline, diesel fuel, ice, water, lobsters, or a pumpout station, go alongside the float at Eaton's Boatyard. Ken Eaton, boatbuilder, seaman, authority on Penobscot Bay lore, can arrange repairs to hull or engine and provide wise counsel on matters marine.

From Eaton's or from the yacht club it is a short walk to the very well-supplied Tarratine Market where groceries, meats, produce, wine, and beer are available. The market is also an Agency liquor store. It will deliver an order dockside.

Next to the market is a laundromat.

There is a restaurant on Dennet's Wharf next to Eaton's. Craft and variety shops abound.

Castine is historically an interesting town. Restored Fort George on the hill behind the town gives a perspective on its military history. The Unitarian church with a Bulfinch tower, a Paul Revere bell, and its original box pews is worth a visit, and there are museums, old houses, and much to see in the town.

Castine, Maine. The entrance from the Penobscot River is at the top left. The Maritime Academy's *State of Maine* is lying alongside their wharf. Vessels lying off Hospital Island are shown. This picture, taken at high water, does not show the shoals in Smith Cove, but the anchorages here and south of Nautilus Island are clear. *Courtesy James W. Sewall Co.*

When you have completed your errands and seen the sights, withdraw to one of the comfortable anchorages described below, for lying in the tide off the town, even on a mooring, is uneasy.

Hospital Island. A number of local yachts, including the fleet belonging to the Maritime Academy, lie in the cove east of Hospital Island. It is out of the tide but is likely to be crowded.

Smith Cove. Large vessels lie in the mouth of Smith Cove, favoring the west shore. A more picturesque and better-protected anchorage is at the head of Smith Cove south of Sheep Island. In approaching this, beware of a rock marked by a nun, just inside the mouth of the cove, and of another rock west of Sheep Island. This is indicated on the chart by a cross, which means it does not show at low water. The rocks opposite Sheep Island on the western shore extend far to the east.

Holbrook Island. There is excellent shelter south and east of Holbrook Island. The usual course is to enter south of the island. The channel is narrow and deep, with bold water on both sides. Favor the Cape Rosier side. Just beyond Goose Falls, site of an early tide mill, swing south into the first cove. One can continue east of Ram Island and anchor anywhere in the well-protected water inside, but be sure to locate the rock in the middle of the channel south of the long ledge making off from Ram Island. Between Ram and Holbrook Islands is a good berth for a small boat.

The Maine Maritime Academy is situated in Castine. Their classes are conducted aboard their vessel and in their brick buildings, formerly part of Castine Normal School. The academy trains officers for the Merchant Marine and gives them practical experience cruising on their vessel. The vessel is open to inspection by visitors at stated times.

Numerous signs relating to the colorful and significant part Castine played in the early history of the country have been erected around the town. Baron de St. Castin, who married one or more of Chief Madockawando's daughters, had his base and trading post here and gave his name to the town.

In colonial days, Castine was the advance base for French domination of the coast, as Pemaquid was for the English. The two nations, with varying assistance and opposition from the local Indians, mounted raids against each other's forts and settlements, engaging in mutual and reciprocal massacre.

After the French were driven out of North America in 1763 except for St. Pierre and Miquelon, the British tried twice to establish the Penobscot River as the boundary between the United States and Canada. During the American Revolution in 1779, General McLean seized the town and peninsula and began to build a fort on the hill. Massachusetts, of which Maine was then a part, mounted an expedition to retake it led by Commodore Saltonstall, Generals Wadsworth and Lovell, and Colonel Paul Revere. Wadsworth and Lovell established a foothold on the hill, landing at Trask's Rock, a big boulder on the beach north of Dice Head. Saltonstall, however, "hove up his long chin" and said, "I am not going to risk my shipping in that dam' hole." When, after prolonged indecision, a plan of attack was agreed upon, a British fleet of seven sloops of war, frigates, and a ship of the line sailed up the bay. Saltonstall ordered his fleet to run up the Penobscot River where they were run ashore and burned to prevent their capture. Until Pearl Harbor it was the worst naval defeat in United States history. A full account of the defeat can be found in *General Solomon Lovell and the Penobscot Expedition 1779* or in *Rise and Fight Again*, Flood (Dodd, Mead, New York, 1976).

With the British in control at Castine, many Tories moved their families there and built homes. In 1783, when it appeared that the Saint Croix and not the Penobscot would be the boundary, they moved to Saint John, Saint Andrews, Gagetown, and other Canadian towns.

On September 1, 1814, during the War of 1812, the British again seized Castine and drove the American defenders up the Penobscot River, this time after a more determined but equally ineffective defense. The British pushed on to Bangor, made Castine a port of entry for Nova Scotia, and collected customs duties which were later used to found Dalhousie University in Halifax. Again British sympathizers gathered in Castine, and Americans, despite the war, traded food for scarce British manufactures. Again the Saint Croix River was established as the boundary, and again the British sympathizers moved to Canada.

In 1971, David Wyman, an ocean-engineering professor at Maine Maritime Academy, was instructing his students on the techniques of underwater search. They decided to look for the wreck of the 16-gun privateer *Defence*, a member of Saltonstall's force said to have been sunk in Stockton Cove. Wyman had no idea that they would actually find her, but two lumps in the muddy bottom turned out to be her cookstove and two cannon. The vessel, buried in mud, which effectively excluded oxygen, has been remarkably well preserved. Her whole port side is intact. A great many artifacts have been recovered in an excellent state of preservation. Not only have cannonballs, muskets, spoons, and mugs come to light, but even articles made of wood, leather, and cloth have been preserved under the mud. They are treated with chemicals to prevent their rapid disintegration in air. Many details of the vessel's gear and construction have been recorded and her lines have been taken off. Much of what has been recovered is on display in the Maine State Museum in Augusta.

Castine was fortified against Confederates in the Civil War, but no attack was made against it. The history of the town since then has been commercial rather than military. Recently the fort on the top of the hill has been restored as have some of the breastworks along the shore. Numerous signs indicate points of interest, and the Wilson Museum has relics from three hundred years of the town's history.

Weir Cove, Cape Rosier, Maine (13309). This is a quiet anchorage on an ordinary summer night, but it would be rough in a heavy southerly. In entering from the southwest, leave Buck Island to starboard, giving the mainland a generous berth. The chart does not show all the ledges here, but if you keep clear of shaded areas you will be all right. After passing Buck Island, head straight up the cove and anchor just south of a small island with a house on it, connected to the mainland by a footbridge.

There are several private floats on the west side of the cove. One may land at F. F. Clifford's float, off his boardinghouse, Cedar Cottage. This is the only wharf on the west side and is just above the small island.

Weir Cove is usually a placid and unfrequented anchorage, but should the weather look ugly, go into Horseshoe Cove, Orcutt's Harbor, or Bucks Harbor.

Horseshoe Cove, Maine (13309). This is an easy harbor to enter for the second time, but the writer got cold feet the first time he entered, on finding himself rushing up a narrowing inlet studded with ledges before a smoky sou'wester, with a green crew adorning the foredeck. However, it is such a good place when you are in and it is really so easy to make that it is well worth the few nervous moments you may have at the start. Seal Cove Boat Yard maintains aids to navigation in this cove.

This first marks at the entrance are Dog Island to port and a privately maintained beacon on a ledge making out south from Howard's Point, the eastern point of the cove. This is on station from June 1 to September 15, or later. Continue up the cove, favoring the eastern shore. Pass a wharf and float with several boats moored off it and continue up the eastern shore. Keep Eagle Island Light to the east of Dog Island. Near another clump of moorings you will see a red triangle on an iron pole on the southern end of Cowpens Ledge. Pass between the beacon and the black spars, keeping away from the beacon and close to the spars. Run up the cove, parallel to the ledge, *keeping at least 75 yards west of it.* About halfway up the ledge there is a rock awash at low water, which extends somewhat to the westward. As you converge with the high shore to the west, you will see several moorings. All but the outer one belong to the Seal Cove Boat Yard. Take one of these and prepare to spend the night in quiet comfort. Nothing can touch you here, as has been amply demonstrated in recent hurricanes.

Note that the buoys and beacons are privately maintained, but they are indicated on recent charts. Mr. Robert Vaughan, owner of the Seal Cove Boat Yard, who maintains these marks, has asked the Coast Guard to replace spar 3 with a beacon showing a square dayboard.

If you are in need of boatyard assistance, *row in your dinghy* farther up the cove to Mr. Vaughan's yard. Mr. Vaughan writes, "Some people have, on the strength of the *Cruising Guide's* information, attempted to get to the yard itself in large boats; about one in five makes it. It should be emphasized that passage beyond our outer moorings is not recommended in a large boat." Mr. Vaughan refers to an earlier edition of the *Guide*.

The yard, despite its tortuous approach, is a busy place. There is a 20-ton lift and a 30-ton railway which can haul any boat which can get to the yard. About 130 boats are hauled and stored here in the winter. The yard makes a specialty of the repair and restoration of both wooden and fiberglass boats. Work goes on all winter in a heated and humidified shop for working on wooden boats up to 50 feet.

If no one is at the yard, walk up the road about half a mile to a farmhouse set in a large field. Mr. Vaughan is an enterprising, ingenious, and energetic entrepreneur and a most interesting authority on all aspects of boating and local conditions.

Take the dinghy, with oars or outboard, and run up the creek about one and one-half hours before high water. You will have an utterly wild 2-mile prowl between clean granite shores, with the trees almost meeting overhead, and the fun of shooting small rapids. Have a warm swim

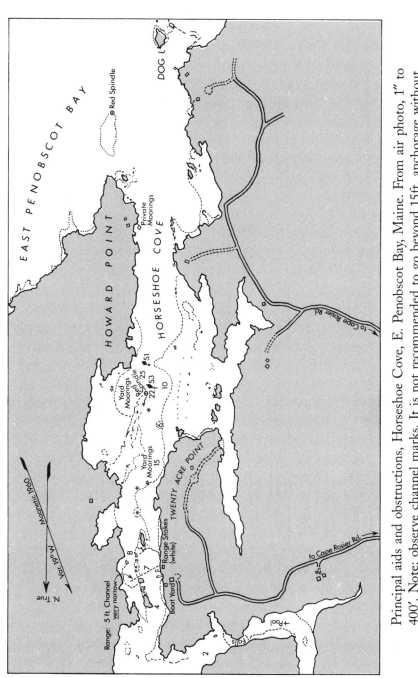

Principal aids and obstructions, Horseshoe Cove, E. Penobscot Bay, Maine. From air photo, 1" to 400'. Note: observe channel marks. It is not recommended to go beyond 15ft. anchorage without local pilot except in tender.

on the rocks of the little lake at the head. Then follow the tide out about an hour after high water.

Orcutt Harbor, Maine (13309). Although perhaps not quite so well protected in heavy weather as either Horseshoe Cove or Bucks Harbor, this is a placid and peaceful anchorage on a summer night. A good anchorage is behind the small islet on the west shore, but anywhere near the head of the harbor is good. A small storage and maintenance yard here skids boats up the beach on cradles without a railway. Otherwise the harbor is without commercial interests.

It is a short walk to the four corners at South Brooksville where supplies can be obtained.

Bucks Harbor, Maine (13309). Buck Harbor on the chart and in the *Coast Pilot* is almost universally referred to elsewhere as Bucks Harbor. There seems little danger of confusing it with Bucks Harbor in Machias Bay.

Situated at the western end of Eggemoggin Reach, Bucks Harbor is a convenient stopping place, well sheltered and easy of access. In the fog or at night, make bell "ER" off Cape Rosier. From here it is a clear course ENE (067 degrees) to the flashing bell "EG." Thence proceed cautiously toward either entrance to the harbor. The depth sounder will keep you in the deep and narrow path. In clear weather, leave all the cans to starboard and the nun off Spectacle Island to port, or thread your way among the cans. The rocks they mark are all isolated pinnacles and quite near the buoys. Changes in buoyage have been proposed. Consult the latest *Light List.*

Enter either east or west of Harbor Island but keep away from its southern shore from which ledges extend farther than appears from the chart. Also there is a notorious dead spot off the island. The best breeze seems to favor the western entrance to the harbor, but it is a gamble.

The harbor is crowded with private moorings, but the yacht club, situated prominently on the northern shore, maintains several for guests. Inquire at the float.

The quietest berth is in the eastern cove. There are several moorings here without pennants, usually available for visitors. Check by radio with Bucks Harbor Marine located on the easterly granite wharf. Cruise schooners often lie alongside this wharf, but in their absence it may be possible to tie up and plug into shore electricity. Granville Henthorne, the current owner, sells gasoline, diesel fuel, and ice at the float. There is a water hose as well. In the store on the wharf he has a few groceries, beer, and basic marine supplies. He can call a mechanic to attend to engine troubles. A yacht with a long keel can ground out against a crib on the north side of the wharf. If you join his "club" for a reasonable fee, you get a mooring, fresh water, a place to tie your dinghy, trash disposal service, hot showers, and a parking space. This is a daily membership, but there are special rates for extended membership.

From Bucks Harbor Marine it is a short walk to the four corners, the hub of South Brooksville. Here is a post office and an adequate grocery store which also serves light meals. Condon's Garage, prominently labeled, can advise on inboard and outboard engine repairs, and across from the garage is the post office.

The yacht club runs an active social and racing program during the season and welcomes visitors. There is a telephone on the porch and a water hose on the float. Do not plan to lie alongside for long, however, as it is a busy place. Tie your dinghy to the back of the float. Many who use the float have no engines in their boats and many of those who do have power are loath to use it so the harbor and the front of the float are likely to be busy with yachts under sail.

Close to the yacht club is the Bucks Harbor Cafe serving breakfast and lunch on the first floor. Above it is the Landing Restaurant serving gourmet dinners.

Repairs to hull, spars, or engine can be arranged through Robert Vaughan at Seal Cove Boat Yard in Horseshoe Cove or through Mr. Henthorne. Donald Hale in Sargentville close to the north end of the Deer Isle bridge is a reliable sailmaker.

Follow the road to the east from the four corners up the hill to Kench's Ledge for a grand view of Penobscot Bay, an experience well worth the walk.

Note on the Sequence of Harbors

Having been up the west side of the bay and the Penobscot River and down the east side to Cape Rosier, we now take the reader down the bay to North Haven, Vinalhaven, and off to Matinicus. Thence we proceed to Isle au Haut and up East Penobscot Bay to Eggemoggin Reach.

As one goes down the bay from Cape Rosier, he passes a number of islands, most of them uninhabited, where reasonable shelter and a degree of privacy is possible. Hog, Pickering, Bradbury, and Butter are examples. Beach Island and Eagle Island are inhabited. Great Sprucehead has a summer place on it as does the largest of the Barred Islands. Of course one can anchor in any cove he chooses. However, all the islands, whether inhabited or not, are private property and must be treated with respect. Most of Bradbury Island is the property of the Nature Conservancy.

Barred Islands, Maine (13305). There is a quiet and snug anchorage in the midst of the archipelago between Butter and Great Sprucehead Islands. Enter from the northwest, passing between the high peak of the northernmost island and a privately maintained beacon off a ledge on the southern side of the entrance. Follow the shore of the peaked island, giving it 150 yards berth, and swing to starboard, keeping about halfway between the big island to port and the smaller one to starboard. Ledges make out from both islands, and there is a 5-foot spot to be avoided. This is usually well marked with lobster buoys. Proceed with care and keep a good eye out for bottom.

Once up to the middle of the big island, you are in about 3 fathoms, with mud, clay, and gravel bottom. Anchor anywhere short of the bar. The green fringe on the west side of the big island indicates ledges bare at low water and is to be taken seriously.

The big island is inhabited in summer by the Schauffler family. Their house is on the southern end of the island but out of sight of the anchorage. They are glad to have you explore the island but are justly concerned about fire. Light no fires ashore and do not smoke in the woods.

Great Sprucehead, Maine (13305). This island is owned by the Porter family and is the source of many of Eliot K. Porter's magnificent photographs in *Summer Island*, published by the Sierra Club. There is fair anchorage off the Porters' float, but of course the island is private property and one should not land without permission.

Butter Island, Maine (13305). This island is privately owned through the Maine Coast Heritage Trust and is under the watchful eyes of the Island Institute and the Maine Island Trail Association. This fragile island has been "discovered" by cruising people, kayakers, and picnickers, and there is a real danger of its being loved to death. Camping areas have been designated and are assigned to applicants, who must have written permission to camp. The owners urge visitors to stay on the trails which have been flagged and for the most part cleared and to avoid irresponsible bushwhacking. Build no fires and, of course, leave no trash.

Of course a visitor is free to anchor wherever he can find a lee. There is an anchorage off the beach on the north side of the island, but be sure your anchor is well set. There have been reports of weed and kelp on the bottom. The beach is quite smooth for a Maine beach, and the water is temperate if not warm.

For a lunch stop one can anchor north of the southeast or southwest tip of the island. There is a steep bluff on the south side and a fairly good beach in front of it. Note that the bar on the northwest corner of the island dries out at low water. At high water one can creep through the passage north of the largest of the Barred Islands into the harbor. Depending on the draft of one's boat, it might be a good idea to view the scene from the dinghy at low water before making the attempt.

There used to be a town, Dirigo, on Butter Island, with a post office, summer hotel, and other evidences of civilization. Gradually it shrank and at length was abandoned, and one winter the whole village was removed. Only cellar holes remain.

Pulpit Harbor, Maine (13305). This harbor is the goal of many a cruising man, typical still of what yachtsmen seek in Maine. When the skipper from busy Long Island or sandy Cape Cod furls his mainsail in Pulpit Harbor and contemplates the granite shores, the skyline spiked with spruce, the sunset behind Pulpit Rock and the Camden Hills, he can say truly he has arrived.

The principal problem with Pulpit Harbor is to find it. When one is running up the bay before the afternoon southerly, Pulpit Rock melts into the shore behind it. If you are close to the bold shore, however, you will identify the second point after Bartlett's Harbor. As you pass it, look back and you will notice a mowed field among the spruce trees. This was used as landing field by Charles Lindbergh, who owned a house there. Soon after, you may see the sun shining on masts of anchored yachts behind the ledge. If you miss these marks, continue until you see a large house with two gables facing the water and three dormer windows between them. Run in close to the shore, and as you follow the shore back to the southwest, you will run right into Pulpit Harbor and wonder how you failed to see that huge rock on the end of the ledge.

In the fog, plan to make the shore northeast of the harbor and work back. The shore southwest of Pulpit Harbor abounds in ledges and boulders, and the points run out under water far enough to make it a difficult shore to follow in really thick weather.

Inside the harbor the shores are fairly steep except off the first two points on the northeast shore. The sight of a large motor-sailer flat on her side leaking diesel fuel from her capacious tanks was all the warning the writer needed.

Anchor wherever inclination dictates. It is all very well protected. The cove to the southwest of the entrance is a snug spot but likely to be crowded with the fleet of the family which owns the shores, and there is no public landing here. Most yachts anchor along the eastern shore and in the northeast cove. There are a few moorings here, some rental moorings marked "Y KNOTT," but plenty of room to anchor. Near the head of the northeast cove is a public landing with a water hose. There is a telephone at the head of the wharf.

If the family of ospreys is in residence on Pulpit Rock, do not disturb them. They had nested there for over a century and left a few years ago. At last reports they had returned, it is hoped, to stay.

Pulpit Harbor is attractive, said one visitor, for the things it lacks. There is no fuel wharf, no marina, no place to lie alongside and plug in a TV set, no repair facilities, no launch service, not even a yacht club.

If you are in need of supplies, you will find it a pleasant 20-minute walk through island countryside to the Island Store, a rather complete grocery carrying produce, meat, wine, and beer. Turn right at the head of the landing.

If you are desperate for repairs, J. O. Brown's boatyard in North Haven can be of help.

A ferry runs several times a day between North Haven and Rockland.

Fox Islands Thorofare, Maine (13308) (13305). This deep and narrow thoroughfare lies between North Haven and Vinalhaven Islands and is the shortest route east from Rockland to the harbors on Mount Desert. Consequently, in fair weather or fog it is constantly agitated by coastal traffic of all kinds, from bouncy Boston Whalers to heavy diesel sardine-carriers. One must be especially vigilant in the fog when making a buoy. One thick summer morning the writer encountered, off the red-and-white bell outside the western end of the Thorofare, a small sloop, a lobster boat, a motor-sailer, and the North Haven ferry.

The principal marks for approaching the Thorofare from the west are the square granite monument with a pointed top on Fiddler Ledge off Stand-in Point, and the cylindrical standpipe on the hill behind North Haven. Note that there is a string of ledges running southward from the bell. They are marked by nuns and must be treated with respect.

On the run up the bay from Marblehead Island or Fisherman Island Passage, the flood tide will set you toward them somewhat and the ebb tide will set you away from them even more. The depth sounder will warn you when you are getting too far to the eastward, even if you do not find one of the nuns. On the run across from Owls Head figure on about $1/4$ knot of tide, more during the times of new and full moon at the strength of the tide.

On the flood tide run for the bell, and on the ebb run for the gong. In either case, you will be set into the channel. If you miss to the north, you will see the Drunkard or the Fiddler before you hit it. If you miss to the south, you will see a nun or at least a big clump of lobster traps.

In the Thorofare the tide sets east on the flood and west on the ebb.

From the bell or the gong, run for Browns Head Light. With reasonable visibility, the white tower and buildings are very obvious. In the fog, be particularly alert. The wind will breeze up as you come in on the shore and the thin bleat of the horn does not carry well to windward. Thence make the gong and follow the shore, east of the Sugar Loaves, around the corner into the Thorofare off North Haven.

Beyond North Haven there is a narrow spot between Iron Point and a green beacon. Leave the beacon to starboard bound east and the nuns to port. The dangers are well buoyed past Calderwood Point, Goose Rocks, Widow Island, and Channel Rock. From the bell on Channel Rock you can set a course for Mark Island and Deer Island Thorofare.

Coming in from the east on a clear day, there will be no trouble in finding the entrance. Goose Rock Light is quite prominent, and there is nowhere else to go but up the Thorofare. In the fog, you can expect a scale-up as you get in by Calderwood Neck on any except the darkest days.

There are several anchorages in the Thorofare.

Southern Harbor is open to the southwest and on a rough day would be uncomfortable, but it is so narrow that in ordinary conditions it is quiet enough. You are unlikely to find much company here. The head of the harbor is shoal and there is no public landing.

Good anchorage can be found on the south side of the Thorofare opposite North Haven, although passing vessels create an occasional wash. Be sure to anchor clear of the ferry slip, where cars are loaded on a scow for transportation to North Haven.

North Haven. This is a convenient place at which to stop for supplies, water, and fuel as it is on the direct route east and west. Anchor anywhere off the town except in front of the ferry wharf, identified by a small house high in the air over the slip.

The North Haven Yacht Club and Brown's boatyard maintain guest moorings marked with orange balls. Brown's are lettered "J.O.B." "Y KNOTT" also maintains rental moorings, so marked. You can land at the yacht club wharf, the second west of the ferry slip, but note that the buildings on the wharf except for the one on the outer end are private cottages. Brown's wharf is just east of the ferry wharf and is well set up for yachts. The float has 8 feet at low water and the tide runs surprisingly fast by its outer end. Brown's has gasoline, diesel fuel, ice, water, marine hardware, charts, and lobsters. There is also a travelift with a gate which can haul masted vessels up to 15 tons. A mechanic can do basic repair work requiring standard parts. Special parts can be delivered quite quickly from Rockland. The yard has a laundry machine and showers. It builds wooden lobster boats in the winter and is the North Haven center for storage and repair work.

There is a pleasant restaurant on the wharf east of Brown's.

On the street east of the boat yard is a grocery store with adequate supplies for a cruising yacht. Here also are showers and a laundry machine. Across the street are the post office and a snack shop. There is a public telephone on the ferry wharf.

Calderwood Hall a few yards east of the town is now an attractive art gallery and craft shop run by Herbert Parsons, a local resident, artist, and craftsman. He is particularly interested in the productions of North Haven people.

North Haven is a quiet community, disinclined to make a stir about visitors. The king of Thailand dropped in one summer not long ago and was delighted that no one paid the slightest attention to him. The people you will see on the street are mostly summer people in from their cottages on the shore to shop or to meet the ferry. There is little nightlife at North Haven.

When your shopping is finished, it is well to move along to one of the other anchorages in the Thorofare and leave the North Haven fleet to roll in the wash of skylarking outboards and passing sardiners.

A story is told of a distinguished Harvard professor, long a summer resident of North Haven. Two fishermen were watching him sail a small boat in the Thorofare. The professor was having a good deal of trouble keeping clear of anchored yachts. Said one to the other, "Old Professor— *knows* an awful lot, but he don't *re-al-ize* nothin'."

The sign on the shore advising of the presence of a water pipe crossing the Thorofare should be taken literally. The writer anchored in a state of excitement one day and fouled it. Gentle twitching, brute strength, and deep diving failed to dislodge the anchor. A passing fisherman tried his hand, with no better success. Finally exercising a "kill or cure or break the water pipe" philosophy, he let out the entire scope of the line and calling on every ounce of horsepower his boat possessed, described huge circles around the anchor at high speed. Just before we got seasick from our own wash, the anchor broke the surface. We hastily gathered in the line and departed, leaving the pipe intact, I am told.

This pipe was laid under unusual circumstances. The residents on the south side of the Thorofare live too far from Vinalhaven to be on town water. In dry summers, they eyed the North Haven standpipe with longing. At last, money was raised to lay a water pipe under the Thorofare. Several mainland contractors and one North Haven resident bid on the job. The latter's bid was much the lowest. The committee raised grave doubts as to whether the job could be done at the bid price, and asked the local man how he proposed to do it so much more cheaply than experienced contractors who owned barges, derricks, and heavy equipment. He refused to tell, but the contract was awarded him as it appeared that he knew what he was doing.

During the winter he laid the pipe across the Thorofare on the ice and made up the connections. Then he sawed a trench in the ice and lowered the pipe safely to the bottom.

One of the hardest tasks for the yachtsman coming from the west, unable to go farther east than North Haven, is to turn back at that point. To the east and north of North Haven lies the eastern paradise: Isle au Haut, Eggemoggin Reach, Blue Hill Bay, and the waters about Mount Desert. Not until he has pushed the prow of his boat to the head of Somes Sound or dropped anchor in Northeast Harbor can any yachtsman say he has seen the best of the coast of Maine. But West Penobscot

Bay is a good start, and will only increase his determination to return down east another year.

Perry Creek. This is a small, tight, and possibly crowded anchorage. The entrance is a bit tricky and the dangers are unmarked. Furthermore, there is a cable right through the anchorage. It was picked up by a cruising man's anchor in 1992 and dropped again only after considerable difficulty. It is still there.

There are no facilities ashore and no public landing. The shores are owned by a conservation group.

To enter, round the small island off Hopkins Point, giving it as much berth as you can without getting afoul of the long unmarked ledge on the south side. Edge up the cove, favoring the southern shore, for the 2-foot spot marked on Chart 13305 does indeed exist despite reports to the contrary. Anchor where you can find room and make a small libation to whatever trolls inhabit the bottom to keep your mudhook clear of the cable.

Seal Cove. If you can avoid the deep hole in the entrance and the shoal in the middle, Seal Cove is a good anchorage. Press well up into the head of the cove as far as your draft permits or until you find less than 2 fathoms. Do not count on going ashore here as there is no landing and the shore is privately owned.

On the west side of the cove about 150 yards south of the southern point of Perry Cove where the chart shows a 6-foot sounding is a ledge with about $2^1/_2$ feet running north and south. It is about 60 feet long and 20 feet wide. People living nearby usually put a white plastic pipe on it in the summer. Inside the ledge there is 10 to 12 feet of water and good anchorage, especially in a heavy northwester.

Waterman Cove. This will get you out of the tide; it is well protected, but not particularly attractive. Take the dinghy and explore the Cubby Hole at the head of the cove.

Kent Cove. This is not as well protected as some of the other coves described above, but on a quiet night is entirely satisfactory, especially if it blows from the north or east.

Carver Cove. This snug shelter behind Widow Island is probably the most attractive anchorage in the Thorofare. It is well protected, quiet, and usually secluded, and the surrounding open fields and woods are pleasant indeed to contemplate at sunset. There is no landing, and if there were, there is no source of supplies nearby. However, for an overnight anchorage far from the outboard menace of North Haven or the wash of passing powerboats, it is superb. Anchor in the southwest corner under the high bluff.

Note that when fog is thick in East Penobscot Bay, it often scales up north of Calderwood Neck as one approaches Channel Rock.

Little Thorofare. Although the tide runs through this passage north of Stimpson's Island, and although the western end is obstructed by ledges, this is an attractive anchorage and a shortcut to islands up the bay. Pass north of Goose Rock Light, close to Indian Point, to avoid the ledges in the middle, one of which usually shows, and cut back into the middle again before reaching the next projection of Indian Point. Move very carefully here.

Vinalhaven Island, Maine (13290). This large island is so cut up with inlets, channels, and ponds that one is seldom more than a short distance from the water. Vinalhaven was settled before the Revolution and has had an eventful history, involving lumber, fish, and granite, with occasional excursions into privateering. This story is told in *Fish Scales and Stone Chips,* by Sidney L. Winslow. The chapters on the granite boom are most interesting. The pillars for the Cathedral of St. John the Divine in New York were quarried in Vinalhaven. It was intended that each pillar should be cut from one piece of granite. After three had broken on the lathe or in transport, the idea was abandoned and the pillars were made in sections. But the broken pieces of the huge monoliths still lie in a Vinalhaven quarry. One is on Sands Cove Road near the ferry landing. The old granite quarries on Hurricane Island are conspicuous. Fifty years ago, a thousand men were working in them, and it was a wild place; Hurricane Island granite was known everywhere. The waters around Vinalhaven abound in unusual tales, too.

The full-rigged ship *Hualco,* 1,086 tons, had been launched in Belfast in 1856 just as the 1857 depression was coming on. She lay at anchor in Belfast Harbor for six months, unable to get a charter. Then she sailed, ostensibly for New Orleans, but no one knew her business. She was heavily insured.

She sailed from Belfast one morning, and ran down the Eastern Bay with all sail set before a northwest breeze. Approaching Saddleback Shoal, the story goes, the helmsman, a young fellow who had just been fishing off Saddleback, protested to the captain. "You are heading right for Saddleback Shoal, Captain!" "Mind your business, damn you, and I'll mind mine!" roared the captain.

The *Hualco* struck the needlepoint of Saddleback Shoal going about 8 knots, knocked her bottom out, went over the shoal, and sank in twenty minutes in deep water. Within half an hour the crew, all natives of Belfast, were in the longboat heading for home, and the ship had disappeared.

More recently, the mail boat from Rockland to Vinalhaven was lost. One February day in 1946 she left Vinalhaven for Rockland. Apparently her forward hatches were not tightly secured, for when a heavy northwest squall struck, she took water over the bow and filled her foc's'le and forehold. Down by the bow, she could not be steered; and as the squall developed into a full gale, she filled and sank, leaving three men adrift on a raft in subzero cold. They made Leadbetter Island at last and attracted the attention of people on Vinalhaven and so were rescued.

Little do we realize, as we run up the bay before a 20-knot southwester, what double the velocity and winter cold can do to Penobscot Bay. Every winter Maine men are lost at sea.

Vinalhaven is a week's cruise in itself. Hoping not to dim the joy of such a cruise, the author lists a few shelters on Vinalhaven. Let us start from the western end of Fox Islands Thorofare and circumnavigate the island.

The west side of Vinalhaven on a clear day is Maine cruising at its best. White granite islands, some high, bold, and spruce-forested, others bare and grassy, provide shelter from the sea and seem to warm and strengthen the wind. To beat from Fox Islands Thorofare to Carvers Harbor is a challenge to pilot, helmsman, and sail handlers and is a delight to photographer, artist, and poet. In the fog, however, even with a fair tide, it can be worse than confusing. The tide runs very hard through Leadbetter Narrows, Laireys Narrows, and the Reach. Except for the bell outside Laireys Narrows, there are no sound signals. The area is peppered with low, humpy islands and half-tide rocks, which all look the same looming through the fog. Even the bold shore of Leadbetter Island, the one sure guide on the west, has several nests of half-tide rocks pretty well daubed with the bottom paint of yachts that found them the hard way. Furthermore, the channel is churned many times daily by the ferry from Rockland. Monitor VHF-13 and identify yourself if you hear her blast in the fog. Remember that she heads for the same buoys you do and frequently in the fog has to stop and let yachts get out of the way.

With the wind to the east of south, one could reasonably expect the fog to scale up through the passages, but with the wind to the west of south, the fog is packed in even thicker. Indeed, one day in 1985 the fog was so thick that the ferry, which had come all the way from Rockland on radar, got lost briefly in Carvers Harbor looking for her own slip.

On the passage south, green buoys are to be left to starboard and red buoys to port. This is true for Leadbetter Narrows, so narrow that the chart is necessarily unclear. At the southern end of the passage as one comes out of the Reach by Green's Island, there may be a moment of confusion. The green beacon and the green flasher east of the ledge off Green's Island are to be left to starboard going south, and red nun 2 is to be left to port. However, red flasher 4 is to be left to starboard by one entering Carvers Harbor, to port by one bound up East Penobscot Bay. The red beacon on Green Ledge, the red beacon on Point Ledge, and nun 8 are all to be left to port. Nun 2 on Sheep Island Ledge should be left generously to starboard by one following the line of nuns up the Vinalhaven shore, but to port by one bound across the bay. Finally, can 5 on Triangle Ledge, at the end of a line of nuns all to be left to port, is also to be left to port. With a brisk southerly astern, the pilot may have to think quickly. There are several well-protected anchorages on Vinalhaven, most of them attractive and not heavily used.

Crockett Cove. This is a pleasant and secure anchorage and is, comparatively speaking, unfrequented. Protected by Dogfish Island and a half-tide ledge, it is a quiet spot in anything but a heavy southwester. One can enter either north or south of the three half-tide rocks off Crockett Point. From the south, simply hug the steep bluff on the southern shore and run up the middle of the cove. Anchor under the northwestern shore as far up as draft and inclination dictate.

Coming from Browns Head, you will see a string of high, bold ledges off the Vinalhaven shore. At anything but high water, even in the fog, they are excellent guides to the bold shore of Crockett Point.

From the west, an old yearbook of the Cruising Club of America advises, "Stand for the end of Crockett Point with the North Haven monument (square stone beacon off Crabtree Point) astern. Keep a distance of about 100 feet off Crockett Point and head for a small red house on the opposite side of the cove until the center of the cove is opened; then head straight up the center until abeam of the float on the port hand."

In 1992, the beacon, the red house, and the float were still there and brought us to a quiet anchorage.

Long Cove. This anchorage is bottle-tight, easy of access, and only a little disturbed by tidal current. Hence it is likely to be crowded, especially on weekends when cruise schooners and yachts chartered out of Camden find it convenient for a first or last night.

From the knob on the Vinalhaven shore at the south end of Leadbetter Narrows, head about east-southeast for a high little island with a cliff on its south side. Round this and head up the middle of the entrance. The shores are bold so an ambitious sailor can beat in or out with a handy vessel. Anchor on the western side, out of the tide if possible. The eastern side is shoal and rocky. There are a number of moorings in the cove, all privately owned. The shores, too, are privately owned by people who value their privacy.

There is a ledge across the cove above the anchorage, which makes a small reversing fall. A row up the cove in a dinghy is a pleasant excursion with due attention to the tide table.

There are no supplies or facilities ashore nor any public landing. The nearest supplies are at North Haven, 3 1/2 miles away. There is no telephone connection at the cove.

The Basin. There is an attractive anchorage north of Barton Island, and tales abound of intrepid yachtsmen who have entered the Basin. Tales also abound of those who have tried and did not make it. It is a pleasant excursion on a flood tide in a stout dinghy, but one may not get out again until slack water. One may anchor outside the basin itself in a small cove to the south. However, this puts one embarrassingly close to a summer cottage on the bluff.

Cedar Island. There is a snug little anchorage between Cedar and Laireys Islands. In 1994 there was one mooring here and little room to anchor. Enter from the south and proceed cautiously. Beware of ledges on the northwest and northeast sides of the harbor. The writer found Irving Johnson's old *Yankee* in here once, but another time he found bottom startlingly close. Laireys Island is clean, smooth, white granite and affords what Samuel Johnson, in his *Journey to the Hebrides,* called "wild and noble prospects."

Hurricane Island, Maine (13305). This account of the Outward Bound School was contributed by Ms. Joan Welsh, the president.

The island, formerly the scene of a profitable granite quarry, is now the site of the Hurricane Island Outward Bound School.

The first Outward Bound School was established at Aberdovey in Wales in 1941 to help reduce the alarming loss of young British sailors on merchant ships following sinkings by German U-boats. Lawrence Holt, head of the Blue Funnel Line, had noted that, while younger and physically better-equipped men succumbed, the older and more experienced officers survived. He reasoned that success in meeting severe challenge depends more on attitude than on physical prowess. He turned to Dr. Kurt Hahn, headmaster and founder of the Gordonstoun School, who had succeeded in putting physical challenge into his curriculum as a means of developing character in his students. Together, Mr. Holt and Dr. Hahn organized the first four-week course for young seamen, "Outward Bound," for the fleet and for life. The Aberdovey Sea School more than fulfilled the hopes of its founders in developing an individual's initiative, resourcefulness, and individuality. It was apparent by the end of the war that supervised exposure to a series of testing and hostile situations was indeed a successful approach to the difficult transition from youth to manhood.

The idea spread rapidly, and there are now thirty-four Outward Bound Schools . . . the one at Hurricane Island being the only Outward Bound sea school in the Western Hemisphere.

During the months of May through September, hundreds of young men and women aged fifteen and older are exposed to a program of increasing challenges for two to four weeks at Hurricane Island. Up to 30 percent are on scholarship, assuring a variety of cultural and economic backgrounds. The students are divided into watches of twelve each with two instructors: a watch officer and an assistant. The watch officers are mature men and women and technically proficient. All possess U.S. Coast Guard sailing licenses and are skilled in other areas, such as ecology, rock climbing, fire fighting, and emergency medical care. Their extraordinary experience assures a high standard of instruction and safety.

The Hurricane Island program, founded in 1964 by Peter O. Wellauer, is not limited to young people. In 1992, 5,431 adults participated in courses varying in length from five to twenty-six days. Specific courses are designed for businessmen, teachers, and college students (both graduates and undergraduates, with credit available), women over thirty, men over forty, and community and youth workers.

One of the most important components of an Outward Bound School is its Rescue Services. There is always someone on duty at the island. They monitor channel 16 twenty-four hours a day, and are also in telephone communication with the Coast Guard and the hospital in Rockland. The school is well equipped to perform search and rescue services in the Penobscot Bay area, as well as fire-fighting aid and emergency medical care. Four powerboats (*Hurricane, Reliance, Mallard,* and *Vigilant*) are completely outfitted with radar, VHF radios, fire-fighting equipment, diving gear, and first-aid materials. A doctor is usually in residence on the island.

The school also has sixteen 30-foot, open, ketch-rigged pulling boats. These wooden strip-built craft are light enough and long enough to be rowed by twelve students, but also go well to windward under sail. Early training includes a capsizing and righting drill, and the whaleboats, full of water, and with twelve students on board, still have 6 inches of freeboard due to the 32 cubic feet of styrofoam flotation. Basic instruction in these boats emphasizes navigation, sail-handling, and, above all, safety. The instructors are on board at all times, but students soon learn to handle the boats by themselves. They take long cruises under a variety of conditions, including fog and night running, and you may see them as far east as Cutler.

About halfway through the course, and after several ecology lessons, the students are each placed on an uninhabited island for three days and three nights. Equipped with a line and hook, sleeping bag, eight matches, a 12-foot-square plastic sheet, a Hibachi stove fashioned from a #10 can, a first-aid kit, a gallon can of water, a knife, and a journal, every student has his hours of self-appraisal, of seeing himself in unique perspective. With a little ingenuity, one can eat well on the Maine islands, but who has ever been really alone for three days? The solo is a test of the mind and the spirit of each individual in relation to his environment. If you come across one of these students on solo, he or she would prefer to be left alone!

By all means pick up the guest mooring off the old granite wharf next to the large mess hall on the east side of the island at the south end of the anchorage, or anchor, being careful to avoid the half-tide ledges just east of the anchorage, the northeasternmost marked by a small iron spike.

A board with information and a map for a self-guided tour is located at the rescue station. Please refrain from smoking or drinking while ashore, and leave pets on board. You are welcome to observe groups of students for a few minutes on the ropes course and while they are rock climbing in the old quarry, and then move on. An audience tends to make people more nervous.

For those returning to the mainland, you are also welcome at the school's headquarters along Rockland's waterfront located just west of Atlantic Point in the southern end of Rockland Harbor adjacent to the Rockland Marine Corporation. Water, telephone, and other facilities are available.

(Here Ms. Welsh's account ends.)

Some visitors have found the anchorage off the wharf rather rolly if there is much of a southerly swell outside. One might profitably spend a few hours visiting ashore and then move on to Green's Island or Long Cove for a quiet night.

A local authority claims that the ball bearing was invented on Hurricane Island. A derrick was being built to handle heavy blocks of granite. The boom had to turn in order to swing the blocks off the wharf to the holds of vessels alongside. The ingenious foreman had the plate at the base of the derrick grooved to form a raceway, set several iron cannonballs in the groove, clapped a similar plate on top, and erected the spar on the upper plate. When the cannonballs were slushed with grease, the derrick operated with great ease and precision.

There is much abandoned and rusted machinery on the island, including the remains of huge stationary steam engines. There is also considerable beautifully fashioned cut stone abandoned near the wharf. The scenery is magnificent, and the view from the cliff overlooking the southern end of the island is particularly superb. Should you want a good idea of what Hurricane Island must have been like when the quarries were running, read Ruth Moore's *Speak to the Winds*.

Old Harbor. This harbor is well protected but it is shoal and the bottom is rocky. There are no facilities ashore.

Green's Island Cove. There is a well-protected cove on the north side of Green's Island. The island is sparsely inhabited and the anchorage peaceful. The island takes its name from its first settler. He was the son of

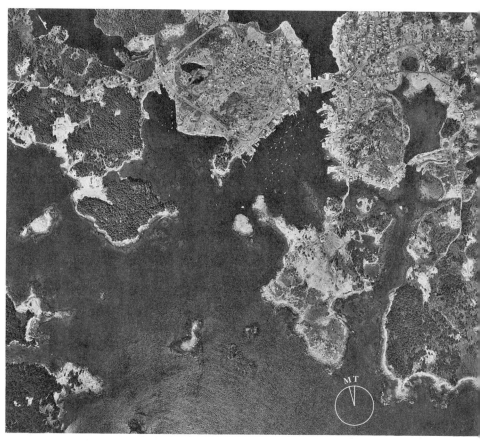

Carvers Harbor, Vinalhaven, Maine. The island at the end of the Reach is on the left and beyond it is Green Island Knob. With a glass, the beacon on the end of Green Ledge is discernible. *Courtesy James W. Sewall Co.*

Mrs. Ebenezer Hall of Matinicus by a former marriage. In 1757 Indians seeking revenge for two of their friends killed by Hall, raided his Matinicus house, shot him, and carried off his wife and four young children. Green escaped through a window and fled to Green's Island, where he settled. Hence the name Green's Island, distinguished from the Green Islands between Matinicus and Two-Bush.

Carvers Harbor. When people speak of going to Vinalhaven, they usually mean Carvers Harbor. This is essentially a lobstering town, not a yachting town or a vacation town. No effort is made to accommodate yachts and yachtsmen. Nevertheless, some cruising people like the busy atmosphere, and Carvers Harbor has the advantage for the westward-bound mariner of being well to windward in the usual summer south-wester. Also it is a good place from which to depart for Matinicus. The waters to the southwest, south, and east are beset with bleak islands, ledges, and half-tide rocks through which the tides run hard. The whole region is wide open to the North Atlantic Ocean. In fog or heavy weather it is no place to be. However, in ordinary summer weather, it is both challenging and interesting country.

The approach to Carvers Harbor from the northwest down Hurricane Sound and the Reach is described on page 593.

From the southwest, run for Heron Neck Light, leaving the can on James and Willies Ledge to port. The ledge is high and prominent and the rock off it usually breaks. From Heron Neck Light follow Green's Island around to the east, passing between it and Folly Ledge, and run up the harbor, giving the lighted beacon on Green Ledge a good berth to starboard.

There is a buoyed channel between Arey Ledge and The Breakers, but to penetrate the cordon of ledges extending from nun 2 on Colt Ledge to Roberts Island in any other place on a rough day requires close attention to chart and depth finder and just a dash of good luck.

Coming from Isle au Haut and the east, make Saddleback Ledge. Leave Diamond Rock to port. This is a prominent mark, steep-to and standing 40 feet high. Pass between Carvers Island and nun 2 on Sheep Island Ledge, leave nun 8 and the beacon on Point Ledge to starboard, and run for the lighted beacon on Green Ledge. This course is not easy in the fog, for to one unacquainted with the landmarks, all the islands except Diamond Rock look the same and the buoys are very silent.

When you are coming down the bay from Stonington or North

Haven, Coombs Hill and Barley Hill stand up boldly. What seems like a long way beyond Barley Hill and too far offshore, you will find the small can on Triangle Ledge. From there, simply follow the string of nuns by Sheep Island, Bunker Ledge, Point Ledge, and in to Green Ledge. Give Green Ledge and nun 4 a reasonable berth to avoid the rock behind the nun.

The bottom in Carvers Harbor is very soft mud and wiry grass. The author and his wife plowed it up thoroughly one windy August night. Do not anchor in Carvers Harbor on any but the quietest of summer nights. Pick up a mooring without a skiff. Of course you do this at your own risk, not knowing what is on the bottom of it or whether the owner will return and require it or charge you for it, but the odds are that the latter contingency will be the worst that will occur. In 1994 there was a rental mooring marked with a yellow ball on the east side of the channel near the head of the harbor. The lobster boats in Carvers Harbor are big, heavy vessels designed for offshore winter fishing, and their moorings hold them in winter gales. Usually when they go out to haul traps, they do not tow their skiffs but leave them on their moorings.

Hopkins' boatyard has a small railway and can make repairs to hull and engine.

A narrow unmarked channel with 6 feet at low tide has been dredged to the town wharf. Proceed slowly and watch for bottom. Better yet, row in.

The main street runs around the head of the harbor. Here you will find an excellent grocery store, restaurants, post office, and a telephone. A ferry runs to Rockland several times a day from a wharf on the west side. About a mile and a half from town is an airstrip serviced by planes from Rockland where one can connect with planes to Boston and Bar Harbor.

Medical help is available at the local clinic.

The business of the town is primarily fish and lobsters. Lobstermen fish the rough waters off the island summer and winter in big, able boats with the most reliable modern engines and power winches, with radar, loran, electronic depth finders, radios, and the most efficient and advanced fishing gear. They are energetic, intelligent, active people engaged in a business both financially and physically risky. Many of the lobsters are sold to Claw Island Foods, a North Carolina firm which has developed a process for quick-freezing whole lobsters. These lobsters can be shipped anywhere in the world at far less expense than shipping live lobsters and with no loss. This opens up markets in Hawaii, Japan,

Europe, and other distant places. A Vinalhaven selectman is quoted as saying that he could not tell the difference between a Claw Island frozen lobster and a fresh one boiled live. Frozen lobsters have a shelf life of at least nine months. The plant can use all the lobsters Vinalhaven fishermen can catch and is actually trucking in lobsters from elsewhere. This appears to be a vast expansion of the market for a limited resource, certainly of immediate benefit to Vinalhaven lobstermen and Raleigh, North Carolina, entrepreneurs.

For many years Vinalhaven derived much prosperity from the many granite quarries in the neighborhood. This stone was shipped in barges to Boston, New York, and Philadelphia. Much of it was for paving blocks in New York, but it had other uses. The huge pillars on three sides of the altar of the choir of the Cathedral of St. John the Divine in New York, each more than 54 feet in height and weighing approximately 120 tons, came from Vinalhaven. Likewise, the massive stone eagles adorning the post office in Buffalo, the granite of the State Capitol in Albany, Grant's Tomb, the Philadelphia Mint, and several large government buildings in Washington and Annapolis all came from Vinalhaven. One could spend an interesting day roaming over the quarries of this section, especially on nearby Hurricane Island.

On the main street at Vinalhaven stands a granite eagle said to have adorned Pennsylvania Station in New York. The eagle is unquestionably a most evil-tempered fowl, who is determined to take no backwash. He fiercely turns his back on the harbor to face the monoxide fumes to which he is accustomed.

Vinalhaven's East Side—Winter Harbor and Seal Bay There are several coves and harbors in this broken coast, none of which the writer has visited and on which no cruising man has contributed information. Roberts Harbor, Arey Cove, and Smith Cove are challenges to the explorer. However, inside Coombs Hill, there are two very attractive bodies of water, Winter Harbor and Seal Bay.

Penetrating deep into the northeast corner of Vinalhaven Island are Winter Harbor and Seal Bay. Here is excellent protection in beautiful surroundings very little visited. What few houses there may be on the shores are not obvious from the water and the high-pressure cruisers en route to Northeast Harbor seldom take time to explore these waters. Yet from those who do, the writer has a file of enthusiastic letters.

One enters north of the Hen Islands behind Bluff Head. To starboard is Winter Harbor with a snug little cove under Starboard Rock. One shoal-draft yacht with an anchor out ahead and a line to a tree ashore can just squeeze in. The view from the top of the cliff is well worth the scramble. The 2-foot spot farther up must be respected, despite rumors that it does not exist. One can press on farther, proceeding with great caution to several quiet anchorages. The bottom in Winter Harbor is very soft mud, good enough holding ground on a quiet night but not at all good in a heavy southwest on northeast breeze.

Seal Bay, to port as one rounds the Hen Islands, is a real challenge to the "gunkholer" but with commensurate rewards.

The section of this *Guide* on Fox Islands Thorofare deals with anchorages between Calderwood Neck and Browns Head. We now take the reader offshore to the Green Islands and Matinicus.

Green Islands, Maine (13303). These two low, grassy islands lie east of Metinic and south of the Northern Triangles. If you are approaching from the west, keep well away from the Southern Triangles. Note that most of the ledges lie N.N.W. from the can and at a considerable distance, but that one lone rock lies half a mile to the westward of the buoy and is unmarked. It usually breaks. The Northern Triangles are an unmarked menace. Parts of the ledge often break. Little Green, the westernmost of the two, appears to be uninhabited, although there are a few shacks on it. Large Green has a cove on the northern side, with several large winter moorings described as "piles" on the chart. If they are still there, pass a line to one. On any day on which you might be likely to visit, the mooring should hold you.

Residents of the island are lobstermen who come out from Sprucehead or Rockland for the summer's fishing. Unfortunately, some visitors to the island have wantonly damaged houses and fishing gear. You may get a cool reception, but it is important to stop in at one of the houses and make clear your purposes before exploring around.

The middle of the island is grass, eaten quite smooth by sheep. All around the shore is a windrow of driftwood composed of odd boards, pulpwood, and the drifting detritus of modern civilization. In among it all, though, you may find a treasure.

The island is a nesting place for gulls, terns, petrels, and other seabirds. Be careful not to disturb them or tread on their eggs.

There isn't much on the Green Islands; and in the fog, the whole area is very dangerous, with the perils badly marked. However, on a warm

Matinicus Harbor, Maine. Rental moorings extended from the rock in the
middle of the harbor toward the shore of Wheaton Island in the lower
right corner, in 1993. What appear to be experimental salmon pens were
not there in 1994. *Courtesy of James W. Sewall Co.*

summer day they are pleasant places from which to contemplate the Camden Hills.

It is a short run to Matinicus or Home Harbor for the night.

Matinicus, Maine (13303). The Matinicus group is unique. The islands lie far offshore and off the usual course of coastal cruising yachts. Matinicus inhabitants make no effort to attract yachtsmen. There is no marina, no deep-water wharf, not even a float at which to land from a dinghy. Nevertheless, to some cruising people the islands have a strong attraction.

Leaving Vinalhaven for Matinicus on a typical summer day, one heads offshore for an empty horizon. There are five lighted buoys more or less on the course: Old Horse bell, Bay Ledge whistle, Penobscot Bay bell, Zephyr Rock flasher, and a lighted bell west of No Man's Land and north of Matinicus. As you run down this line, Matinicus and Wooden Ball appear on the horizon, the latter easily distinguished by a large knob on its northern end. The course from Vinalhaven is roughly south-southwest, which means that most sailing yachts with a southwest breeze will fetch well to the east of Matinicus. A flood tide setting roughly northwest should be of some help. The adventurous navigator can make bell "9MI" and pass north of Matinicus and Beach Ledges, and east of the Barrel, which almost always breaks and usually shows. Then leave Harbor Ledge bell to starboard and run in to the harbor. The usual course is to give Zephyr Rock flasher a good berth to avoid Zephyr Ledges, make the can on Mackerel Ledge and then the bell on Harbor Ledge. Note the big can buoy close east-southeast of Green Ledge. It marks nothing of concern to a yacht on a summer day but is a useful reference point.

The ledges east of Matinicus are all bold, always break, and most of them stand well up out of the water. The sound of the surf is as good as a fog signal. If the sun is shining over the fog, expect a scale-up north of Matinicus. However, in the fog or in a heavy easterly, this is dangerous country. One experienced and capable skipper, running in from offshore at dusk in a mounting southeasterly, struck Mackerel Ledge. His sloop broke up quickly on the weather side of the rock. He and his crew of one hauled the dinghy over the ledge, launched it on the lee side, and tried for Matinicus. They did not make it, spent a long night in the dinghy, and were picked up off Isle au Haut in the morning.

Anyone in distress can call on channel 16 and expect someone to answer; then shift to channel 6. The Matinicus pilot boat listens to 16 and talks on 10, but should only be called in an emergency.

Such an emergency broke on the night of January 16, 1992 in a subzero gale. The tug *Harkness,* iced up, leaking badly, her pumps frozen, and her propeller fouled in a hawser, was sinking off Matinicus. Her MAYDAY call to the Rockland Coast Guard was overheard on Matinicus, much nearer the *Harkness* than Rockland. Three fishermen in the rugged lobster boat *Jan-Ellen* headed for *Harkness'* last position through heavy sea smoke with only a dim hope that they could find her in time.

Harkness sank and left her crew of three adrift on a wooden ladder that had floated clear, but life expectancy in January water is very short. The Rockland Coast Guard boat arrived, and the two crews poked about in the sea smoke and heavy seas. *Jan-Ellen* caught the gleam of a flashlight through the mist and pulled aboard two of the men. The Coast Guard got the other.

The mate's daughter had given him the flashlight for Christmas. One of the men, as *Harkness* was sinking, grabbed it from the shelf in the wheelhouse and turned it on. When his hand became too cold to hold it, it froze to his glove, and it was this light the rescuers found.

Matinicus Harbor lies between Wheaton Island and Matinicus. The inner harbor is protected by a breakwater but it is shallow, crowded with local boats, and obstructed by occasional boulders and a big ledge with an iron spike in the top. A visitor must anchor in the outer harbor, which is entirely satisfactory except in an easterly gale. In January 1978 such a gale piled solid water over the breakwater and destroyed many of the wharves.

In 1994 there were several rental moorings with yellow-and-white lobster buoys. Pick one up. The owner will stop by and collect a fee. They are attached to a heavy ground line running across the harbor. Seiners sometimes maintain big moorings here. Keep off them unless you get permission, for a seiner returning at 4 A.M. after a night's work to find a yachtsman asleep on his mooring may be a bit surly.

The bottom of the harbor is rocky. If you must anchor, use a trip line attached to the crown of your anchor and floated with a buoy, so the anchor may be capsized if caught down. You will notice that the lobster boats lie in orderly lines. Instead of each boat's having a mooring of its own, each is moored to a heavy nylon line running across the harbor from shore to shore. The ends are chain to resist chafe on the rocks. Each boat is attached to this line with a heavy nylon painter. Nylon has lots of stretch, every bit of which is needed in a heavy northeasterly. One fisherman observed "Don't they ride some easy!" Useful and efficient as they are, an anchor fouled in one of these lines is as good as lost without a trip line.

Occasionally herring school in the harbor. The fishermen will then stop off the harbor with a net stretching completely across it and extending to the bottom. If you approach the harbor and find it stopped off, be patient and someone will appear in a dory and press down the head rope with an oar to let you in. Let him know when you are ready to leave, and he will let you out. One impatient yachtsman tried to cross the net, got his propeller fouled in it, tried to anchor, and dropped his anchor right down through the twine. He was, not surprisingly, very unpopular ashore.

There is no public float at Matinicus. Row up the inner harbor and either land on the beach west of the granite steamboat wharf or climb a ladder on the west side. Near the head of the wharf are the post office and a public telephone, which connects with the mainland via microwave. There is no store on the island. Mail now comes to Matinicus by air in planes flown by Herb Jones and his son Charlie from the field at Owls Head. In 1994 *Mary & Donna* ran daily from Rockland. The Maine Department of Transportation sends the motor ferry *Silsbee* to Matinicus once a month unless she is filling in for some other ferry. *Silsbee* can carry trucks, which can drive directly from her deck onto the steamboat wharf at high water, thus making possible deliveries of lumber, cement, hay, and other bulk supplies without transshipping. A small oil tanker fills the tanks by the store when necessary. The island's generator runs on these. Occasional lobster smacks call at the island.

South of the old store is a ferry wharf owned by Mr. and Mrs. Burr. A farmers' market is held here from 11 A.M. to 1 P.M. on Mondays and Fridays in July and August. Local vegetables, crafts, and sandwich lunches are sold.

The roads on the island are gravel, not tar, and make pleasant walking. North of the harbor are the airfield and a pretty sand beach. On the hill behind the harbor are the church, the school, the radio tower, and most of the dwellings. It is said that the schoolteacher went on strike some years ago, objecting that the ancient building was cold and that when the wind was to the northwest, the sanitary facilities were too obvious. The School Committee found another teacher. When he approached the school, the lone striker asked, "Are you going to cross my picket line?" "Yes," announced the scab. He did, he rang the bell, and education resumed. However, the next year a pleasant, efficient, and more modern building was constructed.

There is no regular minister for the church, but the Maine Sea Coast Missionary Society supplies a minister as often as possible via the mission boat *Sunbeam.*

Matinicus has been inhabited since early in the seventeenth century. Captain John Smith speaks of sending a vessel there from Virginia to dry fish, and there were year-round residents on the island in 1671. In 1750 Ebenezer Hall had a fundamental disagreement with the local Indians over burning grass on Green Island and sealing and fishing rights. In 1751 he shot two Indians on Matinicus and buried them in his garden. Other members of the tribe sought legal redress and in April 1753 wrote to Governor Phipps objecting to Hall's activities, particularly to his murdering their two friends, concluding, "If you do not remove him in two months, we shall be obliged to do it ourselves." Finally, on June 10, 1757 Hall was shot and his wife and four children carried off to Bangor. Joseph Green, a son of Mrs. Hall by a previous marriage, got out a window and hid. He went to Pemaquid, returned to Matinicus, and finally settled on Green's Island off Vinalhaven. Mrs. Hall was ransomed in Quebec but the children were never heard of.

The history of the island has been written up to 1925 by Charles A. E. Long in *Matinicus Isle: Its Story and Its People,* published by Lewiston Journal Print Shop in 1926. At that time, Matinicus and Criehaven were busy, prosperous communities. There is space here for only one more incident from Mr. Long's account: In 1845 two teen-agers named Lohman and Philbrook took the 15-ton schooner *Rainbow* to the West Indies and returned with a cargo of rum. At least one barrel was in a store on a wharf on Wheaton Island. Some thirsty rascals got under the wharf, bored a hole up through the rum barrel, and filled a bucket. However, as there must have been a space between the bottom of the barrel and the wharf, they could not stop the flood and all was lost.

The community now is in a difficult position. No longer is living on an offshore island close to the fishing grounds a great advantage. The population has declined as young people have left, first to go to high school and then to work ashore. Their parents have moved with them. There are now about forty winter residents and five children in the school with an inspired and innovative teacher. There is no longer a store. Lobstermen sell their lobsters and buy bait, fuel, and groceries on weekly runs to Tenants Harbor, Sprucehead, Rockland, or Vinalhaven. People remaining would like to see the old days return when the church, the school, and the lodge were vital organizations, but new families of lobster fishermen are not encouraged. The young men who come as sternmen do not fit into the community and seldom stay long. Much of the island has been bought up by summer people although the fishermen hold tenaciously to shore property around the harbor. Matinicus people look at Monhegan and its summer business with horror and at the declining state of their island with concern.

Still, to the cruising man willing to be self-sufficient and to take his time, Matinicus is fascinating. The fog sifts through the spruce trees, the dark weed swings to the tide, and the distant surf on the ledges underlies the clang of the bell buoy and the distant horn on the Rock. The gentle motion in the harbor reminds him he is far offshore, on the edge of a life beyond his own.

Criehaven, Maine (13303). The Indians called the island Raggertusk. Early settlers corrupted it to Ragged Arse, its common name for two centuries. The government, in a burst of modesty, changed it to Ragged Island when it printed the chart.

This tiny offshore harbor is on the northwest corner of Ragged Island about a mile south of Matinicus. In clear weather Criehaven is easy to enter. From the north and east, pass west of Mackerel Ledge, between East Black Ledge and West Black Ledge, and leave the Hogshead to port. All these ledges show at high water and break noisily. However, it is a bold and careful navigator who sails these waters in thick weather. Unless there is a big sea running, pass close to Pudding Island, and round the high knob on the northwest corner of Ragged Island. From the west, be sure to locate the big nun on Bantam Rock and the small one on Harbor Ledge. Note that a direct course from the latter nun to the breakwater comes dangerously close to the ledge. If you elect to approach west of Matinicus, beware of the long ledge making off the Black Rocks.

Inside the breakwater the harbor is safe enough in summer weather unless it blows hard from the northwest. The water is clear so one can see bottom. The best water is on the north side of the harbor, but notice the half-tide rock, clearly marked on the chart, well off the north shore. There are several moorings in the harbor attached to lines running from shore to shore on the bottom. Inquire of anyone within hail about their use. If no one is around, take one without a skiff on it and be sure someone is left aboard who can move the yacht if the owner should return and need the mooring. Ordinarily, many fishermen go to Tenants Harbor or Sprucehead on weekends to sell lobsters and to buy fuel, bait, and groceries, leaving moorings temporarily available for visitors. Do not anchor as the holding is terrible, and you will get tangled up in the ground lines that crisscross the harbor.

Land on the beach at the head of the cove. The wharves are all privately owned. The visitor would do well to stop at one of the houses near the shore, get acquainted, and inquire as to the current situation on the island. Most of the island is owned by a family "from away," but visitors are not unwelcome if they stay on the paths and respect the privacy of the owners. Do not leave any trash ashore, and remember that fire is a constant danger.

There is a path leading through the woods toward the south end of the island, but the last of it is badly overgrown. However, you can't get lost on Ragged Island. Stop and listen for the sound of surf. The southern end of the island is bare and cliffy with a wide view of the Atlantic Ocean, Matinicus Rock, and small islands, ledges, and breakers nearer at hand. To some people the scene is well worth the considerable effort to get there.

Another path leads to the north end of the island by several houses occupied in the summer.

For many years Criehaven was a prosperous, active community. It was established as a town by Robert Crie of Matinicus, who settled here in 1848. He was a very active man, raising sheep and much of his own food and shipping lumber, salt fish, and live lobsters to Boston. He was joined by others and in 1896 Criehaven was incorporated as a town with a population of about 40. Robert Crie died in 1901, leaving an active community with a sound economy based on subsistence farming, fish, and lobsters. The town supported a school, a store, a post office, a number of good wharves, and a steamer running to Matinicus and Rockland.

The greatest threat to Criehaven's prosperity at this time was the weather. The harbor was wide open to the northwest, and winter gales occasionally wrecked boats and wharves. Matinicus, open to the northeast, got its breakwater in 1911, but not until 1938 was the breakwater built at Criehaven. The 1938 edition of this *Guide* speaks of a population of 55, a store, telephone connection, a gasoline float, and a steamer from Rockland.

Now, however, Criehaven is essentially a summer fishing community. With declining winter population, the town charter was given up, and Criehaven reverted to plantation status. Fishermen continued to live on the island during the summer and to maintain their rights to their traditional fishing grounds against encroachment from Matinicus. By 1940 the winter population had become so small that it was impossible to find a teacher for the few children left in school and the children were boarded on the mainland. The next year the mothers moved ashore to be with them and the war called the men away. After the war an effort was made to reestablish the winter community, but the same economic and social changes which plague Matinicus made it very difficult. Then in 1978 two fierce winter storms breached the breakwater and wiped out some wharves. The wharves were rebuilt, but only occasionally does anyone stay for the winter.

During the summer and fall, however, the fishermen live on the island in houses ashore and set lobster traps in the rough waters around the island, then return to the mainland for the winter.

High Tide at Noon, Storm Tide, and *The Ebbing Tide* give a picture of life on Criehaven early in this century, although the plots are fictional. Elizabeth Ogilvie, the author, knows Criehaven well. She is a resident of Gay Island at the mouth of the St. George River.

Matinicus Rock, Maine (13303). The lighthouse on Matinicus Rock was made automatic in 1985 and Coast Guard personnel were taken off. The only inhabitants now are occasional Audubon Society observers. There may still be a Coast Guard mooring on the west side of the Rock. Anchoring is difficult in deep water with rocky bottom. Without a dory or a stout peapod, landing on the boathouse skids is wet and difficult, for the surge of the offshore swell, even on a calm day, can bilge or capsize a yacht dinghy.

If you do get ashore, be very careful where you walk. Common and Arctic terns nest in the grassy meadow on the northwest side. The chicks and eggs are so well concealed that it is easy to step on them. Also the Leach's petrels nest in burrows dug in the shallow turf. If you step on a burrow and cave it in, you bury the chicks inside. Just standing around on the Rock observing can keep the birds from their nests and young.

Sailing around the Rock is the best way to see the birds anyway.

Puffins and guillemots, which nest among the boulders on the north end of the Rock, can be approached quite closely as the shore is bold, and they can be easily observed as they fly off to fish in the nearby waters.

As you sail gently by the steep east side of the Rock, think of the March gale in which solid water broke ¼-inch plate glass in the lantern 90 feet above high water. Seas carried away the breakwater of 12- by 12-inch timbers around the engine house and drove the building, the heavy diesel engines, the compressors, and everything else down the lee side of the Rock and overboard. The keepers fled to the granite dwelling where they had to bail to keep the water level down. One keeper said that the roar of each sea breaking on the eastern side of the Rock and tumbling great boulders as big as a small house was the most terrifying sound he had ever heard.

Fixed white lights were established in two wooden towers on the Rock in 1826, and in 1846 the present stone towers and the granite dwelling were built. In 1923, the north light was discontinued and a flashing light installed in the south tower.

In January 1856, the keeper, Samuel Burgess, was away when a heavy storm struck. His wife was sick and had four children to care for. Their seventeen-year-old daughter, Abby, kept the lights burning every night during the four weeks before her father could get back with supplies. She later married Isaac Grant, son of her father's successor, and had four children born on the Rock before 1876.

Wooden Ball, Seal Island, and No Man's Land (13303). Wooden Ball lies east of Matinicus, a high grassy island with bare bones of ledge showing through. It is distinguished by a high knob on the northern end and a dangerous unmarked rock just off it. The island was occasionally inhabited by fishermen in the days before marine engines when being near the fishing grounds was a great advantage; but its coves offer poor protection and only the occasional camper visits it now. In 1823 a ship loaded with iron bars was wrecked on the island and one of the crew, a Frenchman, was drowned. His body is buried in Frenchman Cove on the northeast shore. During the Revolution the United States frigate *Raleigh* was overpowered by several British vessels. Her crew ran her ashore on Wooden Ball, but the British refloated her and took her into the British navy.

Seal Island is a most forbidding island of tumbled granite boulders as big as houses, and a dusting of vegetation. Against the cliffs on the southern side the North Atlantic seas slam in, even on a moderate day. The northern side offers some slight protection and there are steep rocky beaches. People have been known to camp here long ago, and in 1994 two young women occupied a small house on the easterly end. They were observing bird life for the Audubon Society. In the 1860s, *Neptune's Bride* struck Malcolm Ledge in the fog and sank. The crew got out on the ledge but all drowned except one man, who clung to the topmast, just showing above high water, for two days and three nights until rescued by campers from Seal Island.

The island was a gunnery and bombing range for the Navy before and after World War II—without suffering significant damage. In 1978 the grass on the island caught fire. Volunteers from Hurricane Island Outward Bound School went out to fight it but were dismayed by several explosions and had to leave. The island is now controlled by the Fish and Wildlife Service as part of the Petit Manon Refuge with headquarters in Milbridge. Ordinance disposal teams have searched the island but cannot guarantee that it is entirely safe. Prominent signs erected by the Fish and Wildlife Service warn visitors not to land. Efforts are being made to establish a breeding colony of puffins on Seal Island. For a vivid account of the herring fishery around Seal Island, read Joe Upton's *Amaretto* (International Publishing Co., 1986).

No Man's Land, a bare island north of Matinicus, is a nesting place for innumerable seabirds including guillemots and possibly puffins, petrels, and auks. In 1830 the sloop *Darling* was wrecked here. A barrel of rum was recovered from her cargo and consumed at once in a cove shown on old charts as Rum Guzzle.

In 1911 an imaginative entrepreneur bought No Man's Land and put foxes on it to eat the gulls and multiply. The foxes ate the sheep instead. He shot the foxes and was surprised to find them all of the same sex; which sex is not stated by the historian.

Isle au Haut, Maine (13303, 13313). No Maine cruise can ignore Isle au Haut. The eastward-bound mariner can see its blue ridge from the cliffs of Monhegan. He can glimpse it as he rounds Two-Bush; when he emerges into East Penobscot Bay through Fox Islands Thorofare, Isle au Haut dominates the eastern horizon, high, darkly wooded, aloof.

The thoughtful cruising man will add much to his enjoyment of Isle au Haut by reading *Sailing Days on the Penobscot* by Wasson and Colcord, now out of print, and *Here On This Island* by Charles Pratt (Harper &

Row, New York, 1974). The latter book particularly emphasizes the fragility of the island.

A century ago about 250 people lived on the island, farmed, fished, and made it their home. Now the winter population is about 75. Recently there were only 5 children in school. Before the invention of marine engines, it was a great advantage to be near the fishing and no great advantage to live on the mainland. Transportation was primarily by steamers, which called at most islands. Now, however, most residents of Isle au Haut live there because they want to live there, even though they sell their lobsters and buy gasoline, bait, and groceries in Stonington. A successful effort is being made to attract new year-round residents to the island and to maintain a vigorous community life. The complicating factor is the visitor.

During the last century, Indians came down from Bangor hunting gulls and porpoises. Crowds of mainland people, known contemptuously as "plummers," came to pick blueberries, tramped all over residents' property, and raised the risk of fire, but they were a temporary annoyance.

In 1880 Mr. Ernest W. Bowditch of Boston established the Isle au Haut Company and bought a house at Point Lookout for members. No women, no children, no dogs were the cardinal rules. Later these were relaxed, the Point Lookout Club was built, and a number of families of summer people built substantial cottages. There are about 300 summer people, many of whom represent the second or third generation on the island. They are to be distinguished from the tourists, for they are really a part of the Isle au Haut community.

In 1945 and 1946 a large part of the island was given to Acadia National Park. National prosperity, the Deer Isle bridge, the Maine Turnpike, the Maine Publicity Bureau, and a great deal of hotel-motel advertising attracted crowds of visitors to Isle au Haut, crowds which made the "plummers" look minor. At the same time the mail boat, the principal access to the island, was run by a motel owner in Stonington who advertised his services. The park administration encouraged people to visit. The 350 islanders were overrun by 3,000 visitors a year. Part of this was because the mail boat landed at the Thorofare. The visitors did not know where to go or what to do, wandered about people's yards, fouled their wells, left trash, camped where they felt like it, and started fires. "The people of Isle au Haut found that they were being reduced to the status of exhibits in a public zoo," said one summer resident.

There followed a series of conferences between park officials and a committee of residents, both summer and winter people, at which it was agreed that a ranger would be stationed on the island, that camping would be limited to park land at Duck Harbor, that the mail boat, taken over by a corporation of islanders and operated as a public service, would land visitors at Duck Harbor, and that visitors would be limited to those who could enjoy a wilderness experience without getting in their own or the islanders' way and who would not damage the environment.

The only factor the committee and the park cannot control is the visitor who comes in his own boat. It was estimated in 1984 that about 1,800 yachtsmen visited the island. A summer resident, and a sailor himself, said in that year, "Yachtsmen who got as far as Isle au Haut used to be few in numbers and generally good sailors. Now they are far more numerous; they seem more incompetent as well as worse-mannered." Surely we can do better than that.

Isle au Haut was named by Champlain in 1604 and means, of course, High Island. The pronunciation of the name, however, is not as obvious as its meaning. On the lobster cars in Stonington you will hear it called "Aisle au Holt" by fishermen, as it was written in early deeds. Summer people, masters of high school French, favor "Eel-a-Ho." One fisherman in an effort to please, called it "Eely-Oley." The late Dr. Howard Sprague, who lived for many summers near Point Lookout, contributed the following authoritative information:

I have just been looking over my 1961 edition of the *Cruising Guide* and want to give you some definitive information about the naming of Isle au Haut, based on some research I did a couple of years ago in Houghton Library. I wanted to find out what name appeared in Champlain's original accounts and on his early maps. (I suppose one calls them "maps" rather than "charts.") The corruption Isle *au* Haut comes from the carry-over of the accenting of the "e" in *Isle* in Isle Haulte and its transformation into a separate and meaningless extra word "au." This was pointed out some years ago by Mrs. Bowditch. The "au" is meaningless in this context. Champlain called it the "high island" and the translation of Isle au Haut would, of course, be "the island of high."

On page 86 of Volume I of *The Voyages and Explorations of Samuel de Champlain,* translated by Bourne-Allerton Book

Co. in 1922, it says, "And nearly in the middle of the sea there is another island which is so high and striking that I named it Isle Haute."

These spellings of Haute and Haulte appear in the original French accounts.

The earliest Champlain map, of which I have a Xerox copy, shows the island with a key reference letter F and the key shows the spelling *Ille Haulte*. Mount Desert is *Ille des mont desertz*. This map has the title "Carte Geographique De La Nouvelle Franse Faiette Par Le Sieur De Champlain Saint Tongor's Captaine Ordinaire Pour Le Roy En La Marine" (all capital letters), published in 1612.

Nowhere in Champlain's accounts have I found the corruption *Isle au Hault*. Mrs. Sprague tells me the accenting or stressing of the final "e" is common in southern France and Canada and the development of this "au" must have come about from the pronunciation by those who were ignorant of French.

Head Harbor. This is an offshore harbor in a wildly dramatic setting and little used by yachts. The southern end of Isle au Haut is high and cliffy, the rocks running in no regular formations but chaotically as if they might have burst molten from the earth and cooled only yesterday. Spurs and boulders hung about with black weed run out into the heavy surf. Some of the dangers are marked. To approach Head Harbor, make the bell off Roaring Bull, a ledge which almost always breaks. This will keep you between Cape Ann Ledge with 4 feet off Eastern Head, and Western Ear Ledge off the Western Ear. Leave Roaring Bull Ledge to starboard, generously, and run in toward the shore west of Head Harbor. This will keep you away from the extensive ledges on the east side of the entrance. They extend much farther to the westward than appears from the chart, and anyone coming in directly from the bell at high water might find himself in trouble.

As you run into the harbor, favoring the western shore, the swell dies down, the cliffs open out into a meadow at the head of the harbor, and several farmhouses appear backed against the woods. A shingle beach slopes down to the water. There are several moorings near the head of the harbor. Proceed slowly with an eye on the depth sounder and anchor where depth and inclination dictate. There will be some motion here, even on a quiet night, but nothing disturbing. However, in a hard southerly it would not be a comfortable anchorage.

There is a small settlement of fishermen here but no facilities whatever. A jeep road, on which walking is pleasant, leads through the woods westward to Duck Harbor. A well-worn trail marked by orange discs leads up Duck Harbor Mountain to the left. The road continues up the west side of the island to Moore's Harbor and the Thorofare. From Head Harbor the road runs north by Long Pond.

Duck Harbor. This is a narrow slit in the west shore of Isle au Haut well to the south with room for only two or three yachts. Entrance requires careful attention to the chart, for the ledges are unmarked. From Saddleback Light, make the Brandies, a prominent ledge of tawny rocks. It is in two parts. Pass west of the northern part, giving it a generous berth of perhaps 150 yards, and head for the prominent white rock at the entrance to Duck Harbor. The ledge with an 11-foot sounding ENE of the Brandies is usually indicated by a clump of lobster traps. The constellation of half-tide rocks to the south may not be breaking, but Duck Harbor Ledge usually breaks. This, and a bearing of ESE on the entrance to the harbor, should take you in safely. Haddock Ledge always shows.

In 1993 there were several moorings in Duck Harbor. The park maintains a long float projecting from the southern shore. The best anchorage is just inside this float, favoring the northern shore. Stay north of a range bearing 265 degrees magnetic from the end of the wharf to the bare rock on the south side of the harbor mouth. Only shoal-draft yachts can go as far up the harbor as the rocky knob on the south shore.

From the head of the float a path leads east to the road north to the Thorofare. A short distance to the left on this road is a water tap. To the right the road leads to Head Harbor. The trail up Duck Harbor Mountain, marked by orange discs, leads off to the right. The view from the top of the mountain includes all the lower half of Penobscot Bay. It is very well worth the effort. The dense woods are inhabited by deer and by many species of birds. Farther east, a spur road leads off to the right to Deep Cove east of Western Ear, a rugged scene indeed.

Acadia Park maintains several campsites near the float. Reservations for these open on January 1, and are usually filled for the season the same day. Campers come by ferry from Stonington, which brings them directly to the Duck Harbor float. It also brings a substantial number of picnickers and other day visitors. The yachtsman will do well to complete his sojourns ashore before the ferry arrives.

Moore Harbor. Thanks to a weir near the head of the harbor and to outlying ledges, Moore Harbor is much better than it appears to be on the chart. Leave nun 4 on Rock T to starboard. Do not count on seeing Rock T on a calm day. Moore Head is a high, light-colored ledge, an excellent landmark. Keep well away from the half-tide rock in the middle of the harbor. It is much bigger than the little star on the chart suggests. The range used by local people is to keep the little white boathouse in Moore Harbor on the end of the east point of the harbor. This takes you clear of the ledge and up to the weir. Enter east of the weir and anchor well up between the wings on the eastern side. The weir affords considerable protection. The bottom is rocky. There are boulders and ledges as you go farther west and inshore.

There are no facilities here. One can land on the beach and follow the jeep road north to the Thorofare or south to Duck Harbor, Duck Harbor Mountain, and Head Harbor.

Seal Trap. This is an interesting bit of gunkholing to try on a rising tide in a shoal-draft boat or on foot from Moore Harbor. The swimming inside is reported to be warmer than elsewhere. One correspondent suggests that the name has nothing to do with seals but is a corruption of the French *ciel,* meaning sky or heaven. A bit of one or the other is trapped here between the wooded shores.

Isle au Haut Thorofare. This is the harbor with the best protection and the site of the island's principal settlement. The store and church are here too.

In entering the Thorofare from the west, first make Kimball Rock, which lies about a mile to the westward of Kimball Head. It is awash at high water and stands up boldly at low water. Then make the can on Marsh Cove Ledge. Give this corner of the island a good berth, for it is a savage lee shore. A course for Robinson Point Light will clear the outlying dangers on the Kimball Island shore. They deserve plenty of room so give the green beacon on the Kimball Island shore a berth of at least 50 yards. Note that Robinson Point does not have a fog signal but shows a white sector to the southwest, which will lead one safely into the Thorofare at night.

There were four rental moorings on the Kimball Island shore opposite the Isle au Haut wharf in 1994. If you must anchor, favor the Kimball Island shore but beware of outlying ledges and boulders, one of the biggest marked by a black-and-white barrel on a pipe, crowned with an osprey nest. There is another ledge southeast of Moxie Island, the tiny island west of can 5. It drops off and then rises up again as a flat rock with about 3 feet on it.

Kimball Island is privately owned.

At the northern end of the harbor is a mussel bar with a dredged channel through it. It was dredged with a suction hose, so the boulders never were taken out. The edges have sagged in a bit. It is best negotiated on the high side of half-tide. There is a beacon on a rock at the southeast edge of the dredged channel. Give it a good berth. The rock makes out. Favor slightly the western side of the narrow channel. One correspondent recommends keeping the light on Robinson Point in range with the rockweed line on the point on the east shore next to the 15-foot sounding on the chart. On coming out the north-eastern end of the channel, bear a bit to the westward to avoid Eustis' Rock. The writer carried $5^1/_2$ feet through the bar at low water in 1992.

The principal wharf at the Thorofare has about 5 feet at low water. There is not much reason to go alongside in a yacht as there is no fuel and no water hose here. In an emergency one can buy gasoline in a can and lug it from the store. However, if you must go alongside, explore first in a dinghy as there are boulders on both sides of the wharf.

The store is a short distance to the north on the road which passes the wharf. The necessaries are available here, but it does not support the population as many people do their shopping in Stonington.

Beyond the store a path leads up to the right to the church. Services are held here on summer Sundays and at such other times as a minister from the Maine Sea Coast Missionary Society visits the island in the *Sunbeam*. It is all an island church should be, its austere white steeple a landmark from far offshore against the wooded mountain. The stained-glass window over the altar is a work of art.

The tiny post office is next to the store. For many years Miss Lizzie Rich was the postmistress. In what many people would call her old age she was permitted to continue beyond the prescribed retirement age by a special dispensation. When she fell and broke her hip, she made her way to her telephone, called for help, was taken ashore to the hospital, and after a quick recovery resumed her duties. At the age of 83 she retired and took a trip around the world. As a tribute to her faithful and generous nature, the mail boat was named for her.

Do not leave trash ashore on Isle au Haut. It is with difficulty the residents can cope with their own trash problems.

Point Lookout. This anchorage behind Flake Island is the most popular with visiting yachts. Some of the principal dangers are marked, but beware of the big ledge north of Kimball Island. It makes off surprisingly far. In entering from the north, if you pass east of Flake Island, proceed with great caution. The legend on the chart "Rks rep. 1965" should be heeded. They have been reported many times since that date. The ledge off the northeast side of Flake Island extends at least halfway to Birch Point.

In 1994, there were several guest moorings off the granite wharf. If they are occupied, there is usually ample room to anchor between the shore and Flake Island.

The land at Point Lookout, formerly a club, is now all privately owned, but one can follow the road to the Thorofare, about a 40-minute walk. You may see a sign on the left indicating a trail up Mount Champlain. It provides a pleasant walk through the woods to the summit, but the trees have grown so that the view is restricted. There is an enormous cairn of rocks, from the top of which one can peer through the trees and see something of Penobscot Bay. The energetic may climb a tree for a better view. However, Duck Harbor Mountain provides a far more satisfactory prospect.

Burnt Island Thorofare. This narrow and tortuous channel is not difficult at half-tide or less, when the dangers are exposed, but at high water it is considerably more difficult. Entering from the west, make the shore of Burnt Island at a stony beach near the west end, and hug this shore until you are up to the peak of the island in order to pass north of the half-tide rock shown between the figures 26 and 16 on Chart 13313. Then line up the northeast corner of a wharf on Isle au Haut with the south corner of the house behind it. When just west of a line between the ruined wharf on Burnt Island and the wharf on Isle au Haut, drop the hook and snug down to enjoy a beautiful and secluded anchorage. One cruising man, on attaining this goal, was moved to quote the following devout prayer of thanksgiving:

> Lord, we thank Thee that thy grace
> Has brought us to this pleasant place,
> And most earnestly we pray
> That other folk will stay away

To continue to the eastward, head for the big rock blocking the opening. When less than 100 yards from it, turn south and round the south end of it. If the tide is high and the ledge is covered, edge up to it very cautiously until you see it. It is dangerous to proceed without locating this mark. Once by this ledge, proceed to the eastward, favoring the Isle au Haut shore heavily. Move slowly and watch for bottom.

Pell Island Passage. If Burnt Island Thorofare looks complicated, pass between Pell Island and Burnt Island. From the west go close to Mouse Island, avoiding a rock about 50 yards from the shore at low water. Head for the beach on the southwest end of Wheat Island, bending away from Pell Island. When about 100 yards off the beach, follow the shore of Wheat Island. This is an easier passage than the chart suggests, but the ledges off Pell Island make out a long way. Watch for Channel Rock, unmarked, to the eastward. It usually breaks, but on a quiet day at high water would be hard to see.

East Side of Isle au Haut. This is wild, rough country, frightful in fog or storm, but in good weather a most attractive place to explore. Yachts have anchored in Rich's Cove, but there is an uncharted rock in the middle of it submerged at low water.

There was once a settlement and farm on York Island, but the island is now owned by people who value their privacy. The anchorage provides good shelter in anything but a northeasterly gale. The best anchorage appears to be where Chart 13313 shows 6 feet. Enter south of Dolliver's Island, which lies west of the north end of York Island.

The views of Isle au Haut from the east are impressive and well worth a sail down the shore. White Horse, Black Horse, Great Spoon Island, and Little Spoon Island are bare and bleak. A great many birds nest here and can be seen fishing in nearby waters. Great Spoon Island is owned by the Audubon Society.

Isle au Haut to Stonington. This country is the best of the Maine coast, equaled only by the west shore of Vinalhaven and Eastern Bay between Great Wass Island and Head Harbor Island. Small islands and big are bare and grassy or covered with a heavy growth of dark spruce to the edge of clean, white granite rocks. Little beaches among the ledges support clams and mussels. The bulk of Isle au Haut cuts off the ocean swell, dries up the fog on a sunny day, and stimulates the summer southwester. There are many harbors among the islands, more than one can visit on any one cruise.

The only tarnish on the brilliance is that this paradise has been discovered—thoroughly. Except for a few islands owned by The Nature Conservancy or the Friends of Nature, all the islands are privately owned. The owner is likely to regard his island as his personal kingdom, his escape hatch from a frenetic world, and he is unlikely to welcome uninvited visitors. Then there are other yachts, a great many of them, each seeking the seclusion of a quiet anchorage among uninhabited islands and finding only each other. Lastly the cruise schooners, with a week to fill between Camden and Bar Harbor, gather here in midweek looking for a place to hold a lobster feed ashore. Solitude is a shy girl; she is never found where many seek her.

Nevertheless, there are several places which the newcomer to this land might enjoy looking into. Merchant's Island, named after the Merchant family which owned it in the eighteenth century, has a snug cove on the north side behind Harbor Island. The passage between McGlathery Island and Round Island is a popular anchorage. Enter from the north and favor the Round Island side. The grave of Peter Eaton, patriarch of a once-busy community on McGlathery, is on a headland overlooking this anchorage. If approaching from the eastward, beware of the half-tide rock shown on the chart north of the north point of McGlathery Island. It is no doubt correctly charted, but to one sailing west along the McGlathery shore it appears to be far out indeed. It is awash at high water. The cove on the north side of McGlathery is another popular anchorage. Hearing that McGlathery was to be "pulped" in 1954, Martin R. Haase, then a summer resident of South Brooksville, organized the Friends of Nature to buy it and preserve it in its wild state. He writes:

> We let nature maintain the island and are happy to have people enjoy it properly by appreciating its beauty. Incidentally, we pay . . . taxes on the island and would gratefully accept contributions (tax deductible) from those who like the island to be preserved in its wilderness state.

There are coves north of Spruce Island, Devil Island, and Camp Island and another west of St. Helena Island. Many others could be described, but perhaps that is neither necessary nor desirable.

The remains of quarries can be seen on these islands for Deer Isle granite was of excellent quality and great beauty. From the 1870s until World War I quarrying employed hundreds of local people, and stone-cutters were imported from Scotland, Ireland, Sweden, Italy, and other countries. Some stayed after the quarries were closed. The Crotch Island quarry cut a huge granite bowl in one piece, 22 feet in diameter and weighing 50 tons, for the Rockefeller estate in Tarrytown, New York, and John Kennedy's grave in Washington is fashioned of Crotch Island granite. In 1993 Crotch Island was again an active quarry despite objections of Deer Isle neighbors to the noise of stonecutting machines. On the other islands nothing remains but piles of grout and a few granite wharves where schooners and barges were loaded.

The pleasure of exploring all of the Penobscot and Blue Hill Bay islands is much increased by reading *Islands of the Mid-Maine Coast* by Charles B. McLane (Kennebec River Press, Woolwich, Maine).

Deer Island Thorofare (13315). In navigating Deer Island Thorofare and Merchants Row, it is well to use Chart 13315, a large-scale chart which gives much more detail than 13313.

The approach to Deer Island Thorofare is easy. Mark Island Light has a horn which operates continuously. Although it emits but a thin bleat and sounds far away when one is right under it, it provides a sufficient guide for the entrance. The run to the first can is the most diffi-cult, but if you miss, you may find Bay Ledge, an obvious landmark, or you can go back to the horn on Mark Island, still audible, and try again. Yellow Rock is big, bold, and yellow. From here on, the tide runs pretty much parallel to your course and the buoys are close together. Isle au Haut and the islands to windward often dry up the fog in the Thorofare.

Moose Island. Here is Billings Brothers, one of the best shipyards on the coast. It maintains big draggers and lobster boats as well as yachts, so it lacks some of the spit and polish of Wayfarer and Hinckley, but provides any service a yacht may require. Its railway can haul any yacht on the coast. The *Mayflower II* was towed all the way down here from Plymouth to be hauled and repaired. Carpenters, mechanics, machinists, electricians, and riggers can make all kinds of repairs. Moorings, dock space, gasoline, diesel fuel, water, ice, laundry machines, and showers are available at the yard. It is a busy place and may be noisy during working hours. It could not be described as picturesque, but it is a good place to get what you need and depart. There is more water here than the chart shows—ample for most yachts among the moorings and in the basin inside the outer wharf.

Stonington. The town is the distribution point for a number of small Deer Isle communities. As such it is not particularly attractive. It was once a fishing town, then a granite town, now a lobster town.

Gasoline and diesel fuel are available at the long wharf west of the dilapidated cannery wharf. West of that is the Isle au Haut ferry wharf with a gift shop–hardware store at its head. West of the ferry wharf is a public landing with rest rooms. On the main street behind the wharves is a well-supplied fisherman's hardware store, Bartlett's Market, and an Agency liquor store among others.

Green Head Cove is much used by lobster boats but shoal and foul; its principal danger is a half-tide rock marked with a radar reflector nearly awash itself at high water.

With good roads and the Deer Isle Bridge, Stonington is readily accessible by land and by sea.

Webb Cove. This large, open cove is better sheltered than it appears to be and is easy of access. Dow Ledges, Humpkins Ledge, and Channel Rock are easily seen at any tide and are quite bold. Anchor off the old-quarry wharf and watch the ospreys which nest on the old quarry derricks. One can land at the wharf but there are no facilities ashore whatever and only a rough road into the old quarry building. Webb Cove is an attractive anchorage on a quiet night and is seldom crowded although some local yachts moor here.

Should it come on to blow from the south, go around the point at the head of the cove. The ledge off the point has a big boulder on the end of it. There seems to be more water inside than the chart suggests, but the edges of the deep water are abrupt and the north side is all mussel flats. Anchor beyond the house just inside, westerly, of a big black ledge. You must move cautiously in here, but the protection is perfect. Landing is impossible as the shores are all mud and mussels. It is a long way to the road, and a considerable hike to Stonington.

Southeast Harbor. This is a large, little-used, and well-protected harbor with many coves and passages worth exploration. Mud flats and ledges fringe the shores, there are no facilities, and the landing is not easy. There are a few summer homes and a few wharves and floats, but the region is still "unspoiled."

A correspondent familiar with Deer Isle after several visits writes:

> Not that I am trying to lure anyone else in there—it is near perfect in its solitude.
>
> From the can on Whaleback it is an exciting sail into Southeast Harbor through a steadily narrowing passage. Things really get interesting after passing the prominent clump of rocks just past the entrance to Pickering Cove.
>
> The turn is about $8/10$ mile farther on. Steer roughly southwest, leaving the four rocks marked on the chart and the small island with several stunted spruces to port. There is 20-plus feet of water with mussel shoals to either side.
>
> The best anchorage is about 100 yards beyond the small island just before a lobster car and two lobster boat moorings. The bridge will bear about 255°, a gray shed about 175°, and a white house about 050°.
>
> We have seen other boats anchored just before the small island. One year we headed in toward Hawley Deep Hole, but found a number of small boats moored to stakes at the edge of the channel and not much room to anchor, so headed back to Inner Harbor where we had a quiet night, in the heart of the island.

Sylvester Cove, Deer Isle, Maine (13305). This is a pleasant anchorage on the west shore of Deer Isle south of Dunham's Point. The entrance is marked by a nun on the end of Pigeon Island Reef. In a brisk southerly the anchorage is uneasy at high water, but once the reef is exposed, it acts as a breakwater. There is a float maintained by the Deer Isle Yacht Club on the north side of the cove, and in the past there has been a guest mooring. It is a pleasant walk to the village of Sunset. The Camden Hills stand up boldly from the anchorage at sunset.

Northwest Harbor (13305). This harbor, well protected in anything but a northwest gale, is easy of access and comparatively unfrequented. On the northerly shore are a long wharf and a float, privately owned.

About 100 to 150 feet southeast of the float is a ledge, which bares only at moon low tides. It is unmarked and is not shown on the chart. Anchor well to the south of the float or out to the west of it.

The only public landing is in the cove at the head of the harbor, which bares out at low tide. Row up in the dinghy. Here is the village of Deer Isle, with a bank, hardware store, grocery store, post office, and telephone. A local resident writes: "Northwest Harbor is a quiet anchorage averaging about one cruising boat each night and we welcome visitors."

In the days of sail, Northwest Harbor had a ropewalk and sail loft. Vessels wintered here and fitted out in the spring. Now it is quiet and almost deserted, except for an eagle that the writer observed one night, presiding over ospreys, gulls, and a few cottages tucked among the trees.

Billings Cove, Sargentville, Maine (13316). This cove affords adequate shelter and greater seclusion than can be expected in Bucks Harbor. If it blows, one can work well up into the cove for protection, but anchorage off the old clam factory/ex-blueberry factory is good on a quiet night.

Land at the town wharf or on the beach next to it. It is a pleasant walk up the road to a country grocery in Sargentville. Or one can land on the western shore, climb to the road where it comes off the bridge, and walk a short distance north on the road to an old schoolhouse, now the Hale sail loft. It was founded by Clarence Hale, who went to sea in schooners, sloops, and yachts. His son Donald has learned the trade and operates the business with skill and efficiency.

Deer Isle—Sedgewick Bridge (13316). On the Deer Isle end of the bridge at the west side is the Bridge Marina and Motel. There is a float here with 2 feet at low water for the convenience of restaurant patrons. Gas, diesel fuel, and deep-water moorings were promised for ensuing years. However, most of the restaurant's customers appear to arrive over the road, so it would be well to check by telephone before counting on the facilities.

The bridge appears to be broken-backed. The story goes that, after it was started, they found it necessary to increase the clearance so they shortened up on the cables. It swings violently in heavy winds and is said to be the last bridge still standing of several that were built from the same design. However, if it stood the Ground Hog Day gale of 1976 and the winter gales of 1978 and 1993, it may be good for a while yet.

It was said that there were no skunks on Deer Isle until the bridge was built. Can you imagine two skunks, paw in paw, setting out across that bridge to a new land?

Benjamin River, Maine (13316). This is one of those places, like Burnt Island Thorofare, that is much easier at half-tide or less, when the dangers are exposed. On entering, favor the eastern shore a little, as both shores consist of flats studded with boulders, but the channel is not quite in the middle. It is marked by small summer buoys. From the east side, a long bar makes out with a big boulder *almost* on the end of it marked by a locally maintained spindle. The spindle carries a red triangle but it is small, shows little above high water, and for the stranger, is hard to find. There may be a guest mooring available inside. If not, anchor off the town dock, on the west side. This harbor is perfectly protected in anything but a very heavy southerly at the top of the tide. In 1982 the Cruising Club of America constructed a sunflower raft here with well over 100 yachts. Despite some strain here and there, the raft survived a 30-knot northerly during the night.

The Benjamin River Boat Yard may be able to help in an emergency.

The Sedgewick General Store is quite a walk from the town wharf, but your chances of getting a lift from a passing pickup truck are said to be excellent in this hospitable part of the world.

The afternoon southwester is often very light off the mouth of the Benjamin River. Experienced skippers favor the Deer Isle shore.

Center Harbor, Brooklin, Maine (13316). This is a pleasantly neglected harbor in the north shore of Eggemoggin Reach about 3 miles east of the Benjamin River. From the west, leave the nun off Chatto Island to starboard and the beacon inside the harbor to port. The rock on which the beacon stands is quite steep. One can approach it closely and is likely to do so as the southwest wind is light and fluky behind Chatto Island.

From the east one can round Torrey Castle and Torrey Ledge, but if the tide is foul or the wind is light, one can sail north of the Babson Islands and Torrey Islands where there is much less tide. The ledge southeast of Babson Island is prominent and so is the one north of Babson Island except at the top of the tide. Be sure to locate the rock on the *end* of the long ledge making out to the SSE of High Head and NNE of Little Babson between the "2" and the "10" on Chart

13316. The ledge is jagged with boulders, and the outer one seems much farther from shore than one would think from a glance at the chart. There is plenty of water halfway between the ledge off High Head and Torrey Island.

Inquire at the yacht club or at Steve White's boatyard for a vacant mooring. Otherwise, anchor anywhere west of the cove in Chatto Island. Cruise schooners sometimes anchor on the edge of the deep water outside Chatto Island.

The Center Harbor Yacht Club has a clubhouse and float on the north shore. Unless you need water, there is not much point to taking a yacht alongside. There is only about 4 feet alongside, there are no facilities for visitors, and the store is closer to the boatyard than to the yacht club. The club is hospitable but is busy about the affairs of its members.

At the head of the harbor is the boatyard founded by Joel White and now operated by his son, Steve. The yard can haul, repair, or store almost any yacht under 40 feet. There is an excellent mechanic at the yard and both Joel and Steve are helpful and ingenious when confronted with a repair problem. They specialize in problems of wooden yachts. The yard is not a marina and has no fuel or water on the float.

Joel White can deal with fiberglass hulls but is well known for fine work in wood. He has built elegant yawl boats for cruise schooners, peapods, and small boats for Mystic Museum. Also he has built a number of cruising sloops and ketches.

WoodenBoat. On the mainland north of Babson Island is the headquarters of *WoodenBoat* magazine and its summer school. A granite wharf, a float, and several moorings mark the shore facility of the summer school. The anchorage is ordinarily a quiet one unless it blows hard from the south. Then seek shelter behind Babson Island. The editorial offices of the magazine are located in the white mansion on the hill. Visitors are welcome to take a mooring and to visit ashore. The summer school is an interesting project. Courses are conducted in such subjects as small-boat construction, yacht surveying, canoe repair, and kayak building. This is hands-on teaching. You may see a person who started as a complete klutz finishing a neat little skiff. In 1992 the school launched a Friendship sloop. And if you see a vessel out in the Reach reefing her mainsail on a moderate day or maneuvering madly to pick up a cushion, you may be watching a class in seamanship. There are no facilities ashore except in case of emergency.

Naskeag, Maine (13316). A gravel bar divides this harbor into an eastern and a western part. Most boats lie in the eastern part, which is easily entered from the east. The passage between the two anchorages is extremely narrow and should not be attempted at low tide without local knowledge. The western half of the harbor is rather well filled with ledges; caution is advised. The Triangles do not show, even at low water.

The village is on the north side, but there is no dock. There is a public beach, approached by a road running north.

Hog Island is an attractive island with a few small beaches. Devils Head at its southern end affords a good view to the eastward.

A good anchorage is north of the middle of Hog Island.

Swans Island, Maine (13313). This island, not to be confused with Swan Island in the Kennebec, was named for Colonel James Swan. He was born in Scotland, emigrated to Boston at the age of eleven, and became a clerk in the office of Thaxter and Son. He wrote a book on the African slave trade, assisted at the Boston Tea Party, was wounded at Bunker Hill, and advanced in the Continental Army to become a major in the cavalry. He became secretary to the Massachusetts Board of War and adjutant general of the Commonwealth. He speculated in land in Virginia and Kentucky and became a wealthy man. In 1784, he bought Burnt Coat Island, gave it his name, established sawmills, encouraged settlers, and was on his way to establishing a feudal empire. However, he happened to be in France at the time of the French Revolution and devoted his energies to saving his friends, among them Marie Antoinette. He loaded their property aboard a vessel in charge of Stephen Clough of Wiscasset. At the last minute, however, the aristocrats, including the queen, were arrested and guillotined. Captain Clough brought the furnishings and clothes to Wiscasset, where some of them still may be seen. Colonel Swan was accused of owing a debt of two million francs, which he denied, and he was jailed. Being a man of principle, he refused to pay, although he could have raised the money. He was released in 1830 by Louis Philippe and died very soon after.

The island, bereft of its squire, grew in a more democratic way and became prosperous through the sale of lumber, fish, and, finally, lobsters. Now there is a growing income from summer people. The island has a population of 350 in the winter and at least ten times that in the summer.

Mackerel Cove. This is a pleasant, uncrowded, well-sheltered harbor at a convenient place. If you pass Mackerel Cove bound east late in the day, you have 10 miles to go to a good harbor on Mount Desert.

From the north, entrance is easy. Make the lighted gong off North Point, leave nun 2 to starboard and can 3 to port. The rock off Roderick Head is extensive, and there is another one east of it. At high water both are totally invisible except for a little nub on the western edge. Leave the nub to port, pass between it and the bold shore of Roderick Head, and anchor in the cove east of Roderick Head. It really is not necessary to go in that far, however. The whole harbor is well sheltered and shallow enough for anchoring.

There are no facilities here. The *Captain Henry Lee,* the ferry from Bass Harbor, docks at the slip on the west shore, and although there has been a float there in former years, there was none in 1985. It is a 40-minute walk to the store in Minturn.

One can also enter from Casco Passage, passing between Orono Island and Swans Island, favoring the bold shore of Swans Island. Note that the rock which nun 4 marks is north of the buoy so it must be left close to *port* as there is another ledge south of it. There is good anchorage either side of Phinney Island, better on the east side. Professor McLane in *Islands of the Mid-Maine Coast* tells us that Phinney Island was probably named for an Irishman named Jack Finney who lived there in the summers during the last century. A more recent owner named Asa persuaded the Swans Island town meeting to change the name of Phinney Island to Asa's Island in return for a contribution to the school fund. McLane adds, "There the matter rests. The name on coastal charts is still Phinney Island, and if I have any understanding of these affairs, it will remain that way." The 1990 edition of Chart 13313 names it Asa Island. There is still a pleasant anchorage east of it, whatever its name.

Buckle Harbor. This is another convenient stopping place off York Narrows. Favor the Buckle Island shore. There are no facilities whatever here. Buckle Island is privately owned. The Swans Island shores are mud flats punctuated with boulders.

Seal Cove. This large, shallow cove offers good protection and a chance of solitude. Enter close to the ledges off Swans Island Head, between them and the half-tide rock in the middle of the entrance. As you get into shoal water, you will notice clumps of rockweed. Keep away from them. The weed is growing on boulders. The shores are muddy, there are no facilities, and there is little point in going ashore.

Burnt Coat Harbor. An early French explorer, probably not Champlain, named Swans Island Brûle Côte, by which it was known for years until corrupted by English-speaking settlers to Burnt Coat.

Entrance is not difficult. It is a clear course from the bell off Halibut Rocks to the bell outside Burnt Coat. It passes over a 16-foot spot, which should trouble few yachts in protected water. The tide runs through Toothacher Bay with considerable vigor but more or less parallel to the course. The ebb would make little difference. The flood would set one sailing against it to the north, where he would probably see nun 4 and would surely see or hear High Sheriff before he was in trouble. In recent years there have been salmon pens in Toothacher Bay and may well be again. There were none in July 1993. The light on Hockamock Head is now automated. The building is being well maintained and is an excellent landmark. The gong in the harbor entrance is in such sheltered water that it seldom rings except when a lobster boat passes.

One anchorage is off Harbor Island near the private landing on the north side. There is some motion here and the shores are not really bold, but it is a quiet and usually secluded berth. The owners of the island request no camping or fires, and that people who come ashore stay on the trails near the shore.

The usual anchorage is up the cove to the north and below the wharves. There are several moorings here, some used in the winter for lobster cars. If no mooring is available, one can anchor. Some yachtsmen have declared the bottom is foul with kelp and wiry grass. The author watched a yacht drag a Bruce anchor through it several times, but the yacht's plow anchor took hold, as did the author's. A local fisherman ashore declared the holding ground to be good.

Gasoline, diesel fuel, and marine supplies are sold at the fishermen's cooperative, the wharf with the red houses, the first on the western shore. There is 5 feet at low water at the float. The next wharf is the center for IAC salmon operation at Swans Island and Frenchboro. This was started several years ago and failed, was taken over by the bank and failed again, and finally in 1993 it was bought by Swans Island people assisted by the Island Institute and others. It is hoped and firmly believed that with efficient operation gained from past experience and with the processing plant at Minturn, it will do well this time and contribute substantially to the economy of both Swans Island and Frenchboro. Russell Burns has a small railway which can haul lobster boats and small yachts. Land at the first wharf and walk up the road, bearing to the right, and in about half a mile you will come to the fire station where there is an outdoor telephone. Down the first paved road to the right is the post office.

On the east side of the harbor in Minturn is a grocery store run by Nancy and Jerry Smith, open 10 to 6 on weekdays and 3:30 to 6 on Sundays. It was the only store on the island in 1993 for most people drive onto the ferry and do their shopping in Ellsworth once a month. The Smiths will deliver an order to the wharf if it amounts to $40 and will deliver a smaller order for a slight extra charge. A restaurant, The Old Salt, on the road above the wharf in Minturn was opened in 1985 by Dick Jellison. Reservations can be made by radio. Land by dinghy in the cove, on the east side of the harbor except at very low water.

For a freshwater swim, try the old quarry. There is a lifeguard on duty there during the day.

The eastern entrance to the harbor looks difficult on the chart but presents no serious problem. It is narrow, but an able vessel well handled can beat through. With the usual southwest wind, one can fetch either way. Bound east, leave the two cans close to starboard and favor the Swans Island shore slightly after you pass can 3. The tide does not run hard through here, but out in the Southwest Passage between Swans Island and Long Island the tide runs vigorously.

Passages from Jericho Bay to Blue Hill Bay

Casco Passage and York Narrows. These are the most commonly used passages north of Swans Island. One would use Casco Passage going to and from Eggemoggin Reach and York Narrows in connection with Deer Island Thorofare. Both are deep enough for most yachts and clearly marked with buoys. The tide runs pretty hard to the east on the flood and west on the ebb. Approach to Casco Passage from the west is marked only by a nun, but York Narrows has a lighted bell. At the eastern end, the two passages join at can 1 and the red-and-white bell outside it. On the ordinary southwest breeze, one can usually fetch through Casco Passage. York Narrows is wide enough to beat through. There is excellent shelter at Buckle Harbor and Mackerel Cove on the south, and between Black and Opechee islands on the north.

Pond Island Passage. This is an easy and well-buoyed passage north of Pond Island. It might be more favorable than Casco Passage if one were bound east on an ebb tide.

Outside. Go down Toothacher Bay, between John Island and Swans Island and east of the Sisters, Black Island, and Great Gott. This route has the advantage of avoiding Bass Harbor Bar and of a dramatic approach to the hills of Mount Desert, but it is not recommended in thick weather. Note that the ebb tide sets to the southeast out of Blue Hill Bay, making real dangers of the Drums, Horseshoe Ledge, and South Bunker Ledge. Watch the way the tide sets by pot buoys. A skiff adrift off the Drums in a southerly breeze and a flood tide was found under a wharf in Bass Harbor.

Frenchboro, Long Island, Maine (13135). Since it has been dredged, this is a pleasant offshore harbor except in a strong northeasterly breeze. It is one of those places which every skipper is going to visit on his next voyage but almost always postpones for one more year.

Entrance from either west or north is simple with a bell to the west and a lighted gong to the north.

The harbor has been dredged to 10 feet up to the first wharf on the west side, Lunt & Lunt's, and to 6 feet all the way up beyond the big ledge. There is no apparent need for a yacht to go that far up, but in 1993 the ledge was unmarked and at high water would be a menace. Favor the western side of the channel slightly.

A number of rental moorings are maintained by Lunt & Lunt and by Crossman Crab Co., the wharf on the east side just above the ferry wharf. Crossman is reported to put out superior crabmeat. Call either wharf on channel 80 or 81.

There is no store on the island. People go ashore in their own boats or take the ferry to Bass Harbor and shop in Ellsworth. There is a post office on the east side of the harbor.

Just east of the tar road near the head of the harbor is an interesting museum and library presided over by Vivian and Lillian Lunt. The former has written two thorough books on island history and has corrected some of this writer's misconceptions. The library has a good selection of Maine books for all ages, and the museum has tools, fishing gear, and a great many photographs of the way things were.

There are many deer on the island and they are unusually tame.

In a bog on the southwest part of the island is said to grow a rare orchid, pogonia. Years ago they were very numerous, but now their number has diminished considerably. If you do find any, enjoy them where they are. They will not survive transplanting, and picking one is an act of vandalism.

Professor McLane in *Islands of The Mid-Maine Coast* deals at length with Long Island but defers to Mrs. Lunt for the most part. This leaves many amusing and dramatic details of Long Island's history to these able writers. However, one recent development must be recorded: In the fall of 1969, the Department of Education in Augusta declared that there were so few children on the island that no teacher would be sent to teach such a small school. The children would have to board on Mount Desert for the winter. The people of Frenchboro at once set about increasing the number of children on the island by taking into their homes fifteen state wards. This swelled the school to the required number, a teacher was sent, and the arrangement worked out well. All but a very few of the children adjusted happily to island life and to their new families. As of 1976 all of the children had moved ashore to go to high school. The elementary school was still flourishing in 1992 with twelve scholars and several pre-schoolers coming on.

Unlike many islands which once supported vigorous communities, Frenchboro seems determined to survive. Seven new houses have been built and new settlers have "come aboard." Some have had a difficult time lobstering in the winter, but in 1993 there was only one unoccupied house.

The salmon pens west of the island represent another resource. This is to be run in connection with the Swans Island operation. In the winter of 1992 a storm tore up the net and let many fish out and seals damaged parts of the net. Also many fish froze in the unusually cold weather. However, prospects for the future are encouraging.

Blue Hill, Maine (13316). Blue Hill is a fitting climax to a pleasant sail up the bay with inspiring views of Western Mountain and the islands. Entrance is easy from the chart, but note that the first three cans *must* be left to port. In thick weather, and seldom is it thick this far up the bay, one might follow the 5-fathom curve westward along the shore of Woods Point and make can 1.

The Kollegewidgwok Yacht Club maintains nine guest moorings. Hail the steward at the float or call him on VHF-9. He is on duty daily and Sundays from 8 A.M. until 6 P.M. If there is no vacant mooring, anchorage is good anywhere in the triangle indicated by nun 6, can 7, and the yacht club float. Although yachts have survived hurricanes in this anchorage, one can go farther up the harbor between can 7 and nun 8 and anchor in the inner pool.

Merrill and Hinckley's supermarket in the village will deliver a substantial order to the yacht club in response to a telephone call (374-2721). They supply groceries, meats, produce, bakery goods, and liquor.

Gasoline, diesel fuel, water, and ice are available at the yacht club float. Raynes Yacht Yard has a mechanic and a small railway that will haul boats up to about 30 feet. Captain Robert Gray and Captain Murray K. Gray are experienced compass adjusters. Any damage to sails can be repaired by Donald Hale in Sargentville or Robin Lincoln in Brooklin. In other emergencies, consult the steward at the Kollegewidgwok Yacht Club. The name means "mixed rapids" or "salt-fresh falls" and refers to the falls between the headwaters of the Benjamin River and long, narrow Salt Pond on the west shore of Blue Hill Bay. On the ebb tide the water at the falls is fresh, and on the flood it is salt. This and much more information on place names is found in *Indian Place Names of the Penobscot Valley and the Maine Coast* (Fannie H. Eckstrom, University of Maine, Orono, 1974.)

The yacht club is a station of the Cruising Club of America and maintains an active program from June 15 to September 15 including the Danforth Cup Race from Blue Hill to Schoodic bell, Mount Desert Rock, and return. Perhaps as a symbol of the club's vigorous activity, a gun is fired every morning promptly at 0800.

It is about a 2-mile walk to Blue Hill, most of it along a rather uninspiring tar road. Or you can row in a dinghy up to the town wharf where there is 5 feet at *high* water. The town is quite interesting. Beyond the Blue Hill Inn, an attractive place to dine, is Rowantrees Pottery started by ladies in the 1930s as an educational venture. The manganese deposits found on the slopes of Blue Hill are used to make the lavender-and-black glaze characteristic of Rowantrees products.

There are several other interesting places to dine. Jean Paul's Bistro, all the way from the French Riviera, offers lunch 11 to 5. Jonathan's Restaurant is also well known for fine dining. The John Peters Inn offers showers and dinner for cruising people. It is well to call ahead if possible (374-2116).

The Blue Hill Historical Society has acquired the Jonathan Fisher house and keeps it open to the public in the summer. The Reverend Fisher was an eighteenth-century graduate of Harvard who took his bride to Blue Hill and served there as a very active minister for the rest of his long life. His biography has been written by his descendant Mary Ellen Chase. Her own autobiography, *Windswept*, tells of her early life in and near Blue Hill.

Also in Blue Hill are the Kniesel Hall Music School and a golf course.

Blue Hill itself, 934 feet high, dominates every view of the town. If you want to climb it because it's there, take Route 15 north from the town for about a mile and turn right on a road to the east, which in 1993 bore a sign: The Mountain Road. The trail leaves the left (north) side of the road at a yellow sign: Trail to Lookout Tower. It is a steep trail through the woods and up the shoulder of the mountain. About halfway up, it is joined by an old jeep road. This is the easier and longer way; but a short, steep path cuts off to the right.

Near the top, the blueberries are magnificent. The view from the tower on a clear day stretches from Rockland to the Mount Desert hills and south to Isle au Haut and the islands down the bay.

If it is a dry time, there may be a watchman on duty keeping an eye open for forest fires and helping to triangulate them.

The Gazetteer of Maine states:

> The name Blue Hill comes from a commanding elevation of land near the center of the town. It was formerly covered with trees—principally evergreens—which, at a distance, gave a very dark blue tint—whence its name.

East Blue Hill, Maine (13316). This little bight is the home of Webbers Cove Boat Yard, operated by John Cousins. The yard builds a basic fiberglass powerboat hull and will finish it or ship it for the owner to finish up. The yard also does repair, maintenance, and storage work. The yard has a 12-ton railway and a lift.

The upper parts of Blue Hill Bay, Morgan Bay, Patten Bay, and Union River Bay are well protected and free of dangers and afford beautiful prospects, pleasant sailing, and little fog.

Prettymarsh, Maine (13316). This harbor is large, easy of access, and as one can anchor under whichever is the weather shore, well protected. Somes Cove provides excellent shelter in a heavy southwesterly. Avoid the 3-foot spot northeast of Folly Island and keep well off the shore of West Point. Seal Ledges project 300 yards from the western shore and provide shelter for three guest moorings north of the ledge. The shores are privately owned, but cruising people are welcome to land at the small float and telephone from one of the cottages in emergencies. The cove north of Prettymarsh is a pleasant anchorage. Beware of an uncharted rock, bare at half-tide, south of the 25-foot sounding.

Bartlett Narrows, Maine (13316). This is a deep and easily negotiated passage of surpassing beauty. There is good shelter in Great Cove. Bartlett's Island is now occupied by summer cottages. Visitors may use the beaches but may not build fires or camp without permission of the owners. There is a float landing maintained by Acadia National Park on the Mount Desert shore opposite Bartlett Island. However, there is little reason for the cruising man to go ashore here as it is a long walk to a store.

There are several other shelters on the west side of Mount Desert Island. The best is probably the cove north of the bar behind Moose Island. Seal Cove, Goose Cove, and Duck Cove all have small settlements of summer people and are pleasant places from which to view the sunset on a summer evening. Do not count on them for protection in a storm or for extensive supplies.

Bass Harbor Bar, Maine (13318). This rocky bar, strewn with boulders, can be crossed under ordinary conditions anywhere north of the middle, but the best water is close to the channel buoys. Bass Harbor Head Light no longer has a fog signal.

The tide runs hard across the bar and reverses the usual rule for Maine passages. It floods west into Blue Hill Bay and ebbs east. With the tide ebbing south in the Western Way and flooding north, it seems likely you will have to buck it one place or the other. Bound west, one may do well to avoid the bar altogether and use the ebb tide to beat down to Burnt Coat Harbor, thus getting well to windward. Bound east, it is much more important to have a fair tide through the Thorofares and in the Western Way than it is across the bar.

Bound east from Bass Harbor for Petit Manan and the Bay of Fundy, you would do well to start on the ebb, have a fair tide across the bar, be set to windward as you cross Frenchman's Bay, and have the full strength of the powerful flood beyond Schoodic, where it really counts.

When the wind is blowing hard against the tide, the rip on the bar can become very unpleasant and even dangerous for a small boat. Under these circumstances, wait in Bass Harbor or go out around Placentia and Gott's Islands. A hard southerly and an ebb tide in the Western Way can build up a dangerous rip between the gong and the bell.

Under most conditions, however, there is no problem in crossing the bar, finding the gong on Long Ledge, and running up the Western Way. The first real view of the hills as you come by Long Ledge on a summer afternoon is one you will long remember.

Mount Desert Island, Maine (13318, 13316). Mount Desert Island is the culmination of many a cruise. After a day among the granite and spruce islands to the westward, to round Long Ledge and see the panorama of the Mount Desert hills in the afternoon sun is breathtaking. As you sail up the Western Way, they grow higher, more distinct, and more impressive until you tuck into Northeast Harbor at night, with the hills rising steeply around you.

The island was rediscovered in 1604 by Champlain on his cruise westward from St. Croix Island. He named it *L'isle des Monts Désert,* the island of the barren mountains. To be logical, one should pronounce the name of the island in French, with the accent on the last syllable, or in English with the accent on the first syllable. But to mix the two and call it Mount De*sert* suggests the last course at a banquet. There is nothing logical about the English pronunciation of foreign words, however, so do as you like. Some local people still refer to their home as Mount *Des*ert, as did the late President Eliot of Harvard.

The island affords excellent anchorages, better-than-adequate shore facilities, and good communication. There are miles of sailing in protected waters with superb mountain views. The trip up Somes Sound is an example of this. Here is the only fjord on the Atlantic Coast of the United States. The mountains drop sharply into the sea, just as they do in Norway. And at the head, the mountains give way to a lovely valley with a snug harbor at the foot of it.

Do not neglect the trails. Most of the island is now part of Acadia National Park. The Park maintains trails and carriage roads and publishes a map, available at the stationery store on the west side of the main street in Northeast Harbor or through the Mount Desert Chamber of Commerce. The trails are, on the whole, well marked, but some of them are very rugged indeed, leading up over almost vertical ledges by means of iron ladders set into the rock. A good day's walk is from Northeast Harbor, by the Asticou Inn, and up the trail toward Jordan Pond. Swing left up the south shoulder of Jordan Mountain. The trail soon comes out on bare ledge, so that as you climb, you gain changing views of Sargent, Pemetic, Jordan Pond, and the islands to the south. From the top of Jordan on a clear day one can see Mount Desert Rock to the south and Mount Katahdin to the north.

Cross over to the top of Sargent Mountain, stopping for a quick dip in Sargent Pond. Then return down the south side of Sargent to the Jordan Pond trail. The writers have seldom made this trip without seeing deer in the woods and a variety of birds, including ravens and eagles, on the upper slopes.

One might vary the trip by stopping at the Jordan Pond House, at the south end of the pond, widely renowned for delicious popovers.

Do not leave Mount Desert without hiring a car and driving to the top of Cadillac (locally, Green) Mountain at sunset. From Rockland to beyond Petit Manan the coast lies at your feet, fading in outline as the lights wink on.

History is all around you here. Champlain writes of seeing the island in 1604. The Jesuits visited the island in 1613 and settled at the foot of the field on Fernald's Point. Here they found a spring between high and low water that runs freely today. East of Bass Harbor Head is Ship Harbor, dry at low water, where an American privateer is said to have escaped a British warship during the Revolution. In Somes Sound at the foot of Acadia Mountain is a brook where French naval vessels used to fill water casks. Whether Norsemen actually lay alongside the cliffs of Flying Mountain and fought the Indians coming down the Sound in canoes is doubtful, but the scene is not hard to imagine. Indians, Frenchmen, and Englishmen, fishermen, seamen, pirates, and farmers have rowed and sailed these waters for centuries. Only recently has it become a "vacationland." Still in the recollection of many are the days of steam yachts and great schooners at Seal Harbor, fifty-room "cottages" with formal gardens, stables, and battalions of servants at Bar Harbor, and ladies of leisure with parasols and flowered sun hats enjoying it all. A minor theme was the plain living and high thinking of President Eliot of Harvard and a number of his modest and distinguished colleagues.

Characteristic of him is the story told of one of his journeys from Rockland to Northeast Harbor on the steamer *J. T. Morse:*

As the president was leaning on the rail, contemplating the unfolding beauties of Blue Hill Bay, a member of the crew stood beside him a moment and said, "We've been talking about who was the smartest man that travels on this boat. We concluded it was you, but what we don't know is—if you're so smart, why ain't you rich?" To which Mr. Eliot responded with a characteristic blend of wisdom, modesty, and wit, "I guess I never had time."

Visit the Sawtelle Museum on Cranberry Island for more detailed information on the island's history.

For more modern developments, visit the Jackson Laboratory south of Bar Harbor, where continuing work is done on hereditary aspects of cancer. The College of the Atlantic, in Bar Harbor, is doing advanced ecological studies. The Maine Sea Coast Missionary Society's *Sunbeam* is based on Northeast Harbor and is busy helping people in isolated communities to live richer and better lives. There is a great deal to see and do on Mount Desert, and a summer is not time enough in which to do it.

Bass Harbor, Maine (13316). The outer part of this harbor is wide open to the south and the inner basin is likely to be crowded. However, it is a good hour or more farther west than Southwest Harbor or Northeast and is usually less disturbed by the snarling outboard or the incessant ringing of wire halyard on aluminum mast.

Entrance is easy. Simply avoid the well-marked Weaver Ledge. There is an anchorage on the west side of the outer harbor off a stony beach. This is much the best berth in a westerly. The float, lift, and other moorings for Bass Harbor Marine are on the eastern shore outside the ferry wharf. Hail the float or call on channel 9 or 71. These moorings are likely to be uneasy if the afternoon southerly persists into the evening and they are downright uncomfortable if it blows hard, but they are safe enough. There are also moorings in the inner harbor, which offers much better protection. Bass Harbor Marine will know about these. In much of any breeze at all, a berth alongside the float is difficult, but one could lie on the lee side long enough to take aboard gasoline, diesel fuel, water, or ice. The tide runs by the float to the south on both flood and ebb. There is a laundry machine, telephone, and shower in the yard and a good marine store. Pumpout service is available, and both propane and CNG tanks can be filled. Repairs of all kinds can be made here, and there is a travelift. The yard conducts an extensive charter business and is likely to be a busy place on the weekend.

Close to the yard is a restaurant with an excellent reputation on Mount Desert Island. A short walk north on the road and to the right at the first corner is the post office. There is no grocery store nearby.

There are a few private moorings north of the ferry wharf where the boat to Swans Island lands and then a dredged channel running northerly into a dredged basin beyond. This is a well-protected berth frequented largely by lobstermen, but there are several moorings for transients maintained by Bass Harbor Marine on the west shore.

Bass Harbor, unlike the other towns on Mount Desert Island, subsists more on fish, lobsters, and boatbuilding than it does on tourism. Its atmosphere is a little less hurried and less sophisticated.

The Great Harbor of Mount Desert, Maine (13318). This is the name given to the confluence of the Eastern Way, the Western Way, and Somes Sound. It is a well-protected anchorage for large vessels and a good place to sail small boats. It has two entrances.

The Western Way is marked by a lighted gong on Long Ledge and a beacon on South Bunker Ledge. The tide runs briskly along the course from the gong to the red-and-white bell, northeast on the flood and southwest on the ebb, but seems to set one to the side very little. There is a bar between Seawall Point and Great Cranberry Island, with a passage marked by a can and a nun. The tide runs harder here—perhaps 3 knots—and in the shoal water, with the wind against the tide, it can get quite lumpy. Once over the bar, however, conditions improve, and one can run for red-and-white gong "SP" and thence follow the shore, respectfully, into Southwest Harbor or run for the buoys off Northeast.

The Eastern Way is marked by a lighted gong and a beacon on East Bunker Ledge. The beacon is a squatty pyramid painted white with a red-and-white checkered dayboard on it. It has been the writer's experience that when approaching the Eastern Way from Schoodic toward the end of the day, it is well to get to windward and come in south of East Bunker Ledge under the Cranberry Island shore. There is likely to be a fresh little breeze under the shore when it is calm and rolly off Otter Cove. The passage south of Sutton Island is to be preferred.

Southwest Harbor (13318). Although open eastward, Southwest Harbor is well enough protected in ordinary summer weather. Entrance is easy. From the red-and-white bell in the Western Way, follow the southern, Kings Point shore until you are in among the moorings off the yard of Henry R. Hinckley, Inc.

Formerly Mount Desert's principal commercial harbor, Southwest Harbor is now devoted almost entirely to yachting. There is little room to anchor, for the harbor is heavily salted with moorings. As you approach, call the harbormaster, Gene Thurston, or the Hinckley yard on channel 9 for a mooring. The berth off the Hinckley yard is more exposed than the moorings farther up the harbor and subject to wash from passing ferries and fishermen, but it affords an inspiring view of the mountains and of Somes Sound. Also it is convenient to washrooms, showers, and the marine store at the yard, available to those on the yard's moorings.

The Hinckley yard builds fiberglass yachts of the highest quality, elegantly appointed and magnificently equipped, and can do repair work of all kinds on hull, rigging, engine, and electronics. The front of the float is kept open for transients in need of diesel fuel, water, ice, stove fuel, and marine supplies. Gasoline is not available. Do not plan to lie at the float any longer than necessary. Take a mooring and row ashore to do your shopping at the Double J store, a short walk up the hill on the road west of the Hinckley yard. Although crowded, this store carries an adequate supply of groceries, bakery goods, fruit, produce, limited meats, and beer. If business is not pressing, you may get a ride back to the shore with your order.

On the shore west of Hinckley's is Manset Marine Service selling marine supplies and J-boats and renting small power- and sailboats. Farther west is a town wharf with the harbormaster's office, a nice restaurant, and several private wharves. East of Hinckley's is The Moorings, a pleasant place to dine.

The first wharf on the north side of the harbor is the Coast Guard base where buoys are repaired, cleaned, and painted. Next is the wharf of H. R. Beal. Here gasoline, diesel oil, ice, lobsters, and limited marine supplies are available, and Beal also serves lobsters and light lunches on the wharf. The float is much frequented by fishermen in a hurry to buy bait and fuel and to sell their catch. Do not plan to stay long alongside.

Westward of Beal's is a town wharf, near the head of which is Downeast Diesel and Marine, an engine repair service. Here also is the

Oceanarium with interesting oceanographic exhibits. Farther up the harbor on the north side are several private wharves and another town float where one can tie a dinghy and walk the short distance to the town of Southwest Harbor. From this float ferries run to the Cranberry Isles.

West of the town float is the small yard of Ralph Stanley where he builds wooden boats, both yachts and commercial vessels. He has built and rebuilt a number of Friendship sloops as well as other sloops, ketches, and schooners. Some of the handsomest lobster boats in the harbor were launched from his yard. He also makes beautiful and accurate half-models, and he has built his own violin. Besides being an artist and craftsman in wood, he has written a number of articles on maritime history.

West of Stanley's is Morris Yachts, which can perform all kinds of repairs and has finished out many fiberglass hulls.

At the head of the harbor is the Hinckley Great Harbor Marina with about 100 slips. Call on channel 9. The outer slips have at least 10 feet at low water and the inner ones about 4 feet. Each slip has a "power pedestal" dispensing water, electricity at 30 or 50 amps, and cable TV, but no fuel is available here. On the wharf are toilets, showers, washing machines, a pumpout station, and a telephone. Near the head of the wharf is a lobster shop, a restaurant, and several marine-related stores. Here also is Shore Sails Acadia, which can repair a torn sail or in short order build a new one.

On the main street of Southwest Harbor, to your right as you leave the marina, is Sawyer's Market, offering free delivery in response to a telephone call. Also in town are restaurants, a hardware store, a drug store, two clothing stores, a bookstore, a post office, a library, and several gift and specialty shops. Beyond the stores, about half a mile north, is a state liquor store and a small shopping mall.

Somes Sound, Maine (13318). This is the only fjord on the East Coast of the United States. Here the mountains on both sides rise steeply from deep water. Near the head of the Sound the mountains open out into more gentle slopes and a perfectly protected harbor behind Bar Island. It is a delightful sail before a southwest breeze and far preferable to a dank and anxious trip outside should the day be foggy. A northwest breeze can be very puffy under the mountains. Plan for a fair tide through the Narrows.

On the beach at the foot of a large open field on the west side north of can 5 is Jesuit Spring, a natural spring of freshwater bubbling up below high-water mark. Here in 1613 a party of French Jesuits established a mission. It lasted only a few weeks, however, until Governor Dale of Virginia heard of it and sent Samuel Argall to destroy it and to erase all French presence in New England. He succeeded in the former effort but failed in the latter. The story is told in colorful detail in *Coastal Maine,* pp. 70–71.

The first indentation on the west shore above the Narrows is Valley Cove, sheltered by Flying Mountain, Valley Peak, and St. Sauveur Mountain. The shores, too steep in some places for trees, drop off sharply into deep water, leaving a narrow shelf close to the beach on which to anchor. From time to time moorings have been established here. If you find one and want to take a chance on its quality, take it. It is much easier than anchoring in deep water on what is likely to be rocky bottom. Leading south from the beach is a trail with a branch off to the west up St. Sauveur Mountain affording excellent views of the Sound, the cove, and the islands to the south. It leads down into the gap under Acadia Mountain whence one can turn left to Echo Lake for a freshwater swim or right to go back to the shore and south on a trail through the woods and over rock slides to Valley Cove again. Acadia Mountain is a good climb and affords a good view. From the brook at its foot naval vessels used to fill water casks. It is still called Man o' War Brook.

Above Acadia Mountain is a boatyard at Hall's Quarry, and on the east side behind nun 10 is Abels' yard, largely devoted now to building fiberglass boats. In the northeast corner of the Sound is John Butler's Mount Desert Boat Yard with facilities for hauling, repairs, and storage. The yard does admirable work and the management is skillful, ingenious, and friendly. The yard has several moorings. There are no facilities ashore beyond those connected with the yard.

In Somes Harbor there is excellent shelter in peaceful surroundings. There is a landing on the west shore and a path leading to the tar road. To the left is Port in a Storm Bookstore, an excellent resource for a depleted book locker. It is particularly strong on children's books and Maine books but has a more-than-adequate supply of light paperback reading. About $1/2$ mile to the right is Fernald's store, a very general store ready to supply any reasonable need. There is a telephone outside the store and a post office nearby.

Northeast Harbor. This picture, taken in April, gives no idea of how crowded Northeast Harbor is in the summer. However, it does show the Clifton Dock on the west side of the entrance, the Town Wharf, the marina, and the Mt. Dessert Yacht Yard wharf. The tip of Bear Island appears at the bottom. *Courtesy James W. Sewall Co.*

Northeast Harbor, Maine (13318). As you sail up the Western Way on a summer afternoon before a pleasant southwest breeze, Northeast Harbor looks like what you have dreamed about all winter. It lies tucked in under the mountains, with Bear Island Light at its entrance, perfectly protected and easy of access. As you get closer, however, there are a few practical details to be observed.

Bear Island Light has been officially discontinued but shows a flashing white light. Close south of the island is a flashing red bell (4 seconds). West of the island is another flashing red bell (2½ seconds) marking a half-tide rock. Leave both of these buoys to starboard.

There is a notorious dead spot off Sargeant Head which can be avoided by keeping to the east near nun 4.

There is a channel through the thicket of masts and moorings, but there is no room to anchor. If you call the harbormaster on the radio, he will refer you to the mooring agent on channel 9. This busy person circulates through the harbor in a small powerboat with a hand-held radio. He will materialize, apparently miraculously, and either lead you to a mooring or do his best somehow to accommodate you.

The buoyed channel leads to the public dock and marina in the cove on the west side of the harbor. As this dock is heavily used by ferries, excursion boats, and fishermen, there is a 2-hour tie-up limit and a 15-minute loading and unloading zone. Although the slips at the marina are crowded with large motor yachts and auxiliaries, bristling with antennas, their decks gleaming with polished chrome, several transient berths are available for visiting yachtsmen. Advance reservations are encouraged. Call on channel 9 or consult the harbormaster in the gray building between the public dock and the marina.

North of the marina is the Northeast Harbor branch of the Mount Desert Yacht Yard, with a travelift and facilities for the repair of hull, engine, rigging, and electronics. South of the public dock is a hard-surfaced launching ramp.

Gasoline, diesel fuel, water, ice, stove fuel, and limited marine supplies are available at Clifton Dock, the prominent wharf on the west side near the entrance. This is a tidy, well-maintained, and efficient operation dedicated to serving the cruising yacht. One can telephone a grocery order to Pine Tree Market or Provisions and have an order delivered. Advice on repairs and restaurants is free. However, do not plan to lie alongside longer than necessary.

To visit the town of Northeast Harbor, land at the dinghy float north of the marina. You will be confronted by a huge parking lot. To your left is the harbormaster's office, a dumpster for your trash, and a battery of outdoor telephones. To your right is another telephone. Ahead of you lies Sea Street, which takes you up the hill to the town. On a knoll to your right is a small gray building providing a shower on the deposit of four quarters. Change is immediately available at the Chamber of Commerce office in the same building. If it is necessary for you to leave Northeast Harbor by land, consult the bulletin board in the lounge and ask at the office about taxi service and airplane and bus schedules. These are subject to frequent change. One can call the Chamber at (207) 276-5040.

Farther up the hill is a simple restaurant serving seafood on a takeout or eat-in basis. Sea Street delivers you into the midst of a Maine resort town. To the right is an elegant clothing store, F. T. Brown's hardware store with a wide selection of marine supplies including charts, the post office, and Provisions, a store planned to meet the needs of the cruising yachtsman. They will deliver an order to the shore for you, and if you are doing extensive provisioning, this beats lugging paper bags and boxes down the hill. Visit Provisions last, and include your other *impedimenta*.

Down an alley between the post office and Provisions is Shirt Off Your Back. Here you can leave your laundry and recover it clean in a short time. Essentially it is a laundromat, but the management operates the machines.

To the left on the main street is the Pine Tree Market, familiar now to generations of cruising men. It has an excellent variety of groceries, meats, fruits, wines, beers, and hard liquor. If business is not too pressing, someone may be free to deliver you and your purchases to the shore.

Farther to the left are numerous gift shops, art and craft stores, restaurants, and branches of well-known city stores.

There is a medical center in Northeast Harbor.

Northeast Harbor is the base for *Sunbeam*, the Maine Seacoast Missionary Society's vessel, known as God's Tugboat. See the article about the society in the section on Bar Harbor.

This is also the approach to the Asticou Terraces, a unique memorial park left to the town by the late Joseph H. Curtis of Boston. The trip ashore, with a short walk to the top of Asticou Hill, is one of the most rewarding side jaunts of a cruise to Maine. Take it at sunset, or by moonlight. At the top is Thuya Lodge, the old Curtis house, containing the noted Curtis collection of botanical books, open 10 A.M. to 6 P.M. daily. A famous botanical collection has recently been transplanted to the Terraces. At the Asticou Inn, Charles Savage has developed a beautiful Japanese garden.

It is also a good walk on a well-traveled trail from the red-roofed Asticou terrace to the Jordan Pond House. The trail starts at the head of the harbor.

The Northeast Harbor Fleet has its clubhouse and dock at Gilpatrick's Cove, just west of Northeast Harbor. Don't try to get to the club by water! The anchorage is small and very poor. Cruising yachts are extended a cordial invitation to join the fleet's numerous special races and cruises.

The road skirting the eastern shore of the harbor has been named Peabody Drive in honor of the late Dr. Francis Greenwood Peabody of Harvard University, who, throughout a long life, cruised these waters. Once, when asked his occupation, Dr. Peabody replied, "I stay ashore winters."

The authors are indebted to the late Mr. W. Rodman Peabody of Boston, son of Dr. Peabody, for the following story concerning President Eliot of Harvard University:

There is a crop of interesting stories about President Eliot, who, you may know, was a very skillful sailor and who sailed the Maine coast with a good deal of regularity from the end of the 1860s to the time of his death. For many years after his first wife died his summer home was a little sloop called the *Sunshine* and his headquarters were at Calf Island in Frenchman Bay.

President Eliot was, as you may guess, an imperturbable person even when fate was against him. I remember once as a small boy sailing from Bar Harbor to Northeast Harbor with my father, who was preaching at Northeast Harbor. We lunched with President Eliot and then started home for Bar Harbor. You may recall that at the mouth of Northeast Harbor there is a ledge with a high rock at each end. It is now protected by red and black buoys, so that there are two entrances to the harbor. In those days the ledge was unbuoyed.

As the President walked with us to the float, my father asked him for the bearings of the ledge which was directly in front of his house and dead to windward. He immediately got in his rowboat and said: "I will sail you out until you are clear and then row home."

We got under way in a stiff southwester and were swinging to it well when we came up with a crash. The boat stopped, slid off, hit again, and went free. The President, who was steering, without a gesture of concern, then turned the wheel over to my father and said: "Those were the two high points of the ledge. If you will take a careful bearing, you will always know their exact location in the future. Good-by. You preached a good sermon." Without another word he hauled in his painter and rowed away.

Seal Harbor, Maine (13318). This harbor offers adequate protection on an ordinary summer night. There will be just enough motion to rock you to sleep. But in a heavy southerly or southeaster, Seal Harbor can be very unpleasant.

Water is available at the town landing. Whether you need supplies or not, take the short and pretty walk to the village. There is a thoroughly adequate store.

The summer homes of Fords and Rockefellers overlook the harbor. The late Mr. John D. Rockefeller was glad to make available to horseback riders and hikers the carriage roads and trails on his extensive estate. The family continues this hospitable tradition.

Great Cranberry Island, Maine (13318). Spurling Cove on the north side is a good anchorage in southerly weather. For those passing through, it saves time. There are several moorings here and a restaurant on the shore. The island is not particularly interesting, though the view is superb.

The Pool, entered from the northeast side, is an excellent anchorage for shoal-draft boats. With a draft of more than 3 feet, it is necessary to leave and enter with half-tide or more. When entering, follow the southeast side of the channel and, while rounding the little point, keep only a few yards off the beach. Anchor where the fishing boats are moored; there is about 6 feet at mean low water and a soft mud bottom.

Great Cranberry Island has claim to fame as the birthplace, on February 22, 1822, of John Gilley, Maine farmer and fisherman, immortalized in "John Gilley" by Charles W. Eliot, available in his *The Durable Satisfactions of Life* (Thomas Y. Crowell & Co., New York, 1910). The piece has been reprinted in a booklet, *John Gilley of Baker's Island,* by the Eastern National Park and Monument Association in cooperation with

Acadia National Park. Anyone cruising these waters will be moved by this simple account of the life and death by drowning of a Maine islander.

Islesford, Little Cranberry Island, Maine (13318). Islesford is an excellent place from which to depart for eastern Maine waters. Stock up in Southwest Harbor or Northeast, spend the night at Islesford, and leave on the last of the ebb tide the next day. You will be set to windward down Frenchman Bay and then have the full flood with you from Schoodic past Petit Manan and Mistake Island where it really counts. And Islesford provides a stimulating change from the "yachty" atmosphere of Northeast Harbor.

With the bell on Spurling Rock, the harbor is easy to find under almost any conditions. There is plenty of room to anchor off the wharves and there are several rental moorings so marked. Fuel and lobsters are available at the Co-op wharf and there is a hardware store.

Islesford somehow gracefully absorbs its 500 summer people into a population of 90 year-rounders. The houses along the road leading back from the shore are the traditional Maine farmhouses, standing firm against winter. They are well maintained, their lawns are neatly mowed, and some of their flower gardens stop the sailor ashore in his tracks. About a quarter mile up from the wharf, near a prominent white church, is Islesford Stores, Inc., carrying a variety of groceries.

The Sawtelle Museum has a number of old charts and many relics of the French days. A walk across the island to the abandoned Coast Guard station, marked "Tower" on the chart, is a refreshing change from the carefully cultivated paths around Northeast Harbor. You are again on a Maine island, with granite ledge, huckleberry, and sweet fern giving way to a stony beach, a view of Bakers Island, and the sea breaking heavily on the offshore ledges.

Get back aboard in time to enjoy the sunset behind the mountains. This is the best place from which to see it.

Bar Harbor, Maine (13318). Bar Harbor is a better harbor than most cruising people give it credit for. True, it is deep, the holding ground is poor, and there is usually some motion in the harbor. However, the breakwater protects it from any dangerous sea from the south, and the town provides a number of stout moorings. It is easy of access. One can enter between the beacon on the west end of the breakwater and the Mount Desert shore, being careful to give the beacon a good berth to starboard.

The entrance from the east is wide open. From the north, enter either side of Sheep Porcupine, leaving the bell to starboard on the east side and the ledge off Bar Island to port on the west side.

Note that on a southerly breeze, while it may be gentle offshore, very often it will be blowing very much harder between Ironbound Island and Bald Porcupine.

Call the harbormaster on channel 9 or 16 for a mooring or possibly slip space with water and electricity, or just pick up a town mooring and visit the harbormaster at his office on the town wharf. There is a water hose on the town float. Also on the same wharf is the Information Center where one can pick up printed information on the facilities of the town and Acadia National Park, hiking trails, bus tours, and transportation by bus and air. Any further questions can be answered by well-informed and helpful attendants.

Just inside the town wharf is Harbor Place, which monitors channels 9, 16, and 80. Some moorings are available with slightly better protection than the town moorings, and there is some room to lie alongside with water and electric connections. Gasoline, diesel fuel, water, ice, and pumpout service are available at the float. Showers, a laundromat, and a marine store which also sells charts are situated either right at Harbor Place or close by, and there is a restaurant as well.

The very name Bar Harbor has an aura of romance, now sadly tarnished. Campers and motor homes from distant states prowl the streets. Tired-looking visitors stroll about with the slightly disappointed air of one who has come a long way and found it scarcely worth the trip. The glamour is gone. The great "cottages" of the past were destroyed in the fire of 1947, torn down, or converted to motels. No lofty schooner yachts lie in the harbor. No sleek steam yachts with clipper bows and twinkling brass are anchored off. No carriages take flanneled youths and butterfly girls to dance beneath crystal chandeliers. Now Bar Harbor is a busy tourist center, the terminus of the Bar Harbor–Yarmouth ferry, a good place to stock up or change crews or from which to climb a mountain. Dorr Mountain is within walking distance.

North of the harbor is the conspicuous landing of the ferry *Bluenose,* which makes daily trips to Yarmouth, Nova Scotia, leaving about 8 A.M. and returning around 9:30 P.M. Her route runs by Egg Rock and then about southeast by east for Yarmouth. She moves at an uncompromising speed.

The Jackson Laboratory, located about 2 miles south of downtown

Bar Harbor on Route 3, is an internationally recognized center for mammalian genetics research. The laboratory has a threefold mission: biomedical research, scientific training and education, and animal resources. Its research is relevant to cancer, heart disease, diabetes, anemias, birth defects, aging, and normal growth and development. Over three million genetically defined inbred, mutant, and hybrid mice are reared and distributed annually to the world's scientific community.

During the summer the laboratory presents a one-hour summary of its program with multi-media illustration in the auditorium. The public is invited. There is no admission charge. The program is presented on Tuesday and Thursday at 4 P.M. from June 16 through August 28 except during the week of August 11. The laboratory is not open to the public on weekends and holidays. The dates may vary slightly from year to year.

The Maine Sea Coast Missionary Society

The diesel motorship *Sunbeam,* owned and operated by the Maine Sea Coast Missionary Society of Bar Harbor, is a unique vessel which may be seen in almost any harbor of the Maine coast. Known as God's Tugboat, the *Sunbeam* is easily distinguishable because of the white cross on either side of her bow, denoting the practical Christian service in which she is engaged.

The *Sunbeam* is 65 feet long, powered by a 225-horsepower diesel engine, and draws 7 feet. The vessel is built of steel, and the bow section is reinforced with extra-heavy steel plate and frames for ice-breaking purposes. The *Sunbeam* was built in Warren, Rhode Island, in 1964 and is the sixth in the succession of vessels that have served the mission since it was founded in 1905.

The mission's work is interdenominational, with the objective of providing Christian leadership and pastoral care along the coast and on the islands of the Maine coast and of engaging in all efforts that are calculated to contribute to the moral and spiritual welfare of the inhabitants. The *Sunbeam* is used as transportation for mission workers and as a lifeline for isolated families and communities, especially in frigid winter weather. This splendidly equipped small ship symbolizes in its ready and able service the total program of the mission, which comprises Christian work in uncounted, practical ways: preaching, teaching, aid to the sick and the unfortunate, encouragement of young people, visitation and ministry to the lonely, and much more.

A new *Sunbeam* built in 1995 by Washburn & Doughty in East Boothbay is The mission is now well along in a capital campaign to build a new *Sunbeam,* bigger and better suited to changed conditions in its salt-water parish. Instead of the extensive medical equipment of the present *Sunbeam,* it has more conference, meeting, and passenger space. It will carry the same cross on its bow to symbolize its continuing work.

The mission has an embrace large enough to take in all members of its widespread parish, regardless of their estate, whether clean and scrubbed or spattered with mud from the flats, yet intimate enough to call each one by name. At present, mission workers are stationed either full or part time in the following places: Jonesport, Masons Bay, Cherryfield, Ashville, Vinalhaven, North Haven, Islesboro, Swans Island, and Bar Harbor. In addition, services are held either regularly or on a seasonal or itinerant basis in the following: Islesford, Frenchboro, Matinicus, Monhegan, Isle au Haut, and Loudville. Visitors are always welcome at the mission stations and churches as well as on board the *Sunbeam* and at the Mission Headquarters, 127 West Street, Bar Harbor, where items relating to the history of the mission are on display in a small museum.

The mission's annual reports and bulletins constitute an offshore saga full of salty incident and color. Any yachtsman interested in keeping in touch with the Maine coast throughout the year would do well to subscribe to the mission and receive its unique publications.

These, plus the newsy monthly *National Fisherman,* published at Rockland, serve to brighten the long months of those who, like the late Dr. Francis Greenwood Peabody of Harvard, "stay ashore winters."

Sullivan, Maine (13318). The Sullivan anchorage is exposed to the south. There is a strong tide in the river, and there is a narrow and rocky place that forms rapids. It is not recommended for strangers.

Sullivan is a small village on the north side of the harbor, 3½ miles above the entrance. There is a privately owned wharf that bares at extreme low tides.

It was on the western side of Hancock Point that a German submarine landed two spies on a snowy winter night in 1944. As they walked up the road, the sheriff's son noticed them, lightly clad in city clothes. He became suspicious, followed their tracks, and notified the FBI. They were located in Bangor and followed until they revealed their "contacts" and then were arrested.

On the eastern side of Hancock Point is a dock with about 6 feet at low water and a guest mooring. It is a pleasant place to spend a night in quiet weather.

On the west side of Hancock Point facing Sullivan Bay is the former site of Mount Desert Ferry, once the busy terminus of the Maine Central Railroad. Here passengers and freight were transferred to three ferry steamers for points inside the bay and to Bar Harbor and other harbors along the ocean side of Mount Desert Island. The amount of traffic can be visualized if one remembers that at that time there was only a clay-and-dirt road from the mainland, over a bridge, to the island, and almost everything that went onto and from the island went by boat, either from Mount Desert Ferry or from Rockland. Mr. Dean K. Worcester describes the scene in the early days of this century as follows, in the *National Fisherman:*

> Mount Desert Ferry, of which no trace remains, was a place on the mainland where the railroad track came down alongside deep water, so that the Bar Harbor Express, with its dozen or more sleeping cars, could lie at one side of the dock, while *Norumbega* lay at the other, rising and falling in the 10′ tide.
>
> The train used to arrive about 7 A.M. and when the passengers and their baggage had been put aboard, *Norumbega* would shove off for Bar Harbor, nearly an hour's journey. There was a restaurant in the forward deckhouse, where you could have breakfast and at the same time see where you were going. The course lay nearly due south, and since Mount Desert Island's abrupt mountain ranges and valleys, carved by glaciers, also run more or less north and south, their endwise profile as seen from the steamer was particularly dramatic. After having left New York on a hot summer evening, it was a pleasure to watch the island approaching in the clear cool morning light, gently suffused with eggs and bacon and coffee.
>
> At least that's how I remember it, 50-odd years later.

Sorrento, Maine (13318). Well sheltered and with inspiring views of the Mount Desert hills to the south, Sorrento is an attractive harbor. Enter midway between Dram and Preble Islands or between Dram Island and the mainland. Favor Dram Island in either case as a long ledge, visible at low water, extends halfway across the entrance, and the shore of Preble Island is less than bold.

There are three guest moorings in the outer part of the harbor, one bearing the legend:

In Memory of
Robert M. Lewis
1886–1958
He Cruised

Captain Lewis was a New Haven doctor who served with the Grenfell Mission in Labrador and cruised the New England coast extensively.

If it comes on to blow from the south, one can have an uncomfortable night on the guest moorings. Withdraw into the southeast corner of the harbor as far as draft and moored boats will permit. Eastern Harbor and Flanders Bay are also acceptable refuges.

West Cove Boat Shop in Back Cove offers storage and repair service.

A few fishermen work out of Sorrento, but the harbor is largely used by the summer population. The Sorrento Yacht Club uses the town wharf and float. Except in such a dire emergency that one must borrow a jerry can and lug gasoline a considerable distance, do not count on buying fuel here. The nearest store is about 4 miles away. There is a telephone on the wharf and a post office nearby. Sorrento is a pleasant town of winding streets and gracious cottages, a good shelter for the night and a pleasant place to remember.

Stave Island Harbor, Maine (13318). This is a large and well-protected harbor on the east side of Frenchman Bay. The best place to anchor appears to be under the steep northeast side of Jordan Island. There was what looked like some kind of cannery in South Gouldsboro in 1981, but aside from that and an unobtrusive summer cottage or two, the shores seemed delightfully deserted.

Winter Harbor, Maine (13318). Easy of access, deep, and clearly marked, Winter Harbor is an excellent place to spend the night for yachtsmen bound east or west. Bound east, it cuts the run from Mount Desert to Mistake Island enough to make it an easy day's run even in a modest breeze. Bound west, it postpones until next day what can be a long beat across Frenchman Bay in the chill of a late afternoon.

Entrance from the south and east is easy with a gong off Turtle Island Ledge, the conspicuous abandoned lighthouse on Mark Island, and the lighted bell off it. From the east, one need simply follow the bold shore of Schoodic Point at a respectful distance.

From Frenchman Bay the entrance is perhaps confusing to the stranger, but it is easier than it looks from the chart. It amounts essentially to following the bold shore of Grindstone Neck. Leave can 5, Pulpit Ledge, and beacon 3A to starboard and nun 2 to port. Grindstone Ledge may be crossed at high water about midway between the beacon and Grindstone Point.

From the west, either go south of the gong off Turtle Island or pass between Turtle Island and Spectacle Island. Pass about 20 yards south of the stone pier on Spectacle Island and head for the red-and-green nun on Roaring Bull Ledge, leaving it to starboard and can "GL" to port. There are three anchorages in Winter Harbor:

Henry Cove. This cove on the east side of Winter Harbor is wide open to the southwest and is not at all a comfortable berth. The only reason for considering it at all is the Winter Harbor Marine Trading Corporation at the head of a heavy granite wharf on the east side. They have several moorings and a float with 7 feet at low water. They have a Brownell trailer and can make repairs to hull, spars, and engines. The yard is closed on Saturdays, Sundays, and holidays.

Inner Winter Harbor. This narrow cove is much better protected than Sand Cove, and although it is crowded with fishermen and local yachts, you may find a vacant mooring. Hail a fisherman and inquire. The cove has been dredged to a depth of 10 feet as far as the Co-op wharf, where gas and diesel fuel are available.

Land at the heavy float on the east side. It is a pleasant walk through the eastern Maine countryside to Winter Harbor. There is a telephone on the corner of the main street. Turn right for the store, post office, and restaurants. The atmosphere of the road, fields, town, and harbor provides a refreshing change from the harbors of Mount Desert.

The cove may be noisy in the early morning with departing fishermen, but you will want to get along anyway.

It was here that I first heard of fishing for herring with piano wire. One man rows a dory or a peapod quietly up a cove. Another drags over the side a length of piano wire too short to reach bottom. There is a weight on the end of the wire. If herring are in the cove, they will brush against the thin wire and their number can be estimated by the frequency of the jiggles on the wire. If there are enough, the cove is stopped off and seined.

Sand Cove. This is a deep cove on the west side of the harbor. On the west side stands Winter Harbor Yacht Club, built in the gracious tradition of the century's early years. The club is still hospitable to cruising people but cannot offer the facilities it once did.

Call on VHF 16 or 9 for a mooring between 9 A.M. and 5 P.M. Launch service runs until 4 P.M. Ice may be available, but there is no fuel and the pool is off limits to visitors. However, there are a few guest moorings, a water hose, and an outdoor telephone. The town of Winter Harbor is a pleasant walk from the yacht club or the town landing at Inner Winter Harbor. There is a grocery store, a dry-goods store, and a hardware store with limited marine supplies, and several restaurants in town.

Chapter XII

Schoodic Point to
West Quoddy Head

General Conditions. To be headed east by Schoodic bell before a summer sou'wester with Mount Desert fading astern and the lonely spike of Petit Manan Light just visible on the port bow is about as close to perfection as a man can expect to come on this imperfect earth.

Astern lie supermarkets, yacht clubs, water skiers, high-charged power cruisers, the pageantry associated with racing and day sailing. Ahead lie cold waters, racing tides, and the probability of thick fogs and delightful scale-ups. The islands and most of the mainland shores are mostly uninhabited except for small communities of lobstermen. The long, low, wooded promontories keep one well offshore in rounding them, but between, once east of Petit Manan, are islands, coves, and quiet creeks.

For the experienced navigator with a touch of the explorer, this country is the Promised Land, and for the "cricker," it is a happy hunting ground. The gregarious, the inexperienced navigators, and those who like to dress up and go ashore for dinner at the yacht club will be happier west of Schoodic.

There are a few cautions to bear in mind. Perhaps the first is to be sure that you have proper charts. Charts 13327, 13326, 13324, 13312, and 13325 are essential. An accurate compass in which the navigator can have implicit confidence is necessary. Log, lead, and lookout are never to be neglected. Those with loran will find the 5930 chain more precise than the 9960 chain used farther west.

Next, *be careful.* Careless errors may exact their price very quickly on this lonesome coast.

Thirdly, be prepared to stay a while. You may be fogbound or windbound, but be sure that you will have to wait out tides. A tide setting against the wind on this coast can raise a dangerous sea in short order. To beat against a Fundy tide is a losing battle, and even motoring against the tide is slow work.

Alternate Routes. From Schoodic bell to Cutler there are several routes, more or less overlapping and appropriate for different weather conditions.

The easiest in thick weather or in heavy seas is the outside route. From Schoodic bell go outside Southeast Rock whistle 3 miles outside Petit Manan, thence outside Mistake Island, outside Libby Islands and Cross Island, and up the shore to Cutler. Petit Manan, Mistake Island, and Libby Islands have lights with powerful horns. The course avoids all shoals and navigational hazards. For one in a hurry to traverse the coast and "get somewhere," it is the preferred course, but it is supremely dull and the skipper who has come east to see Maine will be disappointed.

The next course leads from Schoodic bell to the nun off Petit Manan, thence between Tibbett Rock and the nun south of it to Seahorse Rock, past Egg Rock, the high bold shores of Crumple Island and Red Head to the entrance to Eastern Bay where there are several excellent shelters— the Mudhole, the harbor behind Knight Island, and the Cow Yard. All of these are down-east Maine at its best, and they are not the only possibilities. The course would then round Black Head, pass inside the Libby Islands, across Machias Bay, through Cross Island Narrows, and on to Cutler. This course is not difficult to navigate and offers much more interesting country. Nevertheless, the marks are far apart and there are considerable stretches of open water. The tide is probably more significant on this course than on the ones farther inside. Against the tide, even with a fair wind, one seems to be sailing through glue. Beating against the tide is often just a slow way to lose ground.

For a vessel with a mast over about 45 feet high, another course is to run from Schoodic bell to Moulton's Ledge and to the bell on Petit Manan Bar. Note that the buoy on Moulton's Ledge is southwest of the rock so that one passing close to the buoy on a course for the bar would come very close to the rock. Give buoy and rock a wide berth.

The coast between Schoodic Point and the bar looks desolate in the extreme. The harbors are some distance from the course and are either tricky to enter, like Corea, or exposed, like Prospect Harbor. The mouths of Dyer and Gouldsboro Bays are obstructed by ledges and islands. When a heavy sea is running, this is an awesome piece of coast. In thick weather, with a strong and unpredictable tide running, it can be a horror. For instance, the tides here appear to change direction during the ebb or flood. I have noticed the ebb tide still running west at the first of the flood and well around to the southwest a few hours later.

Petit Manan Bar can be an ugly experience with the wind against the tide, especially if there is any sea running. However, under ordinary conditions it presents no problem. From the bar one can cross to Seahorse Rock and join the course described above or run up to Trafton's Island or Cape Split, explore Pleasant and Narraguagus Bays, and thence go out around Seahorse Rock and Great Wass Island. The explorer can then duck in again, either at Channel Rock or through Main Channel Way, and work up through Eastern Bay. This is beautiful country, equaled only by the islands between Isle au Haut and Stonington, and much less frequented. Some of the islands are high and wooded, with white granite shores. Others are bare and grassy, humped and domed. The bottom is uneven, the bay peppered with half-tide rocks and unmarked ledges, but there are enough buoys to guide the newcomer through. There used to be a great many weirs but now almost all are abandoned, leaving the possibility of old weir stakes to keep the lookout alert.

From Eastern Bay one can cross to Roque Island, cross Englishman Bay, traverse Foster Channel, and run up Machias Bay to Cross Island Narrows and out into the Bay of Fundy. This course is a lovely sail on a clear day, an experience to be treasured always, but in the fog it would be a real challenge and not to be undertaken by the inexperienced navigator coming east for the first time.

The inside passage from Petit Manan Bar to Cape Split through Moosabec Reach is limited by the height of the bridge, 39 feet above *high* water. With a 12-foot tide, a boat with a 45-foot mast should be safe enough. The upper parts of Pleasant and Narraguagus Bays are well protected and delightful. Moosabec Reach is well buoyed and easily negotiated, although the tide runs hard by Emms Rock and runs crossways between Shabbit and Hardwood Islands. Roque Island is well worth exploring. The skipper visiting for the first time will probably want to pass through the Thorofare between Great Spruce Island and

Roque Island, possibly stopping at Pattens Cove or Bunker Cove, and then anchor off the great beach for a quick walk ashore. Look in at Lakeman's Harbor, cross Englishman Bay, run up Machias Bay by Starboard Cove and Bucks Harbor, and cross over to Cross Island Narrows and on to Cutler.

On any of the inside courses the tide is important, but the delay occasioned by having to wait out a head tide in this delightful land affords time for exploration of many coves, inlets, and islands on which this *Guide* declines to comment.

Fish Weirs. Among the islands down east where the tide runs hard and the waters are well protected, herring are trapped by means of weirs (pronounced "wares"). A weir consists essentially of a circular fence of brush supported by poles 4 to 6 inches thick driven into the mud. The fence has an opening on the side facing the ebb tide. From this opening one or two or sometimes three leaders or wings run off at a broad angle to each other. Each wing extends a few yards inside the weir.

The herring run up the bay with the tide and on the ebb "settle back" between the wings and work into the trap. At low water a day or so later, when they have "worked the feed out of them," the fish are seined; and if the haul is good, a carrier is called. This big vessel, perhaps 70 feet long, is equipped with a powerful pump. This sucks the fish out of the seine, scales them, and dumps them into the hold. They are lightly salted and rushed to the factory to be canned as sardines. The scales are sold for "pearl essence," for shirt buttons, for making fire-extinguisher foam, and—it is said—for clearing beer.

This method of catching herring is now almost obsolete. There are very few working weirs on the Maine coast, and only a few in New Brunswick. Most of the old weirs have rotted away or been removed although an occasional weir pole broken off by the ice may remain. Airplanes now spot schools of herring and talk the seiners to them.

Salmon Pens. Salmon pens in eastern Maine and New Brunswick are proliferating annually. Aquaculture is becoming as important as fishing and lobstering. Fish farming, however, is an expensive and risky business. First, the leasing of a site requires a great deal of legal work. Local, state, and federal governments must be convinced that endangered species, both above and below water, are not further endangered. The environment must not be unduly polluted. Other businesses—fishing, lobstering, tourism—must not be threatened. Navigation must not be unduly impeded. And permits must be obtained attesting to these considerations. "A new finfish farming enterprise had better have access to upwards of a million dollars in order to get a profitable business under way," writes Frances Koch in *The Working Waterfront,* June 1993.

Then the operation itself is expensive to start and risky to operate. The pens must be constructed and moored securely. Small salmon are purchased from a hatchery at just the right stage in their development, when they can go into salt water. They must be fed regularly and watched for the development of diseases, and their food must be doctored to cure them. If the winter is unusually cold, many are frozen. The nets must be kept clean so the circulation of water is not obstructed lest they suffocate for lack of oxygen or poison themselves with their own waste. Then they must be harvested, transported, processed, and sold at a profit.

At any time a heavy gale or a hurricane may set the whole operation adrift or tear up the nets and let the fish escape. Nevertheless, prospects of a profitable business are great. American, Canadian, and Norwegian companies, some with complicated international corporate structures, are making heavy investments and developing a new industry in a region which has been suffering economically.

Bunker Harbor, Maine (13324). Closer than Winter Harbor to the direct course down east, this is a convenient overnight stop and a pleasant place. It is much neglected because the entrance appears difficult on the chart. However, it is not as bad as it looks.

From Schoodic bell follow the east shore of Schoodic Island. The shore shown in green is exposed at about half-tide and breaks on all but the calmest days. Make the short run to the whistle off Brown Cow and follow the shore respectfully. Pass about halfway between the high pyramidal rock on the point and Bunker Ledge. The rock is indicated by a tiny circle on Chart 13324 and the ledge is shown in green. It almost always breaks and usually shows above the surface. The chart shows 7 feet in this passage, but it is by far the easiest entrance and is commonly used except in very rough weather. You may see kelp at low water.

From the east, leave can 1 well to starboard, make the bold shore westward of it, and run in as above.

Anchorage in the outer harbor is perfectly satisfactory on a quiet night although there will probably be some motion. The inner harbor has been dredged to 10 feet. Favor the east side and keep close to the lobster boats.

There are ledges on the west side. At the Co-op wharf one can buy fuel and lobsters and inquire for a vacant mooring or a chance to lie alongside a lobster boat.

It is a pleasant walk of about a mile to Chipman's Grocery in Birch Harbor. Here also are a laundromat, post office, gift shop, and liquor store.

Birch Harbor, Maine (13324). This is not nearly as good as it looks on the chart. It is open to the south and east, and much of it dries out at low water.

Prospect Harbor, Maine (13324). This is the easiest harbor to make in the fog on this part of the coast. From the west, make Schoodic bell "8S," and follow the sound of the surf on Schoodic Island until you can steer a course for bell 2 on Old Woman. This ledge is high and breaks noisily, but is fringed with perils. Leave the bell to starboard and run for the gong in the harbor entrance. The light on Prospect Harbor Point has no fog signal but in clear weather is a good landmark. It is part of the naval-communications establishment, whose antennas are prominent over the dwelling.

From the east there is a bell on Moulton's Ledge, but notice that a course from Petit Manan Bar to that bell leads very close to the ledge. There is a bell off Cranberry Point. Little Black Ledge almost always breaks and is bold so one can leave it to port and continue for the gong on Clark Ledges.

Anchor off the wharves and out of the channel as far up the harbor as draft permits. Avoid a small ledge (4 feet) about 200 yards northwest of the fish-plant wharf. In the event of really heavy weather, get behind the cannery wharf but beware of a 4-foot rock in here.

The Laughing Lobster, the northerly wharf, is owned by Scott Davis. With his or Don Smith's permission, one can land there in a dinghy. Here are a telephone, water, and a small art gallery. In 1994 Davis plans to supply gasoline and diesel fuel. Don Smith, who also may be found at The Laughing Lobster, has been a resident of Prospect Harbor for many years and is a reliable source of local information.

Near the head of the harbor is Ray's Deli, a sandwich and pizza shop run by a refugee from New York City who declares his Prospect Harbor product to be the equal of anything "Little Italy" in New York can produce.

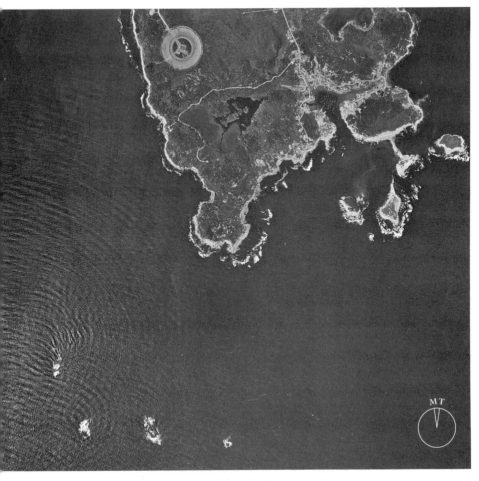

MT

Corea, Maine. Corea is on the right with Western Island, Outer Bar
Island, Bar Island, and Sheep Island protecting it. Observe that after
passing the northwestern point of Western Island, one must head for the
north end of the bar until the harbor opens up clearly and then head in.
The edges of the dredging in the harbor are clear. The ledges in the lower
left are, left to right, Old Woman, Old Man, Big-Black Ledge and Little-
Black Ledge. All are quite bold. *Courtesy James W. Sewall Co.*

About a mile and a half westward at Birch Harbor is a "mini-mart" with a grocery store, variety store, liquor store, restaurant, and post office.

Corea, Maine (13324). Corea is a picturesque harbor, well protected, and nearer Petit Manan Bar than Prospect Harbor. The approach from Schoodic bell is easy. Follow the eastern shore of Schoodic Island, respectfully, and run for bell 2 on Old Woman. Pass between Old Woman and Old Man, both of which are bold and almost always break. Then, if visibility is good, run for Western Island; if it is not, make the gong off Western Island and then run in for the bold shore of the island.

From the western end of Western Island, run for the bar between Bar Island and Youngs Point. Proceed cautiously and watch for bottom. The water is clear, and at low tide you will probably see some of it. When you are up to the end of the trees on Outer Bar Island, head for the big yellow ledge on the east side of the entrance. Favor the eastern side of the channel. Hail the Co-op wharf on the eastern side of the harbor for a vacant mooring. Some of the moorings are designed to hold only lobster crates so be sure you are on to something solid. The area where the lobster boats are moored has been dredged to 8 feet, but the edge of the basin is sharply defined and the flats bare out well before low water. There is scant room to anchor, but the best place appears to be in the southern part of the harbor.

It can be rough in the harbor in a heavy southerly.

The Co-op wharf sells gasoline and diesel fuel but has no water hose.

It is a pleasant walk around the head of the harbor through eastern Maine countryside with views of Gouldsboro Bay to the east, but there is no store within walking distance.

Dyer and Gouldsboro Bays, Maine (13324). These bays are generally neglected by cruising men and hence will be attractive to a few. One experienced explorer's notes on this region read typically, "Ran aground here 8/9/53 and again 8/4/80." "There is a middle ground here." ". . . on 8/9/53 we nicked a small no-account rock about 50 to 100 feet off Lobster Ledge. Hit it again 8/4/80 or a little south of it."

The bays abound in old weirs, half-tide rocks, herons, seals, shorebirds, and mud flats. In the upper reaches of the bays one must proceed with greatest caution as the charts show only some of the rocks and these in approximate locations. Nevertheless, an unhurried day or two around Jetteau Point, Joy Bay, or Smelt Brook might be well worth the time. The pleasure of a cruise may not always be measured by the distance covered.

Note on Petit Manan, Maine (13324). Three factors make Petit Manan a difficult point to round. The tide running east and west along the coast meets tidal currents running in and out of Dyer and Gouldsboro Bays on the west and Pigeon Hill and Narraguagus Bays on the east, producing a confused sea and more or less unpredictable tidal set off the light. Secondly, the bottom between the whistle on Southeast Rock and the light is very uneven, rising steeply in some places from far over 100 feet to within a very short distance of the surface. This makes the depth sounder of somewhat limited value and further disturbs the seas. Finally, when fog shuts down over these waters, all other difficulties are compounded. Although there is a powerful horn on the light which is clearly audible for miles to the eastward, it is often inaudible only a short distance to the west. A low reef extends nearly half a mile offshore from the light. In 1985 one yacht was set inside the nun by the tide and struck without seeing either the nun or the loom of the island. One should plan to pass well outside the nun, and in rough weather, outside the whistle. With a strong wind against the tide, a very unpleasant, confused sea builds up.

Once by the light, one can run for Nash Island whistle, a course on which the tide will affect you little, and on to Cape Split or Trafton's Island. Or go outside to Seahorse Rock, outside Crumple Island, and on to the Mudhole, the Cow Yard, or Roque Island. This course passes between the two red-and-green nuns on Tibbets Rock. If you find one of them in the fog, it will be difficult to tell which one it is, for neither has a number. Whichever it is, give it a wide berth.

Petit Manan Bar. Between Petit Manan Point and the light there is a long bar scattered with boulders. There are two passages across it. The inner passage close to Petit Manan Point is unmarked and beset with dangers. The outer passage, about halfway from Petit Manan Point to the island, is marked with a bell on the western side and a gong on the eastern side. There is about 12 feet of water between them. This is enough water for most yachts, but with the wind against the tide, a very short, unpleasant sea builds up. In a real breeze, it can be dangerous. One man cruising in a powerboat writes:

I have always known about the Petit Manan Bar problem, but on a strong southwest day, perhaps a 25-knot breeze and with a strong ebb against the breeze, I went across it, to my strong regret. I examined it closely first from the east side, looked at the rows of whitecaps in the standing waves just west of the bar, and thought they could be negotiated as they appeared about one foot high with whitecaps. We were tired (always a bad time to make decisions) and did not want to go all the way around the lighthouse. When we crossed the bar, we were all right until we had passed the shallowest spot. Then we met the standing waves. Their height was deceptive and the 1-foot whitecaps were concealing 4-foot troughs between them. The whitecaps were perhaps 30 feet apart measured against our 29-foot boat. While she never buried her bow, being somewhat bluff, she pitched to the extent that the coiled anchor line strapped down on the foredeck was standing straight up in the air and the rowboat on the stern was pitched off its chocks into the cockpit, being tied down only on the inboard side. A thoroughly uncomfortable and undesirable experience. I guess my point is that the waves are so close together as to be deceptive and look smaller than they really are.

Because it is occasionally pleasant to have the rocks and shoals of the coast peopled by figures of the past, the authors venture to repeat here a story told by the late W. Rodman Peabody of Boston, son of Dr. Francis Greenwood Peabody of Harvard University, regarding Petit Manan Bar. Having to do with the nautical adventures of the late President Eliot of Harvard, this story may be put down as a companion piece to another yarn related by Mr. Peabody and included under Northeast Harbor:

I shall always remember another fresh southwest afternoon when, although he was of advanced age, the President had gone cruising with us as far east as Cutler. We were standing across 'Tit Manan Bar heading for the opening which was marked only by a fisherman's buoy. It was blowing freshly and as we approached the Bar there was a heavy rip. My father, whose boat was one which was characterized by a friend as having "rather long spars for a parson," stood in the companionway watching his whipping topmast with grave concern. Forty years of deference, however, left him tongue-tied. From my position by the mainsheet I recognized that he was praying for the best but without much hope. Obviously the topsail ought to have come in. Not a word came from the President, but I saw him glance at my father, take in the situation and give one long and careful look at the whipping spar and then I thought I saw a slight wink from an almost imperturbable face.

We came through whole and the President remarked casually: "If you don't mind taking the helm now, Frank, I think I will take my afternoon nap." No reference to the sea, the wind, or the spars was ever made by either of them, but the younger generation clinging to the weather rail had a thoroughly enjoyable fifteen minutes.

Pigeon Hill, Narraguagus, and Pleasant Bays, Maine (13324). These bays are well worth exploring in a leisurely way, under sail if possible. The shores and islands are thickly wooded and bold, the channels between them deep. The bays are spattered with ledges and half-tide rocks but are threaded with buoyed channels. The tides run strongly but not fiercely, and the sheltered anchorages are largely unfrequented.

Dyer Island, Maine (13324). There are two coves on the west side and one on the east that are picturesque and quiet anchorages for small boats on a calm night. None would be much good in a blow. Apparently Northeast Cove is the best. A correspondent reports 8 feet in the middle and 5 feet near the shores. The bottom is mud. A small ledge makes out from the south side about halfway in. The tide runs about $1/2$ knot through this anchorage. Beware of mosquitoes.

There is a camp for underprivileged children on the island.

Flint Island, Maine (13324). One can anchor with safety in Flint Island Narrows. The tide runs vigorously. Flint Island itself is a delightful island, much like Trafton. Notice the cliff on the southwest corner of Shipstern Island. The rock looks strikingly like the stern of an eighteenth-century warship.

Both Flint Island and Shipstern Island are now owned by the Nature Conservancy. Ospreys and petrels nest here and occasionally a pair of eagles. Several subarctic species of plants are also native to these islands.

Trafton Island, Maine (13324). This island is the nearest good shelter east of Petit Manan and is not hard to find in the fog. Follow the bold eastern shore and anchor on the east side of the cove.

You can carry 6 feet at low water south of the prominent white rock, but not above the little cove beyond it. Most people anchor too far out. The island is occupied in the summer by Mrs. James Rae and her family. If you wish to go ashore, it is appropriate to identify yourself and ask permission. The anchorage is still as lovely as ever and, being on the far side of Petit Manan, may be uncrowded.

The island is wooded, but there are open glades in the woods, patches of birch, and thickets of alder. The woods are grown up enough so that walking is not difficult. The south end of the island is covered with huge boulders of white granite, which lie in confused masses, making caves and passages among them. There is a rocky beach in the southern cove. At high water on a warm day, the swimming on the beach in the northern cove is good. The anchorage is quiet and protected. It is supervised during the absence of the Rae family by the owners: an osprey, a family of seals, and a supercilious shag. It was much used years ago by coasters waiting for a "good chance" down the bay.

Ports Harbor (13324). This cove on the east side of Pleasant Bay above Cape Split is not at once easy to find for the high wooded shores on both sides blend. A course from high, bare Nightcap Island will take you in. There is more water in here than the chart suggests. One could probably anchor with 6 feet in as far as the east end of John White Island. There were no moorings here in 1993 and no signs of activity on the silent shores except for the presence of two large houses, one high on the hill on the north side and one on the south.

Cape Split Harbor, South Addison, Maine (13324). This harbor, properly called Eastern Harbor and widely known as Cape Split, is comparatively easy to make from Petit Manan, and for anyone bound through Moosabec Reach it is a convenient stopping place. From the west, run for the lighted whistle off Nash Island. From Petit Manan the tide runs almost parallel to your course. From Petit Manan Bar be sure to clear the nun off Egg Rock and the beacon on Jordan's Delight Ledge. Jo Leighton's Ground will break in heavy weather. In the fog one would do better to go outside and around Petit Manan light.

From Nash Island whistle pass west of Pot Rock and The Ladle. Both stand high out of water, are well described by their names, and have half-tide rocks east of them which do not break at high water on calm days. From The Ladle it is a short run to the buoys at the entrance to the harbor.

From Seahorse Rock, particularly in poor visibility, run for Black Rock, which is high and bold and on which the surf breaks heavily enough to serve as a fog signal. Keep far away from Flat Island, from which extend frightful ledges. From Black Rock, run for Nash Island whistle. Its peculiar tone, its location, or the sea conditions around it make it heard all over the bay. From the whistle, it is easy to make Pot Rock, The Ladle, and the buoys at the entrance to the harbor. Look to see if there is a beacon on The Ladle. Recently two Coast Guardsmen sent to set up a beacon were chased off the rock and over a 15-foot cliff by two enraged sheep.

Under most conditions the best anchorage is in Otter Cove. Here is a guest mooring maintained by the Moose Neck General Store and several others labeled "Petit Manan Yacht Club." If you must anchor, get as far inshore as possible to keep out of the tide. There is more water here than the chart indicates, but remember that there is a good 12 feet between high and low water—more at new and full moon.

There is an anchorage across the harbor in the western cove, which would be excellent in a northwester but rolly in a southerly. Also one can go up the harbor and anchor off the wharves. There is quite a strong tidal current here which can swing you broadside to a roll coming up the harbor.

When the writer climbed the ladder to the top of the wharf in 1985, he met a local man of whom he asked some questions about store, post office, telephone, and other facilities. After replying in the negative to all inquiries, he volunteered, "This ain't the end of the world, but you can see it from here."

Now, less than half a mile up the road is the excellent Moose Neck General Store run by Mary and Robert Lappeus. They arranged for the mooring in Otter Cove and will provide a ride to the shore with your purchases if business is not pressing. They have a telephone for collect or credit-card calls and will hold mail for yachtsmen as there is no post office in South Addison. They write: "Having been live-aboard cruisers for several years, we understand some of the often unusual needs that cruising folks may have. We will do whatever we can to assist folks and accommodate their needs. Just ask at the store, and if it is at all possible we'll make it happen."

The harbor is now a busy place. Besides the large lobster business, fishermen drag for quahaugs and ship them out by the truckload. There is also a factory for smoking salmon and for smoking and canning mussels, which due to the great range of tide can be gathered in quantity at low water.

A few summer people live in cottages near the shore, and retired people are beginning to find Cape Split, but it is still a fisherman's town. The people are very friendly and helpful. The countryside is beautiful and the walking untroubled by much traffic. If you turn right at the garage, the road soon becomes gravel and leads south through the woods to the shore behind Tibbets (Tabbott's) Island.

The late Mr. Delbert Look of Cape Split was a man of energy and vision. It was he who, back in the thirties, developed the method of transporting lobsters in crates. It had been the practice to dump lobsters into the hold of a smack, which was bulkheaded off and bored with holes to provide circulation. The motion of the vessel killed some lobsters and broke claws off others. However, if the lobsters were crated, there was insufficient circulation of water and they died from lack of oxygen. Mr. Look bought an old schooner, *Verna G.*, lined her hold with cement, and installed powerful pumps so that water could be circulated under pressure. Then he loaded her with crated lobsters and, with pumps running constantly, shipped lobsters to Boston with very low mortality. The method was soon imitated and prevailed until it became cheaper to ship by truck. The wreck of *Verna G.* is rotting on the beach at Cape Split.

During World War II, Delbert's son Oscar was reported missing after Bataan. The father believed firmly that nothing serious had happened to his son and refused to shave his beard in token of it until his son's safe return.

Oscar returned, survived his father, and built the tremendous lobster pound just above the wharf. The project, now managed by others, involves hundreds of thousands of dollars and great risk. The idea is to hold lobsters over a period of low price until the price rises. The difficulty is that lobsters are delicate creatures. If it rains heavily so that the salinity of the water is affected, they will die. If they are fed too much, the food will rot and poison them. If fed too little, they will cannibalize each other. They do not eat with their claws but with very hard "teeth" in the mouth under the proboscis. These teeth can easily grind up another lobster's shell. Of course, if the price fails to rise, the whole scheme is a failure.

Jonesport, Maine (13326). The approach to the town for most masted vessels is from the east. Moosabec Reach is well buoyed starting with the

Anchorages in Eastern Bay, Maine. *Map drawn by Jane Crosen*

bell off Mark Island. The tide runs roughly parallel to the course and the buoys are close together. At Emms Rock the tide runs hard so it is well to have it with you. Off the points there are shelving gravel beaches so keep out close to the line of the buoys.

The usual anchorage is in Sawyer Cove, now dredged to 8 feet and protected by a breakwater apparently consisting of huge steel tubs. When the breakwater was first built, freshwater running into the head of the cove was held there by the breakwater and the concentration of freshwater was raised to the point where it killed lobsters in the lobster cars. Therefore several of the tubs were removed to improve circulation. Nevertheless, the breakwater provides excellent protection.

On the western shore is a wharf and float built by the state as a "marina" with $7^1/_2$ feet near low water. However, there are no facilities whatever. There is a launching ramp north of the wharf.

Farther up the cove is the Jonesport Shipyard run by Patricia and Sune Noreen with laundromat, showers, water, and rental moorings. By 1995 the yard expects to have floats extending into deep water. It might be well to row ashore and investigate, to walk up from the state pier, or to call on a cellular telephone (207) 497-2701. The yard also has facilities for storage and repair.

Gasoline and diesel fuel are available at Look's wharf south of the state wharf, but there is only about 3 feet there at low water and a big ledge next to it. Line up the wharf with the building behind it and come straight in. With a 12-foot run of tide, there should be water for most yachts before half-tide.

Take the second left on the road behind the state wharf. This is Jonesport's main street on which are Church's True Value Hardware store, a well-stocked I.G.A. store, a post office, and a restaurant. Coastal Auto and Diesel across from Church's can help an ailing engine (telephone (207) 497-5603. West of the bridge is a Coast Guard station whence one entering from Canada can call the Custom Office in Lubec at 733-4331. Beyond the Coast Guard station is a grocery and liquor store, and an outdoor telephone is by the fire station.

An alternative to Sawyers Cove is the lobster co-op just east of the bridge. It is a busy commercial wharf, but gasoline, diesel oil, and lobsters are available. There is plenty of water alongside. There is no gangway. You will have to climb a ladder.

Jonesport is a clam and lobster town with little in the way of summer business. Since the herring left the coast and the sardine factories have not been working, it seems less busy than it was and several of the wharves are deserted. However, if you are there on the Fourth of July, it will be lively enough for the annual lobster-boat races are held in the Reach. Competitively minded fishermen and builders of stock fiberglass boats have raised the competition to truly terrifying levels with ultra-light boats and "souped-up" engines.

Moosabec Reach, Maine (13326). Until 1959, Moosabec Reach was the common way for yachts to go east and west along the coast. With the construction of the Beals Island Bridge, with a clearance of 39 feet above high water, only the smaller yachts, sardiners, and old-fashioned gaff-rigged boats can use the Reach. It was reported that in 1986 a yacht with a mast 46^1/2 feet above the water passed under the bridge. The seventh timber from the top of the fender on the bridge pier was showing. The bridge has speeded up the tide by ^{1}/2 knot and formed a powerful back eddy on the north side west of the bridge during the ebb tide. Do your calculating on the bridge in advance. If the tide is running with you, it is difficult to change your mind at the last minute. The tide in the Reach is said to turn about 1^1/2 hours before high and low water.

The approach to Jonesport from the west is easy. Tibbett (usually called "Tabbott") Narrows is buoyed. The tide runs right along the channel, except between Shabbit Island Ledge and Fessenden Ledge. Here there seems to be a cross tide. Allow for it.

The Mudhole, Great Wass Island, Maine (13326). Almost any cruising boat can get into or out of the Mudhole at half-tide or better. It is by all odds the best protection short of Roque Island to one bound east and is a beautiful spot.

From the west, round the high and prominent Freeman Rock and then Channel Rock. The latter is just a star on the chart but it usually breaks and at low water stands up very obviously. In thick weather, after passing Channel Rock, one could make the shore of Great Wass Island south of the entrance and follow the shore in. Hug very close to the southern shore. The rock in the entrance is actually a rather extensive pile of boulders. Continue to favor the southern shore strongly. There is another big rock extending about halfway across from the northern shore well inside. There has for many years been a big winter mooring in the middle of the hole. Take it, or anchor nearby.

The steep shores inside the second ledge are fringed on both sides with

The Mudhole, Great Wass Island, Maine. Observe the wisdom of staying close to the southern shore and anchoring in the middle. *Courtesy James W. Sewall Co.*

mud flats bare at low water. Anchor more or less in the middle, favoring the southern shore. You will not need much scope in this quiet harbor, but sound around the limits of your swing to be sure you will be afloat at low water. Allow for at least 12 feet of tide.

The calm water is disturbed only by the ripple of a seal or shag. An eagle may be perched on a nearby tree. Kingfishers rattle; a blue heron stands in the shallows. The sound of offshore surf filters through the trees and pervades the scene.

A dirt road runs by the head of the cove down toward the end of the island and up to Beals. If the tide is going, leave your dinghy on the north shore on the edge of the deep water. The island now belongs to the

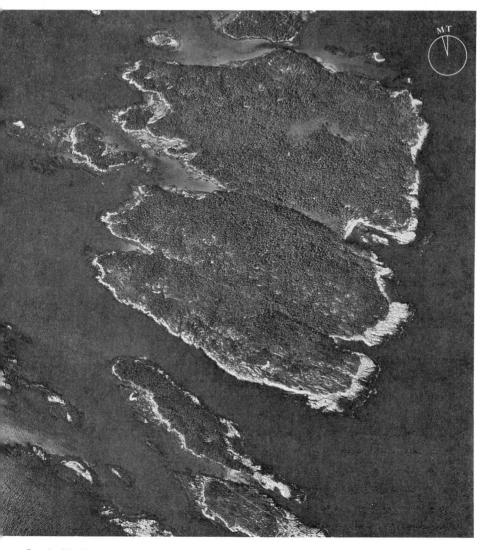

Steele Harbor Island, Maine. At the bottom of the picture is Mistake
Island with Knight Island and the Main Channel Way above it. There is
good anchorage south of the rock west of Mistake Island. At the top right
is the entrance to Head Harbor with Man Island just showing on the right.
Notice the passage north of Black Island at the top. *Courtesy James W.
Sewall Co.*

Nature Conservancy. Visitors are welcome to walk on the road and observe but not disturb the wildlife.

Head Harbor and the Cow Yard, Maine (13326). Head Harbor is just an anteroom to the Cow Yard, and although no doubt acceptable to a coasting schooner, it is no place for a small yacht. To run in here in the fog before a brisk breeze and any considerable sea takes a certain amount of resolution. However, note that the shores of Man Island to starboard are in the main black, and those of Steele Harbor Island to port are white. The shores are fringed by steep rocks hung with black weed, which extend quite far from high-water mark but drop off steeply at low water. Stay in the middle.

Round the high black rock making out from Head Harbor Island to starboard at the entrance to the Cow Yard and anchor as much behind it as you can get. The bottom all through the harbor is good mud.

The cottage near the black rock at the entrance belongs to the owner of Head Harbor Island. Before you explore the shore, it would be well to ask permission. The view from the hill northeast of the anchorage is superb, stretching from Mount Desert to the cliffs of Grand Manan, but it is quite a bushwhack to achieve the summit.

There is an inside passage between Head Harbor Island and Steele Harbor Island close to Crow Point leading out into Eastern Bay. It is strictly a local-knowledge operation, but if you are beset by fog or a foul tide in the Cow Yard, it would be interesting to sound it out in a dinghy. It is a perfectly practicable channel when you know it and is much used by local fishermen.

A visitor to the Cow Yard wrote: "Desolate and beautiful, it is an almost secret place known to few yachtsmen. Most prefer the lovely coves and sandy beach of Roque Island, five miles to the north. At any rate, the usable anchorage is so small that there's barely swinging room for four or five boats. . . .

"It turns out that we have the Cow's Yard to ourselves for only about ten minutes, for in quick succession three other vessels come in through the narrow passage to join us: two 30-foot sloops and a fancy power cruiser."

That's the way it goes, Tom.

Mistake Island Harbor, Maine (13326). This is an easier harbor to make than the Cow Yard. The approach is more sheltered, and the anchorage is quieter and less frequented.

Run up Main Channel Way between Moose Peak and Steele Harbor Island. This is a very deep channel with high white cliffs on the eastern side. The tide runs hard here with swirls and eddies; and with an ebb tide and a southerly wind, it can be rough at the entrance. However, inside, the sea quickly dies down. Round the north end of Knight Island and work up its west side. The rocks shown on the chart are there and they are not alone. There is a rock making off to the southeast of Green Island. Favor the Mistake Island shore and work up close under Mistake Island near the old Coast Guard boathouse. There is a rock which the Coast Guard marked with an iron beacon when Moose Peak was a manned light.

The light was automated in 1970, and in 1982 the Special Forces demolished the dwelling as an exercise. There is still a boardwalk from the old boathouse to the light. It is well to stay on this walk or on the bare rocks because there are swampy places, and also the island supports a variety of rare and delicate plants which grow only under the rugged climatic conditions of this island. The island is now owned by the Nature Conservancy except for the area around the light.

Roque Island, Maine (13326). From Black Head on Head Harbor Island, make the gong on Little Breaking Ledge. You will usually find the sea less, the wind stronger, and the fog less dense as you run up in the lee of Head Harbor Island. There is a bell off Mark Island, whence it is well even in clear weather to take a compass course for the entrance to the Thorofare, for it is a narrow entrance and difficult to pick out. One can, of course, enter through any of the passages among the islands east of Great Spruce Island. The rock between Great Spruce and Anguilla may have less than its charted 7 feet.

Roque Island is both a symbol and a delightful fact. Situated far east of Schoodic and 'Tit Manan, shrouded by Fundy fogs and scoured by icy Fundy tides, it is the goal of many east coast yachtsmen; but few of the rocking-chair sports get by Schoodic. To clear 'Tit Manan and Moose Peak in a fog choking thick and to make a landfall on the back side of Roque is no feat for a mere church-steeple navigator.

Equal to the difficulties of getting to Roque are the delights of being there. Roque Island itself and the islands surrounding it are owned by the Gardner and Monks families. The Gardners and Monkses, like the Forbeses of Naushon, have owned their island for generations. In 1806, Joseph Peabody and a partner, both of Salem, bought the island and built

Roque Island Thorofare, Maine. Entrance from Chandler Bay and Moosabec Reach is at the left. The rock on the south side of the entrance shows clearly and to the east is Bunker Cove with the anchorages under the cliff. Patten Cove extends northward. The shoal in the middle of the Thorofare shows as a faint cloud. *Courtesy James W. Sewall Co.*

several vessels near the tidal mill dam at the head of Shorey Cove. In 1864, Peabody's daughter Catherine bought the shares of the other owners and with her husband, John L. Gardner, took title to the entire island. Except for the years 1870 to 1882, when it was owned by Longfellows and Shoreys, it has been in the family ever since. Subsequent generations have added the neighboring islands and have preserved the group as nearly as possible in a natural state. Over the last five years the present owners have embarked on an ambitious conservation program in cooperation with public and private entities. They have catalogued a number of rare flora (some not found elsewhere in Maine), and are dedicated to preserving the environment as a natural habitat for migratory and resident birds. A number of eagle and osprey nests have been successfully encouraged. Preservation of archaeological sites, particularly relating to the Penobscot Indians, is also being undertaken. For these reasons, on the advice of experts, the owners request that visitors restrict their landings to the north end of the Great Beach and not advance inland on either Roque or on any of the outer islands in the archipelago. Signs have been strategically posted and should be carefully read.

Of course the great white beach is the central feature at Roque. The sand is soft and fine and in certain parts of it are found large white clams, the pursuit of which, while not always productive, is excellent exercise. In the middle of a sunny summer day, the water is warm enough for a brief ceremonial dip, but few will stay in very long.

Anchorage off the beach is usually satisfactory on a quiet night, but if there is a sea outside, one may roll a bit. There is a cove on the south end of the beach that offers fair protection. The charted depth is about right. However, the two best anchorages are Bunker Cove at the west end of the Thorofare, and Lakeman's Harbor between Lakeman Island and Roque.

Bunker Cove. There is excellent anchorage just inside the western entrance to the Thorofare in the mouth of Bunker Cove, but there is room for only two or three boats. The entrance to the Thorofare is not easy to see from Mark Island or the end of Moosabec Reach, but it will open up as you approach. The shores are quite bold and the surf makes ample noise to warn you of your approach.

Round the end of Little Spruce Island, keeping far enough off to avoid the 3-foot spot on which many a tired skipper has stubbed his toe at the end of a long day. Bunker Cove opens up to starboard, looking deceptively quiet and attractive, especially at high water. However, it is only about 3 feet deep at low water. If you are the first one in, go close under the cliff on the easterly side of the cove, just far enough in to get out of the tide. If you are second in, you may be able to get your anchor down on the edge of the mud without getting into the shoal water. Those who come later either ground on the mud at low water or anchor on the edge of the channel where the bottom slopes down steeply in a gravelly bank. It is hard to get a bite in the gravel and you will swing with the tide. However, many yachts so admire the beauty of the spot that they stay anyway. There are several acceptable alternatives.

Patten Cove. This cove lies north of the entrance to the Thorofare. Follow the eastern shore just outside the line of lobster traps. Anchor when the inner end of the islet protecting the cove bears WNW. The bottom is mud. There is almost no current and the surroundings are lovely.

Roque Island Thorofare. This is a comparatively shallow passage leading to Roque Island Harbor and the beach. There has been a good deal of controversy about a rock in the middle of the passage marked on Chart 13326 as "Rep." It certainly has been reported and there can be no doubt that yachts have bumped over it. A sardine-boat skipper told the writer that there is a bar with about 6 feet between the little island off Roque and Great Spruce Island and that he does not use the passage at extreme low water.

The late Mr. Orin Leach of West Southport, Maine, sent the writer a fathometer tracing of his passage of the Thorofare at 2 hours and 45 minutes after low water. It shows a level hard mud or gravel bottom at 14 feet. About 75 yards to the west of where it begins to deepen, a sharp rock rears up to exactly 14 feet, the same level as the gravel bar. So the rock definitely *is* there, but the part of it that Mr. Leach went over is no shoaler than the controlling depth in the passage.

Mr. Ken Rich, formerly caretaker on Roque Island, wrote, "As for the rock in the Thorofare, I'll only say that in ten years I have not found it. I have tacked through in *Advent* at low water a good many times. I have looked, but it has eluded me."

Roque Island Harbor. The most attractive anchorage here, of course, is off the beach. The owners ask that visitors use only the north end of the beach and obey instructions on the prominent signs. In spite of the cold water, the swimming is good.

Note the 7-foot spot between Double Shot and Great Spruce Islands. This often breaks at low water in rough weather.

One yachtsman, having made his difficult way at last to Roque Island, saw several boats anchored in the cove off the south end of the beach and headed that way. People in an anchored powerboat gestured, but he could see nothing about which to be alarmed. After he had anchored near the powerboat, the people aboard explained that there was an old weir off the point at the south end of the beach. They referred to the old stakes as "the little people," and as they watched the tide ebb, the little people showed their heads in considerable numbers. In the case of this weir, one of the poles inside the weir used to show at high water and was thus most deceptive. Give the little people plenty of room. They were still present in 1993.

Lakeman Harbor. In entering, move very cautiously. The ledges, particularly those on the Roque Island shore, run far out at high water. A correspondent writes:

> We stayed between one hundred and one hundred fifty feet from the high-water mark on the Lakeman's Island side of the entrance. The depth sounder gave us 20 feet all the way in. It was just above half-tide. Less than half the ledge which runs out from the north side was showing.

One can carry 6 feet at low water as far as the white boulder with a cleft on the Roque Island shore.

Inside, the best water seems to favor the western shore slightly. A shoal-draft boat could find good protection on the eastern side of the harbor.

For many years there was a colony of fishermen from Jonesport on Lakeman Island. The Carver family maintained a tattered logbook, a photostat of which is now in the possession of the Cruising Club of America, in which visitors registered, wrote comments, and drew sketches. It is a most interesting memorial, extending over several generations.

Shorey Cove. This cove on the north side of Roque Island is little used as it is out of the usual course of coastwise cruisers. For the leisurely, it has much to recommend it. The scenery, although still dramatic, is gentler than that on the south side of the island. The cove is well protected from the usual southwest wind and from the roll coming up the bay from outside. A hard northerly could raise a chop, but one could creep under one point or the other to avoid a northeasterly or north-westerly. The holding ground is good, there is little tidal current, and there is plenty of room to swing.

On the west side of the cove stand the wharf, homes, and farm buildings of the owners, who value their privacy. There are no facilities ashore whatsoever for visitors.

The authors of this *Guide* have been cursed on many accounts, one of the most valid of which is that they have "spoiled" Roque Island with their unbounded enthusiasm for it. We regret it if it be true, but we reply that it will not be spoiled by considerate and appreciative visitors. It can be spoiled, as any place in the world can be spoiled, by selfish, careless, and lazy people who litter the shores, pollute the water, burn the woods, and assault the sensitivities of others. We believe that if you are seaman enough to bring a boat to Roque, you are sportsman and gentleman enough to preserve it.

The curious may wonder at the name of Halifax Island. In February 1775 the schooner *Halifax*, sent to intercept vessels smuggling ammunition to the American Army, struck the rock south of the island and broke up. Her guns were salvaged by the people of Machias and were in the hold of *Margueritta* when she was captured by the O'Briens and Foster in June. A more complete account of the incident can be found in *Coastal Maine: A Maritime History*.

At Roque Bluffs there is a substantial wharf maintained by the owners of Roque Island. Yachtsmen are welcome to use it, but there are no supplies or facilities here and little protection.

Machias Bay, Maine (13326 304). This bay would be crowded with yachts all summer if it lay farther to the westward. The shores are high, for the most part bold, and heavily wooded. The islands are dramatic. The harbors are well protected. The bay is sheltered from the sea by the bulk of Cross Island and the long ridge of Libby Islands. Dangers are well marked. The bay abounds in wildlife, from mackerel and codfish to ospreys and eagles. Furthermore, it is frequently clear in the bay when the fog hangs wetly outside.

However, most of those yachtsmen who do see the bay see it only in crossing from Foster Channel to Cross Island Narrows. On this run, notice Stone Island, a lovely wooded, cliffy island, on which ospreys nest.

The drawbridge above Machiasport has been replaced with a fixed bridge. It has a vertical clearance of 25 feet above high water.

Expect to find the can north of Cross Island much farther off the island than it appears.

Speaking generally, it is better to go inside of Cross Island through the Narrows than it is to go outside. The wind is likely to be light outside and the sea rough. The tide runs hard both inside and outside and there is less likely to be fog inside.

Foster Channel is a little difficult to pick out because all the islands are grassy, with occasional big domes of black rock. Foster Island has a white house and a barn on it and Scabby Island has the highest dome. Ram Island is peaked.

Beware of a rock north of Scabby Island. It is about 3 feet underwater at low tide. The writer spoke with a man who had sounded it with an oar. If you can see Libby Island Light through Foster Channel, you will be clear of the rock.

Machias Bay was the site of the first naval battle of the American Revolution, fought in June 1775.

Starboard Cove, Machias Bay, Maine (13326). For anyone seeking a quiet overnight anchorage in calm weather, not far from the alongshore course, this is a good spot. There is little shelter in northeast or easterly winds. But the convenient cove between Starboard Island and the mainland is perfectly protected by a bar until two hours from high water. Then a sea might roll in from the south, but the ground is so broken in that direction that it would not be dangerous in the summer.

North of Starboard Island is a large salmon pen. Just inside the point of Starboard Island is an old weir, and there is another across from it. Beware of old stakes. Anchor outside the 5-foot spot on Chart 13326 as far to the south and east as you can get.

There is no gasoline or store at Starboard.

Starboard Creek dries out at low water. It can then be forded by the few summer residents living at Point of Main, whence there is a gorgeous view on a clear day.

Anyone visiting Starboard Cove should not fail to go ashore to the impressive hogback shown on the chart at the northeast shore of the creek. It is heaped high with small pebbles of jasper, "a compact, opaque, often highly colored, cryptocrystalline variety of quartz, commonly used in decorative carvings." To the layman, jasper is a stone of extraordinary smoothness.

Richard and Nettie Pettegrow have a boatyard at Starboard with the only marine railway in Washington County.

Bucks Harbor, Maine (13326). In anything but a fresh easterly, Bucks Harbor is well protected. Bucks Head is high and easily recognized. The harbor is occupied by lobster boats, a number of local yachts on moorings, and several larger fishing vessels. Favor the southern side. Land at the large lobster pound on the south side and inquire of Harbormaster

Dana Urquhart for a mooring. Gasoline and diesel oil are available, but only limited fresh water and no ice. There is a small store on the road near the head of the harbor.

This appears to be a small, low-key community, busy about its own constructive business and making little obvious effort to attract visiting yachtsmen. Therefore, some will find it a very pleasant atmosphere.

Machiasport, Maine (13326). This used to be an important lumber port and shipbuilding center but now has only a cannery and a small boatyard. There is plenty of water in the Machias River for most yachts to get to Machiasport, but above the town is a fixed bridge and the river is badly silted up.

Machias, Maine (13326). This is an important distribution center for Washington County. Almost anything you may need to buy is available here, but you will have to get to it by car from Jonesport, Roque Bluffs, Machiasport, or Cutler. There is a hospital at Machias and an outpost of the University of Maine.

The most interesting thing about Machias is its history.

The Battle of Machias

In May 1775, Admiral Graves in Boston, besieged by American minutemen and militia, gave Ichabod Jones permission to carry cargoes of food and supplies home to Machias in his sloops *Polly* and *Unity* on condition that he return with cargoes of firewood and lumber with which to build barracks for General Gage's soldiers. To be sure that Jones returned as agreed, he sent to convoy Jones the armed schooner *Margueritta* under Midshipman Moore and, second in command, Midshipman Stillingfleet.

Many citizens of Machias, inflamed by the news of Concord and Lexington, objected strongly to sending lumber to Boston to house British soldiers, yet the supplies aboard the sloops were badly needed in Machias. A special town meeting voted by a narrow margin to accept the supplies and send the lumber, but Jones refused credit to those who had voted against him, further inflaming the patriotic element.

The Sons of Liberty, led by Benjamin Foster and the fiery Jerry O'Brien, resolved to seize Moore, Stillingfleet, and Jones in church and to capture *Margueritta* and the two sloops. The three in church, seeing the Sons approaching armed with pitchforks, axes, and a few muskets, leaped out a window and fled, Jones to the woods and the other two aboard *Margueritta*. After mutual threats and some firing at each other across the water during the night, Moore made sail in the morning and headed for Boston, pursued by O'Brien in *Unity* and Foster in *Falmouth Packet*. Near the head of Machias Bay *Margueritta* jibed and broke her boom and gaff. Moore seized the boom and gaff from an anchored sloop and also her skipper, Captain Avery. *Margueritta* cut away her boats and fired muskets and swivels at her pursuers, but as O'Brien came up on her port quarter, a musket shot from *Unity* killed her helmsman and she swung into the wind. *Unity*'s bowsprit drove through her mainsail, and the Sons, led by John O'Brien, Jerry's brother, swarmed aboard at the same time that Foster and *Falmouth Packet*'s crew boarded over the starboard bow. Moore was mortally wounded, Stillingfleet and the British crew fled below, and the first naval battle of the Revolution was over with the loss of four of *Margueritta*'s crew, one of whom was the unfortunate Captain Avery.

A fuller and more colorful account of the battle and attendant circumstances can be found in *Coastal Maine: A Maritime History* (W. W. Norton & Co., New York, 1992).

Northwest Harbor, Cross Island. In anything but really heavy weather, there is good shelter just inside Northwest Head off a steep stony beach. The entrance to the cove is occupied but not obstructed by a large raft of salmon pens, including a floating house. There is ample room to anchor inside the pens, and they might provide some protection in a northwest breeze. If you can stand the unromantic prospect of the salmon pens, this is a snug and pretty spot.

Cross Island Narrows, Maine (13327). The argument has almost always favored going through the Narrows rather than out around Cross Island. It is harder to buck an ebb tide in the Bay of Fundy than it is in Machias Bay, and the wind is likely to leave you slopping around off the cliffs in a confused sea. With a fair tide, you get a fine boost through the Narrows, and the breeze will be better inside. In the fog, Machias Bay is often clear when it is thick outside and there is likely to be a scale-up in the Narrows. If you are beating west with a fair tide, it might be better to stay outside and get a powerful lift to windward down Grand Manan

Channel. However, stand well off the cliffs to avoid a soft spot that often develops there.

Bound east from Foster Channel, look for can 7 at the entrance to the Narrows much farther off Cross Island than you expect. You will find it nearly in range of the powerhouse on Thornton's Point. It usually appears more white than green, as the gulls and shags seem to give it special attention.

The usual course is north of Mink Island. However, there may be less tide south of the island. The wind in Northeast Harbor may be fluky, but it seems to draw across the channel very nicely. One can usually fetch through either way.

There is good anchorage in Northeast Harbor. Work as far south as your draft will permit and get out of the tide. Do not let the children row around here in the pram. If they get in the tide near Mink Island, you may have a rescue operation in hand.

The anchorage off the old Coast Guard station, now occupied by a detachment from the Outward Bound School, is less sheltered but perfectly satisfactory.

There are several moorings here in the summer for pulling boats, probably not designed to hold a cruising yacht. If the Hurricane Island base is occupied, they can provide a map of the trails leading to the impressive cliffs on the south coast and to the lookout tower at the summit, whence the view is breathtaking.

The radio towers on Thornton Point can no longer be ignored. There are twenty-six of them. Almost 1,000 feet in the air, they spread a net of copper wire, so that someone in Washington can talk to someone underwater in a submarine in the North Sea. If the station is broadcasting when you go by, your loran will probably turn belly up and die. However, it will recover outside Old Man or in Machias Bay.

It is pleasant to remember Thornton Point heavily wooded, and to recall the feeling that as one passed through Cross Island Narrows, one was way down east in primitive surroundings and a long way from civilization.

On emerging from the Narrows and passing the bell, one enters Grand Manan Channel, which is part of the Bay of Fundy. The character of the coast changes abruptly. The shore consists of steep, bold, black cliffs, in places covered with greenish lichen. There are no off-lying islands. The seas roll up from the south, troubled by tides. On several occasions the writer has left the mild sunny waters of Machias Bay with a pleasant southwest breeze, and, in the few minutes it took to traverse Cross Island Narrows, found himself rolling almost becalmed in a confused chop with a graying sky, the feel of fog in the air, and the sea breaking heavily on the forsaken cliffs of the Old Man. It is a short run to Cutler.

Cutler, Maine (13327). This is the first harbor in the Bay of Fundy, the best shelter between Machias Bay and Passamaquoddy Bay, and a good place from which to take off for Grand Manan, Head Harbor, or Saint John. Yachts returning from Canada often make Cutler as their first American port. On almost any summer night, you are likely to see several American or Canadian yachts in here.

Coming from the west in clear weather one can follow the shore up from Cape Wash. In thick weather this is difficult, for the shore is deeply indented and there are several shoal spots, outcrops, and half-tide rocks. In the fog, one can steer a compass course of about east magnetic from outside Cape Wash and count on hearing the horn on Little River Island when it comes out by Western Head.

From the east the light is not visible or audible until one is by Long Point. One can follow the 20-fathom curve down the American shore of Grand Manan Channel, around Long Point, and right in to the bell buoy off Cutler Harbor. There is sometimes a very uncomfortable tide rip off Long Point.

The usual entrance to Cutler is north of Little River Island. There is an old weir west of nun 2 which projects beyond, south of, the nun. There is a dead spot off the light in the usual southwester in which one can slat about uncomfortably for quite a while. The entrance south of the island is likely to afford a better breeze. It is shoal, but at least 6 feet can be carried through. Inside the harbor are three old weirs and a raft of salmon pens on the south side. As soon as you are by the island, swing into the middle of the harbor.

Inquire at the Little River Lobster Co. located at the wharf beyond the big black ledge on the north side for the availability of a mooring. Or you can anchor west of a line from the wharf to the farmhouse across the harbor. East of this line, the holding ground is poor. Shoals less than 6 feet at low water have been reported off the wharf. In the event of a really heavy easterly or a hurricane, one can go far up the harbor between two great boulders and lie in the mud at low water.

Gasoline and diesel fuel are available at Little River Lobster run by Dean and Susan Crosman, but water is not because some thoughtless cruising people, perhaps accustomed to unlimited supplies to the west-ward, have abused the privilege.

The best place to land in a dinghy is either at Little River Lobster or at a float alongside a wharf in front of a large white building near the east side of the cove on the north side of the harbor. There is no gangway at either float so you will have to climb a ladder. One can avoid the ladder by landing on the launching ramp east of Little River Lobster behind a big black ledge. At the Little River Lobster wharf there is a line on a derrick for hoisting lobster crates, convenient for lowering whatever you are carrying.

East of the Little River Lobster wharf on the road is the Village Market run by Bill and Debbie Holmes. They carry a good selection of groceries, some meats, wine and beer, dairy products, and ice. They also serve light lunches. There is an outdoor telephone on the west side of the store. Ask at the store about a well-marked trail to Western Head, now owned by the Maine Coast Heritage Trust.

Up the hill beyond the flagpole and the bell from Little River Light is the post office and the Cutler General Store, which carries some gro-ceries, cold cuts, and a wide variety of other wares including books, "gifts," and T-shirts.

Up the road to the west of the store is Little River Lodge. They offer bed and breakfast and, for yachtsmen, showers.

Cutler is an active lobstering town and in a good year does well seining herring. The salmon pens are a developing resource. Those in the harbor in 1993 were owned by a Norwegian company employing local people to care for the fish. The salmon are shipped directly to Europe. You can't buy a salmon in Cutler although thousands are splashing in the pens.

A correspondent writes: "Boatbuilder, fisherman, machinist, Norbert Lemieux knows all and can fix anything and everything. His small shop, Little River Boat Yard, about a mile up the road from the fish piers is a living monument to those gifted people who just don't know that certain things can't be done and then proceed to accomplish everything in record time and start searching for more challenging tasks."

Some income in Cutler is derived from the radio base, and summer people are coming in small numbers. An increasing number of people interested in ecology and bird life are making Cutler a base.

Machias Seal Island (13327). This bare rock belongs to the United States but the Canadians operate the lighthouse on it. It is interesting to the navigator principally as a good place to keep away from as there are frightful shoals and tide rips to the east and northeast. To the ornithologist, however, Machias Seal Island is magnetic. A visitor writes:

> Although our interest in birds is fairly casual, we were fascinated by the bird life there—the place is jammed! A steady stream of puffins returning with small fish in their great beaks and making a complete low circle before landing on the rocks and disappearing in the crevices. Razorbills, with their black backs, white fronts, and upright stance, looking like penguins. Terns, both common and arctic, trying to drive us off, while we tried to avoid stepping on the young. Add to this the shore birds, feeding on the wave-washed rocks, and a sprinkling of land birds—swallows were nesting under the porch steps to the keeper's house. There are several observation blinds. The reason for the request that visitors keep to established paths is obvious—there are nests and eggs even on the paths. Pets are forbidden for equally obvious reasons.

Indeed, the island has proved so fascinating to bird-watchers that heavily loaded excursion boats make frequent visits, in addition to yachts which stop by occasionally. A quota has been established limiting the number of people allowed to land on the island each day. As the regular excursion boats use most of the quota, the visiting yacht would do well to call ahead by radio.

Do not try to land on the island in anything less seaworthy than a stout skiff, dory, or peapod. Even in calm weather, there is a surge, and the tide runs hard. If landing conditions are difficult, one can still see a great many birds by sailing around the island. Beware of the rock off the northeast corner of the long ledge extending to the northeast.

Grand Manan Channel, Maine (13327). This is a deep and tide-scoured channel between sheer cliffs. There are almost no off-lying dangers on either side, except Sail Rock and Morton Ledge, and there is a good fog signal at each side of the eastern end. The tide runs from 2 to 3 knots and even faster at times. Therefore, it is scarcely worthwhile beating against it. However, as the turn of the tide approaches, back eddies begin to build under both shores, and it is possible to creep along close to the cliffs with a favorable current an hour or two before it turns in the channel.

The time of the moon makes a great deal of difference in the strength of the tidal current and in the duration of slack water. At the time of full moon and new moon, the tide will run at a full 3 knots, with no more than a half hour of slack between tides. At first quarter and last quarter, the tide may run no more than half as hard, with as much as an hour to an hour and a quarter of reasonably slack water.

An experienced correspondent from New Brunswick writes: "When crossing Grand Manan Channel, the tide allowance can be as high as 3+, but the rate is available in the Atlantic Coast tide tables under 'Grand Manan Channel' and gives time of turning and maximum flow. I would never venture across in a fog without consulting it, as there is a difference of from 1 knot to well over 3 from neap to spring tides."

Beware of this stretch of water in a small boat with a heavy southwester against an ebb tide. It can get dangerous quite quickly, and refuges are not as close as they are among the islands to the westward.

In the fog, navigation is fairly simple because of the steep shores and the fog signals, but be alert for sardiners heading for the factories at Eastport and Lubec. They are big, heavy vessels and can move at a rate to inspire caution in any yachtsman.

A radar reflector is a sensible if not a necessary precaution, as these vessels rely heavily on radar to enable them to keep moving at top speed in thick weather. It is vital to them that they get their fish to the factory as fresh as possible.

Be particularly careful of heavy logs and other debris adrift in this channel. The tide seems to keep it on the move.

Indians from Passamaquoddy Bay were accustomed to paddle down Grand Manan Channel on an ebb tide during the morning calm and cut sweet grass behind Western Head, where it grows abundantly. Then, with a spruce tree in the bow and flood tide under them, they sailed back in the afternoon. A fisherman hauling a trawl one blowy day beheld a spruce tree bearing down on him with a great collar of foam below it, nearly obscuring the bow of the canoe in which it stood. The Indian, unable to go forward without swamping the light craft and unable to bring her to the wind with his sail plan so far forward, hunched in the stern, clutching his paddle and bailing for his life. As he flashed past, he waved his bail dish and with the gift for brief and pithy expression for which his people are noted, shouted, "Too much bush!"

Many a racing yachtsman lugging a spinnaker in a squall may have felt that he was carrying "too much bush."

Haycock Harbor taken near low water, this picture shows very well the channel into the tiny anchorage. Two boats are moored under the cliff. On the right is Balch Head and the west side of Bailey's Mistake. *Courtesy James W. Sewall Co.*

There is no shelter on the Canadian side of the channel and only two possible shelters on the American side: Haycock Harbor and Bailey's Mistake.

Haycock Harbor, Maine (13327). This shelter is about 6 miles from West Quoddy Head. The harbor itself is exposed to the south, but there is a small gut leading out of the west side of it opening into a small basin with a few wharves and farmhouses.

The harbor is hard to pick out from offshore, but is marked by a sort of "double-shot" headland on its east side. Enter halfway between the "double-shot" headland and the one to the west on a northerly course and favor the north and northwest shore until you can see straight up the gut for several hundred yards to where it turns into the basin. Sighting straight up the gut, turn west and place the south end of a small gravel beach dead astern. There is a mess of bad boulders covered by only 1 foot of water at low tide before you reach the bar.

If you can clear the boulders, you can make it; but don't forget to allow for the ground swell if any if running. The tide runs strongly over the bar, but there is more water than over the boulders. The only spot inside where there is more than 2 feet of water at low tide is close under the cliffs on the north side. It's a 9-foot hole at low water, but you'll need a bow-and-stern line to keep your keel fitted into it. This is a pleasant and remote little eel rut, where you will not be disturbed by any sounds except the surf on the ledges outside. Those who like to go into small unmarked places should not miss it if the tides are right.

This harbor is a possible refuge in case one is caught by an adverse tide, but it is interesting principally as an example of what pleasure a thorough exploration can yield. The sketch below was made in August 1980 by the late Mr. Alan C. Bemis after several visits over a number of previous years and was amended by another visit in 1982. Some of the landmarks may have changed by the time you read this, but most of them remain.

On 8/2/80 *Cirrus* . . . entered Haycock on the afternoon high tide. No trouble though we saw bottom by being too close to N shore at point A. We found Almon Farmer fussing with his lobster boat. He suggested we tie alongside a big weir boat that was at C. We did, but then the owner showed up to go out. He was very friendly too and suggested we drop a hook farther north to haul us

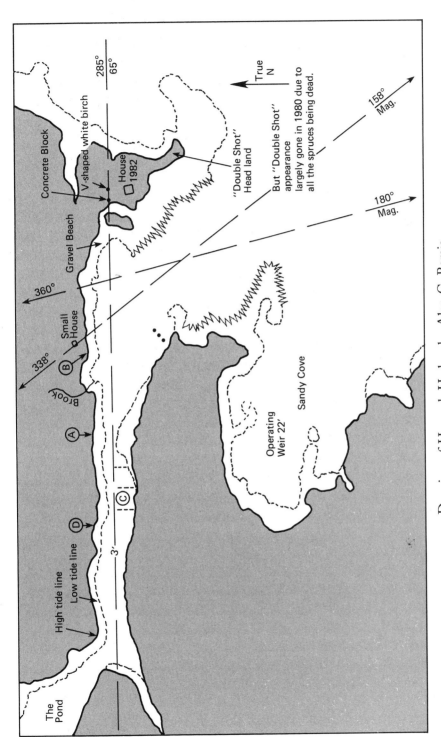

Drawing of Haycock Harbor by Alan C. Bemis.

into deeper water. Only 5′ at C at low tide. Only place with more than 6′ at low tide is half way between the area of the stakes and the N shore. There is 8′ or 9′ there. The cliff is very steep and the broken rock below goes down very steeply, too. Bow & stern anchors are necessary when tide turns, or careful readjustment at high tide.

At low tide we rowed out to outer harbor. The ledges are terrifying! They are shown on my chart as sharp jagged lines. *Very* important to avoid them when covered. Enter on the 360° magnetic line until you intersect the 338° line and head for the small house. Then transfer to the 285° line with the concrete block in the middle of the gravel beach astern.

The bottom and steep walls of the harbor from A to B are *very* coarse gravel and broken rock—mostly broken *rock*. From A to B the channel is only 30′ to 50′ wide and 6″ to a foot deep at low tide. Shoalest area is off where the little brook comes in.

On 7/30/82 we entered Haycock with quite a big SW sea running, real messy outside. Before we passed "Double Shot Headland," the seas calmed down, and by the time we turned to heading 285° the water was absolutely flat. We grounded on rocky bottom by getting too close to the N shore between "Brook Cove" and point A. This was 3¹/₂ hours after low tide. If we had kept a little farther S, we could have got in, but we bumped along gently from rock to rock for ¹/₂ hour before we got into deeper water at A and then on in. Best not to try it until 2 hrs. before H.T. (Tides were neap on 7/30/82.)

Thomas Cabot tells of how he anchored his 50-foot yawl *Avelinda* in the slot off the cliff in Haycock Harbor. She swung in the turning tide and was set down on the ebb with her skeg in a cleft in the cliff. To hold her upright as the tide fell, they rigged lines from her masthead to tall spruce trees ashore. That night, when the tide came, in the dark and rain they could not remember to which trees they had tied the lines. "All hands spent the next two hours climbing like monkeys among the branches and groping for knots in the heavy rain," writes Mr. Cabot. The whole story and much more is told in Cabot's book, *Avelinda* (The Island Institute, Rockland, Me., 1991).

The writer will be delighted to receive detailed accounts of seldom visited harbors such as this.

Bailey's Mistake, Maine (13327). Marked by a whistle and a can buoy, the harbor is easy to make but, except on a quiet night, likely to be rolly. Leave the can, the ledges, and an old weir to port. Anchor under the high land on the western side of the harbor where Chart 13327 shows 15 feet. Beware of old weir stakes.

On the high water, it is possible to penetrate far up into the northwestern cove, but this dries out at low water.

The picturesque name of this harbor refers to an error in judgment on the part of one Captain Bailey, skipper of a four-masted coaster bound for Lubec before the middle of the last century. He miscalculated the tide, perhaps, and instead of rounding West Quoddy Head and running into Quoddy Roads, he rounded Eastern Head and struck the ledges off Balch's Head. The legend goes that he and his crew were so pleased with the town and surroundings when the fog lifted that they built houses from the schooner's cargo and settled there. The Portland *Press Herald* for September 30, 1966, in commenting on this happy ending, observes: "But lumber to Lubec in the 1830s? Who said coals to Newcastle?"

An earlier shipwreck was said to have been behind the first settlement. Captain Congdon, skipper of a privateer in the War of 1812, ran his vessel ashore here to prevent her seizure by the British. After the war he returned with his bride, settled, and established a profitable lumber mill. He was frozen to death with his two oxen in a blizzard in 1822 on the road to Lubec.

Sail Rock, Maine (13327). The easternmost point in the United States, Sail Rock is appropriately named. It is marked by a flashing whistle to the southeast. Here the ebb tide running out of Quoddy Roads meets the tide running southwest down the channel and creates quite a bobble. To approach it in the fog is unnerving, for it sounds like surf breaking on the shore. As you approach, dimly looming through the fog appears a line of breakers. Sailing vessels do well to stand well clear of the rock in light weather, for the tide could set a vessel ashore here.

One often finds a good breeze under Quoddy Head when it is calm outside.

Chapter XIII

Grand Manan

Everything about Grand Manan was magnificent—
a very moving experience.

A reader of the Guide

Although not a desperate seafaring adventure, the voyage to Grand Manan can be exciting in itself, and it brings with it all the fun of "going foreign." Foreign charts, foreign money, a different cast to the language, different time (Atlantic), Customs formalities, and the Canadian flag at the starboard spreader give the trip glamour, especially if you are going for the first time.

Preparation. No notice need be given to American Customs of your departure. However, it helps to have positive identification for each member of your crew in anticipation of your return. New and expensive foreign items like cameras might be registered, or a bill of sale by an American firm provided. Very seldom, however, is a yacht questioned, and the writer has often checked in by telephone.

The navigator should have Canadian Charts 4340 and 4342 and the Canadian Tide and Current Tables. The Canadian *Coast Pilot, Nova Scotia SE Coast and Bay of Fundy,* is very helpful. These can be obtained from the Hydrographic Chart Distribution Office, Department of Fisheries and Oceans, 1675 Russell Road, P.O. Box 8080, Ottawa, Ontario, CANADA KIG 3H6, telephone (613) 998 4931, fax (613) 998 1217. They will take Visa or MasterCard. Write for the *Catalogue of Nautical*

Charts, Sailing Directions and Tidal Information, order specifically what you want, and include payment, with due regard for the exchange rate. This should be done well in advance, as delays are frequent and the materials are indispensable.

Canadian charts are also available at a number of United States chart outlets such as Chase-Leavitt's Chart Room on Dana Street in Portland and L. J. Harri, Nautical Booksellers, 120 Lewis Wharf, Boston, MA 02110, telephone (800) 242-3352, fax (617) 248-5855. See Chapter II.

The easiest way to make the crossing is to leave Cutler on the first of the flood tide and steer for the bold west shore of the island south of Dark Harbour. The only available chart showing both Cutler and Dark Harbour is Canadian 4011. The tide will vary in strength with the phase of the moon, but something like 1^1/$_2$ to 2 knots is about right. It isn't very important anyway, because your course converges with a bold shore and you can't very well miss the whole island. If the weather is clear, there is nothing to be concerned about. If it is thick, beware of sardiners, keep the radar reflector in evidence, and watch the clock. When time runs out, stop and listen for surf. Expect to see the top of the cliff first, surprisingly high off the water. On a sunny day with a low fog, the tops of the cliffs will appear clearly long before the base is visible.

When you make the shore, follow it up at a reasonable distance offshore. There are occasional irregularities, so don't get in too close. If the fathometer reads over 15 fathoms, you are surely safe.

Dark Harbour. This is a dramatic and tempting spot, but the cautious skipper will have no trouble in resisting the temptation. Between a rocky bar, bare at high water, and the cliffs is a deep lagoon. There is a low place in the bar over which a small torrent pours into the sea. As the tide rises in Grand Manan Channel, it reaches the level of the water in the lagoon. At this moment there is said to be 6 feet over the bar so one can nip in. However, at the time of high water when the water is deepest in the entrance, the current is still running in vigorously. Inside is a perfectly protected lagoon with depths up to 10 fathoms and several moorings. Once inside, however, you may have to stay a while. A heavy sea outside makes the gap impassable, and the heavy current running in when the water is the deepest may slow you up. And it is possible that winter gales since 1985 have reduced the depth in the gap.

The principal occupation at Dark Harbour is raking dulse. Dulse is a seaweed that grows below the ordinary low-water mark. At moon tides it is raked up and spread out to dry on flat rocks near the top of the bar. The dried weed is dark purplish, of a leathery consistency, looking and tasting rather like the tongue of an old shoe rescued from a bait barrel. However, it is much esteemed as a delicacy by some, is said to "go good with the beer," and is consumed by health-food zealots for the vast quantities of vitamins and minerals stored in it. It is shipped to Saint John, packed in plastic bags, and sold in supermarkets.

When the dulse rakers are not harvesting, spreading, or packing dulse, they are relaxing in the little camps and shacks spread along the bar. Moon tides are a very social time at Dark Harbour.

If you are exploring ashore, do not try to climb the cliffs. They are composed largely of loose rocks and grow steeper as you go higher. Near the top, the climb is precipitous and the footing most unstable.

Having found the cliffs near Dark Harbour, follow along the shore, keeping off far enough to maintain a depth of 10 fathoms. At Money Cove there is a break in the cliffs and the shore begins to trend more to the eastward. The horn on Northern Head is so far around the corner that it is often inaudible close to the cliffs when the wind is to the south. As you approach Long Eddy Point, a beach begins to build out at the foot of the cliff. Stand well offshore here as a vigorous little rip can build up off the end of the bar. You will probably see the old fog signal station at the base of the cliff.

After you round Long Eddy, the fog will probably scale up and it will be an easy sail up the shore, by Whale Cove to Swallowtail. In the boiling tide around the northern end of the island you are likely to see porpoises, seals, and many different kinds of birds fishing in the disturbed waters. The writer met a whale here on one occasion. Terns, shearwaters, phalarope, and puffins are often seen here. Ashburton Head, where the vessel *Lord Ashburton* was lost in a winter gale many years ago, is a most impressive headland.

Whale Cove is well protected in the usual summer weather. There is a concrete launching ramp here but no wharf.

Continue around Swallowtail, a picturesque lighthouse held to the rock against the winds of winter by a web of steel cables. If you are coming in from the north, from Saint John or Blacks Harbour, you may have trouble hearing the horns on Swallowtail and Northern Head. The reason is that the horn is started automatically. The mechanism depends on two parallel tubes. In the upper one is a bright light. The lower one has a sensing device. If a certain percentage of the upper light returns through the lower tube, the horn starts. Particles of snow, rain, or fog will produce such reflection. Sometimes the fog will hang a mile offshore and lie thick all the way to Saint John, but the light doesn't know that and fails to react. If you don't hear the horn as you approach the island, you will probably break into the clear well before you get dangerously close.

From Swallowtail, make Net Point bell and run in for the made harbor at North Head. The lights shown on the chart are no bigger than light bulbs and make very little impression on a foggy night.

North Head Harbour, Grand Manan, New Brunswick (4340, 4342, Canadian). You can lie in one of the harbors behind the government wharf. These, of course, are perfectly protected, whereas there will be some motion on the moorings outside in a southerly blow. The easterly basin is not as deep as the westerly one although entirely sufficient for most yachts, and it has recently been dredged. Pass close to the corner of the wharf.

The westerly basin is deeper as can be inferred from the larger vessels there. In this basin there is a float with a gangway to the top of the wharf. In the easterly basin you must climb a ladder, a long ladder at low water. In either basin try to tie up to a boat not actively fishing. If you can lie alongside a pile driver or the Canadian fisheries vessel, *Cumella,* you will be well set. If you lie alongside the wharf, you will need very long bow and stern lines to allow for the range of tide and may well have company lying outside you and tramping across your deck. If you do tie up to a boat which has to leave, you will find that its crew is careful to make you fast to the next inside as they slip out.

In 1993 there was extensive blasting and dredging in the western basin to extend its inshore area considerably. Floating catwalks have been installed where vessels can lie alongside without having to tend long lines. This is being done, of course, primarily for fishermen. If yachtsmen take advantage of it, they should understand that fishermen have priority. In 1994, a $20 fee was charged for tieing up at North Head.

In North Head Harbour, the writer was lying alongside a sardiner in a little 28-foot sloop with three boys. It was a black night, thick o' fog. I came on deck in my pajamas about 9:30 to look around before turning in and heard a heavy motor running outside the breakwater and the rush of a bow wave. It came rapidly closer, rushed through the narrow gap. Navigation lights glowed through the fog, the reverse gear roared and ground; the heavy sardiner, still going a good 6 knots, swung, and headed straight for us. I grabbed the boat hook and felt very foolish with it as a head appeared over the bow, now frightfully close, and shouted, "Cut him in half."

More violent reversing churned the water in the little harbor; the great presence swung sideways and stopped alongside without even squeaking the tire that the fierce character forward dropped over the side as he shouted, in a cheerful New Brunswick burr, "Wouldn't crr-ack an egg, skipper-r. We ain't dr-runk, but we ben drr-rinkin'."

I put on my pants and found the rest of the evening most instructive.

Your first stop ashore must be at the Customs Office at the head of the road leading up from the wharf. The necessary formalities being completed, the officer will issue you a cruising permit for as long as you wish to stay in Canadian waters. You will find him a ready source of local information.

One can walk eastward to Swallowtail, a pleasant walk to a dramatic lighthouse whence one can see on a clear day a long stretch of the New Brunswick coast and a bit of Nova Scotia.

Westward on the road is a gasoline station, and about a mile farther west is a grocery. Along this road in both directions from the post office and Customs Office are several bed-and-breakfast houses and snack shops.

Up the hill to the north is the Marathon Hotel, an inn of long standing recently taken over and to some extent modernized by Jim Leslie. He has had the good taste to preserve much of the attractive early-century atmosphere. Here one may get a bath or shower, a drink, and an excellent dinner. Reservations are recommended. Note that in using credit cards or traveler's checks, one must make allowance for the exchange rate.

The Shore Crest Inn also has an excellent reputation with cruising people.

During the summer there are two ferries plying between North Head and Blacks Harbour. They are both drive-on vessels. Klaus Sonnenberg runs an air charter service from an airfield in the northern part of the island.

There is a hospital at North Head.

You should certainly see Grand Harbour, Seal Cove, Southwest Head, and the museum at Grand Harbour Village. This was built, financed in part by the provincial government, on the occasion of the three hundredth anniversary of the founding and settlement of New Brunswick. The principal exhibit in the museum is a magnificent collection of stuffed birds, gathered by the late Allan Moses from the island and adjacent waters.

In 1913, Mr. Ernest Joy, a naturalist friend of Mr. Moses, saw and shot an albatross in the waters of this northern clime, and Joy gave the rare specimen to Moses, who mounted it. The American Museum of Natural History in New York offered to buy it at a great price, but Moses would not sell. However, he traded the bird for a place on an African safari as taxidermist. The expedition was conducted by Sterling Rockefeller to search for the rare green broadbill. After searching for a long time with no success, Moses contracted a fatal case of dysentery. He looked up from his sickbed one day and saw the object of the expedition on a tree overhead. He shot it, and as he lay dying himself, with the bird in his arms, Rockefeller promised him anything he wanted. Moses was distressed that so much was spent scouring distant lands for rare specimens while species were becoming extinct in his own country. He asked that Rockefeller purchase Kents Island off Grand Manan as a sanctuary.

On his return, Rockefeller bought the islands and gave them to Bowdoin College, which now administers them as a sanctuary and research site. Dr. Charles E. Huntington, a Bowdoin professor of biology, is now the director.

It is reported that twenty-one petrels were trapped at this station and taken to England to be released. Nineteen of them showed up back at Kents Island in a short time.

Allan Moses' collection of Grand Manan birds was housed in the schoolhouse and was not easily available to the public, but now the birds are beautifully displayed in lighted cases. There is a good exhibit of the geology of Grand Manan in the basement, and there are interesting displays of tools and of relics from wrecks that have come ashore on the island. In front of the museum is the main yard of a sailing vessel, which gives some notion of how heavy was the gear in commercial sailing ships.

Mr. Eric Allaby is now in charge of the museum. He is a most interesting person, well informed on Grand Manan history, and a very capable artist.

As lobstering is off season in Canada during the summer, the principal occupation is seining herring. The use of spotting planes is impractical here because of fog. The seiners use sophisticated sonar gear, which can detect a school as much as half a mile away. They use big purse seines with power haulers, pump the fish into the hold, scaling them on the way, and rush them to factories, where they are made into fish meal for fertilizer. Some of them are taken to Blacks Harbour, where they are smoked and canned, and some to Seal Cove, where they are salted and smoked. As the government has imposed a quota on herring as a conservation measure, some fishermen supplement lobstering by trawling and handlining for ground fish, and a few draggers work out of Grand Manan.

At North Head, the writer was cautioned not to sail down the eastern side of the island, even with a fair wind and tide. The bottom is very rough and the tide runs hard. Bulkhead Rip is especially dangerous. In the days of sail, fishermen used to anchor there and fish on the flood tide, where the bottom rises from 40 to 4 fathoms in a very short distance. When the tide began to slack, they left at once, for if caught here in the ebb they would cut an anchor line rather than lie there with the heavy ebb tide pouring over the submerged cliff and backing up against a southerly sea.

The skipper bound for Saint John should plan to leave North Head on the last of the ebb tide, moving in the slack water as he leaves the island. The full force of six hours of flood tide will then boost him up the New Brunswick shore at 2 knots or better. Grand Manan authorities recommend running across for Lepreau and then running up the shore, rather than going directly for Partridge Island in order to catch the stronger flood current close to the New Brunswick cliffs. Keep well off Lepreau or else get close under the shore, for a nasty rip develops off the light. There is also a rip eastward of the Wolves. The direct course for Partridge Island avoids these but should bring you close enough to the shore to hear the horns at Lepreau and Musquash. If you are coming west from Saint John, there is a good deal to be said for making North Head rather than Head Harbour, Campobello, for there are good horns at Swallowtail and Northern Head. Another alternative is Blacks Harbour. If you make Lepreau and the whistle inside the Wolves, it is an easy run to Pea Point, with an excellent horn to run for.

Seal Cove, New Brunswick (4340). Make the whistle off Southwest Head and then the bell east of it. This will take you clear of Buck Rock, marked only by a can. However, it breaks noisily and can usually be identified thus. Do not try to follow the shore inside Buck Rock, because you will run into one of Grand Manan's most productive weirs. Round the breakwater into the made harbor at Seal Cove.

The heavy government wharf at Seal Cove now has a hook on the north end of the ell and another wharf north of it so the basin is completely enclosed and perfectly protected. Seek a berth alongside a vessel not actively fishing, alongside the pile driver used to set weir stakes, or alongside one of the lobster cars. Do not try to pass between the cars as they are joined by chains and fuel hoses. There is a float landing in the harbor, but one can probably not lie alongside it over night. Avoid lying against the wharf directly because of the long lines needed to allow for the considerable tidal range.

There is no Customs Office at Seal Cove now. Call the office at North Head.

The northerly harbor at Seal Cove is also very well protected, but it dries out at low water. The boats ground out alongside the wharf. It is not a comfortable place for a yacht.

Serious efforts are being made to conserve herring resources with a quota system. Lobsters can be taken only in the winter, when the price is high and the lobsters are hard. One Grand Manan fisherman was reported to the writer as having brought in 3,600 pounds of lobsters in one day—an almost incredible catch. The waters around Grand Manan are not easily accessible, are highly productive, and are so rough, tide scoured, and obscured by fog that few but Grand Manan people fish them. One Grand Manan resident declared flatly, "There are no poor fishermen." Despite this categorical statement, it is worth remembering that a boat rugged enough for these waters is expensive. When one adds to the cost of the hull the cost for a reliable engine, radar, loran C, sonar, radio, and all the electric and hydraulic gear necessary for modern fishing, one has a tremendous capital investment. The educational qualifications necessary to operate and maintain it are not inconsiderable and are not all acquired in school. It might not be unfair to refer to a modern fisherman as an engineer in charge of a fish delivery system.

Seal Cove is a delightful town, busy in an unhurried way. There is a store that is a pleasant gathering place as well as a source of food and refreshment. The business of the town is fish—principally herring. There is a sardine factory and there are several smokehouses. The latter can be identified at once by the vents along the ridgepole, sheltered by a little roof above them, and by the spicy aroma of driftwood smoke and salt herring. The fish are first heavily salted for a week or less according to taste and then strung on sticks run in through the gills and out the mouth. The sticks are hung on racks in the bottom of the smokehouse over a driftwood fire built on the dirt floor. Day by day they are moved to higher racks until they are finished just under the roof. When the fish come out, they are a beautiful red-gold color. To prepare a smoked herring, cut a strip off the belly, remove the head, and wiggle the fish as if it were swimming. This loosens the flesh from the bone. Open the creature up, remove the two sides of meat, peel off the skin, and store in sealed Mason jars. Smoked herring can be eaten "as is" with beer or soaked out and either fried or boiled.

Herring is the economic mainstay of the island, and in recent years the herring run has been thin. More visitors have come with the new car ferry, but Grand Manan has had some hard times. One ingenious resident, alongside whom the writer lay in 1968, was doing a profitable business searching for wrecks among the ledges to the southeast of the island. With an electronic device to indicate the presence of metal and with information from draggers who had fouled their gear, he went out and salvaged what he could find by scuba diving. He had just recently found a steamer loaded with copper rods. Only gold could have been more valuable.

The vessels you will see at Grand Manan are heavy Nova Scotia–built craft. The lobstermen and fishermen use a big broad-sterned boat with high bow and low waist, heavily powered and equipped with good electronic gear. Sardine carriers are usually double ended to render them easier to maneuver in the weirs and are equipped with pumps like great vacuum cleaners to suck the fish out of the seines and scale them. The scales are used for pearl essence, which is used in shirt buttons and fire extinguisher foam, among other things. These vessels are built heavily of knotty spruce and designed to navigate the Bay of Fundy in winter—a rugged assignment.

From Seal Cove it is possible to explore Wood Island and the Kent Islands, where Bowdoin College maintains an ornithological and oceanographic station. Also one can run up the east side of the island on the flood tide to Grand Harbour and on to North Head, but the navigator must be alert here. These are dangerous waters, with very uneven bottom, violent tides, and dense and frequent fog. Some of the channels are dry at low water, the buoys lying high and dry.

If your schedule affords a day ashore, Seal Cove is an excellent place to spend it. Call Mrs. Green (662-8212) for an automobile tour of the island or walk south on the tar road through pretty rolling country, by snug houses, to the point where the road crosses quite a big brook and turns to gravel. Here there is a wood road to the right that leads across to the cliffs. On the way, it becomes a trail and pretty nearly peters out, but it will get you there. The cliffs are breathtaking, especially with the fog blowing up over them and the black water below. The rock is crumbly and breaks off in long vertical slivers, so take no chances on these cliffs. It is not difficult to follow the shore south toward Southwest Head. You will find a sign marking the spot where William and Lucas Jones were wrecked in February 1963. After a snowstorm they were raking moss off Haycock Harbor when their outboard motor died. The wind came off northwest and bitter cold. In their open skiff they drifted across the channel and struck close to Southwest Head. Their skiff was destroyed, and they were nearly drowned. However, William managed to scale the cliff and get to the lighthouse through the heavy snow, whence help was sent to his brother. Vernon Bagley, the game warden, went down the cliff on a rope, got Lucas under his arm, and was hauled up. He was awarded the Andrew Carnegie medal. Few men wrecked on these cliffs are so lucky.

It is a long walk back to Seal Cove, but you may be fortunate enough to get a ride.

In addition to its natural charm for the casual visitor, the island is of unique interest to the geologist and historian. Grand Manan comprises two great and widely differing sections, dividing it almost from end to end: the western section identified in 1839 by Dr. Abraham Gesner, provincial geologist, as trap rock, and the eastern as schistose rock. The actual contact of the two sections is visible at Red Point, near Seal Cove, but cannot be seen at Whale Cove at the north, as it is buried under the beach. The formations of the eastern section range in age from twice to many times that of the western. The latter is of the Triassic period, extending from 160 to 185 million years ago; the eastern section is of the Palaeozoic and Pre-Cambrian eras, extending from 360 to perhaps 1,500 million years ago. The western section constitutes the only extensive example of Triassic igneous rock in New Brunswick, and Red Point affords one of the few easily accessible views of these geological formations in contact.

Grand Manan is one of the few unspoiled spots on the continent. It has a simple charm unmatched along the coast.

The amateur sailor with a staunch and well-equipped boat and a competent navigator would add great interest to his cruise by spending a few days at Grand Manan.

Chapter XIV

West Quoddy Head to Calais, Maine

General Remarks. The waters described in this chapter are shown in detail on Charts 13398 and 13394 and on Canadian Charts 4114, 4124, and 4332. Notice that soundings on both sets of charts are in meters and decimeters and the scales are 1/50,000 rather than 1/40,000. The charts include Cobscook Bay, the St. Croix River, Deer Island, Campobello Island, and the passages into Passamaquoddy Bay. Campobello Island, Deer Island, and the northern and eastern shores of Passamaquoddy Bay and of the St. Croix River are Canadian territory and on Atlantic time. Although it is all interesting country, the best cruising ground is "the blue Passamaquoddy."

This large protected bay is something quite unexpected to one coming in through Lubec Narrows or Letete Passage out of the cold Fundy fog. It is likely to be warm and sunny with much less fog and tidal current. The shores are high and bold with dramatic cliffs, jutting promontories, and steep beaches. There are few yachts, some sardiners, frequent Canadian ferries, and a great deal of bird life. There are several pleasant anchorages in the bay.

Tidal Conditions. Anyone navigating the waters to the north and west of Campobello Island should realize that the tides in those waters are controlled by the stream that enters and leaves north of Campobello, rather than by that which enters and leaves through Lubec Narrows.

The flood south of Campobello Island sets to the northeast. In Quoddy Roads and Lubec Narrows the current starts to run south one and one half hours before high water and north at about low water. It attains a velocity of from 4 to 8 knots. North of Campobello the flood sets in a southwesterly direction and splits, going south of Moose Island into Cobscook Bay and north through the Western Passage. Hence, when bound north from Lubec, after passing Treat Island, head over toward Campobello Island on the flood tide. The flood runs southwest along the eastern side of Deer Island. The floods in the Western Passage are stronger than the ebbs, attaining 6 knots during spring tides. There is a strong whirlpool just southwest of the southern point of Deer Island. The current runs for three-quarters of an hour after the tide table shows high and low water. Through Letete Passage the flood sets to the north, and the ebb the reverse. This current meets the current through Head Harbour Passage, about halfway between Head Harbour and the White Horse. There is said to be good fishing in the Head Harbour eddy.

An experienced correspondent writes: "Head Harbour Passage develops into a dangerous breaking inlet off the light during and after northeast storms. I have cruised extensively in both oceans and never seen rougher water for a cruising boat."

In proceeding northward through the Western Passage, one will find that the tide swirls off Eastport. A small boat going north against the tide should stay close to the west shore. By going up the west shore, one profits by the eddies behind the points. Avoid the old weir off Kendall Head, covered at high water. The best general rule for this passage is to hug the American shore on all tides if bound north, the Deer Island shore if bound south.

If you are forced to make this passage with an overnight stop, Clam Cove on Deer Island is possible, open only to the south, but there are no supplies. Farther up on the west shore is North Harbour, a good anchorage. Anchor southeast of where Chart 13328 says 27.

The waters of the narrow passage between Moose and Deer islands are frequently white with thousands of gulls and terns snatching fish from the boiling waters.

Customs and Immigration. Yachts leaving the United States do not have to inform the Customs Office of their departure. However, to make re-entry easier, each member of the crew should have positive identification such as an old passport or a birth certificate. Expensive new merchandise like a camera can be registered before leaving so there will be no question about its having been purchased abroad on the cruise.

On entering Canada, one must enter Customs and get a cruising permit. One can enter at the Lubec bridge, North Head on Grand Manan, Saint Andrews, or Saint John. At Saint John, call Fundy Traffic on channel 16 and make arrangements for a Customs officer to meet you at Market Slip float or at the Royal Kennebecasis Yacht Club in Millidgeville. There is no charge for entering between 8 A.M. and 12 midnight. One can spend the night at Head Harbour, Dipper, or Chance and enter the next day at Saint John, as there is a 24-hour grace period if no one goes ashore.

To re-enter the United States, one must clear with both Customs and Immigration. The official procedure is to call the port director of Customs at Lubec (709 733-4331), Bangor (207 947-7861 or 207 945-6320), Belfast (207 338-3954), or Portland (780-3352 or 780-3228). Tell the office what port you are entering and approximately when, and at the same time ask them to inform Immigration. You will be met and you may be thoroughly inspected.

In practice it is sometimes easier. If you come alongside the wharf at Eastport or Lubec, you can walk to the Customs Office at the bridge, check in, and depart in 15 minutes if you have not bought much Canadian merchandise, liquor, or tobacco and if all the crew are United States citizens. Call the Lubec office from Cutler or Jonesport; you may be fortunate enough to be cleared by telephone. On the other hand, with the vastly increased smuggling of drugs taking place on the Maine coast, some of which is being done in yachts, you may be detained and searched thoroughly. It is something of a gamble. The proper and legal procedure, however, is to call the Customs Office in advance, ask them to inform Immigration, and proceed as directed. You will be required to buy a User's Fee Decal for $25, good for one year. This can be done in advance. It makes entry by telephone possible. Apply by mail.

Quoddy Roads, Maine (13394). Anyone caught by the tide can anchor behind Quoddy Head, passing north of Wormell Ledge and working to the south as far as draft permits. It is not a peaceful anchorage. There is a park at West Quoddy Head Light with interesting trails through the woods and along the cliffs.

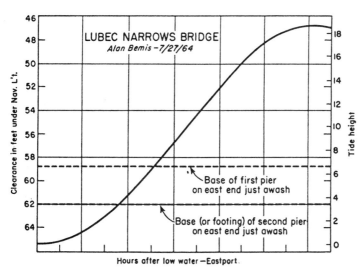

Tide at Lubec Narrows Bridge.

Lubec Narrows, Maine (13394). This is the usual way by which yachts enter Passamaquoddy Bay. With a fair tide and moderate winds, it is ordinarily an exciting but not a dangerous trip. At moon tides, especially after strong winds, the tide can run up to 6 knots or better through the bridge. A correspondent who saw it under difficult conditions writes:

> I would suggest a very strong word of caution to all regarding the tidal current under the Lubec-Campobello bridge. We ran through with the tide behind us and had all we could do to prevent piling up on the supporting piers. The eddies on the bay side are fierce, and even the sardine carriers have difficulty getting through. The tidal current is reported to be slack $1/2$–$1^1/2$ hours before high water.

There are several things to keep carefully in mind if you are planning to enter Passamaquoddy Bay under the Lubec bridge, which has a vertical clearance of 47 feet above high water.

  1. Measure accurately the height of your mast *above the water.*
  2. Remember that the tidal current ceases to run north and becomes slack half an hour to an hour before high water and shortly

begins to run south, even though the tide is still rising. The current is slack again at about the time of low water. Of course these times vary with the phases of the moon and with the wind.

3. Consult the chart on page 709 and determine the clearance under the bridge with respect to mean low water.

4. Consult the tide table and correct the clearance for the height of the tide on the date in question.

5. If it is going to be a very near thing, note that the curve gives height under the navigation light, which hangs about 18 inches below the underside of the bridge.

6. Check your arithmetic. If the calculations are all correct and if you have forgotten nothing, you will have an uneventful passage. Good luck.

You may have implicit confidence in the chart. The late Mr. Alan Bemis constructed it, and his account of its construction is printed below.

With more fixed bridges crossing our waterways every year (and dynamite hard to come by), it is helpful to know their vertical clearance precisely. Published clearance is usually figured at mean high water, and down Fundy way the stage of the tide makes all the difference. We all need to know our exact mast height too. Height above the water seems to be the only parameter not included in the CCA Measurement Rule so many owners don't know it exactly.

Last July, *Cirrus*, with Dwight, Helen and Davie Shepler, and myself aboard, decided to determine some of these half-knowns under the new Lubec Narrows bridge, which allows landlubbers to roll on four wheels from Lubec to Campobello Island. Luck made our calibration easy with a 0.0 low tide at Eastport that morning, i.e., mean low water. We ran up a whisker pole on the flag halyard flying 8.4 feet above any more permanent part of the rig and cruised up and down stream under the center span until, as the tide rose, the whisker pole finally struck the green center navigation light.

We kept a log on the time of day; observed various markers awash and such, providing data for the clearance chart submitted herewith; then departed speedily on the flood, to run Cobscook Falls before the puzzled Lubec populace sicked the Harbor Master on us.

The published figure is 47 feet at mean high. Our calibration indicates this is the correct figure for clearance under the green navigation light, which seemed to hang down about 18 inches below the bridge structure. Please note that there are wide departures from mean high and mean low. The bridge has seven piers, three east of the channel and four west. The pair on either side of the channel carry big steel and timber fenders, which throw huge bow waves in the tide and leave turbulence and back eddies below them. Placing your ship in the center of the span is easier going downstream, and will be more exciting as you wonder if Bemis' calibration is correct. (No guarantee made or implied.) However, it is a long way around Campobello Island even with your rig still standing.

Lubec, Maine (13394). The best anchorage at Lubec is in Johnson Bay, west of the town. Snug up as close as possible under the western shore of the point to keep out of the tide. There is a big L-shaped pier and a float on the north shore of the Lubec peninsula where the *Coast Pilot* says there is from 6 to 14 feet. The town of Lubec, the most easterly in the United States, has a supermarket, hardware store, restaurant, and the usual facilities. At the western end of the bridge to Campobello there is a United States Customs Office open at all times.

The principal industry in Lubec is canning and smoking herring and processing salmon. In addition to these mainstays, R. J. Peacock Co. processes, cans, freezes, transports, or markets sea urchins, scallops, lobsters, mackerel, and other seafoods, arranges export of forest products, and provides pilots for incoming vessels.

Gasoline and diesel oil must be lugged in cans unless enough is needed to warrant calling a tank truck.

There is an airstrip to the west of the town.

In the event of a heavy westerly or a northwesterly blow, cross Johnson Bay and anchor southwest of Rogers Island.

In going from Lubec to Eastport, note that the flood tide runs south through Friar Roads and northwest into Cobscook Bay. A flood tide is a head tide. Hug the eastern shore for less tide and back eddies.

Federal Harbor (13394). Those bound up Cobscook Bay or seeking a quieter anchorage than Lubec or Eastport should investigate this harbor on the east side of Denbow Neck below Horan Head. The upper part of the harbor dries out, but there is good anchorage between Black Head and Horan Head or behind Hog Island or Long Island. Avoid a mooring spar nearby, floating horizontally at low water.

Cobscook Bay, Maine (13394). Cobscook is a large bay full of islands and narrow passages, and very pretty. On account of the heavy tides, which in some places attain the force of rapids, it is not much frequented by strangers. But, aside from the falls west of Falls Island, there is nothing that ordinary care cannot overcome.

Note that nun 8 on Birch Point Ledge between Birch Point and Seward Neck usually tows under on every run of tide.

One can go almost to Dennysville on the high water but must anchor 1¹/₂ miles below the town to stay afloat at low water.

There is a good anchorage between Birch Islands and Williams Island, where Chart 13394 gives a 3-meter depth or west of Birch Island. Leighton Point Cove, called Schooner Cove on the chart, is a good anchorage outside the falls. It is said to be quite a trick to get in here at the full force of the tide, for the tide runs by Denbow Point about as hard as it does through Lubec Narrows.

There is said to be good anchorage off Coffins Point, south of Falls Island.

Cobscook Falls, Maine (13394). These are reversible falls, located just west of Falls Island, where Chart 13394 reads 12.8. They run 10 knots at full run and are something to see. Only crazy men, like the one who provided these data (and who prefers to remain anonymous), run them at full run. He reports that the safest time for sane folk to pass through is at low slack, because all hazards are well above water. The maximum strength of flood current occurs about two hours before high water at Eastport.

The inward run of tide is much more turbulent than the outrun, due to the rock formation. On the inward run the current flows straight past Falls Island to a large ledge, Roaring Bull, which makes out from the western tip of Falls Island. This forces the current violently over toward the north shore, from which it swirls back south to meet the current coming around the south side of the island. This southbound current carries one's boat off Government Rock, located just north of figure 12.8 on Chart 13394. Two Hour Rock is just to the southeast. It uncovers two hours after high water. In the lee of Roaring Bull a big whirlpool develops.

On the outward run, however, the current follows a much straighter course.

A more cautious approach is south of Falls Island.

Because of the interest of venturesome cruisers in running the falls, the following is presented from an experienced cruising man, who has been running them for many years in a 45-foot yawl:

Water is swift, with plenty of huge haycocks, and tosses one around plenty. Skipper should proceed up the bay on the rising tide from Eastport. As he approaches the falls, he should place himself in the middle of the stream. The detail chart is quite accurate. Stream will carry one around Roaring Bull, then one must starboard the helm to avoid points of rock to starboard. A large swirl carries one to port after passing Roaring Bull. Beware of the big whirlpool west of the Bull. There are no particular difficulties about going out with the tide if one places oneself in the center of the stream above the rapids. Current runs 10 to 12 knots; should not be attempted in dinghies or small boats, which whirlpools suck down. Dennys River is a charming, isolated spot.

An equally experienced authority adds: "I would discourage this. For anyone unaccustomed to these tides, it's fearsome."

Eastport, Maine (13394, 4114). Between Eastport and Deer Island is a tidal commotion truly frightening to the skipper unprepared for it. It is caused by the tide coming in north of Campobello meeting the tide running up Lubec Narrows. Huge whirlpools 30 feet in diameter and 3 or 4 feet deep spin even big sardiners halfway around. Great boils rush up, making mounds off which a yacht slides sideways. The whole maelstrom is in constant motion, so passage through it, especially in light weather, can be very exciting. With a fair current and with power or a working breeze, there is no great danger to a seagoing yacht, but a small open boat might find it very dangerous indeed. In rough weather or in a storm, it is too furious to approach, and under any weather conditions it is best taken at slack water.

Eastport has a heavy wharf and breakwater that provides a protected place to tie up out of the tide. Inside the "L" there are likely to be many fishing boats tied up and there is a float on the northern end of the basin. One can lie briefly at the float while checking in with the Customs officer in the building close to the head of the wharf. One must check in in person here; telephone calls are not acceptable. There is a $25 overtime charge for service after business hours. Then move alongside a fisherman. Be careful not to obstruct the Coast Guard boat usually berthed in the northeast corner. There is an IGA market ¹/₂ mile up the hill, and Moose Island Marine has a shop near the head of the wharf for hardware and engine repairs.

There is no gasoline, diesel fuel, or water to be had at the wharf.

Northeast Marina, located ¹/₄ mile south of the breakwater, sells fuel and has a few slips and moorings—also a water hose and showers and a small store. West of the town around the southerly end of Moose Island in Deep Cove is the Marine Trade Center where the Washington County Vocational Training Institute is located. This is a school teaching engine repair for gasoline and diesel engines, hull repair, and boatbuilding. There is a travelift at the school which is also used by Moose Island Marine whose boatyard is next to the school. Repairs to all types of boats can be made here. Call ahead on channel 16 or 10.

Eastport has been primarily a herring town, but is now vigorously expanding its wharf facilities to bring in large vessels for the export of forest products, seafood, and general cargo. It is to be the largest deepwater port in Maine, to rival Portland and Searsport.

During his administration, Franklin Roosevelt started the Quoddy Project to generate electricity by impounding water in Cobscook Bay at high tide. It was never completed, but is periodically revived and reconsidered.

Welshpool, Campobello, New Brunswick (13394). This fishing village, across Friar Roads from Eastport, is on the north side of Friar Bay. There is a summer colony, including what was for many years the summer home of the Franklin D. Roosevelt family.

In the summer of 1966, President Johnson and the Prime Minister of Canada met at the Roosevelt house to dedicate a memorial to the memory of President Roosevelt. The Roosevelt estate is now open to the public and is well worth a visit.

There is good protection behind a big government wharf with 14 feet at low water and a light on the end of the wharf. One can enter Canadian Customs at the end of the Lubec Bridge. Note that Campobello is on Atlantic time, one hour ahead of Eastern time.

Harbour de Lute, Campobello, New Brunswick (13394). Though not so snug or picturesque as Head Harbour on the north end of the island, this anchorage on the northwest side is excellent and well protected. After entering, proceed south, leaving the green buoy to port. Anchor south of the point and weir making out from the west shore, off two houses on the west bank. The harbor was reported to be crowded with salmon pens in 1993.

Head Harbour, New Brunswick (13394). One coming east from Cutler will find Head Harbour a convenient stop and a good place from which to take off for Saint John. It is easy of access and perfectly protected. Coming up from Cutler, make Sail Rock whistle and set a course to parallel the Campobello shore. When you think you are by Eastern Head, edge in toward the shore until you hear the surf or see the loom of the cliffs. Beyond Nancy Head, as the shore tends more northward, you are likely to get a scale-up. If you do, pass between Head Harbour Island and the end of Campobello, leave all green buoys close to port to avoid old weirs, and run up the harbor. A direct course from "S91C" to "S93C" crosses an old weir. At least three stakes are outside this line. If there is no scale-up, keep off the shore until you hear the siren on East Quoddy Head on a bearing north of west. Then run for it and follow the Campobello shore into the harbor. The entrance is quite narrow. As he followed the procedure above, the writer was once confused by soundings of over 100 feet and found that he was following the outer shore of Head Harbour Island. The harbor was obstructed but not closed by salmon pens in 1993.

On the north side of the harbor is a big government wharf much used in the summer by seiners. The wharf on the south side and the big building behind it were built for a fish-meal plant, which for a few years rendered the region most unattractive. It has now been dismantled. Anchor south of the wharf or tie up to an idle pile driver. There is little reason to go ashore. There is no fuel, no water, no store, no telephone.

John and Charles Greenwood were brothers who owned a farm together on the northerly side of the harbor. John disliked Charles extremely. Indeed he disliked him so much that one day he sawed their wharf in half down the middle and bade Charles stay on his own side. Later, incensed at Charles's walking to the shore through a field that John thought was his, John bought a wild bull and pastured it in the field. Charles, by judicious use of apples, sugar, carrots, and a charitable disposition, made friends with the bull, who made no objection to his walking through the field. On one occasion when John entered the field, the bull nearly killed him. John set out moorings, planning to rent them out to sardiners for winter lay-up. However, it appeared that under Canadian law this was illegal, for everything below high water is public property. John, accordingly, neglected the moorings.

In due course he died, leaving his property to the church with the proviso that on no account was Charles ever to get any of it. However, Charles, for reasons not stated, bought the moorings from the church, figuring perhaps that they did not come under the ban. He held them for a while and sold them to Ira Dugay, his son-in-law. Dugay used them for a time but ceased to maintain them in the mid-seventies.

A local authority said that it didn't matter much because the shores were steep and smooth and no sea ever built up in Head Harbour so a boat ashore could be easily pulled off. A correspondent who knew the Greenwoods and Dugay writes: "John was a bit irritable at the best of times. Varn Fletcher got his old pinkie *Pelican* into John's weir one time when trying to beat up the harbour. The weir was in front of John's house and wharf. John sat on the shore with a shotgun and proceeded to blow the jib off the old *Pelican* as Varn tried to sail out of the weir."

It is a pleasant walk along the west shore, past John's house, up through the woods to Charles's house and along the road to Wilson's Beach where there is a store. There is a post office at Wilson's Beach but none at Head Harbour.

If opportunity offers, explore the south side of Head Harbour. There are excellent and abundant raspberries around the old fish factory.

From Head Harbour it is about 40 miles to Saint John, a reasonable distance to make in six hours with a 2-knot tide running with you.

Wilson's Beach, Campobello, New Brunswick (13394, 4340). There is a heavy government wharf affording shelter. Ashore are a store, a post office, and a small marine supply store. Otherwise Wilson's Beach offers little to attract the cruising man. There is a considerable raft of salmon pens. The Canadian chart shows the wharf and a fixed green light.

Northwest Harbour, Deer Island, New Brunswick (13394). This is a well-protected and very attractive harbor with high, wooded shores dropping steeply to the water; in places there are impressive cliffs. In clear weather, entrance is easy. Often when it is thick offshore, there will be a scale-up north of Campobello that will carry you all the way to Deer Island. Note that the flood tide runs south around the end of Deer Island.

The flashing beacon is on a high girder, which does not look like a conventional beacon. Give buoy "VPA" a generous berth as the ledge extends beyond the buoy. In 1993 there was a beacon on the ledge south of Mink Island. There was an abandoned weir off Dinner Island and another farther in on the south side. On the north side at the entrance was an active weir, and an abandoned one at the entrance to the inner cove on the north side.

Run up the middle of the harbor. The writer anchored off the cove on the north shore in front of the ledge on a quiet night, and all was well. A later visitor reports the bottom is smooth rock there and suggests going farther up the harbor among the old moorings where the bottom is soft. There is a small settlement at the head of the harbor, but the nearest store is at Richardson.

In getting out of the harbor, especially in the fog, you may find the tide very confusing. The writer found the first of the ebb setting northeast much earlier than expected.

Lords Cove, Deer Island, New Brunswick (13394, 4124). Although one visitor reported 20 feet between St. Helena Island and Bean Island, the best entrance seems to be up the buoyed channel between St. Helena and Deer Island. When you pick up the range, as shown on Chart 4124, run in. The range is two green lights, but there is a red light on the wharf low down, in front of the other two. The range is marked by day with two white boards. Do not get off the range to port. If you must err, edge to starboard. The range leaves the white beacon close to port and brings you into a bottle-tight little anchorage with 3 fathoms, mud bottom, and several apparently unused moorings. Running this range calls for a little resolution as the channel is narrow, but the writer did it close to low water and got no sounding less than 3 fathoms. The ferry lands at the wharf on the east side where there is a landing float. There are several moorings and a weir on the west side.

Approaching from the north, the navigator will find the shores bold and the dangers exposed at low water. Halibut Rock is big, flat on top, and grassy. There are two weirs on Bean Island, one right under the ledge, which makes out from the easterly point. There is plenty of room to beat in through this entrance and run up the range as described above. North of Lord's Cove are salmon pens.

It is a short walk to Richardson, where there is a village and a government wharf with 6 feet at low water.

Old weir stakes extend to the east of the current weir on Fish Island.

Letete Passage, Deer Island, New Brunswick (13398, 4124). This is the principal deep-water entrance to Passamaquoddy Bay. The tide runs through here with considerable violence, making swirls, eddies, and boils. However, with power or a fair wind, one can run through with a fair tide. There is no difficulty about making the run at slack water. There is a light on Greens Point and a flasher on Morgan Ledge. From here the passage is well marked.

The tide runs southeast on the ebb out of Passamaquoddy Bay and then pulls southerly down the Deer Island shore, making it a short beat down to Lord's Cove, Northwest Harbour, or Head Harbour. Mr. Gerry Peer of Saint John, who has cruised this region for many years, writes: "Having used both Letite and Little Letite passages for years as a means to Passamaquoddy Bay, I find they are an interesting and fascinating area to sail, either charging through with the current or plying your wits against it, but it is no place for a vessel with limited navigation equipment in a fog. Mohawk Ledge has had its share of boats and I don't know of any area I treat with more respect in a fog." There is a good back set along the north shore of the passage on the flood tide, a great advantage to the eastbound yacht.

Little Letete Passage, Deer Island, New Brunswick (13398, 4124). This is a narrow passage from Passamaquoddy Bay running south of McMasters Island into Letete Passage with 14 feet at low water. It is not recommended for strangers.

A correspondent writes as follows about this district:

> I cruised all these waters last summer. Grand and Little Letite Passages are blemished by the big high-tension line to Deer Island. Do urge all to run Little Letite Passage, which is good fun and perfectly safe on half-tide or better. Wonderful climb and view at McMaster Island. Anchor at Red Pebble Beach, west side of island, at the south of Sea Cave.

Another correspondent adds: "Not good fun if the tide is strong." Still another correspondent declares that there is 6 to 8 feet at low water and notes that the ferry runs without reference to the tides. He prefers it to Letete because it is so narrow that even in the fog both sides are visible.

Another correspondent confirms this:

I concur with the above. The tide pool on Pendleton Beach at the entrance to Little Letite is well worth a visit and a good lay in a southwest wind. It is excellent swimming after about half-ebb.

Magaguadavic River (13398, 4331). This river is easily located by the high land at Midjik Bluff. Here the river is wide and deep, but it quickly narrows. One can go up as far as St. George on the tide and lie over in a basin there. A correspondent writes:

The river itself is everything which your *Guide* [1983 edition] suggests—a very pretty, wild-seeming and adventurously narrow river with just enough difficulty in navigation to add spice to the trip. In fact, the Canadian chart and the spars in the river make the voyage up after half tide very easy, and I would not hesitate to recommend it to anyone who finds himself in Passamaquoddy Bay.

The problem comes when a visiting yachtsman decides to spend the night at St. George's, lured perhaps by a summer's evening and the sight of a bald eagle overhead. Contrary to the impression of the *Guide* and the chart, there is no really safe anchorage in the so-called mill pond for a vessel which is not equipped to dry out on the mud flats. While a local told me that the harbor had once been dredged, it is now decidedly shoal, and on a moon tide, dries out with the exception of the area directly in front of the now-abandoned wharf. This might suggest that a safe anchorage can be found by fitting into the narrow pocket in front of the wharf. Unfortunately, the current of the Magaguadavic River flowing into the mill pond is very strong and the wharf creates a back eddy requiring a stern anchor to hold the yacht off the wharf and a line from both bows to the wharf to prevent her from swinging across the current as it surges. Since the current's direction changes as the lowering tide squeezes into smaller and smaller channels, the evening can be remarkably uneasy for the watchkeepers. A further note about the bottom to correct the impression in the present edition

[1983] of *The Cruising Guide*. While there *is* water in the mill pond, the bottom consists of sharp-cornered granite tailings from the old granite mill rather than the soft mud which one might expect, and the river current is so strong that an anchor can be almost literally washed out of the granite when the scope is shortened to the extent necessary to stay in the area of the mill pond covered by water at low tide.

In conclusion, this is a pleasant day trip, but I would strongly recommend against anchoring in the mill pond. For what it is worth, the town is pleasant, and there is a very tasty bakery on the street leading from the wharf to the town square.

A recent visitor to the lower reaches of the river said there were no significant changes and reported that the shores are more built up than formerly.

Digdeguash Harbour, New Brunswick (13398). This harbor, not named on the recent edition of Chart 13398, lies north of the Magaguadavic River on both sides of Long Island. It is a pleasant anchorage and well protected except in a heavy southerly. Notice the rock just east of the little island in the western entrance. It shows at half-tide. The government wharf which used to stand on the west shore is now gone, and the bridge across the head of the harbor is a fixed bridge. There are old weir stakes off the point on the northwest side of the entrance. Good anchorage may be found east of Long Island near the "4.4" sounding.

Chamcook, New Brunswick (13398). A correspondent writes:

Chamcook Harbor, New Brunswick, is an excellent though deserted anchorage. It is large but secure, with excellent holding ground. The entrance to the outer harbor, between two buoys, is very narrow, and the tide runs like a trout brook for a few hundred feet, but there is little current inside.

Entrance to the inner harbor is a gap not over 100 feet wide between two sandbars. We draw 4 feet and entered on the bottom of the tide, using the color of the water as a guide. We used the lead to find a sheltered berth at the head of the inner harbor and spent a couple of pleasant hours toward high water watching the automobiles driving across the sand spit to Ministers Island. It was early evening of a very Canadian Sunday, and competition was keen to see which would be the last car that could possibly make it before high tide covered the road.

This is one of the few really secure small-boat anchorages in Passamaquoddy Bay.

Chamcook is much to be preferred to St. Andrews in any kind of a heavy blow.

St. Andrews, New Brunswick (13398, 4332). This is the principal yachting center in Passamaquoddy Bay. It is a good place to replenish supplies and to change crews as there is bus transportation to Saint John and to Calais and Bangor.

The preferred approach is from the east and is easy once you find Tongue Shoal marked by a flashing light on a pole. Simply run in the line of red buoys. Notice especially nun S x 8 on the southern side of the channel. It shows clearly on the insert on Chart 13398. Do not expect much from the red light at the entrance. It is a light bulb mounted on a white pole.

The western entrance is narrow and at low tide rather shoal, but it presents no insuperable problems. There were no guest moorings in 1993. However, call the wharfinger on channel 16 and he may be able to direct you to a vacant one.

The government wharf burned in 1994, so you will have to land at the temporary wharf. If you have not previously secured a Canadian cruising permit, your first stop is the Custom House at the head of the wharf. Remember that St. Andrews is on Atlantic Daylight Time, one hour ahead of Eastern Daylight Time. Do not stir up the Customs officers on Sunday as it will cost overtime pay.

Water will probably be piped down the wharf, but unless you have considerable length of hose, you may have to lug it in buckets to your tank. There is no gas or diesel oil. Ice is available at a convenience store or the supermarket. Also to the right are a good market and a laundry. The liquor store is on the main street to the left. The Sea Breeze is a good casual restaurant. For fine dining, try L'Europe.

The town of St. Andrews is essentially one long street, with all necessary and many interesting stores. Besides grocery, meat, liquor, and drug stores and restaurants, there is the County Craft Shop famous for hand-knit sweaters, each in a unique pattern.

There is a large hotel overlooking the town and another on the main street. Bus and air connections are easily made from St. Andrews.

Because cruisers from "the States," having come to St. Andrews, may wish to have some of the historical background of this most attractive region, the following footnote is taken from an article by Earl M. Benson in *The New York Times:*

> Among the town's early settlers were Loyalists who came in 1783 in square-rigged vessels from Castine, Me. They thought Castine, on the eastern bank of the Penobscot River, would be in British territory. When they learned that the St. Croix River was to be the boundary line, they sailed farther east to what is now St. Andrews. Some of them even took down their houses in sections and towed them in scows behind the ships. There are still many descendants of these Loyalists living in the town.
>
> These pioneers believed in town-planning. Before building began, the land was surveyed and laid out in squares. The thirteen side-streets, which begin at the water front, were named for King George III and his twelve children.
>
> At the wharf head the visitor will find one of the most rewarding spots in St. Andrews, the County Craft Shop, where the yard is bright with yarns drying in the breeze from the bay. Inside the wide door are the articles made in local cottages and farmhouses.

Two china shops display sets of Wedgwood, Chelsea, Royal Doulton, and Belleek that are as complete as those in many large cities. Another shop offers the products of various New Brunswick handicrafts— pottery, wooden ware, hand-wrought iron, and homemade jams, jellies, and cheeses.

The story of the building of Greenock Church is a strange one. In the early days there was but one church in the town, the Church of England, and the rector offered his church to the Presbyterians who had no place to worship. At a public meeting a townsman arose and charged the Presbyterians with being "too mean to build a church of their own." This aroused the ire of Christopher Scott, a wealthy sea captain, who came from Greenock, Scotland. He declared that the Presbyterians would have a church like the one in his native town and he would pay for it all himself. He kept his word, and the church was built in 1824.

This church, with its Christopher Wren spire, is remarkable for its fine proportions and excellent design. It is unique in that it was constructed without nails or any other metal except that which was used in the locks and door hinges. All woodwork was fastened together by wooden pegs, and today the church appears to be as sturdy as when it was built. Below the steeple clock is a colored bas-relief of a green oak tree, the coat of arms of Greenock. The three-deck pulpit of Honduras mahogany and curly maple, its panels edged with small hand-carved acorns, is a masterpiece.

Guides will take fishing parties for landlocked salmon and lake trout on Chamcook Lake. Small-mouth black bass are found in Wheaton Lake, and there is good fly-fishing for speckled trout and Atlantic salmon in the Digdeguash River.

There are two golf courses, one a tricky nine-hole and the other an eighteen-hole course overlooking Passamaquoddy Bay. Lunches are served at the golf clubhouse.

St. Croix Island, Maine (13398). Though there is no harbor here, the island affords an interesting stop on the way upriver. It was on this island that Pierre du Guast (Sieur de Monts) and Champlain and their men celebrated their first Christmas in the New World in 1604.

They remained only one winter, and then moved on to Port Royal, now Annapolis, Nova Scotia. Professor W. F. Ganong, who has written the best history of the island, has said, "From the day the keel of her small boat grated on the beach of Dochet [St. Croix] Island, this continent has never been without a population of those races which have made the history of the principal part of America—the French and the English." The island was made a national park in July 1949.

Anchor about 100 yards west of the white conical building on the west shore. The bell on the structure's west side is no longer used. There is no fog signal. Watch for a ledge, covered at high water, just northwest of this spot. Approach cautiously.

In a ledge at the highest spot on the island is a small metal marker with the legend "International Boundary." This may have been true once, but today the boundary between the United States and New Brunswick is in the middle of the river to the east. The United States Government owns part of the island, but not all of it. The light is unwatched.

The only historical marker is a metal plaque on a boulder on the northeast side of the island reading as follows:

To Commemorate
The Discovery and Occupation
of this Island by
De Monts and Champlain
Who Naming It
L'Isle Saincte Croix
Founded here 26 June 1604
The French Colony of Acadia
Then the Only Settlement
Of Europeans North of Florida
This Tablet is Erected by
Residents of the St. Croix Valley
1904

The French had a hard winter on the island; thirty-five of the original band of seventy-nine died of scurvy.

The burying ground, where a few skeletons have been unearthed, is in the plateau at the south end of the island, but there are now no traces of it.

Anyone interested in the historical background of this region should read the references to St. Croix Island in *Voyages of Samuel de Champlain* by W. L. Grant (Charles Scribner's Sons, New York, 1907).

There is an excellent account of the settlement in *St. Croix—the Sentinel River* by Guy Murchie (Duell, Sloan and Pearce, New York, 1947). See also *Coastal Maine: A Maritime History* and Francis Parkman's *Pioneers of France in the New World* (Little, Brown & Co., Boston, 1898).

A fitting conclusion to any reference to St. Croix Island is a few lines written by Henry Milner Rideout for the Tercentenary of St. Croix as an example of how one great line of poetry can spring out of a stanza of unremarkable verse.

Into the hill-cleft waterways
With ceaseless ebb and flow astir,
Into the sunset blaze
Craftily steering,
High on her mast
They bore the banner of Old France
To the new Land Acadia, and cast
Their anchor by this island of the bays

At the commandment of Pierre du Gast
And merry, brown Champlain, the King's geographer.

The river above St. Croix Island is reported to be very pleasant sailing, especially if it is thick down the bay. The St. Croix Yacht Club has a landing behind Todd's Point and may have an available mooring. Oak Bay is said to be pretty with what weir stakes there are visible at all tides. Anchor behind Campbell's Point.

Calais, Maine (13398). It is a long way up a narrow channel to Calais, only to be negotiated under sail with a fair wind. However, Calais and its opposite town, Saint Stephen, are good sources of supply and are on the bus line east to Saint John and west to Bangor. A considerable effort is being made to make Calais more attractive to yachtsmen. There is a landing at Saint Stephen and stores within easy reach.

Chapter XV

The Coast of New Brunswick and the Saint John River

Although the writer has cruised the New Brunswick coast and the Saint John River a number of times, most recently in 1993, he has relied heavily on the advice of other visitors from the United States and of Canadian yachtsmen, notably Mr. Gerry Peer. As contributors are not always named and quoted, the style of this chapter is varied, but the information is believed to be reliable.

General Conditions. The 40 miles between Head Harbour or Letete and Saint John can assume a variety of disguises according to the conditions. Usually in the summer the trip is a featureless grind, started at an inconvenient hour to catch the tide and completed under the tension of entering a harbor threatened by ocean-going vessels. If you are lucky enough to catch a northwest breeze, it is a magnificent sail at an incredible speed by a panorama of cliffs, hills, and forests broken by occasional tiny harbors. But run into a head wind, rain, or a real blow and the trip can be an absolute nightmare, especially when the tide turns against you. Shelters are few and widely spaced. In thick weather or heavy seas they are hard to find, and with a $3^1/2$-knot tide running, one's reckoning is soon only a little better than guesswork.

The first 10 miles, from Head Harbour to The Wolves, offers several harbors: Bliss Harbor, L'Etang, Black's Harbour, and Beaver Harbour on the north, and North Head Harbour on Grand Manan to the south. The whistle northeast of The Wolves is an excellent guide and easily found as the tides run generally east and west between Campobello and The Wolves. There are three powerful fog signals along this run—East Quoddy Head, Bliss Island, and Pea Point—not to mention the powerful horn on Lepreau.

The second 10 miles, from The Wolves to Lepreau, is dominated by the horn and whistle buoy at Lepreau. The armchair navigator, scanning Chart 4011 or 4116, would assume that little difficulty would be encountered here. The horn is positively shattering. The point on which it stands is high and bold. The whistle is well offshore and is big enough and loud enough to be worthy of its position. However, bending over the cabin table on a small boat bound E ³/₄ S from The Wolves, the situation looks very different—what you can see of it. Many cruising men aver that the fog factory, located on Point Lepreau, turns out a concentrated product experienced at its thickest in this region. Many cruising men who have been by Lepreau frequently have never seen it. The tide runs to the eastward in the first part of the course but soon sets heavily to the north into Mace's Bay. Off the point you will find, even on a still day, a very active tide rip, with short breaking seas and vigorous swirling currents. Standing on the plunging bowsprit, choked by fog, blasted by the horn blowing from a bearing it should not occupy, looking and listening for an elusive whistle—this is not quite the same as studying the chart before that comfortable fire at home.

Once you are well by Lepreau, however, the worst is over. On the run to Split Rock and thence to Saint John, the tide will affect your course but little. In the absence of the bell formerly off Split Rock, you will have to rely on the horn on Musquash, dead reckoning, or electronic navigation systems to tell when to turn the corner for Partridge Island, but the exact turning point is not crucial.

From Lepreau to Saint John there are three possible shelters: Dipper, Chance, and Musquash. Any of these will do for an anchorage to wait out an adverse tide. Beating against a Fundy tide is impossible, and even motoring against one in a low-powered auxiliary is a slow and tedious business. Each of these three harbors has a bell at the entrance. Dipper has an excellent breakwater, Chance has a government wharf, and the outer harbor at Musquash, although rolly on a southerly breeze, is just tolerable. The inner harbor is bottle-tight, but it is a long way in.

Once at Saint John, go up the falls as soon as the tide serves. See the article under Saint John for a more complete treatment of this subject.

With the falls astern, you have before you many miles of pleasant river, lovely coves, farmland and wooded hills, lakes, and pretty towns. Dangers are fairly well marked now—no more black cows to port and brown cows to starboard. The swimming is warm. Fog is nearly unknown. The people you meet are almost without exception hospitable. It is nearly perfect cruising ground. Only those cussed ones among us who don't like lotus as a steady diet yearn to get back to salt water.

Preparations. The wise skipper will not leave Grand Manan or Passamaquoddy without the basic equipment recommended in Chapter II. Of these, a reliable and accurately compensated compass is a *sine qua non*. You should also have channels 12 and 14 on your radiotelephone in order to receive information and instructions from Fundy Traffic in Saint John. The following charts are necessary:

U.S.	13394	Grand Manan Channel
Canadian	4001	Approaches to Bay of Fundy
	4116	Approaches to St. John
	4124	Harbours in Bay of Fundy
	4117	Saint John Harbour

Also you will need the latest editions of 4141 and 4142, charts of the Saint John River being revised in 1995.

One should also have a copy of the *Nova Scotia and Bay of Fundy Pilot*, *The Atlas of Tide and Current Charts: Bay of Fundy and Gulf of Maine*, the Canadian Tide and Current Tables, *Saint John River* (1994 edition), and for preliminary planning purposes, *Scotia/Fundy Marine Weather Guide*. All of these can be purchased from the Hydrographic Chart Distribution Office, Department of Fisheries and Oceans, 1675 Russell Road, P.O. Box 8080, Ottawa, Ontario, CANADA KIG 3H6, telephone (613) 998-4931, fax (613) 998-1217. Write and ask for a catalog. With your order send the exact price of your purchase by International Money Order in Canadian money. Allow plenty of time as it may be a slow business.

There are now a number of chart outlets in the United States which carry Canadian charts, among them L. J. Harri, Nautical Booksellers, 120 Lewis Wharf, Boston, MA 02110, telephone (800) 242-3352, fax 617-248-5855, and Chase-Leavitt & Co., 10 Dana Street, Portland, ME 04112, telephone (207) 772-3751.

Communications and Provisions. On the New Brunswick coast you are far out of range of Camden Marine Operator. One can call Yarmouth VAU on channel 16 and be switched to channel 26 to arrange a call, but it would be well to get in touch with VAU before departure. Most harbors have an outdoor pay telephone near the shore from which one can make calling-card calls.

Few indeed are the small village stores which used to exist alongshore. Local people drive to supermarkets inland. Blacks Harbour has the only one you can be sure of short of Saint John.

Following are some notes on the passage from Passamaquoddy Bay to Saint John, contributed by Mr. Gerry Peer of Saint John. He has cruised widely on this coast and elsewhere and has proved most hospitable to the writer and to many other yachtsmen who visit these waters.

My Thoughts on Going up the Bay: When I want to go up in one day to Saint John, I usually leave from Blacks or Beaver Harbour. I do not recommend going up to the head of Blacks but behind the Grand Manan Ferry Wharf at the entrance to L'Etang. This is an easy place to get in and out of in a fog and there are a number of winter moorings for yachts, which are usually available. A half-mile walk will give supplies. Because of the unpleasant smells in this berth, I have been using Fisherman's Cove behind Bliss Island lately. The run from here or Blacks Harbor will cut 10 miles off the run from North Head or East Quoddy and many times is the difference in trying to make slack tide at the Reversing Falls.

Beaver is another 4 miles up the coast and is that much closer, but does have a fish factory in it. It is easy to get in and out of and well marked, but watch the weirs to port on entering. A couple of times I have found them in my way when coming in in a fog or at night. The harbour has provided a surge the odd time, as it is wide open to the southeast.

A good suggestion is to take a day from North Head Harbour or St. Andrews and stop in at the Wolves for a couple of hours, ending up at Blacks or Beaver for the run to Saint John the next day. If beachcombing and remote areas are your thing, the Wolves are a delight. East Wolf has about three or four fishermen shacks, which may or may not be occupied, in a cove on the north side, offering good protection from the prevailing southwester. There are some large rocks well up in this cove, but the water is so clear they can easily be sighted if one proceeds slowly. There is a path from this cove to a pebble beach on the other side, where the beachcombing is excellent. The birds, animals, and vegetation are uniquely interesting. The other islands are equally interesting and uninhabited. The light on South Wolf is now unmanned and automatic.

Pt. Lepreau now has a very conspicuous structure in the reactor building of the new nuclear power plant on the point. It is well lighted. The other structure that marks the horizon on the way to Saint John is in the cove about 3 miles up the bay from Split Rock. One can see the stack and the smoke it spews out from Grand Manan on a clear day.

It perhaps should be pointed out that to go inside the whistle buoy off Pt. Lepreau with any sea running at all can be a smashing experience. The seas in the rip are as close to being a vertical wall as I have seen, and more water goes over the boat than under it.

Tiner's Point horn is no more. It is now on Musquash Light around Split Rock Point and is not nearly as good.

Saint John River Weather: One last comment—the weather in the Saint John River Valley and adjacent area is generally fine in the summer months, a fact that may seem unbelievable after what may often be a long run through dungeon fog to get up the coast to Saint John. Once through the falls, even with the most solid fog condition outside and in the harbor, I have never seen a zero visibility condition in the river proper. There are low ceilings and rain occasionally, as anywhere else in the East, but the weather is generally sunny, warm, and dry. Swimming is superb, as the water is considerably warmer in the river and lakes than the Bay of Fundy. The winds prevail from the south and west, with occasionally fresh northwesters when a front has gone by. This makes for ideal sailing along close shores with no sea. Nothing is pleasanter than scudding along among verdant farmlands at 7 knots with not a ripple underneath. The height of the river varies from time to time but only through a foot or so, and I have found the soundings on the charts excellent.

L'Etang Harbour, New Brunswick (4124). Although the entrance is nearly choked off with salmon pens and at times rank with the effluvia from Blacks Harbour, L'Etang's upper reaches are wild and beautiful, well worth exploring, particularly if the fog lies thick outside. Finger Bay and the L'Etang River are pleasant, protected, and secluded. L'Etang Head and McCann Island would be wonders of the world if they were located west of Schoodic.

Back Bay, New Brunswick (4124). This snug little anchorage is one of the few secure harbors with supplies between Campobello and Saint John. It is protected by a ruined breakwater built in 1962. Behind it is a wharf to which a visitor can tie. There are also likely to be vacant moorings. Inquire at the wharf.

There is a sardine factory here and a number of salmon pens. Near the wharf are two small stores with such provisions as will keep a crew alive. No fuel is available unless enough is needed to justify calling a tank truck from St. George.

Mr. Philip Hooper, who supervises the salmon and the processing plant nearby, is a good source of local information. His father, Sylvester Hooper, former owner of the store and now retired, is eager to be of help.

Bliss Harbour, New Brunswick (4124). This is a well-protected harbor between Bliss Island and Frye Island, often clear when it is thick outside. There are good anchorages in Fisherman Cove on the southern side and between Fox Island and Frye Island on the north. In 1994 there were salmon pens on the northwestern side.

Explore some of the other coves around McCann Island with which the writer is unacquainted.

Blacks Harbour, New Brunswick (4124). This harbor has some advantages for the cruising yacht, but the factory smell and the filth on the water are so bad that they very nearly eclipse whatever is to be gained.

It is nearer to Saint John than any other good harbor west of Lepreau.

It is easy of access even under adverse conditions, with a powerful horn on Pea Point, a bell outside, a light on Roaring Bull, and a wide entrance with a bold shore on the northerly side. About a mile from the ferry wharf are a thoroughly adequate grocery store, a hardware store, a telephone, and a post office in the Oceans and Fisheries building. The town is on the main road from Saint Stephen to Saint John, over which run buses several times a day. The ferry to Grand Manan runs from the first wharf on the south side. Ice is available at Daley's Convenience Store on the road to town.

However, you may not want to go in beyond the ferry wharf. There are a few moorings in a cove east of the wharf and a telephone on the wharf available 8 A.M. to 5 P.M.

Above this cove the water is a filthy brownish gray, with a layer of grease on top that prevents a ripple from appearing on its surface. It smells foul.

This is the site of the Connors plant, said to be the world's biggest sardine cannery. Connors also smokes and cans Kipper Snacks and processes salmon from the numerous pens.

Once you are off the Connors wharf, the stench fades and the country becomes quite attractive. The town is said to be a company town, most of it owned by Connors, not very picturesque but entirely adequate as a supply center. However, once you have seen it and accomplished your purpose, you will do well to depart for one of the lovely anchorages up the L'Etang River or in Bliss Harbour.

Beaver Harbour, New Brunswick (13398, 4124). With a bell outside, a light on Drews Head, and another at the entrance and with a substantial government wharf to protect its anchorage, Beaver Harbour is a possible alternative to Blacks Harbour and much more pleasant. Although it is somewhat off the direct route to Saint John, it is the closest shelter to Lepreau on the west. There are several salmon pens in the harbor, but there are moorings and some room to anchor. Ashore there is a post office, grocery store, and telephone but no fuel or water at the wharf.

Point Lepreau, New Brunswick (4128). This promontory, about halfway between Head Harbour and Saint John, is marked with a light, a whistle buoy, and a powerful fog signal. It is further identified by a huge nuclear-generating plant behind it. Coming east on the flood tide, you will be sucked into Mace's Bay and hear the horn to starboard. In coming out to find the whistle buoy, you will encounter the worst of a nasty tide rip. Better go well outside the whistle or *close* inshore—within 200 yards of the shore. On the last of the flood there is a strong back set close to the shore east of the light.

Dipper Harbour, New Brunswick (4116). About halfway from Head Harbour to Saint John, this is a good stopping place for the yacht bound either east or west if the tide is wrong. It is an attractive harbor under any circumstances.

There is a bell outside only a short run from Lepreau whistle. The course thence to the light on the end of the breakwater takes one just clear of the wicked ledges off Fishing Point. Notice that the rocks west of Dipper Harbour are red and those east of it are black or gray, a help in finding the entrance. There is a can well inshore to port and a nun to starboard before one comes to the breakwater. Inside the breakwater the dredged area extends a short way inside the wharf and the lobster cars, but it has silted up to about 6 feet at low water. Move cautiously and allow for about a 20-foot range of tide.

There are two floats alongside the wharf so one need not climb a ladder, but there is no gasoline, diesel oil, or water. Fuel trucks come to supply the fishermen on Friday and Saturday.

There is an outdoor pay telephone near the head of the wharf but no store within several miles.

Near the head of the harbor is a large lobster pound which ships lobsters, refrigerated, packed in wood chips in cardboard boxes. The survival rate is excellent and the weight of the box is so much less than if the lobsters were packed in rockweed and ice that air transport is practical.

A short walk up the road from the wharf is the Fundy Haven Dining Room, a restaurant specializing in local seafood locally cooked. It is well spoken of.

Anyone bound west can leave Dipper on the last of the flood and find a strong back set up the shore to Lepreau. On a smooth day the outer edge of this westerly current is clearly defined against the easterly current outside.

Chance Harbour, New Brunswick (4116). Although not so well protected as Dipper, Chance offers a satisfactory refuge from a head tide. There is a bell outside and a can off Reef Point, which does not always appear to be precisely in its charted position. There is a mean little rip inside it. To starboard is a yellow daymarker. There is no charted light on the end of the government wharf, but a powerful streetlight serves the purpose. There is no really satisfactory anchorage in Chance, but with permission one can tie up to one of the fishermen berthed at the outer end of the wharf on the inside. There is a small dredged area inside the wharf, but it does not extend far from the wharf and its edge is precipitous. Move cautiously as you turn to come alongside.

There is no fuel or water at the wharf and no store within walking distance.

Musquash Harbour, New Brunswick (4116). This is another possible anchorage in which to wait out a foul tide. It is well marked with a lighthouse and a horn on Musquash Head and a bell, which in 1993 appeared to be where Chart 4116 shows can "KT1." Anchorage in the outer harbor near can "KT3" is not too bad in ordinary weather, but can be very uncomfortable in a strong southerly at high water. Five Fathom Hole at the head of the harbor has a 6-foot buoyed channel and is perfectly protected but is a long way from the direct course alongshore.

Saint John, New Brunswick (4117). Saint John is a major seaport, Canada's only ice-free Atlantic seaport except for Halifax, and is much frequented by large commercial vessels. There is a formal traffic-separation scheme here which yachts should avoid entirely. As traffic in this busy port is controlled by radio, you should call "Fundy Traffic" on channel 16 as you pass Lepreau. You will be switched to channel 14 west of Lepreau and to channel 12 east of Lepreau and in Saint John Harbour. Mr. Gerry Peer, who sails the Fundy coast extensively, contributes the following notes:

> If it is at all foggy, I usually call them (Fundy Traffic) to say where I am going and my ETA. They will give a run-down on the ship movements expected and those holding at anchor outside. Also once you have reported and identified yourself, they track you to your destination. As they have receivers at three points in the Bay, they can also do a radio fix on you if your navigation is off and your position is unknown. I think I would have to be quite desperate before I resorted to asking where I was, but I know of some who, en route to Digby from Saint John, did not know if they were east or west of it and Fundy Traffic not only gave them a position but course and distance and talked them in.
>
> It is also worth noting that Saint John Coast Guard Radio VAR is now shut down and all calls for land links are made through Yarmouth VAU who have a repeater at Saint John. One calls on channel 16 and will be asked to switch to 26 international to arrange for the call. Also Fundy Traffic, who will also answer on 16, get a little owly when asked to arrange a phone call as they cannot and it is not their job.
>
> Fundy Traffic will sometimes call Customs if you get a friendly operator.

If there is concern over barge traffic in the Falls, the pulp mill fuel barge for instance, Fundy Traffic will on contact give commercial traffic expected.

The New Brunswick shore is a good bold shore all the way to Negro Head. A course from Split Rock to Partridge Island runs just outside the 20-fathom curve, which gives a good check on position. A yacht need not go out to Black Point whistle but can run for the Partridge Island radio beacon and horn and make the flashing bell southeast of it. Thence run up the line of buoys. Even if you have a flood tide, you may encounter a head current as the fresh water from the river rushes out over the incoming salt water from the Bay of Fundy. If there is a large vessel in the channel, a yacht does well to leave the green buoys close to starboard and keep out of the way. You will come right up on the stern of the Digby ferry at the first wharf in West Saint John, a startling experience in the fog if you are not prepared for it.

Just above Saint John Harbour, at the gateway to the river, lie the Reversing Falls. This is a ledge over which the river falls into the harbor at low water. As the tide in the harbor rises, it reaches the level of the water in the river. At this time the current over the falls is more or less slack. As the tide continues to rise, the Bay of Fundy pours up over the ledge into the river. The slack is repeated again as the tide falls. The duration and exact time of the slack varies with the height of the water in the river and the tide in the harbor. With the river low, a spring tide and a southerly wind, for instance, the slack on the rising tide will come early. Normally slack water occurs 2 hours and 25 minutes after high water and 3 hours and 50 minutes after low water.

If the tide is favorable, one can proceed directly to the Reversing Falls; if not, one will have to wait in Saint John Harbour. If you have not cleared Canadian Customs in St. Andrews, North Head, or Welshpool, you can use the layover time to do so at Market Slip on the east side of the harbor just above the Coast Guard wharf and in the shadow of the Hilton hotel, the first tall building as you scan the Saint John skyline from west to east. Mr. Peer writes:

A large Hilton hotel now prominently occupies the north side of Market Slip with a large Heritage area and a shopping plaza. A floating wharf is located at this point and can be used for access to the downtown area and Customs. There is room for a number of boats, but it gets shoal at the inner end on a spring or moon tide (3–4 feet).

One also must be careful approaching or leaving the float as it sits in non-tidal water except for the last 20 feet which has about a 2-plus knot tide upstream across the end and under the float. I have seen a number of unsuspecting skippers put on an unwonted show when coming to or leaving the wharf.

This wharf is also used for tour boats so those lying at the wharf may find they are asked to move up or out to let a boat in. If one moves up as far as the depth will allow, it is best, and it is better to lie out of the tide run. It does tend to be a bit public as you become the local tourist attraction with people staring down. At low tide there is not much privacy when they look down your main hatch as you eat dinner. But each to his own. Some may like the convenience of the many shops and restaurants only a stone's throw away.

I still prefer to wait out the tide anchored between piers 1 and 2 or 3 and Rodney Terminal on the west side.

If Fundy Traffic is not too busy, they may be willing to give you the time of slack water at the falls for the particular day, allowing for the height of the river and the time of the moon.

As slack water approaches, move up the middle of the river under the first bridge; and as you approach the sharp turn by Split Rock and the second bridge, keep over to the right where there is an eddy and slack water. If the tide is running out, wait until the current appears to moderate enough for you, crack the throttle wide open, and try it. If you can get up by Split Rock and under the bridge, you can make it. If you can't, the current will carry you back and you will have to wait. If it is a near thing, drop back and wait.

When the tide looks to be as slack as it is going to be, which is not really slack but an uneasy swirling equilibrium between the river current and the Fundy tide, pass close to Split Rock and under the middle of the bridge. Then edge over close to the pulp mill. You will see a great boiling and swirling to starboard. This is the "pot." Avoid it. Sometimes pulp logs, pulled under by whirlpools, are shot up by boils and their own buoyancy with force enough to bend a propeller or start a seam. Also, the surface is often covered with thick suds from a detergent used in the mill, so you can't see the logs. Move cautiously.

Coming down the river, arrive in plenty of time and wait at the Saint

John Power Boat Club. Here you will find slips with water and electricity, 5 to 6 feet of water at low tide, a hospitable welcome, and reliable advice. When the time of slack water approaches, edge down the river and wait on the edge of the cove just above the mill until conditions are right.

Remember that, even if the tide in the harbor below the bridge is supposed to be flooding, the fresh water may be running out over it. You may be shot down the harbor a lot faster than you intended and plunged from the bright warm sunshine of the river into a choking thick bank of cold Fundy fog.

The following notes were written by Mr. Gerald Peer for the guidance of visitors:

My Thoughts on the Falls: I have found over the last few years that if one calculates the slack by *Eldridge* it can be as much as 20 minutes out, coupled with a variance of up to 20 minutes either side of the calculated slack. Depending on the height of the river, this could give a run of water that could make passage through either impossible or a bit hair-raising.

The slack is calculated on the normal summer low. With the advent of the Macdaquack dam above Fredericton and after a heavy rain, the river can be 4 feet above normal summer low in July or August. In May, at the height of the spring runoff or freshet, slack is at high tide if there is one at all. Just keep in mind, if the river is high, the slack is early on a high slack, i.e., 2 hours and 10 or 15 minutes, instead of 2 hours 25 minutes after high tide; and it is late on a low slack, i.e., 4 hours and 5 or 10 minutes after low tide, instead of 3 hours and 50 minutes.

My boat *Keloose* can do about 6½ knots with the safety valve tied down, and I stand still at 30 minutes after the slack. The fastest run is at the mill, with under the bridge a close second. If I can get by the mill, I can make it.

If one goes through the falls at dead slack, it is no trick at all. If in doubt about the time, go up about 20 minutes early and keep on the north side next to Ocean Steel. You can proceed right up to a point where you can see Split Rock under the bridge. When the water stops running by the rock, proceed. There is very little current in on that shore on a flood or an ebb. On going out, after passing Kingsville and Indian Town Harbour, head for the chipping machine on the pulp mill. You can go right up to the mill in quiet water and watch the rip around the mill until it stops. In my own boat I leave the RKYC 1 hour before the slack and do 6 knots. This gives me about 10 minutes to wait for the slack. The run at the mill can be deceiving. It is usually running a little harder than it looks.

The height under the bridges is inches less than 80 feet at summer low, with the railway bridge the lowest. There is more clearance on a low slack. I took *Running Tide* through some years ago with a 78-foot mast. During her stay we had a heavy rain, and we went down through early on a low slack so we could make it. The next day the river went up 3 inches, which would have given us problems. That is the highest mast I have put through the falls.

By giving oneself lots of time and with careful calculations and observation at either end, no one should have any problems with this stretch of water.

Saint John Power Boat Club. This is a small, hospitable, and handy stopping place on the eastern shore just above the falls. It is essentially a do-it-yourself powerboat club with no pretensions to yachty elegance. It exists primarily as a base for its own members. It has no telephone listing and no one monitors VHF radio. However, a slip is often open for a visitor, and gasoline, diesel fuel, and water are available.

The entrance is marked by a flashing red light on pilings, which is to be left very close to starboard. There are said to be waterlogged timbers on the bottom not far from the pilings, over which one informant bumped several times. The dredged channel is marked with spars, each with a band of red. Inside is a constellation of slips, one of which is likely to be open.

There is an outdoor telephone up a flight of steps on the side of the clubhouse from which one can call a taxi. There is a gate at the head of the float which is supposed to be kept locked. Therefore it is well to row across the little cove to avoid being locked out should a member remember.

It is about a half mile walk to a shopping mall where everything is available.

For one going down the falls, this is a good place to wait although it lacks the romantic quality of places farther up the river.

Royal Kennebecasis Yacht Club, Millidgeville, New Brunswick (4319). Once by the falls, continue up the river through the dramatic clefts in the rocky hills, round Boars Head (aptly named), and anchor off the Royal Kennebecasis Yacht Club in Brothers Cove at Millidgeville. There is a buoyed channel up to the club, marked at the outer end with a red spar and a flasher and from there with red and green spars. Head for the flasher and then for the red flash on the club. This will take you right up the middle of the channel to the corner of the wharf. There is about 7 feet at the front of the wharf. Tie up here and inquire for a mooring or anchorage. Slips with water and electricity may be rented. There is a dinghy landing behind the wharf and a launching ramp.

At the club wharf one can buy gasoline, diesel fuel, and ice. A water hose is available and a pumpout station. Inside are showers, a telephone, and a substantial bar, open traditionally at five o'clock. Light meals are served Monday through Friday. There is a small marine railway next to the club, and nearby an excellent marine supply store, which also sells charts. There is no longer a grocery store in Millidgeville, but Saint John is only a ten-minute taxi ride away and everything is available there. Investigate the situation on buying bonded liquor. If you agree not to broach it until you leave Canada, there may be a substantial saving.

The members of the Royal Kennebecasis Yacht Club are without doubt among the friendliest and most hospitable people in the yachting world. They will do anything they can to make your visit pleasant. There are a few amenities that seem minor, but that the considerate yachtsman will follow. For instance, you should fly the Canadian flag, the maple leaf, at your starboard spreader on entering Canadian waters and the United States ensign at the staff astern or on the leach of the mainsail. When you take in the American flag at night, take in the Canadian one, too. Bring along an extra club burgee, especially if you belong to a club whose members do not often visit Saint John. Always write out "Saint John"— don't abbreviate it. And remember that St. Johns is in Newfoundland, not New Brunswick.

We who have been treated so hospitably in Canada await the opportunity to return the hospitality at our own yacht clubs and in our own harbors.

The Royal Kennebecasis Yacht Club is a center for yachting on the river, not only for visitors, but for local people as well. On one occasion, the Cruising Club of America, an assemblage of salt-water, stick-and-string gentlemen accustomed to Bermuda and transatlantic passages, visited the Club. They proceeded from Massachusetts in a seamanlike manner through all kinds of weather. From Mount Desert on they had it thick all the way, but being accomplished navigators, they all made it without serious incident by means of compass, chart, fathometer, RDF, and all the best equipment and judgment. At Saint John, a local pilot met them. At just the earliest reasonable time, they passed the falls and proceeded triumphantly through the last of a sunny summer day to the peaceful anchorage at Millidgeville. As they were snugging down, a power cruiser came roaring in, flying the American yachting ensign and bearing a nondescript pennant at her bow staff. The owner bumped up to the wharf. A member of the Cruising Club, thinking perhaps the new arrival had been a little late for slack water at the falls, asked, "How did you make it coming up the falls?"

"What falls?" inquired the new arrival.

He had come all the way from New York on an oil-company chart; and, without any advance planning, or even knowledge of their existence, had hit the falls at exactly slack water.

Kennebecasis Bay. This is a very pleasant and unfrequented cruising ground, at the entrance of which is the hospitable Rothesay Yacht Club. The bay is well worth exploration. Some of the nicer summer homes of Saint John residents are situated in the communities along the shore, and much of the sailing activity of the various clubs is carried on in this area. Forester Cove, at the entrance to the Kennebecasis River, is large and deep but gives good protection. Attractive sand beaches can be found on the north end and in the cove at the south end of Long Island.

The river itself is well buoyed for 5 feet of draft to Hampton, a very interesting trip of bends and oxbows to the town itself for those who like gunkholing. If the river is low, 5 feet is a bit tight before the bridge in sight of Hampton.

If one does not want to stay in the RKYC area but be close to the city, there are a number of good anchorages around Kennebecasis Island. Milkish Channel is a quiet area with Keith Cove just beyond the island cable ferry, an excellent shelter. If the wind is in the northeast, a berth off the RKYC can be uncomfortable. McCormacks Cove provides excellent shelter and good holding.

The Saint John River. To one just up the falls from cold Maine waters, double-digit tides, and Fundy fogs, the river experience is almost unreal. There is no tide, and the water is fresh and warm, ideal for swimming above Kennebecasis Island. In the lower part of the river, the shores are mountainous, dropping in cliffs into deep water. Above Grand Bay the mountains step back from the shore and become more gentle. The shores are at first suburban, then give way to forested hills with small settlements where tributaries enter. Beware of bars off these. Then the valley widens above Long Reach, and the river flows in gentle bends between grassy islands fringed with maple trees. Cows graze near the shore. Overhead soar ospreys and the occasional eagle. From the main river, channels lead off to interesting coves and bays, not all of which are mentioned later.

No longer are logs brought down to the mill in booms, as they used to be. The logs are now reduced to chips and taken down in a barge. If you meet the barge in a narrow place, you will do well to give it all the room you can.

Do not pass close ahead or astern of ferries. They progress by winching themselves across the river on a cable, which is close to the surface forward and aft. At Westfield at the foot of the Reach and at Gondola Point on the Kennebecasis pay particular attention to this for there are two ferries often passing each other in midstream.

The waters are protected enough so no sea ever makes up, and a breeze usually draws up from the south. Fog is almost unknown. An occasional salmon leaps, and local yachts add interest to the scene, especially on weekends.

Whelpley Cove is a good spot except in a northwest or easterly breeze. Catons Island off the cove is now a church youth camp. They are most hospitable in allowing visitors to walk the trails on the island. Land on the point and speak to one of the supervisors. There is also a cove at Oak Point. However, it is not a particularly attractive place to stay because of the current. Chub Channel to the east of Grassy Island is narrow, well buoyed, and an interesting deviation from the Oak Point side.

Beyond the dramatic Gorham Bluff one can follow the chart sharply to the right or proceed north along the river and enter the narrower and deeper channel between Pig and Hog islands and get into Kingston Creek and Belle Isle Bay, one of the most beautiful and desirable cruising areas on the river.

On the right around Gorham Bluff is Shamper Cove. The channel through Shamper Cove is very weedy and no longer buoyed. It is all right under sail, but under power it does a number on fouling your propeller. Turning right to the s'uthard brings one into Kingston Creek, one of my favorite spots. The west side of the cove is bounded by high granite bluffs and, farther in, a steep hillside down which a rocky brook falls with a fine soft music on quiet nights. On the east side the cove is bounded by steep meadows and farmlands, both sides affording fine shelter except in the case of strong winds out of the north or south. About ten years ago Kingston Creek was navigable for a distance of almost 2 miles, but, due to continued logging operations in the surrounding woods, it is difficult to carry 6 feet more than a mile in, which is far enough. The rest of the cove provides good anchorages along the shores and great exploring country and is quiet and peaceful.

It is reported to be windy in strong southwest weather as the wind funnels through the anchorage.

Belle Isle Bay

From Kingston Creek, exploration of Belle Isle Bay is a *must*. It has bold shores, and from our experience it is navigable for a distance of about 5 miles for drafts of up to 10 feet. Several points make out from the shores, and small sandbars can be found off these, but they are clearly identifiable. When entering Belle Isle Bay, either enter through Shamper Channel, a route much used by local boats, or continue north past Shamper Cove and make a U-turn to the east at the north end of Belle Isle (Hog Island). (See inset on Chart 4141.) At that north end is a red-and-green spar and a red spar. Go between them. Continue south through the buoyed channel into Belle Isle Bay and turn northeast for Ghost Island, on the east side of which appears to be a naturally formed obelisk of rock. The island is steep-to and you can tie right up to the trees on most of it, except where the beach lies on the west side. The scenery at this point is grand with high granite bluffs giving way to thick woodlands and occasional farms.

Around the next high bluff on the left lies one of the best coves I have ever been in. It is Jenkins Cove, named for the family owning and still operating the farm on the north side. The cove is spacious but well protected, with good holding ground. There are three houses in the little cove at the entrance. Here are moored a number of high-speed motorboats and a plane, whose pilot, up for an evening flip, sometimes has trouble landing because of the traffic in the cove. Farther up, the cove is still unsettled, the only other house being above the old wharf. Moose and deer are a common sight in the old pasture near the wharf. The road passes close to the westward of the cove. The store is a good mile up the road to the north.

Urquhart's Cove, just beyond Jenkins Cove, is not nearly as scenic and, being a V-shaped cove and open to the south, it does not afford very much protection in strong winds. A little way down the bay on the opposite side is Erbs Cove, which we have looked into but never entered. While it appears to be deep, it is another wide-mouthed cove with no particular attraction. Another mile up the bay is Long Point, beyond which 8 feet can be carried up to Grey's Point, a half mile from Hatfield Point, the end of the bay. Six feet can then be carried to the Hatfield Point wharf. Here is a very pretty town, well worth the trip.

As you come out of the bay to go on up the river, the natural track would be up the Hog Island Channel. The red buoy about halfway up the eastern side of Hog Island must be left to starboard and rounded sharply. The channel lies close to Hog Island until nearing the north end, where it swings over to Pig Island, passing between Hog Island and a green buoy as it enters the river proper.

Navigation and Canadian Buoyage

Since we are moving well up the river now, it may be appropriate to have a few remarks on navigation and buoyage from here on. The Hydrographic Office in 1994 was doing a complete review of the buoyage in the river with decisions available in 1995. Navigators using old charts should expect to find buoy numbers, colors, and locations changed although most of the channels are much as they were. An exception is Shamper channel, now almost closed by weeds and unbuoyed. If the river is high, as it sometimes is during the summer months, spars showing on the charts often project above the surface only a little, even 6 inches. These sometimes have to be sought out, but with no tide, smooth water, and only a moderate current, you can usually go right up to where you think something should be and look around. What looks like a dead tree stuck in the bottom should not be disregarded. It may replace a spar buoy. Now, however, most of the spars have been replaced with Ottawa Valley buoys, metal buoys with wooden tops, a great improvement.

In some areas, such as Chub Channel behind Grassy Island at Oak Point, the thoroughfares to the upper lakes and the upper Kennebecasis are marked by small buoys.

The channels among the islands are relatively easy to follow, in that most of the islands are low and grassy, and the weeds and aquatic plants seem to grow toward the surface up to a depth of almost exactly 5 feet. If uncertain, follow the water clear of growth and it will almost always be deep. A great many cattle, sheep, and some hogs graze on the islands in the river and along the grassy shores. However, the old tale that the brown cows will always be to starboard and the black-and-white ones to port when entering just isn't so.

Things indicated as lights with varying characteristics on the chart may be almost invisible by day because of foliage and location. By night, with a few exceptions, these lights will average what appears to be about 25-watt intensity.

Lastly, we mention the matter of birch and spruce stakes with the foliage still attached used in the Maquapit and French Lake area. Softwood, spruce, or pine stakes are to be treated as green; hardwood, birch, or maple, are to be treated as red. The depths may vary somewhat from the charts, but I have found that in most periods when we have visited the river, the charted depths are conservative. As mentioned above, the Canadian authorities have taken definite steps to improve the aids in the river and have done a great deal, particularly in the lower portion. In most places local bush stakes have been replaced with Ottawa Valley buoys.

Tennant Cove to Grand Lake

Tennant Cove, just beyond the entrance to Belle Isle Bay, is a poor one, having a bad entrance and being shoal. Gas may be purchased at Evandale at the wharf north of the ferry landing on the west bank of the river. Euleigh Hotel serves meals.

Our next run would be up the right side of the river, passing either side of Spoon Island and bearing right to go up the east side of Long Island or up the west side of Long Island to Queenstown, where there is a public wharf, a store, and Broadview Farm Restaurant. The owners will, on call, pick up guests at the wharf. There is an anchorage for those drawing 5 feet or less in the creek leading into Musquash Lake on Lower Musquash Island. Just before coming to the end of this sizable island, one should enter Washadamoak Creek, passing along the east side of Lower Musquash Island until the entrance to Washadamoak Lake appears. It is buoyed and, though narrow, can easily be followed, bringing the cruising man into a lovely, long lake with numerous coves and bays and fine cruising country. This lake is now accurately charted.

Many New Brunswick yachtsmen recommend the anchorage at Colwell's wharf up the Lawson River beyond the entrance to the lake. At Colwell's there is an excellent German butcher shop that has buffalo meat, good sausage, and Black Forest cake, by order.

A little farther along one comes to Lewes Cove, known locally as Big Cove, on the southern shore of the lake about 3 miles from the entrance. Go *well* in, past the little island, and anchor at the end off the last farmhouse to port. Draft of 6 feet is all right, but anchor to starboard and well in. There is a lovely granite bluff and two small wooded islands, Spruce and Birch. It affords protection from all directions and is an excellent spot. About 3 miles beyond is the town of Cambridge, with the village of Narrows on the opposite side of the lake. Here limited supplies may be secured. There are two good restaurants at Narrows.

The bridge at Narrows blew down in the Ground Hog Day gale. A new bridge has been built, but the charted clearance of 45 feet is optimistic. Thirty-nine feet would be a safe figure.

I am told the lake is navigable for considerable draft as far as Cole's Island, another 10 miles. Though the scenery is not quite as dramatic as Belle Isle Bay, this lake definitely should not be missed, the hills rising to several hundred feet on either side.

If one is leaving Washadamoak Lake and going on north, the narrow, deep channel reminds one of the European canals. On leaving Colwell's Creek, one should be careful not to continue to the north of Upper Musquash Island, as a bar obstructs this channel about halfway out to the river. Round Killaboy Island. If one goes up to the cardinal buoy, "JTK" in Lawson Passage, depths are 6 feet or less in summer low water. There is, however, an uncharted deep channel carrying 10 feet around Killaboy Island, not between Killaboy and Musquash, 75 to 100 feet off the grass. If you look carefully, you can see it as it is grass-free and the shoal is not. Turn south and head for the open river, turning north when in the mainstream. Continuing north, we enter Gagetown Creek and tie up at Gagetown, where limited supplies and fuel may be had.

Gagetown is one of the principal towns on the river for yachtsmen. Here is a long float with 7 feet alongside and a number of rental moorings owned by K & W Quality Meats, successors to the well-known Tom Colpitts, who sold out and went to Florida. At the float one finds gasoline, diesel fuel, water, and ice. Toilets are available, but no showers—scarcely needed as the water in the river is warm and fresh. The K & W market a step to the left on the main street has an adequate variety of canned provisions, fruit and vegetables, dairy products, beer, wine, hard liquor, and of course, quality meats. One can call ahead—(800) 263-4830—and supplies will be delivered to the float. Credit cards are acceptable. There is a bank a little farther along the main street and a post office. There is also a craft shop featuring New Brunswick gifts.

The village, established soon after 1758, was populated largely by Loyalists from the United States shortly after 1783. It maintains into our century a well-planned, leisurely, and dignified air.

One can lie at the float or at one of the K & W moorings, but some prefer to seek greater peace and perhaps solitude in Mount Creek about half a mile above Gagetown. The chart shows no water in it, but proceed slowly with depth sounder or sounding pole and anchor in 8 feet well inside the trees on the left. Should you be concerned about swinging ashore, run a line to a tree. Row up the creek another half mile to the ruins of the oldest house in New Brunswick, but do it before dusk, for the mosquitoes are numerous and bloodthirsty.

Our plans would now take us south on Gagetown Creek again and up the river proper to the almost invisible entrance to the Jemseg River, where one passes between shores about 75 feet apart to enjoy a 3-mile run up to the highway bridge at the village of Jemseg. This is a new high-level bridge with 75-foot clearance, replacing the old drawbridge. There is a restaurant and store at Jemseg and gasoline stations along the highway. The Saturday morning Farmers' Market at Jemseg Bridge is well worth a visit from 7 A.M. to 12 P.M. Breakfast is available, and it offers a variety of baked goods, meats, vegetables, and crafts.

If the chip barge, which runs between Chipman and Saint John, is in the channel, it is advisable to wait until it clears the channel before proceeding. It is on a tow line and can fishtail and drive you out of the channel when passing. It looks like a hotel going by.

After successfully negotiating the bridge, we make for Grand Lake, following the marked channel out of the Jemseg River and across Purdy Shoal at the lower end of the lake. This channel is well marked, and with a few obvious places easily identified on the chart excepted, the whole area of Grand Lake is a fine cruising ground, with ample depths, sheltered coves and bays, and fine beaches. The water is generally clear and clean enough to drink, and we have often filled our tanks with it. It is suggested that this be done above Grand Point Bar.

Grand Lake, New Brunswick

The lake averages 3 miles in width and is about 25 miles long. In my opinion, no trip to the Saint John River should fail to include a run into Grand Lake. There is a marina with showers, laundry, and fuel supplies at Jemseg Bridge.

In Grand Lake the first important spot is Douglas Harbor on the northwest shore. This is a lovely series of coves shown in a detailed inset on the Canadian chart. Straight up the harbor toward the wharf will be found a long sand spit, which serves as a dandy swimming beach. We usually moor about halfway between the spit and the wharf in about 8 or 9 feet.

The cove on the left as one enters the harbor looks fine, but, though deep inside, has a 1-foot bar across the entrance and must be explored only in dinghies. The cove on the right, known as Bedroom Cove, is a beautiful place but crowded with moorings. There is usually room to anchor on the outside.

Up the shore from the wharf is a general store, which sells gasoline and ice, among many other things. Across the street is a public telephone.

Mill Cove and White Cove, on the southeast shore of the lake, are perfectly good anchorages, though wide coves, not very snug, and close to the Trans-Canada Highway. The same is true of Young's Cove about halfway up the lake, where we have been a couple of times when we wanted to get near the highway from Saint John in order to swap crews. Though we have never used it, the small cove inside Fanjoy Point near the village of Waterborough can also be used for the crew-shift problem. Cumberland Bay is a large bay running west-southwest to east-northeast and, having a wide mouth, is likely to be choppy with the prevailing winds.

As one enters the northeast arm between Goat Island and Cox Point, there are two coves on the left and one on the right. Barton Cove on the right is deep, but, again open to the southwest; Flowers Cove on the left is interesting and completely snug. Though the inner portion of Flowers Cove is blocked by a power line with a clearance of 38 feet, the outer cove is fine. We anchored in the center of a circle passing through the numerals 11, 14, 12, and 10. Favor the north shore. There was a bar in the middle where the chart shows 12 feet in 1977. The cove north of Flowers Cove is attractive and likely to be uncrowded. The entrance is well to starboard going in and is now buoyed. It is a very quiet place with only one camp on the shore. Fishing is reported to be good near the hatchery outfall at the cove end. At Newcastle Creek, a couple of miles farther up the left side of the lake, there is a small but deep harbor, a large power station, and a small town, the only sign of anything resembling big industry for miles. This is not a good place to lie but can be used for supplies if the charm of Grand Lake extends one's visit.

Into the North Woods

From here we embark on another delightful adventure by following the marked channel around Lead Island and Moray Points into the mouth of the Salmon River, a fine north-woods stream in which one can carry 6-foot draft for about 11 miles upriver to the town of Chipman, pretty nearly into the deep woods of central New Brunswick.

The banks of the Salmon River are thickly wooded, and when one can make the run upstream under sail, as we did, a sense of departure from the conventional cruising atmosphere is most evident. There is the delicious north-woods smell of pine and wild flowers, and the only sound is an occasional birdcall or the scurrying of animals in the woods. There is no sign of civilization, except at Camp Wesegum, a Canadian religious camp about halfway to Chipman.

After this peace and solitude we finally made the turn at Davis Turn and with some surprise saw three bridges, a dam, and a busy sawmill. You can tie up to the wharf at the foot of the bridge or to one of the scows tied along the bulkhead. This is a lumber town and railhead, with both Canadian Pacific and Canadian National railroads crossing the river at this point. All kinds of supplies are available in the town, and the people are most friendly and helpful. Our 40-foot cutter was the first masted vessel they'd seen in town, and we had a large number of visitors, adult and youthful, the latter bearing most welcome gifts of fresh blueberries and home-grown lettuce.

A local authority reports that RKYC cruises have been going regularly to this town for the last eighty years, sometimes with yachts up to 65 feet.

However, you can't take a tall-masted vessel all the way to Chipman, as there is a high-voltage line with a clearance of 54 feet just south of Iron Bound Cove, but it was a nice trip to that bend.

Another interesting side trip from Grand Lake is described below by Mr. Love in an excerpt from his account of a cruise in these waters in 1965 and is still accurate:

> While on this cruise I had occasion at the time of the Douglas Harbor rendezvous to make an investigation of the chain of lakes which run in a westerly direction from the southwest end of Grand Lake. We had towed a Boston Whaler along as tender, and I was able to make an extensive run in comparatively little time.
>
> The entrance to this fascinating waterway is at Indian Point 2.3 miles northwestward from the mouth of the Jemseg River and is marked by red-and-black spar buoys and bush stakes. One must stay close to in rounding Indian Point, and immediately behind it one finds a very neat cove with about 9 feet of water. At normal river height, 6 feet can be carried in.
>
> I had a beautiful trip through Maquapit Channel, or thoroughfare across Maquapit Lake, through French Lake Thoroughfare, across the bottom of French Lake and a short distance up to the Portobello River a distance of about 10 or 11 miles. What the status of the one highway bridge is I don't know, but it seemed operable, clearance being about 15 feet closed. [The French Lake bridge does not swing, but there is a depth of at least 5 feet for a considerable distance beyond. Ed.] This is a real gunk-hole trip, but perfectly beautiful. Another correspondent made this trip as far as the bridge in 1982 in a 38-foot ketch drawing 5 feet.

Note: A canoe trip of historic interest, one of the favorite water routes of the Indians in the early days, may be had by portaging at Maugerville from the Saint John to the Portobello River, a distance of one to two miles. French Lake is reached by descending the latter river and thence the various water areas just described through a channel to Grand Lake. The shores of the latter may be skirted throughout, if so desired, before rejoining the Saint John at Lower Jemseg. In very dry seasons sufficient water even for canoes may not be found in some parts of the Portobello River.

The low marshland and numerous ponds surrounding Grand, French, and Maquapit Lakes are the feeding grounds for large flocks of black ducks, whistlers, teal, and other water fowl. Each autumn brings numerous hunters to the vicinity for the annual duck shooting.

On to Fredericton, New Brunswick

This is the story of the "Rhine of North America," and obviously I am enthusiastic about it. The Saint John River, of course, continues in a northerly and westerly direction for many miles. It is navigable from where we left it at Lower Jemseg as far as Fredericton, with drafts as deep as 6 feet. This latter run I have never made because I have felt other parts of the river and area are more attractive. Fredericton itself is a small city bustling with business activity and a very active chamber of commerce, which puts on a prominent outboard and small-boat regatta every year. Fredericton Airport, only about 4 miles from Oromucto, is handy for crew changes. The air schedules are more reliable than at Saint John as there is much less chance of fog at Freedericton. For the average cruising man I think there are years of fascinating cruising to do in the area we have described.

Appendix A

Wildlife from the Deck:
An Introduction to the Birds and Mammals of the New England Coast by William P. Hancock, Maine Audubon Society

Few activities lend themselves better to an appreciation of wildlife than does ocean cruising. The sailor's lines of sight are long and unobstructed, affording opportunities to see and study birds and mammals that are unmatched in most terrestrial habitats. But perhaps even more significant is that cruising allows one the long periods of time so necessary to really observe wildlife in their natural habitat. Outside for the better part of every day—and sometimes well into the night as well—those who cruise the New England coast are a captive audience to a host of fascinating animals.

The New England coast straddles portions of two relatively distinct biogeographical regions, each of which is distinguished by its own geologic and oceanographic characteristics. And though a detailed discussion of these characteristics goes beyond the scope of this article, it is important to note that the distribution of the fauna along New England's coast and offshore waters is largely determined by them. The boundary line dividing these two regions is Cape Cod. South of the Cape and stretching to Cape Hatteras, North Carolina, is the Mid-Atlantic (Virginia) region, influenced by the Gulf Stream. The waters of this region

759

are characteristically warm and salty, particularly in the summer months. This encourages marine and bird life more commonly found in Southern waters, such as the blue crab and the black skimmer.

North of Cape Cod and reaching all the way to Labrador is the Boreal region. Here the water is more uniform in temperature throughout the year; as anyone who plunges in knows, it is cold even in the summer. The cold-water Nova Scotia current, flowing southwest along the coast of that province, turns into the Gulf of Maine and sets up a counterclockwise circulation that keeps cool water flowing south from the Bay of Fundy to Cape Cod and then east over Georges Bank. This nutrient-laden cold water, coupled with a large tidal range, supports ecosystems rich in wildlife diversity.

The birds and mammals to be seen while cruising New England's waters can be broadly divided into those which are found primarily along the immediate coastline and those which live offshore. But birds and sea mammals are also highly mobile and considerable overlap is commonplace; a tiny warbler or hummingbird may land on your boat 40 miles or more offshore, and whales may strand themselves on an outgoing tide—often with tragic results. Being alert for the unexpected—particularly during migration seasons—can turn up some unusual and exciting sightings of animals that "shouldn't be there."

Although many people don't think of gulls as "wildlife," they are the most visible and in some ways most characteristic animals of the New England coast. Extolled by some, scorned by others, gulls perform a valuable function for humans as scavengers of our species' ubiquitous wastes. Gulls have flourished on what we have thrown away to the point that their numbers now have to be selectively controlled on the breeding grounds of less aggressive species such as terns and puffins. It is sometimes hard to imagine that the herring gull—the most common species in this region with 30,000 breeding pairs in Maine alone—had been so persecuted for its eggs that, at the turn of the last century, it was uncommon to see one.

While the herring gull is the most numerous, there are a number of other gull species to be found along the New England coast as well. The great black-backed gull is a large, boldly patterned bird that only began breeding in Maine in the 1920s; there are now at least 9,000 breeding pairs. Another expanding species is the ring-billed gull, which formerly bred primarily in the Great Lakes region and now is seen commonly from Casco Bay south. Look also for smaller numbers of laughing and Bonaparte's gulls; both have black heads during the breeding season.

Yet not every different-looking gull is a separate species. Like most seabirds, gulls are slow to mature and relatively long-lived. One wild bird is known to have lived at least 31 years, and a captive bird to age 49. A herring gull, for example, first takes to the air as a mottled, dark-brown bird. By the time it acquires the characteristic white, gray, and black look of an adult three-and-a-half years later, it will have molted through several different plumages. Many field guides do an excellent job of portraying these plumages.

Closely related to the gulls, and nearly as familiar, are terns. Four species of these graceful, acrobatic birds breed along New England's coast—the Arctic, common, roseate, and least. Though more or less similar in appearance, each of the four "mackerel gulls," as fishermen sometimes call them, has its own unique life history. Most exceptional is the Arctic tern, which holds top honors among all birds for the greatest distance covered in a year. From their breeding colonies on Matinicus Rock, Petit Manan, and several other islands off the Maine coast, the birds fly east to Europe, then south along the coast of Africa to Antarctica where they spend a second summer. They then return to their North Atlantic breeding colonies, completing a total journey of 22,000 miles. Widely persecuted for the millinery trade 100 years ago, terns made a comeback from the edge of extinction after they gained protection in the early part of this century. However, for a variety of reasons, including competition with gulls, terns have recently been declining again, and both the roseate and the least are listed as endangered species.

From Massachusetts north and east along the Maine coast, the dark, reptilian-looking double-crested cormorant is a common sight as it perches on buoys and ledges, holding its wings out to dry. Unlike other diving birds, cormorants' feathers are not waterproof. This is advantageous in that it allows the bird superb maneuverability underwater to pursue fish as deep as 100 feet. When its feathers are dry, the cormorant is a surprisingly strong and versatile flyer, able to beat rapidly into a stiff sea breeze or, while migrating, to sail on thermals like a hawk. Although almost totally extirpated from New England by 1900, the population of double-crested cormorants, or shags as they were traditionally called, rebounded dramatically, causing concern from fishermen who feel the species is depleting commercially valuable fish. In some instances this concern may be valid, but studies of cormorant feeding habits have demonstrated that cunners and sculpins—neither of which are commercially harvested—constitute 80 percent of the cormorant's diet.

Gulls, terns, and cormorants were not the only species to benefit from conservation and protection. In 1904, only four adult common eider ducks were to be found along the entire Maine coast. The following year, the National Audubon Society leased the island on which the remaining birds were nesting, thus opening the way for the eider to resume its former abundance. Today, Maine's breeding eider population exceeds 20,000 pairs nesting on 239 islands.

After mating, the showy black-and-white drake eiders usually flock off together, leaving the brown-mottled females to tend to the nesting duties alone. When the ducklings hatch, during June and early July, they immediately take to the water and are gathered with the broods of several other females to form what is termed a crèche. The combined efforts of the females are necessary to shepherd the dozen or more ducklings in the crèche and protect them from marauding gulls. Still, many are lost to predation, though it is interesting to note that gulls and eiders often share the same nesting islands, and their populations have flourished side by side. When cruising close to an island—and especially when walking around on one—take care not to startle the females away from the crèche. Unprotected ducklings are easy prey to the ever-present gulls.

With all birds, care should be taken not to disturb them while they are on the nest or in their breeding colonies. If done in the wrong place, seemingly innocent activities like having a picnic or letting a dog go unleashed can jeopardize the success of a nest for that year. As New England's islands come under mounting recreational pressure, the need for caution and respect for wildlife grows.

While they aren't seabirds, both ospreys and bald eagles are closely associated with the coastal environment. Both of these birds of prey suffered grievously from the side effects of DDT and other pesticides that came into widespread use in the 1950s and 1960s. DDT is passed up the food chain, coming to rest at the top where it accumulates in the fatty tissues of predators. In birds, DDT causes a deficiency of calcium, resulting in eggs being laid with shells so thin they break under the weight of the brooding bird. Since DDT was banned in 1972, both osprey and bald eagles have responded favorably. About 700 pairs of osprey and 110 pairs of eagles now breed along Maine's coastline and at least another 150 osprey pairs can be found nesting along southern New England's shoreline.

Protection has not only been a benefit to birds; the Marine Mammal Act of 1972 has made the sighting of harbor seals an everyday event for those cruising New England's boreal coast. Once routinely shot by fishermen who feared the animals were eating commercially valuable fish, harbor seals had become relatively uncommon along the Maine coast west of Mount Desert Island. Now their population numbers more than 15,000 individuals, and it is not uncommon to see 50 or more at a time basking in the sun on a rocky ledge. Harbor seals' coats are somewhat variable in color, depending on age, molt, and whether the animal is dry or wet; seals basking on a favored haulout ledge may range in color from a creamy buff to brown, pale silver to dark gray, spotted or plain. Pups are born from late April to mid-June and weigh about twenty pounds. During the first several months females may leave their young alone for short periods on a beach or ledge while they pursue fish. Many people who find these pups think they have been abandoned, when in fact, the mother is usually nearby. As a result, the best thing to do is to leave the pup alone and move away from the area. Seals make poor pets. If you are sure that the pup has been abandoned and feel compelled to take some sort of action, call the New England Aquarium in Boston, at (617) 742-8830. They can put you in touch with people who know how to handle these animals.

Cruising a little farther offshore brings the sailor in contact with some of the most interesting and sought-after birds and mammals in New England. Among them is the Atlantic puffin, a chicken-sized bird with colorful clownlike facial markings. Atlantic puffins are a member of the alcid family, a group of chunky, largely black-and-white birds, somewhat similar in appearance to the penguin family of the southern hemisphere and filling a comparable ecological niche. This similarity is an example of convergent evolution, for the two families are unrelated, the alcids actually being relatives of the gulls, terns, and shorebirds. Except for the black guillemot, which is commonly seen close to the New England shore, the alcids are pelagic in character, spending all but the breeding months at sea.

One hundred years ago, puffins were harvested extensively as a source of food and bait. Puffins excavate a burrow in which to lay their single egg. By spreading nets over the entrances to these burrows, it was easy to catch a boatload of the birds when they emerged in the morning. Not surprisingly, puffins were greatly reduced and even eliminated from some of their nesting islands.

Happily that situation is being corrected. Thanks to the watchful care of some lighthouse keepers on Machias Seal Island and Matinicus Rock, a breeding core there was maintained. Since 1981 the National Audubon Society has transplanted over a thousand puffin chicks from the massive Newfoundland colonies to Eastern Egg Rock, an historical puffin colony in Muscongus Bay, and to Seal Island in outer Penobscot Bay. The transplanted chicks are placed in artificial burrows and hand-fed until they fledge in early August. At that time, the young birds go to sea where they will spend the next four or five years before returning to land to breed. During the summer of 1991, sixteen pairs returned to Eastern Egg Rock to nest. The colony on Penobscot Bay's Matinicus Rock is somewhat larger with over 100 breeding pairs, and Machias Seal Island off Jonesport is home to approximately 900 pairs.

Although landing on both Matinicus Rock and Eastern Egg Rock is prohibited, one can easily see puffins from the water between late May and early August. Machias Seal Island is managed by the Canadian Wildlife Service so anyone landing there should check with the warden before striking off across the island. For those who do not want to venture that far offshore on their own, there are several charter boats to Machias Seal from either Jonesport or Cutler almost every day throughout the summer. Call Barna Norton at (207) 497-5933 or Andrew Patterson at (207) 259-4484 for information.

Other species of alcids one may encounter off the New England coast—particularly during the spring and fall—are razorbill, common murre, thick-billed murre, and dovekie. Poor flyers, the alcids spend their time on the water diving for small fish. Exactly why all these birds—and most other seabirds—are black and white is still largely a matter of speculation. Clearly, however, there is some beneficial significance to this widespread adaptation among so many different species.

Though the alcids may be poor flyers, the majority of offshore seabirds are not. Almost constantly on the wing, gannets, shearwaters, storm petrels, and jaegers spend most of their lives at sea taking advantage of the omnipresent wind and surface turbulence to glide and soar over the waves. Most spectacular among this group for sheer flying ability is the northern gannet. The gannet's long, narrow wings span 72 inches from tip to tip and are held stiffly as it banks and veers over the water in search of fish. Seeing one, the gannet wings over and plunges straight down into the water in perfect diving form, disappearing below the surface. A flock of gannets plunge-diving on a school of fish is a spectacle not soon forgotten. Though gannets breed off Newfoundland and Quebec, they are regular visitors to the Gulf of Maine throughout most of the year.

New England's two most abundant shearwater species—the greater and the sooty—are actually natives of the southern hemisphere. Breeding off the Antarctic and South American coasts during the austral summer, these species fly north to our coasts to "winter." As such, they are among the handful of birds that migrate north from their southern nesting grounds to spend the off-season in our hemisphere.

Shearwaters, like the smaller storm petrels, are often referred to as "tubenoses" because of the paired, tubed nostrils lying along the ridge of their bills. Like humans, birds must limit the salinity of their body fluids to about 1 percent. Their kidneys are, however, not nearly as efficient as ours. To compensate for this, ocean-dwelling birds, which must drink seawater, have developed a salt gland located in the back of the nasal area to filter out the excess salt. It is from the nostrils that they excrete this salt. Interestingly, many seabirds are so accustomed to drinking salt water that they will actually die of thirst if placed in a freshwater environment.

Tubenoses have acute senses of smell, a fact which can be used to a bird-watcher's advantage. If, while cruising over an offshore bank, you pour out five or more gallons of fish oil sprinkled with a few bags of puffed rice or popcorn, you should begin to draw in scores—and at times thousands—of seabirds. By slowly circling the slick, you will have an opportunity to view a number of interesting birds at very close range.

The most numerous of these birds will, in all likelihood, be Wilson's storm petrels. These small black-and-white seabirds, which swoop swallowlike over the waves, are thought to be the most abundant species of bird on the planet. Breeding off the Antarctic coast, Wilson's storm petrels spend the summer months at sea feeding in these North Atlantic waters. Wilson's storm petrels were once called "Mother Cary's chickens" (from *Mater Cara*, the Holy Virgin) by sailors because they are very active before storms and thus thought to be foretellers of bad weather. On the Grand Banks of Newfoundland the birds were once widely used for bait. Fishermen would attract them close to a boat by spreading fish gurry on the water and then kill them with whips. In fact, so oily is their flesh that when attached to a stick, the bird's body could be ignited and used as a torch.

The closely related Leach's storm petrel looks similar to the Wilson's but has a subtly different flight style and does not patter with its feet on the surface while feeding. Leach's petrels breed on a number of New

England's outer islands where they have formed large colonies. However, because they nest in burrows and are largely nocturnal, Leach's petrels are not usually seen near their colonies.

A group of birds difficult to identify as to species but nonetheless thrilling to watch are the jaegers. Members of the gull family, the three species of jaegers are superlative flyers that make their living by chasing other seabirds and forcing them to regurgitate their recent catch. Breeding in the high Arctic, jaegers are usually seen in the Gulf of Maine in the late summer and early fall. Adult birds often have long tail streamers, but the immature birds do not. Only years of experience can tell these young birds apart.

Where there are large concentrations of feeding seabirds, one is also apt to find cetaceans. This order of mammals includes whales, dolphins, and porpoises, and the Gulf of Maine is home to quite a variety of species.

Though the finback's numbers are still far below what they were in the pre-whaling days (from 50,000 to 8,000 in the North Atlantic alone), this whale is a common sight in offshore New England waters. Measuring up to 80 feet in length, finbacks often "sound" (dive) on close approach, but it is still possible to get excellent views of these mammals as they feed on small fish near the surface.

At 30–60 feet in length, the humpback whale is smaller than the finback, but because of its dynamic activity and relative tameness, it is the favorite among many whale watchers. Humpbacks are relatively common in the Gulf of Maine, to which they migrate every spring from their breeding grounds off the Dominican Republic. Humpbacks exhibit a number of interesting and sometimes dramatic behavioral characteristics worth watching for. Most prominent is their habit of raising their tail flukes clear of the water as they sound for a dive. Since every humpback has a unique pattern of black and white on the underside of its tail flukes, scientists have been able to catalog and keep track of individual animals. Humpbacks are also known for their acrobatics, at times leaping almost clear of the water in a breathtaking display of size and power. At other times humpbacks may wave their enormous white flippers in the air, perhaps to herd fish or show aggression. On a warm summer day, humpbacks can often be approached quite closely as they doze on the surface (called "logging").

The right whale—so named because its large quantities of blubber, long pieces of baleen, and tendency to float when dead made it the "right" whale to hunt—is one of the rarest whales on earth. Once common off the New England coast, right-whales were severely decimated from overharvesting. Despite full protection since 1937, however, right-whale numbers have only rebounded slightly. Exactly why the species has not made a stronger recovery is still a mystery. Probably the most reliable place to see right-whales is in outer Passamaquoddy Bay during the late summer. Other excellent whale-watching locations for all three of the large species mentioned here, plus the smaller minke whale and several dolphin species include Browns Bank, off Mount Desert Rock, Jeffrey's Ledge, Stellwagen Bank, off Cape Ann, Cape Cod Bay, and on Georges Bank.

No article of this length could presume to be anything more than a brief sampling of the wildlife to be found while cruising the New England coast. This margin of land and sea is so rich in different life forms that learning to find, identify, and understand the behavior of the many species here could easily occupy a lifetime or more. There are many ways to appreciate this wildlife; for some it will be enough to sit on deck in the evening and listen to the rich, ethereal song of the Swainson's thrush echo across a spruce-lined cove, while others may want to venture to the edge of the continental shelf in search of an albatross or a sperm whale. But ultimately it is not seeing every species or knowing all their names that really matters; what is important is the recognition that New England's wildlife is a unique and irreplaceable part of our heritage and is inseparably linked to our future.

Suggested Books for Further Study

Bent, Arthur C., *Life Histories of North American Diving Birds*. New York: Dover, 1986.

Bent, Arthur C., *Life Histories of North American Gulls and Terns*. New York: Dover, 1986.

Bent, Arthur C., *Life Histories of North American Petrels and Pelicans and Their Allies*. New York: Dover, 1964.

Berrill, Michael and Deborah, *A Sierra Club Naturalist's Guide to the North Atlantic Coast*. San Francisco: Sierra Club Books, 1981.

Finch, Davis W., William C. Russell, and Edward V. Thompson, "Pelagic Birds in the Gulf of Maine." *American Birds*, Vol. 32, No. 2 (1978): 140–55, and Vol. 32, No. 3 (1978): 281–94. (Reprinted in booklet form.)

Gosner, Kenneth L., *A Field Guide to the Atlantic Seashore*. Boston: Houghton Mifflin, 1978.

Harrison, Peter, *Seabirds: An Identification Guide*. Boston: Houghton Mifflin, 1983.

Katona, Steven K., Valerie Rough, and David T. Richardson, *A Field Guide to the Whales, Porpoises and Seals of the Gulf of Maine and Eastern Canada*. New York: Charles Scribner's Sons, 1983.

Leatherwood, Stephen, and Randall R. Reeves, *The Sierra Club Handbook of Whales and Dolphins*. San Francisco: Sierra Club Books, 1983.

National Geographic Society, *Field Guide to the Birds of North America*. Washington, D.C.: National Geographic Society, 1983.

Peterson, Roger T., *A Field Guide to the Birds East of the Rockies*. Boston: Houghton Mifflin, 1980.

Pierson, Elizabeth Cary and Jan E., *A Birder's Guide to the Coast of Maine*. Camden, Me.: Down East Books, 1981.

Appendix B

A Guide to the Geology of the Maine Coast
by Olcott Gates

Wiscasset, Maine

The coast of Maine is a cruising paradise (barring a little fog now and then) which has been 600 million years in the making. The history of these 600 million years is written in the rocks of Maine's green islands and bold headlands. I hope the following explanation of the geology of the Maine coast will heighten your joy in this pleasant land and your interest in its origin.

Before we begin our geological cruise, we need a geological framework to guide us in understanding the rocks of Maine. The framework the geologists use to interpret the rocks they study is a process called plate tectonics. Crystal plates 40 or so miles thick under the oceans and 60 or so miles thick under the continents move at rates of 1 to 4 inches a year perhaps dragged along by convection currents caused by heat rising from the earth's interior through the mantle between the core and the crust. The collision of continents on plates raises mountain ranges such as the Alps (the Eurasian and African plates) or the Himalayas (Asian and Indian plates). From Chile to New Zealand the floor of the Pacific Ocean is colliding with and diving below the surrounding continents and islands along a subduction zone. The subducted ocean floor partially melts, producing magmas (molten rock) that feed the volcanoes bordering the Pacific rim. On the other hand, Europe, Africa, North America, and South America once were joined as part of a huge continent. About 200 million years ago, a great crack or rift split the continent. Basaltic magma from the mantle erupted through the crack and solidified, wedging the crack apart. Continued eruption and freezing in the crack wedged Europe and Africa farther apart from North and South America, formed the basaltic floor of the Atlantic, and built the mid-Atlantic Ridge on which the volcanoes of Iceland sit. The spreading continues, and currently the Atlantic is widening about an inch a year. The Pacific and Indian Oceans also formed by spreading. This colliding and spreading of crustal plates has gone on for at least several billion years at different places and between different plates.

Let us begin our geological cruise in Casco Bay and sail downwind to Cutler, observing as we go the metamorphic, volcanic, granitic, and gabbroic rocks that make the "rockbound" coast of Maine and looking in them for the imprint of past plate tectonics in now-eroded mountain ranges and vanished ocean basins.

Our geological cruise ends with the most recent events: the sculpturing of the bedrock first by streams and then by the continental glaciers of the Ice Age, which together with a very rapid rise and fall of post-glacial sea level, made the delightful configuration of bays, islands, and peninsulas that is coastal Maine.

Our first chart, that of Casco Bay, shows a very striking northeasterly alignment of peninsulas, bays, and islands. This alignment parallels the orientation of vertical layers in the metamorphic rocks underlying the bay. For millions of years, streams eroded valleys in the weak layers leaving the resistant layers as ridges. The continental ice sheets then further scoured the stream valleys and rounded the ridges. Finally the sea drowned the valleys to make the bays while the ridges became islands and peninsulas, all mimicking the original trend of the metamorphic rocks.

The layered metamorphic rocks (crystalline schists) of Casco Bay began as layers (beds) of sand, mud, and limey mud deposited on the shelf and slope of an ancient continent bordering an ocean basin long since destroyed. As the pile of sediments thickened, the sand beds compacted and lithified to sandstone, the mud to shale, and the limey mud to limestone. The collision of two plates of the earth's crust perhaps

450 million years ago then buried the pile of sedimentary rocks perhaps 5 or 6 miles deep beneath an ancient mountain range raised by the collision, a depth where high temperatures recrystallized (metamorphosed) the sedimentary rocks to schists and where tremendous pressures tightly folded the layers like the bellows of a closed accordion. Deeper still beneath the recrystallizing sedimentary rocks, temperatures were high enough to melt the underlying continental crust to molten rock (magma) which permeated the hot overlying schists as lenses, fingers, and pods, eventually cooling to form granite.

The schists and intercalated granites continue eastward through the Boothbay region to Muscongus Bay and the Port Clyde area, generally maintaining their northeasterly trend. The most spectacular display for the passing sailor is on Pemaquid Point and along its steep shore to New Harbor and beyond. The layering of the dark schists is accentuated by the lenses and layers of white granite. The narrow southeast entrance of Townsend Gut where the channel runs close to the southwest shore provides a closer look. Keep one eye on the lobster pot buoys that clog the channel and the other eye on the layered schists and intermixed white granite on the shoreline ledges an oar's length away.

For a close-up inspection of typical metamorphic rocks, take a walk along the shore almost any place between Portland and Port Clyde where bedrock is exposed. The minerals, black platey mica and elongate hornblende, white blocky feldspar, and gray translucent quartz, tend to be aligned parallel to the layers. The layers, in turn, are distinguished by differing proportions of black minerals (mica and hornblende) to the light-colored minerals (feldspar and quartz) and by lenses and streaks of the latter. The minerals of the schists are aligned because they crystallized from minerals of the original sedimentary rocks in the solid state under great pressure directed perpendicularly to the layers. The granite, in contrast, consists of blocky white feldspar and gray irregular quartz with few if any dark minerals and is massive without layering or mineral orientation. The minerals of the granite crystallized from a magma that injected the schists and then cooled, and liquids do not transmit directed pressure.

Metamorphic rocks of geological groups different from the Casco Bay schists but sharing the same general origin make the rocky shorelines from Owls Head to Belfast, of the Islesboro islands, of the east side of Benjamin River and eastward along the north side of Eggemoggin Reach, and generally around Blue Hill Bay.

Because metamorphism destroyed any fossils the original sedimentary rocks may have contained, the age of the schists is uncertain. Geologic relationships to other rocks in coastal Maine and nearby regions suggest an age of sedimentation and eventual metamorphism any time from the late Proterozoic Era about 600 million years ago to the early Paleozoic Era about 450 million years ago. (See the Geologic Time Scale at the end of this appendix.)

Just south of Tenants Harbor, the schists are abruptly cut off by pink, coarse (large-grained) granite, part of a large mass that makes up the islands of the Muscle Ridge. Other large masses of granite continue eastward, as we shall see, to the Cows Yard on Head Harbor Island. These massive pink granites are younger than the white granites that permeate the schists. They form oval-shaped bodies called plutons ranging from 2 to 10 miles in diameter and extending downward to unknown depths.

Any granite ledge displays the minerals typical of granite: pink blocky potassium feldspar (oxides of silicon, aluminum, and potassium), white calcium feldspar (oxides of silicon, aluminum, and calcium), and translucent gray to colorless glassy-appearing quartz (oxide of silicon). Some granites have black platey biotite mica (oxides of silicon, aluminum, iron, magnesium, potassium, and hydrogen) and black elongate hornblende (oxides of silicon, iron, magnesium, and hydrogen). Most granites have numerous fractures (joints) but lack the layering and alignment of minerals typical of schists.

Great variety in the textures and colors of Maine's granite plutons combined with easy shipment by schooner from shoreline quarries made granite quarrying a booming industry in coastal Maine from about 1830 to World War I. Charles B. McLane in his fascinating history *The Islands of the Mid-Maine Coast* recounts in detail quarrying operations on many of the islands of Penobscot Bay. Large quarries on Clark, Dix, Hurricane, Vinalhaven, and Crotch Islands supplied the granite for such prominent structures as the Library of Congress, the Treasury Building, the Naval Academy, the New York and Philadelphia post offices, the Brooklyn and Manhattan bridges, and the grave of John F. Kennedy in Arlington Cemetery.

The interlocking of crystals in granite make it resistant to erosion, and hence it holds up many of the peninsulas, headlands, and islands of Maine. If from the Muscle Ridge we take the outside route eastward, we sail past granite on Vinalhaven, the Deer Island Thorofare, Merchants Row, much of Isle au Haut, Swans Island, Long Island, Matinicus, the great mass of Cadillac Mountain on Mount Desert, Schoodic, Corea, Petit Manan, Trafton Island, Great Wass Island, Steele Island, and part of Head Harbor Island.

Granite plutons rise upward in the crust of continents as masses of magma and then cool slowly several miles deep so that large crystals have time to grow. Northeast Harbor on Mount Desert is an excellent place to see evidence that granite is emplaced as a liquid. The contact between the granite pluton of Cadillac Mountain and the volcanic rocks (to be described shortly) into which the magma intruded runs north-south across the harbor. Part of the east shore and the highway above it are in pink granite. The west shore from the fuel dock to the town marina has white to gray, locally layered, volcanic rocks. The contact between granite and volcanics can be studied on the shoreline ledge just south of the paved launching ramp at the marina complex and also in the fresh cut made for a small parking lot on the north side of the new town office building. Angular blocks of layered volcanic rocks are scattered through and enclosed by a matrix of white to pink granite. Clearly the magma was a liquid which worked its way into the volcanic rocks by fracturing, breaking away, and engulfing the volcanics, a process frozen when the liquid magma crystallized to granite.

Dating—by measuring the ratio of parent radioactive atoms in a granite to non-radioactive daughter atoms to which the radioactive atoms decay and applying to this ratio the known rate of decay of the given radioactive parent atoms—indicates that the granites of coastal Maine crystallized during the middle of the Paleozoic Era about 400 to 350 million years ago.

Throughout the world, most granite plutons are confined to former mountain ranges where the collision of two continents riding on large crustal plates (modern examples include Africa colliding with Europe to raise the Alps or India colliding with Asia to raise the Himalayas) have squeezed and greatly thickened downward the crustal and surface rocks caught in the viselike collision zone. If buried deep enough, the squeezed rocks melt to granite magma which rises upward through the overlying thick prism of deformed and metamorphosed rocks.

Many of the largely granitic islands of Maine also have dark-green, brown, or black massive rocks that contrast with the pink granite. This dark massive rock is gabbro. Like granite, gabbro rises through the crust of the earth as liquid magma; but unlike granite, it is low in silicon and potassium and high in calcium, iron, and magnesium which crystallize to the black mineral pyroxene and gray calcium-rich feldspar. Gabbroic magmas result from the melting of the iron and magnesium-rich mantle which underlies the thick granite and metamorphic continental crust or the thin basaltic oceanic crust. Melting of the mantle to gabbroic magmas may also cause melting of the overlying crust to granitic magma, and the two types may commingle when erupted. The spectacular "zebra" rocks of white granite and black gabbro along the shore of Morton Point on the Reach near Carvers Harbor are of mingled granitic and gabbroic magmas. On the other hand, later granitic dikes (narrow tabular bodies) commonly cut many gabbro masses; or gabbro dikes cut granite as on Schoodic Point and are hence younger than the latter.

Once through the Muscle Ridge, if we decide to take the inside route eastward, such as through the Fox Island Thorofare or up Penobscot Bay to Bucks Harbor and down Eggemoggin Reach, the rocks of the shoreline ledges are very varied. Colors may be white, gray, maroon, black, or mixed; some rocks are layered, others unlayered; some are tilted, others flat-lying; fractures are numerous; and thin dikes of gabbro are common. These are volcanic rocks produced by eruption of magma to the land surface. Because the magma cooled quickly, volcanic rocks are generally glassy with scattered small crystals in contrast to the interlocking large crystals of granite and gabbro. Some magmas pour out on the land surface as lava flows. Other magmas highly charged with gasses erupt violently, such as those at Mount St. Helens, spewing out avalanches of angular volcanic fragments and lava bombs (blobs of magma solidified in the air) to make volcanic agglomerates and also shooting eruption clouds miles high into the atmosphere from which crystals and solidified droplets of magma settle out on land and in the sea as beds of volcanic ash (tuff). When granitic magmas erupt, the resulting volcanic rock is called rhyolite. The volcanic equivalent of gabbro is basalt.

The north shore of the Fox Islands Thorofare from the steamboat dock to Iron Point has many outcrops of steeply tilted maroon and purple beds of agglomerate and tuff testifying to violent volcanic explosions. The south side of the Thorofare is a gabbro sill injected between beds of volcanic ash. The brown rocks of Pulpit Harbor are basaltic lava flows. Along the east shore the basaltic lavas form football-shaped or pillowlike masses. Pillow lavas are common where basaltic lavas erupt on the sea floor and are quickly chilled. The west shore of Harbor Island at Bucks Harbor has gently tilted beds of volcanic ash.

Similar kinds of volcanic rocks are exposed on most of the islands of Penobscot Bay from North Haven to Bucks Harbor, on Cape Rosier, and on the islands south of Castine. Along our route eastward, Eggemoggin Reach is lined largely by granitic and metamorphic rocks. The islands of Casco Passage and Bass Harbor Head are granite. Volcanic rocks appear again on the Cranberry Islands and in the Northeast Harbor and Bar Harbor areas. From there eastward granite predominates as far as Trafton Island. Shipstern, Flint, and Nash Islands are of volcanic rocks. The shores of Cape Split and the north shore of Moosabec Reach at Jonesport are part of a very large intrusion of gabbro. The south shore of the Reach is part of the large Great Wass Island granite pluton, part of whose south margin runs about through the center of the Cows Yard on Head Harbor Island. The small islands on the north side of the Cows Yard are of granite. The south-side entrance ledge, Man Island, and Black Head consist of gabbro intruded into bedded volcanic rocks.

Roque Island not only has a lovely beach but also the best exposed pile of basaltic lava flows east of the Rocky Mountains. The graceful curve of Roque and associated islands from Squire Point to Halifax Island out-lines a broad shallow fold marked by resistant lava flows stacked one above the other. The cliff at your stern in Bunker Cove is cut into a lava flow. The point at the south end of the beach near the old weir consists of basaltic flows with dark-green or white spots. These once were bubbles of gas that evolved from the magma as it cooled rapidly on the surface. Subsequently circulating groundwater deposited white (calcite) and green (chlorite) minerals in the bubbles. On the steep cliff at the north end of the beach, slightly tilted beds of volcanic ash contain fossil clams and snails. The overlying thick massive rock is a lens of gabbro. The colorful maroon beds of Lakeman Island were once mud and sand on a mud flat where periodic exposure to the air oxidized iron minerals.

Volcanic rocks continue eastward on the shores and islands of En-glishmans and Machias Bays, Cross Island, and the Navy radio station. From the Double Shot Islands to West Quoddy Head the steeply cliffed shoreline exposes mile after mile of a very large intrusion of gabbro, well exposed for a close look on the shores of Cutler Harbor. If we were to continue our cruise into Passamaquoddy Bay, we would sail past volcanic rocks on Campobello and Deer Islands, Lubec and Eastport, and on the shores of Cobscook Bay.

The volcanic rocks of the Maine coast called the coastal volcanic belt are remnants of a chain of volcanoes that rose from the sea, probably along a continental margin, and once extended at least from present New Brunswick to present Boston. In places the volcanic pile is at least 4 miles thick. Abundant fossils indicate a middle-Paleozoic age of about 425 to 400 million years ago. The volcanic rocks are thus younger than the schists. Along the narrows of the Bagaduc River up from Castine, volcanic rocks rest on the eroded upturned edges of schist along a bed of lithified stream or beach gravels containing pebbles of the underlying schist. The volcanic rocks thus must have been deposited on the schists after the latter had been metamorphosed, folded, uplifted, and subsequently beveled by erosion. On the other hand, the volcanic rocks are older than the gabbro and granite that intruded them.

The late-Proterozoic to early-Paleozoic schists and the middle-Paleozoic volcanic rocks are a geological enigma. They are confined to the coastal area and are unlike rocks of similar ages in interior Maine. Less-metamorphosed rocks of early-Paleozoic age near Saint John, New Brunswick, near Boston, and on islands in Narragansett Bay, rocks that appear to belong to the same general geological terrain as those of coastal Maine, have fossil trilobites (ancestors of the horseshoe crab) commonly found in rocks of the same age in central England, France, and Spain but which are totally different from trilobites of the same age in rocks of the Appalachian Mountains and the Champlain and St. Lawrence valleys. The most commonly accepted explanation is that the two different trilobite faunas evolved independently on opposite sides of an ancient ocean basin named the Ancestral Atlantic. The rocks of the coastal terrain were then part of central Europe along the east side of the Ancestral Atlantic. The North American continent, including the Appalachian area and the Champlain and St. Lawrence valleys, lay along the west side. How wide the intervening ocean was is unknown, but it must have been wide enough to keep the two trilobite faunas from mixing. Some time during the middle Paleozoic the intervening ocean basin closed. Some geologists have interpreted the coastal volcanic belt as a chain of volcanoes like that around the Pacific that overlay a subduction zone as the Ancestral Atlantic ocean basin closed, resulting in the eventual collision of the European and North American continents. The metamorphic and highly folded rocks formed deep beneath the mountain range then formed are now exposed by uplift and erosion in the mountains in western Maine, New Hampshire, and Vermont. Early in the Mesozoic Era the two continents began to split apart, forming the present Atlantic ocean basin. However, what is now Maine's coastal terrain remained stuck to the North American continent. The Bay of Fundy is underlain largely by red rocks and basalt (visible along the cliffs of Grand Manan) that filled a basin produced when the crust began to stretch during the early stages of the split. Thus our cruise through the rocks of coastal Maine has also perhaps been a cruise through ancient rocks of the European continent.

Except for the early-Mesozoic rocks of Grand Manan and the Bay of Fundy, we have no rock record for the Maine coast during most of the Mesozoic and Cenozoic Eras. Millions of years of erosion have worn away, perhaps to depths of several miles, any rocks that may once have overlain the schists, volcanics, gabbro, and granite now exposed by erosion at the present land surface. Before the continental glaciers of the Ice Age blanketed the land, coastal Maine was a rolling upland of broad river valleys and low rounded hills, precursors of the present bays and islands. Above this subdued topography stood a few high hills of particularly resistant rocks, the granites of Mount Desert and Isle au Haut and the metamorphic rocks of the Camden Hills and Blue Hill.

Beginning about 1.5 million years ago, continental ice sheets spread southward from centers in Canada into the United States four different times, but in coastal Maine there is a record of only the last advance. The ice sheet moved across the rolling upland and the present floor of the Gulf of Maine as far south as Georges' Banks and was thick enough to completely bury Mount Desert and the Camden Hills. Rocks and sand frozen in the base of the ice acted like the teeth of a gigantic rasp, scouring stream valleys and smoothing and rounding hills and knobs. Many smooth rock ledges show south-trending grooves and striations cut by rock fragments embedded in the ice. Somes Sound, originally a deep V-shaped stream valley, was scoured to a U-shape by glacial erosion, the most spectacular example of a glaciated valley east of the Rocky Mountains. In some places a mixture of clay, sand, pebbles, and boulders (glacial till) was plastered on bedrock beneath the ice. Some large glacial boulders left stranded by the ice (erratics) can be traced to outcrops in northern Maine.

About 14,000 years ago a slight global warming, perhaps no more than 5 or 6 degrees Fahrenheit, caused the margins of the glaciers to melt more rapidly than ice was delivered from the centers of accumulation. In Maine, the edge of the ice retreated northward leaving its load of clay, sand, and boulders as long looping moraines marking places where the margin of the ice temporarily halted its retreat. Streams of melt water choked with sand and gravel built deltas and spread outwash plains of glacial debris in front of the retreating glaciers. The sand and pebble beaches of Maine, such as that at Roque Island, accumulated where waves cut into (and continue to do so), sorted, and redistributed the unconsolidated clay, sand, and gravel left behind by the glaciers. The bars of Bass Harbor Head and Petit Manan are of glacial deposits concentrated in bars by tidal currents.

While continental glaciers melted all over the glaciated world, sea level rose as water, once stored in the ice, returned to the oceans. The crust of the continents depressed by the weight of the miles-thick continental glaciers rebounded more slowly than the ocean filled. In Maine the retreating ice front was closely followed by the sea which flooded as much as 50 miles inland up the Kennebec and Penobscot river valleys. As crustal rebound continued after the ice disappeared, the sea drained from interior Maine, the entire cycle of marine advance and retreat taking less than 1,200 years. Today marine clays with subarctic clam fossils are at elevations of at least 400 feet inland and 200 to 240 feet along the coast. The advancing and retreating ocean waters left a blanket of blue-gray thinly bedded clay in low areas. Erosion and redeposition of this clay by present waves and tides has produced the black mud that makes such good holding ground in Maine's harbors, such a mess of the topsides when the anchor comes aboard, and such fragrant mud flats at low tide.

Currently, sea level worldwide is rising about 4 inches per century. In addition, the ground surface in the Machias-Eastport-Calais area is warping downward at the astonishing (geologically speaking) rate of 3 feet per century, accompanied by many local earthquakes. From Addison eastward, century-old shipyards, wharves, and salt-marsh dikes are now at or below high-tide level; shoreline waves are cutting back salt marshes to mud flats or covering them with sand and gravel beaches; and Indian shell heaps are rapidly being washed away. The rise of sea level relative to the land, both global and local, threatens the real estate of those foolish enough to build on beaches and sand dunes; but the Maine coast should continue to be a cruising paradise for sailors of many future generations, provided we can control condominiums, pollution, and the atom.

GEOLOGIC TIME SCALE

Era	*Begins (millions of years ago)*
Cenozoic	67
Mesozoic	250
Paleozoic	580
Proterozoic	2,500
Archean	3,800
	(oldest rocks known)

Appendix C

New England Coastal Pumpout Stations

Here is a selected list of New England and New York State marinas that, at the time of writing, have pumpout facilities for use by boats equipped with approved marine toilet pollution control devices.

Hudson River

Weehawken, NJ	Port Imperial Marina
Haverstraw, NY	Haverstraw Marina
Kingston, NY	Rondout Yacht Basin
Catskill, NY	Riverview Marine
Troy, NY	Arrowhead Marina

Long Island Sound, North Shore

Mamaroneck, NY	Mamaroneck Boat & Motors
Greenwich, CT	Greenwich Fuel Dock
Stamford, CT	Harbour Square Marina
Milford, CT	Port Milford Marina
Clinton, CT	Cedar Island Marina
	Clinton Harbor Marina
Westbrook, CT	Harry's Marine Repair

Long Island Sound, South Shore

Glen Cove, NY	Glen Cove Yacht Service

Huntington, NY	West Shore Marina
Mount Sinai, NY	Old Man's Boatyard
Shelter Island, NY	Coecles Harbor Marina
Shinnecock Canal, NY	Shinnecock Canal Boat Basin
Montauk, NY	Gone Fishing Marina

Fishers Island Sound to Buzzards Bay

Noank, CT	Spicer's Noank Marina
Mystic, CT	Mystic Cove Marina
Stonington, CT	Dodson Boat Yard
Block Island, RI	Champlin's Marina
Barrington, RI	Stanley's Boat Yard
Sakonnet River, RI	Lighthouse Marina

Buzzards Bay and the Elizabeth Islands

Marion, MA	Burr Brothers Boatyard
Wareham, MA	Warr's Marine
Fiddlers Cove, MA	Fiddlers Cove Marina
Onset, MA	Onset Bay Marina

Vineyard and Nantucket Sounds

Waquoit, MA	Edwards Boat Yard
Hyannis, MA	Lewis Bay Marina
	Hyannis Marina
Bass River, MA	Bass River Marina
Martha's Vineyard, MA	Martha's Vineyard Shipyard
Nantucket, MA	Nantucket Boat Basin

Cape Cod to Cape Elizabeth, Maine

Bourne, MA	Bourne Marina
Boston Harbor, MA	Constitution Marina
	Shipyard Quarters Marina
	Marina Bay
	Hewitt's Cove Marina
	Quarterdeck Marine Corp.
Annisquam, MA	Cape Ann Marina
Essex, MA	Essex Marina

Kittery Point, NH	Kittery Point Town Pier

Portland to Rockland

Portland, ME	Spring Point Marina
Robinhood, ME	Robinhood Marine Center

Rockland to Eastport

Southwest Harbor	*Hinckley Great Harbor Marina*
Southwest Harbor	Dockside
Northeast Harbor	Northeast Harbor Marina
	Mt. Desert Yacht Yard
Bar Harbor, ME	Frenchman's Bay Boating Co.

Millidge, N.B.
Royal Kennebecasis Yacht Club

Appendix D

Hospitals

Almost every city along the coasts of New York, Connecticut, Rhode Island, and Massachusetts has a hospital. In Maine, however, they are less frequent. Hospitals are located in the following towns and cities:

Kittery

York Harbor

York Village

Biddeford

Saco

Portland

Brunswick

Bath

Boothbay Harbor

Damariscotta

Rockland

Camden

Belfast

Bangor

Castine

Blue Hill

Ellsworth

Bar Harbor

Machias

Eastport

Calais

Appendix E

Fog

"Are you cruising down east this summer?"
"I rather doubt it. Too much fog down there you know. Treacherous stuff."

Fog is not treacherous; it is not produced magically by a malevolent Caliban to entrap, entangle, and undo the mariner who fails to make the appropriate sacrifice. Fog is a natural phenomenon, the result of physical laws operating predictably. It can be dealt with by the use of reason and arithmetic applied to known physical conditions.

Fog develops when warm air lying over warm water south of New England moves northerly over the colder coastal water—colder because a branch of the Labrador Current runs close to the coast and because tidal stirring never lets sun-warmed water lie on the surface. When the warm, saturated air is cooled, the invisible transparent water vapor condenses in tiny droplets to produce most opaque fog. If the temperature rises, the fog evaporates into transparent water vapor again.

Thus when fog blows over an island or a cape, it is warmed by the land, dries up, and leaves a window or scale-up on the lee side. One can usually count on such a window north of Grand Manan, Isle au Haut, Cape Elizabeth, Cape Ann, Cape Cod, and Nantucket. On a warm day with the sun shining above the fog, it will scale up to leeward of any island and in the passages like Muscle Ridge Channel, the Thorofares, Eggemoggin Reach, and Casco Passage. The islands at the entrances to bays and rivers and the surrounding land very often warm the air enough so that one can enjoy pleasant sailing up the Damariscotta or Penobscot Rivers when it is thick outside. Visit Bath, Castine, or Somesville on a foggy day.

Conversely, fog will pile up heavily on the weather side of an island and will lie heavily over the cold water in the middle of a bay when it is less dense under the shore.

If you notice late in the afternoon that you can see your breath, that towels or sneakers once wet with salt water are damp and clammy, that the wind is far out to the south or east of south, the fog will probably shut down at night. In the morning, make a slow start to let the day develop. When you come on deck, if you find the sky quite bright, if there are dry spots on the deck despite the fog dew in the rigging, if you can make out the loom of the shore 100 yards away, make a start. It will probably burn off.

You will need a large-scale chart, a reliable compass properly compensated, and a clock. A depth finder is very useful, and a log giving speed or distance through the water is a great help at guessing your speed.

Take off from a known position on a course for something that makes a noise. A bell, gong, or whistle is ideal. Lacking that, the bold shore of an island will do very well. You will surely hear the surf and see the loom of the shore before you are in trouble. Make some allowances for tide, a bit less than you think you should.

Use your crew. Let one person steer, his business not to watch where he is going but to keep the lubberline steadily on the compass course. Assign another to stand forward away from conversation and engine noise, if any. He must look, smell, and above all, listen. It will do no harm if he blows the horn occasionally. The navigator watches clock and compass, depth finder, and log. He is alert to use every resource available and to note it in the logbook. Change lookout and helmsman at least every half-hour. Both are tiring jobs.

The lookout may report a clump of pot buoys. Notice the speed and direction of the tide running by them. Remember that in summer lobster traps are generally set in no more than 10 fathoms on rocky bottom. Check chart and depth finder to identify the spot. A buoy, ledge, or island may swim into the edge of the lookout's circle of visibility just long enough to give a check on position. Sometimes a high island or a distant mountaintop will show over the top of the fog, looking very high in the sky, and the treetops on a near shore will appear against the sky before the shoreline itself becomes visible.

Sometimes the sense of smell will help. Surf and bare rockweed has a characteristic sour smell. A smell like a henhouse on a wet day drifts to leeward of ledges where gulls and shags nest. A wooded island on a warm day smells of spruce, sweet fern, wild roses, and raspberries.

The lookout's most important reports, however, will be of what he hears. For this reason, given any kind of a fair wind, it is much better to sail in the fog than to motor. Almost any sound is important. Surf, the wash of calm water on a steep shore, screaming of gulls on a ledge, song of song sparrow or white-throat in the trees, crows, an automobile horn, even the slam of a screen door can tell you how you are coming on. Of course a bell, gong, whistle, or foghorn is most useful.

When you have almost run out your time, stop and listen. Don't just slow down and slide into neutral. Shut off the engine and drift, or slack sheets and heave to so there is not even the sound of a wash under the bow. Listen for a full minute. You will probably hear the moan of the whistle or clang of the bell you seek or the rumble of surf on a bold shore. Note the time-out in the log.

If you hear nothing, press on and run out your time. Listen again. If still nothing, run on another 5 minutes. If still nothing—and this seldom happens—turn 90 degrees and run another 5 minutes and listen. Then turn 90 degrees again for 5 minutes. Turn again and run 5 minutes. You have now "made a box" and come back nearly to where you were when you ran out your time. If still nothing, make another box on the other side of your course.

While this is going on, review your logbook, checking your course, your allowances for tide and leeway, your estimates of time and speed, and all the hints that came in from the lookout. You may even find an egregious error in arithmetic. By this time you have either found an error you can correct or someone will have heard, smelled, or seen something. If not, I suppose you can make two more boxes and then anchor and wait for a scale-up. Never in my experience has it come to this.

Of course if you have a loran in working order, your problems are much simplified. As you pass significant buoys in clear weather, write down the coordinates which your set gives. Even though they do not agree precisely with the charted position of the buoy, if you return to those coordinates in thick weather, you can reach out and touch the buoy.

Radar, too, is a great help once you have tamed the beast and learned how to look at it. Be sure that the blip or squeak ahead is the buoy you seek and not someone else seeking the same buoy. You could home in confidently on each other while the buoy floats elsewhere—laughing.

GPS, Geographic Positioning System, is another electronic miracle which requires a little practice to get it under control.

All three are delicate and complex machines easily put out of action by a loose connection, dampness, dirt, or unforeseen circumstance. Also they demand practice in clear weather if they are to be useful in the fog. If on a good day you would rather sail your boat than fuss with electronics, you can always depend on compass and clock, on log, lead, and lookout.

There is always the possibility of collision in the fog, most likely near a significant whistle or bell. Again, listening is your best defense. Also it is helpful and reassuring to hang a big radar reflector as high in the rigging as possible and to blow a powerful horn as required in the Navigation Rules—one long blast for a vessel under power and a long and two short for a sailing vessel. If the bearing of an approaching vessel does not change appreciably, call on the VHF radio. Commercial vessels and many yachts listen to channel 13 and all are supposed to monitor channel 16. Often, big vessels will make a "Securité" call on channel 16 from time to time to give their position, course, and speed for the benefit of small boats nearby.

If you are the burdened vessel under the right-of-way rules or if you decide to change your course anyway to avoid peril, make the change significant and decisive, for a small change is often not noticeable, especially on a radar scope.

After a few hours of fog, how cheered will all hands be to see a scale-up, warm sun, and a pleasant afternoon. Sometimes it will come like walking out a door. Sometimes the fog lifts and curls away from ledges, islands, and distant shore. If no scale-up comes, the relief of making a safe harbor and the satisfaction of having met a challenge make a day to be remembered. With caution, care, confidence, and a dash of good fortune traveling in the fog will give another dimension to your cruise.

However, if you come on deck in the morning to find the sky dark, the decks wet, a cold southerly breeze driving the fog through the nearby spruce trees and swirling it choking thick between you and the mast, have a slow and luxurious breakfast, take a walk ashore, pick blueberries, visit the local museum, go up to the store, explore the waterfront, gam with the yacht anchored near by, and enjoy a day at anchor.

Index

Acabonack Harbor, N.Y., 234–36
Allen Harbor, Mass., 370–71
Allen Harbor, Narragansett Bay, 274
Allen Island, Me., 535–39
Allerton, Mass., 396
Alpine Boat Basin, N.J., 53–54
Annisquam, Mass., 410–13
Annisquam River, 408–9
Appledore Island, N.H., 435–38
Apponaug Cove, Narragansett Bay,
    276–77
Aquebogue, N.Y., 226–27
Aquidneck Island, R.I., 282–87
Athens, N.Y., 78–79

Back Bay, N.B., 739
Back Channel, N.H., 430
Back Narrows, Me., 502–3
Bailey Island, Me., 462–63
Bailey's Mistake, Me., 703
Bangor, Me., 582, 584
Bar Harbor, Me., 657–58
Barlows Landing, Mass., 322
Barnstable, Mass., 379
Barred Islands, Me., 592
Barrington River, 293–94
Bartlett Narrows, Me., 644

Barton Cove, N.B., 755
Basin, The, Me., 464–65, 602
Bass Harbor, Me., 647–48
Bass Harbor Bar, Me., 644–45
Bass River, Mass., 368–70
Bath, Me., 475–76
    inside passage from Boothbay
        Harbor, 481–82
    river to, 474–75
Battery, The, New York, N.Y.,
    49
Bayside, Me., 579
Bear Mountain, N.Y., 34
Beaver Harbour, N.B., 740
Belfast, Me., 579–80
Belle Isle Bay, N.B., 752–51
Benjamin River, Me., 634
Beverly, Mass., 405
Biddeford Pool, Me., 446–47
Big Cove (Lewes Cove), N.B., 753
Billings Cove, Me., 633
Birch Harbor, Me., 670
Birds, 759–60
Black Rock Harbor, Conn., 127–29
Blacks Harbour, N.B., 739–40
Bliss Harbour, N.B., 739
Block Island, R.I., 4, 259–66

Block Island Harbor on East Harbor, R.I., 264–66
Blue Hill, Me., 641–42
Blue Hill Bay, Me., 13
Blynman Canal, Mass., 408–9
Boothbay Harbor, Me., 489–93
    inside passage to Bath, 479–80
Boston Harbor, Mass., 395–99
Boston Harbor Islands, Mass., 399
Boston Inner Harbor, Mass., 397–99
Boxer, 517–21
Branford, Conn., 136–37
Bridgeport, Conn., 127–29
Bridges, 42–43
Bristol, Narragansett Bay, 291–93
Brooklin, Me., 634–35
Buckle Harbor, Me., 637
Bucks Harbor, Me., 590–91, 691–92
Bucksport, Me., 581
Bullock Cove, Narragansett Bay, 278–79
Bunker Cove, Me., 687
Bunker Harbor, Me., 669–70
Burnt Coat Harbor, Me., 6–7, 638–39
Burnt Island, Me., 542
Burnt Island Thorofare, Me., 627–28
Butter Island, Me., 592–93
Buzzards Bay, Mass., 9
    harbors on mainland, 304–37
    route to, 303–4
    tidal currents, 302–3
Byram Harbor, N.Y., 104–5

Calais, Me., 733
Calf Pasture Point, Conn., 119
Camden, Me., 571–76
Camden Hills, Me., 6
Campobello, N.B., 722–23, 724
Canada
    buoyage in, 751–52
    Customs and Immigration, 715–6
    see also New Brunswick
Canapitsit Channel, Mass., 332

Cape Ann, Mass., 413
    leaving bound east, 415–16
Cape Ann Marina, Annisquam, Mass., 409–10
Cape Cod, 3, 5, 19
    Monomoy and beyond, 374–77
    South Shore of, 358–74
Cape Cod Canal, 13, 319–20, 378–79
Cape Elizabeth, Me., 378
Cape Neddick Harbor, Me., 440
Cape Poge Light, 5
Cape Porpoise, Me., 443–45
Cape Rosier, Me., 587
Cape Split Harbor, Me., 677–79
Carlisle Island, Me., 504
Carver Cove, Me., 598–99
Carver's Harbor, Me., 607–9
Casco Bay, Me., 6
Casco Passage, Me., 639–40
Castine, Me., 584–85
Castleton-on-Hudson, N.Y., 82
Catskill, Catskill Creek, N.Y., 34, 75–78
Cedar Island, Me., 602–3
Center Harbor, Me., 634–35
Chamcook, N.B., 728–29
Champlain Barge Canal, 84–86
Chance Harbour, N.B., 741
Chart Kits, 16
Charts, 14–16
Chatham, Mass., 372–74
Chester, Conn., 162–64
Christmas Cove, Me., 497–99
City Island, N.Y., 32, 89–92
    to Hudson River, 39–46
Clark Cove, Me., 504
Clearwater, 3–4
Clinton, Conn., 144–45
Coasters Harbor, Narragansett Bay, 289–90
Coast Guard, 16–21, 26, 48
Coast Pilot, 12, 35
Cobscook Bay, Me., 720
Cobscook Falls, Me., 720–21

Coddington Cove, Narragansett Bay, 289–90

Coecles Harbor, N.Y., 221–22

Coeymans, N.Y., 81–82

Cohasset, Mass., 393–95

Cold Spring, N.Y., 66–67

Cold Spring Harbor, N.Y., 185–86

Cole River, 298

Compass, 14

Conanicut Island, Narragansett Bay, 287–89

Connecticut River, 149–77

Connecticut River Marina, Chester, Conn., 162–64

Conservation, 23

Corea, Me., 672

Cornwall-on-the-Hudson, N.Y., 67–68

Cos Cob (Riverside), Conn., 107–8

Cow Yard, Me., 684

Coxsackie, N.Y., 79–80

Cozy Harbor, Me., 483–84

Cranberry Island, Me., 542

Cranston, R.I., 279–81

Criehaven, Me., 616–18

Crockett Cove, Me., 601–2

Cross Island, Me., 693

Cross Island Narrows, Me., 693–95

Cumberland Bay, N.B., 755

Cundy's Harbor, Me., 464

Current, in Hudson River, 39–41

Customs, 715–16

Cutchogue Harbor, N.Y., 222–24

Cutler, Me., 695–96

Cuttyhunk, Mass., 333–37

Damariscotta River, 501–9

Damariscove, Me., 495–97

Darien River, 114–15

Dark Harbour, N.B., 705–7

Deer Island, N.B., 724–27

Deer Island Thorofare, Me., 6, 630–32

Deer Isle-Sedgewick Bridge, Me., 633–34

Dering Harbor, N.Y., 213–15

Digdeguash Harbour, N.B., 728

Dipper Harbour, N.B., 740–41

Dix Island, Me., 559–60

Dodge Lower Cove, Me., 506

Dorchester Bay, Mass., 397

Douglas Harbor, N.B., 755

Duck Harbor, Me., 624–25

Duck Island Harbor, N.Y., 192–93

Duck Island Roads, Clinton, Conn., 145–47

Dutch Island Harbor, Narragansett Bay, 271–72

Duxbury, Mass., 387–86

Duxbury Pier Light, 5

Dyckman Marina, N.Y., 53

Dyer Bay, Me., 672–73

Dyer Island, Me., 676

Eagle Island, Me., 462

East Blue Hill, Me., 643

East Boat Basin, Sandwich, Mass., 320, 378–79

East Boothbay, Me., 500–501

East Branch, Norwalk Harbor, 121

Eastern Point, Gloucester, Mass., 406–8

Eastern Way, Great Harbor of Mount Desert, Me., 648

East Greenwich, Narragansett Bay, 274–76

East Haddam, Conn., 164–65

East Harbor, Fishers Island, N.Y., 245

East Norwalk, Conn., 117–23

Eastport, Me., 721–22

East River, N.Y., 13, 32, 44–46

East Side, Isle au Haut, Me., 628

Eaton's Neck, N.Y., 192–93

Eatons Neck Basin, N.Y., 195–96

Ebenecook Harbor, Me., 484–85

Echo Bay, 96–97

Edgartown, Mass., 351–53

Edgewater, N.J., 51–52

Edgewood, Narragansett Bay, 279–81

Eel Pond, Waquoit Bay, Mass., 364

Eel Pond, Woods Hole, Mass., 329
Eggemoggin Reach, Me., 13, 569
Egg Rock, 13
Eldridge Tide and Pilot Book, 17, 338
Electronic equipment, 18–21
Elizabeth Islands, Mass., 330–37
Englewood Boat Basin, N.J., 53
Enterprise, 517–21
EPIRB (Emergency Position Indicat-
    ing Radio Beacon), 20
Erbs Cove, N.B., 751
Esopus Creek, N.Y., 74–75
Essex, Conn., 156–60
Essex, Mass., 417–19
Etrusco, 392–93
Evandale, N.B., 752

Fairhaven, Mass., 307–9
Fall River, Mass., 298–99
Falmouth, Mass., 360–61
Falmouth Foreside, Me., 455–57
False Whitehead Harbor, Me., 558
Fathometer, 18–19
Federal Harbor, Me., 719–20
Federal Lock, Troy, N.Y., 84
Ferry Point Marina, Old Saybrook,
    Conn., 154–55
Fiddler's Cove, Mass., 323
Finger Bay, N.B., 738–39
First Aid Afloat (Sheldon), 21
Fishers Island, N.Y., 242–45
Fishers Island Sound, N.Y., 242–43
Five Islands, Me., 477–79
Fivemile River, 116–17
Flanders Bay, N.Y., 225–27
Flauters, N.Y., 227
Flint Island, Me., 676
Flowers Cove, N.B., 755–56
Flushing Bay, N.Y., 43–44
Fog, 10, 555, 784–87
Fogland Harbor, Sakonnet River, 296
Fort Popham, Seguin Island, Me.,
    472–74
Fox Islands Thorofare, Me., 594–95
Fredericton, N.B., 758

Frenchboro, Me., 670–71
Friendship, Me., 526–28
Friendship Museum, 533
Friendship sloops, 528–32
Friendship Sloop Society, 532–35
Fundy, Bay of, 3, 7, 12, 22

Gagetown, N.B., 753–54
Galilee, R.I., 267–68
Gardiners Bay, N.Y., 232–36
Garrison, N.Y., 65–66
Geology, 769–79
Georges Harbor, Me., 533–34
Gilkey Harbor, Islesboro, Me., 576–
    77
Glen Cove (Hempstead Harbor),
    N.Y., 180–83
Gloucester, Mass., 405–6
Gloucester Harbor, Mass., 407–8
Goodspeed's Landing, East Haddam,
    Conn., 164–65
Goodwives River, 114–15
Gosport Harbor, N.H., 433–34
Gouldsboro Bay, Me., 672–73
GPS, 20–21
Grand Lake, N.B., 755–56
Grand Manan, N.B., 704–13
Grand Manan Channel, Me., 697–
    700
Grassy Point, N.Y., 61–62
Great Bay Marine, Portsmouth, N.H.,
    433
Great Chebeague Island, Me., 461–62
Great Cranberry Island, Me., 656–57
Great Harbor, Woods Hole, Mass.,
    328–29
Great Harbor of Mount Desert, Me.,
    648
Great Peconic Bay, N.Y., 225, 227–28
Great Pond, *see* Montauk
Great Salt Pond, Block Island, R.I.,
    260–64
Great Sprucehead, Me., 592
Great Wass Island, Me., 681–84
Green Harbor, Mass., 388

Green Islands, Me., 610–12
Greenland Cove, Me., 539
Green Pond, Mass., 361–62
Greenport, N.Y., 211–13
Green's Island Cove, Me., 605–7
Greenwich, Conn., 105–7
Greenwich Cove, Conn., 108–9
Gregory Point, Conn., 119
Guilford, Conn., 143–44
Gurnet Point, 5

Hadley Harbor, Mass., 4, 330
Hamburg Cove, Conn., 160
Hampden, Me., 582
Hampton, N.H., 424–25
Harbor Cove, Gloucester, Mass., 408
Harbor Island, Me., 523–25
Harbor One, Saybrook Point, Conn., 152
Harbour de Loutre, N.B., 723
Harlem River, 32, 33, 34, 37, 39, 41, 42–43
  Hudson River above, 53–83
  Hudson River below, 46–53
Harmon Harbor, Me., 476–77
Harpswell Harbor, Me., 462
Harwich Port, Mass., 371–72
Hastings-on-Hudson, N.Y., 54
Haverstraw, N.Y., 58–60
Haycock Harbor, Me., 700–703
Hay Harbor, N.Y., 243
Hay Island (Ziegler's Cove), Conn., 115–16
Head Harbor, Me., 624–25, 684
Head Harbour, N.B., 723–24
Hell Gate, 13, 32
Hempstead Harbor (Glen Cove), N.Y., 180–83
Hen Cove, Mass., 323
Henry Cove, Me., 663
Heronway Marina, Rust Island, Mass., 409
Herring River, 388–89
High Head, Me., 503
Hingham, Mass., 396–97
Hog Island, Me., 540–41

Holbrook Island, Me., 585–87
Home Harbor, Me., 560
Horseshoe Cove, Me., 587–89
Hospital Cove, Mass., 322
Hospital Island, Me., 585
Hospitals, 783
Housatonic River, Conn., 129–31
How to Use Your Marine Radio-telephone (FCC), 20
Hudson Harbor-79th Street Marina, N.Y., 52–53
Hudson River, 3–4
  canalized, 84–86
  City Island to, 39–46
  at Federal Lock, Troy, N.Y., 83–84
  above Harlem River, 53–83
  below Harlem River, 46–53
  introduction to, 31–39
Hull, Mass., 395–96
Hunters Landing, Me., 506–7
Huntington, N.Y., 189–91
Hurricane Island, Me., 593–95
Hurricanes, 11–12
Hyannis, Mass., 365–68

Immigration, 715–16
Indian Kill, N.Y., 70–72
Inner Winter Harbor, Me., 663–67
Island Institute, 565–66
Islands in Time (Conkling), 23
Islands of America (Department of Interior), 23
Isle au Haut, Me., 620–30
Isle au Haut Thorofare, 625–27
Islesboro, Me., 576–77
Islesford, Me., 657
Isles of Shoals, N.H., 6, 433–38

Jamestown, Narragansett Bay, 287–89
Jemseg River, 754
Jenkins Cove, N.B., 750
Jericho Bay, 6, 13
Jersey City, N.J., 49–50
Jewell Island, Me., 457–60
Jonesport, Me., 679–81

Kennebecasis Bay, N.B., 748
Kennebec River, 468–72
Kennebunkport, Me., 441–43
Kent Cove, Me., 598
Kickamuit River, 298
Kingston, N.Y., 72–74
Kingston Creek, N.B., 749–50
Kittery Landing, Portsmouth, N.H., 431–33
Kittery Point Yacht Club, Portsmouth, N.H., 430

Lakeman Harbor, Me., 689
Lake Tashmoo, Mass., 344
Lake Tear of the Clouds, N.Y., 31, 35
Larchmont, N.Y., 97–98
Leets Island, Conn., 142
L'Etang Harbour, N.B., 738–39
Letete Passage, N.B., 726
Lewes Cove (Big Cove), N.B., 753
Light List, Volume I, 17
Lincolnville Beach, Me., 577–78
Linekin Bay, Me., 493–95
Little Cranberry Island, Me., 657
Little Harbor, Conn., 142
Little Harbor, Portsmouth, N.H., 427–28
Little Harbor, Woods Hole, Mass., 329–30
Little Letite Passage, N.B., 726–27
Little Neck Bay, N.Y., 88–89
Little Peconic Bay, N.Y., 222–25, 230–31
Little River, 497
Little Thorofare, Fox Island Thoro- fare, Me., 599
Lloyd Harbor, N.Y., 188–89
Lloyd Point, N.Y., 186–88
Local Notice to Mariners, 48
Logbook, 18
Londoners (Lunging Island), N.H., 437–39
Long Cove, Me., 602
Long Island, Me., 640–41
Long Island Sound, 3, 4, 10, 13

North Shore, 87–177
South Shore, 178–241
Long Ledge, 13
Loran, 20–21
Lords Cove, N.B., 725–26
Louds Island, Me., 540
Louds Island East Cove, Me., 540
Lowes Cove, Me., 505–6
Lubec, Me., 719
Lubec Narrows, Me., 717–19
Lunging Island (Londoners), N.H., 438–39

McFarland's Cove, Me., 509–10
Machias, Me., 692
Battle of, 692–93
Machias Bay, Me., 690–91
Machiasport, Me., 692
Machias Seal Island, N.B., 696–97
Mackerel Cove, Bailey Island, Me., 462–63
Mackerel Cove, Swans Island, Me., 637
MacMahan Island, Me., 481
Magaguadavic River, 727–28
Maine
courses and routes in, 569–71, 639–49, 665–68
fish weirs in, 668
fog in, 561
general conditions, 449–52, 561, 665–66
harbors in, 591–92
islands in, 563–65
lobstering in, 565–67
salmon pens in, 668–69
supplies and repairs in, 568–69
Maine Island Trail Associates, 564–65
Maine Sea Coast Missionary Society, 659–60
Majors Harbor, N.Y., 218
Mamaroneck, N.Y., 98–101
Mammals, 759–67
Manchester, Mass., 404–5
Manhasset Bay, N.Y., 178–80

Manhattan Island, 33, 34
Manomet, 5
Maplejuice Cove, Me., 549
Marblehead, Mass., 399–402
Marion (Sippican), Mass., 312–16
Marsh Harbor, Me., 537
Martha's Vineyard, Mass., 344, 349
Mason Island, Conn., 246–53
Matinicus, Me., 612–16
Matinicus Rock, Me., 618–19
Mattapoisett, Mass., 310–12
Mattituck, N.Y., 225
Mattituck Inlet, N.Y., 204–7
Maurice Marine, Conn., 121
Meadow Cove, Me., 502
Mears Cove, Me., 506
Medomak River, 525–26
Megansett, Mass., 323
Menemsha, Mass., 342–43
Mere Point, Me., 461
Middletown Yacht Club, Conn., 164
Milford, Conn., 131–33
Mill Cove, N.B., 755
Mill Creek, N.Y., 231–32
Millidgeville, N.B., 746–48
Millstone Point, Conn., 171–72
Milton Harbor, N.Y., 101–3
Mistake Island Harbor, Me., 684–85
Monhegan Island, Me., 542–48
Montauk (Great Pond), N.Y., 3, 4,
    237–41
Montrose, N.Y., 62–63
Moore Harbor, Me., 625
Moosabec Reach, Me., 681
Moose Island, Me., 630–31
Mosquito Island, Me., 553–54
Mount Desert, Me., 6, 7
  Great Harbor of, 648
Mount Desert Island, Me., 645–47
Mount Hope Bay, 298
Mount Sinai, N.Y., 203–4
Mudhole, The, Me., 681–84
Muscle Ridge Channel, Me., 555–60
Muscongus, Me., 523
Muscongus Bar, Me., 523

Muscongus Bay, Me., 512–14
  anchorages in, 538–55
Musquash Harbour, N.B., 742
Mystic, Conn., 246–53

Nantucket, Mass., 5, 351–58
Nantucket Sound, Mass., 4–5, 338–
    42
Napeague Harbor, N.Y., 236–37
Narragansett Bay, R.I. and Mass.,
    269–71
  East Passage, 281–82
  Mount Hope Bay, 298
  Sakonnet River, 294–98
  West Passage, 271–81
Narraguagus Bay, Me., 676
Naskeag, Me., 636
Navigating equipment, 14–18
Navigation, 751–52
Navigation Rules, 17–18
Newagen, Me., 486–89
New Baltimore, N.Y., 80
New Bedford, Mass., 307–9
New Brunswick
  communications and provisions, 737
  general conditions, 734–36, 737–38
  preparations, 736
  tidal conditions, 714–15
  see also Canada
Newburgh, N.Y., 34, 68–69
Newburyport, Mass., 420–24
Newcastle, Me., 507–9
Newcastle Creek, N.B., 756
New Hamburg, N.Y., 69
New Harbor, Me., 515–17
New Haven, Conn., 133–36
New Inlet, Mass., 388–90
New London, Conn., 172–76
Newport, R.I., 4, 282–87
New Rochelle, N.Y., 92–97
New Suffolk, N.Y., 224–25
New York Bay, N.Y., 35
New York Skyports Marina, N.Y., 44
Niantic River, 169–71
NOAA charts, 16

Noank, Conn., 245–53
No Man's Land, Me., 619–20
Noroton, Conn., 114–16
North Cove, Conn., 152–53
Northeast Cove, Dyer Island, 676
Northeast Harbor, Me., 653–56
North Haven, Me., 596–98
North Head Harbour, N.B., 707–10
Northport, N.Y., 193–95, 196–97
Northport Basin, N.Y., 196–97
Northport Bay, N.Y., 191–92
North River, 389–90
North Sea Harbor, N.Y., 230
Northwest Harbor, Cross Island, Me., 693
Northwest Harbor, Me., 632–33
Northwest Harbor, N.Y., 232
Northwest Harbour, Deer Island, N.B., 624–25
North Woods, N.B., 756–58
Norwalk Cove Marina, Conn., 122–23
Norwalk Yacht Club, Conn., 118
Norwest Marine, Conn., 121
Norwich, Conn., 176–77
NOS charts, 16
Notices to Mariners, 16
Nova Scotia, approaching from, 548
Noyack Bay, N.Y., 231–32
Nyack, N.Y., 56–57

Oak Bluffs, Mass., 349
Oak Leaf Marina, Old Saybrook, Conn., 154
Oar Island, Me., 542
Old Harbor, Me., 605
Old Lyme, Conn., 155–56
Old Saybrook, Conn., 153–55
Onset, Mass., 317–18
Orcutt Harbor, Me., 590
Ossining, N.Y., 57–58
Osterville, Mass., 362–63
Otter Island, Me., 542
Oyster Bay, N.Y., 183–85

Padanaram, Mass., 304–7
Palisades, 34
Parkers River, 368
Patchogue River, 147–49
Patten Cove, Me., 687–88
Patten's Yacht Yard, Portsmouth, N.H., 433
Pawtuxet Cove, Narragansett Bay, 279
Peach Island, Conn., 119
Peconic Bays (Great and Little), N.Y., 222–41
Peekskill, N.Y., 63–64
Pell Island Passage, Me., 628
Pemaquid Harbor, Me., 510–11
Pemaquid Point, Me., 511–12
Penikese Island, Mass., 332–33
Penobscot Bay, Me., 621
Penobscot River, 581
Pepperrell Cove, N.H., 428
Perkins Cove, Me., 440–41
Perry Creek, Me., 541
Petit Manan, Me., 673
Petit Manan Bar, Me., 673–76
Pigeon Hill Bay, Me., 676
Pilgrim Monument, 5
Pine Orchard, Conn., 137–38
Playland, Rye, N.Y., 103
Pleasant Bay, Me., 676
Pleasant Cove, Me., 504
Pleasant Point Gut, Me., 548–49
Plum Gut Harbor, N.Y., 207–8
Plum Island Sound, Mass., 419–20
Plymouth, Mass., 5, 385–87
Pocasset, Mass., 320–21
Point Judith Harbor of Refuge, R.I., 266–67
Point Lepreau, N.B., 740
Point Lookout, Me., 627
Pollution, 22
Pond Island Passage, Me., 640
Poole's Landing, Me., 505
Popponesset Bay, Mass., 364
Port Chester, N.Y., 104–5
Port Clyde, Me., 552–53
Port Harbor, Me., 677

Port Jefferson, N.Y., 197–203
Portland, Conn., 166–67
Portland, Me., 26, 452–55
Portsmouth, N.H., 427–33
Portsmouth Yacht Club, N.H., 428–30
Port Washington, N.Y., 178–80
Potato Ledge, 14
Potter Cove, Narragansett Bay, 290–91
Potts Harbor, Me., 462
Poughkeepsie, N.Y., 70
Prentiss Cove, Me., 507
Prescott Park, N.H., 430–31
Prettymarsh, Me., 644
Price Bend, N.Y., 192
Prospect Harbor, Me., 670–72
Prouts Neck, Me., 448
Providence River, 278–81
Provincetown, Mass., 5, 381–84
Prudence Island, Narragansett Bay, 290–91
Publications, 17–18
Pulpit Harbor, Me., 593–94
Pump-out stations, 780–82

Quahog Bay, Me., 463–64
Quicks Hole, Mass., 331–32
Quincy, Mass., 397
Quissett (Quamquissett), Mass., 325–27
Quoddy Roads, Me., 716

Radar, 20–21
Radio direction finder, 19
Radiotelephone, VHF, 19–20
Ragged Rock Marine, Old Saybrook, Conn., 153
Red Brook Harbor, Mass., 321–22
Red Creek Pond, 227–28
Reed's Almanac, 17
Rensselaer, N.Y., 82–83
Reversing Falls, 3, 7
Rex Marine Center, Conn., 120–21
Richmond Island Harbor, Me., 448

Riverhead, N.Y., 227
River Landing Marina, Old Saybrook, Conn., 154
Riverside (Cos Cob), Conn., 107–8
Robinhood, Me., 480–81
Robinsons Hole, Mass., 330–31
Rockland, Me., 558–60
Rockport, Mass., 413–15
Rockport, Me., 413
Rocky Hill, Conn., 167
Rondout Creek, N.Y., 72–74
Roque Island, Me., 685–87
Roque Island Harbor, Me., 688–89
Roque Island Thorofare, Me., 688
Round Pond, Me., 521–23
Rowayton, Conn., 116–17
Royal Kennebecasis Yacht Club, Millidgeville, N.B., 746–48
Rust Island, Mass., 409
Rye, N.Y., 101–3
Rye Harbor, N.H., 425

Sachem Head, Conn., 142–43
Sachuest Cove, Sakonnet River, 296
Saco Bay, 13
Saco River, 447
Safety equipment, 21
Sag Harbor, N.Y., 218–21
Sail Rock, Me., 703
Saint Andrews, N.B., 729–31
St. Anthony's Nose, N.Y., 34
St. Croix Island, Me., 731–33
St. George River, 549–52
Saint John, N.B., 742–46
Saint John Harbor, N.B., 7
Saint John Power Boat Club, 746
Saint John River, 3, 738, 748–50
Sakonnet Harbor, Narragansett Bay, 295–96
Sakonnet River, 294–98
Salem, Mass., 402–4
Salem Bay, 10
Salmon River, Conn., 165–66
Salmon River, N.B., 756
Salt Marsh Cove, Me., 505

Sand Cove, Me., 664
"Sand Hole," at Lloyd Point, N.Y., 186–88
Sandwich, Mass., 376–77
Sandy Bay, Mass., 413
Saquatucket, Mass., 371–72
Sargentville, Me., 633
Saturday Cove, Me., 578–79
Saugatuck, Conn., 123–25
Saugerties, N.Y., 74–75
Saybrook, Conn., 149–51
  see also Old Saybrook
Saybrook Marine Service, Old Saybrook, Conn., 154
Saybrook Point, Conn., 152–53
Saybrook Point Inn Marina, Saybrook Point, Conn., 152–53
Schoodic Point, Me., 666–67
Scituate, Mass., 390–93
Seal Bay, Me., 609–10
Seal Cove, Damariscotta River, Me., 503
Seal Cove, Fox Islands Thorofare, Me., 598
Seal Cove, N.B., 710–13
Seal Cove, Swans Island, Me., 637–38
Seal Harbor, Me., 557–58, 656
Seal Island, Me., 619–20
Seal Trap, Me., 625
Searsport, Me., 680
Sebasco, Me., 465–67
Sebonac Creek, N.Y., 229–30
Seguin Island, Me., 472–74
Selden (Shirley) Creek, Conn., 161–62
Sesuit, Mass., 379–80
Setauket, N.Y., 201–3
Shabby Island, 14
Shamper Cove, N.B., 749–50
Sheffield Island, Conn., 118–19
Shelter Island, N.Y., 208–11, 213–15, 216–18, 221–22
Shelter Island Sound, N.Y., 208–11

Shinnecock Canal Basin, N.Y., 228–29
Shirley (Selden) Creek, Conn., 161–62
Shorey Cove, Me., 689–90
Silting, 14
Silver Beach, Mass., 323
Silver Eel Cove, N.Y., 243
Sippican (Marion), Mass., 312–16
Small Point Harbor, Me., 467–69
Smith Cove, Mass., 407
Smith Cove, Me., 585
Smith Cove, N.Y., 217–18
Smuttynose Island, N.H., 435
Somes Sound, Me., 650–51
Sorrento, Me., 661–62
South Addison, Me., 677–79
Southampton, N.Y., 229–30
South Bristol, Me., 499–500
South Dartmouth, Mass., 304–7
Southeast Harbor, Deer Isle, Me., 632
Southern Harbor, Fox Islands Thorofare, Me., 595–96
South Freeport, Me., 460–61
South Harpswell, Me., 462
South Jamesport, N.Y., 225–26
South Norwalk, Conn., 17–23
South Norwalk Boat Club, Conn., 119–20
Southold, N.Y., 215–16
Southport, Conn., 125–27
South River, 390
South Street Seaport, New York, N.Y., 44–46
Southwest Harbor, Me., 649–50
South Wethersfield, Conn., 167–68
South Yarmouth, Mass., 369
Staatsburg, N.Y., 70–72
Stage Harbor, Mass., 372–74
Stamford, Conn., 109–14
Starboard Cove, Me., 691
Star Island, N.H., 434–35
Stave Island Harbor, Me., 662
Stockton Harbor, Me., 580–81

Stonington, Conn., 253–56
Stonington, Me., 628–30, 631
Stony Creek, Conn., 138–42
Stony Point, N.Y., 34, 35, 61–62
Storm King Mountain, N.Y., 34
Stratford, Conn., 109–29
Sullivan, Me., 660–61
Swans Island, Me., 636–39
Sylvester Cove, Me., 632

Tarpaulin Cove, Mass., 343–44
Tarrytown, N.Y., 55–56
Tenants Harbor, Me., 513, 554–55
Tennant Cove, N.B., 752
Thacher Island, 6
Thimble Islands, Conn., 138–42
Thorofares, Me., 569–70
Threemile Harbor, N.Y., 232–34
Throgs Neck, N.Y., 87–88
Thunderstorms, 10–11
Tidal Current Tables for the Atlantic Coast of North America, 35
Tides, 12–14, 176, 445–46, 714–15
Tiverton, Sakonnet River, 296–98
Townsend Gut, Me., 485
Trafton Island, Me., 676–77
Troy, N.Y., 83–84
Turkey Cove, Me., 549
Two-Bush Channel, Me., 13, 555–56

United States Coast Pilot, 17
Urquhart's Cove, N.B., 751

Vinalhaven Island, Me., 599–602
Vinalhaven's East Side, Me., 609–10
Vinco Marine, Conn., 120
Vineyard Haven, Mass., 344–47
Vineyard Sound, Mass., 338–42

Wadsworth Cove, Me., 505
Wakefield, R.I., 268–69
Waquoit Bay, Mass., 363–64
Wareham, Mass., 316–17
Warren River, 293–94

Warwick Cove, Narragansett Bay, 277–78
Washadamoak Creek, N.B., 752–53
Watch Hill, R.I., 256–57
Water, fresh, 27
Waterman Cove, Me., 598
Watervliet, N.Y., 83
Weather, 8–12
Webb Cove, Me., 631
Weehawken, N.J., 50–51
Weir Cove, Me., 587
Wellfleet, Mass., 380–81
Wells, Me., 441
Welshpool, N.B., 722
Westbrook, Conn., 147–49
Westcott Cove, Conn., 113–14
Westerly, R.I., 257–59
Western Way, Great Harbor of Mount Desert, Me., 648
West Falmouth, Mass., 324–25
West Harbor, Fishers Island, N.Y., 244–45
West Harpswell, Me., 462
West Neck Harbor, N.Y., 216–17
West Point, N.Y., 34
Westport, Mass., 299–301
Wethersfield Cove, Conn., 168–69
    see also South Wethersfield
Weymouth, Mass., 397
Weymouth Back River, 397
White Cove, N.B., 755
Whitehead Island, Me., 513–15, 556
Wickford, Narragansett Bay, 272–74
Wild Harbor, Mass., 323
Wildlife, 759–67
Wilson's Beach, N.B., 724
Winter Harbor, Me., 609–10, 662–63
Winterport, Me., 581–82
Wiscasset, Me., 481–83
Wooden Ball, Me., 619–20
WoodenBoat, Me., 635
Wood Island, Me., 446–47
Woods Hole, Mass., 4, 327–30
Wooley Pond, N.Y., 230–31

Worlds End, Mass., 396
World's Fair Marina, New York, N.Y.,
    43–44
Wychmere Harbor, Mass., 371

Yarmouth, Me., 457

York Harbor, Me., 439–40
York Narrows, Me., 639–40
Young's Cove, N.B., 755

Ziegler's Cove (Hay Island), Conn.,
    115–16

M   A   I   N

River

Penobscot

Bangor •

Winterport •

Belfast • •

Androscoggin

Kennebec River

Blue Hill •
Castine • •
Bucks
Hbr.

*FRENCH-
MAN*

Bar
Harbor •

Eggemoggin

Deer
I.

BLUE HILL BAY

PENOBSCOT

Camden •

Rockland •

Friend-
ship •

Stoning-
ton •

BAY

SWANS I.

River

*Merrymeeting
Bay*

Bath •

North
Haven

Vinalhaven

ISLE AU
HAUT

Freeport •

*MUSCONGUS
BAY*

Tenants Harbor •

Matinicus
I. •

Gulf

Portland •

of

Pemaquid
Pt. •

Monhegan
I. •

ATLANTIC

CASCO BAY

Small
Pt.

Boothbay
Harbor